OECD
ECONOMIC
OUTLOOK

59

JUNE 1996

ORGANISATION FOR ECONOMIC CO-OPERATION AND DEVELOPMENT

The Organisation for Economic Co-operation and Development (OECD)

was set up under a Convention signed in Paris on 14 December 1960, which provides that the OECD shall promote policies designed:

- *to achieve the highest sustainable economic growth and employment and a rising standard of living in Member countries while maintaining financial stability, and thus to contribute to the development of the world economy;*
- *to contribute to sound economic expansion in Member as well as non-member countries in the process of economic development; and*
- *to contribute to the expansion of world trade on a multilateral, non-discriminatory basis in accordance with international obligations.*

The original Member countries of the OECD are: Austria, Belgium, Canada, Denmark, France, Germany, Greece, Iceland, Ireland, Italy, Luxembourg, the Netherlands, Norway, Portugal, Spain, Sweden, Switzerland, Turkey, the United Kingdom and the United States. The following countries became Members subsequently through accession at the dates indicated hereafter: Japan (28 April 1964), Finland (28 January 1969), Australia (7 June 1971), New Zealand (29 May 1973), Mexico (18 May 1994), the Czech Republic (21 December 1995) and Hungary (7 May 1996). The Commission of the European Communities takes part in the work of the OECD (Article 13 of the OECD Convention).

FOREWORD

The *OECD Economic Outlook* provides a periodic assessment of economic trends, prospects and policies in OECD countries. It appears twice a year, in June and December.

Each issue contains an overall analysis of the latest economic trends and short-term projections. This survey is the joint work of members of the Economics Department. The journal also occasionally contains special studies by members of the Department or other divisions of the Organisation designed to assist the interpretation of economic trends. Reference statistics are included. The French version of the *OECD Economic Outlook* is entitled *Perspectives économiques de l'OCDE.*

The *OECD Economic Outlook* is published on the responsibility of the Secretary-General of the OECD. The assessments given of countries' prospects do not necessarily correspond to those of the national authorities concerned.

TABLE OF CONTENTS

NOTE ON STATISTICAL TREATMENT OF HUNGARY

In this issue, aggregate measures for OECD Europe and total OECD do not include Hungary.

LIST OF BOXES

OECD ECONOMIC OUTLOOK AND POLICIES

General Assessment of the Economic Situation

DEVELOPMENTS IN INDIVIDUAL OECD COUNTRIES

DEVELOPMENTS IN SELECTED NON-OECD COUNTRIES

LIST OF NUMBERED TABLES AND FIGURES

OECD ECONOMIC OUTLOOK AND POLICIES

General Assessment of the Economic Situation

Table

Figure

The Influence of Financial Market Fluctuations on the Current Economic Expansion

Figure

The Experience with Fiscal Consolidation in OECD Countries

Table

Interactions between Structural Reform, Macroeconomic Policy and Economic Performance

DEVELOPMENTS IN SELECTED NON-OECD COUNTRIES

Central and Eastern European Countries, Russia and Ukraine

Dynamic Asian Economies and China

Central and South America

ANNEX

Reference Statistics and Annual Projections

LIST OF OTHER TABLES AND FIGURES

INTRODUCTION

GENERAL ASSESSMENT OF THE ECONOMIC SITUATION

DEVELOPMENTS IN INDIVIDUAL OECD COUNTRIES

DEVELOPMENTS IN SELECTED NON-OECD COUNTRIES

ANNEX

CONVENTIONAL SIGNS

$	US dollar	.	Decimal point
c	US cent	I, II	Calendar half-years
£	Pound sterling	Q1, Q4	Calendar quarters
mbd	Million barrels per day	Billion	Thousand million
..	Data not available	Trillion	Thousand billion
0	Nil or negligible	s.a.a.r.	Seasonally adjusted at annual rates
--	Irrelevant	n.s.a.	Not seasonally adjusted

Summary of projections[a]
Seasonally adjusted at annual rates

	1995	1996	1997	1995 I	1995 II	1996 I	1996 II	1997 I	1997 II
				Percentage changes from previous period					
Real total domestic demand									
United States	2.1	2.2	1.8	1.5	1.5	2.5	2.3	1.5	1.9
Japan	1.6	3.3	2.6	0.5	4.5	3.3	2.0	2.8	2.9
Germany	1.7	0.0	2.1	1.6	−0.1	−0.7	1.5	2.3	2.3
OECD Europe	2.8	1.7	2.6	2.9	2.4	1.2	2.1	2.7	2.9
Total OECD	1.8	2.1	2.4	1.2	2.0	2.1	2.4	2.3	2.5
Real GDP									
United States	2.0	2.3	2.0	1.2	2.0	2.4	2.5	1.8	2.0
Japan	0.9	2.2	2.4	0.0	2.8	2.2	1.7	2.5	2.7
Germany	1.9	0.5	2.4	2.0	0.8	−0.3	1.9	2.5	2.6
OECD Europe	2.7	1.6	2.7	3.0	1.4	1.5	2.2	2.8	2.8
Total OECD	1.9	2.1	2.5	1.4	1.7	2.0	2.4	2.4	2.6
				Per cent					
Inflation[b]									
United States	2.4	2.1	2.2	2.7	2.1	2.1	2.0	2.2	2.2
Japan	−0.5	−0.3	0.3	−0.6	−0.1	−0.4	−0.5	0.6	0.6
Germany	2.2	1.5	1.3	2.4	2.3	1.2	1.4	1.3	1.4
OECD Europe (excluding Turkey)	3.1	2.6	2.2	3.2	3.3	2.4	2.2	2.2	2.3
Total OECD (excl. Mexico and Turkey)	2.2	1.9	1.9	2.4	2.3	1.8	1.7	2.0	2.0
Total OECD	4.5	3.7	3.2	5.0	4.1	3.8	3.3	3.3	3.1
				Per cent of labour force					
Unemployment									
United States	5.6	5.5	5.6	5.6	5.6	5.5	5.5	5.6	5.6
Japan	3.1	3.3	3.2	3.0	3.3	3.3	3.2	3.2	3.2
Germany	9.4	10.3	10.4	9.3	9.5	10.2	10.5	10.5	10.3
OECD Europe	10.3	10.5	10.4	10.4	10.3	10.5	10.6	10.5	10.3
Total OECD	7.6	7.7	7.6	7.6	7.6	7.7	7.7	7.6	7.5
				Per cent of GDP					
Current balances									
United States	−2.1	−2.0	−1.8	−2.3	−1.9	−2.0	−1.9	−1.8	−1.8
Japan	2.2	1.8	1.6	2.2	2.1	1.8	1.8	1.7	1.6
Germany	−0.7	−0.5	−0.3	−0.6	−0.8	−0.5	−0.4	−0.3	−0.2
OECD Europe	0.9	0.9	1.0	1.0	0.7	0.8	0.9	1.0	1.1
Total OECD	0.0	−0.1	0.0	0.0	0.0	−0.1	0.0	0.0	0.0
				Per cent					
Short-term interest rates[c]									
United States	5.5	5.1	5.3	5.7	5.3	5.0	5.3	5.3	5.3
Japan	1.2	0.7	0.9	1.8	0.7	0.6	0.7	0.8	1.0
Germany	4.5	3.3	3.5	4.9	4.2	3.4	3.2	3.4	3.6
Major 4 European countries[d]	7.0	5.8	5.5	7.1	6.9	6.0	5.5	5.5	5.6
				Percentages changes from previous period					
World trade[e]	8.6	6.9	7.8	8.8	6.5	6.8	7.6	7.8	7.9

a) Assumptions underlying the projections include:
   – no change in actual and announced policies;
   – unchanged exchange rates from 2 May 1996; in particular $1 = ¥ 105.3 and DM 1.53;
   – dollar price (OECD cif imports) for internationally traded oil of $18.6 per barrel for 1996 I, $16.6 for 1996 II, and rise in line with OECD manufactured export prices thereafter;
   – the cut-off date for other information used in the compilation of the projections was 10 May 1996.
b) GDP deflator, percentage changes from previous period.
c) United States: 3-month Treasury bills; Japan: 3-6 month CD; Germany, France, United Kingdom: 3-month interbank rates; Italy: interbank deposit rate.
d) Unweighted average of Germany, France, Italy and the United Kingdom.
e) Growth rate of the arithmetic average of world import volumes and world export volumes.

Introduction

Cyclical divergence in the economic situations of Member countries has remained as their economic expansions have evolved: the economy of the United States has experienced a ''soft landing'', characterised by sustainable growth and stable inflation; activity picked up in late 1995 in Japan, reflecting supportive monetary and fiscal policies and the correction of the yen's excessive appreciation last year; and growth slowed significantly in key European countries in the second half of the year as domestic demand weakened.

The short-term outlook is for greater convergence across the main OECD regions, with continued sustainable growth in the United States, a more sustained recovery in Japan and a pick-up in Europe. In the United States, the recent rise in long-term rates will help to hold growth to a sustainable pace. In Japan, short-term interest rates remain low, and the return of the value of the yen to levels more in line with fundamentals has effectively eased monetary conditions. In Europe, short-term interest rates have fallen significantly in many countries, the lagged adverse effects of the worldwide run-up in long-term rates in 1994 and of currency tensions in Europe in 1995 have passed, and the inventory cycle that contributed to weakness in several countries in late 1995 and early 1996 appears to be spent. However, the recent rise in long rates may damp activity. Outside the OECD area, growth is expected to be buoyant, particularly in the dynamic Asian economies and China, but increasingly in other areas as well, and consequently export opportunities remain favourable.

Most OECD countries have come close to achieving the medium-term goal of price stability: in 1996, inflation should be below 3 per cent in 19 OECD countries. It remains important for monetary policy to safeguard the gains made on this front. One of the important lessons from macroeconomic management during the past decades is that the primary objective of monetary policy should be the achievement and maintenance of price stability over time: ''fine-tuning'' real economic activity runs the risk of compromising this ultimate goal. However, in a situation where there is significant slack in output and labour markets, little prospect of inflationary pressures and a pressing need for fiscal consolidation – a situation that appears to exist in some key countries in continental Europe – judicious use of monetary easing could help to raise output and employment without generating inflationary pressures. To avoid possible turmoil in financial markets, such easing can be justified in a way that places it in the medium-term context of price stability. Improved institutional frameworks for monetary policy – including, in some countries, greater central bank independence and accountability or a more explicit medium-term framework for monetary policy – could help to enhance and sustain the credibility of monetary policy and reduce the risk that a cut in policy-controlled interest rates would adversely affect medium- and long-term market interest rates or put unwanted strong downward pressure on exchange rates. On the other hand, in a situation where the economy is operating, and is projected to remain, at or very close to its potential – a situation that appears to exist in countries such as the United States – the central bank should err on the side of caution, bearing in mind that monetary policy affects the real economy with a long and variable lag and that there is uncertainty about the magnitude of monetary policy effects on real activity and inflationary pressures. In Japan, the easy stance of monetary policy should be maintained, given the prospect of continued large output gaps, despite the projected recovery of domestic demand.

The most urgent macroeconomic policy requirement in most OECD countries is to intensify the process of restoring the health of public-sector finances. Reducing budget deficits and reversing the rise of debt-to-GDP ratios would re-establish the sustainability of fiscal policies, which will help to reduce long-term real interest rates and ease the persistent tensions that have resulted from an imbalance between monetary and fiscal policy. However, the pace of deficit reduction in the short term depends to some extent on current and prospective economic conditions:

- In the United States, plans have been formulated to balance the budget by early in the next decade and it will be important that the Administration and Congress follow through by agreeing on the specific measures that will ensure success. Given the favourable cyclical position of the economy, there would appear to be little short-run risk in implementing such measures as quickly as possible. Indeed, putting concrete measures in place would enhance the credibility of fiscal consolidation, with favourable effects on real interest rates that would be beneficial to the United States and to the rest of the world. Canada has already made significant progress in its ambitious programme of deficit reduction at a time when economic activity appears to be recovering.

- In Japan, substantial discretionary fiscal expansion has helped to sustain demand for some time, but the deficits and public debt levels that have resulted are unsustainably high and they will have to be corrected over time, particularly in view of population ageing, which will strike Japan sooner and more sharply than elsewhere. Deficit reduction should begin soon, and proceed as rapidly as the underlying strength of domestic demand allows.

- EU countries need to be firmly and jointly committed to reducing structural budget deficits beyond 1997 to well below 3 per cent of GDP. With such commitments ensuring the credibility of fiscal policy, governments can use automatic stabilisers to deal with short-term economic weakness without undermining the process towards European monetary union.

In many countries, tax burdens and the distortions they cause are already high. When this is the case, the scope for further increases in tax rates is limited and the burden of fiscal adjustment will therefore have to fall to a large degree on expenditures, including transfer programmes. In most countries, increases in transfer payments have contributed importantly to the progressive deterioration of fiscal positions and, in the years ahead, population ageing will put significant further upward pressure on certain programmes, particularly public pension plans but also, in some countries, public-sector health care financing. Moreover, in many cases, the design and generosity of transfer systems, as well as the taxes needed to pay for them, have undermined economic incentives, including the incentives to work, to hire workers and to acquire skills. One result has been an erosion of the tax base and pressure on outlays, contributing to further fiscal deterioration and pressure on tax rates.

It will be important, however, to ensure that fiscal consolidation is carried out in a manner that is fair and efficient. Policies must ensure that the benefits of economic growth are shared by all and, in particular, those most in need must continue to be protected to prevent the emergence or exacerbation of poverty and social exclusion. The quality of public outlays must also be improved. Some government expenditures, including some investments in human capital and infrastructure, promote productivity increases in the longer term. Reforms to the structure of expenditures should be part of a wider effort to improve the performance of the government sector more generally. Reform of governance and management would help to ensure that government programmes are responsive to social needs and that the public receives the best possible services at the least cost.

Measures to reduce unacceptably high unemployment are also urgently required in many OECD countries, particularly in Europe, as described in the OECD *Jobs Study*. Although in several countries unemployment is still cyclical to some degree, the bulk of it is structural in nature and must be dealt with by accelerating the pace of structural reforms. Such reforms include: reducing barriers to employment and labour market flexibility; reducing both employment costs and the overall disincentives to work by reforming tax and transfer systems; enhancing the effectiveness of active labour market policies; and promoting dynamism in product markets through greater competition, entrepreneurship and effective innovation.

Structural reform in a broad range of other areas will also be important to raise medium-term growth of output and employment, and to enable OECD countries to exploit the opportunities provided by an increasingly open world economy. Currently, reform has progressed the furthest in financial markets. Even so, further measures to promote efficient transactions both internationally and within countries should be combined with measures to strengthen prudential oversight, competition and consumer protection. In other areas, notably the provision of public services (as well as labour markets), reform is far less advanced, and many regulatory barriers to both domestic and international competition still exist. Further progress in these areas, along with measures to protect those that might be seriously adversely affected by reforms, would improve economic flexibility and performance over the medium term.

The economies of the OECD are becoming increasingly integrated as a result of technological developments and of large increases in flows of international trade, financial capital and foreign direct investment. Many economies in the non-OECD area are also maturing and their role in international trade and finance is growing rapidly. These developments – which have been described by the term ''globalisation'' – will continue to have far-reaching implications for economic policy. Restoring the health of public finances and ensuring low and stable inflation will increase confidence in macroeconomic policy and help to ensure stability in global financial markets. Reforms to labour and product markets will enable economies to better exploit the benefits of increased international trade and investment opportunities. Multilateral approaches to the reduction of remaining barriers to trade and investment and to the resolution of problems common to OECD (and, increasingly, non-OECD) economies offer the best way to further expand those opportunities.

30 May 1996

OECD ECONOMIC OUTLOOK AND POLICIES

GENERAL ASSESSMENT OF THE ECONOMIC SITUATION

Output in the OECD area rose modestly during the early part of 1996, as differences in the cyclical situations of the major regions have persisted. Growth in the area is likely to average 2 per cent during the first half of this year, but should strengthen during the second half to around 2½ per cent, a pace which should be maintained during 1997. Unemployment will remain close to current levels in the United States, and will decline modestly in Japan, but it will persist at high rates in Europe. Inflation is low and should remain low nearly everywhere. Some further narrowing of current account imbalances is likely. Given the paramount priority which must be attached to restoring sound public finances, medium-term fiscal consolidation is on the agenda nearly everywhere. Consequently, the task of supporting output and employment without rekindling inflation will fall primarily on monetary policy in the years to come. Labour market performance must be improved, especially in Europe, to reduce the waste of resources and social costs which high unemployment implies and to make it easier for governments to achieve fiscal objectives. In this regard, particular attention should be paid to reform of social transfer programmes, both to improve the incentives which operate in the labour market in order better to encourage high levels of employment and to ensure control of spending as populations age.

RECENT DEVELOPMENTS AND PROSPECTS

Cyclical divergence continues in major OECD regions

Economic activity in the OECD area continued to expand at a modest pace in the early months of 1996 and real GDP growth in the area is likely to be around 2 per cent at an annual rate in the first half of this year (Table 1; see also the box ''The impact of US national accounts revisions''). Employment growth has remained weak in many countries and unemployment in the area as a whole has edged up, after having fallen in 1995, while inflation continues to be low.

This overall picture, however, embodies continued important divergences in economic developments across major OECD regions since late 1995. In the United States, a number of one-off factors that contributed to the slowdown in the final quarter of 1995 (the government shut-down, bad weather, strikes in some key industries) were no longer operating by the spring of 1996. Real GDP resumed growing at above its potential rate, underpinned by strong private consumption and continued buoyant business investment. The unemployment rate remained near 5½ per cent, and there was some pick-up in wages. Nevertheless, underlying inflation remained low and steady, reflecting slower growth in non-wage labour costs as well as stepped up labour productivity gains and a stabilisation of mark-ups. In Japan, recent indicators suggest that the expansion of demand which became apparent in the last quarter of 1995 has broadened, as a pick-up in private sector spending has reinforced public investment as a source of growth. Residential and corporate investment have grown rapidly, as profitability has continued to improve partly due to a lower cost of borrowing, correction of the earlier overvaluation of the yen exchange rate and business restructuring. Industrial production has accelerated and new orders for machinery and equipment have increased markedly. Downward pressure on prices has weakened. Despite an increase in overtime work, unemployment has started to decline. Strong import growth and an easing in the pace of stockbuilding have been the only moderating factors.

In contrast, economic activity in Europe has weakened, notably in most countries participating in the Exchange Rate Mechanism (ERM), mainly due to the lagged effects of the rise in long-term interest rates in 1994, the loss of competitiveness in many ERM countries which resulted from the turbulence in foreign exchange markets during the first half of 1995 and, in some countries, high short-term interest rates required to support exchange rates. As a result, aggregate European output fell in the last quarter of 1995, industrial production fell during the early months of 1996 in many countries and business confidence has continued to deteriorate. Growth of output in Europe in the second half of 1995 now appears to have been only 1.4 per cent of an annual rate, a significant downward revision from 2.4 per

Table 1. **Demand and ouput**

Percentage changes from the previous year, in volume

	1995	1996	1997	1996		1997	
				I	II	I	II
United States							
Final domestic demand	2.5	2.5	1.8	2.9	2.1	1.6	1.8
of which: Business fixed investment	9.7	7.3	4.8	8.8	7.3	4.1	3.6
Stockbuilding*a*	−0.4	−0.3	0.1	−0.4	0.2	0.0	0.1
Net exports*a*	−0.1	0.1	0.2	−0.2	0.1	0.3	0.1
GDP	2.0	2.3	2.0	2.4	2.5	1.8	2.0
Japan							
Final domestic demand	1.4	3.3	2.5	3.4	2.2	2.6	2.8
of which: Business fixed investment	2.9	5.2	5.6	5.0	5.2	5.7	5.8
Stockbuilding*a*	0.2	0.0	0.1	−0.1	−0.1	0.2	0.1
Net exports*a*	−0.7	−1.0	−0.2	−1.0	−0.3	−0.2	−0.2
GDP	0.9	2.2	2.4	2.2	1.7	2.5	2.7
OECD Europe							
Final domestic demand	2.3	1.9	2.6	1.9	2.2	2.7	2.7
of which: Business fixed investment	6.2	3.7	5.0	3.9	4.2	5.3	5.4
Stockbuilding*a*	0.4	−0.3	0.0	−0.8	−0.2	0.1	0.1
Net exports*a*	0.0	0.1	0.2	0.4	0.3	0.1	0.1
GDP	2.7	1.6	2.7	1.5	2.2	2.8	2.8
Total OECD							
Final domestic demand	1.7	2.3	2.3	2.5	2.4	2.3	2.4
of which: Business fixed investment	6.0	5.5	5.4	6.6	6.3	5.2	4.9
Stockbuilding*a*	0.2	−0.1	0.1	−0.2	0.1	0.0	0.1
Net exports*a*	0.0	−0.2	0.1	−0.3	0.0	0.1	0.1
GDP	1.9	2.1	2.5	2.0	2.4	2.4	2.6

a) Contributions to changes in real GDP (as a per cent of real GDP in the previous year).

The impact of US national accounts revisions

Data and projections for US national accounts series in volume terms reported here are based on the chain weights now used by the Bureau of Economic Analysis (BEA), rather than the fixed 1987 weights used previously. Chain weights change over time as relative prices and production patterns change, and tend to generate lower growth rates relative to those reported under the fixed-weight method. Data and projections reported here for the United States are, therefore, not comparable to similar data and projections reported in previous issues of the *OECD Economic Outlook* since they reflect this change in statistical procedure, as well as revisions to underlying data and changed OECD Secretariat assessments of the economic situation. For each of 1993 and 1994, the impact of this statistical change was to lower the reported growth rate of GDP in the United States by 0.6 per cent, and on the basis of the first three quarters of 1995, for which the BEA reported the growth rates on both the old and new bases, the impact for 1995 appears to have been to lower reported growth by around 0.9 per cent. A rough estimate of the impact, on average, for 1996 and beyond is to lower reported growth by ½ to ¾ per cent per year. Since the weight of the United States used to calculate area-wide aggregates is 0.37, the impact on total OECD growth might be to lower it by around 0.2 per cent or so, on average, at an annual rate.

cent estimated in *OECD Economic Outlook 58*, published last December, and for the first half of 1996 it is estimated to have been only 1.5 per cent, compared to 2.6 per cent projected previously. In this environment, unemployment has increased in many countries and inflation has declined further. In Germany, the combination of the substantial wage settlements agreed in 1995 and, until recently, the strength of the Deutschemark in effective terms has put pressure on profit margins, especially in small and medium-sized enterprises. Germany's industry has been under heavy pressure to restructure and, while direct investment by German enterprises abroad has been strong, the business investment boom in Germany itself which was expected to sustain the recovery has not materialised. In France, too, business investment has been weak, and in both countries household spending has remained subdued as consumer confidence has dropped against a background of rising unemployment. To some extent, the slowdown in activity in non-ERM countries in Europe appears to owe more to weakness in exports to ERM countries than to domestic demand. Inventory adjustments, however, have also been contributing factors in several countries, as firms have adjusted their stocks to more subdued prospects for final sales.

Against the background of weakness of activity that became increasingly apparent late last year in continental Europe, and to a lesser extent in North America, monetary conditions have eased. Short-term money market interest rates have come down since last autumn by about 2¾ percentage points in France and 1 percentage point in Germany and Italy, while in the United States they have also declined slightly (Figure 1). In Japan, they have remained around the record low levels in nominal terms that they reached last October. Margins over German rates have narrowed in France, Italy and several other European countries, while short-term interest rates in Canada have fallen below comparable US rates. In contrast, long-term interest rates, which had declined steadily during 1995, generally increased during the early months of 1996. The rise in US rates, which appears to have reflected market disappointment over the lack of budget agreement and renewed strength in economic activity, has spread to some European countries – notably Germany and the United Kingdom – and, to a lesser extent, to Japan. In Europe, long-term interest rate differentials *vis-à-vis* Germany have been reduced in many countries and those between French ten-year government bond rates and German ones have virtually disappeared for the first time since the early 1970s.

The reversal of many of the exchange rate movements of early 1995 which occurred during the second half of last year has continued, as the dollar has firmed against the Japanese yen, the Deutschemark and the Mexican peso (Table 2). Within Europe, there has been some easing of the Deutschemark against most other European currencies, especially some non-ERM currencies. Notwithstanding these recent movements, however, the real effective exchange rates of the Japanese yen and the Deutschemark in the first quarter of 1996 were still nearly 25 and 20 per cent, respectively, above their 1991 average levels, as measured by relative unit labour costs

in manufacturing (Table 3). On the other hand, in real effective terms the US dollar was some 8 per cent below its 1991 level. In Italy, the United Kingdom, Spain and Sweden, real effective exchange rates remain substantially below their 1991 levels since these countries have succeeded in preserving most of the competitiveness gains that they achieved following the European exchange market turbulence of 1992 and 1993.

Growth is set to converge across OECD regions to similar, modest rates

According to the central projections (based on a set of assumptions described in the box "Policy and other assumptions underlying the projections"), economic activity in the area as a whole in 1996 should increase at a pace similar to that of last year (2 per cent) and rise somewhat faster in 1997 at a rate of about 2½ per cent (Table 1). Growth of output in the OECD area is projected to converge, as activity in Europe picks up starting in the second half of 1996 and reaches 2¾ per cent in 1997, provided currently depressed confidence recovers rapidly. Business investment is expected to strengthen, and to be the most buoyant component of final demand growth, reflecting lagged effects of lower interest rates, a brighter export outlook and a continuing need for rationalisation. Housing investment may also recover somewhat in response to relatively low mortgage costs, government incentives and, in some countries, a stabilization of house prices. At the same time, consumer spending may grow only moderately in many countries, as real household disposable incomes are projected to grow slowly and saving behaviour is affected by continuing concerns about job prospects and future levels of taxation and social benefits. A small positive contribution

Table 3. **Changes in real effective exchange rates**[a] **in selected OECD countries since 1991**

Percentage changes between 1991 and first quarter 1996 averages

United States	−7.8
Japan	24.5
Germany	18.8
France	4.6
Italy	−28.3
United Kingdom	−10.3
Canada	−18.1
Austria	3.7
Belgium	3.3
Mexico	−14.4
Netherlands	3.5
Spain	−14.7
Sweden	−20.7
Switzerland	17.3

a) As measured by relative unit labour costs in manufacturing.

Table 2. **Movements in nominal exchange rates of selected OECD countries**

Percentage changes between second quarter 1995 and 2 May 1996[a]

	Vis-à-vis the US dollar	*Vis-à-vis* the Deutschemark	In effective terms
United States	–	9.9	9.7
Japan	−19.8	−11.8	−17.9
Germany	−9.0	–	−3.4
France	−5.3	4.1	0.5
Italy	6.4	16.9	14.7
United Kingdom	−6.0	3.3	−0.2
Canada	0.6	10.6	3.0
Austria	−9.2	−0.2	−2.7
Belgium	−8.8	0.2	−2.9
Mexico	−18.1	−10.0	−16.3
Netherlands	−8.8	0.2	−2.7
Spain	−3.1	6.5	2.6
Sweden	6.4	17.0	14.2
Switzerland	7.3	1.8	1.4

a) 2 May 1996 corresponds to the date chosen for fixing exchange-rate assumptions underlying the projections reported in this issue of the *OECD Economic Outlook*.

Figure 1. **Interest rates**

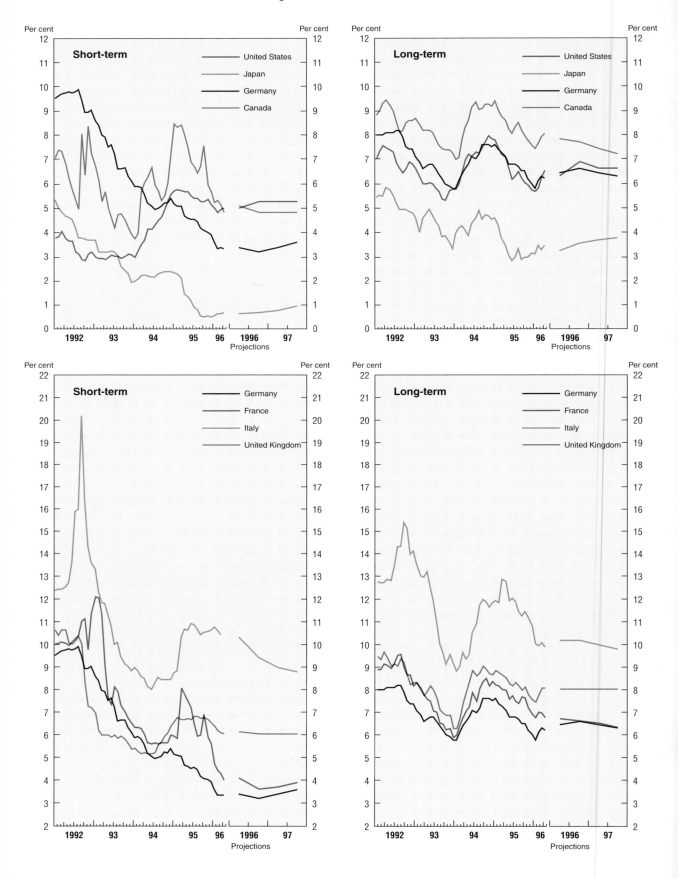

Policy and other assumptions underlying the projections

Fiscal policy assumptions are based on announced measures and stated policy intentions, where they are embodied in well-defined programmes. Members of the European Union intending to proceed with monetary union in 1999 are expected to take measures to reduce general government financial balances to 3 per cent of GDP by 1997, but this is not reflected in the projections unless the necessary concrete measures have been taken. In particular, at the time the projections were finalised, not all elements of the plans recently announced in Germany that envisage substantial net budget savings from 1997 onwards had been enacted or legislated, and therefore have not been incorporated into the projections; and for France, the Government's intention to freeze State expenditures in nominal terms has not been taken into account, as the specific measures required to achieve this had not yet been announced. For the United States, fiscal policy assumptions do not include any changes proposed by either the Administration or Congress designed to achieve a balanced budget early in the next century, pending agreement on the details of such a plan. For Japan, fiscal assumptions include an increase in the consumption tax from 3 to 5 per cent, which should yield 0.8 per cent of GDP, and termination of temporary income tax cuts, amounting to roughly 0.4 per cent GDP, in spring 1997. No further supplementary budgets are assumed, which results in a fall in public works expenditure in the second half of 1996.

Policy-controlled interest rates are assumed to be set in line with the stated policy priorities of the national authorities with respect to inflation (and in some cases to support recoveries). In Japan, a slight upward drift is built into the projection for both short- and long-term rates in 1997. In the United States, a small rise in short-term rates is assumed during the course of 1996 while long-term rates are assumed to remain around recent levels during the rest of 1996 and to ease during 1997. Among the major European countries, short-term interest rates are assumed to remain low in Germany during 1996, before rising slightly in 1997. Long-term interest rates may fall back somewhat this year and next. For some European countries (notably France), premia over German rates are assumed to decline over the projection period, while for others they are assumed to remain roughly constant.

Other important assumptions and external factors which affect the projections are the following:

- The projections assume unchanged exchange rates from those prevailing on 2 May 1996; in particular, one US dollar equals ¥ 105.3 and DM 1.53. The fixed exchange rate assumption is modified for Greece and Turkey to allow for continuous exchange rate depreciation, reflecting the OECD Secretariat's interpretation of ''official'' exchange rate policies.
- The average dollar price (OECD c.i.f. imports) of internationally traded oil is estimated to be $18.6 in the first half of 1996 and to fall back to $16.6 in the second half, a level consistent with underlying oil market conditions. In 1997, the OECD oil import price is assumed to rise in line with OECD manufactured export prices.
- Non-oil commodity prices are projected to continue to increase until end-1996, reflecting rising grain prices, and to remain broadly constant in real terms in 1997.

to growth may come from net exports, although this would be much less important than it was from 1993 to 1995.

In North America, real GDP growth is projected to proceed at a rapid pace during the course of this year before slowing to 2 per cent in 1997, mainly because of a slowdown in the United States in late 1996 and early 1997. In that country, the recent rise in long-term interest rates should moderate growth to a sustainable pace by restraining interest-sensitive components of demand. Public sector demand should also continue to act as a drag on domestic demand as fiscal policy remains tight. However, bolstered by good profits, business fixed investment should remain strong and the contribution from net exports is expected to turn positive from the second half of 1996 onward, so the economy should continue to operate near full capacity with real GDP growth averaging 2¼ per cent in 1996 and 2 per cent in 1997. In Canada, domestic demand should respond positively to lower interest rates, and net exports should continue to benefit from the lower exchange rate. Growth of real GDP could reach 3½ per cent (at an annual rate) in the second half of this year and next year. Mexico appears set to recover from the 1994 exchange-rate crisis and after a fall of almost 7 per cent in 1995, real GDP growth could rise to 4 per cent in 1997.

While recent data suggest that the recovery phase of business investment is now being established in Japan, the expansion of aggregate demand is expected to be relatively moderate by past standards, at an annual pace of about 2¼ to 2½ per cent over the next 18 months. Business investment should continue to expand at a 5 to 6 per cent rate, as the reversal of the rise in the value of the yen should contribute to improve the profit situation in key manufacturing industries. Some stimulus to private consumption growth may come from lower household saving rates, as consumer confidence strengthens. On the other hand, the drag from the foreign sector on output growth is likely to remain significant throughout 1996. However, it will be substantially reduced in 1997, as improved international competitiveness should bolster exports and with the impact of recent domestic reforms on imports gradually diminishing. This projected reduction in the drag from the foreign sector should be sufficient to offset the negative demand effect of fiscal tightening, and aggregate demand should accelerate somewhat to 2¹/₂ per cent in 1997.

Inflation should remain low nearly everywhere while high unemployment will persist in Europe

With output growth projected to average below potential rates in most countries during 1996-97, pressures on capacity should continue to ease, ensuring that inflation remains modest or continues to fall (Table 4). Thus, inflation in the OECD area (measured by the GDP deflator and excluding Turkey and Mexico) may stay at about 2 per cent both this year and next. In the United States, with the projected easing in capacity constraints

due to rapid investment growth, the absence of tensions in the labour market and favourable import price developments as a result of the dollar's recent strength, inflation is likely to remain at or around current levels of around 2¹/₄ to 2¹/₂ per cent. Inflation in Europe should stabilize over the next 18 months. In Japan, the price level may continue to fall slightly in 1996, before stabilizing in 1997 as indirect taxes rise.

Against the back-drop of modest economic growth over most of the projection period, overall OECD employment growth is likely to be weak and the OECD unemployment rate is projected to stay close to 7³/₄ per cent in both 1996 and 1997. The rate of unemployment is likely to remain close to current levels over the projection period in the United States, while it will decline modestly in Japan. In Europe as a whole, however, it is now expected to rise again to 10¹/₂ per cent this year with no improvement in prospect for 1997. For the European Union, the overall employment level in 1997 is now expected to be 2 million lower than projected six months ago in *OECD Economic Outlook 58*; the increase in total employment between 1993, a recession year, and 1997 is now projected to be less than 1 per cent. In several countries (Germany, Italy, Austria, Belgium and Portugal), employment next year is expected to be lower than it was three years ago.

World trade remains robust and international imbalances should narrow

World trade growth is now expected to slow slightly, to around 7 per cent in 1996 (from around 8¹/₂ per cent in 1995), and to re-accelerate modestly again to nearly 8 per cent in 1997 (Table 5). Trade with the non-OECD areas may continue to expand more rapidly than this, while growth of trade between OECD countries may ease in 1996 to around 3¹/₂ per cent, reflecting slower expansion of economic activity in Europe, before picking up again in 1997. Current account surpluses and deficits narrowed rapidly during the latter part of 1995. In particular, a sharp deceleration of import growth in the United States has produced a reversal of the previous increasing trend in the US deficit. Further, albeit smaller, narrowing of international imbalances is likely during the projection period, reflecting increases in US net exports and continuing falls in net exports in Japan. The United States' current account deficit is projected to decline to 1³/₄ per cent of GDP (slightly below $140 billion) and the Japanese surplus to about 1¹/₂ per cent of GDP (about $75 billion) in 1997. Europe as a whole is expected to have a stable external surplus, at around 1 per cent relative to GDP in both 1996 and 1997 (or $80 billion and $95 billion, respectively), although in Italy and some smaller countries surpluses will be considerably larger as a share of GDP.

Table 4. **Inflation and labour market developments**

	1995	1996	1997
	Per cent		
Inflation[a]			
United States	2.4	2.1	2.2
Japan	–0.5	–0.3	0.3
Germany	2.2	1.5	1.3
OECD Europe (excl. Turkey)	3.1	2.6	2.2
OECD (excl. Mexico and Turkey)	2.2	1.9	1.9
Total OECD	4.5	3.7	3.2
Employment growth			
United States	1.6	1.1	1.1
Japan	0.1	0.1	0.4
Germany	–0.2	–0.9	0.2
OECD Europe	0.8	0.3	0.8
Total OECD	1.0	0.6	0.9
	Percentage of labour force		
Unemployment rate			
United States	5.6	5.5	5.6
Japan	3.1	3.3	3.2
Germany	9.4	10.3	10.4
OECD Europe	10.3	10.5	10.4
Total OECD	7.6	7.7	7.6
	Millions		
Unemployment levels			
United States	7.4	7.4	7.5
Japan	2.1	2.2	2.1
Germany	3.6	4.0	4.0
OECD Europe	20.5	21.0	20.9
Total OECD	33.2	33.8	33.7

a) Per cent change in the GDP deflator from previous period.

Table 5. **World trade and payments summary**

	1995	1996	1997
	Percentage changes from previous period		
A. Merchandise trade volumes			
World trade[a]	8.6	6.9	7.8
of which: Manufactures	9.9	7.1	8.0
OECD exports	7.6	5.4	7.2
OECD imports	6.8	5.4	6.8
Non-OECD exports	11.3	10.3	9.0
Non-OECD imports	12.8	10.8	9.9
Memorandum items:			
Intra-OECD trade[b]	5.6	3.6	6.3
OECD exports to non-OECD	12.9	10.6	9.4
OECD imports from non-OECD	11.1	10.0	8.5
B. Trade prices[c]			
OECD exports	4.3	2.0	1.4
OECD imports	4.7	1.9	1.5
of which: Energy	4.0	2.2	0.5
Non-energy raw materials	5.1	3.8	2.7
	Per cent of GDP		
C. Current account balances			
United States	−2.1	−2.0	−1.8
Japan	2.2	1.8	1.6
OECD Europe	0.9	0.9	1.0

a) Growth rates of the arithmetic average of world import volumes and world export volumes.
b) Arithmetic average of the intra-OECD import and export volumes implied by the total OECD trade volumes and the estimated trade flows between OECD and the non-OECD areas. Data are based on the 1991 structure of trade by value, deflated by total OECD export prices.
c) Average unit values in local currency.

Risks and uncertainties surrounding the short-term outlook

In the near term, the risks to this outlook are relatively balanced. Several forces operating could lead to stronger activity than projected. Falling household saving rates are not an important factor in the central projections, providing significant support for demand in only a few countries, and that largely in 1997. Hence, there is scope for them to decline as activity picks up and confidence improves, making for stronger household spending in the OECD area as a whole. Furthermore, the recent decline in inventory accumulation represents a correction from the exceptionally high rates reached earlier in both Europe and the United States. Much of this fall was a reaction to the weakening in final demand, further aggravated in some countries by a high real interest rates. With tighter management of business inventories in relation to sales than in the past, inventories may now serve as less of a buffer against unanticipated fluctuations in final demand. As final demand strengthens, therefore, production may respond more quickly than in the past. Further-

more, if the inventory correction which is now ending has gone too far in recent quarters, a sharp stimulus from renewed stockbuilding could occur.

Particularly in Japan and some European countries, where final domestic demand has been weak for several years, there may be more pent-up demand for durable goods such as cars than is reflected in the central projections. In Japan, the improving business environment points to an upside risk regarding business investment, in particular if the decline of the yen from earlier overvalued level resumes, for example in response to the projected further reduction of the Japanese current account surplus. A further weakening of the Deutschemark and other ERM currencies against the US dollar from their levels of 2 May 1996, on which the central projections are based, may also tend to boost business investment in ERM countries. Finally, in the United States, the recent hike in long-term interest rates could be an indicator of stronger activity in the short term than projected (although it also poses a downside risk of slowing activity later in the projection period, cited below).

On the downside, business and consumer sentiment have deteriorated in continental Europe during the past year, particularly in France, but also in Germany and some smaller EU countries (Figure 2). The subjective nature of confidence and the difficulty of measuring it raise questions about how to interpret movements of these indicators. Nevertheless, experience suggests that the recovery projected for later this year may not occur unless it is accompanied by a rapid turnaround in these indicators (see box "Confidence indicators and economic activity").

Although to some degree it may reflect non-economic factors which do not affect economic behaviour, much of this "feel-bad" factor can be traced to the current economic situation itself and could threaten to restrain private consumption and investment demand in the short term:

- In continental European countries, rising unemployment rates – with over 50 per cent of the unemployed having been without work for more than a year – are clearly a contributing factor. Job turnover rates have increased in many countries and, except in the United States, the probability of a prime age male worker becoming unemployed has been rising in all major OECD countries. In the United States, the drop in voluntary quits among white-collar workers during this recovery suggests that individuals feel less secure about their professional future than in the past.
- Reduced wage and employment security have extended to sectors and population segments that have been historically considered "safe", such as public sector employees and executive and managerial workers. In all countries, the nature of employment is changing, with an increasing share of total employment accounted for by part-

Figure 2. **Business climate and consumer confidence**

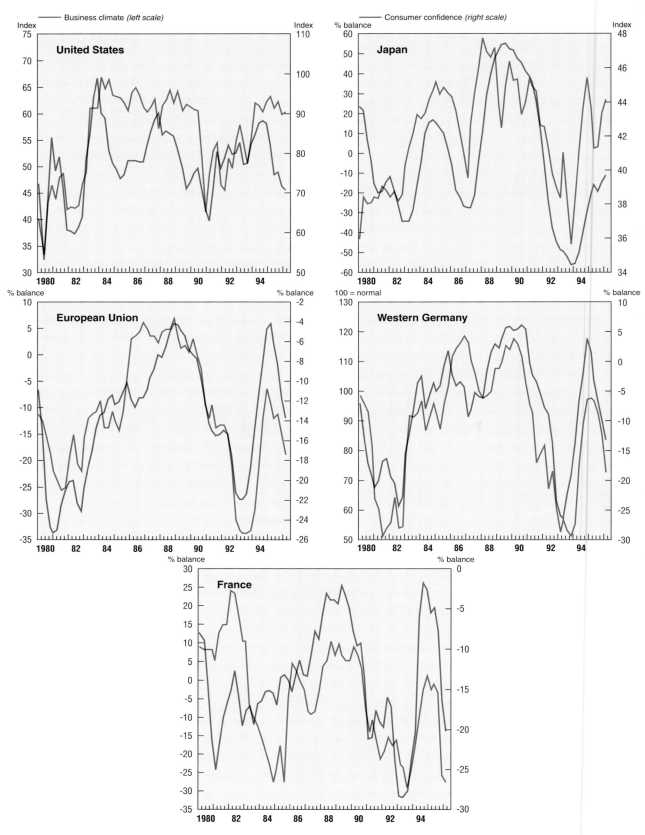

Sources: *Main Economic Indicators*, OECD and EUROSTAT.

Confidence indicators and economic activity

Confidence indicators often play a prominent role in assessments of current economic developments. However, the subjective nature of confidence raises questions about how much weight can be placed on such assessments. Confidence cannot be observed or measured directly, so applied economic analysis must rely on indicators which are often partial, qualitative and subject to various interpretations. Business and consumer sentiment measures derive from simple and rapid surveys containing a small number of questions, generally of a qualitative nature, which can be quickly answered by managers and households. By far the most important advantage of these "sentiment" measures is rapid availability, processing time in most countries being less than a month as compared to two or three months for "hard" economic data. Such indicators are useful from a "storytelling" point of view, as they sometimes appear to offer support for assertions or projections not otherwise based on very solid evidence, and large movements are often indicative of significant changes in the economic situation. But to some degree they just reflect other available information and minor fluctuations should be assessed very cautiously.

The table below shows the correlation of business and consumer sentiment indicators with the broadest measure of economic activity, real GDP growth, leading and lagging up to four quarters. The highest correlation coefficients, which are highlighted in bold in the table, indicate that there is considerable variation in the time-relationships across countries. Furthermore, consumer confidence indicators generally show less correlation with output and major demand components than do business indicators, making them a less useful tool for macroeconomic analysis.

While confidence indicators in the European Union have fallen to levels which in the past have prevailed in periods with growth below trend, they have not reached the absolute low-points that they reached in the recessions of the early 1980s or 1993 (Figure 2). However, unless a rapid turnaround is registered in the coming months, the evidence summarised in this box suggests that the hoped-for recovery in the latter part of the year could prove elusive. In Japan, while consumer confidence is buoyant, business confidence has recovered only slowly from its 1993 low, and now stands only marginally above the levels to which it fell during the slowdowns of 1983 and 1986. This suggests, here too, that the recovery could be more fragile than recent output data would suggest.

Correlation between business and consumer confidence and output[a]

The figures highlighted in bold indicate the timing relationship for which the correlation is highest in every country

	Business confidence (t) and GDP						
	GDP_{t-3}	GDP_{t-2}	GDP_{t-1}	GDP_t	GDP_{t+1}	GDP_{t+2}	GDP_{t+3}
United States	−0.04	0.17	0.46	0.74	**0.86**	0.77	0.55
Japan	0.78	0.82	**0.83**	0.78	0.72	0.65	0.56
Germany	0.25	0.40	0.52	0.60	**0.64**	0.64	0.59
France	0.40	0.65	0.85	**0.90**	0.77	0.58	0.36
Italy	0.24	0.29	0.40	0.55	**0.56**	0.48	0.36
United Kingdom	0.74	0.84	**0.90**	0.87	0.76	0.62	0.47
Canada	0.17	0.43	0.68	0.86	**0.88**	0.74	0.50
Belgium	−0.01	0.12	0.29	0.45	0.56	**0.58**	0.46
Denmark	0.41	0.41	0.58	**0.60**	0.41	0.31	0.21
Netherlands	0.22	0.36	0.50	0.60	**0.62**	0.58	0.51
Spain	0.42	0.57	0.68	0.73	**0.74**	0.71	0.65
	Consumer confidence (t) and GDP						
United States	0.50	0.60	0.67	**0.73**	0.72	0.58	0.39
Japan	0.60	0.70	0.75	**0.79**	0.79	0.74	0.72
Germany	0.16	0.22	0.32	0.37	0.39	0.46	**0.49**
France	0.38	0.53	**0.57**	0.56	0.42	0.27	0.10
Italy	0.54	0.59	0.60	**0.56**	0.52	0.45	0.36
United Kingdom	0.53	0.62	0.67	0.69	**0.71**	0.68	0.65
Canada	0.32	0.42	0.52	0.65	0.74	**0.76**	0.70
Belgium	0.52	0.58	**0.60**	0.58	0.53	0.46	0.39
Denmark	0.65	**0.68**	0.51	0.28	0.07	−0.20	−0.49
Netherlands	0.53	**0.55**	0.54	0.54	0.54	0.47	0.41
Spain	0.89	**0.91**	0.90	0.84	0.76	0.65	0.54

a) Quaterly data, year on year growth for GDP. Confidence indicators are from OECD, *Main Economic Indicators*, and Eurostat.

Figure 3. **Real money market interest rates**

Per cent

—— Short-term interest rate less core consumer price inflation[1]   —— Short-term interest rate less producer price inflation[2]

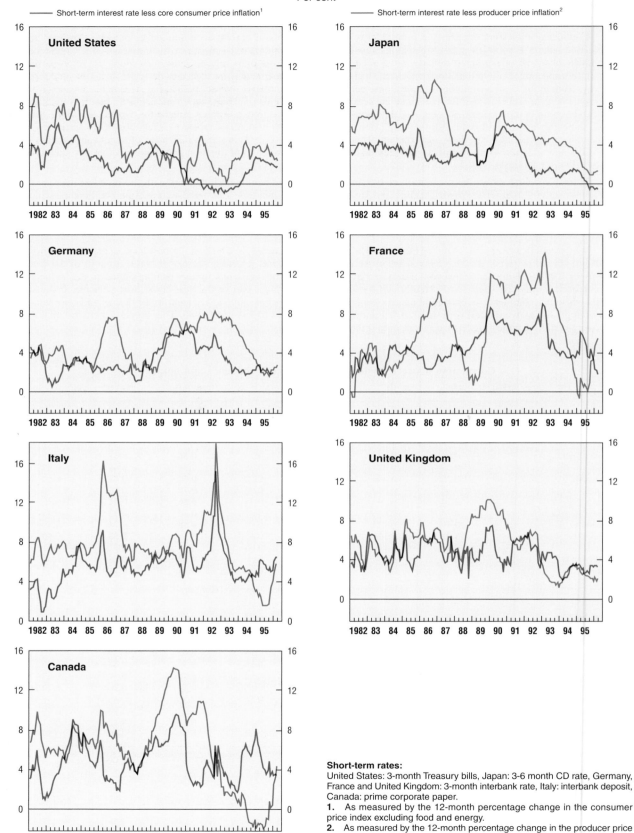

Short-term rates:
United States: 3-month Treasury bills, Japan: 3-6 month CD rate, Germany, France and United Kingdom: 3-month interbank rate, Italy: interbank deposit, Canada: prime corporate paper.
1.   As measured by the 12-month percentage change in the consumer price index excluding food and energy.
2.   As measured by the 12-month percentage change in the producer price index.

time work and temporary contracts. While for some workers this reflects lifestyle choices and increased flexibility, the share of involuntary part-time employment has been increasing in almost all countries – although research indicates that for an individual, involuntary part-time employment is a temporary phenomenon, leading to full-time or voluntary part-time work (with more hours).

– A number of governments have reacted, or are considering reacting, to unsustainable fiscal positions by reducing the generosity of unemployment insurance and other income-support systems. In addition, the realisation that population ageing will significantly raise expenditures on public pensions over the longer term contributed to decisions to reduce the generosity of public pensions. Ageing populations are also placing pressures on medical care outlays in some countries, which have probably intensified concerns about the prospects for public finances and the viability of government programmes. Although many countries have begun to address these problems, households and businesses are concerned about how further necessary measures will affect them.

In view of the urgent need for fiscal consolidation in most countries, there is a likelihood that some – especially members of the European Union intending to participate in monetary union in 1999 – will implement restrictive budgetary measures in the near term, over and above those that are already incorporated in the projections. While such measures would be strongly beneficial over the medium term, they would pose a downside risk to the projections by operating as a restraint on demand and activity in the short run, particularly if many countries acted this way at the same time (for more elaboration, see below).

A number of recent financial market developments may also represent downside risks to the projections. To the extent that the rise in long-term interest rates which has occurred in recent months reflects higher real growth prospects in the United States, stronger demand there may offset the depressive effects on other countries. However, to the degree that the rise reflects a higher risk premium because of changing perceptions about the commitment of the US authorities to agree on specific measures which would achieve a balanced budget, or about US inflation prospects, then it may have negative demand effects on the rest of the world. Moreover, higher long-term interest rates could lead to knock-on-effects in the US stockmarket, where prices have risen rapidly during the past 18 months. If these effects were severe, they could quickly affect equity prices in Japan and Europe. Particularly in Japan, this could in turn adversely affect banks' balance sheets and increase the cost of bank credit to small and medium-sized enterprises.

While the trilateral currency relationships have returned to levels more consistent with fundamentals, they could be affected by changes in market expectations of relative monetary conditions among the three largest countries. They may also be affected by uncertainties about the progress towards European monetary union. Within Europe, nominal long-term interest rates are relatively high in countries where exchange rates have depreciated against the Deutschemark and other ERM currencies closely linked to it, suggesting that the credibility of macroeconomic policy is not fully established. Any renewed exchange rate weakness in these countries would tend to redistribute demand in Europe away from countries whose exchange rates remain firm, while putting unwanted upward pressure on prices, and probably interest rates, in these depreciating countries.

MACROECONOMIC POLICY REQUIREMENTS IN THE CURRENT SITUATION

The task of supporting output and employment without rekindling inflation will fall primarily on the monetary policy authorities in the years to come. Fiscal flexibility will be very limited, since restoring sound public finances stands out as a paramount priority in a large majority of OECD countries and, indeed, medium-term fiscal consolidation is on the agenda nearly everywhere.

Nominal money market interest rates, which the authorities can strongly influence, are at historically low levels in a number of OECD countries. However, it is important not to focus on these alone in assessing the thrust of monetary policy. Given that overall inflation is now lower than it has generally been during the past quarter of a century, real money market rates, *i.e.* nominal rates adjusted for a broad measure of underlying inflation, stand out as unusually low – beyond what cyclical considerations might suggest – only in Japan (Figure 3). If nominal rates are adjusted for producer price inflation, which, from the point of view of assessing business borrowers' demand for funds to finance inventories – a demand component whose variation has acted to influence activity fairly significantly over the past few years – may be more appropriate, implied real costs are somewhat higher in some countries, notably Japan and France. More significantly, the degree to which movements in key inter-bank rates are reflected in what is occurring to actual financing costs of the non-financial business sector varies across countries. In the United States, Italy, the United Kingdom and Canada, spreads between indicators of bank credit costs to business borrowers and key nominal inter-bank money market rates have not displayed important trends since the early 1980s (Figure 4). However, in Japan, Germany and France,

Figure 4. **Differentials between lending rates and money market rates**
Percentage points

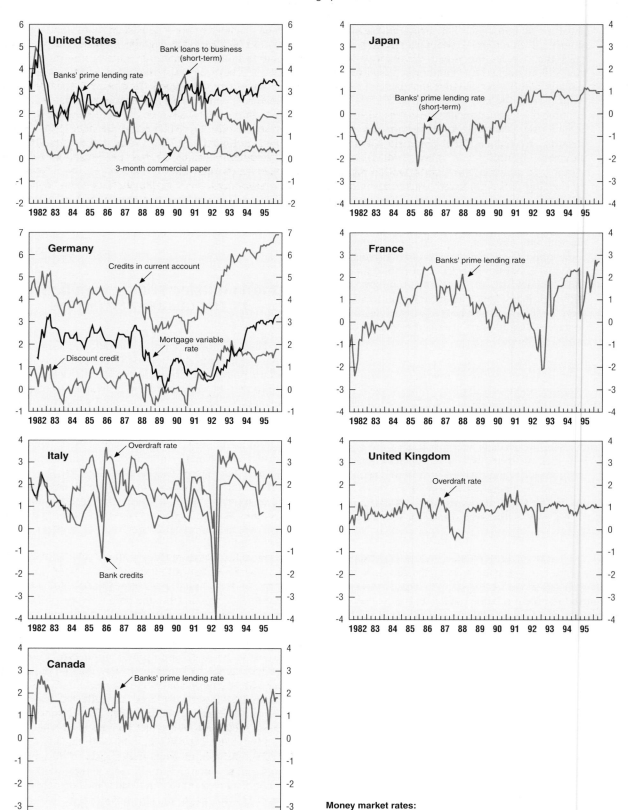

Money market rates:
United States: 3-month Treasury bills, Japan: 3-6 month CD rate, Germany, France and United Kingdom: 3-month interbank rate, Italy: interbank deposit, Canada: prime corporate paper.

these spreads have drifted up during the 1990s. Low nominal levels of inter-bank money market rates in these countries, therefore, may overstate the degree of effective monetary ease at the level of the non-financial business sector.

In the United States, given that the economy may be operating slightly above capacity, the rebound in activity during the early part of 1996 points to the need for cautious monetary policy to safeguard the progress that has been made in achieving the medium-term goal of price stability. In this regard, the substantial rise in long-term interest rates should prove to be a stabilizing force, as should the further modest fiscal tightening that is projected for 1997 (Table 6). However, if inflation pressures

start to emerge, more monetary tightening than the modest adjustment assumed in the projections is likely to be necessary.

As regards medium-term budgetary policy, the most important priority is to agree on the structural changes to entitlement programs which are ultimately necessary to put federal finances on a sound basis over the longer term. Furthermore, given reasonably strong activity, and the history of ambitious consolidation programmes that have conspicuously failed, there could be some advantage – in terms of increased credibility – in front-loading the necessary adjustments, in particular as current plans rely to some degree on lower interest rates in the future. This should ensure that projected savings

Table 6. **The fiscal outlook**

As a percentage of nominal GDP

	Financial balances[a]			Structural financial balances[b]			Gross financial liabilities[c]			Gross public debt (Maastricht criteria)[d]		
	1995	1996	1997	1995	1996	1997	1995	1996	1997	1995	1996	1997
United States[e]	−2.0	−1.9	−1.8	−2.1	−2.0	−1.8	64.3	64.1	63.8	..	..	..
Japan	−3.9	−4.8	−3.7	−2.4	−3.1	−2.0	81.3	88.8	95.4	..	..	..
Germany[f]	−3.5	−4.1	−3.6	−3.2	−3.1	−2.8	61.6	64.4	65.7	58.1	61.0	62.4
France	−5.0	−4.3	−3.7	−3.9	−2.9	−2.5	57.9	60.3	62.1	52.4	55.0	56.9
Italy	−7.2	−6.7	−6.4	−6.6	−6.1	−5.8	123.0	123.1	123.3	124.7	124.8	124.8
United Kingdom	−5.7	−4.8	−3.7	−4.6	−3.7	−3.0	57.6	60.7	62.0	54.0	57.2	58.7
Canada	−4.2	−2.9	−1.8	−2.8	−1.3	−0.6	99.1	99.4	97.9	..	..	..
Total of above countries	−3.5	−3.4	−3.0	−2.9	−2.8	−2.3	71.9	73.9	75.3	71.0	73.3	74.5
Australia[g]	−2.4	−1.9	−1.6	−2.3	−1.9	−1.6	43.8	43.0	42.0	..	..	..
Austria	−6.2	−4.0	−3.2	−6.0	−3.4	−2.3	69.4	72.3	73.9	69.4	72.3	73.9
Belgium	−4.4	−3.2	−3.7	−3.0	−1.1	−1.9	133.5	132.4	131.1	133.5	132.4	131.1
Denmark	−1.8	−1.5	−0.8	−1.1	−0.2	0.2	80.1	80.0	78.3	72.0	72.1	70.9
Finland	−5.6	−3.2	−1.2	−3.6	−1.8	−0.4	63.0	64.1	64.2	59.5	60.8	61.0
Greece[h]	−9.2	−8.0	−6.8	−8.3	−7.2	−5.9	111.5	109.4	107.3	111.5	109.4	107.3
Iceland	−3.4	−2.3	−1.9	..	..	..	55.2	54.6	53.7	..	..	..
Ireland	−2.4	−2.7	−2.6	−2.1	−2.8	−2.7	85.8	82.2	79.9	86.3	82.7	80.3
Netherlands	−3.3	−3.2	−2.7	−3.1	−2.4	−2.0	79.1	78.6	78.2	79.1	78.6	78.2
Norway[i]	3.1	3.9	3.7	−2.3	−1.3	−1.5	39.7	37.7	36.5	..	..	..
Portugal	−5.1	−4.4	−4.2	−3.9	−3.2	−3.1	70.7	71.7	72.5	70.7	71.7	72.5
Spain[j]	−6.2	−5.2	−4.7	−5.0	−3.9	−3.5	71.1	73.6	75.5	65.7	68.5	70.7
Sweden	−8.1	−5.5	−3.1	−6.7	−3.9	−1.8	81.8	83.2	81.5	79.9	81.3	79.8
Total of above EU countries	−5.3	−4.8	−4.1	−4.5	−3.7	−3.2	76.3	78.1	79.0	73.6	75.5	76.5
Total of above OECD countries	−3.6	−3.5	−3.0	−3.1	−2.8	−2.3	72.4	74.2	75.4	..	..	..

a) General government fiscal surplus (+) or deficit (–). Members of the European Union intending to proceed with monetary union in 1999 are expected to take measures to reduce deficits to at most 3 per cent of GDP in 1997, but the projections reported here only reflect concrete measures that have so far been announced.

b) OECD Secretariat estimates of the structural component of general government financial balances as a per cent of potential GDP. The estimates are surrounded by large margins of error, reflecting uncertainty as to the present size and future growth of potential output, and the degree to which elimination of the output gap into enhanced tax revenues and reduced expenditure. For a discussion of the methodology, see ''Potential ouput, output gaps and structural budget balances'', Giorno, C. et al., OECD Economic Studies No. 24, 1995/1.

c) General government gross financial liabilities according to SNA definitions.

d) The Maastricht definition of gross public debt is based on data provided by the Commission of the European Communities for 1995, projected forward in line with the OECD Secretariat's projections for GDP and general government financial liabilities while taking into account, to the extent possible, of governments' policies for acquisitions of financial assets.

e) Financial balances exclude deposit insurance outlays, but includes cash flow surplus of federal, state and local government employee pension schemes.

f) Includes balance and debt of the German Railways Fund and of the Inherited Debt Fund.

g) Debt data refer to fiscal years data ending June 30. Includes indebtedness of local government towards other levels of general government.

h) The financial liabilities shown are not fully consolidated within general government sector.

i) The structural balances exclude revenues from oil production, and are shown as a percentage of mainland potential GDP.

j) Social security payments and contributions are included on a cash basis. The Spanish authorities estimate that if an accruals adjustment were made, which would be more consistent with the principles of the System of National Accounts, the financial balance would be 5.8 per cent of GDP in 1995.

Table 8. **Long-term interest rate differentials**[a] *vis-à-vis*
Germany in EU countries

Average of 24 and 27 May
Percentage points

Netherlands	–0.13
France	–0.01
Austria	0.02
Belgium	0.24
Finland	0.80
Denmark	0.94
Ireland	1.00
United Kingdom	1.62
Sweden	2.00
Portugal	2.52
Spain	2.71
Italy	3.16

a) Redemption yield of 10-year benchmark government bonds.
Source: Datastream, Financial Times for Portugal.

ities based on the assumption that it might be abandoned. This option would probably lead to unwanted exchange rate turbulence within Europe.

Although some interest rate differentials at short and intermediate maturities persist, there has been a convergence of long-term bond rates in several ERM countries, notably Germany and France, to levels considerably below those in other EU countries (Table 8). This suggests that markets regard as fairly likely a scenario in which several countries proceed more or less on schedule to monetary union, including some countries where underlying fiscal positions are improving at a satisfactory pace and which have low inflation and stable exchange rate relationships, even though their actual budget deficits may not be reduced to 3 per cent of GDP. Should the process evolve along these lines, it will be important that it include specific measures or arrangements which ensure that governments will improve their underlying fiscal positions after 1997 in all participating countries beyond what is required by the Maastricht criteria. Such arrangements, together with credible commitment to price stability in monetary union, would bring about greater convergence of interest rates throughout the maturity spectrum in these countries at low levels and help to improve debt dynamics, further improving the sustainability of fiscal positions over time.

MEDIUM-TERM MACROECONOMIC POLICY ISSUES

Monetary policy and OECD-wide fiscal consolidation over the medium-term

Budget deficit reductions are already under way in North America and Europe, and are likely to be on the agenda in Japan now that the recovery appears well established. If programmes are successfully implemented in all three major regions to make substantial progress towards balanced fiscal positions, this will represent a unique situation in recent history where fiscal consolidation will take place simultaneously in virtually all OECD countries, and for several successive years. A policy challenge will be to ensure that simultaneous fiscal consolidation – which could amount to around 3 per cent of OECD GDP between 1996 and 2001 (slightly more than 0.5 per cent of OECD GDP a year) – does not have substantial adverse short-run effects on activity in the OECD area and generates longer-term gains smoothly. Monetary policy will have to be used to avoid this short-run risk, but care will have to be taken to avoid jeopardising the progress that has been made in bringing down inflation.

Adjustment mechanisms

There is no clear agreement about how fiscal retrenchment affects the economy. One generally-held view is that, while it reduces aggregate domestic demand in the short term in the country undertaking it, over the longer term, the downward pressure on interest rates and exchange rates associated with weaker demand work to offset the original negative impact on demand. This simple analysis is however subject to several qualifications. If confidence improves (say because the consolidation is seen to be addressing an unsustainable public finance position), private expenditure may be favourably affected even before taking account of financial market reactions to the prospect of lower budget deficits. Expectations can – and usually do – also play a very important role in the adjustment process, by inducing a very rapid reaction in financial markets, which may in turn affect the balance of importance of the various adjustment mechanisms. A highly credible commitment to reduce budget deficits could, for example, favourably affect long-term interest rates and at the same time lead to a stronger, rather than a weaker, exchange rate as market expectations take account of future improvements in the current account. In this case, private investment would play a greater role in sustaining output and activity, and in improving current account positions through enhanced non-price competitiveness. This, together with any initial terms-of-trade gains, would work to offset the negative effects of currency appreciation on net export volumes. On the other hand, if markets focus on the prospects for interest rates, rather than external adjustment, the exchange rate may depreciate immediately, crowding in net exports in volume terms even before the effects of fiscal consolidation on aggregate domestic demand are actually felt. Despite initial terms-of-trade losses, current account positions might improve, as currency depreciation and stronger business investment might strengthen price and non-price competitiveness, respectively.

The prospect of simultaneous fiscal consolidation in all major regions implies that in each region these adjustments will occur against the background of similar adjustments taking place internationally. Thus, the scope for exchange rate depreciation to crowd in net exports in individual countries is likely to be considerably reduced – and in some countries may not even play a role. Ultimately, offsetting the direct negative demand effects of generalised fiscal contraction may require substantially lower interest rates than when consolidation is pursued unilaterally. The risk of negative effects on activity is correspondingly much greater in the context of joint, as opposed to individual, fiscal contraction, as some important adjustment mechanisms may be less reliable.

The design of monetary policy

Determining the appropriate response of monetary policy in each region will depend on the extent, pace and credibility of consolidation, both at home and internationally. The main issue with respect to timing are whether some monetary policy easing and, if so, how much, should take place in advance of consolidation, *i.e.* as a "down payment" on fiscal consolidation once the relevant budget measures have been announced. The case in favour of such early monetary policy response is that, particularly where consolidation is fully credible, an immediate easing, by offering the prospect of a rapid decline in real short- and long-term interest rates, might nearly completely offset any short-run negative domestic demand impact of budget deficit cuts. Because monetary policy stimuli appear generally to take longer to affect demand than fiscal restriction, monetary easing should come sooner rather than later to support activity.

There are however several reasons why it might be more advisable to phase in the easing of monetary policy in line with the progress of fiscal consolidation. First, a fully pre-emptive shift in monetary policy could raise questions about credibility, in particular when announced fiscal consolidation programmes are not seen as fully credible by the markets; in such a situation an easing of monetary policy might lead to higher long-term interest rates with potentially damaging effects on the economy. Second, other forces are always operating on the economy – among them, fiscal consolidation in other countries and developments outside the OECD area. These forces are likely to influence the extent of any monetary policy adjustments that are appropriate and, conceivably on some occasions, the direction. Third, the extent to which an accommodating shift in monetary policy is likely to be necessary will be influenced by the degree to which financial markets reduce long-term interest rates in anticipation of consolidation. The fall in long-term interest rates in 1995 in the United States, for example, appears to have been at least partly in anticipation of a credible deficit reduction plan, and the recent increase in bond yields as the economy has strengthened illustrates the extent to which financial market behaviour can at times be a stabilising macroeconomic force, limiting the need for specific action by the monetary authorities.

Illustrative scenarios

To illustrate the potential interactions between monetary and fiscal policies and their implications on the economic performance of OECD countries, a series of simulations has been run with the OECD Secretariat's INTERLINK model to the year 2001 (Figure 5). The first of these simulations is a "non-consolidation" scenario in which countries are assumed to take no further measures beyond the ones incorporated in the short-term projections.[4] Two alternative scenarios have also been built,[5] both of which assume that measures will be taken in all countries to achieve broadly balanced budget by 2001. These measures incorporate a reduction in income transfers in the United States and the European Union, and indirect tax increases in Japan. The two "consolidation" scenarios differ in that fiscal consolidation is assumed to take place either unilaterally or simultaneously in the three major OECD regions. In the two consolidation scenarios presented here, it has been assumed that pursuit of sound fiscal policies will entail substantial credibility gains, in terms of falls in long-term interest rates (Table 9), especially in countries where the current fiscal situation is clearly unsustainable. This assumption is crucial in cushioning the response of domestic demand in the short run and in generating the ensuing recovery. If credibility gains were assumed to be less important, the adverse effects on aggregate demand would be more pronounced in all regions and a more aggressive monetary policy easing would be necessary to achieve the same performance for real GDP and unemployment as in a fully credible consolidation scenario.

Comparing the scenarios suggests that:

- fiscal consolidation will adversely affect aggregate demand in the short run, the more so if pursued simultaneously in many OECD countries;
- while the exchange rate plays an important role in single-country consolidation, simultaneous fiscal consolidation largely rules out the mechanism for crowding in net exports to stabilize aggregate demand;
- a decline in interest rates is the main mechanism generating a recovery in aggregate demand when all countries pursue fiscal consolidation simultaneously;
- the decline in interest rates *per se* makes a substantial contribution to fiscal consolidation in European countries because it will reduce the burden of servicing the large public debt;
- monetary policy could be used to offset the adverse short-run effects of fiscal consolidation on aggregate demand without endangering inflation objectives;

Figure 5. **Impact of fiscal consolidation**

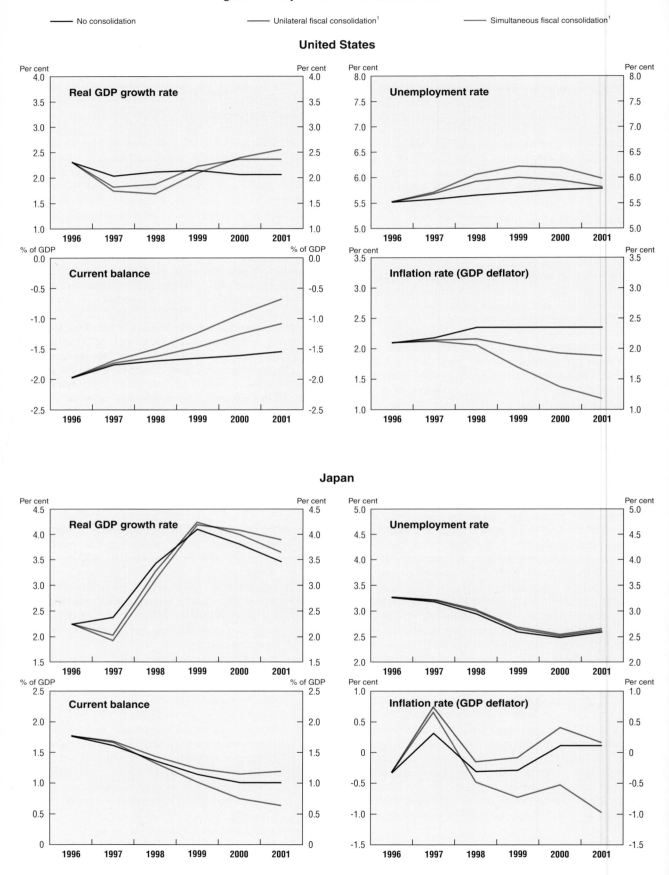

— No consolidation   — Unilateral fiscal consolidation[1]   — Simultaneous fiscal consolidation[1]

Figure 5. *(cont'd)* Impact of fiscal consolidation

—— No consolidation   —— Unilateral fiscal consolidation[1]   —— Simultaneous fiscal consolidation[1]

European Union

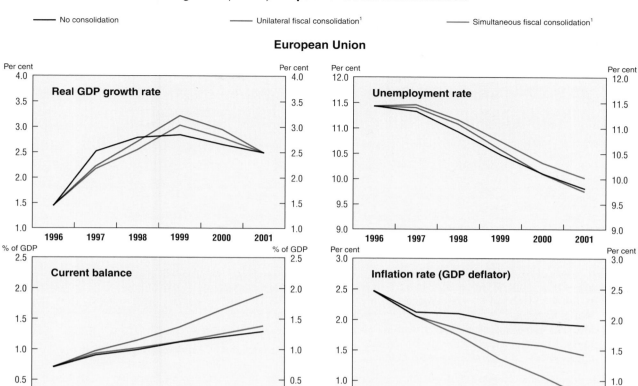

Memorandum item : General government financial balances

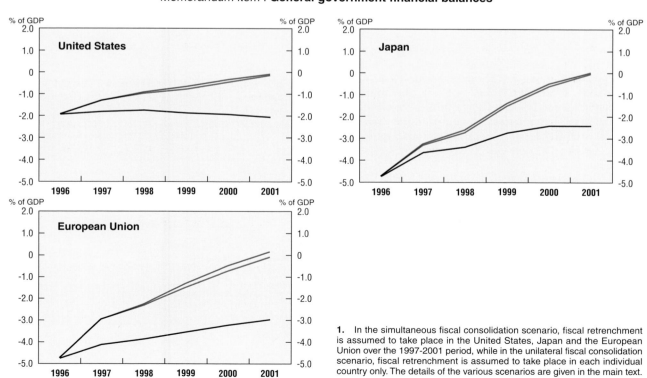

1. In the simultaneous fiscal consolidation scenario, fiscal retrenchment is assumed to take place in the United States, Japan and the European Union over the 1997-2001 period, while in the unilateral fiscal consolidation scenario, fiscal retrenchment is assumed to take place in each individual country only. The details of the various scenarios are given in the main text.

Table 9. **Interest rate assumptions in alternative fiscal consolidation scenarios**

Per cent

	No consolidation[a]			Simultaneous fiscal consolidation[b]			Unilateral fiscal consolidation[b]		
	1997	1999	2001	1997	1999	2001	1997	1999	2001
Short-term interest rates									
United States	5.3	5.1	5.1	4.9	3.2	2.6	5.0	3.6	3.4
Japan	0.9	4.5	4.0	0.8	3.1	2.0	0.9	3.9	3.2
Germany	3.5	4.7	4.7	3.2	3.0	2.9	3.2	3.2	3.4
Long-term interest rates									
United States	6.6	6.6	6.6	6.3	5.1	4.5	6.4	5.4	5.2
Japan	3.7	4.6	4.4	3.6	2.9	2.1	3.7	3.7	3.3
Germany	6.4	6.5	6.2	5.9	4.5	3.7	6.0	4.7	4.2

a) This scenario assumes no change in fiscal policy beyond what is implied by legislation already in place in the short-term projections.

b) In the simultaneous fiscal consolidation scenario, fiscal retrenchment is assumed to take place in the United States, Japan and the European Union over the 1997-2001 period, while in the unilateral fiscal consolidation scenario, fiscal retrenchment is assumed to take place in each individual region only. The details of the various scenarios are given in the main text and the results are reported in Figure 5.

– a given amount of monetary easing in response to fiscal consolidation is less successful in stabilizing aggregate demand when other countries also are pursuing fiscal consolidation; accordingly, monetary policy must be eased more aggressively to smooth aggregate demand.

The results also suggest that the choice between tax increases and expenditure cuts in implementing fiscal consolidation may have important implications for aggregate demand in the short run, and hence for the response of monetary policy. In particular, where increases in indirect taxes are reflected in future wage settlements and the general price level, they offset any tendency for real exchange rate depreciation to crowd in net exports.

Linkages with the non-OECD area

Another important element that OECD policy makers will need to consider is the extent to which non-OECD countries might be affected by widespread fiscal consolidation in the OECD area and how this might in turn generate second-round effects in OECD countries. Given the rising importance of a number of non-Member countries as OECD countries' trading partners, spillovers between OECD and non-OECD regions may be potentially large.

An important channel through which OECD and non-OECD countries' economic situations might interact is the exchange rate. Even if OECD-wide fiscal consolidation were not to result in large variations in exchange rates within the OECD area, it may nevertheless induce a real appreciation in the exchange rates of non-OECD countries.[6] This loss in non-OECD competitiveness, in particular by countries which currently represent important competitors in world markets such as those in Southeast Asia, could allow a crowding in of net exports in the OECD area (see box "The effects of exchange rate appreciation in the Dynamic Asian Economies" in the chapter "Economic Developments in Selected non-OECD Countries") and help dampen the negative demand effects of simultaneous fiscal contraction.

Over the longer term, the widespread decline in interest rates that is expected to accompany fiscal consolidation in the OECD area might lower the cost and increase the availability of funds on international capital markets and thus *inter alia* facilitate the financing of spending by non-OECD countries, with potentially favourable consequences for OECD export market growth for capital goods. Moreover, lower OECD-wide interest rates should work to improve the foreign debt dynamics of the many non-OECD countries with large external indebtedness. This would ease the balance of payments constraint that a number of them are currently facing and further increase their ability to import, again

Table 10. **Impact on non-OECD regions' current account of simultaneous fiscal consolidation in OECD countries**[a]

$ billion

	Difference from "non-consolidation" scenario		
	1997	1999	2001
Current account			
Total non-OECD	–6	8	18
of which: Four Asian NIES	–3	2	7
Other Asian countries	–2	2	4
South and Central America	0	3	3
Investment income balance			
Total non-OECD	2	20	33
of which: Four Asian NIES	0	–1	–3
Other Asian countries	1	7	13
South and Central America	1	11	17

a) Details of this simulation are given in the main text and results are reported in Figure 5.

20

favourably affecting OECD export market growth. The positive effects stemming from lower OECD interest rates are likely to be more important in South and Central America and some lower income Asian countries which have a larger foreign debt and rely more on international capital markets to finance domestic investment than other non-OECD countries, *e.g.* in South-east Asia where rates of domestic saving are higher (Table 10). Overall, given the high degree of integration of European trade and hence the relatively smaller importance of Asian and South and Central American countries as trading partners,[7] the burden of adjustment in European countries is likely to fall somewhat more on lower domestic interest rates to generate a recovery in aggregate demand than is likely to be the case in either the United States or Japan.

Ensuring monetary policy credibility

Credible commitments to non-inflationary monetary policies, can favourably influence nominal wage and price formation throughout the economy, lead to lower inflation premia in market interest rates and thereby contribute to a favourable environment for decisions about current resource allocation and new investment. A number of things can be done to enhance the credibility of these commitments.

First, changes in monetary policy frameworks which convince financial markets that the likelihood of establishing a stable non-inflationary environment has increased may assist in enhancing credibility. Such changes may be institutional, involving strengthening or clarifying the central banks' mandate to achieve medium-term price stability and establishing its autonomy with regard to its operations. There has been a general trend in this direction, as several central banks have become more independent of political control over their operating decisions, either formally (as in New Zealand) or de facto. The legal framework on which the European System of Central Banks is being established is built along these lines and the Maastricht process has already led to greater central bank operating independence and clearer emphasis on price stability as central banks' ultimate goal. Even in some countries where adjustments of the basic monetary policy stance continue to reserve an important role for the Government (for example, in the United Kingdom), greater transparency about the decision making process, explicit government recognition of the need to direct monetary policy toward inflation control, and a framework which requires the authorities to be forward looking appear to be contributing to improved performance. In Japan, the revision of the current central bank law, introduced during the war period and modified only partially in the immediate post-war period, is now under discussion.

Second, approaches to policy formulation which increase the pressure that monetary authorities apply to themselves to pursue non-inflationary policies may also enhance credibility. These approaches usually involve the announcement of price objectives specified in nominal terms. Particularly where countries have been unwilling to commit themselves to exchange rate objectives, this has increasingly taken the form of adopting explicit inflation targets (Table 11), as most countries have found monetary aggregates difficult to control and only loosely related to inflation performance. Numerical inflation targets, often combined with periodic publication of inflation reports and forecasts, have advantages in terms of framing the public debate about monetary policy in terms of its ultimate policy objective and offering a transparent means for the public to judge monetary authorities' performance. Substantial progress toward price stability has been made in countries where such practice has been used. However, many other countries which have not introduced inflation targets have also made significant progress toward price stability. Many of the countries which have adopted inflation targets have histories of high inflation, and current levels of nominal long-term interest rates generally remain high relative to reasonable estimates of potential output and targeted inflation rates. This suggests that targets are not yet fully credible. For this approach to be fully effective, it will be important that targets are regularly achieved over a sustained period, so that clear non-inflationary track records are built up over time.

Table 11.   **Numerical inflation objectives: selected countries**[a]

Per cent

Italy	2.5	Target by 1998
United Kingdom	2.5 or less	Target over a two-year horizon
Canada	1 – 3	Target range through to 1998
Australia	2 – 3	"Central tendency" for inflation over the business cycle
Finland	2	Current target
New Zealand	0 – 2	Current target range
Spain	3	Target by 1997
Sweden	2 ± 1	Current target range

a) The price indexes that these objectives refer to are as follows:
Italy: Private consumption deflator;
United Kingdom: Retail price index excluding mortgage interest payments;
Canada: The consumer price index is the official target, but an underlying consumer price index excluding food, energy, and temporary effects of indirect taxes is used as an operational objective;
Australia: Consumer price index adjusted for interest rates, energy, food and certain public sector goods;
Finland: Consumer price index excluding indirect taxes, subsidies and housing capital costs;
New Zealand: "Underlying" consumer price index which excludes "significant" changes resulting from changes to indirect taxes, government charges, the terms of trade, direct effects from interest rates (mainly effects from mortgage interest rates) and as might results from a major natural disaster;
Spain: Consumer price index;
Sweden: Consumer price index.

Productivity growth and employment

Generating the resources necessary to achieve social objectives and raise living standards over the medium term will require steady improvements in productivity. Equally important, it will require effectively mobilising a large part of the potential labour force which is willing to work. The *OECD Jobs Study* identified a number of structural rigidities that reduced employment opportunities for low skill workers and which have been associated with declining employment rates (the ratio of employment to the working-age population) and rising unemployment rates. These developments are consistent with the observed paradox that a number of countries with high productivity growth as measured by output per worker have been characterised by low productivity growth as measured by output per working-age person.

Figure 6 compares average growth over the past 15 years in output per employed worker (a common measure of productivity) with output per working-age person (a measure that is constructed by assuming constant participation and unemployment rates). Countries above the 45° line had rising employment rates, while countries below it had falling employment rates over this period. Falling employment rates in Europe and a rising employment rate in the United States help to explain why output per working-age person grew less rapidly in Europe than in the United States despite relatively high productivity growth.

In this context, countries that succeed in increasing employment rates by eliminating structural rigidities and, in particular, barriers to the employment of low-skill workers may experience a slowdown in average productivity growth even as output per working-age person increases. But this slowdown will only be temporary, reflecting the effect on average productivity levels of a rising proportion of low productivity workers in total employment. Once the process of re-integration is complete, this transitional effect on average productivity will come to an end, and the higher underlying trend growth of productivity will be re-established.

Japan has enjoyed rapid growth of output per working-age person and a rise in the employment rate over the past 15 years, although employment growth has been restrained during the most recent years due to the protracted cyclical downswing. This points to this country's success in adapting to technological progress and creating more skilled jobs.

Figure 6. **Output per working-age person and per employed worker, 1980-95**

Annual average growth rates

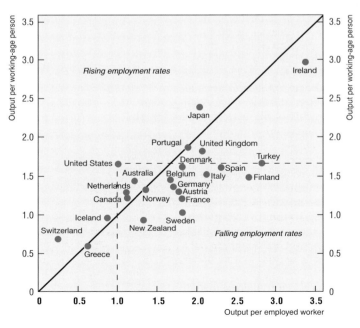

1. Western Germany.

22

Third, restoration of sound fiscal positions, which would raise national savings, reduce interest rate pressure and encourage private investment, would have a favourable effect. In the context of non-inflationary monetary policies, large budget deficits can lead to high real interest rates, exchange rate pressure, rapid increases in public debt and allocative distortions. These may lead to market doubts about the monetary authorities' ability to persevere with policies geared to price stability.

Fourth, improved structural policies, particularly as they affect labour markets, would reassure financial markets that non-inflationary policies can be sustained. Particularly in Europe, structural rigidities that have resulted in high unemployment have affected the credibility of monetary policy.[8] Doubts about the resolve of governments to persevere with non-inflationary policies in the face of high unemployment have on several occasions required large interest rate premia to fend off currency speculation. The fact that on some occasions these doubts have proved to be correct has made these premia difficult to avoid, particularly in countries which have not yet established non-inflationary track records.

LABOUR MARKET PERFORMANCE, BUDGET CONTROL AND SOCIAL TRANSFERS

Improved labour market performance and fiscal implications

Labour market performance remains unsatisfactory in many OECD countries, especially in Europe. The persistence of high unemployment, the large number of long-term unemployed and the high incidence of youth unemployment impose hardship on many households and individuals and adversely affect the social cohesion of many European countries. High levels of unemployment also entail high costs in terms of waste of human resources and lost output. The challenge ahead in many countries will be to implement reforms that educate and mobilise the working-age population effectively in order to promote a high level of employment, while ensuring that incentives are in place to utilise available human resources in the most effective and productive way (see box ''Productivity growth and employment''). Provided such reforms are complemented by flexible product markets, open to competition which encourages the development and diffusion of new technology, OECD countries will be able to enjoy the combination of higher output growth and higher employment, while at the same time generating the resources needed to achieve better distribution of income and other social goals.

Improved labour market performance will also assist greatly in meeting fiscal policy objectives. First, it will reduce the need for income support and unemployment insurance programmes, allowing governments to cut budget deficits or lower tax rates more easily. Direct costs of unemployment, measured by public spending on various labour market programmes including unemployment benefits, have risen considerably since the early 1980s in many European countries (Figure 7, panel A). Given that such measures of direct unemployment costs represent only part of the expenditures which result from high unemployment levels,[9] significantly reducing the number of unemployed could entail important government savings in countries such as Germany, Belgium, Denmark, Finland, Ireland, Spain and Sweden, where direct costs exceed 4 per cent of GDP.

Second, increased participation in the labour market will enhance government revenues by raising the overall tax base. Based on a very simple set of assumptions, OECD Secretariat estimates suggest that each 1 per cent increase in employment might on average raise government revenues by about 0.2 percentage point of GDP.[10] This means that in the European Union, if employment were raised to achieve the stated policy goal of halving the current unemployment rate by end-century, which would also normally involve a rising participation rate, the implied widening of the tax base could bring in additional tax revenues amounting to perhaps 2 per cent of GDP.[11] The employment-induced improvement in public finances might also allow for a reduction in the high marginal tax rates prevailing in a number of countries. More generally, the overall fiscal gains induced by improved labour market performance would allow crowding in of private sector investment or help reduce the labour supply and demand distortions associated with high tax rates, in both cases raising potential output.

Implications of budget control for labour markets and social transfers

While better labour market performance might positively contribute to budget reductions, it is also clear that, likewise, the process of budgetary restraint in which most Member countries are engaged will impinge on the functioning of labour markets. Experience with previous episodes of fiscal consolidation shows that governments have usually resorted to increases in taxation to cut budget deficits (see the chapter ''The Experience with Fiscal Consolidation in OECD Countries''). Between 1965 and 1995 tax receipts in the OECD as a whole rose from 26 to 35 per cent of GDP and from 30 to 41 per cent in Europe.

Both taxes and the transfers they are partly used to finance have an impact on labour market outcomes. On the tax side, there is considerable cross-country variance both in overall levels and in structures, *i.e.* in the extent to which taxes are levied on businesses, household incomes, consumption expenditure or other items. Nevertheless, one way or another most taxes insert a wedge

Figure 7. **Labour market performance, public expenditure and taxation**

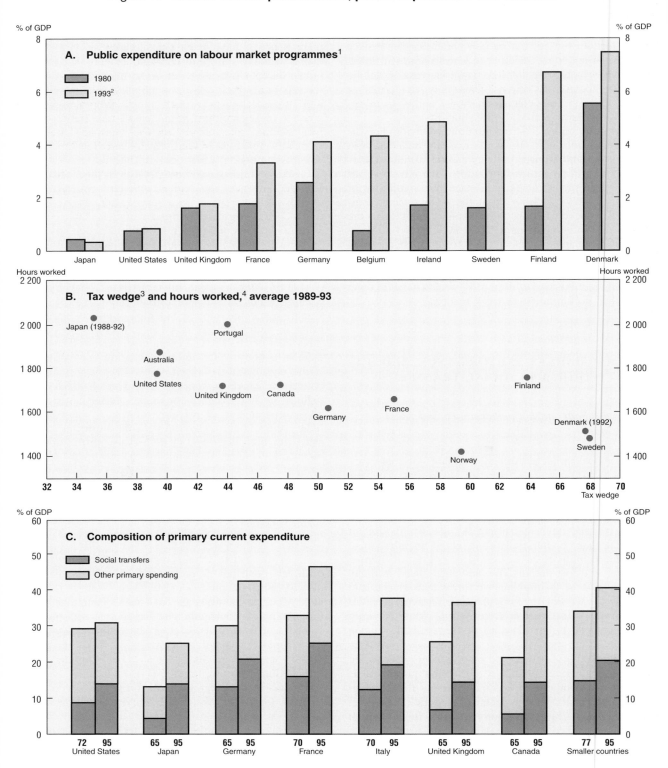

1. All government spending on active and passive labour market measures.
2. 1992 figures for Belgium and Japan.
3. The tax wedge is the difference between the costs for employers of hiring labour and the purchasing power of wage earners. It can be expressed as $[1 - (1 - t_1)(1 - t_2)]$ where: $t_1 = $ (Employers' + employees' social security contributions + household direct taxes)/(labour compensation); and $t_2 = $ Indirect taxes/private consumption.
4. Hours worked are divided by employed persons.

between the real cost to employers of hiring labour and the purchasing power of wage earners.[12] Over the past two decades, tax increases have often taken the form of rises in social security contributions. Where this has not been accompanied by corresponding real wage restraint, overall labour costs have gone up and labour demand has fallen. Among the factors acting to reduce necessary wage flexibility in many countries are excessive minimum wages and insufficiently responsive wage bargaining structures.

Labour supply is also affected. On the one hand, higher taxes imply that people have to work more to reach a certain living standard. On the other, the return to working an extra hour, or to invest in human capital, is reduced. This may be why countries with a high tax wedge, mainly accounted for by a very high household tax pressure, such as the Nordic countries, combine very high labour force participation rates with a low average number of hours worked, whereas in other countries with equally high labour force participation but a low tax pressure, such as the United States, Japan and the United Kingdom, average hours worked are much higher (Figure 7, panel B).

Maintaining unchanged overall tax pressure, let alone reducing it, will require stepped-up expenditure control, in particular for social transfers which have generally tended to rise more rapidly than other forms of government spending (Figure 7, panel C). In the coming decades, OECD Member countries will have to face the problem of ageing of their populations and under current pension rules, it is clear that meeting pension obligations will entail significant rises in public expenditure. As populations grow older other related expenditure, such as health care, will also tend to rise. Offsetting these additional expenditures by tax increases would require increases in tax-to-GDP ratios estimated at more than 5 percentage points in most OECD countries in 2030 (Table 12). Where tax pressure is already high, such further increases may have repercussions on labour markets and elsewhere which would render them unsustainable.

Reform of social transfer programmes will be important both in order to control government spending and for improving utilisation of labour resources. These programmes perform an important role in limiting individual hardship and thereby helping to maintain social cohesion. But they also involve significant budgetary costs and they may, as a side effect, raise structural unemployment. Where lack of a job is the criterion for receipt of transfers, there is a risk that people become trapped in unemployment. And where transfers are income-tested, people may become trapped in poverty because higher labour income would elicit lower transfers and higher taxes. Shifting transfers towards more income-testing may weaken the unemployment trap but will tend to strengthen the poverty trap. Reducing the generosity of income transfers will weaken both unemployment and poverty traps but may conflict with equity objectives.[13]

Table 12. **Estimated impact of ageing population on government expenditure on pensions and health care**[a]

Per cent of GDP

	2010			2020			2030		
	Pensions	Health	Total	Pensions	Health	Total	Pensions	Health	Total
United States	0.3	0.1	0.3	1.0	0.7	1.7	2.4	1.8	4.3
Japan	3.1	0.5	3.5	6.0	1.1	7.0	6.3	1.2	7.5
Germany	0.2	0.0	0.2	0.7	0.1	0.9	5.0	0.8	5.8
France	0.0	0.2	0.2	1.9	1.0	2.9	3.8	1.8	5.6
Italy	0.6	0.1	0.7	2.6	0.5	3.1	7.7	1.7	9.4
United Kingdom	0.7	0.2	0.8	0.6	0.3	0.9	1.0	1.1	2.1
Canada	0.2	0.3	0.5	1.8	1.4	3.2	3.9	3.1	7.1
Australia	0.0	0.1	0.1	0.6	0.7	1.3	1.5	1.8	3.3
Belgium	−1.0	0.0	−1.0	1.0	0.8	1.8	4.2	2.2	6.4
Denmark	1.2	0.4	1.6	2.9	1.0	3.9	4.5	1.6	6.1
Finland	1.3	0.3	1.6	5.8	1.5	7.2	8.4	2.7	11.1
Iceland	0.0	0.0	0.1	0.7	0.7	1.5	1.9	1.9	3.8
Ireland	−0.3	0.0	−0.3	−0.1	0.4	0.3	−0.1	0.7	0.6
Netherlands	1.0	0.5	1.5	3.7	1.7	5.3	6.9	3.3	10.2
Norway	1.1	0.0	1.1	3.7	0.9	4.6	6.0	1.9	7.9
Portugal	1.2	0.0	1.2	2.7	0.3	3.0	6.1	1.0	7.1
Spain	0.2	0.1	0.3	1.5	0.6	2.1	4.2	1.8	6.1
Sweden	1.3	0.2	1.5	2.8	0.9	3.7	3.9	1.6	5.5
Total OECD	0.8	0.2	0.9	2.1	0.7	2.9	3.9	1.7	5.6

a) Calculated as projected spending on pensions and health, based on current policies and projected demographic changes, minus spending based on no change in the respective expenditure to GDP ratios after the year 2000. For further details, see Leibfritz, W. *et al.*, ''Ageing populations, pension systems and government budgets: scenarios for 20 OECD countries'', *OECD Economics Department Working Papers* (forthcoming).

THE INFLUENCE OF FINANCIAL MARKET FLUCTUATIONS
ON THE CURRENT ECONOMIC EXPANSION

This chapter reviews the impact of developments in securities and currency markets on recoveries in OECD countries during the first half of the 1990s. These markets have undergone a series of fluctuations since 1992 arising in part from changing perceptions about the course of monetary policy, concerns surrounding large budget deficits and external imbalances, and tensions between exchange rate commitments and domestic economic needs in Europe. Overall, these financial market fluctuations have had a stabilising impact on the economic recoveries in the United States and Canada but have hampered the recoveries in Japan and in some members of the European Exchange Rate Mechanism (ERM) – including in particular Germany and France. Financial market fluctuations also have accentuated divergences in economic performances between these and other European countries.

Bond and equity market developments

The synchronised swings in OECD long-term interest rates during 1993-95, which were reflected in most countries in significant changes in real interest rates[1] (Figure 8), accentuated divergences in what were already relatively unsynchronised business cycles in the region. In the United States, the long-term interest rate swings reinforced the impact of changes in policy-controlled short-term interest rates and, overall, have proved to be stabilising for the real economy. Although the decline in long-term interest rates during 1993 contributed to a temporary surge in real growth above a sustainable, non-inflationary pace, the increase in long rates during the following year helped to bring output growth back in line with its long-term potential. Likewise, the subsequent decline in long-term interest rates in 1995 partly offset the slowdown in activity arising from the contraction in exports to Mexico during the first half of the year.

The overall effects of the swings in long-term interest rates were adverse for Germany, France and a number of other countries participating in the ERM, as well as Japan. The 1993 decline in long-term interest rates did reinforce the impact of monetary easing to combat the recession, but the effect was probably blunted by

depressed business confidence and, in Germany, by currency appreciation. However, the 1994 increases in long-term interest rates ran counter to the thrust of monetary policy, came at a very early stage of the recovery, and probably contributed to the weakening in final demand that became apparent in Japan, Germany, France and a number of other European countries the following year.

Equity market developments also had a bearing on the recoveries in several countries. The buoyancy of equity markets in the United States and the United Kingdom, which has out-performed those of most other OECD countries since 1992, has tended to enhance incentives for business investment and helped to improve household financial positions. Evidence suggests that the low inflation environment in the United States, and the improved inflation performance of the United Kingdom, have been important contributors to the strength in their equity markets during this decade.[2] This strength has been further reinforced by improvements in the international competitiveness of these two countries during the 1990s.

In Japan, the depressed level of equity prices following the 1990-92 stock market contraction added to the financial problems of banks by lowering their capital base. The weakness in the stock market also further reduced incentives for business investment by raising the cost of capital, as the higher cost of equity financing more than offset the decline in real borrowing costs. Equity prices in Japan and Germany fell in 1994, due in large part to concerns over the depressing effect on their industries of the real appreciations of the yen and Deutschemark, respectively. However, markets in both countries began to rebound in the spring of last year, reflecting in Japan the reversal of the yen appreciation earlier in the year and in Germany falling interest rates, whose effects were probably reinforced by the abatement of upward pressures on the Deutschemark.

Currency and money market developments

Currency fluctuations had relatively benign effects on the US recovery in the first half of the decade. The depreciation of the real effective value of the dollar between 1990 and 1992, although fairly modest, further

Figure 8. **Real long-term interest rates**[1]

Per cent

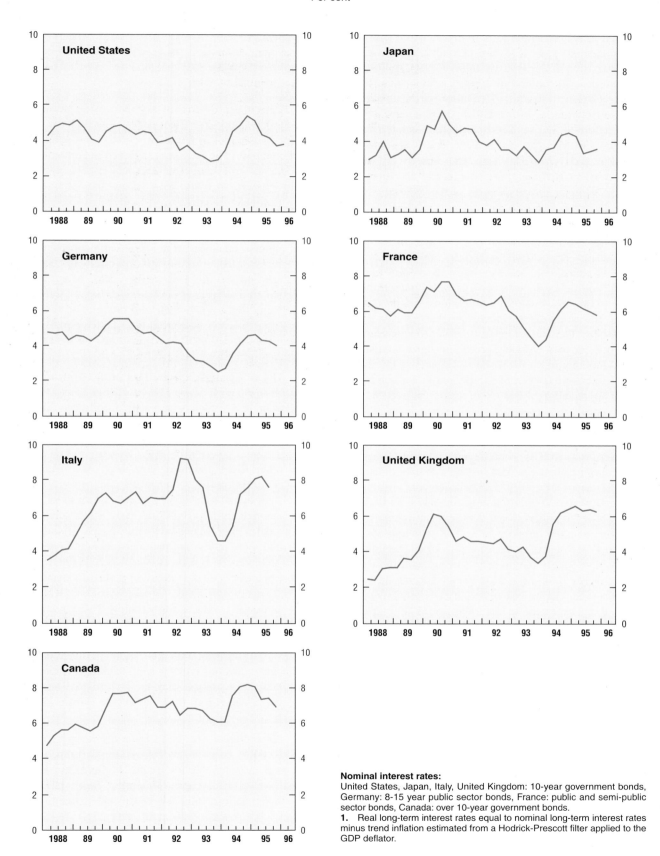

Nominal interest rates:
United States, Japan, Italy, United Kingdom: 10-year government bonds,
Germany: 8-15 year public sector bonds, France: public and semi-public
sector bonds, Canada: over 10-year government bonds.
1. Real long-term interest rates equal to nominal long-term interest rates
minus trend inflation estimated from a Hodrick-Prescott filter applied to the
GDP deflator.

enhanced the already favourable competitive position of the economy and helped to sustain fairly robust export growth throughout the recovery. Since 1992, the dollar has been relatively stable in real effective terms, despite marked changes against several individual currencies. In particular, the dollar's large appreciation against the Mexican peso at the end of 1994 was more than offset by depreciations in early 1995 against the Japanese yen, the Deutschemark, other ERM currencies and the Canadian dollar that stemmed partly from concerns arising from the Mexican crisis itself. The Canadian and Australian recoveries also have been boosted by strong export growth stemming in large part from their real effective depreciations over most of the 1990s.

Japan's economic performance has suffered considerably from the appreciation of the yen since mid-1992. The more than 20 per cent rise in the yen's real effective value between mid-1992 and mid-1993 added significantly to downward pressures on demand and delayed the recovery, both directly and by adding to the excess capacity conditions in industry created by the over-investment during the late 1980s and early 1990s. The factors behind the yen fluctuations are difficult to identify with any precision. Japan's outstanding productivity performance in large parts of the manufacturing sector has been one important factor behind the secular appreciation of the yen in real terms over the past two decades. Some evidence suggests that Japan's rising net foreign asset position, created by its chronic current account surpluses, has also contributed to the secular real appreciation as well as to the renewed upward pressures on the currency that emerged in 1992.[3] While the current account surplus has since declined considerably in real terms and relative to GDP, it has remained high in dollar terms due in large part to the temporary improvement in the terms-of-trade arising from the yen appreciation ("J-curve"). Trade tensions arising from this large dollar surplus, particularly the bilateral surplus with the United States, appear to have been a factor behind the yen's further appreciation in late 1994 and early 1995, which in turn was a key factor in the faltering of the Japanese recovery during the first half of last year.

The currency appreciations in Japan effectively offset the impact of substantial declines in policy interest rates during the recession. Overall monetary conditions, as measured by an index which takes account of movements in exchange rates as well as short-term real interest rates, tightened between mid-1992 and mid-1995, although they did ease noticeably in the latter half of last year (Figure 9). Any expansionary impacts of cuts in policy-controlled short-term interest rates were further blunted by Japanese banks' efforts to offset losses on real estate loans by widening the margin between their lend-

ing rates and other short-term market rates[4] (see Figure 4 in the chapter "General Assessment of the Economic Situation"). As a result, bank loan rates have fallen significantly less than policy interest rates. The scope for further monetary policy easing over the last year has also been limited by the fact that nominal interbank money market interest rates are close to zero.

Currency pressures in Europe arising during and after the 1992 and 1993 ERM crises likewise have tended to depress demand in Germany, France and some other ERM countries. The pressures stemmed in part from concerns about large budget deficits and the weakening of output growth, together with rising unemployment in many European countries at a time when interest rates were still high in Germany. These developments raised market concerns that domestic economic needs in some ERM member countries were becoming inconsistent with the interest rate relationships required to maintain exchange rate stability within the ERM. Moreover, as happened on a number of occasions in the past, repercussions from the renewed downward pressure on the dollar against the yen, and later from the Mexican crisis, seem to have contributed to upward pressures on many ERM currencies in 1994 and early 1995.

The substantial depreciations of the British pound, Italian lira, Spanish peseta, Swedish krona, and Finnish markka in real effective terms that followed the two ERM crises boosted the recoveries in these countries and sustained them into 1995. The corresponding currency appreciations experienced by Germany, France, and some other ERM countries aggravated their recessions and were an important factor in the unexpected weakening of their activity in 1995.[5] The real appreciation of the Deutschemark during 1994 and early 1995, along with unexpectedly high wage settlements in certain industries, weakened Germany's international competitiveness and tended to undermine business confidence. These developments apparently led to a delay in planned expansion of capital expenditures inside Germany that surveys late in 1994 suggested would be forthcoming. There is evidence of German firms shifting capital spending to foreign countries. Business caution in implementing domestic capital spending plans may have been further reinforced by financial positions that rising bankruptcy rates and other indicators suggest may have recovered less from the earlier recession than aggregate profits figures indicated.

As in Japan, the currency movements stemming from the ERM crises have effectively offset much of the effects of monetary policy easing in Germany, France, and several other European countries. Since 1992, currency appreciations have worked to substantially offset

Figure 9. **Monetary conditions indexes**[1]

Index Q1 1990 = 100

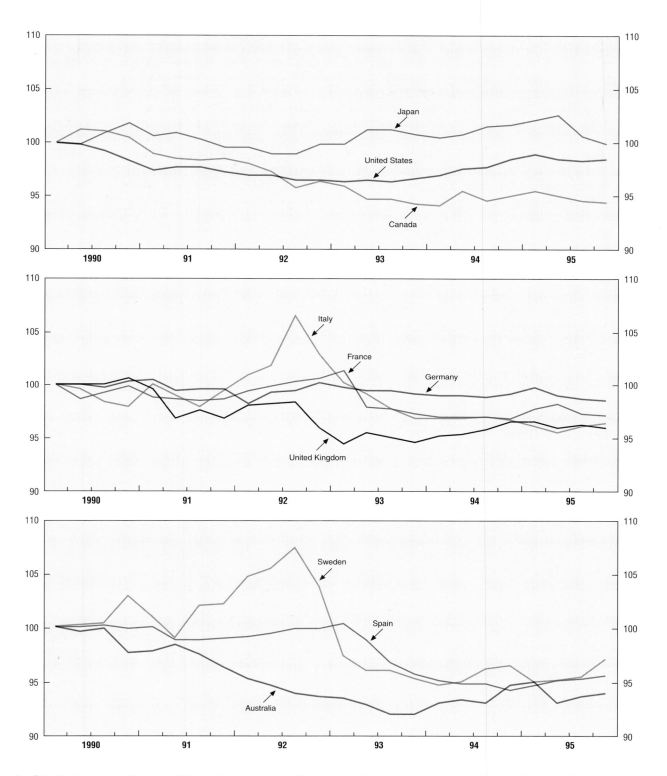

1. Calculated as a cumulative index of the weighted average of: *a)* the change in the real short-term interest rate; and *b)* the percentage change in the real effective exchange rate. A rise in the index indicates that monetary conditions are becoming tighter.
The real interest rate is the 3-month nominal rate less consumer price inflation over the preceding year; the real effective exchange rate is based on relative unit labor costs. The weights on the real interest rate are as follows: United States: 0.9; Japan, Germany, France, Italy, United Kingdom: 0.8; Canada, Australia: 0.7; Sweden, Spain: 0.6. Weights on the real effective exchange rate are one minus the weights on the real interest rate. Weights reflect the relative impact of proportional changes in each component on real GDP and are derived from the OECD Interlink Model.

the effects of the downward trend in policy-controlled interest rates in these countries, notably in 1995.

Monetary policy easing in France has been further impeded by the repercussions of periodic currency pressures on domestic financial markets. Short-term money market interest rates had to be raised sharply in 1992 and again in 1995 to maintain reasonable stability in the French franc-Deutschemark relationship. The overall pace of monetary easing has to a large degree been determined by the progress of easing in Germany. France's relatively low inflation means that although nominal interest rates on average have been close to those in Germany, real interest rates, at least on short-term instruments, remain comparatively high. Increased bank loan rate spreads, which have been noticeably higher during this recovery than during the expansion in the early 1980s, have further blunted the impact of monetary policy easing in France as well as in Germany. As in Japan, the rise in bank loan spreads in France largely reflects banks' attempts to offset losses from non-performing real estate loans.

Several other European countries, notably Italy and Sweden, also had to raise short-term money market interest rates in 1995 to counter currency pressures. Pressures on these currencies, as well as on the Spanish peseta, arose in part from repercussions of the flight to quality that followed the Mexican crisis, which seems to have increased market concerns over large budget deficit and public debt levels. The fact that long-term interest rate differentials with Germany did not narrow nearly as much during the bond market rally in 1995 as they did in 1993 is a further indication of these heightened concerns.

The constraints on monetary policies in many European countries and Japan contrast with the greater flexibility monetary authorities in the United Kingdom, the United States and Canada have had in pursuing domestic policy objectives. The immediate effect of the withdrawal of the British pound from participation in the ERM in late 1992 was to allow authorities to lower short-term money market interest rates considerably, to levels below those prevailing in Germany. This easing was an important factor in boosting and sustaining the recovery in the United Kingdom, since private spending there is more sensitive to short-term interest rates than to long-term interest rates. Despite the improvements that mone-

tary policy in the United Kingdom may have gained since the adoption of inflation targets, however, long-term interest rates remain high relative to those in many ERM countries (see Table 8 in the chapter ''General Assessment of the Economic Situation''). The exercise of monetary policy flexibility afforded by withdrawal from the ERM, therefore, was not without costs.

In the United States, policy interest rates have changed fairly rapidly when warranted by economic conditions. The authorities were able to ease monetary policy substantially in 1992, and to maintain that ease in 1993, to support recovery without undermining the strength in stock and bond markets. The inflation impact of the dollar's depreciation was negligible. Although monetary policy has been somewhat more constrained by exchange rate considerations in Canada, credibility gained through success in reducing inflation to below that in the United States and careful attention by authorities to markets' understanding of policy actions has helped to eliminate the gap between Canadian and US short-term interest rates. As a result, monetary conditions have eased even more than in the United States – a development which would appear to be warranted by the different cyclical positions of the two economies.

NOTES

1. Group of Ten (1995), *Savings, Investment and Real Interest Rates.*

2. See Blanchard, Olivier J. (1993), ''Movements in the equity premium'', *Brookings Papers on Economic Activity*, Vol. 13, No. 2.

3. Farukee, H. (1994), ''Long-run determinants of the real exchange rate: a stock-flow perspective'', *International Monetary Fund Working Paper 94/90*; and Stein, J. (1995), ''Fundamental determinants of the real exchange rate of the US dollar relative to other G-7 currencies'', *International Monetary Fund Working Paper 95/81*.

4. *OECD Economic Surveys, Japan, 1995.*

5. The rise in the real value of the Deutschemark following the crises added to the already substantial real appreciation resulting from the increase in German inflation in the aftermath of unification.

THE EXPERIENCE WITH FISCAL CONSOLIDATION IN OECD COUNTRIES

Summary and main conclusions

Consolidation of government fiscal positions is on the policy agenda in many OECD Member countries. Such action to improve fiscal positions has been clearly necessary for many years to contain and reverse rising indebtedness, and will become more urgent in the years ahead because of the pressures which population ageing will generate. However, concerns about the short-term negative macroeconomic consequences of consolidation have often reinforced political resistance to specific adjustment measures. Hence, governments have often been reluctant to act as early or as forcefully as necessary.

This chapter reviews episodes of significant multi-year fiscal consolidation over the past two decades with a view to assessing the extent to which concerns about such short-term negative consequences are justified. It examines the circumstances in which fiscal consolidation took place; how it was achieved (*i.e.* through increases in revenues or cuts in expenditures); developments in financial markets during the period of consolidation (*i.e.* whether they reinforced or countered the effects of consolidation); and finally, overall developments of key macroeconomic variables: saving behaviour, output, inflation, unemployment; and the external position.

''Significant'' consolidation is defined here as an improvement (*i.e.* positive change) in the general government structural (*i.e.* cyclically-adjusted) financial balance equivalent to at least 3 percentage points of GDP, which takes place continuously over consecutive years.[1] The experience of 18 countries from 1974 is reviewed here, and Table 14 summarises all the episodes of significant fiscal consolidation so defined.[2]

Despite the political difficulties of achieving significant fiscal consolidation, 15 episodes are identified during the period under review. In some countries (Australia, Belgium, Ireland and Italy) there have been two such periods of consolidation, while in others there have been none.[3] The fiscal consolidations undertaken in Ireland, Belgium and Denmark stand out as major episodes in terms of the size of the turnarounds, but there were several other cases of consolidation amounting to considerably more than 3 per cent of GDP. In the review of these episodes below, the country name and the first year of consolidation will be used to identify the individual episodes summarised in Tables 14 to 19.

The key features of these episodes, all of which were also influenced by developments unrelated to fiscal policy, are the following:

- In a majority of cases, fiscal consolidation was undertaken when actual general government balances were in deficit by at least 3 per cent of GDP, and following a deterioration in one or more key economic parameters, frequently rising inflation and widening current account deficits. High and rising levels of gross government financial liabilities were also common, though until recently these appeared to be of less concern than inflation and external problems.

- In all but one case, consolidation involved some increase in revenues as a per cent of GDP, with the emphasis on direct rather than indirect tax increases. Expenditures were cut in two-thirds of the episodes, with the emphasis usually on cuts in government investment spending, followed by cuts in consumption spending; while transfers were also cut, this played a much smaller role.

- In almost three-quarters of the episodes, there was active monetary policy easing (measured by changes in nominal short-term money market interest rates) during the course of fiscal consolidation. However, this did not always translate into effective monetary easing, as falls in real short-term interest rates occurred in just under half the episodes. A broadly similar pattern was evident in changes in long-term interest rates. (Of course, real interest rates would have been higher in the absence of consolidation.)

- Real exchange rate appreciation occurred during just over half the episodes.

- Fiscal consolidation was usually reflected in higher national saving rates by the end of the episode, but the extent of the improvement was limited by a tendency for household saving rates to decline during the course of consolidation; fluctuations in business saving were more variable.

- Fiscal consolidation did not uniformly lead to low economic growth, as average growth rates

government financial liabilities as high as 50 per cent.[4] For several of the consolidation episodes, net indebtedness was quite low: less than 15 per cent of GDP.[5]

How consolidation was achieved

In all but one of the 15 episodes, fiscal consolidation involved at least some increase in the proportion of total revenue to GDP, with the emphasis usually on direct rather than indirect tax increases (Table 16). Only in Ireland (1986), did revenues (as a per cent of GDP) fall. Consolidation involved a cut in expenditure as a proportion of GDP in 10 of the 15 episodes. Expenditure cuts, where they were achieved, usually involved cuts in investment and consumption spending as a share of GDP, particularly the former. Transfers were cut in just under half the episodes, but in general by much less than corresponding cuts in outlays on goods and services. Overall, more than half of the consolidation episodes under review relied more on revenue increases than on expenditure cuts.

The impact of ongoing debt accumulation on fiscal positions is shown by the rise in gross debt interest payments by many governments during the course of (and in spite of) their consolidation efforts. This amounted to almost ³/₄ per cent of GDP or more in around half of the episodes and was particularly large – 2³/₄ per cent of GDP – in Belgium (1982) and Denmark (1983). In most countries, net debt interest payments behaved similarly to gross payments, usually changing by slightly smaller accounts. The notable exception is Japan (1980), where the large increase in the gross debt interest share during consolidation was considerably offset by the significant interest earnings of the Japanese government, leading to a much less significant rise in net interest payments.

Developments in financial markets

Lower fiscal deficits can be expected to reduce real interest rates in the longer term, thereby raising investment, productivity growth and real incomes, which should in turn raise the real effective exchange rate. The

Table 16. **How consolidation was achieved**

	Period of fiscal consol-idation[a]	Change in total revenue as a per cent of GDP[b]	Of which: Direct tax	Of which: Indirect tax	Of which: Other[c]	Change in total outlays as a per cent of GDP[b]	Of which: Transfers	Of which: Consump-tion	Of which: Invest-ment	Of which: Debt interest payments[d]	Of which: Other[e]	Memorandum item: Debt interest, net
Australia	1980-82	3.4	2.2	1.1	0.1	1.5	0.4	1.1	−0.5	0.1	0.2	0.1
	1986-88	1.1	1.4	−0.5	0.1	−2.7	−1.8	−1.3	−0.7	0.4	−0.3	−0.2
Belgium	1982-87	1.6	0.4	−0.1	1.3	−4.0	−1.0	−2.3	−1.7	2.8	−1.8	2.7
	1993-95	1.2	1.6	0.2	−0.6	−1.4	0.1	0.2	−0.1	−1.5	−0.3	−1.1
Denmark	1983-86	7.1	3.9	1.9	1.3	−5.5	−2.3	−4.3	−0.5	2.8	−1.2	2.5
Finland	1975-76	10.6	4.0	0.1	6.7	7.7	3.9	2.8	0.3	0.1	0.7	−0.9
Germany	1980-85	1.2	0.0	−0.6	1.8	−0.2	−0.1	0.4	−1.1	1.3	−0.5	1.2
Greece	1994-95	2.5	1.7	−0.8	1.5	−2.5	0.2	0.3	−0.1	0.1	−3.1	..
Ireland	1982-84	4.2	1.5	1.1	1.7	0.7	2.2	−0.8	−1.7	1.8	−1.0	1.4
	1986-89	−2.7	−0.4	−0.2	−2.1	−11.7	−2.3	−3.2	−2.0	−2.1	−2.2	−0.5
Italy	1976-77	2.0	1.5	1.1	−0.7	−2.3	−0.7	−0.4	−0.2	0.7	−1.7	0.8
	1991-95	2.0	0.1	1.1	0.9	−1.8	1.0	−1.1	−1.1	1.1	1.4	1.2
Japan	1980-87	6.2	2.9	0.8	2.5	1.0	1.7	−0.3	−1.3	1.8	−0.9	0.6
Sweden	1986-87	2.6	2.8	0.8	−1.1	−5.5	−0.1	−1.2	−0.2	−1.9	−2.1	−1.3
United Kingdom	1979-82	5.1	1.0	3.2	0.9	3.1	2.1	1.8	−1.2	0.8	−0.4	0.6

Note: Due to rounding, the sum of the components may not add to the total.

a) Defined as change in general government structural balance of at least +3.0 percentage points of potential GDP.

b) From year prior to consolidation to final year of consolidation.

c) Current transfers and social security items received, property and entrepreneurial income.

d) For some countries this item includes other property and entrepreneurial income paid.

e) Current subsidies and capital transfers.

short-term effects, however, are less clear cut, even from a theoretical perspective. If, under conditions of high capital mobility, the short-run effect of fiscal consolidation were a reduction in aggregate demand, this would result in downward pressure on interest rates and the exchange rate. However, the extent to which the fall in aggregate demand will be offset by lower interest rates or a depreciation of the currency will depend on the exchange rate regime (flexible or linked to other key currencies); the size and openness of the economy; and the degree to which other countries are pursuing similar policies. In addition, expectations are important: the extent to which consolidation had been foreseen, expectations as to the durability of consolidation, and the likely impact of consolidation on actual and expected inflation and interest rates will all influence financial market behaviour. Furthermore, all of these factors affect financial markets with varying lags and to different degrees over time. At the empirical level, different ways of adjusting nominal interest and exchange rates for changes in inflation can yield different assessments of what has occurred. This is particularly a problem as regards long-term interest rates, since good proxies for long-term inflation expectations are not readily available.

The complexity of the relationship between fiscal consolidation, interest rates and exchange rates which should be expected during the consolidation process is reflected in the experience being reviewed here. Nominal interest rates have generally eased in response to fiscal consolidation, but less consistently and uniformly than might be expected. In most cases (11 out of 15) nominal short-term interest rates fell during the course of consolidation as monetary policy was eased (Table 17). However, during some of these episodes – in Germany (1980), Italy (1991) and Japan (1980) – rates rose before falling, and in a few cases nominal short-term interest rates ended the consolidation period higher than they had been the year before it began. In all cases where nominal short-term rates declined, but only in those cases, nominal long-term rates also fell.

When account is taken of inflation movements in a conventional way, by adjusting nominal interest rates for the change in the GDP deflator, the picture of a tendency for easing is substantially modified. In only just under half of the episodes were the demand effects of fiscal policy tightening somewhat offset by monetary easing, as indicated by the changes in real short-term rates. Declines in real long-term interest rates – in six of the 15 episodes – were even slightly more limited. The case of Ireland (1982) is particularly striking. There, small falls in nominal interest rates translated into more than a 9 percentage point rise in real short-term rates and more

Table 17. **Financial market developments**

	Period of fiscal consolidation[a]	Change in nominal short-term interest rates[b] Percentage points	Change in real short-term interest rates[b, c] Percentage points	Change in nominal long-term interest rates[b] Percentage points	Change in real long-term interest rates[b, c] Percentage points	Change in real effective exchange rate[b] Per cent
Australia	1980-82	6.7	5.6	5.5	4.4	9.4
	1986-88	–3.3	–5.6	–1.8	–4.1	–5.7
Belgium	1982-87	–8.2	–5.8	–5.2	–2.8	–0.5
	1993-95	–4.6	–3.2	–1.3	0.1	5.8
Denmark	1983-86	–7.7	–1.6	–11.3	–5.3	8.1
Finland	1975-76	2.0	11.7	1.4	11.1	11.7
Germany	1980-85	–1.3	0.5	–0.4	1.3	–16.2
Greece	1994-95	–5.7	–1.0	–5.7	–1.0	–4.3
Ireland	1982-84	–2.0	9.1	–2.7	8.4	8.8
	1986-89	–1.9	–2.1	–3.7	–3.9	0.3
Italy	1976-77	3.4	1.2	4.7	2.4	–10.3
	1991-95	–1.7	1.2	–1.7	1.1	–24.5
Japan	1980-87	–1.7	0.9	–3.3	–0.7	31.1
Sweden	1986-87	–4.8	–2.9	–1.5	0.3	–0.3
United Kingdom	1979-82	3.1	7.0	1.0	5.0	29.8

a) Defined as change in general government structural balance of at least +3.0 percentage points of potential GDP.
b) From year prior to consolidation to final year of consolidation.
c) Nominal interest rates less inflation, measured by changes in the GDP deflator.

than an 8 percentage point rise in real long-term rates, as inflation fell sharply from 17½ per cent to 6½ per cent. So far as real exchange rates are concerned, no clear tendency one way or the other emerges. Effective exchange rates of consolidating countries appreciated in real terms in eight out of 15 episodes and depreciated in seven. The amounts involved ranged from a real appreciation of around 30 per cent in Japan (1980) and the United Kingdom (1979) to a real depreciation of nearly 25 per cent in Italy (1991).

At least as regards real interest rates, especially long-term rates, this review of consolidation experiences may not seem encouraging. To some degree, the failure of real long-term interest rates to decline more regularly during consolidation probably reflects understatement of real interest rates prior to fiscal adjustment, since actual inflation may have exceeded expected inflation in many cases, especially in periods when inflation was volatile. In any case, long-term interest rates prior to fiscal adjustment would in many episodes have been unsustainably low had inflation not come down. In five cases out of 15, for example, real long-term interest rates were 1½ per cent or less before consolidation began. More generally, the evidence points to the difficulty of establishing credibility in financial markets once it has been lost, and to the overriding influence of international financial conditions on bond markets in most countries.

Saving behaviour during consolidation

An increase in national saving in response to fiscal consolidation would be considered a desirable outcome, as it would allow for greater investment and, in some cases, a reduction in current account deficits. Table 18 shows three indicators of saving behaviour during each episode of consolidation. There appears to be quite a strong correlation between changes in government dissaving and household saving ratios: in 13 out of the 15 cases household saving ratios declined during the period of consolidation, thereby offsetting some of the positive effect of consolidation on national saving. To some degree, this may reflect longer-term trend declines in household saving ratios in OECD countries during the past two decades. However, it is also consistent with theories that suggest that households tend to reduce their saving somewhat in the wake of a rise in taxation or a cut in government spending as a means of maintaining their living standards, as well as providing some evidence in favour of Ricardian equivalence.[6] Alternatively, it is possible that at times the causality works the other way, with fiscal consolidation undertaken in response to a fall of household saving ratios, and in attempt to counter the associated deterioration in external accounts. No similar clear relationship emerges one way or the other between changes in business saving and fiscal consolidation.

Table 18. **Saving behaviour**

	Period of fiscal consolidation[a]	Change in household saving ratio[b, c]	Change in corporate saving as per cent of GDP[b, c]	Change in national saving as per cent of GDP[b, c]
Australia	1980-82	-4.0	..	-4.6
	1986-88	-1.2	0.5	3.5
Belgium	1982-87	-4.1	..	3.3
	1993-95	-1.2	0.4	..
Denmark	1983-86	-15.4	-3.0	4.0
Finland	1975-76	-0.7	..	-6.5
Germany	1980-85	-1.3	9.6	-0.8
Greece	1994-95	-1.2	-0.2	..
Ireland	1982-84	0.4	..	2.8
	1986-89	-3.4	-1.4	1.3
Italy	1976-77	-3.0	..	2.2
	1991-95	-5.1	3.4	..
Japan	1980-87	-4.4	..	1.1
Sweden	1986-87	-5.1	-1.5	0.7
United Kingdom	1979-82	0.4	..	-1.7

a) Defined as change in general government structural balance of at least +3.0 percentage points of potential GDP.
b) Percentage points.
c) From year prior to consolidation to final year of consolidation.

Despite the strong tendency for household saving rates to fall and the ambiguous behaviour of the business sector, lower government dissaving has tended to result in a rise in national saving: national saving increased during the period of consolidation in eight out of the 12 episodes of consolidation for which data are available.

Macroeconomic developments during consolidation

The impact of fiscal consolidation on a range of key macroeconomic variables is summarised in Table 19. Average growth rates during consolidation periods varied but they were always positive, were within 1 percentage point of potential growth rates in six of the 15 episodes, and were above potential growth in four of them. During five episodes, average growth exceeded 3 per cent. Overall, there appears to be little relationship between either the extent or the pace of consolidation and growth rates during the process (Figure 10).

The impact of fiscal consolidation on unemployment largely reflected growth outcomes. In two episodes – Denmark (1983) and Ireland (1986) – economic growth was strong, at just over $3^{1}/_{2}$ per cent, and unemployment fell significantly during consolidation, by

between 2 and $2^{1}/_{2}$ percentage points. In Australia (1986) and Sweden (1986) unemployment also fell modestly, reflecting solid growth of $3^{1}/_{2}$ and $2^{3}/_{4}$ per cent respectively. In another five episodes unemployment was either essentially unchanged (Greece 1994) or rose moderately, by up to $1^{1}/_{4}$ percentage points, during the period of consolidation. With the exception of Italy (1976), these were episodes in which growth was weak or less than potential. In six of the 15 episodes unemployment rose by more than 2 percentage points. Given that economies were usually operating at above their potential output level prior to consolidation (11 out of 15 episodes), it could be argued that the rises in unemployment in two-thirds of the episodes were to some extent inevitable. Only in Italy (1976) and Greece (1994) did a rise in unemployment follow below-potential growth in the year preceding consolidation.

Inflation experiences were generally favourable during the course of consolidation, at least partly reflecting a dampening impact of consolidation on demand which was not offset by easier monetary policy, with falls in inflation occurring in more than two-thirds of the episodes. All cases in which significant rises in unemployment occurred fell into this category. In the cases where the inflation rate actually increased during the

Table 19. **Macroeconomic developments during consolidation**

	Period of fiscal consolidation[a]	Average real GDP growth rate[b] Per cent per annum	Change in inflation rate[c] Percentage points	Change in unemployment rate[c] Percentage points	Change in current account balance/GDP[c] Percentage points
Australia	1980-82	1.8	1.2	1.0	-2.7
	1986-88	3.6	2.3	-1.0	1.4
Belgium	1982-87	1.4	-2.4	1.2	6.4
	1993-95	0.8	-1.3	2.6	3.1
Denmark	1983-86	3.7	-6.0	-2.0	-1.5
Finland	1975-76	0.7	-9.7	2.2	1.4
Germany	1980-85	1.1	-1.7	4.8	3.4
Greece	1994-95	1.7	-4.7	0.3	-1.7
Ireland	1982-84	2.1	-11.0	5.6	8.0
	1986-89	3.6	0.2	-2.4	2.1
Italy	1976-77	4.9	2.2	1.0	1.4
	1991-95	1.2	-2.8	2.9	4.1
Japan	1980-87	3.3	-2.7	0.8	4.5
Sweden	1986-87	2.7	-1.8	-0.8	1.3
United Kingdom	1979-82	0.2	-4.0	5.2	1.0

a) Defined as change in general government structural balance of at least +3.0 percentage points of potential GDP.
b) During period of consolidation.
c) From year prior to consolidation to final year of consolidation.

Figure 10. **Output growth during fiscal consolidation processes**

Growth and the amount of fiscal consolidation

Total positive change in structural balance[1]
as a percentage of GDP

Total positive change in structural balance[1]
as a percentage of GDP

Annual average growth rate of GDP[1]

Growth and the pace of fiscal consolidation

Annual average positive change in structural balance[1]
as a percentage of GDP

Annual average positive change in structural balance[1]
as a percentage of GDP

Annual average growth rate of GDP[1]

1. During respective episodes of fiscal consolidation. In those countries which experienced two consolidation episodes, these are labelled respectively (1) and (2).

course of consolidation, these increases ranged from $1/4$ to $2^1/4$ percentage points, and tended to coincide with strong growth. In three out of these four episodes – Australia (1986), Ireland (1986) and Italy (1976) – recorded growth was close to or exceeded potential growth by up to 3 percentage points. Only in Australia (1980) did inflation rise during the course of consolidation alongside significantly less than potential growth, and this can be partly explained by its positive output gap at the start of consolidation.

The mechanism through which fiscal consolidation affects current account balances inextricably involves the behaviour of interest and exchange rates as well as the reaction of saving balances. Whilst interest and exchange rate developments tended to vary across episodes, the more consistent relationship between consolidation and national saving developments during the course of consolidation, noted earlier, has been reflected in a consistently, if not uniformly, favourable impact on current accounts. In 12 out of 15 episodes current account balances improved as a per cent of GDP during the period of consolidation. The only exceptions were Australia (1980), where expectations of a resources boom led to strong imports which were not followed by the hoped-for boom in exports; Denmark (1983), whose current account was negatively affected by an increasing burden of external debt interest payments and the weakness of household saving; and Greece (1994), where a recovery in domestic demand fuelled an increase in imports, especially of investment-related capital goods.

1. Thus, the consolidation period will vary from episode to episode, both in terms of when it occurred and its length. One-year improvements that are not sustained beyond the year in which they occur (one in Greece and four in Portugal) are not considered.

2. The 18 countries are the seven major countries plus Australia, Austria, Belgium, Denmark, Finland, Greece, Ireland, the Netherlands, Portugal, Spain and Sweden. This covers all countries for which the OECD Secretariat calculates budget balances on a structural basis except Norway, which is an exceptional case due to fluctuations in oil revenues. Among the countries not covered here, Mexico and New Zealand have also had significant episodes of fiscal consolidation since the mid-1980s.

3. Although, on the basis of current OECD Secretariat projections, Canada would be included if the analysis included 1996.

4. There is no definitive rule on what constitutes an acceptable level of public debt, which would anyway vary from country to country. As a guide, however, the New Zealand Government in its Fiscal Responsibility Act defines a ''prudent'' level of net general government financial liabilities as equivalent to or less than 30 per cent of GDP. On this definition, the United Kingdom would also be in the ''high'' category.

5. Although net indebtedness figures may understate a government's underlying financial position, especially in cases where substantial contingent liabilities exist, *e.g.* in relation to future pension payments.

6. Ricardian equivalence argues that the private sector will anticipate the future tax burden associated with government debt service and adjust its saving accordingly.

INTERACTIONS BETWEEN STRUCTURAL REFORM, MACROECONOMIC POLICY AND ECONOMIC PERFORMANCE

Introduction

The past three decades have seen important and fundamental changes to the economic landscape; these present new challenges to both macroeconomic and structural policy. Prominent examples of institutional changes include the dramatic lowering of trade barriers, both within the OECD area and worldwide, regional trade integration (particularly the European Union), the generalised shift to floating exchange rates (along with the arrangements to stabilise some exchange rates within Europe) and the liberalisation of domestic and international financial markets. OECD economies have also experienced a deceleration of underlying, or sustainable, real output growth, rapid technological change at the individual industry level, higher unemployment in many countries, widening income distributions in others, declines in national saving rates and rising public debt. As well, OECD countries are developing closer links with non-OECD economies, several of which have developed strong economic and financial positions.

It has become clear that key macroeconomic issues – notably high unemployment and slow growth – are partly of a structural nature, that the structural reforms necessary to tackle these problems can affect the role and operation of macroeconomic policy, and that, in turn, macroeconomic policy can help to realise the full benefits of structural reform. The structural-macroeconomic challenges facing each OECD country have many common features, but also country-specific elements, reflecting differences in economic structure, macroeconomic situations and approaches to structural and macroeconomic policies.

In the United States, unemployment changes have been largely cyclical in the past 30 years, and the macroeconomic policy challenge has been to reduce inflation while stabilising economic activity near full employment. Although the fiscal and monetary policy mix has become better balanced in recent years, continuous budget deficits since the early 1980s have contributed, along with unfavourable debt dynamics, to the marked rise in government indebtedness, persistent current account deficits, a large change in the US net foreign asset position, a gradual depreciation of the real exchange rate against other key currencies (and particu-

larly the yen) and, at times, pressures on the authorities to be more protectionist. Since the late 1960s, the growth of underlying total factor productivity has been very low in the United States, with the consequence that real wages and incomes have also grown slowly. The adverse effect on take-home wages has been exacerbated by growth in non-wage costs, largely associated with the rapid growth of health-care costs. Technological and, in some measure, trade developments have tended to depress wages of the unskilled even though they have raised aggregate output and incomes. There are concerns about the widening of the income distribution, as well as about job security.

In Japan, unemployment has remained low. Aggregate productivity growth slowed dramatically in the 1970s and 1980s, and may have decelerated further in the 1990s, although the extended recession has made it difficult to separate cyclical changes from longer-term trends. Behind this aggregate productivity picture, export and import-competing sectors (essentially manufacturing) are very productive, whereas in a number of sheltered sectors (largely services and agriculture) competitive pressures are weak and productivity has lagged badly. The role of the banking sector has been key in corporate governance, with equity playing more the role of cementing business links than acting as an instrument of control. However, the asset price bubble and subsequent recession exposed weaknesses in the financial sector, including in its role in corporate governance. Active use of expansionary fiscal policy to deal with the long recession has also resulted in a substantial budgetary deterioration that needs to be reversed, and budgetary pressure threatens to increase sharply as the population ages. The key policy challenge in the longer term is to raise aggregate productivity. Success here should, in turn, strengthen the fiscal position and help the authorities to deal with the expenditure pressures that will arise from population ageing. Deregulation and greater competition in the sheltered sectors would contribute to this goal, while active labour market policies may be required to ensure the adaptability of workers shed in the process of structural change.

In Europe, unemployment rates rose substantially in most countries during the 1970s and 1980s. Although current unemployment rates are still to some extent cyclical, reflecting the as yet incomplete recovery from the recent recession, the bulk of unemployment is structural. The persistence of high unemployment, the large numbers of long-term unemployed and the high incidence of youth unemployment all threaten to aggravate the problems associated with social exclusion. In many countries, the recent recession worsened fiscal positions which had not been sufficiently restored during the previous expansion. Fiscal consolidation now must be stepped up against the background of high unemployment. Several European countries have geared monetary policy to stabilising their exchange rates, and most of these hope to proceed to monetary union by the end of the decade. However, high unemployment and the need for deficit reduction have at times undermined the credibility of monetary policy at times when tightening has been required. As the European Union becomes more closely integrated economically, pressure for harmonisation of tax regimes (through agreement or a less formal process of ''tax competition''), social security systems and private pension arrangements is increasing, not least because of the need to reduce distortions regarding location and to promote geographical labour mobility.

Other OECD countries share these challenges to varying degrees: government deficits have led to the run-up of large government debt and contributed to continuous external imbalances while unemployment has remained high in Canada and Australia; wage and income distributions have widened in these countries as well as in New Zealand; with New Zealand a recent exception, these countries have experienced slow productivity growth while Mexico's catch-up process has been very erratic.

The policy responses to these various challenges have been, in the final analysis, insufficient. The strategy developed in the 1980s combined macroeconomic policies to achieve price stability and strong public finances in the medium term with structural reforms to enhance trend growth, reduce structural unemployment and increase economic flexibility and adaptability. While price stability has largely been achieved, fiscal positions are now generally worse than they were in the late 1970s. Structural reforms have been significant in some areas, notably the financial sector and international trade, but have lagged in others, notably labour markets. In part, this uneven progress reflects uncertainties about the net benefits of structural reform at the aggregate level and concerns about transition costs. As well, the potential costs of reform tend to be easily identifiable and the potential gains tend to be diffuse. These factors have contributed to political resistance to reform.

This chapter discusses several dimensions of interactions between macroeconomic and structural policy. The next section examines the macroeconomic conse-

quences of structural policy reforms in financial markets, labour markets, product markets and tax-expenditure systems. Subsequent sections discuss how macroeconomic policy might react to the successful implementation of such structural reforms; the progress of structural reform to date and ways in which the process of reform could be enhanced; and areas in which further analysis is needed to further articulate and refine structural reform policies.

Structural reform and macroeconomic performance

A key effect of structural reform is the substantial improvement in economic performance on a macroeconomic scale that can result from well designed reform measures. This section focuses on the potential effects of structural policy change – or, equivalently, the costs of structural rigidities – on the levels or growth rates of important macroeconomic variables, including real GDP, productivity, employment and unemployment.[1]

Successful structural reform would not only increase employment or output in the long term, it would also have much broader macroeconomic effects. Increases in employment, for example, would raise output and translate into increased private-sector incomes, saving and capital formation. This would increase the tax base and reduce expenditure on unemployment insurance and other income support programmes, allowing governments to close deficits or lower tax rates more easily. These fiscal gains would allow crowding in of private-sector investment or help to reduce the distortions associated with high tax rates, in both cases further raising output potential.

Structural reforms could also increase productivity and, thereby, longer-term growth by raising the rate of technical progress, most directly by increasing incentives for innovation. Other reforms, however, could have adverse effects on measured productivity even as they raise economic efficiency and living standards. For example, in markets where real wages are too high to be compatible with full employment, reducing labour market rigidities could allow real wages to fall at the margin, which would increase employment and, in the first instance, reduce the marginal product of labour. As suggested above, however, such reforms might have further effects, including higher investment, that would raise output and productivity in the longer run. Other mechanisms, which are associated with theories of ''endogenous'' technical change and remain somewhat speculative, include the possibility that higher investment rates will help to speed the adoption of best-practice technologies, or that there are effectively increasing aggregate returns to scale that would translate a higher investment rate into a higher growth rate.[2]

The process of structural change is now very advanced in financial markets, which to a large extent have been liberalised in the OECD area, with substantial deregulation of domestic financial sectors and the elimination of controls on international capital movements. Liberalisation, as well as the rapid development of information technology, has allowed substantial innovation in the available range of financial products, reduced the costs of financial intermediation, improved allocation of funds both within countries and across the world, and deepened financial markets. The popularity of these new products, the growth of the financial sector and the explosive increase in international capital flows attest to the success of the reforms, at least at the microeconomic level.

However, evidence on the macroeconomic implications of financial-sector structural reform is, so far, mixed. In many countries, reforms in the 1980s were associated with asset-market bubbles, although these appear to have been due to the difficulty policy authorities faced in adapting to the new financial environment. Andersen and White (1996) argue that, in those countries that managed to avoid such crises during the liberalisation process, financial reform appears to have enhanced economic growth. There is widespread concern that financial markets are becoming more volatile, although evidence provided by, for example, Edey and Hviding (1995) suggests that this has not, in fact, been the case.

In general, it seems to be too early to draw firm conclusions about the quantitative macroeconomic importance of financial reform. Andersen and White (1996) argue that the process of financial-sector reform is still continuing, and Winters (1996) notes that, in particular, the process of internationalisation of financial markets remains incomplete, as evidenced by the still limited degree of international portfolio diversification and corresponding divergences in risk-adjusted returns between OECD and non-OECD financial markets.

Because chronically high unemployment rates have come to dominate the macroeconomic policy debate, particularly in Europe where this problem is the most severe, the effects of structural policy on the labour markets have been studied intensively. Although the situation varies significantly from country to country, even within Europe, it is clear that most of the current unemployment represents ''structural'' unemployment, in the sense that expansionary monetary or fiscal policy would have only a limited effect on unemployment rates before inflationary pressures re-emerged. Thus, while macroeconomic policy has a role in absorbing slack in those countries where it still exists, it is clear that, in many countries,

substantial progress in reducing unemployment to acceptable levels will require considerable reforms to the structure of labour and product markets, as well as to tax-transfer systems.

The *OECD Jobs Study* (OECD, 1994) identified several areas for labour market reform and, although the evidence is mixed and there is still room for disagreement about the empirical importance of specific policy measures, the following tentative conclusions could be advanced for some of these areas of reform.[3]

First, there is wide consensus that the generosity of unemployment and other social benefits, in terms of both duration and level, raises structural unemployment by reducing the incentive to find and keep a job. This effect is leveraged if benefits are withdrawn sharply as people begin to receive employment income, or if tax rates on low levels of employment income are high. Estimates by Jackman *et al.* (1996) suggest that reducing the replacement rate by one percentage point would reduce the unemployment rate by about 0.1 percentage point, and reducing benefit duration by one year would reduce the long-term unemployment rate by about 0.5 percentage points. Cross-country time-series estimates by Scarpetta (1996) suggest that a one percentage point reduction in the overall generosity of benefits would reduce the unemployment rate by 0.1 to 0.2 percentage points.[4] OECD (1996a) addresses this issue in detail, recommending that: benefits should not be excessively generous; low wage work should not be highly taxed; job search should be effectively policed for those receiving unemployment benefit; benefits not related to employment should be restricted to those entitled to them (for example, invalidity benefits should be provided only to those unable to work); support programmes and their financing should be made more transparent, so workers and tax payers can better assess them; and incentives for part-time work and for work by spouses of the unemployed should be maintained.

Second, excessive minimum wages can raise unemployment rates by making it unprofitable to hire workers with low marginal product, including the unskilled and youth. Although subject to some recent controversy, a rule of thumb from the US literature has been that a 10 per cent increase in the minimum wage would increase the youth unemployment rate by 1 to 3 percentage points (Brown, 1988), similar to an estimate for France by Bazin and Martin (1991).[5] In general, however, the effects of changes in minimum wages would be expected to depend on their initial levels in relation to the prevailing wage structure. Administrative extension of wage agreements and high social benefits may in some respects have effects resembling those of minimum wages, in that they may set effective floors on the wage distribution. The effects of minimum wages should be seen in conjunction with evidence that youth unemployment has permanent effects on the employment prospects and earnings capacity of the affected persons.

Third, employment protection legislation may reduce employment and labour force participation, but there is disagreement as to whether it raises equilibrium levels of unemployment, perhaps by reinforcing insider-outsider mechanisms. Such legislation is likely to slow adjustment to equilibrium, which complicates macroeconomic policy making. Job protection and, therefore, its effects are intrinsically difficult to quantify. Jackman *et al*. (1996) argue that the effect of employment protection legislation is ambiguous, as it tends to reduce both the flow into and the flow out of employment, thereby raising long-term unemployment but lowering short-term unemployment. Scarpetta (1996), however, suggests that the effects in certain European countries with rigid employment protection legislation could be significant.

Fourth, the employment tax wedge may raise unemployment because it is a disincentive to firms to hire workers, particularly low-wage workers if the tax wedge has a lump-sum component or a cap and therefore falls particularly heavily on them. However, in the long run, the effect of labour taxes on employment depends critically on the extent to which the tax is shifted back to labour in the form of lower wages. If it is fully shifted, then total labour costs for the firm do not rise, but labour supply might be affected. A lower net wage may reduce supply, especially in the presence of generous social benefits. On the other hand, the tax wedge is often linked to pension or healthcare benefits, and labour supply would be raised to the extent these depended on employment. Empirical evidence on the effects of high employment taxes is mixed. Mendoza *et al*. (1993) find that higher labour taxes reduce employment, a result which is supported by Tyrvainen (1995) for some countries. Andersen (1992), Scarpetta (1996) and Jackman *et al*. (1996) find no reliable indication of any effect. Kostoris (1991) finds that such effects have declined over time and ascribes this decline to increasingly open and competitive product markets. Fitoussi (1996) argues specifically for employment subsidies to combat unemployment while maintaining living standards, which would be economically similar to reducing the employment tax-wedge for lower-paid jobs.

Fifth, active labour market policies (ALMPs) could help to reduce unemployment by preparing the unemployed for jobs through training, by helping them find work, and by testing availability for work. The evidence on the effectiveness of such programmes, as surveyed in the 1993 *OECD Employment Outlook*, is mixed and sug-

gests that programme design is very important. Jackman *et al*. (1996) strongly recommend ALMPs, based in part on their empirically estimated effects of ALMP spending on unemployment: European OECD countries on average spent about 1 per cent of GDP on active measures in the early 1990s and a doubling of that spending would be associated with a fall in the unemployment rate of about 1 to 1½ percentage point. Scarpetta (1996) finds some limited effect of ALMPs on unemployment rates, but it is difficult to identify with precision. Based on an in-depth study, OECD (1996*b*) concludes that: training needs to be targeted to those with similar employment handicaps and to focus on specific skills sought by employers; job search assistance is low cost and helps to re-integrate the unemployed into the workforce; employment subsidies result in little net employment gain, although there may be long-term benefits as people remain integrated in the workforce (self-employment subsidy programmes, though very small, have been successful); and public sector job creation has not been successful, although it too can help people remain integrated in the labour force. In terms of improving the effectiveness of active labour market policies, the study recommends: focusing job search and counselling assistance on those most at risk of becoming long-term unemployed; tightening monitoring of job-seeking requirements for benefit receipt; making passive income support conditional on accepting participation in an active programme after 6 or 8 months; but not allowing such participation to establish eligibility for further passive support; avoiding large-scale programmes not geared to specific labour-market needs; focusing public employment agencies on normal job placement, rather than referral to active labour market programmes; and making existing passive programmes more ''active'', using re-employment bonuses, in-work benefits and regular contacts between claimants and public employment services.

Finally, policies to reduce labour supply, such as mandatory reductions in working hours or early retirement programmes, have no substantial direct impact on unemployment, but reduce aggregate output and may, therefore, increase distortions due to taxes.

Regional disparities are an important dimension of sub-par macroeconomic performance in several OECD countries, including Germany, Italy, Canada and Spain. The durability of high unemployment rates in lagging regions points to the structural nature of the problem, and underscores the challenges facing regional development policy. Reducing barriers and disincentives to labour mobility, and encouraging investment and enterprise formation could both help to ease these problems.

Competition in product markets may be enhanced both through application of domestic competition policy and by opening the economy up to foreign trade. The interaction between trade and competition is of increasing policy interest and concern (see OECD, 1996d, for a detailed discussion). Privatisation has been another potential source of competition, although in many markets the effect is as yet unclear. Enhanced product market competition raises living standards by improving the allocation of resources across industries. As initially measured by applied general equilibrium models, however, the gains from doing so may sometimes seem to be small. But by focusing on resource re-allocation alone, such models may underestimate the effects of product market competition. Other important considerations include:

- Interactions with labour market imperfections can magnify the effects of non-competitive behaviour. In particular, labour often receives monopoly rents. If this rent-shifting spills over into other industries, through administrative or less formal extensions of wage agreements, for example, then excess unemployment could result. Policies to increase competition would thus help to reduce unemployment and further raise output. Röger (1996), using a general equilibrium model, shows how increased product market competition can raise demand for labour, both by reducing rent shifting and increasing investment.

- Innovation and technical progress may be affected by competitive forces, although there is an argument that monopoly power raises innovation because the monopoly rents can be used to fund research and development activity. In fact, there appears to be little correlation between concentration, one measure of competition, and innovative activity. However, both Coe and Helpman (1993) and Norman (1996) argue that international trade and foreign direct investment enhance the diffusion of innovation, thereby raising long-term growth. In addition, Manning (1992) argues that higher productivity growth may lead to lower unemployment.

- Increasing returns to scale can combine with barriers to trade and imperfect competition to reduce technical efficiency and in this case rationalisation – brought about by freer trade, for example – could have a large payoff. Using a general equilibrium methodology incorporating returns to scale and imperfect competition applied to Canada, Harris (1984) calculates that multilateral trade liberalisation could increase aggregate labour productivity by some 35 per cent, as opposed to only 8 per cent under the

usual assumptions of perfect competition. Norman (1996), using a broadly similar approach, also shows that economies of scale can greatly magnify the effects of trade liberalisation.

Even abstracting from such wider effects, gains arising simply from improved resource allocation can be significant. For example, Martin et al. (1990) found that the elimination of agricultural support from its 1986-88 levels, which have not changed much since then (Table 20), could raise OECD-wide real income by 1 per cent. That should be seen in the context of agriculture and food processing accounting for only about 6 per cent of total OECD output.

Fiscal reform can also affect macroeconomic performance. Reductions in deficits and ratios of public debt to GDP help to lower real interest rates and crowd in private investment. Furthermore, changes to the structure of taxes and expenditures can also affect macroeconomic performance. Reducing the distortive effects of the tax and transfer structure by avoiding insofar as possible high marginal effective tax rates would improve resource allocation and thereby raise real incomes. The importance of reforms to the fiscal structure has increased in the past 30 years because of the substantial increase in the scale of government activity and the corresponding increase in the tax burden and tax rates. Between 1965 and 1995 tax receipts in the OECD as a whole rose from 28 to 38 per cent of GDP.[6] Because the distortive cost of taxation rises much more rapidly than the tax rate itself, a high overall tax burden puts a premium on allocative efficiency of the tax system.

Table 20. **Producer subsidy equivalents**

Percentage of value of agricultural production

	1979	1986	1990	1994[a]
United States	13	35	23	21
Japan	66	74	65	74
EC[b]	41	50	47	50
Canada	19	47	46	27
Australia	7	14	12	10
Austria	31	45	50	62
Finland	50	65	71	67
Iceland	69	79	84	73
New Zealand	15	33	5	3
Norway	71	75	75	75
Sweden	45	57	58	51
Switzerland	68	78	79	82
Turkey	30	24	31	10
OECD[c]	32	47	42	43

a) Provisional.
b) EC: EC-10 for 1979; EC-12 from 1986; includes total Germany since 1990.
c) Weighted average.
Source: OECD, *OECD Economies at a Glance: Structural Indicators*, 1996.

In recent years many OECD countries have reduced top marginal income tax rates and attempted to broaden the tax base in order to increase work incentives and avoid the costs involved in tax avoidance. In several countries, and recently particularly in the United States, there has been policy interest in shifting the tax base from income to consumption in order to increase saving, capital formation and output. As in the case of product market competition, however, formal evaluations of such moves tend to suggest that they will have relatively modest payoffs, except in certain cases, such as the disincentives to work discussed above.[7]

One structural fiscal policy reform that could have large payoffs is pension reform. Under current pension rules, demographic forecasts and reasonable assumptions about growth, it is clear that the burden of meeting pension obligations as populations get older in all OECD countries will become unmanageable. Most solutions involve reducing the generosity of pension plans, for example by increasing the age of eligibility, reducing payout rates or having less generous indexation of benefits (Leibfritz *et al.*, 1995).

The implications of structural reform for macroeconomic policy

The implementation of structural reforms and their effect on the economy can potentially affect macroeconomic policy in four distinct, but closely related, ways. First, the process of structural change is likely to affect, both beneficially and adversely, the implementation of macroeconomic policy and its transmission to economic activity. Second, against this backdrop, macroeconomic policy needs to respond to changes in potential output and the structural rate of unemployment to maximise growth while ensuring that inflation is contained. Third, macroeconomic policy may have a role in easing the transition costs associated with structural reform. Lastly, macroeconomic policymakers may also have a more active role by attempting to coordinate macroeconomic policy and structural reform or even in gaining political and social support for structural reform by agreeing to a "package" of microeconomic and macroeconomic policy proposals. This section examines these four issues in turn.

The effects of structural reform on the operation of macroeconomic policy

The links between monetary policy and economic activity are typically uncertain and involve long lags, and monetary authorities therefore need intermediate indicators to form opinions about future trends of activity and prices so as to be able to judge the stance and thrust of policy. Short-term indicators of prospective demand conditions and output gaps, such as overtime hours or order books, are helpful. Central banks also typically look at a range of financial market indicators, such as money stocks and interest rates. However, the interpretation of such indicators is likely to change with structural reform. Innovations in financial markets have changed the relationships between money and credit aggregates and economic activity, which have been expressed as unexpected shifts in velocity. Similar problems exist with asset prices. Judging by the past 30 years, real interest rates and exchange rates appear to change significantly over time, for reasons that are only partly understood. Assessing the level of these prices that is compatible with the ultimate goal of policy is therefore bound to be difficult as the markets for the underlying assets undergo structural change.

The liberalisation and internationalisation of economies and asset markets has also changed the transmission of monetary policy to the real economy and, ultimately, prices. In particular, as described by Taylor (1995), the exchange rate has become increasingly important in many countries as a channel for the transmission of monetary policy. The volatility of exchange rates, relative to interest rates, means that the stance of policy is more difficult to assess and to control. In addition, the international ramifications of policy are now more important, partly because exchange rates are determined by both domestic and foreign conditions, but also because international capital market integration implies that interest rates in one region may increasingly respond to events elsewhere.

Fiscal reform involves similar challenges. An important reason for undertaking such reforms is often the macroeconomic objective of ensuring the sustainability of the public finances. Obviously, extensive reforms to the structure of taxes and expenditures will initially introduce uncertainty about the future course of revenues and outlays. They could also affect the cyclical properties of the economy by, for example, changing the strength of automatic stabilisers, which could imply a greater or lesser need for discretionary policy changes to achieve the same degree of stabilisation. In the longer term, deficit and public debt figures can be misleading as to the underlying sustainability of the fiscal position in that they typically do not include future obligations under current programmes, which can be large. Public social security programmes, in particular, threaten to be an increasing source of fiscal strain as populations age, but just how serious a problem they are depends, among other things, on the expected effects of structural reform on real output growth over the next few decades.

Although during the transition phase the changing economic structure may complicate macroeconomic policy, structural reform can be expected to help the implementation of policy in other ways. The growth of global financial markets has in some ways improved policy making by imposing discipline and by forcing necessary adjustments of policies sooner than might otherwise have been the case. This is because, increasingly, macroeconomic policies that are unsustainable or inconsistent provoke reactions in bond and exchange markets that signal the need for policy adjustment. In Europe, structural rigidities in labour markets that have resulted in high unemployment have also reduced the credibility of macroeconomic policy. The resolve of governments to raise interest rate to defend the exchange rate has been put in doubt, particularly in times when domestic considerations pointed to the need for lower interest rates. A study of the European Exchange Rate Mechanism period suggests that unemployment rates have been a factor in triggering currency crises (Funke, 1996). A similar situation exists regarding deficit reduction, the short-term effects of which include a temporary slowing of aggregate demand. When unemployment is already unacceptably high, markets may doubt that governments will carry through. In Japan, underdevelopment of the domestic venture capital and securitised credit markets, which are particularly important for small businesses, may recently have impaired the effectiveness of monetary policy in conditions where the transmission of monetary policy through the banking channel has been weakened by balance sheet problems (Shigehara, 1993).

Maintaining growth and high employment

Macroeconomic policy plays a fundamental role in helping the economy to remain close to its potential output path and to maintain unemployment near its structural level, while at the same time pursuing the longer-term goals of price stability and fiscal prudence. As described in the previous section, structural unemployment and potential output will be moving targets as structural reforms take hold. As explained by Gordon (1996), from a macroeconomic policy point of view, such reforms are analogous to favourable supply shocks that expand output without adding inflationary pressure. Depending on the reaction of the private sector to the new investment opportunities that would be opened up, macroeconomic policy would have to adjust.

Assessing the development of the economy's supply potential is difficult at the best of times. Predicting the timing and the long-term effects of structural reforms is likely to be even more so. Initially as structural reforms take effect, there may be a short-term increase in structural unemployment when resources are reallocated across industries, occupations and regions. Structural reform may also have short-term effects on aggregate demand, including by opening new areas for investment. Fortunately, however, precise measurements and predictions are not needed because as the economy begins to exceed or fall short of its capacity, signs will emerge that suggest a correction in policy settings. For example, excess demand conditions could be reflected in rising overtime work and higher capacity utilisation measures and, eventually, upward drifts in wage growth and inflation.

This line of reasoning suggests that monetary policy that follows an inflation target would be self-regulating, but because inflation responds only with a relatively long lag and, as suggested above, intermediate indicators of future inflation may prove unreliable, the response of monetary policy to the presumed effects of structural reform must be cautious. This is all the more so because inflation is costly to reduce once it has risen (see below). There would appear to be little option other than ''feeling the way'' ahead by allowing unemployment to fall, and output growth to pick up gradually, while maintaining close surveillance of possible inflationary pressures.

Medium-term fiscal consolidation is now required in almost all OECD countries, both to reduce high levels of public debt and also, in the somewhat longer term, to prepare for the expenditure pressures that will arise as populations age. In the medium term, structural supply-side developments are key determinants of the fiscal outlook. A significant reduction in unemployment would allow substantial budgetary saving. Likewise, a fairly small increase in productivity and real output growth – if it were sustained by a durable increase in economic efficiency, even in the face of population ageing and the decline in the working-age population – would greatly help to stabilise the debt-GDP ratio, both mechanically by increasing the denominator and also by raising the tax base. For this benefit to accrue, though, it may be necessary to take action in order to prevent expenditures from rising in line with output growth, because of generous automatic standard-of-living adjustments in transfer payments, for example.

In designing deficit-reduction plans, many of the same cautions raised in the context of monetary policy apply. In particular, predictions of the transition, timing and ultimate effects of specific structural reform measures are bound to be fraught with uncertainty. A prudent fiscal adjustment programme, therefore, would be drawn up on conservative assumptions about medium-term output and unemployment developments, and adjusted over time in the event of higher sustainable output or employment growth.

Can macroeconomic policy help to ease the adjustment costs of structural reform?

The extent to which temporarily expansionary monetary or fiscal policy could, or should, attempt to compensate for transitory adjustment costs that might be brought about by the implementation of structural reform would seem to depend on the precise reform in question. For example, fiscal reforms that reduce industrial subsidies or that change the tax rates on specific goods are likely to result in the decline of some industries and the expansion of others. A by-product of this process may be frictional unemployment. Labour market policies such as retraining or job-matching services would help to eliminate and ultimately absorb this extra unemployment. However, in this case expansionary macroeconomic policies may do little but add to inflationary pressures, because reductions in the frictional unemployment will in any case take some time.

In other cases, however, macroeconomic policy may have a role. In some labour markets real wages may be too high to be consistent with full employment. Reforms might make the reduction of excessive real wage levels possible in these markets, thereby boosting employment, although the need for lower real wages would in any case be reduced to the extent that reforms raised productivity (Gersbach, 1996). But if such reductions were strongly resisted, the adjustment period could be lengthy in an environment of price stability. In such circumstances, a one-off increase in the price level might ease the adjustment. However, even if such a policy response were considered feasible and desirable in the short run, longer-term considerations would militate against it. An initial one-off rise in the general price level could easily translate into higher inflation by feeding through into expectations and aggregate nominal wages. Once such an inflationary spiral had taken hold, it would be costly to reverse. There is evidence, for example, that inflation is an asymmetric process, in that the inflationary impulse when unemployment falls below its structural level is stronger than the disinflationary impulse when it rises above (Turner, 1995). In this case, the transitory gain from macroeconomic expansion would be more than lost in the subsequent contraction.

Can macroeconomic policy help to overcome resistance to structural reform?

It has been suggested that a more active role for macroeconomic policy than just reacting, in an *ex post* sense, to events may help to overcome resistance to structural reform by helping to reach the necessary consensus in favour of structural reform by showing *ex ante* flexibility. On this view, macroeconomic policy and structural reform should be coordinated or even determined jointly in a "package" approach (Gersbach, 1996, and Gordon, 1996). Depending on circumstances, such a package could be either negotiated or unilaterally decided and would involve, for example, a promise by macroeconomic policy makers to ensure that any slack arising as a result of structural reform would be quickly taken up.

The feasibility of negotiating a package evidently depends on the existence of appropriate counterparts and institutions for striking a deal. In many countries, it is not immediately clear who the counterparts to a deal would be. The possibility of negotiated packages may therefore be limited to those countries where strong labour and business organisations act within corporatist institutions or traditions. The striking of such deals may be seen as legitimising and enhancing the influence of such organisations and institutions. Indeed, for such organisations to be able to accept structural reforms, which may well hurt some parts of their constituencies, they may have to be seen to receive something in return – if nothing else than recognition as a valid negotiating partner.[8] There is a risk, however, that such deals may thereby favour the interests of those at the negotiating table – insiders – at the expense of outsiders.

For countries without such organisations and institutions, the authorities still have the option of unilaterally committing themselves to a similar course of action, with a view to persuading all parties that the benefits of structural reform would outweigh the costs. Whether unilateral coordination of structural reform and macroeconomic policy adjustment would be helpful in this regard is, however, not clear. For example, if the problem is not one of attempting to pave the way for the introduction of structural reform, but is rather one of dealing with the risk of subsequent electoral fallout, relying on an *ex post* adjustment of macroeconomic policies may suffice.

Both negotiated "packages" and unilateral coordination involve significant risks. The design of such combined policies is difficult, even in principle, because macroeconomic and structural policy instruments are not commensurable. Because the timing and size of the effects from structural reform are highly uncertain, and because of the asymmetry in the inflation process noted above, macroeconomic policy aimed at maintaining output close to economic potential could prove destabilising. The difficulties in fine tuning macroeconomic policy would increase to the extent structural reform affects the effectiveness of macroeconomic policy levers. Moreover, once macroeconomic policy has been put on the table, its long-term stability orientation may be lost in the course of negotiation.

The risk to macroeconomic stability may be increased in the likely event that bargaining over a package leads to severe restrictions on the flexibility of macroeconomic policy. The macroeconomic policy setting, and in particular the setting of monetary policy, is much more flexible than structural reform. Thus, the authorities may be tempted to pursue time-inconsistent policies, effectively promising more macroeconomic adjustment than they would subsequently want to implement in order to get agreement on structural reform. Bargaining partners perceiving this could insist that the package include specific promises on the setting of macroeconomic policies. While the specific settings agreed may seem reasonable *ex ante*, subsequent unexpected developments could render them much less appropriate *ex post*.[9]

The package approach relies on generating as favourable a macroeconomic climate as possible to enhance structural reform. However, a completely different, and more radical, role for macroeconomic settings could also be envisaged: effectively forcing through structural reform by making it the only feasible mechanism of adjustment. A credible refusal to use macroeconomic accommodation to resolve an impending or existing economic crisis could help to pave the way for structural reform. It has been argued that important structural reforms have often been a response to a difficult economic situation to which there is no other obvious solution. Possible examples include recent changes to labour market practices in Italy and Spain in response to rising unemployment and difficulties in reducing inflation; changes to banking system regulation in Japan in response to the recession and the build-up of problem loans and trade liberalisation; and privatisation and deregulation in Mexico in 1983-89 following the debt crisis. The ''hard currency'' approach of a number of European countries can be seen as an example of such an approach, which would be reinforced by the move to European Economic and Monetary Union. Seen from the point of view of an individual country, it involves the abolition of the exchange rate instrument, the weakening of influence over short-term interest rates and the subjecting of fiscal policy to strict limits on permissible budget deficits. These constraints on macroeconomic policy may expose structural weakness and force adjustment.

Enhancing structural reform

The implementation of structural reforms has been uneven, with considerable progress in financial markets and international trade, but rather less in other areas, especially labour markets. In part, this reflects strong resistance, often at the political level. In some cases, this is attributable to a belief that specific structural reforms may not result in significant economic or social gains in the long term. In other cases, there is concern that important economic and social policy objectives of existing institutional and regulatory structures would not be fulfilled. In particular, as argued by Fitoussi (1996), well functioning markets are not guaranteed to generate income distributions that are socially acceptable. Several types of government programmes are a response to this dilemma, most obviously income transfers and minimum wages. The dilemma need not always arise: there is sometimes the possibility of introducing reforms that attain social objectives but at lower aggregate economic cost; moreover, the extra resources freed by structural reform can be partly devoted to social goals. Nevertheless, in many cases, as the result of the implementation of reforms, some people will lose – and will therefore resist structural reform – even if the aggregate effects are positive. Whether structural reform might conflict with social objectives or not, options for overcoming resistance need to be considered carefully. This section first briefly documents the progress that has been made in structural reforms, then considers ways of improving the reform process, and ends by discussing the possible role of international co-operation.

Progress in structural reform

With most evidence pointing to substantial benefits from structural reform, provided that macroeconomic policy is appropriately set to reap those benefits, substantial progress might have been expected across most areas of structural reform. In practice, however, progress has been very uneven. Most progress has been made in liberalising financial services (Edey and Hviding, 1995). In particular, progress has been important in allowing financial institutions to conduct their business at market-clearing prices:

- Whereas in the 1960s all OECD countries applied restrictions on banks' borrowing and lending rates, only three countries applied such controls in any significant way at the end of the 1980s. Quantitative restrictions on bank lending and its allocation have also largely been eliminated.
- Regulation on securities markets, concerning features such as access to the industry, commission rates, terms of issue for private debt securities and other price and quantity controls, has also largely been abolished, though only relatively recently in some countries.

– Liberalisation of international capital movements has progressed far, though in some countries restrictions remain on foreign ownership of real estate and foreign direct investment, as well as on the international portfolio diversification of pension funds and insurance companies.

In contrast, deregulation has been less rapid in the area of institutional boundaries and barriers to competition in financial markets:

– While there has been considerable liberalisation of cross-border access to foreign banks, many countries require some form of reciprocity of access.
– A number of measures have been taken to reduce line-of-business regulations. Restrictions on ownership linkages nevertheless remain important, owing to complexities associated with competition, conflict of interest, systemic risk and the need for supervision.

Considerable progress has been made in reducing tariff barriers to trade (Table 21) and, with the implementation of the Uruguay Round of tariff cuts, average tariff rates on a most-favoured nation (MFN) basis will fall to very low levels. However, the dispersion of tariff rates, which may give a better impression of their distortive effects, has developed more unevenly across countries. Preliminary OECD Secretariat work suggests that dispersion of tariff rates may actually rise in some cases as a result of the Uruguay Round (OECD, 1996c). As regards non-tariff barriers to trade (NTBs), the proportion of goods (tariff lines) subject to restrictions has generally tended to fall since the late 1980s. In a number of countries, however, the proportion of total imports subject to restrictions has actually risen and in most others, with the notable exceptions of Australia and New Zealand, it has remained almost constant. Trends have been variable across individual instruments with, for example, outstanding anti-dumping actions having risen sharply in some countries (Figure 11). There is also evidence that initiations of anti-dumping procedures have become increasingly counter-cyclical, suggesting that the general political climate may play an increasing role in such actions. In the specific field of agriculture, where government support in many countries relies heavily on border measures, overall measures of producer subsidy equivalents have remained broadly stable since the mid-1980s (Table 20).

In domestic product markets, progress has been more uneven as far as can be judged by available indicators. Regulations concerning ownership, access, price etc., have been considerably reformed in, for example, the road haulage sector and, to a lesser extent, airlines. Much less has happened in electricity generation, transmission and distribution. Restrictions also remain heavy in telecommunications and retail trade, despite some recent progress in those sectors. More generally, evidence on mark-ups in various sectors and across countries suggests that they have tended to shrink only slightly over the past decade, and levels remain high in some sectors and countries (Oliveira Martins *et al.*, 1996). Progress towards privatisation has been uneven across countries and in the provision of public sector services action has generally been modest in terms of exposing producers to competition. For example, while a few countries have introduced reforms to allow greater scope for economic incentives in the provision of health care, others have relied on a command and control approach to limit expenditure growth (Oxley and MacFarlan, 1995). Experience with contracting out also remains spotty. Some progress has been made with public sector wage reform, however. Also, a few countries have or are in the process of raising pension ages, but public pension schemes remain a source of future budgetary pressures.

In labour markets, progress has generally been limited, with the exception of a few countries, such as New Zealand and the United Kingdom. Although the disincentive effects of generous unemployment benefits are generally well understood, most countries have either broadly maintained or, in a few cases, raised the generosity of unemployment benefits over the past decade (Figure 12). Furthermore, when judged net of tax and taking other transfers into account, replacement rates are substantially higher than suggested by standard calculations (OECD, 1996a). Reflecting the fact that countries have generally had little success in reducing the size of public expenditure, overall tax wedges have come down in only a few countries and have risen in others (Table 22). While in some countries legal minimum wages have been allowed to slip relative to average wages, they remain above half the average wage in France and the Netherlands and are only somewhat below that in other countries. Administrative extension of wage contracts continues to be the rule in a number of continental European countries. Some countries, notably Italy and Spain, have reduced the stringency of employment protection legislation in recent years, but such legislation continues to deter hiring in these and in other continental European countries. Despite intentions, governments have not succeeded in re-orienting their labour-market spending from passive income support to active measures.

Can the process of structural reform be improved?

Implementing structural reform involves a number of inherent disadvantages which go a long way to explain

Figure 11. **Anti-dumping actions outstanding**
Mid-years, 1981-95

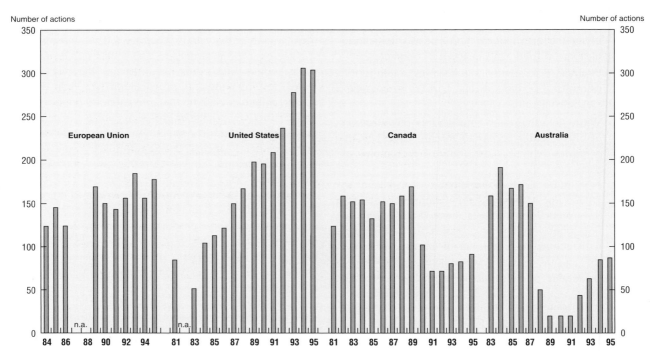

Source: WTO and GATT *Annual Reports* up to 1995.

why progress is sometimes slow and often uneven across different policy areas:

– The adjustment costs are often borne by rather narrow and homogenous groups that are already organised or are easy to organise and that have a strong incentive to resist structural reform. In addition, where reform is seen to break with existing social contracts, such as for example those governing pay-as-you-go pension systems, even the beneficiaries may be hesitant to push for reform, both out of considerations for fairness and for fear that modification of social contracts in one area could generalise into areas where they would stand to lose.

– The benefits of structural reform are often spread widely but thinly, reducing the incentive to push for reform. Moreover, the gains will partly result in the creation of businesses and jobs not yet in existence and hence not forming a constituency prior to the reform. It is notable that reform has progressed most in financial

Table 21. **Indicators of barriers to trade**

	Average MFN tariff rate[a]		Dispersion of MFN tariff rates[b]		Frequency ratio of NTBs	
	1988	1993	1988	1993	1988	1993
United States[c]	4.7	4.9	7.7	8.6	25.5	22.9
European Union	7.3	7.7	6.1	6.1	26.6	23.7
Japan	4.0	3.5	8.8	12.7	13.1	12.1
Canada	9.2	8.9	8.8	8.4	11.1	11.0
Australia	14.4	6.9	14.3	10.1	3.4	0.7
Austria	10.9	9.5	10.1	8.7	65.8	55.6
Finland	9.3	9.5	10.1	10.3	10.6	8.4
Iceland	6.9	6.9	7.5	7.3	. .	3.9
Mexico	11.0	12.9	7.0	5.2	2.0	2.0
New Zealand	13.2	7.1	15.7	10.4	14.1	0.4
Norway	4.4	4.4	6.9	6.9	26.6	23.7
Sweden	3.3	3.3	4.8	5.1	32.6	29.8
Switzerland	3.7	3.6	13.0	11.6	12.9	13.5
Turkey	47.6	12.0	35.7	5.7	0.1	0.3

a)   Applied MFN tariff rates on manufactured products, weight by production.
b)   Standard deviations of applied rates.
c)   First observation is for 1989.
Source: OECD, Indicators of Tariffs and Non-tariff Barriers to Trade in the OECD, forthcoming.

markets and trade, areas where there has been an identifiable constituency benefiting, or at least perceiving to benefit, from reform. Indeed, financial reforms were generally undertaken not because policy makers perceived large gains *ex ante*, but instead because the regulations that had existed in the 1970s – many of which had their genesis in the interwar depression period – were felt by the financial industry itself to be excessively constraining, particularly in view of the rapid pace of technological advance that was occurring and the new opportunities that appeared to be opening.[10]

– There is often less uncertainty concerning sizeable adjustment needs on the part of losers than concerning the gains accruing to beneficiaries from reform. Moreover, adjustment costs are often borne up front, whereas the timing of benefits is more uncertain but usually involves a delay relative to the costs.

– Concerning the timing of structural reform, pressures for change may rarely be as acute as is sometimes the case for macroeconomic policies which may tend to delay action and may often imply that action is taken only at times of serious economic disequilibria where adjustment costs may be particularly high.

Letting reform take effect only for newcomers to a certain activity (''grandfathering'') is an option for overcoming resistance to reform. Examples could be softer job protection rules applying only to new hires or higher retirement ages affecting only new labour-market entrants. With this approach, the government is not seen to break any implicit or explicit promises to groups which may have acted in confidence of such promises and it may therefore ease the process of building a consensus in favour of reform. Among the disadvantages of this approach are that it will slow down the process of reform and that it may be seen as unfair to newcomers. Offering compensation to the losers from reform would be an alternative option to establish consensus. Income transfers to farmers as compensation for reduced direct intervention in agricultural markets is an example of this. But from a fairness point of view this raises the question of whether it is appropriate to pursue reform by effectively bribing groups which have often already been receiving economic rents for extended periods. In addition, budgetary constraints may limit the scope for offering compensation. More generally, however, the issue arises of how to design public transfer systems in such a way as to reduce fear of and resistance to structural change while maintaining appropriate incentives.

Policy momentum may be easier to achieve if reforms in different areas are linked so as to generate expectations of gains among a majority of the population. While this approach may sometimes be effective, it also involves high political risk that no reform at all will be undertaken. A related point is whether the chance of succeeding is best helped by an incremental approach to reform or by very deep and bold reform. It may be argued, for example, that comprehensive structural reform in New Zealand was helped by reforms in each area being very deep, generating a momentum behind reform into new areas and containing resistance by reducing the perceived likelihood that such resistance would meet with success. But, it may also be argued that getting started on reform in the first place would be easier if it were based on an incremental approach. In fact, the correct approach is likely to depend on the prevailing political and social climate.

Introducing reforms in such a way as to avoid negative interactions between reforms in some areas and lack of reform in others could also reduce resistance. For example, financial reform may not have revealed its full potential for enhancing growth and welfare because of the interaction with the lack of reforms in areas such as supervision and taxation, as well as monetary and fiscal policy. Thus, in some countries financial reform exposed weaknesses in both tax systems and prudential supervision. Similarly, increased openness to trade with the non-

Table 22. **Overall tax wedges**[a] 1979-94

Percentage of the earnings of an average production worker

	1978	1985	1994
United States	36	37	35
Japan	21	26	26
Germany	50	53	59
France	37	40	41
Italy	51	56	57
United Kingdom	44	48	44
Canada	31	37	40
Australia	28	30	29
Belgium	57	61	61
Denmark	59	66	63
Finland	52	54	55
Iceland	..	32	36
Ireland	46	55	55
Luxembourg	48	51	52
Mexico	..	..	27
Netherlands	55	58	55
New Zealand	33	33	39
Norway	63	66	58
Portugal	36	40	47
Spain	39	43	47
Sweden	58	63	60

a) The difference between the cost to the employer and the consumption which can be supported from that wage.

Source: OECD, Making Work Pay: A Thematic Review of Taxes, Benefits, Employment and Unemployment, 1996.

Figure 12. **Indicator of benefit entitlements, 1961-95**[1]

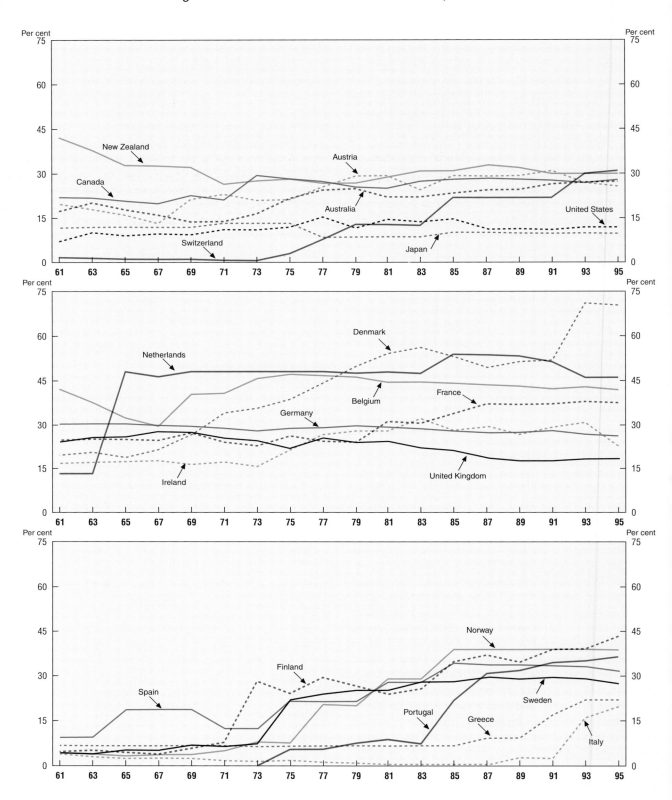

1. Benefit entitlements before tax as a percentage of previous earnings. Average of the unemployment benefit replacement rates for two earnings levels, three family situations and three durations of unemployment. For further details, see OECD, *The OECD Jobs Sudy: Evidence and Explanations*, Chapter 8. The earnings data used to compute replacement rates for 1995 are OECD Secretariat estimates. Final-year data refer to 1994 for the United States.
Source: OECD, *Making Work Pay: A Thematic Review of Taxes, Benefits, Employment and Unemployment*, 1996.

OECD area may, where insufficient up-skilling of labour has taken place, show up as either declining relative wages for low-skilled labour or, in countries with heavy labour market regulation, higher unemployment for this category. Discussion about the economically optimal sequencing of reforms across markets has focused on relative speeds of adjustment, the argument being that slowly adjusting markets need to be liberalised first. However, political realities may in practice make it difficult to pursue such an optimal sequencing. In addition, positive interaction effects between reforms in different areas may exist, such as when product market reform allows the more rapid reallocation of labour set free through labour market reform. Such positive economic externalities or spillover effects between reforms in different areas makes the assignment of certain reforms to deal with problems in specific markets less obvious and thereby complicates the question about an economically optimal sequencing of reforms. However, positive spillover effects between product and labour market reforms could reduce transition costs and thereby help to reduce resistance to reform.

The benefits of international co-operation and coordination

International co-operation and co-ordination may have a significant role to play in helping to advance structural reform. This link is most obvious in areas of multilateral, or even bilateral, negotiation and agreement. Thus, the perceived "fairness" in multilateral agreement, for example on reductions of trade barriers, may help to reduce resistance to reform where unilateral action would not have succeeded, despite its beneficial effects. In many cases gains from structural reform are enhanced by international agreement. For example, the favourable effects of intellectual property rights on innovation will be larger to the extent that foreign producers are covered as well. The more countries co-operate on prudential financial regulation, the more systemic problems are more likely to be avoided. Similarly, international co-operation in tax reform may reduce erosion of the tax bases. And, increasingly, international co-operation on reform of competition law and regulation may give more benefits than when countries act alone since these structural features give rise to steadily more important obstructions to trade and foreign direct investment as traditional trade barriers are unwound. In addition, multilateral agreements, for example in the trade area, are more likely to succeed because they create a constituency (exporters) who stand to gain from reform. In contrast, those gaining from unilateral action, especially consumers, are often less easily identifiable and new competitors may not even be active in the field where gains will appear.

Other structural reforms are more domestic in character. This, however, does not imply that lack of reform in these areas has no international ramifications.[11] For example, lack of labour market reform, which entails weak adaptability to outside shocks, may be a source of protectionist sentiment and may encourage speculative pressures on a country's exchange rate. Also, distortions to domestic resource allocation are likely to spill over into saving-investment balances, real interest rates and real exchange rates with repercussions for other countries. This gives countries a strong incentive to engage in the discussion of other countries' domestic structural reforms and to attempt to exert "peer pressure" to help the process of reform.

International co-operation may also be helpful in generating information about structural reform. Thus, international comparisons may help to identify best practices in the field of structural reform and may help to bring issues onto the domestic policy agenda which would otherwise have received too little emphasis. Indeed, sometimes the use of international evidence may be a pre-requisite for identifying the effects of a particular structural feature. Moreover, experience from other countries may be a valuable tool for convincing a sceptical audience about the merits of structural reform.

Summing up

Across OECD regions, structural reform has become increasingly important for meeting the challenges posed by slow output and productivity growth and unacceptably high unemployment rates. Macroeconomic policies have been able to respond only imperfectly to these problems and, in many cases, the freedom of manœuvre has been constrained by past excesses or political considerations. Well designed and implemented structural reform across a wide range of areas could have significant positive effects on growth and jobs. To reap those gains, macroeconomic policies need to be set appropriately. This is a challenging task, in part because judging the correct setting of monetary and fiscal policy is always difficult, but in part because successful structural change will itself change the way economies react to macroeconomic policies, and in ways that are difficult to foresee. Focusing on achieving the medium-term targets of price stability and fiscal soundness may be the best contribution of macroeconomic policies to advancing structural reform. However, attempts to smooth the transition through expansionary macroeconomic policy or to trade off macroeconomic expansion against the

DEVELOPMENTS IN INDIVIDUAL OECD COUNTRIES

UNITED STATES

The pace of economic growth has picked up since the turn of the year despite continued tight fiscal policy and a number of temporary disturbances. Persistently rapid investment growth has nevertheless allowed capacity constraints to continue to ease. There have therefore been few signs of either excess supply or demand: underlying inflation has been fairly steady, although wage increases have edged up, with the unemployment rate just above a twenty-year low. The current account deficit has begun to narrow due to a favourable cost position and an easing in the growth rate differential between the United States and its major trading partners. The most likely prospects are for a return of output growth to potential rates of about 2 per cent as the effects of higher long-term interest rates work their way through the interest-sensitive sectors of the economy. This growth scenario should allow inflation and unemployment to remain near current low levels and the external deficit to continue to fall slowly. The risks surrounding the central projections for activity appear to be fairly evenly balanced, mainly emanating from possibly weaker private fixed investment on the one hand and stronger household consumption and stockbuilding on the other.

Recent developments

After nearly stalling in the first two quarters of 1995, growth of real GDP picked up during the second half to around potential rates of 2 to 2¼ per cent on the new chain-weighted basis.[1] Throughout the year activity was held back by an ongoing inventory correction, particularly at the retail level, and continuing fiscal consolidation. The revival of growth last summer was sparked by a pickup in exports and residential construction. Exports rose as the Mexican economy began to recover and exporters continued to expand market share, given their favourable relative cost positions. The housing market recovered owing to the sharp reversal of the 1994 increase in long-term interest rates. By year-end, housing construction was again above a pace consistent with trend rates of net household formation. Private non-

UNITED STATES
Demand and output

Percentage changes from previous period, seasonally adjusted at annual rates, volume (1992 prices)

	1992 current prices billion $	1993	1994	1995	1996	1997	1995 I	1995 II	1996 I	1996 II	1997 I	1997 II
Private consumption	4 219.8	2.8	3.0	2.4	2.5	2.0	2.0	2.5	2.7	2.2	1.9	2.1
Government consumption	1 054.6	−0.1	0.2	−0.3	−0.9	−0.5	−1.1	−1.1	−0.8	−0.7	−0.5	−0.3
Gross fixed investment	992.5	5.1	7.9	5.4	5.3	2.7	5.3	2.9	7.0	4.2	2.0	2.5
Public	209.1	−1.2	−1.3	2.0	1.6	1.5	1.5	−1.3	3.1	1.5	1.5	1.5
Private residential	225.5	7.6	10.8	−2.3	2.7	−2.2	−6.6	2.4	5.3	−2.0	−3.4	0.1
Private non-residential	557.9	6.4	9.8	9.7	7.3	4.8	11.5	4.3	8.8	7.3	4.1	3.6
Final domestic demand	6 267.0	2.7	3.3	2.5	2.5	1.8	2.1	2.0	2.9	2.1	1.6	1.8
* stockbuilding	7.0ᵃ	0.2	0.6	−0.4	−0.3	0.1	−0.5	−0.5	−0.4	0.2	0	0.1
Total domestic demand	6 274.0	2.9	4.0	2.1	2.2	1.8	1.5	1.5	2.5	2.3	1.5	1.9
Exports of goods and services	639.4	3.3	8.3	8.3	7.7	8.0	6.1	7.9	7.0	9.0	7.9	7.4
Imports of goods and services	669.0	9.9	12.0	8.0	6.1	5.6	8.6	2.7	7.4	6.9	5.0	5.6
* net exports	−29.6ᵃ	−0.7	−0.5	−0.1	0.1	0.2	−0.4	0.5	−0.2	0.1	0.3	0.1
GDP at market prices	6 244.4	2.2	3.5	2.0	2.3	2.0	1.2	2.0	2.4	2.5	1.8	2.0
Industrial production	−	3.5	5.8	3.3	2.1	2.3	3.2	1.4	2.2	2.5	2.2	2.3

* Contributions to changes in real GDP (as a per cent of real GDP in the previous period).
a) Actual amount.

UNITED STATES
Employment, income and inflation

Percentage changes from previous period, seasonally adjusted at annual rates

	1993	1994	1995	1996	1997	1995 I	II	1996 I	II	1997 I	II
Employment[a,b]	1.5	2.3	1.6	1.1	1.1	1.9	0.1	1.5	1.3	1.0	1.1
Unemployment rate[b,c]	6.9	6.1	5.6	5.5	5.6	5.6	5.6	5.5	5.5	5.6	5.6
Compensation of employees	4.5	5.2	5.0	4.4	4.4	5.4	4.8	4.2	4.4	4.4	4.4
Unit labour cost	2.2	1.7	2.9	2.0	2.3	4.1	2.7	1.8	1.8	2.5	2.3
Household disposable income	4.4	4.9	5.3	4.7	4.7	5.1	4.7	4.7	4.6	4.9	4.3
GDP deflator	2.6	2.3	2.4	2.1	2.2	2.7	2.1	2.1	2.0	2.2	2.2
Private consumption deflator	2.6	2.4	2.3	2.0	2.3	2.5	1.7	2.1	2.0	2.3	2.4

a) Household basis.
b) Break in series as of January 1994.
c) As a percentage of labour force.

residential investment continued to increase at rates well above overall growth, reflecting a healthy overall business financial position, declining relative prices for capital equipment and a falling cost of capital. But a deceleration was clearly evident in the second semester, as capacity utilisation eased. Private consumption rose in line with income. While household finances may have deteriorated somewhat as delinquency rates and debt payment burdens have risen, these are still well below previous peak levels. At the same time, household assets have increased markedly as the equity and bond markets have made substantial gains.

However, as 1995 drew to a close there were once again signs of renewed weakness. Household consumption fell in both September and October, pushing up inventory-sales ratios. Then the partial shutdowns and constrained spending of the federal government further weakened demand and output, as did a major strike in the aircraft industry. Domestic demand actually edged down in the fourth quarter, though with export growth in double digits real GDP managed a tiny gain. January's production was also disrupted by winter storms and a further government shutdown, and March saw an important strike in the auto sector.

Yet ever-confident consumers had by no means abandoned the scene: with strong growth in disposable incomes in the five months to March real private consumption surged at an annual rate of 5.4 per cent, driving the saving rate down 3/4 of a percentage point. Aided by a strong rebound in business new orders and investment and a further rise in housing starts, supply began to respond with the end of the severe winter weather, and real GDP rose 2.8 per cent (annual rate) in the first quarter, despite the (auto-related) slowdown in stockbuilding to the lowest rate since 1992. With a turnaround in auto production and inventories in prospect,

the stage is set for a strong second-quarter outcome as well.

The trade deficit narrowed quite sharply in the second half of 1995 – the first decline since 1991. Export growth strengthened, reflecting both economic developments in some of the United States' largest trading partners and faster market-share gains. Import increases slowed to a crawl, perhaps a payback from the elevated rates in the first half when imports accelerated despite the cooling in domestic demand. The current account deficit also declined to an annual rate of $143 billion (1.9 per cent of GDP) in the second half as the surplus on services increased slightly (attributable to increased earnings from royalties and license fees) and official transfers abroad dipped temporarily due to the budgetary impasse, but the balance on investment income worsened in line with the nation's increasingly negative net international investment position. Thus far in 1996 export growth has slowed again and, with the renewed buoyancy in domestic demand, import growth has picked up, with the result that the trade deficit has widened again.

Employment, as measured by the establishment survey, grew at about a 1 per cent annualised rate in the second half of 1995, roughly equal to trend labour force growth. However, according to the household survey, the labour force and employment grew at only a 0.3 per cent rate. In the first four months of 1996, labour force growth rebounded, bringing the rate back towards trend. But with non-farm job creation at an annual rate of 1.7 per cent, the unemployment rate has remained near 5 1/2 per cent. Labour productivity in the non-farm business sector is estimated to have risen 1.6 per cent over the most recent four quarters compared to only 0.5 per cent in 1994 and 1.1 per cent in 1995, an encouraging performance for this stage in the cycle. This has been a factor in restraining unit labour costs, which rose 2.5 per cent in 1995 and 0.6 per cent (annual rate) in the first quarter.

United States

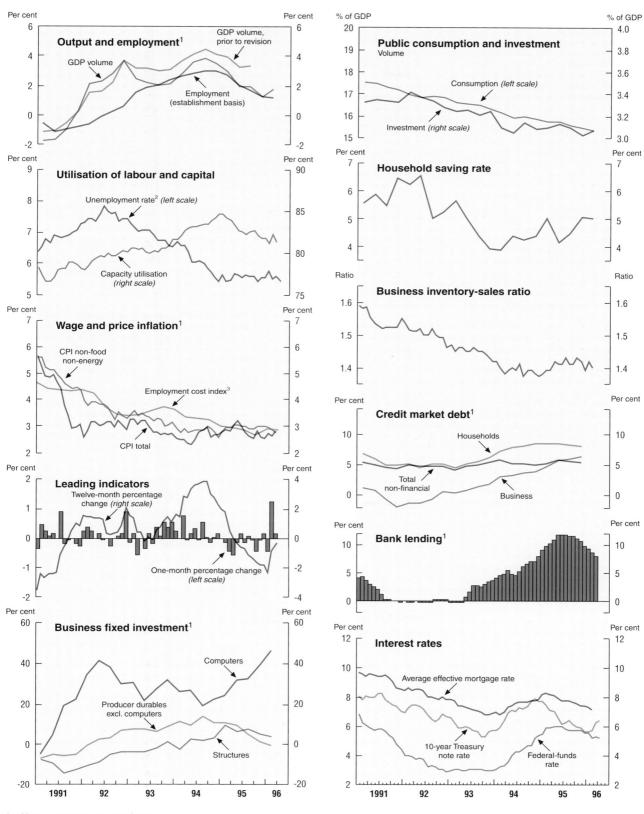

1. Year-on-year percentage change.
2. Break in series. New basis as of January 1994.
3. Total compensation of private, non-farm workers, s.a.

Sources: Department of Commerce; Federal Reserve Board; Congressional Budget Office; OECD, *Main Economic Indicators*.

Financial indicators

	1993	1994	1995	1996	1997	1995 I	1995 II	1996 I	1996 II	1997 I	1997 II
Household saving ratio[a]	4.7	4.2	4.7	4.8	5.0	4.6	4.8	4.7	4.8	5.1	5.0
General government financial balance[b]	−3.6	−2.3	−2.0	−1.9	−1.8	−2.0	−1.9	−2.0	−1.8	−1.9	−1.7
Current balance[b]	−1.5	−2.2	−2.1	−2.0	−1.8	−2.3	−1.9	−2.0	−1.9	−1.8	−1.8
Short-term interest rate[c]	3.0	4.2	5.5	5.1	5.3	5.7	5.3	5.0	5.3	5.3	5.3
Long-term interest rate[d]	5.9	7.1	6.6	6.6	6.6	7.1	6.1	6.3	6.9	6.6	6.6

a) As a percentage of disposable income.
b) As a percentage of GDP.
c) 3-month Treasury bills.
d) 10-year government bonds.

More importantly, labour compensation has not accelerated even though labour markets have remained fairly tight by historical standards. Indeed, the employment cost index for private industry recorded its smallest rise (2.8 per cent over the year to December) since its inception in the early 1980s, due to moderation in non-wage labour costs, especially health insurance premiums. However, there was a noticeable pick-up in wages and salaries in the first quarter. Reflecting the modest compensation gains, a stabilisation of mark-ups as well as falling import prices, price pressures appeared to ease in the second half of 1995, with the consumer price index up only 2.5 per cent for the year to December. This marked the fourth consecutive year at or below 3 per cent, the best performance since the mid-1960s. As a result, the Survey of Professional Forecasters reported that long-term inflation expectations had declined to 3 per cent by the end of 1995. In recent months prices have risen at a 4 per cent annual rate owing to surging energy and food prices, but other consumer prices have not accelerated.

Policies and other forces acting

Efforts by the Administration and the Congress to come to an agreement on a plan to eliminate the federal budget deficit over a seven-year horizon have proved fruitless, and, with the election season underway, the prevailing view in the market is that prospects are dim for any further progress before next year. For most of the current fiscal year many federal departments' discretionary spending has been funded by a series of continuing resolutions which guarantee as little as 75 per cent of previous expenditure levels. It was only in April that a final budget for FY 1996 was agreed, calling for small cuts in nominal discretionary outlays. The result has been weak growth in overall federal outlays and a further substantial cut in the deficit relative to previously expected levels, especially in light of the economy's sluggish output performance thus far this fiscal year; over the first half of FY 1996 the cumulative deficit is down by $18 billion over the previous year's outcome, consistent with the Administration's forecast of $146 billion (1.9 per cent of GDP) for the full year.

Federal borrowing was also disrupted by Congressional unwillingness to increase the debt limit until late in March. Thus, in order to avert default, the Treasury was forced in November 1995 and February 1996 to exchange non-marketable public debt held by certain government trust funds for IOUs not subject to the debt limit. In the context of the budgetary deadlock the Administration has proposed a FY 1997 budget which is very similar to its previous negotiating position with Congress. It calls for a deficit of $140 billion (1.8 per cent of GDP) in FY 1997, falling to a small surplus in 2001. Receipts would be cut marginally, as small personal income tax cuts for middle-class families with young children would be largely offset by higher taxes on businesses. Discretionary spending would edge down in nominal terms until 1999 and then rise by an average of 2¼ per cent (an annual decline of ½ per cent in real terms) until 2002. Transfer programmes (mostly for health care) would be cut by an average of about 4 per cent per year for a seven-year total saving of nearly $300 billion.

Citing primarily lower-than-expected inflation, the Federal Reserve continued to unwind the monetary tightness it had put in place in 1994 and early 1995 by cutting the federal funds rate by ¼ percentage point in both December and January as well as the official discount rate on the latter occasion. Financial markets had been expecting these moves, as short-term Treasury bill rates had been trading continuously below the funds rate. Indeed, for much of this period the very short end of the yield curve was inverted. Long-term interest rates continued their steady decline until January, bringing the cumu-

Recent projections for the federal budget deficit

$ billion, fiscal years except as noted

	1995[a]	1996	1997	1998	1999	2000	2001
Administration[b, c]	164	146	140	98	64	28	(8)
Congressional Budget Office[b, d]	164	144	171	194	219	244	259
Congressional Budget Office[b, e]	164	146	155	152	123	105	54
OECD Secretariat (calendar year)[f]	156	145	141	..	..	..	..
Blue Chip Economic Indicators (calendar year)[f]	164	164	155	..	..	..	..

a) Actual estimates for 1995.
b) Budget basis.
c) Including impact of Administration budget proposals on both budgetary outlays and receipts, and economic assumptions.
d) Assuming that discretionary spending is fixed in real terms after 1998.
e) Including impact of Administration budget proposals on outlays and receipts as well as the effects of balancing the budget on economic assumptions.
f) National accounts basis.

lative decline from the November 1994 peak to that point to nearly 2½ percentage points at the ten-year maturity.

The financial markets persisted in the expectation that further easing was in the offing, but when the Federal Reserve gave no clear indications that such was its intention, the prospects for an agreement to eliminate the budget deficit deteriorated further, and the economy showed definite signs of a rebound, the stage was set for a major reversal in psychology: almost simultaneously, three-month rates rose about ¼ percentage point, futures markets began to indicate expectations of a slight rise in short rates and the yield curve steepened noticeably, with interest rates on ten-year bonds rising a full percentage point from mid-February to early May, before a modest reversal. With lower inflation expectations, a fall in the discount rate applied to the expected stream of earnings has kept share prices on an upward path. The dollar, too, has continued to appreciate, with a cumulative gain of almost 10 per cent on an effective basis since the spring 1995 trough. While M1 growth continues to be weakened by the spread of sweep accounts for large commercial bank customers and reduced demand for US currency from abroad, both M2 and M3 growth have been above the top of their respective targeting ranges (1 to 5 and 2 to 6 per cent, respectively), and bank credit supply has also been increasing moderately, albeit at rates well below those of 1994 and early 1995, as lending standards have been tightened. But consumer credit expansion has remained fairly robust.

The OECD Secretariat's central projections assume that the federal funds rate will rise slightly in the second half of 1996, as the forces playing on the economy are expected to be finely balanced, keeping it on a sustainable growth path near full employment with fairly steady underlying inflation. This rise reflects a tilt in the balance of risks from insufficient demand, which was evident late last year and early this year, towards persis-

tent above trend demand which would put increasing pressure on prices. Long-term rates are projected to remain elevated until demand and output pressures are seen to have eased back to trend rates of growth near the end of this year, and then to fall modestly in 1997. The projections also assume that there will be no change in fiscal policy. Thus, spending will continue to be governed by the provisions of the 1993 omnibus legislation and the spending cuts incorporated in the 1996 appropriations bills. However, the recently passed reform of the regulatory regime in the telecommunications sector – which is already leading to significant restructuring – will probably unleash powerful forces pushing up investment in the years to come. And reforms to the farm and electricity distribution sectors could also stimulate substantial restructuring.

Prospects

The economic outlook continues to be promising, with no strong reason to fear either overheating or prolonged weakness. Thus, the OECD Secretariat's projection calls for real GDP growth of 2 to 2¼ per cent in both 1996 and 1997 with fairly steady, low inflation rates. GDP growth should ease at the end of 1996 under the influence of higher long-term interest rates before firming slightly during 1997 as rates reverse course. Business fixed investment is expected to continue to rise faster than overall growth, buttressed by the reduction in overall capital costs, the continued need for incorporating new technologies, particularly in information processing, and a healthy business financial position. Another source of growth is projected to come from exports, reflecting a pick-up in activity in Canada, Japan and Mexico, as well as increased market shares world-wide, especially in 1996. Weakness in residential construction should hold

UNITED STATES
External indicators[a]
Seasonally adjusted at annual rates

	1994	1995	1996	1997	1995 I	1995 II	1996 I	1996 II	1997 I	1997 II
					$ billion					
Merchandise exports	502.5	575	628	688	562.0	588	611	645	674	701
Merchandise imports	668.6	749	787	839	748.2	750	772	801	825	852
Trade balance	−166.1	−174	−159	−151	−186.2	−163	−162	−156	−151	−151
Invisibles, net	14.9	22	9	12	23.0	20	9	8	14	10
Current balance	−151.2	−153	−150	−139	−163.2	−143	−152	−147	−137	−140
					Percentage change					
Merchandise export volumes[b]	10.1	10.7	9.2	9.3	8.6	9.5	8.2	10.8	9.1	8.3
Merchandise import volumes[b]	13.5	9.1	6.0	6.0	9.6	2.5	7.2	7.3	5.4	6.0
Export performance[c]	−1.0	2.8	1.6	0.6	2.6	2.9	0.9	2.0	0.4	−0.4
Terms of trade	0.0	0.3	1.0	−0.4	1.6	1.6	1.0	0.5	−0.7	−0.6

a) For further detail, see tables in the External Trade and Payments section of the Annex.
b) Derived from values and unit values on a national accounts basis. Certain adjustments to the balance of payments basis are therefore excluded, the most important being the omission of foreign trade of the Virgin Islands.
c) Ratio between the total of export volumes and export market of total goods.

back aggregate demand growth as the rise in long-term interest rates in 1996 and lower demographic requirements depress construction activity. The government sector should continue to be a drag on final demand as pressures to reduce deficits at all levels are maintained. Private consumption should grow in line with household incomes, since saving rates seem near desired levels.

Joblessness should change little over the projection horizon as output grows at near its potential rate. With the unemployment rate roughly in line with the OECD Secretariat's estimate of the structural rate, there should be little pressure for either stronger or weaker growth of real compensation. However, wage gains may pick up somewhat as the recent deceleration of non-wage labour costs is passed through to wages. Consumer price inflation is not projected to stay as rapid as very recent rates, because of the moderate compensation outlook, favourable import price developments and the expected unwinding of the run-up in oil prices.

The external accounts are projected to improve somewhat in 1996 and 1997, with the current account deficit falling from around 2 per cent of GDP in 1995 to 1³/₄ per cent in 1997, reflecting rising national saving rates while nominal investment stabilises as a share of GDP. Most of the improvement would be found in merchandise trade because the rest of the world is projected to begin to grow faster than the United States, while US cost advantages are expected largely to persist. But the deficit on investment income may continue to widen because of the deterioration of the nation's net investment position, with little movement in relative rates of return.

Among the key uncertainties after the major historical data revision are whether the economy is actually at full employment and what is the rate of growth of output at full employment. The OECD Secretariat's estimates of the structural unemployment rate (around 5³/₄ per cent) and potential GDP growth (between 2 and 2¹/₄ per cent) imply that the projected output path should yield little change in unemployment and inflation. But the outlook for output growth is subject to considerable uncertainty. If household spending proves more buoyant due to greater wealth and confidence effects and the recent pick-up in growth proves to be more persistent than projected, then pressures on supply could lead to a noticeable acceleration of inflation, prompting a more substantial tightening in monetary policy. Alternatively, the rise in long-term rates that has already occurred as well as declining capacity utilisation rates, rising consumer debt burdens and tightening bank lending standards could lead to a more rapid slowdown in interest-sensitive demand than projected. But these risks seem to be evenly balanced.

NOTE

1. See the box entitled "The Impact of US National Accounts Revisions" in the chapter "General Assessment of the Economic Situation" in this Outlook for a brief quantification of the effect of these changes on recent and prospective real GDP growth.

JAPAN

The weak recovery in economic activity that started in 1994 gained momentum in the second half of 1995, when output rose by nearly 3 per cent. Aided by strong growth of public investment and low interest rates, domestic demand accelerated rapidly though this was partially offset by a rapid increase in imports. For 1995 as a whole, GDP grew by 1 per cent. The momentum of the recovery is likely to persist, despite the fiscal tightening planned over the next eighteen months. In particular, increased investment stemming from the higher profits associated with continued restructuring, lower financing costs and the correction of the earlier over-valued yen exchange rate should sustain the recovery, yielding output growth of 2¼ per cent this year and 2½ per cent next year. With widespread spare capacity remaining and unemployment still high, the underlying price level should continue to fall, though higher indirect taxes will raise the overall GDP deflator in 1997. The current account surplus may fall to close to $77 billion (1.6 per cent of GDP) by that time.

Recent developments

The hesitant recovery of the economy, which had been interrupted in the first half of 1995 by the effects of the Kobe earthquake and the sharp appreciation of the yen, gained momentum in the second half of the year, with GDP growth picking up to nearly 3 per cent. The added stimulus to demand provided by the easing of monetary policy and two supplementary budgets helped in this regard. Almost half the increase in domestic demand came from public investment, which rose at an annual rate of nearly 25 per cent in the second half of 1995. Lower interest rates appear to have increased private sector demand, with consumption of durable goods, such as autos, rising markedly. In addition, businesses benefited from the orderly reversal in the value of the yen, lower financing costs and continued cost reductions achieved through restructuring. These factors led to a significant increase in the profits of major companies in FY 1995, particularly in the manufacturing sector. As a result, the growth of business investment accelerated in the second half of the year, bringing the growth of private sector demand to 3 per cent. Overall, total domestic demand grew by nearly 4½ per cent.

The expansion of domestic demand was not fully reflected in an increase in output due to a marked fall in net exports. Exports stagnated as the lower value of the yen had not had sufficient time to increase sales by the second half of the year while the increase in imports

JAPAN
Demand and output
Percentage changes from previous period, seasonally adjusted at annual rates, volume (1990 prices)

	1992 current prices trillion Y	1993	1994	1995	1996	1997	1995 I	1995 II	1996 I	1996 II	1997 I	1997 II
Private consumption	272.3	1.2	1.8	1.6	2.4	2.2	0.4	3.6	2.0	2.2	2.3	2.0
Government consumption	43.3	2.4	2.2	2.0	1.7	2.1	5.0	−1.0	2.7	2.3	2.1	2.0
Gross fixed investment	143.5	−2.0	−1.0	0.8	5.6	3.2	−1.2	7.7	6.4	2.0	3.3	4.5
Public[a]	35.3	15.7	2.8	1.4	9.0	0.6	−4.6	24.8	8.9	−4.0	1.8	2.8
Private residential	22.8	2.4	9.2	−6.1	0.8	0.6	−9.4	−11.3	6.2	3.5	−2.0	3.1
Private non-residential	85.4	−10.2	−6.0	2.9	5.2	5.6	3.7	5.5	5.0	5.2	5.7	5.8
Final domestic demand	459.1	0.3	1.0	1.4	3.3	2.5	0.3	4.4	3.4	2.2	2.6	2.8
* stockbuilding	1.5[b]	−0.1	−0.2	0.2	0	0.1	0.2	0.1	−0.1	−0.1	0.2	0.1
Total domestic demand	460.6	0.1	0.8	1.6	3.3	2.6	0.5	4.5	3.3	2.0	2.8	2.9
Exports of goods and services	47.4	1.3	4.5	5.0	5.2	7.5	6.1	2.0	6.0	7.0	7.5	8.0
Imports of goods and services	36.2	1.7	9.0	13.5	14.7	9.5	12.6	17.8	15.7	10.0	9.4	9.3
* net exports	11.2[b]	0	−0.3	−0.7	−1.0	−0.2	−0.5	−1.6	−1.0	−0.3	−0.2	−0.2
GDP at market prices	471.8	0.1	0.5	0.9	2.2	2.4	0	2.8	2.2	1.7	2.5	2.7
Industrial production[c]	–	−4.5	0.8	3.3	5.6	6.3	4.7	−2.4	8.8	7.7	5.6	6.2

* Contributions to changes in real GDP (as a per cent of real GDP in the previous period).
a) Including public corporations.
b) Actual amount.
c) Mining and manufacturing.

JAPAN
Employment, income and inflation
Percentage changes from previous period, seasonally adjusted at annual rates

	1993	1994	1995	1996	1997	1995 I	1995 II	1996 I	1996 II	1997 I	1997 II
Employment	0.2	0.1	0.1	0.1	0.4	0.5	−0.2	0.2	0.4	0.4	0.4
Unemployment rate[a]	2.5	2.9	3.1	3.3	3.2	3.0	3.3	3.3	3.2	3.2	3.2
Compensation of employees	2.3	1.9	1.6	2.0	2.4	3.8	1.7	2.0	2.3	2.5	2.5
Unit labour cost	2.2	1.4	0.7	−0.2	0	3.8	−1.1	−0.2	0.6	−0.1	−0.2
Household disposable income	2.5	1.9	1.9	1.6	2.7	3.6	1.4	1.5	2.0	2.8	3.0
GDP deflator	0.6	0.3	−0.5	−0.3	0.3	−0.6	−0.1	−0.4	−0.5	0.6	0.6
Private consumption deflator	1.2	0.7	−0.5	−0.4	0.6	−0.6	−0.5	−0.4	−0.4	0.9	1.0

a) As a percentage of labour force.

amounted to almost one-third of the rise in domestic demand. A part of this fall in net exports represented a move of production overseas. Japanese car producers filled a growing proportion of overseas demand by using the output of their foreign plants, which also increased their exports back to Japan. In addition, out-sourcing of component production and greater competition in the retail sector have been among the factors leading to a marked increase in imports from Asia. These developments led to a fall in the current account surplus to an annual rate of $105 billion (2.1 per cent of GDP) in the second half of 1995, down from the peak of $131 billion in 1993.

Although the growth of output picked up, capacity utilisation remained low and employment fell, leading to a rise in the unemployment rate to 3.4 per cent by the end of 1995. As a result, the downward pressure on domestic prices and wages continued, with the final domestic demand deflator falling at an annual rate of 0.8 per cent in the second half of the year, despite a marked increase in import prices. The fall in the GDP deflator moderated, however, as exporters increased their domestic currency prices by almost three-quarters of the fall in the value of the yen.

Recent indicators point to a sustained expansion in private sector demand and output in the first half of 1996, notwithstanding a further reduction in the current account surplus, though the momentum may be somewhat less than at the end of 1995. Indicators for investment are buoyant, with new orders for machinery and equipment and housing starts increasing markedly at the beginning of the year, and the strength of retail sales points to a continued expansion of private consumption. On the other hand, the growth of public sector demand is likely to slacken after the strong improvement registered at the end of 1995. The pace of stockbuilding may also ease, especially in the manufacturing sector where the stock-to-sales ratio is particularly high. These last two compo-

nents of expenditure account for nearly all of the slow-down in the growth of domestic demand projected for the first half of this year. While the lower value of the yen should start to narrow the gap between the growth of imports and exports, the expansion of GDP, at 2.2 per cent, may still be slower than that of domestic demand. Nevertheless, output growth has been sufficient to stabilise the labour market. Unemployment fell in the first quarter of the year and the amount of overtime working increased.

Policies and other forces acting

Since the reduction of the Official Discount Rate (ODR) to 1/2 per cent in September of last year, monetary policy has continued to support economic activity. Interest rates in the overnight call market rate quickly fell below the ODR and were gradually reflected in lower rates on three and six-month CDs. The gap between money market rates and the rate of inflation (as measured by the private consumption deflator) fell to slightly over 1 per cent in the second half of 1995, reversing the increase that occurred in the previous year. Since the first half of 1995, the fall in short-term interest rates has been greater than in the United States. This has reinforced the authorities' policy of ensuring a reversal of the earlier appreciation of the yen through intervention in currency markets, which led to foreign exchange reserves increasing by 1.0 per cent of GDP in the second half of 1995. By the spring of 1996, the yen-dollar rate, at around 106, was almost one quarter below its peak level.

Long-term interest rates have increased only slightly since the lowering of the of the ODR. In the first half of 1996, they stood close to 3 1/4 per cent, near to the average of the previous six months. Such stability may reflect, in part, the low risk of the expansion in economic activity generating higher inflation. Moreover, the higher

Japan

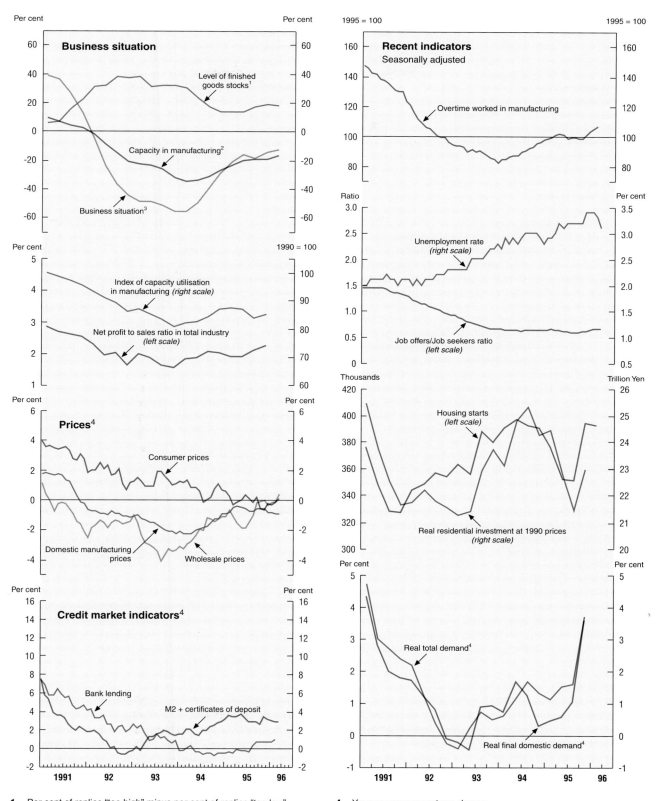

1. Per cent of replies "too high" minus per cent of replies "too low".
2. Per cent of firms with insufficient capacity minus per cent of firms with excessive capacity.
3. Per cent of replies "good" minus per cent of replies "bad".

4. Year-on-year percentage change.
Sources: Bank of Japan, *Short-Term Economic Survey of Principal Enterprises in Japan;* EPA, *Japanese Economic Indicators.*

JAPAN
Financial indicators

	1993	1994	1995	1996	1997	1995 I	1995 II	1996 I	1996 II	1997 I	1997 II
Household saving ratio[a]	13.4	12.8	13.4	13.1	12.9	13.4	13.5	13.2	13.0	12.9	12.9
General government financial balance[b]	−1.6	−2.1	−3.9	−4.8	−3.7	−3.5	−4.2	−4.9	−4.7	−4.1	−3.2
Current balance[b]	3.1	2.8	2.2	1.8	1.6	2.2	2.1	1.8	1.8	1.7	1.6
Short-term interest rate[c]	2.9	2.3	1.2	0.7	0.9	1.8	0.6	0.6	0.7	0.8	1.0
Long-term interest rate[d]	4.3	4.4	3.4	3.4	3.7	3.7	3.1	3.3	3.6	3.7	3.8

a) As a percentage of disposable income.
b) As a percentage of GDP.
c) 3-6 month CD.
d) Central government bonds.

government deficit does not appear to have resulted in higher long-term rates given the rapid increase in holdings of bonds by the non-bank sector. With both a lower yen and lower short-term interest rates helping to boost company sector profits, the stockmarket has recovered substantially from the low levels of the spring of 1995.

Despite the pick-up in economic activity and the fall in short-term interest rates, there has been no acceleration in the growth of credit. The growth of lending by public and private institutions, taken together, has remained stable at a rate of around 2 per cent. However, the market share of banks stopped falling as their lending started to increase once again. Part of this movement reflected a decision of borrowers to move away from public financial institutions as their charges became relatively expensive. This move was facilitated by the change in official regulations at the end of 1994 that allowed banks in 1995 to offer mortgages based on the short-term prime rate.

The easing in monetary policy has not raised the growth of the broad money supply (M2 + CDs) which has expanded only slightly faster than nominal GDP in the second half of 1995. The deposit base of banks became markedly more liquid, with enterprises reducing longer-term deposits and increasing their holdings of demand deposits as interest rates fell. Consequently, the growth of narrow money rose to nearly 15 per cent by March 1996. There was some evidence that depositors were moving towards institutions that were perceived as more secure, after the failure of several credit co-operatives and two second-tier regional banks during the summer of 1995 and spring of 1996. Partially as a result of this trend, postal savings deposits rose rapidly, so boosting the growth of the broadest definition of the money stock (M3 + CDs) to 3¾ per cent.

Although official support to financial institutions had reached ¥ 2.5 trillion ($24 billion) by April 1996, progress in improving the capital position of financial institutions has been slow. While the increase in stock market values and the continued operating profits of most institutions have helped to rebuild the capital base of the banks, the value of the collateral backing their non-performing loans, which are officially estimated at ¥ 38 trillion, has continued to decline as the fall in commercial property prices accelerated. Banks are now beginning to recognise the low value of these loans by increasing write-offs and provisions. The government plans to inject ¥ 685 billion from the general budget into the *Jusen* Resolution Corporation (JRC), which will acquire part of the bad loans of the housing loan companies (*jusen*). Parliament has authorised this expenditure but not yet passed the bill establishing the JRC. This law is being considered along with a reform of the deposit insurance system and a new regulatory framework for financial institutions, permitting prompt corrective action by the authorities when banks have problems. Against this background, the premia which Japanese banks have to pay on their international borrowing started to widen again in the spring.

The stance of fiscal policy became markedly more expansionary in FY 1995 but the emphasis of policy in the FY 1996 budget moved to containing the budget deficit. The stimulus to activity on the 1995 budget initially came from a supplementary budget for earthquake-related reconstruction in the Kobe area. The momentum of spending was increased further by a decision to advance expenditure to the first half the fiscal year. A final boost to spending was given by a second supplementary budget, designed to implement the September 1995 economic package. In total, these two supplementary budgets boosted spending by Y 8 trillion (1.7 per cent of GDP) resulting in an increase in central government net borrowing to 4.2 per cent of GDP. The draft budget for FY 1996 attempts to stabilise the size of the central government deficit. Total expenditure is projected to drop by almost 5 per cent, despite the provision for spending on resolving the *jusen* crisis. Overall, cen-

JAPAN
External indicators[a]
Seasonally adjusted at annual rates

	1994	1995	1996	1997	1995 I	1995 II	1996 I	1996 II	1997 I	1997 II
					$ billion					
Merchandise exports	385.5	429	417	453	436.1	422	406	428	444	462
Merchandise imports	241.3	297	314	351	292.9	301	305	323	341	361
Trade balance	144.2	132	103	102	143.2	121	101	105	103	101
Invisibles, net	−13.5	−20	−21	−25	−24.6	−16	−19	−23	−24	−26
Current balance	130.6	112	82	77	118.7	105	81	82	79	75
					Percentage change					
Merchandise export volumes[b]	1.7	3.3	2.6	6.9	5.0	−2.8	2.1	9.1	6.0	6.5
Merchandise import volumes[b]	13.6	12.5	8.6	10.7	13.4	7.3	7.8	11.5	10.5	10.2
Export performance[c]	−10.3	−7.3	−5.9	−1.5	−5.8	−11.4	−5.9	0.3	−2.2	−1.9
Terms of trade	7.6	−0.4	−2.5	0.5	0.1	−1.5	−4.8	1.4	0.3	0.2

a) For further detail, see tables in the External Trade and Payments section of the Annex.
b) Customs basis.
c) Ratio between the total of export volumes and export market of total goods.

tral government net borrowing is not expected to change in FY 1996, remaining at around 4 1/4 per cent of GDP.

Fiscal policy will become markedly tighter in FY 1997. The government has already passed legislation to allow an increase of the consumption tax from 3 to 5 per cent to be effective in April 1997, and the possibility of raising that tax further is under consideration. In addition, there are no plans to prolong the temporary income tax cut which ends in FY 1996. The higher revenues stemming from these changes should push the central government deficit below 4 per cent of GDP. Even after taking into account the diminishing social security surplus and the local authority deficit, the general government deficit should also decline to 3 3/4 per cent of GDP in 1997 from 4 3/4 per cent in 1996, bringing gross and net government debt to over 95 per cent and 17 per cent of GDP, respectively.

Prospects

The stimulus from economic policy measures and the lower value of the yen appear to have set the economy on track for a modest recovery, with GDP growth expected to average 2.2 per cent in 1996 and 2.4 per cent in 1997. The stimulus to growth coming from improved international competitiveness should be a contributing factor supporting the expansion from the second half of 1996 onwards, through its impact on both foreign trade and profits. Indeed, the drag on activity coming from the continuing fall in net exports may be reduced by more than 3/4 per cent of GDP over the next eighteen months and should be sufficient to offset the tightening of fiscal

policy. The correction of the earlier over-valued yen exchange rate, if sustained, should progressively reduce the loss in export market shares. By 1997, the growth of manufactured exports may be only 1 1/2 per cent below the growth of markets, down from a gap of over 10 percentage points in 1994 and 1995. Import growth should also slacken, though still remaining high compared with the growth of domestic demand, as the restructuring of industry continues. As a result, the current account surplus should decline less rapidly from the second half of 1996 onwards, though still dropping to $77 billion (1.6 per cent of GDP) by 1997.

The reversal in the value of the yen should also help profits in export industries to continue to rise and maintain the strength of business investment, especially in the chemical and car industries. Profitability will also be improved by the efforts that large firms are making to reduce employment. As a result, the upturn in demand should generate the strongest productivity growth since 1991. Small businesses do not, though, have the same excess of labour as large firms, according to business surveys, and this suggests that the projected gains in employment may be mostly in this sector. With the numbers of self-employed continuing to fall in 1996, the unemployment rate is likely to show only a modest decline. Such developments are likely to restrain the rise of real personal disposable income as will the fall in households' interest income, making for only a modest increase in private consumption.

The pick-up in growth will not be sufficient to reduce markedly the extent of spare capacity in the economy. With wages growing by slightly less than produc-

GERMANY
Employment, income and inflation
Percentage changes from previous period, seasonally adjusted at annual rates

	1993	1994	1995	1996	1997	1995		1996		1997	
						I	II	I	II	I	II
Employment	−1.8	−0.7	−0.2	−0.9	0.2	−0.4	−0.3	−1.3	−0.5	0.2	0.8
Unemployment rate[a]	8.9	9.6	9.4	10.3	10.4	9.3	9.5	10.2	10.5	10.5	10.3
Compensation of employees	2.0	2.2	3.3	2.3	2.7	4.3	2.6	2.1	2.3	2.6	3.4
Unit labour cost	3.2	−0.6	1.3	1.7	0.3	2.2	1.8	2.4	0.4	0.1	0.8
Household disposable income	3.9	3.0	3.6	3.0	3.4	5.2	1.9	3.5	3.0	3.3	4.0
GDP deflator	3.8	2.3	2.2	1.5	1.3	2.4	2.3	1.2	1.4	1.3	1.4
Private consumption deflator	4.0	2.8	2.0	1.6	1.5	1.8	2.1	1.4	1.4	1.5	1.5

a) As a percentage of labour force.

unusually harsh weather in January and February, which led to a marked decline in construction activity. The IFO indexes of business expectations and of current conditions continued to deteriorate while business concerns about excess stocks suggest that de-stocking was a continued drag on growth. Consumer sentiment also deteriorated and, for the first time in three years, households became more pessimistic about their future incomes. Western German unemployment surged by 100 000 in the first three months, with construction accounting for about a third of the increase.

In March and April there were the first signs of at least a seasonal recovery: unemployment in western Germany declined in April by a tenth of a point to 8.9 per cent (with a more substantial recovery in eastern Germany) and first estimates point to increased industrial production, including manufacturing. Moreover, abstracting from month-to-month variations, the decline in manufacturing orders appears to have slowed since the last quarter of 1995. Winter sales were also relatively strong, allowing retailers to de-stock, while car sales were up, suggesting that consumers were not immediately reducing spending in line with depressed expectations of income. Nevertheless, excluding weather-related corrections, the majority of indicators point to continued stagnation, and with capacity utilisation declining further.

Inflation has decelerated sharply. At the beginning of 1995, producer price inflation had been running at an annualised rate of some 2½ per cent, but by the end of the year this had declined to around ¾ per cent and in the first quarter prices fell. Construction prices stabilised, and export prices were stagnant. After falling throughout most of 1995, import prices picked up in the first quarter as a result of a stronger dollar and a jump in oil prices. While this will eventually feed through to consumer prices, year-on-year consumer price inflation has slowed to 1.4 per cent, led by slower increases in housing rents and services. Wholesale prices picked up in March but

are still down by some 1 per cent on a year-on-year basis, indicating that downward pressure on tradeable goods prices in the CPI is likely to persist.

Policies and other forces acting

Structural factors seem to be exercising a key dampening role in the current slowdown. In the manufacturing sector, which is relatively large in Germany, stagnant investment in equipment and declining employment are attributable to high wage costs and low rates of return on new investment following the post-reunification investment boom. Although profits recovered somewhat in 1994 and margins may have increased in some sectors in 1995, overall it now appears that their level in relation to capital is low both internationally and in comparison with the past. Output and employment in services have continued to expand, but at a rate inadequate to absorb resources released by the manufacturing sector.

Underlying the trend to industrial restructuring has been the appreciation of the nominal effective exchange rate by some 6 per cent between 1991 and 1994, which has put German enterprises under continuing pressure to cut costs. The further appreciation of the currency by around 5 per cent during 1995 was, in this respect, an important additional stimulus to rationalisation. However, reinforcing the pressure arising from the nominal exchange rate was the development of wages and social charges: in terms of unit labour costs in manufacturing, the currency has appreciated by 20 per cent in real terms since 1991. The 1995 wage round, which increased hourly labour costs in manufacturing by around 5.5 per cent, represented a severe negative shock to the economy. As important as the wage increase itself was the signal that a recovery in profitability, such as occurred in 1994, could be quickly bid away in the form of higher wages. In response, wage settlements in the current round

Germany

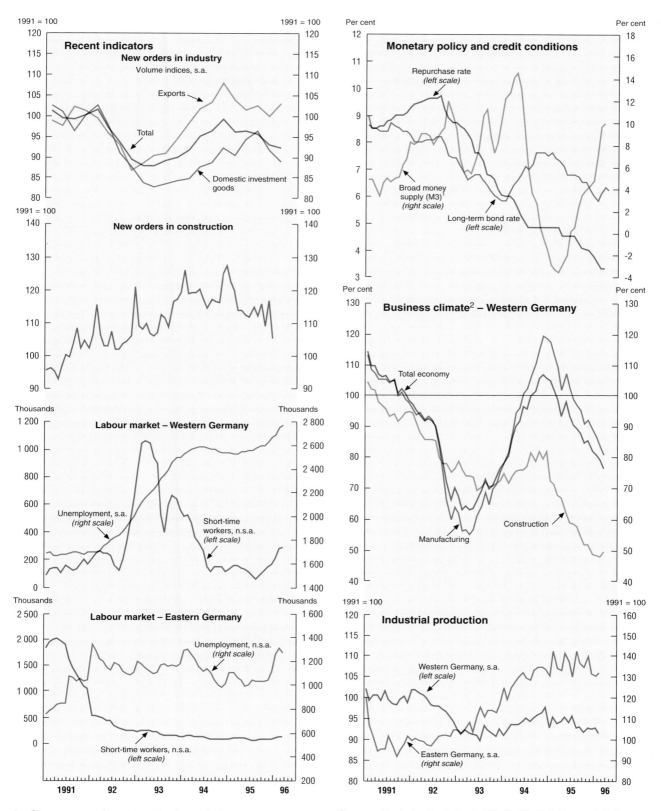

Recent indicators

New orders in industry
Volume indices, s.a.

1991 = 100

Exports

Total

Domestic investment goods

New orders in construction

1991 = 100

Labour market – Western Germany

Thousands

Unemployment, s.a.
(right scale)

Short-time workers, n.s.a.
(left scale)

Labour market – Eastern Germany

Thousands

Unemployment, n.s.a.
(right scale)

Short-time workers, n.s.a.
(left scale)

Monetary policy and credit conditions

Per cent

Repurchase rate
(left scale)

Broad money supply (M3)[1]
(right scale)

Long-term bond rate
(left scale)

Business climate[2] – Western Germany

Per cent

Total economy

Manufacturing

Construction

Industrial production

1991 = 100

Western Germany, s.a.
(left scale)

Eastern Germany, s.a.
(right scale)

1991   92   93   94   95   96

1. Change over previous six months at annual rate.
2. Weighted average of present and future (six months ahead) business situation. A level of 100 corresponds to "normality".

Sources: Deutsche Bundesbank; IFO; OECD, *Main Economic Indicators.*

GERMANY
Financial indicators

	1993	1994	1995	1996	1997	1995 I	1995 II	1996 I	1996 II	1997 I	1997 II
Household saving ratio[a]	12.2	11.6	11.6	11.7	11.5	11.7	11.4	11.8	11.5	11.4	11.6
General government financial balance[b]	−3.5	−2.5	−3.5	−4.1	−3.6	−1.1	−6.0	−4.1	−4.1	−3.8	−3.5
Current balance[b]	−0.9	−1.0	−0.7	−0.5	−0.3	−0.6	−0.8	−0.5	−0.4	−0.3	−0.2
Short-term interest rate[c]	7.3	5.4	4.5	3.3	3.5	4.9	4.2	3.4	3.2	3.4	3.6
Long-term interest rate[d]	6.5	6.9	6.9	6.5	6.4	7.2	6.5	6.5	6.6	6.5	6.3

a)   As a percentage of disposable income.
b)   As a percentage of GDP.
c)   3-month interbank rate.
d)   Public debt securities, 9-10 years.

have moderated to around 2 per cent, but have been associated with undertakings to protect current employment levels and by provisions to compensate overtime with free-time. The agreements run for only a year.

In the face of falling inflation and weak activity, monetary policy has become progressively, if cautiously, expansionary. In December the Bundesbank announced a wider money supply growth target for M3 for 1996 of 4-7 per cent based on the last quarter of 1995. Although no correction was made for the undershooting of the money supply during 1995, the bank took the view that this was due to a shift in money demand at the start of 1995 which corrected a previous liquidity overhang. In support of the new target, the discount rate was lowered by 50 basis points to 3 per cent in December and in April it was cut once again to a record low of 2.5 per cent. With the repurchase rate being held at 3.3 per cent, the gap between the two rates has served as a signal to the markets that a further reduction in policy rates remains possible. After falling rapidly until late January, bond yields have firmed, but this has been due largely to a weakening of world bond markets: the yield on ten-year DM bonds has fallen below that on the US equivalent for the first time since the 1980s. Measured on a six-month annualised basis, the growth rate of M3 has steadily increased since the third quarter of 1995, reaching some 10 per cent in March, although measured relative to the end of 1994, the actual growth rate of money has amounted to only some 4 per cent. The Deutschemark weakened on foreign exchange markets and in effective terms all of the 1995 appreciation was reversed by the end of the first quarter of this year. The combination of a weaker exchange-rate, relatively low policy-controlled interest rates, and moderate growth of monetary aggregates are projected to underpin output growth, while bond yields could ease as inflation expectations adjust to the new conditions of relative price stability.

Despite the reintroduction of the Solidarity tax surcharge and successful attempts to control the growth

of public expenditures, declining tax revenues led to a deterioration of the general government deficit by around DM 16 billion in 1995, raising the deficit by half a percentage point to 3.5 per cent of GDP. Only about one third of the decline in revenues can be attributed directly to the slowdown of growth during 1995, although this understates the role of cyclical factors. A major part of the decline is attributable to difficulties in predicting the cost of tax-incentive schemes, such as those used extensively to support investment in the new states. Such uncertainty is likely to remain for some time to come.

Although the government remains committed to meeting the Maastricht fiscal consolidation targets, the general government deficit is projected to deteriorate further in 1996, to around 4 per cent of GDP. Much of the deterioration will be due to falling employment, which will place important financial strains on the pension and unemployment funds. On the revenue side, automatic stabilisers are expected to support the weak economy, while tax reforms will result in substantial tax losses. However, given the considerable uncertainty about the development of tax revenues, the government has taken action to ensure that slippage of the structural budget balance remains limited: strict spending controls were introduced by the federal government in February, which are expected to reduce expenditures by some DM 8 billion in the course of the year. In addition, the government announced a fifty-point programme of deregulation and liberalisation in January, to promote growth and employment and this was followed up with a detailed action plan in April which envisages budget savings of DM 70 billion from 1997 onwards. Implementation difficulties, however, remain severe, and for this reason only those few measures which have either been agreed with third parties or mandated have been incorporated into the OECD's short-term projections. Legislation to control health costs was finally approved by the upper house of parliament, and the potential savings from this have been incorporated, as have the increases in pension contribu-

France

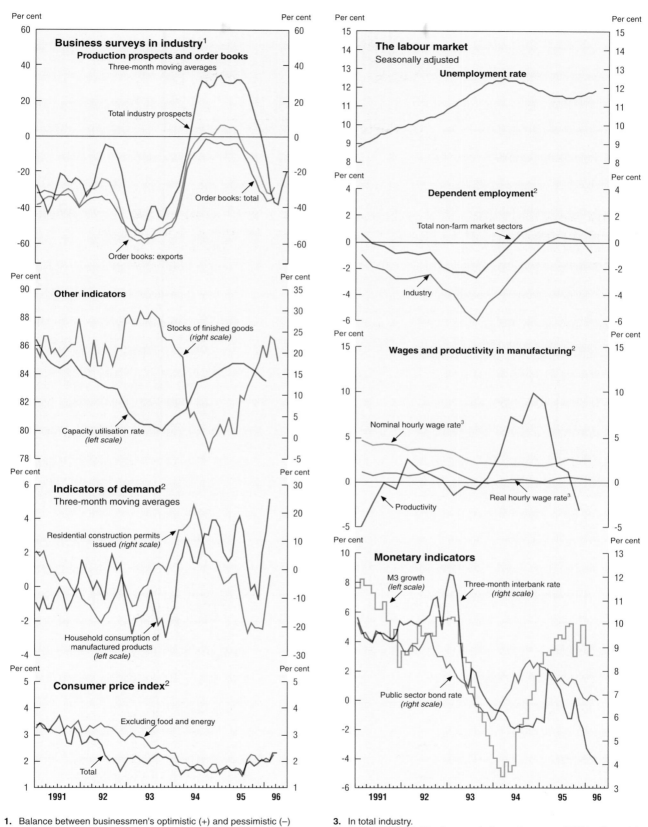

Business surveys in industry[1]
Production prospects and order books
Three-month moving averages

Total industry prospects

Order books: total

Order books: exports

Other indicators

Stocks of finished goods *(right scale)*

Capacity utilisation rate *(left scale)*

Indicators of demand[2]
Three-month moving averages

Residential construction permits issued *(right scale)*

Household consumption of manufactured products *(left scale)*

Consumer price index[2]

Excluding food and energy

Total

The labour market
Seasonally adjusted
Unemployment rate

Dependent employment[2]

Total non-farm market sectors

Industry

Wages and productivity in manufacturing[2]

Nominal hourly wage rate[3]

Productivity

Real hourly wage rate[3]

Monetary indicators

M3 growth *(left scale)*

Three-month interbank rate *(right scale)*

Public sector bond rate *(right scale)*

1991   92   93   94   95   96

1. Balance between businessmen's optimistic (+) and pessimistic (−) answers.
2. Year-on-year percentage changes.

3. In total industry.
Sources: INSEE, *Tendances de la conjoncture;* OECD, *Financial Statistics.*

FRANCE
Financial indicators

	1993	1994	1995	1996	1997	1995 I	1995 II	1996 I	1996 II	1997 I	1997 II
Household saving ratio[a]	14.1	13.6	14.3	13.9	13.9	14.1	14.5	13.9	14.0	13.9	13.8
General government financial balance[b]	−5.8	−5.8	−5.0	−4.3	−3.7	−5.1	−4.9	−4.3	−4.3	−3.9	−3.6
Current balance[b]	0.8	0.6	1.1	0.9	1.2	1.7	0.6	0.8	1.0	1.1	1.3
Short-term interest rate[c]	8.6	5.8	6.6	3.9	3.8	7.0	6.1	4.1	3.6	3.7	3.9
Long-term interest rate[d]	7.0	7.5	7.7	6.6	6.4	7.9	7.4	6.7	6.6	6.5	6.3

a) As a percentage of disposable income.
b) As a percentage of GDP.
c) 3-month interbank rate.
d) Public and semi-public sector bonds.

The State's budget deficit on a public accounts basis was on target in 1995 (at 4.2 per cent of GDP). Revenues (excluding privatisation receipts) rose by 5.3 per cent and expenditure by 2.8 per cent. Expenditure restraint was largely reflected in a sharp reduction in defence spending, while debt interest payments surged by 12.6 per cent. The 1996 budget again aims at expenditure restraint – pay scales for government employees were frozen – and a fall in the deficit to 3.6 per cent of GDP. While revenue measures in this budget were of minor importance, 1996 receipts will benefit from the carry-over effect of the tax rate increases introduced in mid-1995. Since early 1996, several initiatives have been taken in order to boost private consumption and the residential construction sector, and taxation has been lowered for small and medium-sized enterprises. On the other hand, a freeze of FF 20 billion in voted expenditure was announced in order to contain the budgetary effects of the slowdown in economic activity.

At FF 75 billion, the deficit of the general social security scheme was somewhat higher in 1995 than in 1994, largely reflecting a significant acceleration in health spending. In November 1995, the government announced a series of social security reform measures: Parliament will play a greater role in controlling spending and revenue decisions of the social security schemes,[1] and a new tax was introduced in February 1996, the proceeds of which will be used to repay the accumulated debt of the social security system. Health reform has progressed with the implementation of spending caps on health professionals and the reform of public hospitals has advanced. On the other hand, the reform of the "special" pension schemes (largely for public sector employees) was abandoned in the aftermath of the strikes in late 1995.

The OECD Secretariat's projections assume that social security reform will reduce social spending below its long-term trend, but that social spending will be some-

FRANCE
External indicators[a]
Seasonally adjusted at annual rates

	1994	1995	1996	1997	1995 I	1995 II	1996 I	1996 II	1997 I	1997 II
					$ billion					
Merchandise exports	222.9	268	264	283	268.5	267	262	265	277	290
Merchandise imports	215.2	256	253	269	254.9	257	253	254	264	275
Trade balance	7.7	12	10	14	13.5	10	9	11	13	15
Invisibles, net	0.4	6	4	5	11.8	0	4	4	5	6
Current balance	8.1	17	14	19	25.3	10	13	15	18	21
					Percentage change					
Merchandise export volumes[b]	6.5	7.6	1.6	7.0	10.6	−2.2	1.8	5.0	7.4	8.0
Merchandise import volumes[b]	7.3	5.7	2.0	5.9	6.7	0.1	2.1	3.8	6.3	7.3
Export performance[c]	−2.9	0.1	−4.3	0.0	3.6	−8.6	−3.5	−1.2	0.2	0.6
Terms of trade	0.2	−0.4	0.3	0.2	−1.5	1.0	0.0	0.1	0.2	0.2

a) For further detail, see tables in the External Trade and Payments section of the Annex.
b) Customs basis.
c) Ratio between the total of export volumes and export market of total goods.

80

what above the official target. On this basis, the general government deficit could fall to 4¼ per cent of GDP in 1996 and 3¾ per cent of GDP in 1997.[2] For 1996, the projections show a tightening of the fiscal stance of close to 1 per cent of GDP, while cyclical factors could raise the deficit by about ¼ per cent of GDP. Both factors will play a smaller role in 1997. The Government has recently announced that it envisages expenditure cuts of FF 60 billion (¾ per cent of GDP) in order to meet the Maastricht deficit criterion in 1997. In the absence of legislation on specific measures, these expenditure cuts have not been taken into account in these projections.

Prospects

Business surveys suggest a reversal of the current weakness in demand and consumer confidence rose somewhat in early 1996, albeit remaining at a very low level. Fiscal tightening and rising unemployment are likely to restrain consumer spending in 1996. Business investment, however, could rebound, underpinned by better financing conditions and healthy balance sheets. INSEE's investment survey points to a rise in real industrial investment of close to 10 per cent, very similar to the survey on investment intentions of large enterprises covering all sectors. Exports are also likely to show increasing dynamism. Overall, GDP growth in 1996 might only be 1 per cent. In 1997, however, better job prospects should bolster consumer spending and GDP growth could pick up to 2½ per cent. Despite the revival in import demand, the current account should remain in sizeable surplus.

Job losses during 1996 could lead to a rise in the unemployment rate to 12¼ per cent in early 1997. With some rebound in labour productivity, growth in 1997 might just suffice to stabilise the unemployment rate at this level. The rise in unemployment could lead to

somewhat lower wage increases, while inflation could fall to close to 1 per cent, once the impact of the VAT rate hike on consumer price inflation wanes in late 1996. Given substantial cyclical slack and slow rises in labour costs, underlying inflation is likely to drift down over the projection period.

Important risks attach to the outlook. Large uncertainties surround the development of the household saving ratio, which has risen to a high level in recent years. The strength of the recovery will largely depend on whether monetary policy has eased sufficiently to boost private consumption and investment and offset the negative short-run demand effects of the fiscal tightening measures incorporated in the central projections. If fiscal tightening in the short term is more significant than assumed in the central projections, output growth could be slower in 1997, although it would have positive consequences for activity beyond the projection period.

NOTES

1. So far, the social security schemes were managed by the Government and the social partners, with Parliament playing no role.

2. INSEE's national accounts treatment of interest payments does not make an adjustment for the payments corresponding to a premium received by the government when a bond is issued part-way through a standard coupon period. For the first period, the full coupon payment is recorded including the ''coupon couru'', which is in fact a repayment. In principle, the premium should be recorded as an offsetting receipt against the first coupon payment, with the net result that only the interest applying to the period after the bond was issued would be included. From 1992 onwards, data provided by INSEE incorporating this adjustment have been included here.

ITALY

With net exports weakening and last year's stock build-up being reversed, output growth seems set to weaken in 1996 before regaining some strength in 1997. In this setting, unemployment may be slow to fall, remaining well above the structural rate during the projection period. This, together with the stronger lira, should keep inflation on a downward course, creating the opportunity for the monetary authorities to lower interest rates during the second half of 1996. Long-term interest rate premia relative to Germany have already narrowed, partly as a result of the favourable 1995 budget outcome, and this improvement is expected to continue. But with the weakening of economic activity, the 1996 budget deficit could overshoot the target.

Recent developments

A strong build-up of stocks sustained economic expansion in the second half of 1995, pushing the rise in real GDP to 3.0 per cent for the year as a whole, the best result since 1988.[1] At the same time, slower growth in export markets sharply curtailed foreign sales, making for a negative contribution to economic growth from net exports. Final domestic demand also decelerated, as weakening output prospects reduced the buoyancy of investment in machinery and equipment. More recently, a rundown in inventories has depressed economic activity, reducing industrial output. By the first quarter of 1996, industrial production had dropped by an estimated 3.5 per cent from the peak reached in the third quarter of 1995. Output weakness was particularly pronounced for consumer goods and intermediate products.

The seasonally adjusted rate of unemployment remained at the historically high level of 12 per cent in the second half of 1995 and in early 1996, as the re-entry of discouraged workers swelled labour supply, matching overall employment gains. Labour market imbalances thus remain deep-seated. Employment, after shrinking for eight quarters in a row, picked up in the second half of 1995, supported by a rising demand for services and products of small industrial firms. Large industrial firms continued to shed labour as export demand decelerated in response to real exchange rate appreciation. Productivity rises remained strong as a consequence, limiting the rise in unit labour costs and boosting profitability further.

ITALY

Demand and output

Percentage changes from previous period, seasonally adjusted at annual rates, volume (1985 prices)

	1992 current prices trillion L	1993	1994	1995	1996	1997	1995 I	1995 II	1996 I	1996 II	1997 I	1997 II
Private consumption[a]	948.1	−2.5	1.6	1.6	1.4	2.1	1.8	1.2	1.4	1.7	2.2	2.3
Government consumption	267.8	0.7	0	−0.3	−0.1	0.4	−0.5	−0.7	−0.1	0.4	0.4	0.4
Gross fixed investment	287.4	−13.1	−0.1	5.7	5.1	5.2	8.4	4.9	5.3	5.1	5.1	5.4
Machinery and equipment	135.2	−19.3	5.3	10.5	4.8	4.4	14.6	5.1	4.8	4.5	4.2	4.5
Construction	152.3	−6.3	−5.2	0.8	5.5	6.0	2.1	4.8	5.8	5.6	6.1	6.3
Residential	80.3	−0.9	−2.2	1.7	3.6	4.0	3.5	3.6	3.5	3.9	3.9	4.1
Non-residential	71.9	−12.4	−9.0	−0.4	8.2	8.8	0.1	6.4	9.1	8.0	9.0	9.2
Final domestic demand	1 503.3	−4.2	1.0	2.1	1.9	2.5	2.6	1.6	1.9	2.2	2.5	2.7
* stockbuilding	5.1[b]	−1.4	0.8	0.5	0.1	0	−1.9	2.6	−1.0	0.1	0	0
Total domestic demand	1 508.4	−5.5	1.9	2.6	2.0	2.4	0.6	4.2	0.9	2.2	2.4	2.6
Exports of goods and services	274.2	9.4	10.9	11.1	3.4	5.7	16.7	0.7	4.1	4.5	5.8	6.5
Imports of goods and services	278.6	−7.8	9.8	9.8	4.5	5.9	9.1	7.0	3.3	4.5	6.0	7.3
* net exports	−4.4[b]	4.6	0.3	0.4	−0.3	−0.1	2.1	−1.9	0.3	0	0	−0.2
GDP at market prices	1 504.0	−1.2	2.2	3.0	1.7	2.3	2.8	2.3	1.1	2.2	2.4	2.3
Industrial production	–	−2.4	5.2	4.2	2.1	3.6	0.6	3.7	1.3	2.1	4.0	4.4

* Contributions to changes in real GDP (as a per cent of real GDP in the previous period).
a) Final consumption in the domestic market by households.
b) Actual amount.

ITALY
Employment, income and inflation
Percentage changes from previous period, seasonally adjusted at annual rates

	1993	1994	1995	1996	1997	1995 I	1995 II	1996 I	1996 II	1997 I	1997 II
Employment	−2.5	−1.7	−0.6	0.2	0.2	−0.7	0.8	0	0.1	0.3	0.4
Unemployment rate [a]	10.2	11.3	12.0	12.1	12.0	12.0	12.0	12.1	12.2	12.1	12.0
Compensation of employees	1.0	1.7	2.9	4.2	4.8	2.6	3.7	4.4	4.5	4.9	4.7
Unit labour cost	2.2	−0.4	−0.1	2.5	2.3	−0.2	1.4	3.2	2.3	2.4	2.4
Household disposable income	−0.7	4.5	4.9	5.3	5.4	5.7	4.5	5.8	5.3	5.5	5.2
GDP deflator	4.3	3.6	4.8	4.3	3.1	4.2	7.4	3.4	3.0	3.1	3.1
Private consumption deflator	4.8	4.7	5.7	3.9	2.9	6.3	5.7	3.5	3.0	2.9	2.9

a) As a percentage of labour force.

For the third consecutive year, nominal wage growth in 1995 stayed below the rate of consumer price inflation, as indirect tax hikes and currency depreciation pushed consumer prices sharply above initially targeted levels. At 5.7 per cent, the rise in consumer prices in 1995 was more than 3 points above the objective set in the 1994 medium-term stabilisation programme. However, helped by the more recent currency appreciation and decelerating external price trends, the twelve-month rate of consumer prices fell to 4.5 per cent in April 1996, the lowest rate recorded since February 1995.[2] A strong competitive position, reflecting the fall in the lira in 1994 and early 1995, has been a factor behind the widening of the current account surplus to 2.5 per cent of GDP in 1995, the strongest result for Italy in more than twenty years.

Policies and other forces acting

The fact that inflation has stayed well above levels in other European countries has been instrumental in preventing official lending rates from falling since May 1995. At the same time, both short-and long-term market rates have declined substantially over the past few months, reducing the long-term differential *vis-à-vis* Germany to 4 points in early May 1996. While the lira has firmed relative to the Deutschemark since the autumn of 1995, the monetary authorities have made a cut in official rates conditional upon consumer price inflation descending below 4 per cent.

The fall in market interest rates has been facilitated by a favourable 1995 budget outcome, the general government deficit shrinking from L 147 trillion in 1994 to L 127 trillion or 7.2 per cent of GDP – half a point below the original target set for the state sector. A tight mini-budget introduced in February 1995, together with higher-than-expected nominal income growth, accounted for the greater part of this improvement. In the process, the general government primary surplus widened to 3.3 per cent of GDP, arresting the rise in the public debt-to GDP ratio.

The 1996 budget was designed to maintain the momentum of fiscal consolidation, reducing the state sector borrowing requirement to L 109 trillion, or 5.8 per cent of GDP. Relative to baseline, the budget implied a fiscal correction of L 32.5 trillion, of which the greater part was to spring from extra revenues, enlarging the targeted primary surplus to 4.3 per cent of GDP. These budget targets, however, would be unlikely to be met under OECD growth projections, as economic growth will be significantly lower than the rate of 3 per cent initially projected.[3] In addition, payment of pensions arrears ordered by the Constitutional Court (L 23 trillion) will be made over a six-year period beginning in 1996, through direct issues of government bonds to recipients rather than cash payments. Privatisation receipts could also fall short of target (L 10 trillion in 1996), as planned sales of public utilities depend upon the new regulatory authority for ENEL (electricity) which has not yet started to perform its supervisory role. In the case of STET (telecommunications), such an authority has still to be established. Faced with prospects of a significant deficit overshoot, officially estimated at around L 10 trillion, the new government, which took office in mid-May, has announced additional measures of fiscal restraint, as mandated by the 1996 financial law, although details are still to be announced.

Prospects

Available indicators suggest a deceleration in overall activity in the first half of 1996, with both domestic and foreign orders declining and production prospects worsening as inventories are run down. The latest invest-

Italy

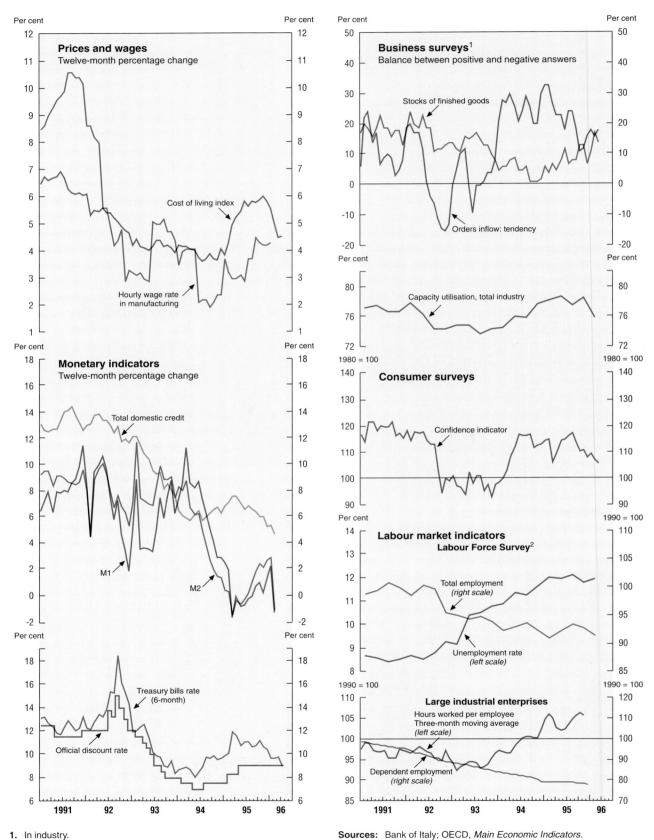

1. In industry.
2. Seasonally adjusted.

Sources: Bank of Italy; OECD, *Main Economic Indicators.*

ITALY
Financial indicators

	1993	1994	1995	1996	1997	1995 I	1995 II	1996 I	1996 II	1997 I	1997 II
Household saving ratio[a]	15.8	14.8	13.1	12.8	13.0	13.5	12.6	12.8	12.8	13.0	13.1
General government financial balance[b]	−9.6	−9.0	−7.2	−6.7	−6.4	−7.6	−6.8	−6.7	−6.7	−6.5	−6.3
Current balance[b]	1.2	1.5	2.5	3.2	3.5	2.4	2.6	3.1	3.3	3.4	3.6
Short-term interest rate[c]	10.7	8.5	10.3	9.9	8.9	10.0	10.6	10.3	9.4	9.0	8.8
Long-term interest rate[d]	11.3	10.6	11.8	10.2	9.9	12.2	11.4	10.2	10.2	10.0	9.8

a) As a percentage of disposable income.
b) As a percentage of GDP.
c) Interbank deposit rate.
d) 10-year Treasury bonds.

ment survey portends a sharp slowdown in capital outlays by industry. Due to weaker export market growth and real exchange rate appreciation the contribution of net export volumes to economic growth is projected to turn negative in 1996, damping business investment despite a further rise in profit shares. Private consumption should gain some strength in the second half of 1996, as the wage accords due to be concluded under the labour agreement of July 1993 restore part of real income losses induced by unanticipated inflation in 1994 and 1995. Nevertheless, since this stimulatory influence will be small compared with decelerating exports and investment, real GDP growth is expected to moderate to 1¾ per cent in 1996.

For 1997 the projections show a recovery in private consumption, stimulated by larger gains in real disposable income. As the negative contribution to economic growth from net exports fades, given a slower pace of real exchange rate appreciation, output growth

could start to firm, rising to around 2¼ per cent by the end of the projection horizon. In value terms, the trade surplus should initially widen with improving terms of trade and this should be followed by stronger export volumes in 1997, as a consequence of stronger growth in export markets. Along with large net receipts from tourism, this should enlarge the current account surplus to around 3 per cent of GDP by 1997.

Given the prospects of only modest output growth, the rate of unemployment is likely to remain at around 12 per cent. At this rate, unemployment would continue to exceed the level observed in 1993, the recession year, by a large margin. Nominal wage growth may rise in 1996, as wage-earners receive compensatory awards, but the resultant acceleration of unit labour costs should be contained by improved productivity, maintaining the trend to higher profitability seen over the past three years. Price inflation is projected to diminish, assisted by weaker price trends on the external side and a temporary

ITALY
External indicators[a]
Seasonally adjusted at annual rates

	1994	1995	1996	1997	1995 I	1995 II	1996 I	1996 II	1997 I	1997 II
					$ billion					
Merchandise exports	189.4	231	249	266	221.3	242	247	251	260	271
Merchandise imports	154.0	187	199	213	178.4	196	198	200	208	218
Trade balance	35.3	44	50	53	42.9	45	49	51	52	53
Invisibles, net	−19.8	−17	−12	−8	−17.3	−16	−13	−11	−9	−8
Current balance	15.5	27	38	44	25.6	29	36	40	43	46
					Percentage change					
Merchandise export volumes[b]	10.5	10.4	6.5	5.8	8.3	13.3	4.3	4.7	5.8	6.7
Merchandise import volumes[b]	10.5	7.7	6.3	6.3	1.2	15.0	3.2	4.6	6.4	7.6
Export performance[c]	1.5	2.1	0.7	−1.3	−0.1	7.2	−1.3	−1.7	−1.4	−0.8
Terms of trade	−1.0	−2.3	1.3	0.3	−2.5	0.8	1.8	0.9	0.1	−0.1

a) For further detail, see tables in the External Trade and Payments section of the Annex.
b) Customs basis.
c) Ratio between the total of export volumes and export market of total goods.

freeze for public fees and charges. Consumer price inflation could decline below the official target rate of 3 per cent in 1997.

Mainly due to weaker output prospects, the projections embody a slower pace of fiscal consolidation than envisaged by the 1996 budget. On the usual unchanged policy assumption, which excludes the supplementary budget measures which have yet to be detailed, the general government deficit might overshoot the target by L 16 trillion or nearly 1 per cent of GDP in 1996, leaving government borrowing at 6.7 per cent of GDP compared with 7.2 per cent in 1995. In this setting, the primary surplus is expected to stabilise at 3.3 per cent of GDP, which is insufficient to put public debt on a downward course in terms of GDP. For 1997, the assumption of unchanged policies implies an estimated slight decline in the government borrowing requirement to around 6.4 per cent of GDP. A fiscal adjustment of nearly 2 per cent of GDP (L 40 trillion) would be required to bring the 1997 deficit in line with the target set under the June 1995 medium-term programme. With fiscal consolidation and disinflation continuing, interest rates should ease further, perhaps reducing the long-term differential *vis-à-vis* Germany to around 3½ points by the end of 1997.

Reduced political uncertainties associated with the formation of a new government could have positive effects on confidence leading to stronger activity than set out in the central projections. The main adverse risk concerns continued job insecurity, which could mean higher precautionary savings and lower consumption than has been allowed for in the projections. The negative impact on output growth would be enlarged if fiscal action were to be taken to correct the resultant cyclically-induced increase in the budget deficit. On the other hand, further progress towards structural budget consolidation could have favourable effects on market confidence and private demand over the longer term.

NOTES

1. From the fourth quarter of 1995, national accounts data published by ISTAT are based upon 1990 prices. OECD data and projections are still based upon 1985 prices.

2. A new index of consumer prices has been introduced, giving a larger weight to large retail outlets and a lower one to food, housing and transportation; this subtracts an estimated 0.3 point from the year-on-year inflation rate measured by the old index.

3. The deficit overshoot thus induced could widen with the suspension of special contributions to be made by certain categories of self-employed persons under the pension reform of 1995.

UNITED KINGDOM

GDP growth stabilised at an annualised rate of 2 per cent during 1995, somewhat below its medium-term trend, and may remain weak until the recent inventory build-up is corrected. But domestic demand is picking up, and activity should gather momentum in the course of 1996, with output growth projected to average 2¼ per cent for the year and 3 per cent in 1997. Unemployment may broadly stabilise during 1996, but decline again in 1997. Together with a continuing output gap, this should suffice to keep inflation on a downward path to below 2½ per cent over the next two years.

Recent developments

GDP grew at an annualised rate of less than 2 per cent in the first quarter of 1996, with non-oil GDP up 1.9 per cent on a year earlier. Service sector output continued to expand, albeit less strongly than in the previous quarter. Manufacturing output was weak in early 1996, possibly reflecting the level of excess inventories. But private consumption growth has remained steady at some 2¾ per cent. Retail sales gathered strength in the last quarter of 1995 and into early 1996, with some recovery in new car sales and signs of a modest pick-up in the depressed housing market, which appears to have passed its trough in mid-1995.

Investment growth has remained subdued in the recovery to date. Although there have been marked differences between sectors, the ratio of business investment to GDP nonetheless remains at a higher level than in the early 1980s. There is evidence that investment has taken place in the areas where capacity utilisation rates are highest (notably in manufacturing). Private non-residential investment (excluding the privatised utilities) rose by almost 5 per cent in 1995; manufacturing investment was up by 7.6 per cent. In contrast, there were substantial declines in the privatised utilities and by general government, while residential investment fell modestly.

Export volume growth slowed sharply in 1995, partly reflecting weaker world market growth. But import growth fell even more, in response to the slower expan-

UNITED KINGDOM
Demand and output

Percentage changes from previous period, seasonally adjusted at annual rates, volume (1990 prices)

	1992 current prices billion £	1993	1994	1995	1996	1997	1995 I	1995 II	1996 I	1996 II	1997 I	1997 II
Private consumption	381.7	2.6	2.7	2.3	3.0	3.2	2.4	2.3	3.2	3.2	3.2	3.2
Government consumption	131.9	0.3	1.7	0.9	0.8	0.8	1.0	1.0	0.7	0.8	0.8	0.8
Gross fixed investment	93.6	0.6	3.0	−0.7	2.2	4.7	0.1	−1.4	3.3	3.7	5.0	5.0
Public [a]	17.2	1.5	4.1	−12.1	−11.7	−4.6	−5.8	−19.0	−9.0	−9.0	−3.0	−3.0
Private residential	16.1	4.3	6.3	1.3	0.6	4.0	11.0	−9.0	4.0	4.0	4.0	4.0
Private non-residential	60.3	−0.6	1.8	2.3	6.5	7.0	−0.9	6.3	6.4	6.8	7.0	7.0
Final domestic demand	607.2	1.8	2.6	1.5	2.4	3.0	1.7	1.4	2.7	2.8	3.0	3.0
* stockbuilding	−1.9 [b]	0.4	0.4	0.2	−0.1	0	−0.9	1.0	−0.7	0	0	0
Total domestic demand	605.3	2.1	3.0	1.6	2.3	3.0	0.8	2.4	2.0	2.8	3.0	3.1
Exports of goods and services	141.8	3.3	9.0	5.7	5.0	6.1	5.0	3.4	5.4	5.8	6.2	6.3
Imports of goods and services	149.9	2.8	5.1	3.1	5.2	5.9	1.1	5.0	5.0	5.7	6.0	6.0
* net exports	−8.1 [b]	0.1	0.9	0.7	−0.1	0	1.0	−0.5	0.1	0	0	0.1
* compromise adjustment	0.0 [b]	0	−0.1	0.1	0	0	0.1	0	0	0	0	0
GDP at market prices [c]	597.2	2.3	3.8	2.4	2.2	3.0	2.0	2.0	2.1	2.8	3.1	3.1
Industrial production [d]	–	1.2	4.3	1.9	1.6	2.5	0.9	1.1	1.5	2.1	2.6	2.7

* Contributions to changes in real GDP (as a per cent of real GDP in the previous period).
a) Including nationalised industries and public corporations.
b) Actual amount.
c) Data for GDP in the past are based on a compromise estimate which is the average of the expenditure, output and income estimates of GDP. The compromise adjustment is the difference between compromise GDP and the expenditure estimate of GDP.
d) Manufacturing production.

UNITED KINGDOM
Employment, income and inflation
Percentage changes from previous period, seasonally adjusted at annual rates

	1993	1994	1995	1996	1997	1995 I	II	1996 I	II	1997 I	II
Employment	−0.8	0.7	0.6	0.3	1.0	0.5	0.2	0.3	0.6	1.0	1.2
Unemployment rate[a]	10.2	9.2	8.2	7.9	7.5	8.3	8.0	7.9	7.9	7.6	7.3
Compensation of employees	2.8	3.4	3.7	4.1	4.6	3.5	3.6	4.1	4.6	4.5	4.6
Unit labour cost	0.5	−0.5	1.3	1.8	1.5	1.5	1.6	2.0	1.7	1.4	1.4
Household disposable income	5.2	3.2	5.6	5.4	5.4	5.8	6.1	5.1	5.4	5.3	5.4
GDP deflator	3.3	1.9	2.4	2.2	2.2	2.7	2.1	2.3	2.2	2.2	2.1
Private consumption deflator	3.5	2.5	2.6	2.5	2.5	2.9	2.0	2.7	2.6	2.5	2.4

a) As a percentage of labour force.

sion of domestic demand, so that net exports continued to contribute positively to GDP. Sterling's sizeable real depreciation has largely been maintained, with relative unit labour costs in manufacturing in the second half of 1995 still some 12 per cent lower than in the first half of 1992. The current account deficit widened slightly to some £6.7 billion (1 per cent of GDP) in 1995, as special factors damped the surplus on investment income.[1]

Inflation rose modestly during the first nine months of 1995, but subsequently fell back. The government's target measure – the 12 month rise in the Retail Price Index excluding mortgage interest payments (RPIX) – peaked at 3.1 per cent in September 1995 and subsequently eased to 2.9 per cent in March 1996. Core producer price inflation[2] declined even more, from 5 per cent in September 1995 to 3.4 per cent in March 1996. Keen competition and a persisting output gap continue to impose discipline on business costs. In particular, labour cost pressures remain remarkably subdued, with the underlying growth of average earnings stable from mid-1995 to February 1996 at around 3½ per cent.

Employment continued to grow in 1995, but with conflicting evidence as to its strength. The Winter 1995/96 Labour Force Survey showed employment up by around 1.2 per cent over the previous year, while the establishment-based survey indicated growth of ¼ per cent in the year to the fourth quarter. Unemployment nonetheless fell for a 29th consecutive month in January 1996, and by some 770 thousand cumulatively over this period to 2.2 million. The number of unemployed rose slightly in February, but resumed its falling trend in March, bringing the unemployment rate down to 7.8 per cent of the workforce.

Policies and other forces acting

The government's fiscal objective is to bring the PSBR back towards balance in the medium term. The November 1995 budget projected the PSBR to decline from 4 per cent of GDP in FY 1995/96 to balance in FY 1999/2000.[3] Some reductions in taxes were judged possible in the context of a neutral budget, with fiscal consolidation achieved primarily through tight control on public spending. Real government spending was projected to decline by ½ per cent in FY 1996/97, and to grow by only ½ per cent in subsequent years.

In the event, the PSBR for FY 1995/96 was £32.2 billion (4½ per cent of GDP) some £3 billion higher than the November 1995 budget estimates and some 1½ per cent of GDP higher than in the previous year's budget. The projected decline in the PSBR to 3 per cent of GDP (£22.5 billion) in FY 1996/97 may also be subject to slippage, as the latest budget's forecast GDP growth of 3 per cent in 1996 carries a downside risk. The OECD Secretariat's estimates suggest that the structural budget deficit in 1996 may be around 3½ cent of GDP, down from 5¾ per cent in 1993. On current policies, the OECD Secretariat projects general government net borrowing (which excludes privatisation revenue) to be 3¾ per cent of GDP in calendar 1997 (somewhat above the Maastricht Treaty reference value of 3 per cent), and gross debt to be around 57 per cent of GDP (somewhat below the 60 per cent reference value).

The government's stated aim for monetary policy is to achieve underlying inflation (RPIX) of 2½ per cent or less, looking ahead two years or so. The new monetary policy framework acts as an early warning system for detecting inflation pressures and meeting the inflation objective. The rise in RPIX has averaged 2.8 per cent over the past three years, the best sustained performance in a generation.

The pick up of RPIX inflation from 2.0 to 3.1 per cent in the year to September 1995 largely reflected a drop in sterling and higher world commodity prices. But there seem to have been no second-round wage effects. With domestic costs under tight control, base interest rates were cut by 25 basis points in December 1995, and

United Kingdom

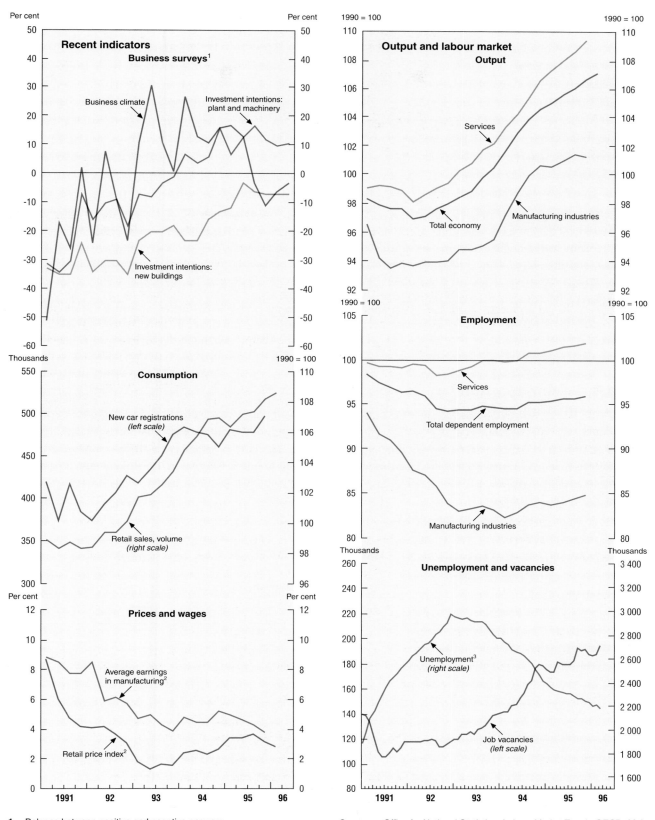

Recent indicators
Business surveys[1]

Business climate

Investment intentions:
plant and machinery

Investment intentions:
new buildings

Consumption

New car registrations
(left scale)

Retail sales, volume
(right scale)

Prices and wages

Average earnings
in manufacturing[2]

Retail price index[2]

Output and labour market
Output

Services

Total economy

Manufacturing industries

Employment

Services

Total dependent employment

Manufacturing industries

Unemployment and vacancies

Unemployment[3]
(right scale)

Job vacancies
(left scale)

1. Balance between positive and negative answers.
2. Change over four quarters.
3. Claimants aged 18 and over.

Sources: Office for National Statistics, *Labour Market Trends;* OECD, *Main Economic Indicators.*

UNITED KINGDOM
Financial indicators

	1993	1994	1995	1996	1997	1995 I	1995 II	1996 I	1996 II	1997 I	1997 II
Household saving ratio[a]	11.4	9.6	10.2	10.1	9.7	9.8	10.5	10.2	10.0	9.8	9.7
General government financial balance[b]	−7.8	−6.8	−5.7	−4.8	−3.7	−5.8	−5.7	−5.1	−4.5	−4.0	−3.4
Current balance[b]	−1.8	−0.3	−1.0	−1.5	−1.7	−0.8	−1.1	−1.4	−1.7	−1.5	−1.8
Short-term interest rate[c]	5.9	5.5	6.7	6.0	6.0	6.7	6.7	6.1	6.0	6.0	6.0
Long-term interest rate[d]	7.5	8.2	8.2	8.0	8.0	8.5	8.0	8.0	8.0	8.0	8.0

a) As a percentage of disposable income.
b) As a percentage of GDP.
c) 3-month interbank rate.
d) 10-year government bonds.

again in January and March 1996 to a level of 6 per cent. Long-term bond yields have generally drifted lower in sympathy with world bond market developments since late 1994, and the slope of the yield curve has become steadily less pronounced. Despite lower bond yields, long-term differentials *vis-à-vis* Germany and the United States have widened erratically since late 1994, although sterling's effective rate has changed very little over the past year.

Prospects

GDP is projected to grow by around 2¹/₄ per cent in 1996 and 3 per cent in 1997. Output growth will be initially restrained as excess inventories accumulated in 1995 are run down. Consumer spending is projected to continue to sustain domestic demand, boosted by lower interest rates, income tax cuts and "windfall receipts".[4] In addition, individuals who opened tax exempt special savings accounts in 1991 can now gain access to their savings without foregoing the tax exemption, which may encourage them to save less out of their regular income. Private sector investment is also likely to pick up as the economy strengthens further, against the background of healthy company finances. Public sector investment will decline sharply, although the government is encouraging private sector participation in areas formerly considered "public sector", *via* the Private Finance Initiative. Net exports are unlikely to contribute further to GDP growth, as imports strengthen in response to higher domestic demand, while exports are restrained in the first half of 1996 by weak market growth in continental Europe.

The OECD Secretariat estimates suggest an output gap of around 2 per cent in 1996 and a structural rate of unemployment of some 7 per cent. Unemployment is

UNITED KINGDOM
External indicators[a]
Seasonally adjusted at annual rates

	1994	1995	1996	1997	1995 I	1995 II	1996 I	1996 II	1997 I	1997 II
	$ billion									
Merchandise exports	206.1	241	252	272	236.2	246	249	255	266	278
Merchandise imports	222.7	259	274	296	252.8	266	270	278	290	302
Trade balance	−16.6	−18	−22	−24	−16.6	−20	−20	−23	−24	−25
Invisibles, net	13.4	8	5	5	7.8	7	6	4	7	3
Current balance	−3.2	−11	−17	−19	−8.7	−13	−15	−19	−17	−21
	Percentage change									
Merchandise export volumes[b]	12.9	5.9	3.6	6.1	6.2	0.7	4.5	4.9	6.4	6.5
Merchandise import volumes[b]	6.3	2.4	5.5	6.2	−0.8	6.5	5.0	5.7	6.3	6.3
Export performance[c]	2.9	−2.7	−2.6	−1.1	−3.2	−5.3	−1.6	−1.8	−0.8	−1.0
Terms of trade	−3.0	−1.9	0.1	−0.2	−3.3	0.8	0.3	−0.8	0.0	0.1

a) For further detail, see tables in the External Trade and Payments section of the Annex.
b) Customs basis.
c) Ratio between the total of export volumes and export market of total goods.

projected to broadly stabilise in 1996 and decline slightly in 1997, although remaining slightly above the structural rate. Hence, inflation could decline to between 2 and $2\frac{1}{2}$ per cent in 1997. The current account deficit may widen modestly owing to a lower invisibles surplus.

The risks surrounding these central projections are balanced and largely centre on the timing and strength of the expected recovery in domestic demand. On the upside, consumer spending and private investment could pick up more sharply – as projected in the November 1995 budget. On the downside, a sharper inventory adjustment and/or a more marked downturn in continental Europe could spill over into exports, business confidence and investment. No allowance has been made for the possible effects of the temporary ban on UK beef exports.[5] Overall, the downside risks – even if they materialise – would be unlikely to lead to a prolonged period of weak output growth. The inflation projection is also subject to uncertainty about the size of the output gap and the structural unemployment rate. But wage inflation remains remarkably low, the most visible sign to date of the positive interplay of microeconomic reform over a number of years and a stable macroeconomic framework.

NOTES

1. In 1994 investment income was boosted by a number of exceptional factors, including a sharp fall in the profits of foreign financial institutions operating in the United Kingdom. In 1995 investment income was depressed by losses associated with the collapse of Barings Bank.

2. Producer prices excluding food, drink, tobacco and petroleum products.

3. Financial years begin 1 April.

4. These include a £50 rebate on electricity bills to consumers and payments to building society members following either take-over or conversion to public limited company status.

5. The recent scare concerning British beef is likely to have minimal effects on the overall economy. Beef production accounts for less than 0.3 per cent of GDP. The cost of compensation to farmers may add around £¾ billion to public spending in FY 1996/97, which is expected to be covered by the "contingency reserve" in the public spending plans. Beef exports amounted to £0.7 billion in 1995. Hence the current account deficit could increase by between £½ billion and £1 billion in a full year, although the actual amount will depend on the duration of the export ban, the reaction of foreign consumers once the ban is lifted, and the effect on UK net transfers to the European Union.

CANADA

Following a period of sluggish growth, the recovery is again gathering momentum. Underlying this development are both the revival in US demand and a pick-up in interest-rate-sensitive spending at home, as well as the completion of the inventory correction that acted as a drag on output growth in the second half of 1995. The decline in inflation towards the lower bound of the target range has led the authorities to allow short-term interest rates to fall below US levels. With monetary conditions – taking account of exchange rate movements – nearly as easy as before the spurt in activity in 1994, economic growth is projected to average 3½ per cent over the next eighteen months, which is more than ¾ percentage point above that of estimated potential output.

Recent developments

After falling in the second quarter of 1995, real GDP grew at an annual rate of around 1 per cent in both the third and fourth quarters of the year. The modest expansion resulted from strongly divergent developments in major demand components: buoyant export growth was to a large extent offset by a sharp inventory correction, while aggregate final domestic sales changed little in volume terms. Export volumes expanded at double-digit rates, reflecting favourable conditions in the United States market, but also gains in export market shares more generally owing to the significant improvement in Canada's relative cost position in recent years. At the same time, however, a sharp slowdown in stockbuilding reduced real GDP growth by around 1½ percentage points in both quarters, as companies worked down excess inventories built up in early 1995 when demand slowed unexpectedly. Moreover, final domestic demand was depressed by an ongoing decline in residential construction as well as fiscal retrenchment. Business investment dropped in the third quarter of 1995 due to the completion of major projects, but rebounded in the remainder of the year.

Recent indicators signal a marked revival in activity growth at the turn of 1996. Despite unfavourable weather conditions at the beginning of the year, employment rose by more than 2½ per cent (annual rate) in the first quarter of 1996. At the same time, the labour force participation rate, which had been trending downward in recent years, increased markedly, suggesting improving

CANADA
Demand and output
Percentage changes from previous period, seasonally adjusted at annual rates, volume (1986 prices)

	1992 current prices billion C$	1993	1994	1995	1996	1997	1995 I	1995 II	1996 I	1996 II	1997 I	1997 II
Private consumption	422.5	1.6	3.0	1.4	2.2	3.0	0.9	1.4	2.1	3.1	3.0	3.1
Government consumption	150.4	0.5	–1.7	–0.9	–1.6	–0.2	0.7	–3.8	–1.0	–0.7	–0.1	0
Gross fixed investment	128.9	0.6	7.2	0.2	2.5	6.2	–0.9	–1.8	3.4	5.2	6.5	6.5
Public[a]	16.1	0.7	5.7	3.1	4.1	3.4	–1.8	3.5	5.0	3.0	3.8	3.2
Private residential	43.8	–4.2	3.0	–13.8	–0.5	5.9	–18.2	–9.5	1.5	5.2	6.0	6.3
Private non-residential	68.9	2.7	9.4	5.2	3.2	6.8	6.3	–0.3	3.7	5.6	7.3	7.2
Final domestic demand	701.8	1.1	2.9	0.7	1.5	3.1	0.5	–0.3	1.8	2.8	3.2	3.3
* stockbuilding	–3.7[b]	0.9	0.3	0.4	–0.4	0.1	1.5	–1.1	–0.4	0.3	0.1	0
Total domestic demand	698.1	2.0	3.2	1.1	1.1	3.2	2.0	–1.4	1.4	3.1	3.2	3.3
Exports of goods and services	181.2	10.4	14.2	11.8	7.1	7.6	7.8	6.5	7.0	7.9	7.5	7.4
Imports of goods and services	187.3	8.8	10.5	9.0	4.9	7.2	9.5	2.2	5.2	7.1	7.2	7.2
* net exports	–6.1[b]	0.3	1.1	1.0	0.9	0.3	–0.6	1.7	0.8	0.4	0.2	0.2
* error of estimate	–1.9[b]	–0.1	0.2	0.1	0.1	0	0	0.3	0	0	0	0
GDP at market prices	690.1	2.2	4.6	2.2	2.1	3.4	1.5	0.6	2.1	3.5	3.4	3.4
Industrial production	–	4.5	6.5	3.9	2.3	4.0	2.9	–0.1	2.5	4.2	4.0	3.8

* Contributions to changes in real GDP (as a per cent of real GDP in the previous period).
a) Excluding nationalised industries and public corporations.
b) Actual amount.

92

CANADA
Employment, income and inflation
Percentage changes from previous period, seasonally adjusted at annual rates

	1993	1994	1995	1996	1997	1995 I	1995 II	1996 I	1996 II	1997 I	1997 II
Employment	1.4	2.1	1.6	1.4	2.1	1.2	0.7	1.5	2.1	2.1	2.1
Unemployment rate [a]	11.2	10.4	9.5	9.3	9.0	9.6	9.4	9.5	9.2	9.1	8.9
Compensation of employees	1.7	3.0	2.9	3.6	4.6	2.6	2.3	3.8	4.6	4.5	4.6
Unit labour cost	−0.5	−1.5	0.7	1.5	1.1	1.1	1.7	1.6	1.0	1.1	1.1
Household disposable income	2.4	1.9	2.4	3.2	4.4	3.7	0.4	3.9	4.6	4.3	4.4
GDP deflator	1.1	0.6	1.7	1.6	1.5	2.0	1.8	1.6	1.5	1.5	1.6
Private consumption deflator	1.7	0.7	1.6	1.4	1.4	1.8	1.5	1.3	1.5	1.4	1.5

a) As a percentage of labour force.

job opportunities. Rebounding housing re-sales and starts, as well as vehicles sales, show that the marked decline in interest rates over the past year is stimulating demand for durables. Nonetheless, real GDP growth may have fallen short of 2 per cent in the first quarter of 1996, given the damping effects of special factors (such as labour conflicts in the auto industry and in the Ontario public sector in March).

Growing excess capacity in the economy over the past year has placed downward pressure on inflation. By the first quarter of 1996, the annual increase in the consumer price index had fallen to below 1½ per cent. This brought inflation near to the lower bound of the official 1 to 3 per cent target range. With persistent labour-market slack – the unemployment rate has stabilised at 9½ per cent – wage growth has remained moderate, although it has picked up somewhat in a lagged response to the temporary import price induced rise in inflation in the first half of 1995. With exchange rate depreciation coming to a halt and world commodity prices weakening, import prices have, however, ceased to put upward pressure on domestic inflation. Import price stabilisation has led to a significant improvement in Canada's terms of trade. Together with the strong increase in real net exports, this has resulted in a rapid narrowing of the external deficit. In the fourth quarter of 1995, the current account deficit stood at just over ½ per cent of GDP, down from nearly 4 per cent in early 1994.

Policies and other forces acting

With the output gap widening, the exchange rate stabilising and inflation falling, the Bank of Canada has allowed interest rates to ease significantly. The latest reduction in the Bank's target for overnight financing rates[1] in April 1995 to a new range of 4½-5 per cent brought cumulative official rate cuts to 325 basis points in just under a year, leaving the mid-point of the target band 50 basis points below the US federal funds rate, a situation that has not existed since 1984. In contrast to earlier easing episodes, this has, so far, not led to significant downward pressure on the Canadian dollar, given increasingly favourable fundamentals (notably shrinking fiscal and external deficits) and reduced political uncertainty. The substantial monetary stimulus to the economy is captured by the Bank's Monetary Conditions Index (a weighted average of changes in short-term interest rates and the exchange rate). The index, which serves as an operational target for monetary policy, has again approached its low level recorded in early 1994. Improved fundamentals have also been reflected in long-term interest rates. Although the latter have firmed recently, long-term interest rate differentials vis-à-vis the United States have continued to decline steadily. Since October 1995 – the time of the Quebec referendum on sovereignty – Canada/US government bond yield spreads have narrowed by about 50 basis points to around 140 basis points.

Fiscal consolidation has made considerable progress. From 1993 to 1995, general government net borrowing (national accounts definition) declined by 3 percentage points to 4¼ per cent of GDP. Two-thirds of this improvement resulted from a discretionary tightening of the fiscal stance, which is to continue on current budget plans. The recent federal budget reconfirmed previously announced deficit targets (3 per cent and 2 per cent of GDP for the fiscal years 1996/97 and 1997/98, respectively, on a public accounts basis). Given the stringent consolidation measures outlined in past budgets, this could be achieved with limited additional spending cuts and a broadly unchanged tax burden. The Government has not yet announced when it intends to meet its ultimate objective of "budget balance" but, on present pol-

Canada

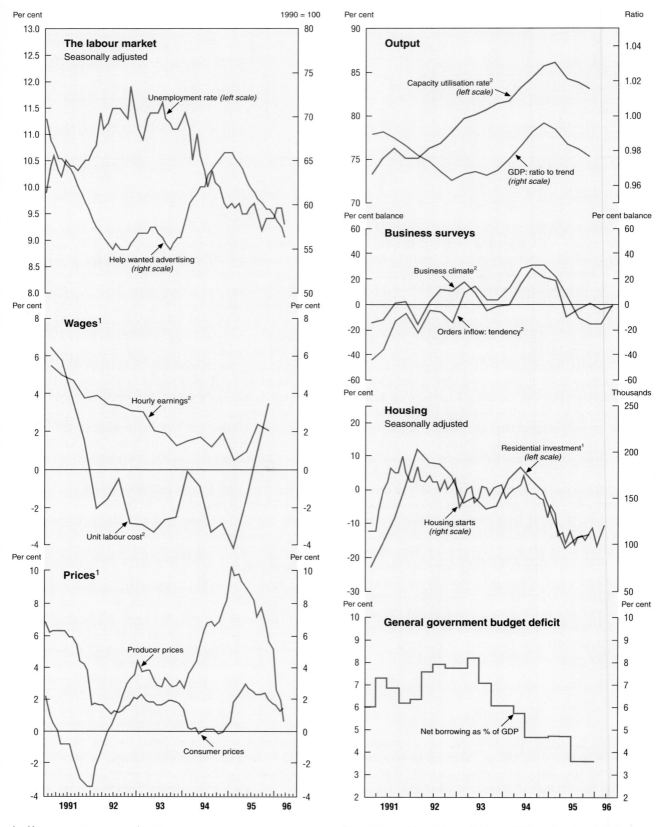

The labour market
Seasonally adjusted

Unemployment rate *(left scale)*

Help wanted advertising
(right scale)

Output

Capacity utilisation rate[2]
(left scale)

GDP: ratio to trend
(right scale)

Wages[1]

Hourly earnings[2]

Unit labour cost[2]

Business surveys

Business climate[2]

Orders inflow: tendency[2]

Housing
Seasonally adjusted

Residential investment[1]
(left scale)

Housing starts
(right scale)

Prices[1]

Producer prices

Consumer prices

General government budget deficit

Net borrowing as % of GDP

1. Year-on-year percentage change.
2. Manufacturing.

Sources: CANSIM, Statistics Canada; OECD, *Main Economic Indicators*.

CANADA
Financial indicators

	1993	1994	1995	1996	1997	1995 I	1995 II	1996 I	1996 II	1997 I	1997 II
Household saving ratio[a]	9.6	7.9	7.4	7.0	6.9	8.0	6.8	7.1	7.0	7.0	6.9
General government financial balance[b]	−7.3	−5.3	−4.2	−2.9	−1.8	−4.7	−3.6	−3.1	−2.6	−2.0	−1.5
Current balance[b]	−4.0	−3.0	−1.7	−0.5	−0.1	−2.4	−1.0	−0.6	−0.4	−0.2	0
Short-term interest rate[c]	5.0	5.4	7.0	4.9	4.8	7.6	6.3	5.1	4.8	4.8	4.8
Long-term interest rate[d]	7.9	8.6	8.4	7.8	7.3	8.7	8.0	7.8	7.7	7.4	7.2

a) As a percentage of disposable income.
b) As a percentage of GDP.
c) 90-day finance company paper.
d) Long-term federal government bonds.

icy settings and cautious economic assumptions, it can expect to have no net borrowing in 1998. Eight (out of twelve) provincial and territorial governments have already balanced their budget or achieved surpluses (on a public accounts basis) and all of them now have legislation or plans committing them to eliminate deficits over the medium term.

In December 1995, the federal Government tabled legislation to change its unemployment insurance system. The implied budget savings would in part be reinvested in labour market programmes. An important feature of the proposed reforms is to discourage frequent use of the system by tying benefits more closely to earnings. The draft legislation goes in the direction of OECD Jobs Study recommendations. It is less ambitious, however, than previous proposals and would remove only some of the incentive distortions inherent in the present system, which have contributed to high structural unemployment in Canada.

Prospects

The recent pick-up in activity is projected to gain momentum during 1996, becoming more broadly based. Nevertheless, given the low starting point, economic growth this year is likely to remain modest at just over 2 per cent. In 1997, however, real GDP should again grow more than productive capacity, which is estimated to be expanding at just over 2½ per cent per annum. Underlying this projection is continued solid growth in the United States and an increasing positive demand impact of the monetary easing that has taken place over the past year. Export growth should be bolstered by continued gains of market share owing to the substantial improvement in Canada's competitive position. Lower interest rates and substantial pent-up demand are expected to stimulate household spending on durables and housing. Business investment should be underpinned by favourable corporate profitability, improved demand

CANADA
External indicators[a]
Seasonally adjusted at annual rates

	1994	1995	1996	1997	1995 I	1995 II	1996 I	1996 II	1997 I	1997 II
	$ billion									
Merchandise exports	163.6	189	206	225	185.4	193	201	211	220	229
Merchandise imports	151.3	167	176	191	167.2	168	172	180	187	195
Trade balance	12.2	22	30	34	18.2	26	29	31	33	34
Invisibles, net	−28.6	−31	−33	−34	−31.6	−31	−32	−33	−34	−35
Current balance	−16.3	−10	−3	−1	−13.4	−6	−4	−2	−1	0
	Percentage change									
Merchandise export volumes[b]	14.7	12.3	7.2	7.8	8.0	6.3	7.2	8.2	7.7	7.5
Merchandise import volumes[b]	13.6	9.8	4.8	7.2	9.2	1.8	5.2	7.2	7.2	7.2
Export performance[c]	2.0	3.3	0.7	1.3	−1.2	2.0	0.1	0.8	1.7	1.0
Terms of trade	0.9	2.4	1.1	0.0	2.6	3.1	0.6	0.1	0.0	−0.1

a) For further detail, see tables in the External Trade and Payments section of the Annex.
b) Customs basis.
c) Ratio between the total of export volumes and export market of total goods.

prospects and a renewed rise in capacity utilisation. Slack in product and labour markets is, however, expected to persist over the next eighteen months, placing downward pressure on inflation which is projected to remain within the lower half of the 1 to 3 per cent target band. Despite a widening invisibles deficit, the current account is likely to move towards balance, given favourable trade performance.

The risks surrounding the above projections appear to be evenly balanced. Consumer confidence is still low, partly reflecting job insecurity associated with economic restructuring and fiscal retrenchment. Thus, households' response to lower interest rates may be weaker, or come later, than expected. On the other hand, there appears to be substantial pent-up demand, and when an upturn takes hold, its cyclical momentum tends to be underestimated. Moreover, the projections assume that short-term interest rates will remain unchanged, while low inflation and improving fundamentals more generally might allow fur-

ther interest rate cuts without significant downward pressure on the exchange rate. Nonetheless, the currently benign environment could also change for the worse, if renewed political uncertainties, or doubts about governments' resolve to tackle fiscal problems, were to trigger financial market concerns.

NOTE

1. Since late February, the bank rate (the rate used by the Bank of Canada for advances to financial institutions) has been set at the upper limit of the central bank's operating band for the overnight financing rate. Before, the bank rate was set at 25 basis points above the average interest rate resulting from the weekly auctions of three-month treasury bills.

AUSTRALIA

The easing of the drought across most of eastern Australia and a pick-up in private consumption contributed to a strengthening in GDP growth in the second half of 1995. Growth has eased, nevertheless, to more sustainable rates compared with the very strong growth experienced in 1994. Output growth is projected to weaken in the first half of 1996 but to pick up subsequently, averaging 3 to 3¼ per cent over the next two years. This outlook reflects the offsetting effects of weaker growth in consumption and stronger growth in exports and investment. Underlying inflation remains close to the 3 per cent upper limit of the authorities' medium-term target band, though it is projected to fall back to 2½ per cent by 1997. The current account deficit is projected to decline somewhat, from 5½ per cent of GDP in 1995 to 4½ per cent in 1997.

Recent developments. Economic growth strengthened in the second half of 1995, reflecting a strong rise in GDP(A)[1] in the September quarter (a 1.6 per cent rise on the previous quarter). This increase was in large part attributable to a recovery in farm production as the drought eased across most of eastern Australia. However, with this effect having largely passed, the quarterly growth rate slowed to 0.5 per cent in the December quarter despite continuing strength in private consumption, a rebound in public consumption and continued growth in non-residential construction. Recent indicators of economic activity are mixed, suggesting a continuation of divergent trends in demand components in the first half of 1996.

Trend[2] annual growth in employment has been around 1.5 per cent in the period since May 1995. This has been just sufficient to absorb growth in the labour force with the trend unemployment rate remaining at 8.4 per cent. With the level of job vacancies remaining high, employment growth has probably continued in the first half of 1996, albeit at a slower pace than in early 1995.

AUSTRALIA
Demand, output and prices[a]
Percentage changes, volume (1989/90 prices)

	1992 current prices billion A$	1993	1994	1995	1996	1997
Private consumption	248.9	2.3	4.4	4.2	2.8	2.7
Government consumption	72.8	0.3	5.1	3.5	1.7	1.5
Gross fixed capital formation	79.3	2.4	12.3	2.1	4.3	9.9
Final domestic demand	400.9	1.9	6.2	3.6	2.9	4.1
* stockbuilding	−1.4[b]	1.0	−0.4	0.7	−0.5	−0.1
Total domestic demand	399.6	3.0	5.8	4.4	2.4	4.0
Exports of goods and services	73.3	7.4	8.5	4.0	9.0	6.0
Imports of goods and services	73.7	5.2	15.3	9.7	6.1	9.4
* net exports	−0.4[b]	0.5	−1.1	−1.1	0.6	−0.7
* statistical discrepancy	−4.4[b]	0.5	0.6	−0.1	0	0
GDP at market prices[c]	394.8	4.0	5.2	3.1	3.1	3.3
GDP implicit price deflator[c]	–	1.3	1.3	2.6	2.7	2.6
Memorandum items						
GDP average measure[d]	–	3.5	5.5	3.2	3.1	3.3
Private consumption deflator	–	2.0	1.4	2.5	3.0	2.6
Industrial production	–	6.1	10.4	4.6	1.5	2.0
Unemployment rate	–	10.9	9.7	8.5	8.7	8.6
Household saving ratio[e]	–	2.7	2.5	1.3	1.3	1.2
General government financial balance[f]	–	−3.8	−4.0	−2.4	−1.9	−1.6
Current balance[f]	–	−3.7	−4.7	−5.4	−4.0	−4.4

* Contributions to changes in real GDP (as a per cent of real GDP in the previous period).
a) Based on seasonally adjusted data for fiscal years. As a consequence of this seasonal adjustment, annual data may differ from annual unadjusted data.
b) Actual amount.
c) The income measure of GDP.
d) Average measure of the expenditure, production and income measures of GDP.
e) As a percentage of disposable income.
f) As a percentage of GDP.

Wage increases accelerated strongly from mid-1994, as measured by average weekly ordinary time earnings of full-time adults (AWOTE), but have moderated recently. AWOTE increased by 0.4 per cent in the March quarter 1996 to a level 4.2 per cent higher than a year earlier, down from the increase of 4.9 per cent in the year to the previous quarter. Inflation also slowed markedly in the March quarter 1996, with both the underlying[3] and "headline" CPI rates falling to 0.4 per cent, giving through-the-year rates of 3.3 and 3.7 per cent respectively.

The current account deficit fell to A$ 11 billion (4.6 per cent of GDP) in the second half of 1995 from A$ 14.5 billion (6.3 per cent of GDP) in the first. This improvement mainly reflected strong growth in export volumes, especially of farm products. Import volumes declined also, notably for intermediate and other goods, and the terms of trade continued to strengthen. In trend terms, the current account deficit has been stable in the early months of 1996 at around A$ 1.8 billion per month, despite a pick up in merchandise imports.

Surveys of intentions suggest that business investment is likely to strengthen in coming months. The Australian Bureau of Statistics' capital expenditure survey in the December quarter reported that many firms had deferred expenditures until the first half of this year, especially for plant and equipment in the manufacturing sector. Moreover, this survey points to strong growth in business investment in FY 1996/97,[4] with the first estimate of expenditure for the year being 27 per cent higher than the first estimate for FY 1995/96. This, together with the probable turning of the stock and residential construction cycles towards the end of this year, points to growth accelerating again as from the second half of this year.

Policies and other forces acting. Following the recent change of government, a revised budget outlook for the Commonwealth Government on the basis of current policies was released. This showed that the Commonwealth Government's underlying[5] budget deficit in FY 1995/96 was estimated to have increased by over A$ 2 billion since the May 1995 budget to A$ 9 billion (1.9 per cent of GDP), mostly owing to downward revisions to the forecasts of economic growth and of growth in certain incomes and prices. For FY 1996/97, economic growth is now forecast to be lower than in the previous medium-term assumptions. The medium-term assumptions for years beyond FY 1996/97 have also been lowered, resulting in less progress in reducing deficits (abstracting from the new Government's announced fiscal tightening). Thus, on present policies a deficit of A$ 3.3 billion (0.6 per cent of GDP) is projected to

remain in FY 1998/99. Although the new Government has undertaken to achieve underlying balance by FY 1997/98 (mainly through expenditure reductions), this commitment has not been taken into account in the OECD Secretariat's projections. The Government will announce the measures to achieve this commitment in the FY 1996/97 Budget which will be brought down on 20 August. On the basis of current policies, the OECD Secretariat projects a fall in the general government budget deficit from 2.4 per cent of GDP in (calendar) 1995 to 1.9 per cent of GDP in 1997. This improvement is estimated to be essentially structural.

There have been no recent changes in monetary policy settings; the official cash rate remains at 7.5 per cent, where it has been since December 1994. Long-term interest rates have increased from just above 8 per cent at the beginning of 1996 to around 8¾ per cent in late April. While this increase has largely been in line with that in US bond rates, better than expected wage and price data in Australia have contributed to a narrowing of the differential on 10-year bond rates from around 250 basis points to around 215 basis points over this period. The new Government has affirmed its commitment to the Reserve Bank of Australia's objective that underlying inflation be between 2 and 3 per cent on average over the course of the economic cycle. Despite the significant appreciation of the exchange rate in recent months (by late May, the effective exchange rate had appreciated by 9 per cent since the beginning of the year), and the slowing of the economy to more sustainable growth rates, monetary policy will need to remain firm if underlying inflation is to be reduced to rates comfortably within the medium-term target band.

Prospects. After slowing in the first half of this year, output growth is projected to pick up, averaging 3 to 3¼ per cent over the next two years. This reflects the offsetting effects of weaker growth in both private and public consumption and stronger growth in exports (boosted in 1996 by the easing of the drought across most of eastern Australia) and, especially in 1997, in investment expenditures. The housing cycle is expected to reach a trough towards the end of this year and to contribute modestly to growth next year. Total employment growth is set to slow from 4 per cent in 1995 to 1½ to 1¾ per cent over the next two years, leaving the unemployment rate stable at around 8½ per cent. A slowing in wage growth, a recovery in labour productivity and lower import prices should contribute to a reduction in the underlying inflation rate to 2½ per cent by 1997. With the slowing in domestic demand growth, the easing of the drought and rising terms of trade, the current account deficit is projected to fall from 5¹/₂ per cent of GDP in 1995 to 4¹/₂ per cent of GDP in 1997.

The major upside risk surrounding these projections is that investment expenditure could rebound more strongly than projected, especially in the mining sector. This risk would be accentuated were the recovery in the OECD area to prove stronger than expected. Even if growth is not stronger than projected, there is a risk that wage and price inflation could accelerate. In particular, there have been a number of recent wage claims which, if successful, would place upward pressure on future wage growth.

NOTES

1. The average of the expenditure, production and income measures of GDP.
2. All references to trend are to the smoothed series calculated by the Australian Bureau of Statistics.
3. Treasury measure. This series excludes from the consumer price index mortgage and consumer debt charges and volatile items.
4. Fiscal year begins 1 July.
5. This is the headline balance less net advances, which consist primarily of asset sales and net repayments of debt by the States.

AUSTRIA

GDP growth declined sharply in the second half of 1995 as exports and business fixed investment weakened. Excess inventories and unemployment increased, while inflation decelerated during the course of the year. The budget deficit worsened much more than expected, reaching some 6 per cent of GDP. Growth is likely to remain weak under the influence of declining construction activity and the temporary effects of sharply curtailed public consumption, but growing export demand should act as a partial offset.

Recent developments. The economy weakened rapidly in the second half of 1995: the growth rate of GDP fell from 2.8 per cent in the first half (s.a.a.r.) to 1.6 per cent in the second. Excess inventories increased significantly during the second half and indexes of business expectations worsened. The sharp deceleration of activity was principally associated with a fall in export demand; in the first half, merchandise exports to the European Union grew at annual rates in excess of 15 per cent, but orders declined from the second quarter, as growth slowed in Austria's export markets. Consumer demand also decelerated in the course of the year, but nevertheless grew by 1.2 per cent in the last quarter. At the same time, construction activity and tourism continued a longer-term pattern of decline, the latter due to continuing competitiveness problems: from November to January overnight stays were down 4 per cent year-on-year. Preliminary information points to very weak economic activity in the first quarter of 1996, exacerbated by poor weather conditions.

Merchandise imports grew strongly in 1995, the first year of membership of the European Union, leading to increased competition in the domestic market, and this contributed to a deceleration in the year-on-year rate of inflation from 2.5 per cent in the first half of 1995 to 1.5 per cent in early 1996. Tourism abroad grew rapidly, contributing to the worsening of the current account. Unemployment, which has been held down by early retirements, reached 7.2 per cent (national definition) in the first quarter, 0.8 percentage points higher than a year earlier.

Policies and other forces acting. The general government deficit reached some 6.2 per cent of GDP in 1995 (Sch 145 billion on a national accounts basis), far above planned levels. Slippage occurred at all levels of government, but was especially pronounced at the Länder and community level, where increased deficits have been driven by rising health costs and by compensation to farmers occasioned by entry into the European Union. The budget for 1996/1997 aims to reduce the federal deficit to 2.7 per cent of GDP in 1997 compared with 5.2 per cent in 1995, and a projection of 6.5 per cent on the basis of unchanged policies. This implies a total saving of some Sch 112 billion compared to baseline in 1997. At the same time, a political agreement has been reached with the Länder that they should run balanced budgets in 1997, and that the combined deficit of the communes should not exceed 0.3 per cent of GDP. Two-thirds of the consolidation is to come from expenditure reductions, which includes a Sch 15 billion payment by the Post Office to the budget – and the remainder from a broadening of the tax base and tax rate increases, notably the extension of an energy tax in 1996 to electricity and gas and the incorporation of overtime earnings and the thirteenth month salary in the wage tax base. It is the intention of the government to stabilise all major expenditure items broadly at their 1995 nominal values, which implies a significant real contraction in public spending.

AUSTRIA
Demand, output and prices
Percentage changes, volume (1983 prices)

	1992 current prices billion Sch	1993	1994	1995	1996	1997
Private consumption	1 133.7	0.7	2.5	1.9	0.8	0.7
Government consumption	374.8	3.1	2.2	2.1	0.3	0.1
Gross fixed capital formation	513.1	−1.6	6.8	2.3	0.4	1.9
Final domestic demand	2 021.6	0.5	3.6	2.0	0.6	0.9
* stockbuilding	6.0[a]	0.3	1.0	0.9	−0.3	0
Total domestic demand	2 027.6	0.7	4.5	2.9	0.4	0.9
Exports of goods and services	791.6	−1.6	5.2	5.0	3.0	3.7
Imports of goods and services	772.0	−0.7	8.2	7.1	2.0	2.3
* net exports	19.7[a]	−0.4	−1.5	−1.2	0.4	0.6
GDP at market prices	2 047.2	0.4	3.0	1.8	0.8	1.5
GDP implicit price deflator	−	3.4	3.4	2.1	1.7	1.6
Memorandum items						
Private consumption deflator	−	3.4	3.0	2.3	1.9	1.7
Industrial production	−	−1.8	3.9	5.4	3.8	3.5
Unemployment rate[b]	−	6.1	5.9	5.9	6.2	6.5
Household saving ratio[c]	−	12.2	13.6	13.4	12.7	12.4
General government financial balance[d]	−	−4.3	−4.4	−6.2	−4.0	−3.2
Current balance[d]	−	−0.4	−0.9	−2.0	−1.7	−1.3

* Contributions to changes in real GDP (as a per cent of real GDP in the previous period).
a) Actual amount.
b) In order to avoid statistical breaks, a new definition of unemployment has been adopted resulting in an increase in the unemployment rate by about 1.5 percentage points in comparison to *OECD Economic Outlook 58* (See data annex for details).
c) As a percentage of disposable income.
d) As a percentage of GDP.

The budget measures include numerous structural reforms covering pension entitlements and access to social programmes and unemployment benefits. However, a significant volume of budgetary savings are of a short-term character: a total of Sch 4 billion will be saved by a wage freeze, for example and around Sch 5 billion of pensions will be saved by forgoing an indexation adjustment in 1997, which is still subject to recommendations of a pension commission. If fully implemented the measures would be sufficient to bring the general government deficit down to within the 1997 Maastricht limit, but those that still require third-party agreement have not been incorporated in the OECD projection. The deficit projection here thus shows a slight overshoot in 1997.

Despite the 1995 fiscal slippage, the Austrian central bank has been able to reduce policy-controlled interest rates in line with those of the Bundesbank, while maintaining the schilling/Deutschemark link. Moreover, the premium on long-term interest rates over German rates, which increased to around 45 basis points in the second half of 1995, fell to more normal levels of around 15 basis points at the start of 1996.

Prospects. Growth is likely to be slow over the projection period, due principally to weak construction activity and the temporary effects of sharply curtailed public consumption. Slower export growth arising from lower levels of activity in Europe will also serve to weaken business investment in the short term, but lower imports and recovering exports should lead to a gradually-increasing contribution from real net exports to demand. Growth could pick up to 1½ per cent in 1997. Employment is expected to decrease markedly in 1996, not only on account of slower-than-potential growth but also due to ongoing structural adjustment in industry. With diminished resort to early retirement, the unemployment rate is projected to rise.

The projections are potentially subject to confidence effects which could prove positive if the 1997 budget target is achieved, leading to higher investment and growth than expected. However, such effects could be attenuated by the fact that further consolidation measures appear to be needed to ensure that the fiscal improvement is not merely temporary. Since projected growth depends on a recovery of exports, any weakening in major European countries also represents an important downside risk.

BELGIUM

The Belgian economy weakened in 1995. Although a sustained recovery is expected to get under way in the second half of 1996, for the year as a whole real GDP growth is projected to decelerate further, to 1 per cent, before rebounding to nearly 2½ per cent in 1997. The unemployment rate is likely to broadly stabilise at a rather high level. Inflation is projected to remain subdued, and the current-account surplus of the BLEU to average nearly 6 per cent of GDP. On present policies, the general government budget deficit is expected to decline to 3¼ per cent of GDP in 1996 but may widen again in 1997. However, the Government has stated its readiness to take further corrective measures, if necessary, to reduce the deficit to 3 per cent of GDP.

Recent developments. Economic activity decelerated sharply during 1995. Real GDP fell between the first and second quarters, and again in the third, before turning-up again in the final quarter. For 1995 as a whole, economic growth declined to just under 2 per cent. The main reason for the slowdown was a progressive loss of buoyancy of exports during the year, reflecting primarily the inventory cycle in neighbouring countries and its impact on intermediate goods which represent the dominant share of Belgian exports. At the same time, imports were buoyed by strong business fixed investment so that,

for 1995 as a whole, the contribution to growth of the foreign balance may have decreased significantly. Economic conditions seem to have broadly stabilised in recent months, with few clear indications of a pick up. In the first quarter of 1996, the conjunctural indicators of the Belgian National Bank – which generally lead industrial production and overall economic activity by only a few months – were at the same low level as in the final quarter of 1995. Car sales rebounded strongly in January-March, but this was mainly accounted for by the biennial "car show". Also, the improvement in some labour market indicators has largely reflected either seasonal factors or administrative measures – *i.e.* the decision to move a number of older unemployed into special programmes, thereby excluding them from the labour force. At 9.4 per cent in April, the standardised unemployment rate was still close to its recent peak. The acceleration in consumer-price inflation in early 1996 – to a little over 2 per cent – reflected the introduction of indirect tax increases at the beginning of the year, notably the increase in the standard VAT rate from 20.5 to 21 per cent.

Policies and other forces acting. Monetary conditions, on balance, have not changed greatly over the past few months. The Belgian franc has remained slightly above its central rate *vis-à-vis* the Deutschemark, and the

BELGIUM
Demand, output and prices
Percentage changes, volume (1985 prices)

	1992 current prices billion BF	1993	1994	1995	1996	1997
Private consumption	4 439.5	−0.7	1.3	1.4	1.1	1.8
Government consumption	1 035.6	0.8	1.5	0.7	0.3	0.6
Gross fixed capital formation	1 354.9	−6.7	0.5	2.7	2.9	4.2
Final domestic demand	6 830.0	−1.7	1.2	1.5	1.3	2.1
* stockbuilding	−3.2[a]	−0.2	0.3	0.1	−0.2	0.1
Total domestic demand	6 826.8	−1.8	1.4	1.6	1.1	2.2
Exports of goods and services	4 977.9	1.6	8.1	8.2	4.6	6.5
Imports of goods and services	4 706.3	1.3	7.2	7.9	4.7	6.2
* net exports	271.6[a]	0.2	0.8	0.3	−0.1	0.3
GDP at market prices	7 098.4	−1.6	2.2	1.9	1.0	2.4
GDP implicit price deflator	–	4.1	2.6	2.2	2.1	2.0
Memorandum items						
Private consumption deflator	–	3.1	3.0	1.5	2.1	1.8
Industrial production	–	−4.9	1.6	1.9	1.0	2.6
Unemployment rate	–	12.1	13.1	13.0	13.2	13.0
Household saving ratio[b]	–	21.0	19.8	19.3	18.5	18.4
General government financial balance[c]	–	−6.7	−5.3	−4.4	−3.2	−3.7
Current balance[d]	–	5.4	5.4	6.1	5.7	5.8

* Contributions to changes in real GDP (as a per cent of real GDP in the previous period).
a) Actual amount.
b) As a percentage of disposable income.
c) As a percentage of GDP. It includes the proceeds of privatisations and sales of other assets.
d) As a percentage of GDP. Balance for BLEU.

Belgian National Bank has continued to lower short-term interest rates generally in tandem with the Bundesbank. Long-term interest rates have rebounded somewhat, following German rates, but in this segment of the market interest differentials with Germany have narrowed to historically low levels. Interest rates in Belgium are projected to be lower in 1996-97, on average, than in 1995, especially at the short end of the market.

Fiscal policy will be somewhat restrictive in 1996. The 1996 budget included a new package of fiscal savings estimated at some 1¼ per cent of GDP and additional measures representing a little over ¼ per cent of GDP were announced in May 1996 in order to reduce the general government deficit to 3 per cent of GDP. On the basis of a weaker economy than assumed by the Belgian authorities, the OECD Secretariat expects the deficit target to be overshot modestly, the deficit declining from an estimated 4.4 per cent of GDP in 1995 to 3¼ per cent in 1996. As about one half of the two 1996 fiscal packages represents one-off measures, the deficit is expected to widen again in 1997. However, the Government has stated its readiness to take further corrective measures (not included in these projections) should the economic slowdown threaten the policy objective of reducing the deficit to 3 per cent in 1996, and the 1997 budget will be drafted to keep the deficit at this level. Reflecting the importance of cyclical factors, the cyclically-adjusted deficit is projected to decline from an estimated 3 per cent of GDP in 1995 to less than 2 per cent in 1997. Proceeds from privatisations were rather modest in 1994-95 but are expected to be of the order of 1 per cent of GDP in 1996. The debt/GDP ratio is projected to continue to edge down, from nearly 134 per cent in 1995 to 131 per cent in 1997.

Prospects. Real GDP growth is projected to decline to 1 per cent in 1996 but to accelerate in 1997, to nearly 2½ per cent, approaching the European average. Both this year's slowdown and next year's upturn are essentially accounted for by external factors, *i.e.* the evolution of economic conditions in neighbouring countries and its impact on exports. Given the openness of the economy, this evolution of exports will strongly affect most sectors of the economy as well as imports, so that the contribution of the foreign balance to GDP growth may not change greatly. The projected pick up in private consumption in 1997 reflects a rise in real disposable income, with the savings ratio likely to remain broadly unchanged, due to the uncertainty generated by soft labour market conditions and fears of new fiscal measures. Both business fixed investment and residential construction may strengthen in 1997: the first supported by high rates of capacity utilisation, good profits, and a better outlook; the second responding essentially to somewhat lower mortgage rates. With real GDP growth well below potential and despite the shift of older unemployed into special programmes, the unemployment rate may rise further this year, on average, and merely edge down in 1997. In these conditions, the end of the two-year freeze of real wages at the end of 1996 is unlikely to produce a major rebound. Nonetheless, the rate of increase of wages may approach 3 per cent in 1997. Consumer-price inflation may average around 2 per cent in 1996-97. The current-account surplus of the Belgian-Luxembourg Economic Union (BLEU) is expected to remain at nearly 6 per cent of GDP. The main risks to these projections are related to the conjunctural pick up in neighbouring countries and in Belgian exports which may not take place as soon and as rapidly as envisaged.

CZECH REPUBLIC

Driven by domestic demand, especially investment and stockbuilding, real GDP growth reached 4.8 per cent in 1995. The foreign balance deteriorated noticeably but strong private capital inflows more than financed the current account deficit. In 1996, economic expansion should continue broadly as in 1995, with the unemployment rate remaining among the lowest in the OECD area but with an inflation rate still higher than that of most OECD Members.

Recent developments. In 1995 GDP grew by 4.8 per cent, driven largely by continuing growth in final domestic demand and an acceleration in stockbuilding. Government consumption continued to decline, partly due to privatisation of state assets, while household consumption rose in line with substantial real income gains. Gross fixed investment rose almost 15 per cent, reaching 32 per cent of GDP. The contribution of stockbuilding (this variable includes errors and omissions, which are not separately identifiable) to total domestic demand growth was very high. Exports continued moderate growth, with an important contribution from exports of services, particularly tourism.

Despite 9 per cent growth in industrial production, strong demand was met by a considerable increase in imports, and the trade balance recorded a $3.9 billion deficit (more than four times the 1994 level), about 8 per cent of GDP. In the first quarter of 1996 the trade deficit was $1 billion. The services balance improved noticeably in 1995, thanks to tourism, limiting the current account

CZECH REPUBLIC
Demand, output and prices
Percentage changes, volume (1992 prices)

	1993 current prices billion Kc	1994	1995	1996	1997
Private consumption	512.6	5.3	6.4	7.5	7.0
Government consumption	215.6	−2.3	−4.3	0	0.5
Gross fixed capital formation	242.7	17.3	16.1	14.5	13.5
Final domestic demand	970.8	6.9	7.2	8.4	8.1
* stockbuilding	−80.6[a]	0.4	5.2	1.4	0
Total domestic demand	890.2	7.3	12.1	9.3	7.7
Exports of goods and services	516.8	0.2	7.9	10.2	10.2
Imports of goods and services	496.4	7.8	19.2	15.0	12.0
* net exports	20.3[a]	−4.8	−7.9	−4.9	−3.2
GDP at market prices	910.5	2.6	4.8	5.6	5.8
GDP implicit price deflator	−	11.1	11.5	11.0	10.5
Memorandum items					
Private consumption deflator	−	10.7	9.1	8.4	8.0
Unemployment rate	−	3.2	3.0	3.1	3.2
General government financial balance[b]	−	−2.0	−1.5	−0.8	0.1
Current balance[b]	−	−0.1	−4.1	−6.0	−5.8

* Contributions to changes in real GDP (as a per cent of real GDP in the previous period).
a) Actual amount.
b) As a percentage of GDP.

deficit to some 4 per cent of GDP. The overall balance of payments was in large surplus, since private capital inflows – encouraged by the fixed exchange rate regime and high interest rate differentials – far exceeded the current account deficit. Total capital inflows in 1995 amounted to close to 20 per cent of GDP and official reserves increased by almost $7 billion. The large capital inflows were relatively successfully (though expensively) sterilised, and money growth exceeded the target only slightly.

Accelerating growth maintained pressure on the labour market. While the average unemployment rate of about 3 per cent is relatively low, in Prague unemployment is practically zero, and the scarcity of labour resulted in substantial real wage increases. The abolition of the excess wage tax (which in practice did not affect many firms) in mid-year had no discernible impact on wage developments. The one percentage point decline in the average inflation rate was obtained partly thanks to a favourable evolution of food prices, and inflation remains relatively high. Consumer prices rose 8.5 per cent in the 12 months to April 1996. Month-on-month data for the beginning of 1996 are difficult to interpret since some controlled prices, as well as indirect taxes on some goods, were increased, as in the past, in January.

Policies and other forces acting. The overall budget was practically balanced in 1995 when privatisation revenue is included, though the figures for government net lending shown in this issue of the *OECD Economic Outlook* treat such revenue, approximately 2 per cent of GDP in 1995, as a financing item. Taxes on corporate profits were lowered at the beginning of

1995 and 1996; a further reduction can be expected in 1997. On current legislation a tendency towards increasing surplus in the state budget can be expected, which in previous years has been corrected by additional expenditure allocations during the course of the year. Neither this nor likely tax cuts are built into these projections, since they are not embodied in current legislation.

After maintaining the exchange rate fixed (against a currency basket) within very narrow limits since 1992, the Czech National Bank moved to a wide fluctuation band (plus or minus 7.5 per cent, around an unchanged central rate) at the end of February. This measure can be expected to reduce somewhat the level of capital inflows motivated by interest rate arbitrage; indeed, inflows had already fallen away sharply in the first two months of 1996. The increased flexibility should make monetary management easier this year, though the central bank has large and expensive sterilisation positions to unwind. The official inflation target is still an annual reduction of one percentage point in the inflation rate, but no supporting monetary targets have yet been announced. The exchange rate has been remarkably stable since the regime was modified; given the still large differences between prices of financial and other assets in the Czech Republic and other countries, and the size of potential related capital flows, active monetary management may be needed from time to time if excessive fluctuation in the exchange rate is to be avoided.

Prospects. Growth will probably remain strong in 1996, with GDP rising over 5 per cent, and gross fixed investment being the most dynamic component of

The Czech Republic

In December 1995, the Czech Republic became the 26th Member of the OECD and the first of the Central European Economies in Transition to join the Organisation.

State ownership and control in the Czechoslovak economy had been practically complete prior to 1990. GDP fell by almost one quarter in the following two years due to the reorientation of trade and adjustment of the economy to new market incentives. The recovery may have been delayed by the dissolution of the Czech-Slovak Federation at the end of 1992, but GDP growth resumed in the Czech Republic in 1994; average real incomes have been growing rapidly as the economy begins to reap the benefits of liberalisation. Czech per capita GDP, about $8 850 at purchasing power parity exchange rates in 1994, is almost half the OECD average. About two thirds of GDP is now generated by the private sector and practically all prices are liberalised. The ratio of gross fixed investment to GDP is the highest among OECD Members, and the unemployment rate is among the lowest.

The Czech economy is very open. The sum of imports and exports of goods and services is about equal to GDP. Average tariffs were reduced to low levels in the early stages of liberalisation and there is no special protection for agriculture. The foreign exchange regime was also liberalised very quickly; full convertibility on the trade account was already introduced in 1991 and full current account convertibility was achieved in September 1995. A high degree of capital account liberalisation was already in place by 1993 as far as transaction by foreigners were concerned, and this was extended to Czech residents in September 1995, with remaining restrictions limited to certain short term transactions.

Trade with developed market economies now accounts for the bulk of external trade. A further sign of the rapid integration of the Czech Republic into the world economy is the substantial inflow of foreign capital. This has mostly been direct investment. In 1995, large inflows of financial investment were superimposed on inflows of foreign direct investment, pushing total inflows to almost 20 per cent of GDP.

With the tax reform implemented in 1993, the Czech Republic introduced a modern and fairly simple system for tax and social security finance, with relatively few special exemptions or allowances. Corporate tax rates and employers' social security contributions are relatively high, but are being progressively reduced, along with the still high share of government spending in GDP. Overall budget discipline has been consistently maintained, although health expenditure has proved difficult to control since the new system was introduced in 1993. Public debt as a percentage of GDP is among the lowest among OECD countries, and declining.

The Czech National Bank is empowered to conduct monetary and exchange rate policy with a high degree of independence. Since 1991 it has maintained a fixed exchange rate, and was largely successful in sterilising enormous capital inflows last year. Experience with the problems of sterilisation contributed to the decision in February 1996 to modify the exchange rate regime to allow wider fluctuation, of +/–7.5 per cent, around the unchanged central rate. Inflation remains high by OECD standards, and the pressure of demand has prevented it from declining very much in the last two years.

The banking system, whose core still consists of banks created in 1990 out of the former state banking monopoly, emerged from the period of central planning with a weak capital base. It has been recapitalised partly from the state budget and partly from privatisation revenues, and provisioning levels for the banking system as a whole are much improved, despite still high levels of doubtful loans. Controlling minority stakes in the major banks are still held by the National Property Fund (NPF). These banks, and other firms with a minority state holding, are classified as private sector enterprises.

Apart from its stakes in the major banks, the NPF also owns a number of other large enterprises that were not included in the first waves of privatisation, mostly in the steel, energy and chemicals industries, as well as small residual shareholdings in many privatised companies. The latter are being sold off progressively, while the former are to be privatised in a rather more deliberate fashion than was the case earlier. One of the legacies of the earlier mass-privatisation schemes was a large number of enterprises with very diffuse ownership (at the peak, 60 per cent of the population owned shares in privatised companies, a proportion now thought to have fallen to about 40 per cent) – a complete contrast with historical experience in the Czech Republic; these shareholdings are being reorganised, though immature and somewhat opaque capital markets make the process difficult to evaluate.

Commercial banks, operating as universal banks, are emerging as very important actors in the market for ownership and control. They are creditors but also shareholders. Bank shareholdings are sometimes direct, but more often indirect through their fund management subsidiaries which control most of the major investment funds which were set up during the privatisation process. Foreign influence is also important, however, through a number of very large capital investments, as well as through a multitude of small scale partnerships and trading arrangements. In addition, thousands of small enterprises have been created through restitution and the small privatisation programme, largely complete by 1993, and through start-ups of new firms. The current government's principal aims are to complete the privatisation process, including disposing of the remaining ''strategic'' holdings of the NPF.

(continued on next page)

(continued)

The Czech economy in perspective, 1994

	Czech Republic (rank among OECD* countries)[1]		25 other OECD* countries		
			Maximum	Minimum	Average
Size					
Area (million square km)	0.079	(20)	9.970	0.003	1.370
Population (million)	10.3	(14)	260.6	0.3	38.9
Labour force (million)	5.2	(12)	132.5	0.1	17.7
GDP ($ billion)	36.0	(24)	6 931.4	6.0	816.0
Structure (per cent)					
Participation rate	78.3	(4)	83.4	54.7	70.2
Unemployment rate[2]	3.5	(17)	23.8	2.9	7.9
Gross public debt/GDP[3]	20.1	(20)	135.0	36.1	69.5
Government expenditure/GDP[3]	50.0	(9)	68.8	33.5	41.4
Government current receipts/GDP[3]	48.0	(8)	59.5	31.5	37.5
Gross fixed investment/GDP	29.7	(1)	28.6	13.7	20.6
Performance					
Average inflation (1991-94)[4]	13.9	(2)	79.9	1.2	4.4
Real GDP growth (1991-94)[4]	−1.6	(26)	4.6	−0.6	1.9
GDP per capita ($'000s) (PPP)	8.9	(23)	29.4	5.3	18.6

* Excluding Hungary.
1. (1) = highest/largest in OECD countries.
2. ILO definition. Data for only 18 other OECD Member countries are available.
3. General government, six OECD countries are not included in the comparison.
4. Average annual percentage change.
Sources: Czech Statistical Office; OECD Secretariat.

demand. Household consumption may accelerate, thanks to continuing increases in real wages. High investment levels should be improving the supply response of the economy and, with a deceleration of stockbuilding, should allow some increase in export growth and a fall in import growth; the latter can be expected to remain high, however, and the current account deficit will likely widen further. The unemployment rate will remain low, exerting pressure on wages. With such pressure, high levels of demand (which unchanged fiscal policy would do little to restrain) and increases in regulated prices continuing to contribute 1.5 to 2 percentage points to annual inflation, the inflation rate is unlikely to fall significantly.

The main risks attached to the projection concern productivity growth and the financing of the current account deficit. High levels of investment should mean high productivity growth provided the investment has been well-directed; if not, net exports could be weaker and GDP growth lower. Even with the projected increasing productivity growth, increases in the current account deficit beyond projected levels might not be sustainable; difficulties in financing it could require an increase in interest rate differentials or put downward pressure on the exchange rate, despite its apparent undervaluation by PPP comparisons. Depending on how such pressures were dealt with, disinflation or growth could be put at risk.

DENMARK

GDP growth has slowed as real net exports have fallen, but domestic demand is being sustained by strong growth in earnings. Combined with the effects of lower interest rates and rising property prices, this underlying strength in domestic demand should lead to a quickening of economic growth once the stock adjustment process comes to an end. With inflation- **ary pressure likely to remain subdued for most of the projection period and the budget position sound, differentials between Danish and German interest rates could narrow.**

Recent developments. The pace of economic expansion slowed in the second half of 1995, as exports were hit by the weakening of growth in Denmark's main

DENMARK
Demand, output and prices
Percentage changes, volume (1980 prices)

	1992 current prices billion DKr	1993	1994	1995	1996	1997
Private consumption	447.1	2.4	6.6	2.3	2.0	2.7
Government consumption	219.1	3.0	1.4	0.2	1.1	1.1
Gross fixed capital formation	133.8	−4.6	3.0	11.0	3.7	5.2
Final domestic demand	800.0	1.3	4.7	3.2	2.1	2.7
* stockbuilding	−2.2 [a]	−0.5	1.0	1.3	−0.6	−0.1
Total domestic demand	797.8	0.8	5.8	4.6	1.4	2.6
Exports of goods and services	309.4	−1.6	7.9	1.0	2.1	5.0
Imports of goods and services	251.1	−3.9	12.3	5.4	3.0	5.0
* net exports	58.3 [a]	0.7	−0.9	−1.6	−0.2	0.3
GDP at market prices	856.0	1.5	4.4	2.6	1.1	2.7
GDP implicit price deflator	–	0.7	1.7	1.7	2.5	2.8
Memorandum items						
Private consumption deflator	–	0.2	1.7	1.7	2.2	2.5
Industrial production	–	−2.6	10.6	5.4	4.2	2.9
Unemployment rate	–	12.3	12.2	10.0	9.2	9.2
General government financial balance [b]	–	−3.9	−3.5	−1.8	−1.5	−0.8
Current balance [b]	–	4.1	2.0	0.9	0.6	1.0

* Contributions to changes in real GDP (as a per cent of real GDP in the previous period).
a) Actual amount.
b) As a percentage of GDP.

trading partners, leading to an unanticipated build-up in stocks. Consumer sentiment remained relatively resilient, although private consumption growth slowed as pent-up demand for durables was satisfied. Housing investment continued to grow at a modest pace, while business investment growth accelerated in response to increasing capacity utilisation and lower capital costs. With domestic demand growth significantly above the OECD average in 1994 and 1995, the current account surplus fell from 4.1 per cent of GDP in 1993 to 0.9 per cent in 1995.

Unemployment fell to just above 9 per cent in early 1996, after peaking at 12.6 per cent two years earlier. This reflected both private sector employment growth of 3 per cent and a 1 per cent government-induced reduction in the labour force, as older long-term unemployed took early retirement in response to a recently terminated scheme. With the output gap narrowing, wage growth accelerated to around 4 per cent. But with low growth in import prices, consumer price inflation has remained low, at around 2 per cent in early 1996.

Policies and other forces acting. Reflecting the focus of monetary policy on maintaining a stable exchange rate *vis-à-vis* Germany, the downward pressure on the krone during the spring of 1995 was met by increases in three-month money market rates of almost 2 percentage points, and the interest rate differential with Germany was kept high into late summer. Subsequently, the Danish central bank has been able gradually to lower interest rates, with short-term interest rates currently below 4 per cent. Since the beginning of 1995 government bond yields have fallen by around 1¼ percentage point to a current 7½ per cent, reducing the differential

with Germany by ½ percentage point. Long-term interest differentials with Germany may be expected to narrow over the projection period, with the firm exchange rate policy being underpinned by budget deficit reductions and continued low inflation.

Tighter fiscal policy and continued economic growth reduced the budget deficit from 3½ per cent in 1994 to below 2 per cent last year. Further fiscal policy restraint is in train, with planned cuts in public investment and modest real growth in government consumption expected to lead to reductions in the structural deficit of ½ per cent of GDP in both 1996 and 1997. However, the weakening of economic activity in 1996 will hamper progress in fiscal consolidation, and on the OECD growth assumptions, the budget deficit is projected to come in at just under 1 per cent in 1997. Thus, the stated objective of balance would not be obtained without further discretionary action and consequently, government net debt would remain close to 45 per cent of GDP.

Prospects. Domestic demand is expected to remain buoyant, since household demand should be supported by resilient consumer sentiment, continued real income growth and an improving financial outlook, while lower interest rates will encourage business investment. The adjustment resulting from the unexpected build-up in stocks in 1995 will contribute negatively to growth in 1996, but exports should recover with the pick-up in market growth from the second half of 1996 onwards. Overall, real GDP growth is projected at around 1 per cent in 1996, rising to 2¾ per cent in 1997.

The consequent tightening of labour market conditions, combined with price impulses of close to ½ a percentage point from indirect tax increases in 1996 and

1997, may raise inflation to 2½ per cent in 1997. In this respect, the risks to the outlook appear to be evenly balanced between a pick-up in inflation which would hamper the ability of the central bank to reduce interest rates, and further short-term weakness, stemming from a more negative export outlook.

FINLAND

The strong export-led recovery from the 1991-93 recession began to lose momentum in 1995 as foreign demand weakened. With domestic-oriented sectors still sluggish, GDP growth is set to slow further in 1996, followed by a pick-up in 1997. After having stalled at 17 per cent since mid-1995, the unemployment rate is expected to resume its downward trend, while the current central pay agreement should contribute to keeping inflation subdued. A projected terms-of-trade loss related to a fall in forestry prices is likely to end the marked improvement over recent years of the external position.

Recent developments. Growth of real GDP reached 4.2 per cent in 1995 – virtually the same as in 1994 – but slowed down during the year as the contribution from foreign trade turned negative. Exports started to decline from record levels in mid-1995 due essentially to a sharp reversal in international forestry markets, while imports continued to rise vigorously. With the economy losing momentum, the unemployment rate stabilised at a seasonally-adjusted 17 per cent in the second half of 1995, after falling from 17.7 per cent at the start of the year. Despite labour market weakness, sharp pay increases carried over from the late 1994 wage round led to an acceleration of overall wage increases from 2 per cent in 1994 to 4.6 per cent in 1995. Consumer price inflation, nevertheless, remained practically unchanged at 1 per cent and, on a twelve-month basis, fell to 0.6 per cent in March 1996 from 1.7 per cent a year earlier – helped by falling food prices consequent on the accession to the European Union and the appreciation of the currency.

The strong export-led recovery from the 1991-93 recession has so far not been translated into a revival of domestically-oriented industries. In particular, while improved profitability and high capacity utilisation boosted fixed capital formation in exporting industries, residential investment has remained sluggish due to a prolonged slump in the housing market. Moreover, a marked rebound in private consumption – supported by strong wage increases, falling food prices and an accumulation of tax refunds – leaked mostly into imports. The external position nonetheless improved, with the current account surplus at 3½ per cent of GDP in the twelve months to February 1996.

FINLAND

Demand, output and prices

Percentage changes, volume (1990 prices)

	1992 current prices billion Mk	1993	1994	1995	1996	1997
Private consumption	272.1	−2.9	1.8	4.2	2.8	2.6
Government consumption	118.5	−5.3	0.9	1.1	1.3	1.0
Gross fixed capital formation	88.0	−19.2	−0.3	8.1	8.0	10.1
Final domestic demand	478.5	−6.8	1.2	4.1	3.4	3.7
* stockbuilding	−5.8[a]	0.5	2.3	0.5	−0.2	0
Total domestic demand	472.7	−6.4	3.7	4.6	3.1	3.6
Exports of goods and services	128.3	16.7	13.3	7.6	3.7	6.2
Imports of goods and services	121.9	0.8	12.6	9.6	5.9	7.0
* net exports	6.4[a]	4.2	1.0	0	−0.4	0.1
GDP at market prices	476.8	−1.2	4.4	4.2	2.4	3.5
GDP implicit price deflator	–	2.4	1.1	3.7	1.5	1.7
Memorandum items						
Private consumption deflator	–	4.2	1.4	1.1	1.5	2.0
Unemployment rate	–	17.9	18.4	17.2	16.4	15.5
General government financial balance[b]	–	−8.0	−6.3	−5.6	−3.2	−1.2
Current balance[b]	–	−1.3	1.5	3.5	3.3	2.7

* Contributions to changes in real GDP (as a per cent of real GDP in the previous period).
a) Actual amount.
b) As a percentage of GDP.

Policies and other forces acting. Macroeconomic policies remain geared towards the objectives of low inflation, sustainable public finances and maintaining confidence of international financial markets. Recently this strategy included a tripartite incomes policy agreement, entailing moderate pay increases of 1.8 per cent in November 1995 and 1.3 per cent in October 1996, and a Convergence Programme detailing the steps to be taken to meet the fiscal criteria for joining the European Monetary Union.

Fiscal policy is set to be less restrictive in 1996 than envisaged in the Convergence Programme, due to automatic stabilisers and measures to stimulate construction – with the general government deficit projected to decline from 5.6 per cent of GDP in 1995 to 2.9 per cent instead of an initially planned 0.7 per cent. The budgetary slippage is planned to be offset by additional fiscal consolidation in the following years in order to stabilise the public debt/GDP ratio at its current level of around 60 per cent.

The prospect of continued low inflation after the incomes policy agreement in October 1995 prompted the Bank of Finland to reduce its tender rate in various steps – most recently in March 1996. The three-month Helibor rate fell accordingly to 3.8 per cent last April after having been around 6 per cent during most of 1995. The monetary authorities thus appear to be confident that the official medium-run target of 2 per cent underlying inflation (measured by the consumer price index less indirect taxes, subsidies and mortgage interest payments) will be achieved. The relevant inflation rate has actually been negative since the summer of 1995 due essentially to the food-price effect. Long-term interest rates have responded favourably to the fall in short rates, declining from 9.3 per cent in the first quarter of 1995 to 6.5 per cent last April. As a result the differential *vis-à-vis*

Germany has narrowed from 180 to 30 basis points. In recent months the markka weakened somewhat, reflecting the sharp turn-around in the forestry sector.

Prospects. GDP growth is projected to taper off to around 2½ per cent in 1996, as exports are expected to remain weak in the first half, reduced growth of real disposable income is likely to dampen consumption growth and housing investment is set to remain sluggish. Business investment, by contrast, will continue to be boosted by high profitability in some exporting industries – metal engineering in particular. With exports rebounding later in 1996, measures to stimulate construction becoming effective and household saving falling to normal levels, economic growth could pick up to some 3½ per cent in 1997. Unemployment is projected to remain high, attaining 16½ per cent in 1996 and 15½ per cent in 1997. Although accelerating somewhat towards the end of the projection period, inflation should stay within a range of 1½ to 2 per cent. After peaking at 3½ per cent of GDP in 1996 the current account surplus is set to decline to 3 per cent in 1997, essentially due to an expected further slide in international forestry prices.

Although the short-term outlook appears favourable, there is a risk of the economy becoming trapped in a vicious circle, with high unemployment and low confidence among households feeding upon each other. Indeed, at this point, the behaviour of consumers appears to be very sensitive to the unemployment situation, interacting with developments in the housing market. Households' saving rates could thus turn out to be higher, and domestic demand accordingly weaker, than projected here. On the external side, the weakness of forestry activity may become more pronounced than presently envisaged, implying a downside risk for exports. On the other hand, Finnish exports could be stimulated by renewed stockbuilding in Europe.

GREECE

Greece is beginning to reap the benefits of several years of perseverance on the fiscal front. In 1995, inflation fell to single digits and interest rates declined by more than inflation; at the same time, an acceleration in investment bolstered output growth. The current momentum of the economy should be sufficient for output to maintain a growth rate slightly above 2 per cent. In the context of accelerating domestic demand, progress in reducing inflation will probably be slower. Fiscal consolidation, which has resulted from revenue enhancement and reductions in interest rates, will continue but – based on announced policies – at a more gradual pace.

Recent developments. Output growth accelerated during 1995, reaching 2 per cent, driven by strong public and private sector investment. The public investment pro-

gramme has been supported by structural funds from the European Union, while business investment has been spurred by a sustained reduction in financial costs. Though the accompanying employment growth was strong – approximately 1 per cent – the unemployment rate rose to about 10 per cent. In 1995 wage increases of the order of 4 per cent in real terms partially reversed a large decline during 1990-93. Despite the persistent high rate of increase of unit labour costs, consumer price inflation declined to 8.1 per cent at end-1995, as the strength of the exchange rate held back import price rises. An increase in administered prices and in excise taxes at the beginning of 1996 pushed inflation back up to 9.2 per cent in April.

The pick-up in aggregate demand has led to an acceleration in imports, mostly of machinery and

GREECE
Demand, output and prices
Percentage changes, volume (1988 prices)

	1992 current prices billion Dr	1993	1994	1995	1996	1997
Private consumption	13 877.3	0.1	1.5	1.6	1.9	2.2
Government consumption	2 561.6	0.7	1.1	1.4	0.5	0.5
Gross fixed capital formation[a]	4 037.1	−2.8	0.5	5.8	9.5	9.2
Final domestic demand	20 476.0	−0.4	1.2	2.4	3.3	3.6
* stockbuilding[b]	124.2[c]	−0.3	−0.1	1.0	0	0
Total domestic demand	20 600.2	−0.7	1.1	3.3	3.3	3.5
Exports of goods and services	3 112.4	0.6	7.7	1.8	5.5	6.0
Imports of goods and services	5 034.6	1.1	4.1	6.2	7.8	8.4
* net exports	−1 922.2[c]	−0.2	0.2	−1.7	−1.6	−1.8
GDP at market prices	18 678.0	−1.0	1.5	2.0	2.2	2.3
GDP implicit price deflator	–	14.0	10.8	9.3	7.6	6.4
Memorandum items						
Private consumption deflator	–	13.7	10.8	9.3	7.8	6.5
Industrial production	–	−1.9	0.6	2.2	2.9	3.0
Unemployment rate	–	9.7	9.6	10.0	10.2	10.4
General government financial balance[d]	–	−14.2	−12.1	−9.2	−8.0	−6.8
Current balance[d]	–	−0.8	−0.2	−2.5	−2.6	−2.8

* Contributions to changes in real GDP (as a per cent of real GDP in the previous period).
a) Excluding ships operating overseas.
b) Including statistical discrepancy.
c) Actual amount.
d) As a percentage of GDP.

equipment, and a marked rise of relative unit labour costs also affected trade adversely. In conjunction with a poor tourist season, the current account of the balance of payments (payments basis) suffered a pronounced deterioration in 1995, (a deficit of 2.5 per cent of GDP from approximate balance in 1994). However, the balance of payments data are generally accepted to underestimate exports, especially as regards drachma-denominated trade with other Balkan countries. In the event, capital inflows have fully financed the current account deficit, leaving official reserves at nearly $16 billion (approximately 8 months of 1995 imports).

Policies and other forces acting. Monetary policy broadly achieved its main intermediate target for 1995: a pre-announced 3 per cent downward crawl of the exchange rate against the ECU during the year. The decline in inflation (which nevertheless exceeded the Government's target of 7 per cent during the year), in conjunction with the increased credibility of the hard drachma policy, permitted a large reduction in interest rates. The headline 12-month Treasury bill rate came down from 17.5 per cent at the beginning of 1995 to 13.3 per cent in early 1996. Nevertheless, interest rate spreads remain high, of the order of 10 percentage points with respect to comparable Deutchemark-denominated securities. In 1996, monetary policy is aiming at keeping the drachma broadly stable against the ECU, with a view to achieving the Government's ambitious convergence programme inflation target of 5 per cent during the year. The interest rate/exchange rate nexus, in combination with heightened international capital mobility, is making liquidity management more difficult, and will require fiscal policy to bear a larger share of the adjustment burden.

The target for the 1995 general government budget was met by a comfortable margin – the outturn being an estimated 9.2 per cent of GDP, as compared with a (revised) convergence programme target of 10.7 per cent. The composition of the deficit was not as expected, as the central government budget experienced revenue shortfalls (albeit from an ambitious target) which were more than compensated by the surplus of the social security funds.[1] For 1996, the budget target is for a general government deficit of 7.4 per cent of GDP, compared with a convergence programme target of 7.6 per cent. The bulk of the consolidation is expected to occur from a lower debt servicing cost and further improvement in revenue collection. On the other hand, primary expenditure is set to retain its share of GDP for a third year in a row, with the investment budget and the government wage bill envisaged to expand and other consumption expenditures to contract as a share of GDP. The OECD Secretariat projections for this year and next are more cautious than those of the Greek authorities on the yield from tax administration reform and the scope for future declines in interest rates, suggesting a general government deficit of 6¾ per cent of GDP in 1997, which would imply a substantial shortfall from the convergence programme target of a general government deficit of 4.2 per cent of GDP in 1997 unless additional measures are taken.

Prospects. The current momentum of the economy should be sufficient for output to maintain a growth rate slightly above 2 per cent during 1996 and 1997, as investment peaks, and consumption and tourism recover. The principal risk to the projections is on the inflation front. The 1996 national collective agreement provides for minimum wage increases of 7.5 per cent during the year; however past years' experience suggests that the drift above the norm could be quite significant. If progress in inflation reduction slows, further reductions in interest rates would be prevented and export performance would also be adversely affected. In addition, measures that would seem to be needed to avoid slippage from the Government's deficit reduction targets and to bring about a fall in the debt burden could be threatened by the political cycle and the need to address structural weakness in the budget which will necessarily strike strong interest groups.

NOTE

1. During 1995, better accounting of the social security funds led to the discovery of additional receipts amounting to approximately 1 per cent of GDP per annum, which derive for the most part from the recent reforms to the social security system.

HUNGARY

Facing an unsustainable situation in early 1995, the Government introduced a stabilisation package. This significantly reduced the budget and current account deficits. Domestic demand fell, but a large swing in net exports meant that GDP rose by about 1.5 per cent in 1995. Inflation, however remained in the 28 to 30 per cent range. In 1996, growth is expected to increase somewhat and inflation will decline. The current account deficit will also decline and be financed by private capital inflows, particularly foreign direct investment.

Recent developments. The stabilisation plan introduced in March 1995 – which included the devaluation of the forint, the imposition of an import surcharge, large real wage cuts in the state sector and other cuts in expenditure, induced a substantial decline in domestic demand, but generated a large positive swing in net exports, so that GDP may have grown by some 1.5 per cent in 1995 (final data for GDP and its components are not yet available). Industrial production grew by 4.8 per cent in 1995 and by 1.5 per cent in the year to the first quarter of 1996. Real wages declined by a larger-than-expected 12 per cent in 1995, contributing to a decline in consumption of as much as 5 per cent. Although private sector investment was buoyant, cuts in public investment meant that there was very little growth in total fixed investment.

Thanks to the devaluation, the import surcharge and falling domestic demand, the current account deficit narrowed to $2.5 billion (5.4 per cent of GDP), from $4.1 billion in 1994. Capital inflows (especially in the form of foreign direct investment) continued to exceed the current account deficit and were partially sterilised by the National Bank of Hungary. These inflows received a boost from the speed-up of privatisation in important sectors of the economy (five regional gas distributors, six electricity distributors and a large share of the telecom-munication company) at the end of last year. Official reserves increased noticeably and the ratio of net foreign debt to GDP declined to some 38 per cent.

Inflation trends have remained disappointing, the year-on-year increase in the CPI remaining in the 28 to 30 per cent range throughout 1995. The adjustment of some administered prices in January 1996 may have contributed to inflation persisting in this range in early 1996. In the year to April, consumer prices rose 24.4 per cent. In the first quarter of 1996, the trade deficit was larger than expected, reportedly affected by higher than expected energy imports due to cold weather. Exports continued to grow. Modest output growth and a 9 per cent decline in real wages in the first quarter of this year (with respect to the same period of last year) had little impact on the labour market, and the unemployment rate hardly changed.

Policies and other forces acting. The general government deficit – excluding privatisation receipts –

Hungary
Output, prices and unemployment

Percentage changes

	1993	1994	1995	1996	1997
GDP	–0.8	3.0	1.5	2.0	3.0
Consumer price index	21.0	21.0	28.0	22.0	18.0
Unemployment, per cent	12.1	10.4	10.4	10.0	10.0
Memorandum items					
Fiscal balance, per cent of GDP	–6.0	–8.3	–6.5	–4.0	–3.0
Current account balance					
$ billion	–3.5	–3.9	–2.5	–2.0	–2.0
Per cent of GDP	9.0	9.5	5.4	..	..

Hungary

In May 1996, Hungary became the 27th Member of the OECD.

Per capita GDP of about $4 000 is relatively low, though purchasing power parity measures put it at about $6 300. Service industries account for over 60 per cent of GDP, including some 17 per cent of GDP accounted for by health, education and public administration. The share of agriculture in GDP has fallen by more than half since 1987, and that of manufacturing by around one third, to about 8 and 20 per cent respectively. (Some of the fall in manufacturing is due to reclassification of service activities previously carried out within manufacturing companies.)

The Hungarian economy appears less open to trade than many other small OECD countries, exports of goods and services in the national accounts representing around one quarter of GDP in 1994 (the share had been over one third in 1991). Customs-free zones are playing a rapidly increasing role in Hungary's foreign trade, however, and this may distort the comparison. Trade with developed market economies now accounts for about 70 to 75 per cent of external trade. The steady integration of Hungary into the world economy is attested to by substantial inflows of foreign direct investment (FDI); over a third of all FDI flows into central and eastern European transition countries since 1990 has been absorbed by Hungary. Hungary's sizeable foreign debt – about 70 per cent of GDP – has always been serviced on time, and is carefully managed to avoid excessive stocks of short-term debt or bunching of principal repayments.

Unemployment is high, though comparable with that in a number of other European OECD countries. Inflation, however, is much higher, and has remained stubbornly in the 20 to 30 per cent range for the last four years. The share of government expenditure in GDP remains high by comparison with OECD countries, partly because of the high level of social transfer payments. This share changed little between 1991 and 1994, but measures put in place in the context of the March 1995 stabilisation package, and further measures under preparation, suggest that this share will resume its downward path.

While Hungary had attempted to implement a market-oriented version of socialism over two decades prior to 1989, it was only from that year that significant private ownership and hard budget constraints began to be introduced. The principal legacies of the attempt to decentralise decision-making without these essential disciplines were the high level of external debt and badly undercapitalised enterprise and banking sectors. These legacies at least partially offset the advantages that Hungary had in other respects: a relatively modern tax system had been introduced in the late 1980s, and a conscious policy of re-directing trade relations towards OECD countries and away from the Council for Mutual Economic Assistance (CMEA) began in 1986. The tradition of gradual change, and protection of potential losers from change through compensation, is reflected in certain constitutional provisions which prevent the government from making too-radical changes to "acquired rights".

Privatisation policy has been through a number of phases. Changes introduced in 1995 led to a burst of activity with sell-offs including a number of key network industries, such as telecommunications and electricity and gas distribution, contrasting with a preceding period of very little activity. Privatisation has accounted for a significant proportion of the FDI inflows. The development of the private sector has been as much due to new firms as to privatisation, although the distinction is not always easy to make. The main commercial banks remain in state hands, although one was privatised in 1995 and another is currently in the course of being privatised.

Macroeconomic policy too has been through a number of phases. Fiscal policy has been handicapped, not only by very high levels of external debt, but also by the existence of complex and overlapping sets of central, local and parastatal institutions; many off-budget funds operate outside the control of the government, most notably the independent health and pension insurance funds, which control a large part of general government expenditure and for whose deficits the government is ultimately liable. A central treasury operation was introduced for the first time in 1996, and reforms are planned to the social insurance arrangements, though this may require constitutional changes.

Monetary and exchange rate policy have been hampered in recent years by conflicting aims – to put downward pressure on prices on the one hand and to stimulate economic recovery on the other – while also funding large budget deficits and attempting to avoid actions that could bankrupt state-owned commercial banks that held both a high level of doubtful loans and considerable foreign-currency denominated debts. These conflicts have become less severe recently owing to the serious efforts to deal with a ballooning general government deficit made in early 1995, some improvement in the health of the banking system and the adoption of pre-announced crawling peg policy for the exchange rate.

(continued on next page)

(continued)

The Hungarian economy in perspective, 1994

	Hungary (rank among OECD* countries) [1]		25 other OECD* countries		
			Maximum	Minimum	Average
Size					
Area (million square km)	0.093	(18)	9.970	0.003	1.370
Population (million)	10.2	(14)	260.6	0.3	38.9
Labour force (million)	6.3	(12)	132.5	0.1	17.7
GDP ($ billion)	41.4	(24)	6 931.4	6.0	816.0
Structure (per cent)					
Participation rate	66	(16)	83.4	54.7	70.2
Unemployment rate [2]	10.4	(6)	23.8	2.9	7.9
Gross public debt/GDP [3]	84.0	(6)	135.0	36.1	69.5
Government expenditure/GDP [3]	56.0	(5)	68.8	33.5	41.4
Government current receipts/GDP [3]	49.0	(6)	59.5	31.5	37.5
Gross fixed investment/GDP	19.6	(11)	28.6	13.7	20.6
Performance					
Average inflation (1991-94) [4]	21.4	(2)	79.9	1.2	4.4
Real GDP growth (1991-94) [4]	–0.3	(24)	4.6	–0.6	1.9
GDP per capita ($'000s) (PPP)	6.3	(25)	29.4	5.3	18.6

* Excluding the Czech Republic.
1. (1) = highest/largest in OECD countries.
2. ILO definition. Data for only 18 other OECD Member countries are available.
3. General government, six OECD countries are not included in the comparison.
4. Average annual percentage change.
Sources: Hungarian Statistical Office; OECD Secretariat.

turned out to be slightly larger than planned in 1995 partly because rulings by the Constitutional Court delayed some expenditure cuts. It nevertheless declined by two percentage points to just over 6 per cent of GDP. Its financing was substantially eased by the surge in privatisation activity towards the end of the year. Further fiscal consolidation is envisaged for 1996 and 1997, in the framework of the Stand-by Agreement with the IMF that was signed in March of this year. Although some steps have been taken to address the problems of an over-large and poorly controlled social security system, the deficit of the social security funds in the first quarter of 1996 has almost reached the target for the whole year. The government is also expected to reduce the import surcharge in 1996 and abolish it in mid-1997.

The National Bank of Hungary continues to follow a pre-announced crawling peg policy for the exchange rate. After a nominal depreciation of the effective rate of 30 per cent between December 1994 and December 1995, a further depreciation of 15 per cent is expected by December 1996, implying a fairly substantial real appreciation of the forint. At the same time, the bank has so far successfully continued to offset the increase in foreign exchange reserves with a lower expansion of net domestic credit. The reduction in the central bank's base rate in the first quarter of 1996 may help to slow down the inflow of financial capital.

Prospects. GDP growth in 1996 is expected to be slightly higher than in 1995. Household consumption will probably fall, though by less than last year, and investment should resume sustained growth. Progress in privatisation should also improve the responsiveness of the supply side. The current account deficit should continue to decline, but not by as much as last year. Fiscal consolidation is expected to continue and the target deficit to GDP ratio for 1996 (4 per cent) should be met, although this may be due to a combination of a smaller than budgeted central government deficit and a larger than budgeted outcome for the social security funds. End-year inflation may, however, exceed the government's target of 20 per cent.

The main risks attached to the projection concern the development of the current account and the path of fiscal consolidation. Real appreciation may lead to a larger than expected current account deficit, depress economic activity and slow down the recent progress in easing the foreign debt burden. Fiscal consolidation is still relying heavily upon some temporary measures (*e.g.* the wage pact in the public sector and the import surcharge) and further action in reining in social security expenditure will be needed.

ICELAND

Real GDP rose 2 per cent in 1995 as a surge in private consumption and a broad based pick-up in business fixed investment generated a 4½ per cent increase in domestic demand. But the current external surplus declined, as exports were plagued by supply constraints. The unemployment rate rose for a fourth consecutive year. Economic growth is projected to pick up, buoyed by further rapid increases in private consumption and investment, especially related to the expansion of the aluminium smelter and brighter prospects for marine exports. As demand pressures begin to emerge, price increases may accelerate and the current account may return to deficit.

Recent developments. Real GDP expanded by 2 per cent in 1995 as strength in domestic demand was partially absorbed by imports. Private consumption rose 4½ per cent, reflecting the increases in wages secured during last year's negotiations and moderate increases in employment. Business investment posted its first substantial increase since 1991. But export volumes declined as the fish catch other than cod fell by more than quotas were cut, less fish was processed from foreign-vessel catches, aluminium output levelled off as production neared capacity and declining activity at the NATO base cut into services earnings. Other manufactured exports rose rapidly, however. Import volumes of goods and services rose at the same pace as domestic demand, shrinking the current account surplus to under 1 per cent of GDP. Despite employment growth of more than 1 per cent, the unemployment rate edged up, as the labour

force recorded its fastest growth since 1987. Consumer prices rose 1¾ per cent in 1995 and have been rising at an annual rate of about 2 per cent in early 1996; this is still below the average outcome for trading partners.

Policies and other forces acting. The marine products sector has been constrained by the catch quotas that have been put in place to rebuild stocks; these appear to be having the desired effect. The cod quota for the 1995/96 fishing season was unchanged from the previous year, the first time since 1988 that the allowance was not cut. While restrictive catch quotas for other species may reduce fisheries export production by nearly 3 per cent this year, this may be offset by increased catches of capelin, herring and shrimp. It now seems likely that cod quotas will be raised substantially for the next fishing year (beginning in September) reflecting improved cod stocks.

While the Treasury deficit edged up on a cash basis in 1995 due to overspending, the general government deficit is believed to have fallen by more than 1 percentage point of GDP. Fiscal policy is slated to tighten this year with the goal of reducing the Treasury's cash deficit by 1 percentage point of GDP through cuts in public investment, transfers and health care outlays. The central government plans to emphasise reductions in government consumption in the 1997 budget in order to reach cash balance in that year. Short- and long-term interest rates stabilised in the second half of 1995 after rising sharply early in the year. More recently, short-term market rates

ICELAND
Demand, output and prices
Percentage changes, volume (1990 prices)

	1992 current prices billion IKr	1993	1994	1995	1996	1997
Private consumption	249.0	−4.5	1.8	4.6	4.5	3.8
Government consumption	80.4	2.3	3.7	2.0	2.0	2.0
Gross fixed capital formation	69.6	−11.5	−1.1	3.0	16.8	7.2
Final domestic demand	399.0	−4.4	1.7	3.8	5.9	4.0
* stockbuilding	−0.4 [a]	0.2	−0.2	0.6	−0.4	0
Total domestic demand	398.6	−4.2	1.5	4.5	5.4	4.0
Exports of goods and services	121.2	6.7	9.7	−2.4	5.0	6.0
Imports of goods and services	121.9	−8.6	4.1	4.4	11.0	8.0
* net exports	−0.7 [a]	5.0	2.1	−2.2	−1.6	−0.5
GDP at market prices	397.9	0.8	3.5	2.0	3.6	3.4
GDP implicit price deflator	–	2.4	2.2	2.9	2.4	2.9
Memorandum items						
Private consumption deflator	–	4.6	1.6	1.8	2.2	2.9
Unemployment rate	–	4.3	4.7	5.0	4.4	4.0
General government financial balance [b]	–	−4.5	−4.7	−3.4	−2.3	−1.9
Current balance [b]	–	0	1.9	0.8	−0.8	−1.3

* Contributions to changes in real GDP (as a per cent of real GDP in the previous period).
a) Actual amount.
b) As a percentage of GDP.

and bank lending rates have edged down in early 1996. The private sector reduced its exposure to foreign debt in 1995, while foreign borrowing by the Treasury continued to rise. A major expansion of the aluminium smelter was announced in November. The project, along with the associated harbour and power infrastructure, is expected to cost IKr 16 billion and to be completed in two years.

Prospects. Real economic growth is projected to be around 3½ per cent in both 1996 and 1997. The pick-up is expected because of a rise in business investment, a rebound in exports, and continued robust private con-sumption fuelled by recent wage increases. Fiscal consol-idation should be a moderating factor. This growth out-look is expected to lead to falling unemployment rates, increasing demand pressures, and some further accelera-tion in wage and price inflation. Strong domestic demand, particularly for imported capital goods, may lead to a deterioration of the trade account and a renewed current account deficit. However, over time the current account should improve as the aluminium plant expan-sion and the continued rebuilding of the fisheries will ease capacity constraints.

IRELAND

Ireland's economic expansion accelerated in 1995, with output growing by almost 8 per cent. Strong employment gains reduced the unemployment rate to under 13 per cent, while inflation remained under control, aided by a central pay agreement limiting wage increases. Robust export growth boosted the current account surplus to about 7 per cent of GDP. The rapid pace of economic activity resulted in a further decline in Ireland's relatively high public debt ratio. GDP growth is expected to remain buoyant at between 5 and 6 per cent in 1996 and 1997, which may lead to some upward pressure on wage rates and domestic prices.

Recent developments. Real GDP increased by an estimated 7¾ per cent in 1995, reflecting both strong domestic demand and buoyant export growth. A decline in interest rates and a high level of business confidence led to a marked acceleration in fixed investment. The resulting expansion of capacity made possible a 20 per cent rise in manufacturing output in 1995, much of which was concentrated in export-oriented sectors dominated by multinational companies. In the first half of 1995, for example, sales abroad of electronic products and office and data-processing machines were up about 40 per cent from year-earlier levels. With the rise in exports, the current account surplus increased to about 7 per cent of GDP despite a double-digit increase in imports for the second consecutive year.

Although the current expansion has proved very strong, there has been little evidence of inflationary pressure. The rise in consumer prices remained steady at 2½ per cent in 1995 before declining to 2 per cent in early 1996. Wages increased in line with the Programme for Competitiveness and Work (PCW), while continued slack in the labour market also contributed to wage sta-bility. The unemployment rate, which fell from slightly over 14 per cent in 1994 to about 13 per cent in 1995, has since levelled off, reflecting the rapid increase of the labour force as a result of demographic developments and an apparent decline in net emigration. In contrast to the relative stability of consumer prices, new home prices rose more than 7 per cent in 1995.

Policies and other forces acting. The unwinding of the hike in interest rates in March 1995 has played a role in sustaining the upturn of the Irish economy, without weakening the effective exchange rate of the Irish pound. The Central Bank cut its lending rate in August and December of 1995, reflecting trends in other EU coun-tries, notably Germany. With the reduction in official interest rates, short-term market rates fell almost 2 per-centage points during the past year, broadly in line with the decline in German rates. While keeping the interest rate differential with Germany at less than 2 percentage points, these developments contributed to an acceleration of the growth of the money supply in the second half of 1995. Long-term rates, in contrast, fell only 120 basis points in the past year, matching the decline in German rates.

Despite a faster-than-expected rise in revenues, the general government deficit remained about 2.4 per cent of GDP in 1995, as the increase in public spending exceeded the 6 per cent nominal target. In the 1996 Budget, spending surpassed the initial objective of a 2 per cent real increase. In addition, the budget reduced some tax rates, in line with the agreement underpinning the PCW, in order to strengthen the incentives to work. As a result, there is likely to be a small rise in the government's actual deficit in 1996 despite very strong growth. Nevertheless, the deficit should remain comfort-ably below the Maastricht ceiling of 3 per cent of GDP in both 1996 and 1997. Consequently, the government debt-to-GDP ratio is projected to fall to less than 80 per cent in 1997 from 91 per cent in 1994.

Prospects. The growth of real GDP is projected to moderate to about 6 per cent in 1996 and 5 per cent in 1997. The major factor will be slower growth of exports, reflecting weaker demand in Europe in 1996. The decel-eration of external demand is likely to be accompanied by slower growth of business investment. However,

IRELAND
Demand, output and prices
Percentage changes, volume (1990 prices)

	1992 current prices million Ir£	1993	1994	1995	1996	1997
Private consumption	17 582	1.4	4.3	3.7	4.7	3.4
Government consumption	4 834	1.3	3.9	3.0	1.5	1.5
Gross fixed capital formation	4 683	–0.8	7.3	10.7	8.2	6.5
Final domestic demand	27 099	1.0	4.7	4.8	4.8	3.7
* stockbuilding	–134 [a]	–0.2	–0.8	0.2	0	0
Total domestic demand	26 966	0.8	3.8	5.1	4.9	3.7
Exports of goods and services	18 823	9.2	13.9	13.6	9.8	9.0
Imports of goods and services	15 817	6.8	11.9	11.6	9.5	8.5
* net exports	3 006 [a]	2.4	3.1	3.4	2.0	2.0
GDP at market prices	29 972	3.1	6.4	7.7	6.0	5.0
GDP implicit price deflator	–	4.1	1.2	1.4	1.5	1.4
Memorandum items						
Private consumption deflator	–	1.7	2.7	2.5	2.3	2.4
Industrial production	–	5.6	11.9	18.0	14.0	10.0
Unemployment rate	–	15.6	14.2	12.9	12.4	12.2
Household saving ratio [b]	–	12.9	11.2	12.0	10.8	10.9
General government financial balance [c]	–	–2.4	–2.3	–2.4	–2.7	–2.6
Current balance [c]	–	6.6	5.8	7.2	7.0	6.8

* Contributions to changes in real GDP (as a per cent of real GDP in the previous period).
a) Actual amount.
b) As a percentage of disposable income.
c) As a percentage of GDP.

residential construction, which registered a record-high number of housing starts in 1995, is expected to remain buoyant, given the low level of interest rates and rising house prices. Continued employment gains may reduce the unemployment rate to about 12 per cent by the end of next year. This should reinforce consumer confidence and help sustain the rise in personal consumption at about the 4 per cent rate recorded in 1995.

The principal risk to this outlook is a revival of inflationary pressure. Although inflation has remained under control despite the very strong growth of the past two years, the prospective termination of the PCW at the end of 1996 has created some uncertainty about wage developments in 1997. The continued decline in the number of jobless might put upward pressure on wage rates, and consequently on domestic prices.

LUXEMBOURG

Economic activity slowed in the second half of 1995, in large part because of weakness in the steel sector. Real GDP growth is expected to decelerate to just under 2 per cent in 1996, but to rebound to 3 per cent in 1997. Unemployment is projected to decline only slightly, as most new jobs may be filled by cross-border workers. Consumer price inflation may average below 2 per cent. The general government budget is likely to remain in surplus.

Recent developments. Real GDP growth was 3¾ per cent in 1995, but activity slowed down in the second half of the year. The steel sector was especially affected by the conjunctural downturn in neighbouring countries and by intensified competition from eastern Europe. Export growth decelerated markedly in the second half of the year. However, imports also lost buoy-

ancy due to the weakness in the steel sector, and the foreign balance still contributed ½ of a percentage point to GDP growth. On the domestic side, business investment was sustained by projects in telecommunications and the steel industry. As in previous years, private consumption lagged behind GDP growth. Employment growth was strong, especially in the services sector. However, as most jobs were taken by cross-border workers, the unemployment rate edged up, to more than 3 per cent at the end of the year. Inflation – measured by the consumer price index – came down to 2 per cent in 1995, partly due to the appreciation of the Luxembourg franc (in tandem with the Belgian franc), which resulted in lower import prices. Wages rose by 3.4 per cent on average in 1995, with wages in the banking and insurance sector progressing by 4.7 per cent.

LUXEMBOURG
Demand, output and prices
Percentage changes, volume (1990 prices)

	1992 current prices billion LF	1993	1994	1995	1996	1997
Private consumption	191.0	−0.9	2.5	2.4	2.1	2.4
Government consumption	58.0	1.8	2.1	2.3	2.0	1.8
Gross fixed capital formation	94.1	3.9	2.4	3.5	3.0	4.0
Final domestic demand	343.1	0.8	2.4	2.7	2.3	2.8
* stockbuilding	8.6[a]	−1.0	−0.1	0.5	−0.2	−0.1
Total domestic demand	351.7	−0.2	2.3	3.1	2.1	2.6
Exports of goods and services	302.5	−2.4	5.0	4.4	3.3	5.4
Imports of goods and services	314.7	−2.5	3.9	3.8	3.4	5.0
* net exports	−12.2[a]	0.2	0.9	0.5	−0.2	0.3
GDP at market prices	339.5	0	3.3	3.7	1.9	3.0
GDP implicit price deflator	–	4.7	1.9	3.1	1.9	1.9
Memorandum items						
Private consumption deflator	–	3.7	1.8	2.0	1.7	1.8
Industrial production	–	−3.2	6.4	1.8	1.2	2.2
Unemployment rate	–	2.1	2.7	3.0	2.9	2.8

* Contributions to changes in real GDP (as a per cent of real GDP in the previous period).
a) Actual amount.

Policies and other forces acting. The Government is expected to maintain a prudent fiscal policy, with a medium-term orientation. According to the 1996 budget, government expenditure is projected to rise by 5.7 per cent, slightly more than the medium-term guideline. The overshooting is due to a government transfer to the social security sector to cover a substantial increase in child benefits. The budget gives priority to investment, notably for environmental works, school building, and rail infrastructure. Government investment is expected to rise to almost 3½ per cent of GDP and government receipts to grow by 6.7 per cent, implying an almost balanced central government budget. The Government expects the public sector to show a surplus of 0.6 per cent of GDP, slightly lower than in previous years, with gross consolidated debt below 8 per cent of GDP. Among the other forces acting, negotiations are currently under way in the steel industry to cut jobs through outsourcing in order to create more flexible and competitive steel plants.

Prospects. As in recent years, the economy is expected to follow a cyclical pattern in line with neighbouring countries, although at a higher growth rate. Real GDP growth is projected to decelerate to a little less than 2 per cent in 1996, before rebounding to 3 per cent in 1997. The foreign balance is projected to make a negative contribution to GDP growth in 1996, notably due to weaker exports of goods. However, following the conjunctural upturn in neighbouring countries, exports in the steel industry are likely to pick up in the second half of 1996 and in 1997. Domestic demand is likely to show a less pronounced cycle. Supported by increases in real wages, private consumption growth is projected to stabilise at some 2¼ per cent. Business investment growth may also remain around recent levels, as some of 1995's investment projects have been shifted to 1996. Residential investment may pick up, supported by lower mortgage rates and lower construction prices, as international competition in this area intensifies. Job creation is projected to remain rapid but, as in the past, cross-border workers may take up most of the new jobs, and the unemployment rate may merely edge down. Consumer price inflation is expected to average less than 2 per cent. The main risk to the projections is that the recovery in neighbouring countries might be weaker than envisaged, in which case the highly export-dependent steel industry would be especially hit.

MEXICO

The Mexican economy experienced a severe recession in 1995. Real GDP fell by close to 7 per cent, although it hit bottom around mid-year. Domestic demand collapsed following the March 1995 stabilisation measures. This, together with improved international com- **petitiveness, brought the current account close to balance. Inflation peaked at 52 per cent in the 12 months to December. With the support of international financial facilities, external obligations were met and foreign reserves built up. Interest rates and**

inflation are coming down, but the recovery is still modest. On the assumption of improved confidence leading to further declines in interest rates, the recovery should become more broadly based, as investment picks up; and inflation should continue to fall.

Recent developments. The 1995 recession proved more severe than had been thought earlier. Total domestic demand fell by 18 per cent in 1995, reflecting the deflationary impact of the stringent stabilisation measures. After a period of some stability in financial markets, renewed turbulence in October and November brought about a further depreciation of the exchange rate, while short-term interest rates rose sharply (to 70 per cent for 28-days Cetes, from a low of 40 per cent in previous months). Recent indicators suggest that the recession may have ended around mid-1995. On a seasonally adjusted basis, real GDP increased in the 3rd and 4th quarter. Labour market conditions began to improve after September, with the open unemployment rate starting to fall and insured employment edging up. The monthly rate of consumer price inflation, which had been declining since May 1995, turned up again in the last months of the year, as public tariffs were raised and the peso depreciated anew. After peaking at 52 per cent on a 12-month basis in December, 10 points above the government's projection, inflation fell to 37 per cent in April this year.[1] Including the in-bond sector, the trade balance recorded a $7 billion surplus over the year, reflecting booming exports and a steep drop in imports; it remained in surplus in the first quarter of 1996, despite a recovery of imports. The current account swung from a deficit of 8 per cent of GDP in 1994 to near balance in 1995.

Mexico has been able to meet its short-term foreign obligations, and by February 1996 it had redeemed all dollar-linked Tesobonos. This was done in part using the credit facilities provided by the United States, the IMF and other official institutions (a little more than half of the available $50 billion was used in 1995). At the end of December, the total public debt amounted to 43 per cent of GDP, slightly down on its level a year earlier, with the net external component at 37 per cent of GDP. Net foreign reserves had risen to $15.8 billion,[2] exceeding the servicing of the public external debt scheduled for 1996. The Mexican government and some public and private enterprises were able to raise funds on international capital markets on an increasing scale in the course of 1995 and in the early part of 1996.

Policies and other forces acting. In 1995, the surplus in the public sector financial accounts was slightly higher than projected (1 per cent of GDP instead of ½ per cent in the March stabilisation programme).[3] The primary surplus amounted to 5.5 per cent of GDP, against a projection of 4.4 per cent. The Social Pact, signed last October, set the base for macroeconomic policies in 1996, including an inflation target of 20 per cent over the 12 months to December, a minimum wage rise of 10 per cent in April and increases in public tariffs. It maintained the floating exchange rate regime. With a balanced budget projected for 1996 and a primary surplus reduced to 4 per cent of GDP, fiscal policy could provide a mild stimulus to the recovery. Expenditure on infrastructure, which was held back in 1995, will be activated this year.

MEXICO
Demand, output and prices
Percentage changes, volume (1980 prices)

	1992 current prices billion P	1993	1994	1995	1996	1997
Private consumption	735.9	0.2	3.7	−12.9	1.0	3.0
Government consumption	102.8	2.0	2.5	−4.1	−4.0	1.0
Gross fixed capital formation	211.9	−1.2	8.1	−30.9	5.3	7.7
Final domestic demand	1 050.5	0.1	4.5	−15.9	1.2	3.7
* stockbuilding	25.3[a]	−0.4	0	−1.8	0.2	0
Total domestic demand	1 075.8	−0.3	4.4	−17.7	1.4	3.7
Exports of goods and services	128.3	3.7	7.3	28.4	12.0	9.0
Imports of goods and services	185.0	−1.3	12.9	−27.6	10.0	12.0
* net exports	−56.6[a]	0.9	−0.9	10.8	1.8	0.7
GDP at market prices	1 019.2	0.6	3.5	−6.8	3.0	4.0
GDP implicit price deflator	–	10.0	7.3	35.4	26.0	15.0
Memorandum items						
Private consumption deflator	–	9.3	6.6	39.1	33.0	17.0
Unemployment rate[b]	–	3.4	3.7	6.3	6.0	5.5
Current balance[c]	–	−6.5	−7.8	−0.2	−1.0	−2.0

* Contributions to changes in real GDP (as a per cent of real GDP in the previous period).
a) Actual amount.
b) Based on the National Survey of Urban Employment.
c) As a percentage of GDP.

Measures put in place in 1995 to provide a safety net for poorer segments of the population will be continued. Some tax exemptions are provided to business to stimulate investment and job creation. There are plans to modernise tax administration and to simplify taxation on smaller firms. At the same time, the ceiling on credit growth by development banks was announced – allowing for a significant expansion in favour of small- and medium-sized enterprises and for exporting firms.

The monetary base rose by 17 per cent in the 12 months to December 1995. Net domestic credit from the central bank (the monetary base less non-borrowed foreign exchange reserves) fell over the same period, as Mexico increased its liabilities to the IMF.[4] M1 increased by only 8 per cent during the year, while M4 rose by 20.8 per cent, largely reflecting the impact of the depreciation on the peso value of foreign-currency deposits. The monetary programme for 1996, announced at the start of the year, follows the line of the policy implemented during 1995, with the pursuit of disinflation as its primary objective. Again a ceiling was set on the growth of central bank net domestic credit (allowing for an increase in line with a projected growth of nominal GDP of 24 per cent). The announcement of the Budget and the monetary programme for 1996 contributed to calming financial markets after the turn of the year. Real short-term interest rates were still high in the first quarter of 1996 (above 15 per cent for the 3-month Cetes), but they have declined since then. At the start of May, nominal interest rates were down to just above 30 per cent for the 3-month Cetes. The OECD Secretariat's projections are based on the assumption that they will continue to decline over the next two years as inflation slows and the risk premium falls somewhat.

The banking sector remains under strain and this may slow the recovery. Restructuring is under way: by the end of 1995, eleven banks, holding more than 70 per cent of the banking system's assets, had been recapitalised. With support from the various schemes put in place the system was able to overcome its immediate liquidity difficulties. The level of past-due loans increased quickly again in October and November with the hike in interest rates. This deterioration, however, seems to have stopped around year-end. Use of the various debt restructuring programmes also contributed to improving the quality of bank portfolios. The fiscal cost of the government support to banks has been officially estimated at around 5 per cent of 1995 GDP, to be spread over many years.

Prospects. With recovery under way, real GDP is projected to grow by 3 per cent on average this year – not a very strong rebound because of still hesitant domestic demand and slower export growth following the 1995 boom. Private agents' uncertainties on future income and the high level of their indebtedness will restrain expenditure, while the fragility of the banking sector will limit lending. In 1997, growth of real GDP

should become more broadly based. Inflation is projected to fall substantially over the projection period under the usual technical assumption of an unchanged nominal exchange rate. On average, inflation may still amount to 33 per cent this year (for the private consumption deflator), coming down to 17 per cent next year.[5] The trade surplus is expected to narrow as import growth picks up; and the current account may return to a moderate deficit of around $6 billion (2 per cent of GDP) in 1997.

The projections hinge on the assumption that improved investors' confidence will allow a reduction of the risk premium currently incorporated in interest rates. Banks' capacity to emerge from their current difficulties largely depends on financial market stability and the level of interest rates. The system's fragility constitutes a major potential restraint on growth. However, should financial and exchange markets remain relatively stable over the projection period, a virtuous circle could start. More dynamic activity and lower interest rates would be rapidly reflected in an improved banking situation. This in turn could be translated into the higher lending necessary for stronger output and employment growth.

NOTES

1. Between 1994 and 1995, the CPI increased by 35 per cent on average, while the private consumption deflator rose by 39 per cent. The Secretariat's projections refer to the deflator, hence are not strictly comparable with official projections.

2. The Bank of Mexico now publishes data on net international reserves according to two definitions: its own legally mandated definition and the IMF's definition which excludes borrowed reserves (notably liabilities to the IMF). Neither definition deducts obligations for emergency financial support from the United States and Canada. On the IMF definition, net international reserves amounted to $1.3 billion at end April.

3. The fiscal outturn takes into account the estimated fiscal cost of the debt relief programme for small debtors (ADE).

4. Net domestic credit fell by 77.7 billion pesos (from a positive 24 billion pesos to a negative 54 billion), while a ceiling of 10 billion pesos was set on the growth of net domestic credit in the March 1995 stabilisation programme. Beginning in 1996, the central bank has changed its definition of net domestic credit to include IMF liabilities, which are now excluded from foreign exchange reserves. The net credit ceiling set in the monetary programme for 1996 is based on the new definition. The monetary base is unaffected by the accounting change.

5. These averages are consistent with a projected 12-month increase of the CPI in a range of 20 to 25 per cent in December 1996 and 10 to 15 per cent in December 1997.

NETHERLANDS

Economic activity weakened in the last quarter of 1995, and annual GDP growth is expected to decelerate to around 1³/₄ per cent in 1996, before picking up in 1997, to 2¹/₂ per cent. This evolution is essentially due to developments in neighbouring countries, but the cycle should be milder in the Netherlands than in the EU on average. The unemployment rate is likely to stabilise at around the current rate of 7 per cent, and inflation may remain subdued. The general government budget deficit is projected to decline to below 3 per cent of GDP in 1997.

Recent developments. Real GDP growth decelerated to 2.4 per cent in 1995, from 2.7 per cent in 1994, as economic growth came almost to a halt in the final quarter of 1995. This weakness seems to have continued in early 1996. The end of the expansion came as export growth decelerated in the second half of 1995, following slower growth in neighbouring countries and an appreciation of the guilder in real terms in late 1994. Also the specialisation of Dutch industry in intermediate goods is not favourable in the current phase of the cycle. On the domestic side, real disposable income rose by over 3 per cent in 1995, boosted by rapid job creation, but private consumption growth remained subdued, at around 2 per cent, with the saving ratio rising. Business investment was the most dynamic spending category in 1995, rising by more than 6 per cent. It was partly influenced by

special factors, like the start-up of a car assembly plant. Compared with earlier cycles, the investment boom seems to have been modest, reflecting the fact that both capacity utilisation and occupancy rates for office buildings have remained well below the peaks reached in the previous expansion. The labour market made a strong recovery in 1995, and employment (in persons) increased by 1.5 per cent. However, employment growth seems to have slowed in the final quarter of the year, bringing to an end an almost two-year declining trend in unemployment: indeed, the unemployment rate has been edging up since mid-1995 – to 7.1 per cent in February 1996. Wage settlements remained moderate in 1995, despite the improvement in the labour market, and are currently running at around 1¹/₄ per cent. Inflation – measured by the consumer price index – accelerated somewhat in the first months of 1996, to around 2 per cent, with prices controlled by the Government (gas, indirect taxes, rents and non-market services) contributing most of it.

Policies and other forces acting. The guilder has progressively strengthened against the Deutschemark, rising to around ³/₄ of a percentage point above its central rate – an unusually large premium. Short-term interest rates have declined steadily, and are more than ¹/₂ percentage point lower than in Germany. In line with global developments, long-term rates have rebounded somewhat in the first months of 1996, but the differential with German rates has turned marginally negative. The OECD

NETHERLANDS
Demand, output and prices
Percentage changes, volume (1990 prices)

	1992 current prices billion Gld	1993	1994	1995	1996	1997
Private consumption	340.9	0.9	2.1	2.1	1.8	1.9
Government consumption	83.0	0.2	0.9	0.5	2.1	1.6
Gross fixed capital formation	113.3	−3.1	3.0	4.9	2.8	2.5
Final domestic demand	537.2	−0.1	2.1	2.4	2.1	2.0
* stockbuilding	3.1 *a*	−1.1	1.1	0	−0.5	0.2
Total domestic demand	540.4	−1.2	3.3	2.4	1.5	2.2
Exports of goods and services	294.9	1.6	5.8	6.1	3.3	5.7
Imports of goods and services	269.2	−1.1	7.5	6.5	3.3	5.3
* net exports	25.7 *a*	1.4	−0.4	0.2	0.2	0.6
GDP at market prices	566.1	0.2	2.7	2.4	1.6	2.6
GDP implicit price deflator	–	2.0	2.3	1.9	1.3	1.9
Memorandum items						
Private consumption deflator	–	2.3	2.4	1.0	1.8	1.8
Industrial production	–	−2.5	3.8	2.6	1.2	2.7
Unemployment rate	–	6.5	7.6	7.1	7.0	6.9
Household saving ratio *b*	–	0.9	0.7	1.8	0.8	0.6
General government financial balance *c*	–	−3.2	−3.2	−3.3	−3.2	−2.7
Current balance *c*	–	3.8	3.8	3.9	3.9	4.0

* Contributions to changes in real GDP (as a per cent of real GDP in the previous period).
a) Actual amount.
b) As a percentage of disposable income, excluding mandatory saving through occupational pension schemes.
c) As a percentage of GDP.

Secretariat expects Dutch interest rates to be lower in 1996-97, on average, than in 1995, especially at the short end of the market, with interest differentials with Germany moving back towards zero. Continuing good wage and price performance and fiscal measures to reduce non-wage labour costs, combined with the modest depreciation of the guilder in effective terms from its peak in early 1995, should help to redress the international competitive position of Dutch firms.

Budget policy is expected to be somewhat restrictive, but the positive effects of the general economic strategy introduced by the 1994 Coalition Agreement should increasingly be felt. Cuts in the volume of public expenditure and structural reforms in the social security area should create room not only for a further reduction in the overall collective burden, but also for selective fiscal incentives and subsidised job creation to promote employment for low-skilled workers, as well as initiatives to boost investment in infrastructure. In the 1996 budget, the general government deficit was projected to fall below 3 per cent of GDP. However, since the budget was finalised, the conjunctural situation has worsened. With unchanged economic policies, the OECD Secretariat projects the deficit to be a little above 3 per cent of GDP in 1996, and to decline to 2³/₄ per cent in 1997. The cyclically-adjusted deficit is estimated to be around 2 per cent of GDP in 1997. The debt/GDP ratio (Maastricht definition) is projected to edge down, from around 79 per cent in 1995 to 78 per cent in 1997.

Prospects. Real GDP growth is expected to slow to around 1³/₄ per cent in 1996 but to accelerate again in 1997 – to a little over 2¹/₂ per cent. The major force behind the projected upturn is more buoyant foreign markets, which will boost exports and hence most sectors of the economy. The net contribution of foreign trade to GDP growth is projected to widen, although import growth is also expected to pick up due to an increase in domestic demand growth and the high import content of exports. On the domestic side, business investment will be supported in 1996 by on-going projects in the energy sector, and in 1997 by the improving economic outlook generally. Government investment is likely to remain buoyant, as construction for some important infrastructure projects gets started. Lower interest rates may lead to a rebound in residential investment in 1997. With the growth of real disposable income constrained by a reduced pace of job creation, wage moderation and fiscal consolidation, households will try to preserve their recent expenditure pattern: the growth of private consumption is projected to dip to just below 2 per cent in 1996-97, and the non-contractual saving ratio to fall to ³/₄ per cent of disposable income, from 1.8 per cent in 1995. The unemployment rate may merely edge down, to just below 7 per cent, thereby remaining slightly above the OECD Secretariat estimate of the structural rate of unemployment. This, combined with a more uncertain outlook for employment and business profits, is likely to keep any acceleration in the growth of wages to a minimum. Consumer price inflation may remain below 2 per cent and the current-account surplus at around 4 per cent of GDP. The main risks to these projections seem to be on the downside, and are related to the conjunctural situation in neighbouring countries which may not improve as soon and as rapidly as envisaged.

NEW ZEALAND

Weakening external demand and high short-term interest rates in response to domestic inflation pressures have led to a slowdown in growth from the high rates achieved in 1993-94. Much of the burden of adjustment has fallen on the traded goods sector as a consequence of a continuing appreciation of the exchange rate. With the Reserve Bank's measure of "underlying" inflation expected to continue close to the upper limit of the target range, monetary conditions will remain tight in order to minimise the risk of a further breach of the inflation target. This should lead to a GDP growth rate which is more sustainable over the medium term, despite the fact that tax cuts, announced for mid-1996 and again for mid-1997, are likely to boost household spending.

Recent developments. GDP growth, based on the output measure, slowed from over 6 per cent in 1994 to 3¹/₂ per cent in 1995.[1] The real foreign balance is increasingly acting as a brake on the real economy. This results from the strong appreciation of the exchange rate, which on a trade-weighted basis has risen almost 15 per cent since the beginning of 1994, as well as from slower export-market growth and supply constraints in the agricultural sector. Thus, export volume growth has shown a marked slowdown, from 9¹/₂ per cent in 1994 to 2 per cent in 1995, while growth in import volumes has remained high at 12¹/₂ per cent. This is reflected in a marked deterioration in the current account, which recorded a deficit equivalent to over 4 per cent of GDP for 1995. Imports have been boosted by domestic demand, which has remained remarkably strong, rising by 7 per cent in 1995, following similar increases in 1993 and 1994. Nevertheless, with an easing in "catch-up" spending by households and businesses, there are signs of a recent slowdown, particularly in fixed investment and stockbuilding: between the first and second half of 1995 the increase in fixed investment was less than 4 per cent (s.a.a.r.), compared with annual growth rates of the order of 20 per cent or higher between 1993 and early 1995; seasonally-adjusted stockbuilding in the final

NEW ZEALAND

Demand, output and prices

Percentage changes, volume (1982/83 prices)

	1992 current prices million NZ$	1993	1994	1995	1996	1997
Private consumption	46 726	3.0	4.4	3.5	4.1	4.7
Government consumption	12 596	−2.5	−2.1	0.9	0.7	0.6
Gross fixed capital formation	12 181	17.7	23.3	18.0	6.4	6.8
Final domestic demand	71 503	5.5	8.3	7.4	4.4	4.9
* stockbuilding[a]	1 395[b]	1.4	−0.2	−0.2	−0.4	−0.2
Total domestic demand	72 898	6.8	8.0	7.1	4.0	4.6
Exports of goods and services	23 087	6.0	9.6	2.2	5.5	7.0
Imports of goods and services	21 636	8.9	17.9	12.6	7.5	8.4
* net exports	1 451[b]	−1.6	−4.4	−5.6	−1.9	−2.0
GDP (expenditure) at market prices	74 349	5.5	4.1	2.2	2.7	3.4
GDP implicit price deflator	−	1.3	1.6	2.0	2.2	1.9
Memorandum items						
GDP (production)[c]	−	4.6	6.3	3.5	2.7	3.4
Private consumption deflator	−	0.3	1.3	1.6	1.9	2.0
Unemployment rate	−	9.5	8.1	6.3	6.2	6.4
Current balance[d]	−	−1.1	−3.0	−4.3	−3.5	−3.3

* Contributions to changes in real GDP (as a per cent of real GDP in the previous period).
a) Including statistical discrepancy.
b) Actual amount.
c) Considered as a more reliable indicator of total economic activity by the New Zealand Department of Statistics.
d) As a percentage of GDP.

quarter of 1995, while remaining positive, was at its lowest level for three years.

It is only recently that the slowdown has become apparent in the labour market, with employment growth in the final quarter of 1995 of 2 per cent (s.a.a.r.) representing the lowest quarterly rate of increase for two years, although employment was still 4 per cent higher than a year earlier. Strong labour force growth, partly explained by a rise in the participation rate, means that the unemployment rate stabilised at just over 6 per cent in the second half of 1995, after falling continuously since the beginning of 1994 and from a peak of just under 11 per cent in 1991. This tightening of the labour market has gone together with a gradual pick-up in nominal wage inflation, with total wage costs rising by 2½ per cent in the year to the fourth quarter of 1995.

Having overshot the target in the second quarter of 1995, the Reserve Bank's measure of "underlying" inflation (which excludes, among other effects, mortgage interest payments from headline CPI inflation) was on the upper limit of the 0 to 2 per cent range in the subsequent two quarters, before marginally breaching the target again in the first quarter of this year. Over the same period, the "headline" CPI inflation rate fell from a peak of 4½ per cent to just over 2 per cent. Price developments have also been dominated by the exchange rate appreciation: in the first quarter of 1996 the annual inflation rate of "tradeable" components of the CPI was slightly negative, whereas for "non-tradeables" it was nearly 4½ per cent. An important contribution to the latter has come from the housing component of the CPI (excluding mort-

gage interest costs), which increased by 5 per cent, reflecting continued strong activity in the construction and property sectors, especially around Auckland.

Policies and other forces acting. In the light of these developments the Reserve Bank made it clear in its end-of-year *Monetary Policy Statement* that it did not see any scope for short-term interest rates, currently at 9½ per cent, to fall below 8½ per cent before 1998, unless the effective exchange rate appreciates more strongly than expected (that is, 1.7 per cent per annum). This is consistent with their latest forecast, according to which underlying inflation would remain "uncomfortably" close to the upper limit of the target range throughout much of 1996.

The government is satisfied that the required fiscal and macroeconomic conditions for tax cuts – in particular a reduction in the net debt-to-GDP ratio to below 30 per cent, no immediate prospect of a return to budget deficits and no risk of the emergence of inflation or balance of payments pressures – will be fulfilled in the fiscal year 1996/97. It has therefore proceeded with its plans to cut income taxes, which will be targeted at low and middle-income earners and implemented in two steps in mid-1996 and mid-1997, amounting to 1 per cent of GDP on both occasions. Recent Treasury projections imply that, even with the announced tax cuts, the "operating surplus" (an accrual-based measure of the budget surplus) will remain at the level of about 3 per cent of GDP recorded in 1994/95 in the short run, before increasing to 5½ per cent in 1998/99, because of continued expenditure restraint. While this suggests that there is ample scope for a reduction of the tax burden on the basis of the foreseeable budgetary situation, the government recognises that macroeconomic developments may require some retailoring of the second set of tax cuts.

Prospects. The OECD Secretariat's projection assumes a continuation of tight monetary conditions, leading to a more sustainable output growth rate of about 3 per cent on average this year and next. High short-term interest rates and the slowdown in aggregate demand are expected to induce a decline in investment growth as well as a negative contribution to growth from stockbuilding. Thus, on the further assumption that the planned tax cuts are fully implemented, economic growth will become increasingly led by consumption rather than investment.

With average GDP growth projected to be close to the estimated 3 to $3^1/_2$ per cent growth rate of potential, it is likely that underlying inflation will remain in the upper half of the target range, with some risk of at least a temporary breach of the upper limit. The above projection may, however, overstate this risk because it is based on the technical assumption of an unchanged nominal exchange rate, whereas continued appreciation of the exchange rate – which is possible given the strong fiscal position, recent credit upratings and high short-term interest rates – would significantly reduce this likelihood. Nevertheless, by the same token, the projection may also understate the continuing burden of adjustment which will be placed on the traded goods sector. In either case, developments in inflation or the balance of payments may lead the authorities to reassess the scale of tax cuts in 1997 in order to avoid excess demand pressures and undue pressure on monetary policy.

NOTE

1. Caution is warranted in interpreting these figures because according to the less favoured expenditure measure of GDP the growth rate is significantly lower, at 4 and $2^1/_4$ per cent in 1994 and 1995, respectively. However, the strong growth in employment (referred to in the main text) gives added credence to the output-based figures.

NORWAY

While remaining stronger than in most other OECD countries, overall GDP growth slowed appreciably in 1995 relative to its exceptional strength in 1994. Mainland economic growth also decelerated in 1995 and is projected to edge down further in 1996 and 1997. Nevertheless, with the economy operating above its potential, the unemployment rate is expected to fall towards 4 per cent and inflation to rise somewhat in 1997. The strength of the recovery from the recession in the early 1990s has prompted the government to restrain public expenditure, which, together with larger-than-expected increases in petroleum revenues, is officially projected to result in a substantial budget surplus for the second consecutive year in 1996.

Recent developments. At 3.7 per cent, overall GDP growth in 1995 was well below the 5.7 per cent peak reached in 1994. The expansion of mainland GDP (which excludes oil and gas production) also declined over the same period, from almost 4.8 to 3.3 per cent. Growth was supported by buoyant mainland fixed investment in the first part of 1995 – spurred by low interest rates, high capacity utilisation, improved corporate profitability, and a sustained recovery in the real estate market – as well as by a sharp pick-up in investment on the Norwegian Continental Shelf later in the year. By contrast, the expansion of private consumption slowed, and foreign demand for traditional goods actually declined from the spring onward. With oil and gas exports surging in 1995 and the terms of trade improving, the current account surplus has been on an upward trend, reaching $3^1/_2$ per cent of GDP for the year. Although weakening somewhat in 1995, retail sales, housing starts and new car registrations have regained momentum in the first half of this year.

The unemployment rate continued to decline in 1995 to an average of 4.9 per cent from the 1993 peak of 6 per cent, and by April 1996 it reached 4.3 per cent. Although labour market conditions have therefore become relatively tight, wage increases have remained stable, with average hourly earnings in the private sector rising by 3.3 per cent in 1995, only a fraction higher than in the previous year. Price inflation has also stayed moderate. While a 1 percentage point increase in the rate of value added tax (VAT) in January 1995 lifted the twelve-month rate of consumer price increases from $1^1/_2$ to $2^1/_2$ per cent, inflation declined steadily thereafter to reach about 1 per cent in the first three months of 1996, when the VAT impact dissipated and lower car registration charges took effect.

Policies and other forces acting. Maintaining stable economic growth with low inflation is, to a large extent, conditional on continued wage moderation and restrained public spending, while monetary policy is geared towards ensuring the stability of the krone's exchange rate *vis-à-vis* other European currencies. Although upward pressure on the exchange rate and a downward revision of official inflation projections

NORWAY
Demand, output and prices
Percentage changes, volume (based on previous year prices)

	1992 current prices billion NKr	1993	1994	1995	1996	1997
Private consumption	394.9	2.1	4.6	2.7	3.1	2.4
Government consumption	172.9	1.0	1.1	0.6	1.1	1.4
Gross fixed capital formation	156.3	1.5	5.5	5.1	6.7	2.3
Final domestic demand	724.2	1.7	4.0	2.7	3.5	2.2
* stockbuilding	5.8 [a]	1.0	0.9	1.1	0	0
Total domestic demand	730.0	2.8	4.9	3.9	3.4	2.1
Exports of goods and services	300.1	2.0	8.5	3.7	8.3	3.8
Imports of goods and services	245.8	4.0	6.6	4.1	6.7	3.3
* net exports	54.3 [a]	−0.5	1.1	0.1	1.1	0.5
GDP at market prices	784.3	2.1	5.7	3.7	4.2	2.4
GDP implicit price deflator	–	2.6	0.2	2.8	2.4	2.2
Memorandum items						
Mainland GDP at market prices [b]	–	1.7	4.8	3.3	2.7	2.4
Mainland GDP deflator [b]	–	2.2	1.2	1.6	3.1	2.6
Exports of energy	–	5.2	12.5	5.7	13.6	3.6
Private consumption deflator	–	2.2	1.3	2.4	1.7	2.4
Unemployment rate	–	6.0	5.4	4.9	4.3	4.1
Household saving ratio [c]	–	5.6	6.3	5.2	4.3	4.9
General government financial balance [d]	–	−1.5	0.4	3.1	3.9	3.7
Current balance [d]	–	3.1	2.4	3.5	4.4	4.3

* Contributions to changes in real GDP (as a per cent of real GDP in the previous period).
a) Actual amount.
b) GDP excluding oil and shipping.
c) As a percentage of disposable income.
d) As a percentage of GDP.

recently prompted the Bank of Norway to ease monetary policy somewhat, the short-term interest rate differential *vis-à-vis* Germany has been on an upward trend in the last twelve months, widening from 40 to 120 basis points. At the same time, the spread between Norwegian and German long-term bond rates has declined from 70 to around 40 basis points, indicating a slightly improved risk assessment in financial markets.

Fiscal policy aims to establish a structural budget surplus which is to be largely invested abroad via the Petroleum Fund, beginning in 1996, with the official objectives of avoiding excessive liquidity in the mainland economy and maximising returns. Moreover, the associated capital outflow has the added benefit of relieving upward pressure on the krone. In 1995, the surplus on the general government account was 3.1 per cent of overall GDP, and is now officially projected to reach 3.9 per cent in 1996. Most of these surpluses are to be invested in the Petroleum Fund. The "non-oil" budget is also improving, with the general government deficit excluding oil revenues projected to decline from 3¾ per cent of mainland GDP in 1995 to 3¼ per cent in 1996.

Prospects. With the boom in mainland capital formation unwinding, and despite a continued resilience of private consumption and an expected pick-up in traditional exports in the second half of 1996, mainland GDP growth should slow down to around 2½ per cent by 1997. Continued buoyancy in oil and gas exports, how-

ever, is projected to raise overall GDP growth to 4.2 per cent in 1996 – slightly faster than in 1995 – and, as the expansion of energy output briefly stalls next year, to converge to about the same rate as mainland economic growth in 1997. Combined with a moderate expansion of the labour force, this should suffice to stabilise the current unemployment rate at 4.3 per cent in 1996 and to reduce it to 4.1 per cent in 1997. With labour market conditions thus tighter, wage growth is projected to accelerate to over 4 per cent and consumer price inflation, after falling to around 1½ per cent in 1996, could pick up to 2½ per cent towards the end of the projection period. A narrowing investment income deficit and rising energy exports are projected to boost the current account surplus to around 5 per cent of GDP in both 1996 and 1997.

Despite strong recent disinflation gains, there is a risk that inflation may pick up more than projected as the Norwegian economy continues expanding at high levels of employment. Given the importance attached to exchange rate stability, the room for further monetary tightening to contain inflation pressure in the period ahead might be constrained by the persistence of upward pressure on the currency in the context of growing external surpluses. This would make inflation control all the more dependent upon government expenditure restraint and continued wage moderation, both of which may slip in the presence of rising petroleum revenues and high corporate profitability, respectively.

PORTUGAL

The recovery slowed in the second half of 1995 and this weakness continued into early 1996. However, wage moderation and the price discipline imposed by the stability of the escudo are sustaining further disinflation, the differential relative to the EU average shrinking to below 1 percentage point in early 1996, a historical low. With confidence in the escudo strengthening, the monetary authorities have continued their policy of gradual easing of official interest rates, and this, together with rising foreign demand, should lead to a pick-up in activity in 1997. Following a significant deficit undershoot in 1995, the 1996 budget envisages a further decline in the deficit/GDP ratio of one percentage point through higher tax receipts, with a fiscal adjustment of similar size scheduled in 1997 in order to meet the Maastricht budget deficit criterion.

Recent developments. Real GDP accelerated to an estimated 2.5 per cent in 1995, underpinned by both private consumption and gross fixed investment, which offset a negative contribution to growth from the foreign balance. However, in the second half of 1995 weakening foreign demand adversely affected both fixed investment and private consumption. The expansion had thus lost momentum entering 1996.

Despite the cyclical rebound, employment fell by 0.6 per cent in 1995, and the unemployment rate increased to 7.3 per cent by year-end, 3.4 percentage

points higher than the low reached in the second half of 1992. Consumer price inflation eased to 4.1 per cent in 1995, well within the official target range of 3.5 to 4.5 per cent. Disinflation, sustained by low increases in import prices and moderate growth of unit labour costs, gathered speed in early 1996, with the 12-month average increase in the CPI index falling to 3.6 per cent in March. The current account deficit is estimated to have moved close to balance in 1995, as the trade deficit narrowed and receipts of official transfers increased.

Policies and other forces acting. The currency has been stable since the March 1995 realignment, and the firmness of the escudo has allowed the monetary authorities to resume their policy of gradual interest rate reduction. Key official lending rates were lowered on four occasions between August 1995 and April 1996. In the process, interest rate differentials relative to Germany have narrowed significantly, the premium on 10-year government bonds falling to 2.4 percentage points in early May, a 2.8 percentage points decline since April 1995.

On the fiscal front, the general government deficit declined to 5.1 per cent of GDP in 1995, undershooting the original target by 0.7 percentage points. This favourable result mainly reflected better-than-expected fiscal receipts, partly due to reduced tax evasion; current expenditure overran initial estimates. The budget for 1996, approved by parliament in March 1996, envisages

PORTUGAL

Demand, output and prices

Percentage changes, volume (1985 prices)

	1992 current prices billion Esc	1993	1994	1995	1996	1997
Private consumption	8 346.9	0.4	0.2	1.7	1.8	2.4
Government consumption	2 142.0	0	1.4	1.6	1.4	1.4
Gross fixed capital formation	3 426.5	−4.8	3.9	5.4	5.0	6.2
Final domestic demand	13 915.3	−1.0	1.3	2.6	2.6	3.3
* stockbuilding	117.4 [a]	0.2	0.2	0.2	−0.1	0
Total domestic demand	14 032.8	−0.9	1.5	2.7	2.5	3.2
Exports of goods and services	3 266.1	−5.1	10.7	11.4	9.7	7.5
Imports of goods and services	4 470.2	−3.2	8.5	8.6	7.5	6.8
* net exports	−1 204.1 [a]	−0.1	−1.0	−0.8	−0.7	−1.3
GDP at market prices	12 828.7	−1.2	0.8	2.5	2.3	2.7
GDP implicit price deflator	−	7.4	5.6	5.8	4.2	3.7
Memorandum items						
Private consumption deflator	−	7.1	4.8	4.1	3.2	2.7
Industrial production [b]	−	−2.4	−0.1	4.3	2.5	3.9
Unemployment rate	−	5.6	6.9	7.2	7.4	7.5
Household saving ratio [c]	−	10.9	11.1	11.0	11.3	11.4
Current balance [d]	−	1.0	−1.2	0	−0.3	−0.3

* Contributions to changes in real GDP (as a per cent of real GDP in the previous period).
a) Actual amount.
b) Industrial production index.
c) As a percentage of disposable income.
d) As a percentage of GDP.

a further fall in the fiscal deficit to 4.2 per cent, structural revenue gains due to better tax enforcement more than offsetting a rise in spending, particularly capital outlays.

Prospects. While the most recent business surveys may foreshadow a further weakening of economic activity in the near term, output growth should pick up in the second half of 1996, in line with the projected recovery in other European countries. For the year as a whole, real GDP growth is projected to ease to 2.3 per cent. The coming on-stream of new capacity in the automobile sector will contribute to further gains in export market shares in 1996, adding an estimated 0.7 percentage point to real GDP growth. Continued buoyancy in public infrastructure works, partly related to EU grants and the 1998 World Fair, together with a moderate strengthening of private consumption, may raise real GDP growth to around 2¾ per cent in 1997. With unemployment well

above its estimated structural level and a new incomes policy agreement in place, nominal wage growth should diminish further. Together with a moderate increase in import prices, this should reduce consumer-price inflation to below 3 per cent in 1997. On the external side, the current account is projected to weaken as the trade deficit widens and private transfers continue to trend down.

A risk attaching to the projections is that export market growth could be weaker, damping industrial investment. Domestically, the main risk is that if the growth assumptions prove optimistic, the budget deficit could be exceeded, eroding exchange-market confidence and putting upward pressure on interest rates. However, prospects for continued disinflation are good, enhancing the stability of the escudo within the ERM and holding out the promise of greater room for interest rate cuts than envisaged.

SPAIN

The macroeconomic fundamentals continued to improve during 1995. Based on strong exports and a pick-up in investment, output growth was relatively high. Moreover a prudent monetary policy, in combination with a narrowing of the budget deficit, facilitated the achievement of a rare current account surplus, and a further reduction in the inflation rate to 3.4 per cent in early 1996 – a 23-year low. However, in tandem with developments in other European countries, the recovery slowed down in the second half of the year, as the rate of consumer spending dropped sharply. The conditions for a pick-up in domestic demand are, nevertheless, in place provided consumer confidence recovers. In part due to the slowdown in output, fiscal policy based on an extension of the 1995 budget would not be sufficient to meet the convergence programme budget targets; however, the new Government has recently announced plans for further budget cuts (which have not been incorporated in the OECD Secretariat projections).

Recent developments. Real GDP registered one of the strongest growth rates in Europe in 1995, increasing by 3 per cent in 1995 compared with 2.1 per cent in 1994. However, growth slowed down significantly during the course of the year, with the annualised half-yearly growth declining from 3.4 per cent in the first half of 1995 to 2.1 per cent in the second half. The main factor behind the flagging output growth was a weakness in private consumption, despite a strong recovery in real disposable incomes. The increase in households' saving rate could be linked to the upturn in interest rates and to the composition of employment creation, which exhibited an increased recourse to part-time and short-term fixed-duration contracts. In response to the slowdown in

demand generally, private sector investment – which had been the most dynamic component of demand – also appears to have peaked during the second half of 1995. A sharp contraction in government projects also had a significant negative impact on overall investment demand.

Employment rose at a rapid pace of about 2½ per cent in 1995, and the unemployment rate declined to 22.8 per cent in the fourth quarter. Nevertheless, in line with the path of the economy, employment creation slowed down during the second half of 1995. In exchange for employment creation workers appeared willing to dampen their wage demands, a tradeoff which probably reflects the still high unemployment rate and the effect of the recent labour market reforms. The purchasing power of wages declined for the second year in a row, while unit labour costs increased broadly in line with inflation (after adjusting for the reduction in social security contribution rates). Moreover, preliminary indications suggest that wage moderation could continue, as collective agreements for 1996 point to relatively low wage increases on the order of 4 per cent.

The headline 12-month rise CPI fell to a 23-year low of 3.4 per cent in March 1996 from 5.1 per cent a year earlier. This development ensued in part from the slowing of demand and in part from the tapering off of the effects of transient cost-side factors: the increase in the VAT rate in January 1995, the reversal in mid-year of the prices of imported intermediate products, and the end of the drought.

In 1995, the current account of the balance of payments registered a surplus for the first time since 1986. Export growth continued to be strong despite the generalised slowdown in Europe. Reflecting the continuing effect of the 20 per cent depreciation of the peseta in 1992-93, Spanish goods captured a further 6 per cent

SPAIN

Demand, output and prices

Percentage changes, volume (1986 prices)

	1992 current prices billion Ptas	1993	1994	1995	1996	1997
Private consumption	37 242.9	−2.2	0.8	1.8	2.3	3.0
Government consumption	10 093.1	2.3	−0.3	0.9	−0.9	0
Gross fixed capital formation	12 916.2	−10.6	1.4	8.4	6.1	5.3
Final domestic demand	60 252.2	−3.4	0.7	3.0	2.6	3.0
* stockbuilding	472.0 [a]	−1.0	0.3	0.2	−0.2	0
Total domestic demand	60 724.3	−4.2	1.1	3.2	2.4	3.0
Exports of goods and services	10 409.8	8.5	16.2	9.3	7.3	7.3
Imports of goods and services	12 052.8	−5.1	10.4	9.7	7.3	8.0
* net exports	−1 642.9 [a]	3.3	1.0	−0.4	−0.2	−0.5
GDP at market prices	59 081.4	−1.2	2.1	3.0	2.3	2.7
GDP implicit price deflator	–	4.3	3.9	4.8	3.4	2.9
Memorandum items						
Private consumption deflator	–	5.5	4.9	4.6	3.5	3.0
Industrial production	–	−4.4	4.5	5.5	4.6	4.2
Unemployment rate	–	22.7	24.2	22.9	22.9	22.7
Household saving ratio [b]	–	12.5	10.6	11.7	11.5	10.9
General government financial balance [c,d]	–	−7.5	−6.9	−6.2	−5.2	−4.7
Current balance [c]	–	−0.8	−1.2	0.2	−0.2	−0.5

* Contributions to changes in real GDP (as a per cent of real GDP in the previous period).
a) Actual amount.
b) As a percentage of disposable income.
c) As a percentage of GDP.
d) Currently the national accounts of Spain include social security payments and contributions on a cash basis, whereas recording them on an acrual basis would provide a measure that was more consistent with the principles of the System of National Accounts. The Spanish authorities estimate that if this accruals adjustment were made, the financial balance would be -6.2 per cent of GDP in 1994 and -5.8 per cent of GDP in 1995.

market share; in addition, the tourist season was very good. However, the improvement of the current account is partly accounted for by higher official transfers from the European Community, reflecting a catch-up in the disbursement of funds under the EU support programmes.

Policies and other forces acting. Following a six-month period of a notably tight monetary policy – at a time when other European countries were easing their monetary stance – policy was relaxed gradually in early 1996. This decision by the Bank of Spain reflects *(i)* the above-mentioned decline in inflation, *(ii)* the reduction in the yield of the benchmark 10-year government bond by about 300 basis points since early 1995, and *(iii)* the appreciation of the peseta *vis-à-vis* the Deutchemark to a level last observed prior to the exchange market turbulence preceding the March 1995 depreciation. Specifically, the Bank of Spain has reduced its intervention rate five times since December 1995, from a peak of 9.25 per cent during the latter part of 1995 to 7.5 per cent in May 1996. Following this last move, the spread on three-month interest rates with comparable Deutchemark denominated instruments has fallen to about 400 basis points while that on 10-year instruments has fallen to about 300 basis points. In view of these developments and inflation prospects which appear to be in line with the Bank of Spain's announced medium-term inflation

target (of below 3 per cent during 1997), the OECD Secretariat projections incorporate a further cautious easing of monetary policy.

The deficit of general government (national accounts basis) is estimated to have been 6.2 per cent of GDP in 1995 compared with 6.9 per cent in 1994. The convergence programme target for last year (5.9 per cent of GDP) was met once the receipts of the social security system are included on an accrual, rather than on a cash basis, with the former accounting principle being consistent with the Maastricht definition and the System of National Accounts. The fiscal outcome in 1995 reflects, most importantly, shortfalls in non-tax receipts, and higher than projected interest servicing of the public debt, which were compensated by cuts in discretionary expenditure, especially of investment. Fiscal policy aims at reducing the deficit of general government to 4.4 per cent of GDP (accrual basis) in 1996, on the way to a convergence programme target of 3 per cent of GDP in 1997. Following the rejection by Parliament of the 1996 budget, the 1995 budget has been prorogued to 1996. To achieve the requisite deficit reduction, royal decrees were used to raise wages, pensions, and income tax brackets by an amount equal to targeted inflation (3.5 per cent), and to cut specific non-discretionary expenditures by about 1 per cent of GDP. For 1997, the OECD Secretariat projects that, at the level of general government, non-wage consumption will remain constant in real terms and government investment and subsidies to enterprises will remain constant in nominal terms. Acknowledging that further measures will be necessary to attain the 1996 convergence programme fiscal target, the new Government has recently announced further cuts in expenditure and an acceleration of the privatisation process, which have not yet been specified and, thus, have not been incorporated in the OECD projections.

Prospects. The timing and the strength of a recovery from the slowdown experienced in the second half of 1995 will depend to a large extent on private consumption behaviour. The sharp drop in the purchase of consumer durables observed during the second half of 1995 may be reversing as new passenger car registrations have picked up rapidly in the first two months of 1996, and the index of consumer confidence has improved steadily since late 1995. The evidence surrounding private investment points to a slowdown from the fast pace registered in 1995, as capacity utilisation has come down.

Nevertheless, business profits are still performing well, and the continued moderation in wage costs and the current level of long term interest rates suggest that investment should remain strong during 1996 and 1997, though less buoyant than in 1995. As a result, overall output growth may fall to 2.3 per cent in 1996, despite the envisaged pick up in consumption, and could recover to 2.7 per cent in 1997. The moderate growth of demand in conjunction with a cautiously restrictive monetary policy, suggest that there should be few obstacles to reducing inflation to 3 per cent in 1997. The main uncertainty surrounding the projections, which are based on a fall in the household saving ratio, is the behaviour of domestic consumer spending. However, if fiscal tightening in the short term is more significant than assumed in the projections, output growth could be slower in 1997, although it would have positive consequences on activity beyond the projection period.

SWEDEN

The expansion has slowed as export demand has faltered. With the private sector benefiting from strong financial balances and rising real incomes, the economy is well placed to sustain a moderate expansion of domestic demand, particularly since inflationary pressures have abated and increased the scope for a more supportive monetary policy. However, with high wage increases embedded in the economy through existing settlements, further inroads into unemployment will be made only slowly.

Recent developments. The Swedish economy slowed in the third quarter of 1995 and activity declined towards the end of the year, as the impulse from net exports, which had sustained the economy since late 1993, died away. Domestic demand was supported by business investment as the investment cycle spread from manufacturing to service sectors. But private consumption has remained weak well into 1996, with household income depressed by higher taxes and cuts in transfers. Although the inflow of orders to industry held up fairly well in 1995, inventory growth continued to outstrip production throughout the year, setting in train a stock correction in early 1996.

Inflation performance has improved. The appreciation of the Swedish krona since early September has served to rein in export and import prices and has fed through to a fall in consumer price inflation to 1.3 per cent in April 1996, from 3.3 per cent one year earlier. An increase in manufacturing labour costs of 6$^1/_2$ per cent during 1995 has been substantially offset by high productivity growth. However, labour cost increases in the ser-

vice sectors, in the range of 4 to 6 per cent, are putting profits under pressure, as consumer prices net of indirect taxes have been virtually stable over the last year.

Policies and other forces acting. At 8.1 per cent of GDP, the budget deficit turned out larger than expected in 1995, reflecting the slowing of economic growth and a temporary weakening of tax receipts. However, progress towards fiscal consolidation has been maintained insofar as the programme of retrenchment adopted in 1994-95 has been reinforced by the adoption of additional measures. Contingent upon the projected expansion of the economy, particularly in domestic demand, the budget deficit could fall to 5$^1/_2$ per cent in 1996 and be close to 3 per cent in 1997, allowing the government debt-to-GDP ratio to fall from 1996 onward.

With inflation having fallen below the official target rate of 2 per cent, monetary policy has been allowed to give support to the economy. So far in 1996 the repo rate has been gradually reduced from 8.9 to 6.5 per cent, and short-term prospects may allow a further reduction of the short-term interest rate differential against Germany, currently at 3 percentage points. The long-term spread against Germany has fallen to 2 percentage points, from a peak of 3$^1/_4$ percentage points in mid-1995. As current yields have to a large extent discounted the improvement in policy fundamentals, further reductions are likely to depend on visible progress being maintained towards medium-term goals.

Prospects. While the overall level of industrial costs is still favourable, the real appreciation resulting from the combination of a firmer krona, relatively high

SWEDEN
Demand, output and prices
Percentage changes, volume (1991 prices)

	1992 current prices billion SKr	1993	1994	1995	1996	1997
Private consumption	777.3	−3.1	0.8	0.3	0.5	1.5
Government consumption	402.5	0.2	−0.5	−2.3	0.9	−1.3
Gross fixed capital formation	244.6	−17.2	−0.2	10.6	9.4	4.4
Final domestic demand	1 424.4	−4.7	0.3	1.2	2.1	1.2
* stockbuilding	−6.7[a]	−0.5	1.5	0.5	−0.8	0.1
Total domestic demand	1 417.8	−5.2	1.9	1.6	1.2	1.3
Exports of goods and services	401.6	7.6	14.1	11.4	4.5	6.0
Imports of goods and services	377.6	−2.5	13.4	8.7	5.0	5.0
* net exports	23.9[a]	2.9	0.9	1.4	0.2	0.7
GDP at market prices	1 441.7	−2.2	2.6	3.0	1.3	2.0
GDP implicit price deflator	−	2.6	2.7	4.1	1.6	2.8
Memorandum items						
Private consumption deflator	−	5.7	3.1	2.7	1.8	2.8
Industrial production	−	−0.2	10.6	9.4	2.5	4.0
Unemployment rate[b]	−	8.2	8.0	7.7	7.6	7.2
Household saving ratio[c]	−	8.3	8.6	8.2	8.4	7.2
General government financial balance[d]	−	−12.3	−10.8	−8.1	−5.5	−3.1
Current balance[d]	−	−2.0	0.4	2.1	2.2	3.2

* Contributions to changes in real GDP (as a per cent of real GDP in the previous period).
a) Actual amount.
b) Based on monthly Labour Force Surveys.
c) As a percentage of disposable income.
d) As a percentage of GDP.

wage growth embedded in the two-to-three year wage agreements concluded in 1995 and slowing productivity growth will reduce the contribution to the economy from foreign demand, implying greater reliance on domestic demand as the vehicle for economic growth. With higher real wage growth and household financial savings amounting to 10 per cent of disposable income, private consumption growth should resume, even if continued high unemployment and weak property prices are likely to limit the fall in the saving ratio. The acceleration of wage growth implies a squeeze on profits which will slow investment growth. But since capacity utilisation in manufacturing is still high and business profits remain healthy, business fixed investment is projected to continue to be the most buoyant demand component. Over-

all, after slowing to 1¼ per cent in 1996, GDP growth may increase to 2 per cent in 1997.

With the combined number of unemployed and participants in government-sponsored employment schemes still above 12½ per cent of the labour force, the Swedish economy should be in a position to respond readily to a faster-than-expected pick-up in external demand, with potential benefits for the budget deficit and interest rates. Conversely, it remains highly vulnerable to a prolonged slowdown, as the inflexibility of wages would leave producers with no alternative but to shed labour to contain costs. This would exacerbate the already serious unemployment and budget situation, calling for further fiscal retrenchment to maintain policy credibility.

SWITZERLAND

Output declined in the last two quarters of 1995, and indicators point to continuing weakness in the first half of 1996. Sluggish economic activity reflected the marked real appreciation of the Swiss franc since 1993, fiscal restraint and ongoing adjustment of the real-estate sector after earlier speculative excesses. The near-term outlook is bleak, but activity may improve gradually from the second half of 1996 onward as the effects of contractionary forces give way to those of lower interest rates and economic

recovery in Europe. Gains in employment are, therefore, expected to be very small, and inflation is set to stay below 2 per cent.

Recent developments. The effects of the Swiss franc appreciation since 1993 came through in terms of a sizeable negative contribution to growth from the real foreign balance in 1995, brought about by very strong imports of goods and services and falling services exports – notably tourism – in spite of the relatively good performance of merchandise exports. Machinery and

SWITZERLAND

Demand, output and prices

Percentage changes, volume (1980 prices)

	1992 current prices billion SF	1993	1994	1995	1996	1997
Private consumption	198.1	−0.6	1.0	0.2	0.5	1.1
Government consumption	49.3	−1.2	0.8	−0.1	−0.2	0
Gross fixed capital formation	80.4	−2.5	5.9	5.3	2.0	2.6
Final domestic demand	327.8	−1.2	2.2	1.6	0.9	1.4
* stockbuilding	−1.0[a]	−0.7	1.5	0.9	0.2	0.3
Total domestic demand	326.8	−1.8	3.8	2.5	1.1	1.7
Exports of goods and services	122.2	1.6	3.3	2.8	2.2	4.5
Imports of goods and services	110.2	−0.8	9.0	6.4	3.2	4.2
* net exports	12.0[a]	1.1	−2.6	−1.8	−0.7	−0.1
GDP at market prices	338.8	−0.8	1.2	0.7	0.5	1.7
GDP implicit price deflator	–	2.0	1.4	1.4	0.9	1.2
Memorandum items						
Private consumption deflator	–	3.1	1.0	1.3	0.9	1.3
Industrial production	–	−0.5	7.9	3.9	4.2	5.0
Unemployment rate	–	4.5	4.7	4.2	4.2	4.0
Current balance[b]	–	8.4	7.1	6.5	6.5	6.5

* Contributions to changes in real GDP (as a per cent of real GDP in the previous period).
a) Actual amount.
b) As a percentage of GDP.

equipment investment was buoyant as companies strove to remain competitive. By contrast, construction investment declined as the stock of unused structures remained high and federal housing loan subsidies and the "investment bonus programme" were phased out. Private consumption broadly stagnated as real disposable incomes of households were weakened by a combination of stagnant real wages, meagre employment growth and rises in taxes and social security contributions. Fiscal retrenchment also resulted in flat real government consumption in 1995. Overall, GDP rose by 0.7 per cent. Current economic indicators suggest that activity remained depressed in early 1996: the business climate index fell further, consumer confidence remained low and other business survey indicators, such as production prospects and both the level and trend of orders, have deteriorated further.

Employment grew only marginally in 1995, but with labour force participation declining further the unemployment rate fell from 4.7 per cent in 1994 to 4.2 per cent; it rose to 4.4 per cent in March 1996. The jump of average consumer price inflation from 0.9 per cent in 1994 to 1.8 per cent in 1995 was entirely due to the introduction of value-added tax (VAT). As the VAT effect dropped out of the statistics in early 1996, 12-month inflation rates fell back to below 1 per cent.

Policies and other forces acting. Marking the more aggressive monetary policy easing during the second half of 1995, the National Bank (SNB) lowered the discount rate in December for the fourth time in the year, by ¹/₂ percentage point to 1.5 per cent, the lowest rate since late 1979. Money market interest rates followed suit: the three-month Euro-Swiss franc interest rate fell to some

1.7 per cent in April 1996. Long-term interest rates continued their fairly steady decline, reaching 3³/₄ per cent at the end of 1995. But bond rates edged up again in early 1996, to around 4 per cent in April 1996, in the face of economic weakness and stable prices.

With the real effective Swiss franc exchange rate now some 12 per cent higher than in 1993, overall monetary conditions remain tight. In view of this and given the expansion of the monetary base still below the medium-term target path, it is assumed that the SNB will bring money market interest rates down somewhat further. This should make for a reversal of the recent rise in bond yields and bring them back to the lower levels observed late last year. A very gradual pre-emptive tightening of monetary policy could occur in the course of 1997, when economic activity is projected to gather strength. This could induce a slight upward drift in short-term interest rates towards the end of next year, but is expected to leave bond yields largely unaffected. Although fiscal policy aims at achieving budget balance over the medium term, a neutral fiscal stance is assumed for this year and next, with further fiscal tightening taking place as from 1998.

Prospects. The forces which have depressed activity in 1995 are still in place, so that economic growth is projected to improve only gradually during the second half of this year, as the lagged effects of monetary relaxation in 1995 come through, fiscal policy ceases to be restrictive, and growth picks up in other European countries. Given the negative carry-over from the second half of 1995, this will be insufficient to raise the growth rate of real GDP in 1996 above that of 1995. With the contractionary effects of the Swiss franc appreciation waning, economic growth may accelerate to 1.7 per cent in 1997. This implies a very small reduction of the large output gap, projected at more than 3 per cent both in 1996 and 1997.

Private consumption will probably remain markedly below its long-term growth trend in 1996 and 1997 as employment is set to improve only a little; in addition, the substantial slack in the labour market will keep a brake on real wage gains. Growth of machinery and equipment investment is set to slow, its ratio to GDP having already reached the high level of the preceding cyclical peak. By contrast, construction investment seems bound to contract further in 1996, in line with recent falls in building permits. But as excess capacity in the real-estate sector is reduced during the year, construction activity could turn around in 1997. Export growth will be damped further this year by the lagged effects of exchange rate appreciation, but will increasingly benefit from robust export market growth in 1997. With import growth largely following domestic demand and the terms of trade unchanged, the current external surplus may stabilise at 6½ per cent of GDP in 1996-97. The very gradual recovery of activity is likely to entail only a small decline in unemployment in 1997, which is consistent with modest wage and price increases.

The risks attaching to the projections appear to be balanced: household consumption could be somewhat weaker than expected if consumer confidence worsened further or employment grew by less than projected. On the other hand, growth could be stronger if the downward correction of the effective Swiss franc exchange rate which began in November 1995 were to continue.

TURKEY

The Turkish economy faces a number of crosscurrents following the severe 1994 external crisis and recession. GDP growth rebounded to over 7 per cent in 1995, but inflation picked up sharply in the six months to March 1996, and the current account moved back into deficit towards the close of 1995. Growth is projected to slow to some 4½ per cent in 1996, in response to an assumed tightening of macroeconomic policies. This should help to rein in inflation and to limit the current account deficit to around 2 to 3 per cent of GDP.

Recent developments. GDP growth was around 7¼ per cent in 1995, rebounding from the sharp 1994 recession; industrial production and retail trade rose particularly strongly. The early stages of recovery were export-led, stimulated by the large real exchange rate depreciation of some 20 per cent dating from early 1994. By mid-1995, buoyant domestic demand was the leading component in the expansion. Survey data indicate a slowing in the growth of domestic demand in early 1996. Labour market data are not available beyond April 1995, when the unemployment rate was reported at 7.2 per cent, down from 8.2 per cent a year earlier.

Inflation fell significantly between March and September of 1995, but picked up subsequently. In the six months to March 1996, wholesale price inflation jumped to an annualised rate of 94 per cent, compared with 40 per cent in the six months to September 1995. Much of this pick-up reflected the strong growth of the monetary aggregates in the first six months of 1995, exacerbated by accelerated exchange rate depreciation in the last quarter of 1995. Inflation in early 1996 was boosted by large public sector tariff increases delayed by the 1995 elections.

Real wages of dependent employees (which make up some 30 per cent of the labour force) may have dropped by some 20 to 30 per cent between 1993 and 1995. By contrast, profits and dividends have risen sharply and real interest rates are very high, resulting in a big shift in factor income shares and a marked rise in income dispersion.

Exports of goods and services rose strongly in 1995 (by some 6.7 per cent), but imports jumped by over 30 per cent, leading to a significant widening in the trade deficit. As a result, although tourism and other invisibles earnings as well as remittances from Turkish workers abroad increased strongly, the current account moved into deficit towards year-end, recording a deficit of $2.3 billion (1½ per cent of GDP) for 1995 as a whole.

External financing constraints eased in 1995, as official borrowing on international capital markets resumed (raising some $2.5 billion). A temporary surge in short-term capital inflows facilitated official debt repayments, but contributed to a rapid rise in foreign reserves to record levels of some $17 billion in October 1995. It proved difficult to sterilise the impact of these inflows on the domestic money supply. Capital inflows reversed in the period surrounding the December 1995 elections.

Policies and other forces acting. The PSBR was originally targeted at some 6 per cent of GDP for 1995. In the event, debt service and real interest rates proved much higher than programmed. But as inflation was almost 50 per cent higher than had been assumed in the budget, the PSBR as a proportion of GDP was held to some 6½ per cent.

The new Government's 1996 budget calls for a consolidated budget deficit of 6½ per cent and a PSBR of some 7½ per cent of GDP. Government revenue is projected to rise by some 2 percentage points of GDP in 1996, as a result of buoyant economic activity in 1995 and improved tax collection. However, tax revenue

TURKEY
Demand, output and prices
Percentage changes, volume (1987 prices)

	1992 current prices trillion TL	1993	1994	1995	1996	1997
Private consumption	734	8.4	−5.3	7.6	5.0	5.3
Government consumption	141	5.4	−3.5	6.7	3.0	3.0
Gross fixed capital formation	251	24.9	−15.9	8.3	7.7	7.8
Final domestic demand	1 127	12.4	−8.2	7.7	5.6	5.8
* stockbuilding	4 [a]	1.2	−4.6	4.7	0	0
Total domestic demand	1 131	13.5	−12.3	12.7	5.5	5.8
Exports of goods and services	157	7.7	15.2	6.7	12.0	12.0
Imports of goods and services	190	35.8	−21.9	30.0	14.5	13.4
* net exports	−32 [a]	−6.2	8.6	−5.1	−1.2	−1.1
* statistical discrepancy	−5 [a]	0.5	−0.9	−0.1	0	0
GDP at market prices	1 093	8.0	−5.5	7.3	4.5	5.0
GDP implicit price deflator	–	67.7	107.0	81.6	70.0	60.0
Memorandum items						
Private consumption deflator	–	67.5	104.1	94.6	70.0	60.0
Manufacturing production	–	9.2	−4.8	8.7	5.0	5.0
Unemployment rate	–	7.7	8.1	7.5	7.7	7.4
Current balance [b]	–	−3.6	2.1	−1.6	−2.3	−2.8

* Contributions to changes in real GDP (as a per cent of real GDP in the previous period).
a) Actual amount.
b) As a percentage of GDP.

will also be hit by the abolition of the Mass Housing Fund and other levies previously charged on imports. At the same time, government spending is projected to rise even more, with a big rise in debt service from 7½ to 10 per cent of GDP between 1995 and 1996. Interest rates have dropped from their January peaks, but remain very high, with rates on 6-month treasury bills at about 120 per cent at end-April.[1] Decisive fiscal and structural action could pave the way for a drop in inflation, lower risk premia on government debt, and thereby a reversal of the rising debt-service burden.[2] Nonetheless, in the near term, the 1996 budget and PSBR targets may be subject to further, albeit modest, slippage.

Turkey entered into a customs union with the EU on 1 January 1996, and this should have positive effects on the economy in the medium term. However, other structural reforms, which are key to exploiting these opportunities, made slow headway in 1995. Some limited progress has been made in restructuring large loss-making state economic enterprises, and privatisation, albeit making progress, has remained plagued by delays. Legislation to reform the tax and pension systems has yet to be passed by Parliament.[3]

Prospects. Measures to restrict the PSBR to some 8 to 9 per cent of GDP in 1996 are assumed in the OECD Secretariat's projections. Under this assumption, GDP growth is projected to slow to some 4½ per cent in 1996, permitting inflation to fall to around 70 per cent in 1996 and 60 per cent in 1997. This scenario would be consistent with a modest pick up in economic activity in 1997 and a current account deficit of around 2 to 3 per cent of GDP.

The risks and uncertainties surrounding these projections are large. External financing constraints are not a near term problem. But large scale currency substitution and the very short maturity of domestic debt has increased the volatility of financial markets. Failure to establish a credible medium-term economic strategy and to restore fiscal stability could trigger a deterioration in confidence and economic instability. By the same token, sharper declines in the PSBR and inflation are also possible. But this would require a greater degree of social cohesion and political resolve to pursue fiscal consolidation and structural reform than has been shown over the past decade.

NOTES

1. Interest rates hit a peak of 240 per cent in January 1996. Although nominal rates dropped to 120 per cent by end-April, this still implies real rates of over 30 per cent, if expected inflation is around 4 per cent a month (60 per cent a year).

2. Falling interest rates can have a big impact on debt service, as the average maturity of domestic debt (carrying market related interest rates) is around 4 months.

3. Pending legislation includes: a special consumption tax to offset a part of the $2.5 billion in revenue losses from lower tariffs and the abolition of the Mass Housing Fund levy; and legislation to phase in higher minimum statutory retirement ages of 50 for women and 55 for men.

DEVELOPMENTS IN SELECTED NON-OECD COUNTRIES

Growth in most countries of central and eastern Europe, propelled by exports and investment, may have peaked in 1995 but is projected to remain robust in 1996. In the former Soviet Union, output generally continued to decline in 1995, but signs of recovery are becoming more tangible. Integration of the region into the world economy gathered pace, with foreign trade booming and capital inflows strengthening. Progress in structural reforms continued, although unevenly and with occasional reversals. The robust macroeconomic performance of the Dynamic Asian Economies (DAEs: Chinese Taipei, Hong Kong, Korea, Malaysia, Singapore and Thailand), was sustained in 1995; GDP grew strongly and inflation fell. In China, inflation also fell and the current-account surplus has increased considerably. Given relatively tight monetary policies and real exchange rate appreciation, average GDP growth in the DAEs is likely to be lower in 1996, also leading to lower inflation. A moderate re-acceleration of growth is expected for 1997 as the effects of the exchange-rate appreciation wane. The Chinese economy, on the other hand, is likely to continue to grow strongly with a relatively high but stable rate of inflation. For both the DAEs and China, the major risk affecting the projections is of further upward pressure on the real exchange rate affecting the competitive position and trade performance. Most Central and South American economies were affected by the consequences of the Mexican crisis in 1995. GDP growth decelerated sharply as monetary policies were tightened in the context of deteriorating fiscal and current-account balances. In most of the region, and particularly in Brazil, the need for fiscal adjustment remains significant. As such, output growth is not projected to pick up significantly until 1997, inflation is likely to continue to fall slowly and the current-account deficit should stabilise at around 3 per cent of GDP.

CENTRAL AND EASTERN EUROPE, RUSSIA AND UKRAINE

Transition trends

Half a decade after the start of major reforms, the countries most advanced in the transition to a market economy had progressed sufficiently with stabilisation and structural change to join the OECD or to approach that stage.[1] Progress was slower, or started later, in Romania, Bulgaria, and the Baltic states (Estonia, Latvia and Lithuania). Russia has also made considerable progress in transition, albeit at times somewhat chaotically, while Ukraine has clearly lagged, despite some belated efforts to speed up reforms. The uneven outcomes of the transition process are rooted in differences in initial conditions and policy choices. Masked by differences in timing, some common features nevertheless emerge, as these countries faced a number of similar challenges.

In most countries of the region, growth performance improved in 1995 (Tables 23 and 24). Preliminary official data indicate that in 1995 output growth approached or exceeded 5 per cent in the most advanced countries. The expansion was less impressive in the rest of the central and eastern European countries (CEECs), with the exception of Romania. In the former Soviet Union, output declines were shallower than in 1994 in Russia and Ukraine, while additional large contractions were observed in several other New Independant States (NIS). The extent of the collapse in the NIS may partly be a statistical artefact stemming from the under-reporting of the activities of the emerging private sector, as officially, if belatedly, acknowledged in some countries, including Russia. It also to some extent constitutes an unavoidable aspect of adjustment to market conditions. Nevertheless, the depth and length of the depression suggest that the collapse was genuine – and larger than can be explained by structural transformation itself.

Among the reasons for the dynamism of output in the most advanced CEECs were, on the supply side, large productivity gains (from an admittedly low base) and recovery from a series of poor harvests. On the demand side, the expansion continued to be driven by exports and, increasingly, by investment, which continued to be financed primarily from retained earnings, although there was also a revival of bank lending. Over time, growth is clearly becoming more dependent on incremental inputs of capital and labour, following an initial phase dominated by the reallocation of existing human and physical resources. In addition, growth is becoming more broadly based sectorally and regionally.

Sustained growth has contributed to a turnaround in employment and to a reversal of the trend of increasing unemployment rates in most CEECs. Nevertheless, registered unemployment rates remain very high, and

Table 23.	**European economies in transition and the Russian Federation: key economic indicators**[a]			
	1994	1995	1996	1997
Bulgaria				
Output	1.4	2.5	2.5	3.0
Inflation	125.0	33.0	40.0	30.0
Unemployment	12.8	11.1	13.0	12.0
Fiscal balance	−5.6	−6.8	−6.5	−6.0
Current account	0.1	0.3	0.0	0.0
Poland				
Output	5.2	7.0	5.5	5.0
Inflation	29.0	22.0	19.0	15.0
Unemployment	16.0	14.9	14.0	13.0
Fiscal balance	−2.7	−2.9	−2.8	−2.5
Current account[b]	−0.9	−2.1	−2.9	−3.5
Romania				
Output	3.5	6.9	4.0	4.0
Inflation	62.0	28.0	25.0	20.0
Unemployment	10.9	8.9	10.0	10.0
Fiscal balance	−1.0	−3.6	−2.5	−2.5
Current account	−0.4	−1.5	−1.5	−1.0
Russia				
Output	−15.0	−4.0	1.0	3.0
Output/revised series[c]	−12.6			
Inflation	226.0	131.0	50.0	30.0
Unemployment	6.0	8.0	9.0	10.0
Fiscal balance	−10.1	−4.0	−4.0	−3.5
Current account	0.0	7.0	2.5	−0.6
Slovak Republic				
Output	4.9	7.4	5.0	5.0
Inflation	11.7	7.2	7.0	7.0
Unemployment	14.8	13.1	12.5	12.0
Fiscal balance[d]	−1.2	0.7	−1.5	−1.0
Current account	0.7	0.5	0.0	0.0
Slovenia				
Output	5.5	4.5	5.0	5.0
Inflation	19.0	9.0	10.0	10.0
Unemployment	14.2	13.5	13.0	12.0
Fiscal balance	−0.2	−0.9	−0.5	−0.5
Current account	−0.5	0.0	0.3	0.1

a) Output data are average annual percentage changes of real GDP. Inflation refers to the year-end per cent change in consumer prices. The fiscal balance is expressed as a percentage of GDP while the current account balance is in $ billion. Except for Russia, unemployment is registered unemployment in per cent of the labour force at year-end, which may differ significantly from other unemployment measures; for Russia, the concept of open unemployment is used.
b) Excluding (large) unrecorded cross-border trade flows.
c) As presented by the World Bank and the Goskomstat of the Russian Federation, *Report on the National Accounts*, Washington DC and Moscow, October 1995.
d) Excluding principal payments on public debt and clearing account transactions.
Sources: National authorities; OECD, *National Accounts Central and Eastern Europe*, May 1995, Paris, and OECD Secretariat estimates.

Table 24.	**Ukraine and the Baltics: key economic indicators**		
	1993	1994	1995
Ukraine			
Output	−14.2	−19.0	−11.8
Inflation	10 155.0	401.0	181.0
Unemployment	0.3	0.3	0.4
Fiscal balance	−12.0	−8.6	−4.0
Trade balance	−0.8	−1.4	−1.3
Estonia			
Output	−7.0	−3.0	3.0
Inflation	35.0	42.0	29.0
Unemployment	4.7	5.1	5.4
Fiscal balance	1.0	3.0	1.0
Current account	0.0	−0.2	−0.2
Latvia			
Output	−15.0	1.0	−2.0
Inflation	35.0	26.0	23.0
Unemployment[a]	7.0	7.0	6.7
Fiscal balance	1.0	−2.0	−4.0
Current account	0.0	−0.1	−0.2
Lithuania			
Output	−30.0	1.0	3.0
Inflation	189.0	45.0	36.0
Unemployment	3.4	4.5	7.3
Fiscal balance	1.0	−2.0	−1.0
Current account	−0.1	−0.2	−0.2

a) In Latvia, the definition of unemployment may be somewhat narrower than in the other two Baltic countries.
Sources: National authorities; OECD, *National Accounts Central and Eastern Europe*, May 1995, Paris, and OECD Secretariat estimates.

labour offices, and contribute to relatively low *de facto* unemployment.

Helped by relatively prudent fiscal policies, disinflation continued in most CEECs in 1995, albeit gradually, and hindered in some cases by the monetary impact of rapid reserve accumulation. In Russia and Ukraine, the 1995 stabilisation efforts had some success, but inflation remains very high. In most other NIS countries as well, inflation performance improved, owing to tightened financial policies.

The rise of the share of the private sector has to a significant extent reflected the growth of new private entities, including those that emerged from the split-up of large-scale enterprises at different stages of the privatisation process. Privatisation has followed many different tracks, and has been pursued with uneven vigour. Even where the formal transfer of ownership title has been effected early on, corporate governance still needs improving. Where the state has retained blocks of shares, the risk of politicisation of enterprise management remains. In contrast, where foreign investors have been

regional disparities within countries are substantial, reflecting different sectoral legacies and local policies. In Russia and Ukraine, by contrast, open unemployment is still rising. Extremely low levels of unemployment benefits discourage the unemployed from registering with

granted access, restructuring has generally been more effective.

Financial fragility remains a feature of many transition countries, notwithstanding the recovery of corporate profits in the more advanced economies and efforts to restructure loan portfolios and increase provisioning levels. Symptomatic in this respect were the banking crises that erupted in several countries in 1995. Notably, inadequate risk management, insider lending, and outright fraud persist in some cases. Entry of, and competition from, foreign banks, coupled with stricter supervision and technological modernisation are necessary to enable banks to play a more active and efficient intermediation role.

Foreign trade boomed in 1995, mainly reflecting the ongoing integration of the countries in transition into the world economy. The revival of trade among countries in transition that started in 1994, after several years of steep declines, also gathered speed. Exports expressed in dollar terms expanded by some 27 per cent on average in the CEECs, but also surged in Russia. Even after taking into account the weakening of the US currency in 1995 and dollar inflation, export volumes rose strongly. At the aggregate level, therefore, there is little evidence that barriers in export markets were a major constraint on the expansion of trade. Imports grew at a similarly brisk pace, often reflecting purchases of intermediary and investment goods, including in the context of relocation of processing operations (*i.e.* the subcontracting to CEECs by firms in the EU of a portion of their manufacturing). To that extent, the increase in measured trade deficits witnessed in 1995 in a number of CEECs could be interpreted as a welcome intertemporal trade-off rather than an unsustainable consumption upsurge.

The ongoing lowering of trade barriers, inter alia in the framework of WTO commitments and of agreements with the European Union, has helped foster competition and spur restructuring. It is also important, however, that domestic competition policies be forcefully pursued, in particular to prevent the resurgence of para-statal monopolistic structures and cartels.

Growing integration into the world economy was also reflected in the opening up of current and capital accounts. A number of countries formally declared their currencies convertible in line with the IMF's Article VIII requirements. Access to the international bond market was regained or consolidated, marked by the emission of eurobonds. Borrowing abroad by banks and enterprises, but also by central and local governments, started or increased. And inflows of foreign direct investment generally picked up. In this process of opening up and joining the world economy, most NIS countries were clearly lagging behind, reflecting in a number of cases a deliberately more inward-looking orientation, with more attention being devoted to restoring some former, non-market based links among themselves.

Country-specific developments

Growth reached 7.0 per cent in 1995 in Poland, fuelled by exports and investments, and is expected to remain above 5 per cent in 1996, with domestic demand becoming a more important driving force. Inflation continued to slow down, but the 12-month rate still exceeded 20 per cent in early 1996. In part, the continuing inflation momentum stems from the ongoing rapid accumulation of reserves, driven by unrecorded exports and, increasingly, by capital inflows. The authorities have reacted with a gradual firming of exchange rate policy coupled with cautious interest rate cuts. In addition, measures to liberalise the capital account were taken, counteracting some of the forces underlying the expansion of base money. In other domains, the pace of structural reforms has remained somewhat hesitant. The distribution of mass privatisation vouchers finally started in November 1995. However, uncertainties continued to linger regarding such key issues as the fate of some large banks involved in a controversial consolidation scheme, the restitution of formerly nationalised property, the status of the central bank, and the much-needed overhaul of the pension system.

Slovakia enjoyed one of the highest rates of output growth among transition economies in 1995, with real GDP soaring by an officially estimated 7.4 per cent. This contributed to bring about a fiscal surplus. Inflation performance was also very good, with consumer prices up only 6 per cent on a 12-month basis in April 1996. Unemployment declined somewhat but remains high. Although the trade and current account balances continued to be in surplus, recent export growth rates may not be sustainable. Moreover, the inflow of foreign capital has been modest thus far. There are also some doubts that the privatisation strategy implemented in 1995 will significantly improve corporate governance. Growth is therefore projected to ease somewhat in 1996.

Growth was also sustained at a rapid pace in 1995 in Slovenia. Export growth accelerated despite a comparatively strong real exchange rate, though imports rose even faster. Inflation was brought down to single digit levels. Joblessness as measured by registrations with labour offices remained high, but in light of survey evidence is likely to overstate substantially the actual degree of labour market slack. A major privatisation programme was launched in 1995, resulting so far mostly in employee buyouts.

In Romania, the current account deteriorated sharply in the course of 1995, which in combination with a general lack of trust in government policies and official data triggered an exchange rate crisis in November 1995. The subsequent tightening of monetary policy should allow further disinflation in 1996. Despite these difficulties, the recovery strengthened in 1995, fuelled by rapid export growth, and unemployment declined. The pace of privatisation and structural reform remains sluggish, diminishing the likelihood that current vigorous growth will be sustained.

In Bulgaria, a recovery of output finally materialised in 1994, and strengthened a little in 1995, pulled in particular by exports. Major structural weaknesses, however, cast doubts on the chances of a more vigorous expansion in 1996. The fiscal deficit widened anew in 1995 and is projected to loom large still in 1996, at 6.5 per cent of GDP. Uncertainties over the direction of policy led to a serious loss of confidence in the currency in early May. Inflation has been picking up following the ending of a spell of tight monetary policy and real exchange rate appreciation in 1994-95, and is projected to be the highest amongst CEECs in 1996. The distribution of mass privatisation vouchers started in January 1996, after much hesitation.

Recorded output may start recovering in Russia later this year, even though real GDP was still down 3 per cent on a 12-month basis in early 1996. Notwithstanding a proliferation of spending promises in the wake of the December 1995 parliamentary elections and in the run-up to the June 1996 Presidential poll, monthly inflation continued to decline slowly during the first four months of 1996, to around 2.2 per cent in April – the lowest rate since late 1991. Prospects for stabilisation received a boost with the approval of a $10.1 billion IMF loan. However, the ambitious 1996 budget already shows some signs of strain, as expenditure commitments have been expanded and revenues in early 1996 were lower than budgeted. Consolidating the reduction in the fiscal deficit will require more revenue to be effectively raised from the energy sector. The controversial "shares-for-loans" privatisation programme, allowing selected banks to be entrusted attractively priced shares in state firms in exchange for credit to the government, was put on hold. At the same time, the stability of the banking system became a major concern, and over 300 banks saw their licenses withheld in 1995, particularly in the wake of a liquidity crisis on the interbank market in August. In the framework of restructuring programmes often initiated by the state, the constitution of large financial-industrial groups has accelerated.

In Ukraine, officially measured real GDP dropped by 12 per cent in 1995. The budget deficit was cut to some 8 per cent of GDP on a commitment basis, and 4 per cent of GDP on a cash basis. As in Russia, however, deficit reduction was partly effected through the default of the government on many of its budgeted expenditures. Inflation slowed in late 1995, rebounded in early 1996, but more recently declined anew. Political struggles continued to disrupt stabilisation efforts and to hamper structural reforms.

Economic outcomes were generally less favourable than hoped-for in the Baltic countries in 1995. Growth remained relatively subdued in Estonia and Lithuania, and output contracted in Latvia partly as a result of a severe banking crisis. Disinflation continued, but prices were still rising at about 2 per cent a month by early 1996. Structural change is most advanced in Estonia, where foreign capital continued to enter in generous amounts, and slowest in Lithuania.

DYNAMIC ASIAN ECONOMIES AND CHINA

Background to the current situation

GDP growth in the Dynamic Asian Economies remained strong in 1995, at around 8 per cent (Table 25). However, activity moderated gradually through the second half of the year in response to monetary tightening and currency appreciation.

Monetary policy was tightened around the end of 1994 in many DAEs because of domestic overheating, mounting current account deficits and inflationary pressures. The effects of this tightening became visible towards the end of last year, although for some countries (Korea and Thailand, in particular) they were mitigated by the persistence of strong capital inflows. After rising sharply at the time of the Mexican crisis, short-term interest spreads vis-à-vis the United States and Japan have remained high in most DAEs, except Hong Kong and Singapore. To some extent, high spreads also reflect efforts to sterilise the effects of official intervention to hold down exchange rates in the face of capital inflows.

More recently, the deceleration in demand has been strengthened by the consequences of the appreciation of the dollar against the yen. Despite differences in exchange-rate regimes,[2] monetary authorities in most DAEs have tried to limit adjustment against the dollar, implying some loss in competitiveness vis-à-vis Japan as the dollar rises. The resulting deceleration of exports and rise in imports has contributed to a further deterioration of overall trade balances for the region, notably so for Chinese Taipei, Hong Kong, Korea and Singapore, whose exports include many close substitutes for

Table 25. **China and the Dynamic Asian Economies:**
key economic indicators[a]

	1994	1995	1996	1997
China				
GNP	11.8	10.2	10.5	10.5
Retail prices	21.7	14.8	9.0	10.0
Current account balance	7.7	18.2	8.0	5.0
DAEs Total				
GDP/GNP	7.6	7.7	6.4	6.6
Consumer prices	5.4	4.7	4.3	4.4
Trade balance	–2.0	–15.7	–14.5	–13.3
Current account balance	3.9	–10.9	–8.5	–8.0
Korea				
GDP	8.4	9.0	6.8	7.3
Consumer prices	6.2	4.5	4.2	4.0
Trade balance	–3.1	–4.8	–4.3	–3.8
Current account balance	–4.5	–8.8	–8.5	–8.0
Chinese Taipei				
GNP	6.1	5.9	5.0	5.5
Consumer prices	4.1	3.7	3.5	4.0
Trade balance	12.0	13.6	14.0	13.0
Current account balance	6.2	5.0	6.3	5.0
Hong Kong				
GDP	5.4	4.6	5.0	5.0
Consumer prices	8.1	8.7	7.5	8.0
Trade balance	–10.9	–19.0	–20.5	–19.5
Current account balance	2.8	–1.5	–1.8	–2.0
Singapore				
GDP	10.2	8.9	7.8	7.3
Consumer prices	3.0	1.7	1.5	1.5
Trade balance	2.1	1.7	2.0	2.0
Current account balance	11.9	15.0	14.5	14.0
Thailand				
GDP	8.5	8.9	8.0	7.5
Consumer prices	5.1	5.8	5.5	5.0
Trade balance	–3.7	–7.5	–6.5	–6.0
Current account balance	–8.4	–13.5	–12.5	–11.5
Malaysia				
GDP	8.7	9.3	8.0	7.5
Consumer prices	3.7	3.4	3.2	3.0
Trade balance	1.6	0.3	0.8	1.0
Current account balance	–4.1	–7.1	–6.5	–5.5

a) The figures given for GDP/GNP and consumer prices are percentage changes from previous period. Trade and current account balances are in $ billion. Current account estimates for Hong Kong correspond to net exports of goods and services on a national account basis and therefore exclude investment income and transfers. The trade balance corresponds to net exports of goods on a national account basis.

Sources: IMF, *International Financial Statistics*; Chinese Taipei sources; Hong Kong Census and Statistics Department, *Monthly Digest of Statistics*; OECD projections.

Japanese goods. At the same time a weaker yen may have discouraged Japanese direct investment, which has been an important source of growth in the region.

In China, tight credit controls since the end of 1993, which provoked a sharp deceleration of economic activity and, in particular, investment demand, have significantly diminished the synchronisation of the Chinese economy with other emerging East Asian economies. At the same time differences in cyclical positions, combined with the bringing forward of exports to avoid the future loss of tax rebates, resulted in a major strengthening of the trade balance in 1995. The degree of desynchronisation may strengthen further in 1996. A selective easing of credit has occurred since the end of 1995 as a means of assisting state enterprises and the temporary easing of retail price inflation, to a little over 7 per cent in February, may permit further relaxation of credit.

For some of the DAEs, the combination of efforts to maintain tight monetary policies and volatile capital movements has complicated exchange-rate management. Difficulties have perhaps been most serious for Malaysia and Thailand, where capital markets have been liberalised somewhat, but the monetary authorities continue to give high priority to control of monetary aggregates. This has been a source of problems: for example, where prolonged use of sterilised intervention during 1995 led to rising interest rates, which only further encouraged short-term capital inflows.[3] Those countries planning further liberalisation of international capital movements in coming years may also attract strong capital inflows which would put upward pressure on the exchange rate. This is particularly the case for Chinese Taipei and Korea, where the process of deregulation has been slow until recently.[4]

The situation differs for Hong Kong and Singapore which are most open to foreign capital and accustomed to changes in real exchange rates. In Hong Kong, the currency board scheme implies that interest rates closely mirror US rates,[5] sometimes resulting in inflation pressure. In Singapore, which follows the most flexible exchange-rate policy among the DAEs, gradual nominal appreciation since the middle of the 1980s has been an important element in the control of inflation, which remains the lowest in the region. Both economies have been able to maintain low, or even negative (Singapore) interest rate differentials *vis-à-vis* the United States, with foreign funds attracted by the soundness of the macroeconomic environment, and neither has resisted appreciation in real terms, either through nominal appreciation or higher prices.

In common with the DAEs, China is exposed to upward risks on the real exchange rate. Already, a rising current account surplus and continued strong inflows of foreign direct investment in 1995 have contributed to a sharp rise in foreign exchange reserves, from an estimated $50 billion to over $70 billion. Positive confidence effects of a move towards full currency convertibility would add further to these pressures.

Notwithstanding differences in exchange rate regimes, a common uncertainty facing the DAEs over the coming period is the extent to which there may be further upward pressure on the real exchange rate. Such pressure might also be intensified if interest spreads widen as a result of lower OECD interest rates, for example in the event of more rapid fiscal consolidation (see the chapter "General Assessment of the Economic Situation"). In the event of significant further appreciation, net exports in the region could be substantially lower in the short term and the current account deficit for the region significantly larger, with corresponding positive effects on OECD exports, GDP and current account balances (see box "The effects of exchange rate appreciation in the Dynamic Asian Economies").

The effects of exchange rate appreciation in the Dynamic Asian Economies

As an illustration of the relative importance of possible further appreciation in the DAEs for trade and output in the OECD area, the table below reports an alternative scenario, based on the OECD INTERLINK model, which assumes a flat 10 per cent nominal appreciation for the Asian Newly Industrialising Economies (ANIEs: Chinese Taipei, Hong Kong, Korea and Singapore) against a basket of OECD currencies, sustained over a four year period.

Impact of a 10 per cent nominal exchange rate appreciation in the ANIEs [1]

Differences from baseline

	Year			
	1	2	3	4
ANIEs				
Imports of goods and services volume (per cent)	3.1	2.9	1.6	0.5
Exports of goods and services volume (per cent)	–2.4	–3.9	–3.7	–2.9
Current account balance				
Billion dollar	–7.0	–32.0	–35.0	–33.0
Per cent of GDP	–0.6	–2.7	–2.7	–2.3
OECD				
Exports of goods and services volume (per cent)				
OECD total	0.7	1.3	0.7	–0.2
of which:				
United States	0.8	1.4	0.9	–0.1
Japan	1.5	2.1	0.9	–0.5
OECD Europe	0.5	0.9	0.5	–0.1
OECD total current account balance (per cent of GDP)	0.1	0.2	0.2	0.1
Real GDP level (per cent)	0.2	0.3	0.1	–0.1

1. This scenario assumes a 10 per cent appreciation of the ANIEs against a basket of OECD currencies. Real interest rates and real government expenditures in OECD countries are assumed to remain unchanged.

As with most industrialised countries, the effects of such nominal appreciation are likely to erode steadily, with a fairly large impact on import and export cost and price competitiveness in the near term, tending to diminish over time as domestic prices and costs adjust to improved terms of trade and lower import costs. The corresponding effects on real trade performance would be expected to build up steadily over the first two years, attenuating thereafter as competitiveness losses are slowly recovered. In the reported scenario, import volumes for the ANIEs rise by up to 3 per cent relative to baseline in the first year, whilst the reduction in export volumes peaks at around 4 per cent after two years, before tailing off. The corresponding effect on the combined current account is an increased deficit, by up to \$35 billion, *i.e.* of the order of 3 per cent of aggregate GDP.

Translated into effects on OECD countries, exports of goods and services for the area as a whole would be up to 1 1/4 per cent higher, more so for the United States and Japan, whose goods compete most actively (in export and domestic markets) with manufactures coming from the ANIEs region. In terms of broad aggregates for the OECD area, the level of GDP might be temporarily boosted relative to baseline by up to one-third of a per cent and the current account by up to 0.2 per cent of GDP within two years. Applying similar competitiveness effects also to the other Asian industrialising countries (including China, India, Malaysia, the Philippines and Thailand) would imply broad impacts on the OECD which were about 60 per cent larger.

Short-term outlook

Over the projection period, monetary policies in the DAEs are assumed to remain relatively tight and fiscal policies prudent (with the aggregate fiscal balance for the region continuing to be in surplus). Export growth may be damped somewhat by a further deterioration in competitive positions, given the technical assumption of unchanged exchange rates and relatively high domestic inflation. Average real GDP growth for the DAEs as a group is projected to moderate to around 6.5 per cent in 1996, with a marked slowdown in the export sector. Growth is expected to accelerate moderately in 1997 as the effects of recent appreciation wane. Slowing economic activity will ease tight labour-market conditions, resulting in some deceleration in the inflation rates, to below 5 per cent per annum on average.

The deceleration in GDP growth for 1996 is expected to be particularly pronounced in Korea, Singapore and Chinese Taipei. For Korea and Singapore, the slowdown should be most marked in the export sector. The deceleration in Korea – to real growth of 7 per cent – could be seen as a "soft landing". The situation is different for Chinese Taipei, where growing political uncertainty and tensions with China in the early months of this year had adverse effects on business confidence and economic activity. As a result, GDP growth is expected to moderate somewhat this year, but rise again to around 5¹/₂ per cent in 1997.

A projected recovery in Chinese import demand (see below) and the pick-up of activity in the OECD area will partially offset the negative effects of the deterioration in competitiveness but some deceleration in exports is expected. Import growth is also expected to slow, reflecting a deceleration in domestic demand and, in particular, imports of capital equipment destined for export-intensive sectors. Overall, trade and current-account deficits for the region are expected to narrow over the projection period.

For China, the present projections are for continued strong growth, with a moderately high but relatively stable rate of inflation of 9 to 10 per cent. With selective credit easing assumed to continue, real GDP growth could rise to around 10.5 per cent this year and next. Stronger investment demand, combined with the implementation of the scheduled plan of tariffs reduction, will likely strengthen import demand. At the same time, export growth is expected to moderate somewhat and a trade deficit of over $2 billion is estimated for the first half of this year. Overall, the current account is expected to remain in surplus this year and next but at levels significantly lower than in 1995.

CENTRAL AND SOUTH AMERICA

Background to the current situation

Most countries in Central and South America were affected by the Mexican crisis in 1995. Interest rates went up sharply at the beginning of the year in the face of large capital outflows. These flows were quickly reversed, but real interest rates remained significantly higher than pre-crisis levels as monetary policies remained tight in the context of deteriorating fiscal and external balances. Country risk premia also increased, while the spread between borrowing and lending rates went up as a result of problems in the banking sector of many countries in the region. As a result, output growth slowed considerably, while inflation rates continued to fall.

Fiscal balances deteriorated throughout the region. Revenues were below budget targets, typically because of lower output growth. Many countries rely heavily on taxing consumption, which was hit by higher interest rates on consumer loans. Outlays, on the other hand, continued to increase at a rapid pace, as debt service costs went up sharply. In some countries, government support for the banking sector, some of it publicly-owned, also played a major role in the increase in outlays.

External balances deteriorated further in 1995. This was in part a lagged response to the significant real exchange rate appreciation of previous years, although the rising cost of external debt service was also an important factor. For the region as a whole, import volumes increased by approximately 13 per cent, while export volumes are estimated to have gone up by only 3 per cent. This was only partly offset by an improvement in terms of trade, as commodity prices were significantly higher than in 1994. Real exchange rate appreciation largely stopped in 1995, mostly as a result of government interventions in foreign exchange markets, which offset capital inflows attracted by high domestic interest rates.

Most countries in the region relied heavily on tight monetary policies to slow the economy and reduce external imbalances.[6] During 1995, monetary policies were particularly tight in Brazil, Colombia and Peru, where external imbalances were large (equivalent to 3, 5 and 8 per cent of GDP in 1995, respectively) and fiscal-balance deterioration was significant. The fiscal problem was most acute in Brazil, where the deficit reached 7¹/₂ per cent of GDP in 1995.[7] The rising cost of servicing the public debt was compounded by an increase in payroll costs, especially at sub-federal levels of government.[8] In Colombia and Peru, fiscal deficits were relatively small in 1995 (between 1 and 2 per cent of GDP), but deteriorated markedly compared with the fiscal surpluses of 1994, largely because of a substantial increase in social expenditure and larger transfers to sub-federal levels of government in Colombia, and increased public investment and a delay in the privatisation programme in Peru.

In all three countries, tight monetary policies have started to have their desired effects: inflation now appears to be falling and external deficits narrowing.[9] This has provided room for a gradual relaxation of monetary policies, which in turn has damped the short-term capital inflows that has at times complicated the management of macroeconomic policies.[10]

The high levels of interest rates in Argentina during 1995 were more directly associated with the Mexican crisis, as capital outflows caused severe liquidity and banking problems which proved difficult to limit under a currency board system. As a result, output dropped by an estimated 4.4 per cent, while inflation approached zero towards the end of the year. However, buoyant exports provided some support for economic activity and helped to narrow the current account deficit from the equivalent of 3 per cent of GDP in 1994 to 1 per cent in 1995. The fiscal deficit was limited to ½ per cent of GDP in 1995, in spite of a significant drop in the tax base. This was achieved by an increase in tax rates, especially value-added tax, and by strict controls on spending, including those made at sub-federal levels of government. The government also succeeded in advancing privatisation and other structural reforms, including a series of measures to make labour markets more flexible.

Two major countries in the region not affected by the Mexican crisis, but for opposite reasons, were Chile and Venezuela. Chile has the highest saving rate in the region and has followed a policy of discouraging short-term capital inflows. A balanced current account and a solid fiscal surplus[11] also made the country less vulnerable to changes in external confidence. Output growth actually accelerated in 1995, fuelled by an increase in investment demand. Venezuela has followed a more interventionist path, including the use of price and exchange controls, some of them introduced as a result of severe problems in the banking sector in 1994. Both the banking crisis and the capital outflows which followed it, preceded the Mexican crisis, meaning that Venezuela was little affected by the latter. In 1995, higher petroleum production and exports led to a mild pick up in output and a positive current account balance. The fiscal deficit remained high, at approximately 7 per cent of GDP; while outlays related to the banking crisis fell, public debt interest increased sharply. Inflation increased further, leading to a major devaluation in December 1995. An adjustment programme, involving further devaluation, the phasing-out of price and exchange controls, strong fiscal adjustment and monetary tightening was announced in April 1996. This programme is expected to receive considerable external support, principally from the IMF, the World Bank and the Inter-American Development Bank.

Short-term outlook: the need for fiscal adjustment

The need for fiscal adjustment is significant in most of the region. Any failure to control budget deficits would increase the medium-term risks of a severely adverse financial market reaction, particularly since domestic savings are still low and external debt levels remain high, both in the public and private sector. This would require a rapid, and disciplined, adjustment of the current account. Furthermore, as last year's Mexican crisis demonstrated, significant problems in any single important country are difficult to isolate, so the entire region could be exposed to contagion effects.

Widespread concern to avoid a financial-market crisis appears to have led to a strong commitment throughout the region to persist with fiscal adjustment. In this environment, output growth in Central and South America is likely to be moderate, in the 2½ to 4 per cent per annum range (Table 26). Inflation is also likely to continue on a downward path, while current account deficits should stabilise at present levels (a little below 3 per cent of GDP) on the assumption of no real exchange rate appreciation. Import volume growth is expected to decel-

Table 26. **Central and South America:
key economic indicators**[a]

	1994	1995	1996	1997
Central and South America[b]				
GDP	6.0	2.2	2.6	4.0
Trade balance	−4.8	−12.8	−11.6	−15.2
Current account balance	−25.3	−34.4	−33.5	−38.1
Argentina				
GDP	7.4	−4.4	1.5	3.0
Consumer prices	4.2	3.4	1.0	2.0
Trade balance	−4.1	2.7	2.5	2.0
Current account balance	−10.2	−3.3	−3.5	−4.5
Brazil				
GNP	5.8	4.2	3.0	4.5
Consumer prices	3 630.0	210.0	18.0	12.0
Consumer prices (Dec./Dec.)	930.0	22.0	14.0	12.0
Trade balance	10.4	−3.2	0.0	−2.0
Current account balance	−1.7	−17.8	−15.5	−18.0
Chile				
GNP	4.1	8.4	7.0	6.5
Consumer prices	11.5	8.2	7.5	6.5
Trade balance	0.6	1.4	−0.5	−1.0
Current account balance	−1.0	−0.4	−2.0	−2.5
Colombia				
GDP	5.6	5.3	3.5	4.5
Consumer prices	22.9	20.9	20.0	18.0
Trade balance	−2.2	−2.4	−2.1	−1.5
Current account balance	−2.9	−4.1	−4.0	−3.5
Peru				
GDP	13.2	6.9	2.5	3.5
Consumer prices	24.3	11.2	13.5	12.0
Trade balance	−1.1	−2.1	−1.8	−1.5
Current account balance	−3.2	−4.9	−5.0	−5.0
Venezuela				
GDP	−3.3	2.2	−1.0	2.5
Consumer prices	59.7	61.2	90.0	40.0
Trade balance	8.0	6.6	8.0	5.0
Current account balance	4.1	1.8	2.5	−1.0

a) The figures given for GDP and consumer prices are percentage changes from previous period. Trade and current account balances are in billions of dollars.
b) The figures for the Central and South America region include Venezuela. In other tables, Venezuela is included in the OPEC aggregate.

erate sharply in 1996, especially in Brazil, where the lagged adjustment to the exchange-rate appreciation which occurred in the second half of 1994 is largely complete.

Brazil accounts for almost half of the zone's GDP, and through its increasing importance as an intra-regional trading partner, is the key to the stability of the region in the next few years. Fiscal adjustment depends in large part on constitutional reforms – affecting the social security and tax systems, and the organisation of the public sector – which are moving only very slowly through Congress. Public administration reform is the most important in the short-run, as it would allow for a reduction of payroll costs, by far the largest expenditure item for both federal and sub-federal levels of government. Beyond the effects of constitutional reforms, the recent drop in domestic interest rates will reduce the cost of servicing the public debt, while a correction in public-sector tariffs is likely to lower the deficit of public-sector enterprises from 1996.

The high level of foreign exchange reserves[12] gives Brazil some time in which to make its fiscal adjustment, but this could be considerably shortened if confidence problems led to large capital outflows. The slow pace of fiscal adjustment also imposes clear limits on the ability of authorities to proceed with the monetary easing which started in late 1995. Real interest rates are thus likely to remain relatively high through 1997, while exchange rate policy will probably continue to aim for a slow nominal depreciation of the currency, in line with inflation rate differentials. As a result, inflation and external imbalances are expected to stabilise at present levels, while output growth is expected to be moderate.[13]

In Argentina, the main problem facing the government is to revive the economy without jeopardising fiscal targets and putting into doubt the government's ability to remain solvent. Public debt remains high and relatively short-term. As a large share of this debt matures in 1997, the country is particularly vulnerable to changes in investors' confidence. Also, government estimates of 1996 revenues look increasingly optimistic so that the authorities are unlikely to attempt to boost activity through a major fiscal stimulus. Indeed, although the fiscal package announced in March 1996 included incentives to the housing sector and measures to reduce interest rate spreads, it should not have a major impact on revenues, in particular as the value added tax, the main source of government revenues, is unlikely to be lowered until it is warranted by the budget situation. Output growth is not expected to pick up significantly until the second half of 1996, as consumer confidence and investment demand increase only gradually. Exports may not grow as rapidly as in the past two years, as Brazilian import demand stabilises. As a result, inflation should remain at low levels, while the trade surplus goes down gradually.

In Colombia, the tax package approved in December 1995, is not expected to be sufficient to bring the budget back into balance. Federal spending continues at high levels and only slow progress has been made on privatisation. As in Brazil, unless significant progress is made on the fiscal front, the central bank is unlikely to lower interest rates much further, and with significant political uncertainty which is affecting investment demand, output growth is likely to slow considerably to about 3.5 per cent in 1996. As a result, inflation and external imbalances are also expected to decline. A large increase in oil production expected for 1997 is likely to impact positively on fiscal and external balances and on GDP growth. In Peru, output is also likely to decelerate sharply in 1996, as fiscal and monetary policies remain tight. Increased exports are expected to sustain output growth in 1997, also helping to close external imbalances.

The main problem now facing Chile is the danger that the economy will eventually overheat, thereby jeopardising inflation targets. Faced with the choice between higher inflation or a faster real exchange rate appreciation, which could lead to larger current account deficits, the government seems to have chosen the latter. External balances will also be affected by the fall in copper prices, which started in late 1995. Fiscal policy is expected to remain tight, with increased social spending being compensated by increased revenues from excise taxes.

In Venezuela, the short-term outlook hinges on the successful implementation of the adjustment programme announced in April 1996. The markets' initial reaction to the programme seems to have been positive. The elimination of capital controls did not lead to major outflows and the currency seems to have stabilised after an initial drop. This gives the government a window of opportunity in which to pursue structural reforms and fiscal adjustment. Without these, interest rates will have to remain tight, with negative consequences for output and the already fragile banking system. On the assumption that the programme is successfully implemented, the fall in GDP will be relatively limited in 1996, followed by recovery in 1997, as capital flows in. Inflation and external surpluses are likely to peak in the first half of 1996, before declining through 1997 as the currency appreciates in real terms.

NOTES

1. The Czech Republic joined in late 1995 and Hungary in May 1996. Poland and Slovakia are engaged in an accession process. In March 1996, Slovenia officially stated its desire to join. The Russian Federation applied for membership in May 1996.

2. Hong Kong has used a currency board scheme to peg to the US dollar since 1983. Malaysia, Singapore and Thailand have adjustable pegs to currency baskets with relatively

high dollar weights, while Chinese Taipei and Korea have managed floats. Dollar weights appear to vary from about 70 per cent (Singapore) to above 90 per cent (Chinese Taipei and Korea).

3. At the beginning of 1994, Malaysia introduced temporary capital controls after a number of attempts to sterilise capital inflows. For a wider discussion of the policies used by Malaysia and Thailand in response to capital flows, see "Emerging markets and the liberalisation of capital movements", *OECD Economic Outlook 58*, December 1995.

4. Korea, for example, has recently launched a four-year programme to liberalise capital movements. For a more detailed discussion of these issues, see *OECD Economic Surveys, Korea*, 1996.

5. Temporary deviations from US interest rates do occur at times of specific tension, for example, during the Mexico crisis.

6. In most cases this was also accompanied by the tightening of restrictions on short-term capital inflows, to compensate for the effect of an increase in international interest rate differentials.

7. Correcting for inflation by counting only the real component of domestic debt service, Brazil's fiscal deficit amounted to approximately 5 per cent of GDP in 1995.

8. The cost of servicing the public debt was equivalent to 8 per cent of GDP. Also contributing to an increase in internal debt were the effects of the sterilisation of foreign reserve accumulation, equivalent to 4 per cent of annual GDP in the second half of 1995. As the local currency denominated domestic debt paid a much higher interest rate than the foreign currency denominated foreign exchange reserves, reserve accumulation sharply increased debt service costs.

9. In Colombia, a major political crisis also had the effect of cooling down the economy by affecting investment demand.

10. In Brazil, new restrictions on short-term capital inflows were introduced in February 1996. They consisted mainly of limits on the purchase of dollar-indexed government bonds and increases in minimum maturity periods for private sector bond placements.

11. Both fiscal and current account balances were positively affected by high copper prices during 1995. Copper mining is in large part controlled by public enterprises.

12. Estimated at $55 billion, equivalent to approximately 10 per cent of GDP or one year of imports.

13. GDP growth for 1996 is likely to be affected by carry-over effects associated with the large drop in output which occurred in the second quarter of 1995.

ANNEX

This Annex contains data on some main economic series which are intended to provide a background to the recent economic developments in the OECD area described in the main body of this report. (A complete list of Annex tables and figures is given beginning on page vii.) It also contains a section describing the OECD Secretariat's projection methods and underlying statistical concepts and sources. Data for 1996-97 are OECD Secretariat projections. The data in some of the tables have been adjusted to internationally agreed concepts and definitions in order to make them more comparable as between countries, as well as consistent with historical data shown in other OECD publications. Regional totals and sub-totals in each table are based on those countries in the table for which data are available. Aggregate measures contained in the Annex are computed on the basis of 1991 GDP weights expressed in 1991 purchasing power parities (see following page for weights). Aggregate measures for external trade and payments statistics, on the other hand, are based on current year exchange rates for values and base-year exchange rates for volumes.

NOTE ON STATISTICAL TREATMENT OF GERMANY AND HUNGARY

In this publication, data up to end-1990 are for western Germany only; unless otherwise indicated, they are for the whole of Germany from 1991 onwards. In tables showing percentage changes from the previous year, data refer to the whole of Germany from 1992 onwards. In this issue aggregate measures for total OECD do not include Hungary.

COUNTRY CLASSIFICATION

OECD

Seven major OECD countries	The United States, Japan, Germany, France, Italy, the United Kingdom and Canada
Smaller OECD countries	Australia, Austria, Belgium, the Czech Republic, Denmark, Finland, Greece, Iceland, Ireland, Luxembourg, Mexico, Netherlands, New Zealand, Norway, Portugal, Spain, Sweden, Switzerland and Turkey
OECD North America	United States, Canada and Mexico
European Union	Germany, France, Italy, United Kingdom, Austria, Belgium, Denmark, Finland, Greece, Ireland, Luxembourg, Netherlands, Portugal, Spain and Sweden
OECD Europe	European Union member countries, the Czech Republic, Iceland, Norway, Switzerland and Turkey

Non-OECD

OPEC[a]	Algeria, Bahrain, Gabon, Indonesia, Iran, Iraq, Kuwait, the Libyan Arab Jamahiriya, Nigeria, Oman, Qatar, Saudi Arabia, the United Arab Emirates and Venezuela
Asian newly industrialising economies (ANIEs)	Chinese Taipei, Hong Kong, Korea and Singapore
Non-OPEC developing countries	
Other Asia	Non-OECD Asia and the Middle East, excluding OPEC countries and the ANIEs
Other Africa	Africa, excluding OPEC countries
Other Latin America	South and Central America, excluding OPEC countries
Central and Eastern European countries	Albania, Bulgaria, Poland, Romania, the Slovak Republic, the Newly Independent States of the former Soviet Union, the Baltic States and, in this issue also, Hungary, which became an OECD Member country in May 1996

a) Historical statistics for OPEC include Ecuador up to and including 1992. Ecuador is included in Other Latin America beginning in 1993.

WEIGHTING SCHEME FOR AGGREGATE MEASURES

GDP weights used in calculating aggregate measures

Per cent

United States	36.83	Australia	1.73
Japan	14.85	Austria	0.84
Germany	8.45	Belgium	1.07
France	6.45	Czech Republic	0.56
Italy	6.06	Denmark	0.56
United Kingdom	5.61	Finland	0.48
Canada	3.25	Greece	0.62
		Iceland	0.03
Total of above countries	81.50	Ireland	0.26
		Luxembourg	0.05
Total of smaller countries	18.50	Mexico	2.73
		Netherlands	1.54
OECD North America	42.82	New Zealand	0.29
OECD Europe	40.32	Norway	0.49
European Union	36.60	Portugal	0.63
		Spain	3.08
Total OECD	100.00	Sweden	0.90
		Switzerland	0.92
		Turkey	1.71

Note: Based on 1991 purchasing power parities (PPPs). The benchmark year for the PPPs is 1990.

REFERENCE STATISTICS AND ANNUAL PROJECTIONS

Annex Table 1. **Real GDP**

Percentage changes from previous period

	Average 1971-78	1979	1980	1981	1982	1983	1984	1985	1986	1987	1988	1989	1990	1991	1992	1993	1994	1995	Projections 1996	1997
United States	3.6	2.9	-0.3	2.5	-2.1	4.0	6.8	3.7	3.0	2.9	3.8	3.4	1.3	-1.0	2.7	2.2	3.5	2.0	2.3	2.0
Japan	4.5	5.5	2.8	3.2	3.1	2.3	3.9	4.4	2.9	4.2	6.2	4.8	5.1	4.0	1.1	0.1	0.5	0.9	2.2	2.4
Germany	2.7	4.2	1.0	0.1	-0.9	1.8	2.8	2.0	2.3	1.5	3.7	3.6	5.7	5.0	2.2	-1.2	2.9	1.9	0.5	2.4
France	3.3	3.2	1.6	1.2	2.5	0.7	1.3	1.9	2.5	2.3	4.5	4.3	2.5	0.8	1.2	-1.3	2.8	2.2	1.0	2.4
Italy	3.7	5.8	4.1	0.6	0.2	1.0	2.7	2.6	2.9	3.1	4.1	2.9	2.1	1.2	0.7	-1.2	2.2	3.0	1.7	2.3
United Kingdom	2.4	2.8	-2.2	-1.3	1.7	3.7	2.3	3.8	4.3	4.8	5.0	2.2	0.4	-2.0	-0.5	2.3	3.8	2.4	2.2	3.0
Canada	5.0	3.9	1.5	3.7	-3.2	3.2	6.3	4.8	3.3	4.2	5.0	2.4	-0.2	-1.8	0.8	2.2	4.6	2.2	2.1	3.4
Total of above countries	3.7	3.8	0.8	1.9	-0.3	2.9	4.8	3.5	3.0	3.1	4.4	3.6	2.5	0.7	1.8	1.0	2.8	1.9	1.9	2.3
Australia	3.1	4.7	2.3	3.6	-0.6	1.0	7.5	4.4	1.8	4.7	4.3	4.2	1.4	-1.6	2.6	4.0	5.2	3.1	3.1	3.3
Austria	3.4	4.7	2.9	-0.3	1.1	2.0	1.4	2.5	1.2	1.7	4.1	3.8	4.2	2.8	2.0	0.4	3.0	1.8	0.8	1.5
Belgium	3.2	2.1	4.3	-1.0	1.5	0.5	2.2	0.8	1.4	2.0	4.9	3.4	3.4	2.2	1.8	-1.6	2.2	1.9	1.0	2.4
Czech Republic	:	:	:	:	:	:	:	:	:	:	:	:	:	:	:	:	2.6	4.8	5.6	5.8
Denmark	2.4	3.5	-0.4	-0.9	3.0	2.5	4.4	4.3	3.6	0.3	1.2	0.6	1.4	1.3	0.2	1.5	4.4	2.6	1.1	2.7
Finland	3.0	7.3	5.3	1.6	3.6	3.0	3.1	3.3	2.4	4.1	4.9	5.7	0	-7.1	-3.6	-1.2	4.4	4.2	2.4	3.5
Greece	4.9	3.7	1.8	0.1	0.4	0.4	2.8	3.1	1.6	-0.5	4.5	3.8	0	3.1	0.4	-1.0	1.5	2.0	2.2	2.3
Iceland	5.7	4.9	5.7	4.3	2.2	-2.1	4.1	3.3	6.2	8.6	-0.1	0.3	1.1	1.3	-3.3	0.8	3.5	2.0	3.6	3.4
Ireland	5.4	3.1	3.1	3.3	2.3	-0.2	4.4	3.1	-0.4	4.7	4.3	6.1	7.8	2.2	3.9	3.1	6.4	7.7	6.0	5.0
Luxembourg	2.9	2.3	0.8	-0.6	1.1	3.0	6.2	2.9	4.8	2.9	5.7	6.7	3.2	3.1	1.9	0	3.3	3.7	1.9	3.0
Mexico	6.3	9.2	8.3	8.8	-0.7	-4.3	3.6	2.8	-3.8	1.9	1.2	3.3	4.4	3.6	2.8	0.6	3.5	-6.8	3.0	4.0
Netherlands	3.1	2.2	1.2	-0.5	-1.2	1.7	3.3	3.1	2.8	1.4	2.6	4.7	4.1	2.3	2.0	0.2	2.7	2.4	1.6	2.6
New Zealand	1.6	1.5	0.4	4.7	3.3	2.4	8.5	1.6	1.0	-0.7	3.9	-1.4	0.1	-3.7	0.3	5.5	4.1	2.2	2.7	3.4
Norway	4.8	5.1	4.2	0.9	0.3	4.6	5.7	5.3	4.2	2.0	-0.5	0.3	1.6	2.9	3.4	2.1	5.7	3.7	4.2	2.4
Portugal	4.4	5.6	4.6	1.6	2.1	-0.2	-1.9	2.8	5.0	5.5	5.8	5.7	4.3	2.1	1.1	-1.2	0.8	2.5	2.3	2.7
Spain	4.2	0	1.3	-0.2	1.6	2.2	1.5	2.6	3.2	5.6	5.2	4.7	3.7	2.3	0.7	-1.2	2.1	3.0	2.3	2.7
Sweden	1.9	3.8	1.7	0	1.0	1.8	4.0	1.9	2.3	3.1	2.3	2.4	1.4	-1.1	-1.4	-2.2	2.6	3.0	1.3	2.0
Switzerland	0.4	2.4	4.4	1.4	-0.9	1.0	1.8	3.7	2.9	2.0	2.9	3.9	2.3	0	-0.3	-0.8	1.2	0.7	0.5	1.7
Turkey	5.5	-0.6	-2.4	4.9	3.6	5.0	6.7	4.2	7.0	9.5	2.1	0.3	9.3	0.9	6.0	8.0	-5.5	7.3	4.5	5.0
Total of smaller countries	4.0	3.5	2.8	2.3	0.9	1.0	3.6	3.1	2.0	3.6	3.3	3.5	3.6	1.4	1.8	1.0	2.3	1.8	2.5	3.1
Total OECD	3.7	3.7	1.2	2.0	-0.1	2.6	4.6	3.4	2.8	3.2	4.2	3.6	2.7	0.8	1.8	1.0	2.7	1.9	2.1	2.5
OECD North America	3.9	3.4	0.4	2.9	-2.1	3.4	6.6	3.7	2.6	2.9	3.7	3.3	1.4	-0.7	2.6	2.1	3.5	1.5	2.3	2.3
OECD Europe	3.2	3.4	1.4	0.4	1.0	1.9	2.5	2.7	3.0	3.2	4.0	3.4	3.2	1.5	1.2	-0.1	2.5	2.7	1.6	2.7
EU	3.2	3.6	1.5	0.1	0.9	1.7	2.3	2.5	2.8	2.9	4.2	3.5	3.0	1.6	1.0	-0.5	2.8	2.5	1.4	2.5
Total OECD less the United States	3.8	4.2	2.1	1.7	1.1	1.7	3.3	3.2	2.7	3.4	4.5	3.7	3.5	1.9	1.2	0.2	2.2	1.8	1.9	2.7

A4

Annex Table 2. Nominal GDP
Percentage changes from previous period

	Average 1971-78	1979	1980	1981	1982	1983	1984	1985	1986	1987	1988	1989	1990	1991	1992	1993	1994	1995	Projections 1996	1997
United States	10.7	11.6	8.9	11.9	4.0	8.4	11.1	7.1	5.8	6.1	7.6	7.7	5.6	3.0	5.5	4.9	5.8	4.5	4.4	4.3
Japan	14.2	8.4	8.4	7.4	4.9	4.1	6.7	6.6	4.7	4.3	6.9	7.0	7.5	6.7	2.8	0.8	0.8	0.3	1.9	2.7
Germany	8.0	8.2	6.0	4.3	3.5	5.1	4.9	4.1	5.6	3.4	5.3	6.1	9.1	9.1	7.8	2.6	5.2	4.2	2.1	3.8
France	13.8	13.7	13.2	12.7	14.6	10.5	8.9	7.8	7.9	5.3	7.5	7.4	5.7	4.1	3.3	1.1	4.4	3.9	2.8	3.7
Italy	19.5	22.2	25.1	19.7	17.5	16.2	14.6	11.7	11.0	9.3	11.0	9.3	9.9	8.9	5.2	3.1	5.9	8.0	6.1	5.5
United Kingdom	16.5	17.6	16.9	10.0	9.5	9.1	7.0	9.7	7.7	10.0	11.3	9.4	6.8	4.4	3.8	5.6	5.8	4.8	4.5	5.3
Canada	13.9	14.3	12.2	14.9	5.2	8.4	9.6	7.5	5.8	9.1	9.8	7.4	2.9	1.0	2.0	3.3	5.2	4.0	3.8	5.0
Total of above countries	12.5	12.2	10.8	11.0	6.4	8.1	9.4	7.3	6.3	6.1	7.9	7.6	6.6	4.8	4.8	3.5	4.7	3.9	3.7	4.1
Australia	15.3	15.3	13.5	13.5	10.6	9.3	14.4	10.6	8.9	12.6	12.9	12.0	5.9	0.7	3.9	5.3	6.6	5.8	5.9	5.9
Austria	10.5	9.0	8.3	6.2	7.3	6.0	6.3	5.6	5.5	4.1	5.7	6.8	7.7	6.9	6.3	3.7	6.5	4.0	2.5	3.2
Belgium	11.6	6.7	8.2	3.7	8.7	6.1	7.5	7.0	5.2	4.4	6.7	8.3	6.5	4.9	5.4	2.4	4.9	4.1	3.1	4.5
Czech Republic	⋮	⋮	⋮	⋮	⋮	⋮	⋮	⋮	⋮	⋮	⋮	⋮	⋮	⋮	⋮	⋮	14.0	16.8	17.2	17.0
Denmark	13.2	11.4	7.8	9.1	13.9	10.3	10.3	8.8	8.4	5.0	4.6	4.8	4.1	3.6	3.4	2.2	6.1	4.3	3.6	5.6
Finland	16.0	16.3	15.6	13.2	12.4	11.5	12.1	8.9	7.0	9.0	12.3	12.1	5.9	-4.8	-2.9	1.2	5.5	8.1	3.9	5.2
Greece	19.7	23.0	19.7	19.8	25.6	19.6	23.6	21.3	19.5	13.7	20.7	18.8	20.6	23.9	15.0	12.9	12.4	11.5	9.9	8.8
Iceland	41.8	47.7	61.2	56.2	56.6	72.4	30.6	35.6	33.2	29.9	22.8	20.1	18.0	9.0	0.3	3.3	5.8	5.0	6.1	6.4
Ireland	20.3	17.2	18.2	21.3	17.8	11.3	11.0	8.5	5.3	7.0	7.8	11.9	7.0	3.9	6.0	7.3	7.6	9.2	7.6	6.5
Luxembourg	10.4	8.8	8.8	6.6	12.1	10.0	10.9	6.0	8.8	1.9	9.9	13.1	6.2	6.1	6.5	4.7	5.2	6.9	3.9	4.9
Mexico	25.0	31.2	39.4	37.1	59.9	82.5	64.7	60.8	67.6	142.9	102.4	30.0	35.1	26.1	17.8	10.7	11.1	26.2	29.8	19.6
Netherlands	11.7	6.4	6.8	4.8	4.1	3.8	4.7	4.9	2.9	0.7	3.8	6.0	6.5	5.0	4.3	2.3	5.1	4.4	2.9	4.5
New Zealand	14.0	17.5	16.2	22.1	15.8	7.2	15.3	17.5	15.3	14.7	10.9	6.5	3.3	-1.1	2.6	6.9	5.8	4.3	4.9	5.4
Norway	13.3	12.0	19.4	15.0	10.6	11.0	12.5	10.6	2.7	9.3	3.9	6.7	5.8	5.7	3.0	4.7	6.0	6.7	6.7	4.6
Portugal	21.7	26.2	26.5	19.5	23.3	24.4	22.3	25.2	25.4	17.2	17.3	17.8	17.7	16.7	14.7	6.2	6.4	8.5	6.6	6.5
Spain	21.0	17.0	14.9	12.4	15.7	14.2	13.3	10.5	14.6	11.8	11.1	12.2	11.3	9.5	7.6	3.1	6.1	7.9	5.7	5.7
Sweden	12.0	12.1	14.9	9.5	9.3	12.0	12.0	8.7	9.3	8.1	8.9	10.6	10.3	6.4	-0.4	0.3	5.5	7.2	2.9	4.8
Switzerland	5.7	4.5	7.4	8.5	6.1	4.0	4.6	6.9	6.8	4.7	5.4	8.2	8.1	5.4	2.3	1.2	2.6	2.1	1.4	2.9
Turkey	30.4	74.7	83.5	51.0	32.8	32.4	58.2	59.6	45.5	46.0	73.7	75.3	73.3	60.0	73.6	81.2	95.7	95.0	77.7	68.0
Total of smaller countries	18.2	22.2	24.1	18.7	21.4	24.3	24.1	22.5	22.6	32.9	30.1	19.8	18.8	14.6	13.5	11.7	16.0	17.7	15.3	13.4
Total OECD	13.6	14.0	13.2	12.4	9.1	11.1	12.1	10.1	9.2	10.9	11.9	9.8	8.8	6.6	6.4	4.9	6.8	6.5	5.8	5.8
Total OECD *less* Turkey	13.3	12.9	11.9	11.7	8.7	10.7	11.3	9.2	8.6	10.3	10.8	8.6	7.7	5.7	5.3	3.7	5.1	5.0	4.6	4.7
OECD North America	11.8	13.0	11.0	13.7	7.6	13.5	14.5	10.6	10.0	15.1	14.0	9.1	7.2	4.3	6.0	5.2	6.1	6.1	6.0	5.3
OECD Europe	15.1	17.0	17.3	12.7	12.1	11.2	11.4	10.8	10.1	8.7	11.5	11.6	11.1	9.4	8.2	6.2	9.8	9.3	7.1	7.5
OECD Europe *less* Turkey	14.4	14.3	14.1	11.0	11.2	10.2	9.4	8.6	8.5	7.0	8.6	8.6	8.5	7.1	5.4	3.1	5.6	5.6	4.1	4.8
EU	14.6	14.5	14.2	11.0	11.3	10.3	9.4	8.5	8.6	7.0	8.7	8.7	8.5	7.1	5.5	3.1	5.6	5.5	3.9	4.7
Total OECD *less* the United States	15.3	15.4	15.7	12.7	12.2	12.6	12.7	11.9	11.3	13.8	14.5	11.1	10.7	8.8	6.9	5.0	7.4	7.6	6.7	6.7

Annex Table 3. **Real private consumption expenditure**

Percentage changes from previous period

	Average 1971-78	1979	1980	1981	1982	1983	1984	1985	1986	1987	1988	1989	1990	1991	1992	1993	1994	1995	Projections 1996	1997
United States	3.8	2.3	-0.3	1.2	1.2	5.2	5.2	4.7	4.0	3.1	3.9	2.3	1.7	-0.6	2.8	2.8	3.0	2.4	2.5	2.0
Japan	4.9	6.5	1.1	1.5	4.4	3.3	2.6	3.3	3.5	4.2	5.3	4.8	4.4	2.5	2.1	1.2	1.8	1.6	2.4	2.2
Germany	3.3	3.3	1.2	-0.6	-1.3	1.5	1.8	1.7	3.5	3.4	2.7	2.8	5.4	5.6	2.8	0.5	0.9	1.7	1.3	2.0
France	3.7	3.0	1.2	2.1	3.5	0.9	1.1	2.4	3.9	2.9	3.3	3.1	2.7	1.4	1.4	0.2	1.4	1.8	1.4	1.9
Italy	3.9	7.1	1.2	1.5	1.2	0.7	2.0	3.0	3.7	4.2	4.2	3.5	2.5	2.7	1.1	-2.5	1.6	1.6	1.4	2.1
United Kingdom	2.1	4.3	0	0.1	1.0	4.5	2.0	3.8	6.8	5.3	7.5	3.2	0.6	-2.2	-0.1	2.6	2.7	2.3	3.0	3.2
Canada	5.5	2.9	2.2	2.3	-2.6	3.4	4.6	5.2	4.4	4.4	4.5	3.4	1.0	-1.6	1.3	1.6	3.0	1.4	2.2	3.0
Total of above countries	3.9	3.8	0.8	1.1	1.5	3.7	3.6	3.8	4.0	3.6	4.3	3.1	2.6	0.8	2.2	1.6	2.3	2.0	2.2	2.2
Australia	3.7	2.8	3.6	4.3	2.7	1.4	2.9	5.1	1.0	2.5	4.1	5.3	2.6	1.0	3.8	2.3	4.4	4.2	2.8	2.7
Austria	3.7	4.4	1.5	0.3	1.2	5.0	-0.1	2.4	1.8	3.1	3.9	3.1	3.3	2.9	2.8	0.7	2.5	1.9	0.8	0.7
Belgium	3.8	4.8	2.0	-1.1	1.3	-1.6	1.2	1.9	2.3	3.0	2.8	3.8	2.6	3.1	2.9	-0.7	1.3	1.4	1.1	1.8
Czech Republic	..	..															5.3	6.4	7.5	7.0
Denmark	2.4	1.4	-3.7	-2.3	1.4	2.6	3.4	5.0	5.7	-1.5	-1.0	-0.4	0	1.2	1.9	2.4	6.6	2.3	2.0	2.7
Finland	3.0	5.5	2.0	1.2	4.7	2.6	2.7	3.2	4.0	5.2	5.1	4.3	0	-3.6	-4.9	-2.9	1.8	4.2	2.8	2.6
Greece	5.2	2.6	0.2	2.0	3.9	0.3	1.7	3.9	0.7	1.2	3.6	6.0	2.6	2.8	1.8	0.1	1.5	1.6	1.9	2.2
Iceland	5.6	2.8	3.4	6.2	4.9	-5.6	3.7	4.2	6.9	16.2	-3.8	-4.2	0.5	4.1	-4.4	-4.5	1.8	4.6	4.5	3.8
Ireland	4.7	4.4	0.4	1.7	-7.1	0.9	2.0	4.6	2.0	3.3	4.4	6.2	1.1	2.0	2.9	1.4	4.3	3.7	4.7	3.4
Luxembourg	4.1	3.5	2.8	1.7	0.4	0.5	1.4	2.7	3.4	5.0	3.9	3.9	4.0	6.5	1.7	-0.9	2.5	2.4	2.1	2.4
Mexico	5.6	8.8	7.5	7.4	-2.5	-5.4	3.3	3.6	-2.8	-0.1	1.8	6.8	6.1	4.9	3.9	0.2	3.7	-12.9	1.0	3.0
Netherlands	4.1	2.3	-0.4	-3.0	-0.5	0.9	1.2	2.8	2.6	2.7	0.8	3.5	4.2	3.1	2.5	0.9	2.1	2.1	1.8	1.9
New Zealand	2.0	1.8	0.3	2.3	0.6	1.4	5.7	0.5	4.6	1.4	2.3	0.8	0.2	-2.0	0.2	3.0	4.4	3.5	4.1	4.7
Norway	3.8	3.2	2.3	1.1	1.8	1.5	2.7	9.9	5.6	-1.0	-2.8	-0.6	0.7	1.4	2.2	2.1	4.6	2.7	3.1	2.5
Portugal	3.7	0	3.7	2.9	2.4	-1.4	-2.9	0.7	6.3	6.0	5.7	3.6	6.9	4.8	3.7	0.4	0.2	1.7	1.8	2.4
Spain	4.4	1.3	0.6	-1.3	-0.1	0.3	-0.2	3.5	3.3	5.8	4.9	5.7	3.6	2.9	2.1	-2.2	0.8	1.8	2.3	3.0
Sweden	2.1	2.4	-0.9	-0.3	0.7	-2.0	1.5	2.7	4.4	4.6	2.4	1.2	-0.4	0.9	-1.4	-3.1	0.8	0.3	0.5	1.5
Switzerland	1.6	1.1	2.6	0.5	0	1.7	1.6	1.4	2.8	2.1	2.1	2.2	1.5	1.5	-0.2	-0.6	1.0	0.2	0.5	1.1
Turkey	5.4	-1.2	5.9	-7.6	6.9	6.7	8.1	-0.6	5.8	-0.3	1.2	-1.0	13.1	1.9	3.3	8.4	-5.3	7.6	5.0	5.3
Total of smaller countries	4.1	3.1	2.6	0.5	1.0	0.4	2.2	3.0	2.4	2.5	2.7	3.8	4.2	2.5	2.3	0.7	1.8	0.5	2.3	2.8
Total OECD	3.9	3.6	1.1	1.0	1.4	3.1	3.3	3.6	3.7	3.4	4.0	3.2	2.9	1.1	2.2	1.4	2.2	1.8	2.2	2.3
OECD North America	4.0	2.8	0.3	1.7	0.6	4.4	5.0	4.6	3.6	3.0	3.8	2.7	1.9	-0.4	2.7	2.6	3.1	1.4	2.4	2.2
OECD Europe	3.5	3.5	1.8	0	1.1	1.7	1.7	2.7	4.1	3.6	3.7	3.1	3.4	2.2	1.6	0.3	1.4	2.1	1.9	2.4
EU	3.5	3.8	1.6	0.3	0.9	1.5	1.4	2.7	4.0	3.9	4.0	3.4	3.0	2.3	1.5	-0.1	1.6	1.8	1.7	2.3
Total OECD *less* the United States	4.0	4.4	1.9	0.9	1.6	1.9	2.2	3.0	3.6	3.6	4.1	3.7	3.6	2.2	1.8	0.6	1.8	1.4	2.1	2.5

Annex Table 4. **Real public consumption expenditure**
Percentage changes from previous period

	Average 1971-78	1979	1980	1981	1982	1983	1984	1985	1986	1987	1988	1989	1990	1991	1992	1993	1994	1995	Projections 1996	1997
United States	0.9	1.0	1.6	1.6	1.9	2.1	1.7	4.8	4.6	2.2	2.0	2.7	2.3	1.0	-0.1	-0.1	0.2	-0.3	-0.9	-0.5
Japan	5.1	4.2	3.1	4.5	2.9	2.5	2.3	0.3	5.1	1.6	2.3	2.0	1.5	2.0	2.0	2.4	2.2	2.0	1.7	2.1
Germany	3.4	3.4	2.6	1.8	-0.9	0.2	2.5	2.1	2.5	1.5	2.1	-1.6	2.2	0.5	5.0	-0.5	0.7	2.1	1.4	1.4
France	3.4	3.0	2.5	3.1	3.7	2.1	1.1	2.3	1.7	2.8	3.4	0.5	2.1	2.8	3.4	3.4	1.1	0.9	1.1	1.1
Italy	3.0	3.0	2.1	2.3	2.6	3.4	2.3	3.4	2.6	3.4	2.8	0.8	1.2	1.6	1.0	0.7	0	-0.3	-0.1	0.4
United Kingdom	2.5	1.9	1.7	0.3	0.9	2.1	0.8	-0.1	1.6	1.0	0.7	1.4	2.5	2.6	-0.1	0.3	1.7	0.9	0.8	0.8
Canada	4.1	0.6	2.8	2.5	2.4	1.4	1.2	3.2	1.6	1.7	4.1	4.0	3.2	2.7	1.0	0.5	-1.7	-0.9	-1.6	-0.2
Total of above countries	2.5	2.2	2.2	2.3	1.9	2.1	1.8	3.0	3.8	2.0	2.2	1.8	2.1	1.5	1.2	0.7	0.7	0.5	0.1	0.5
Australia	5.4	1.2	3.9	3.5	-0.3	5.2	4.6	5.5	4.5	2.0	3.1	2.5	4.5	2.7	1.4	0.3	5.1	3.5	1.7	1.5
Austria	3.9	3.0	2.7	2.2	2.3	2.2	0.2	1.9	1.7	0.4	0.3	0.8	1.2	2.6	2.2	3.1	2.2	2.1	0.3	0.1
Belgium	4.4	2.5	1.5	0.6	-1.3	0.2	0.3	2.5	1.8	0.3	-0.9	-0.1	-0.4	2.4	0.3	0.8	1.5	0.7	0.3	0.6
Czech Republic	:	:	:	:	:	:	:	:	:	:	:	:	:	:	:	:	-2.3	-4.3	0	0.5
Denmark	4.0	5.9	4.3	2.6	3.1	0	-0.4	2.5	0.5	2.5	0.9	-0.6	-0.4	-0.1	0.4	3.0	1.4	0.2	1.1	1.1
Finland	5.5	3.8	4.2	4.3	3.5	3.7	2.8	5.2	3.1	4.3	2.3	2.3	3.8	2.5	-2.2	-5.3	0.9	1.1	1.3	1.0
Greece	7.3	5.8	0.2	6.8	2.3	2.7	3.0	3.2	-0.8	0.9	5.7	5.4	0.6	-1.5	-0.8	0.7	1.1	1.4	0.5	0.5
Iceland	7.8	5.5	2.1	7.5	5.9	4.7	0.6	6.5	7.3	6.5	4.7	3.0	4.4	3.2	-0.8	2.3	3.7	2.0	2.0	2.0
Ireland	6.1	4.6	7.1	0.3	3.2	-0.4	-0.7	1.8	2.6	-4.8	-5.0	-1.0	5.4	2.5	2.5	1.3	3.9	3.0	1.5	1.5
Luxembourg	3.2	2.2	3.1	1.4	1.5	1.9	2.2	2.0	3.1	2.7	3.8	1.9	3.2	3.8	3.5	1.8	2.1	2.3	2.0	1.8
Mexico	8.3	9.6	9.5	10.3	2.0	2.7	6.6	0.9	1.5	-1.2	-0.5	-0.1	2.3	3.9	2.3	2.0	2.5	-4.1	-4.0	1.0
Netherlands	2.7	3.5	1.4	2.8	2.3	2.3	0	2.4	3.6	2.6	1.4	1.5	1.6	1.5	1.7	0.2	0.9	0.5	2.1	1.6
New Zealand	4.3	0.8	-0.3	2.0	0.4	2.7	2.2	1.5	1.9	-0.8	2.7	-1.2	2.0	-0.7	2.3	-2.5	-2.1	0.9	0.7	0.6
Norway	5.4	3.6	5.4	6.1	3.9	4.6	2.4	3.3	2.2	4.0	0.5	2.2	4.1	3.9	5.5	1.0	1.1	0.6	1.1	1.4
Portugal	7.8	6.4	8.0	5.5	3.7	3.8	0.2	6.4	18.6	3.8	8.0	4.4	5.7	3.0	1.4	1.4	1.4	1.6	1.4	1.4
Spain	6.0	4.2	4.2	3.5	5.3	3.9	2.4	5.5	5.4	8.9	4.0	8.3	6.6	5.6	4.0	2.3	-0.3	0.9	-0.9	0
Sweden	3.2	4.8	2.3	2.3	1.0	0.8	2.2	2.2	1.3	1.0	0.6	2.1	2.6	2.8	0	0.2	-0.5	-2.3	0.9	-1.3
Switzerland	2.1	1.6	0.9	2.5	1.1	3.9	1.2	3.3	3.7	1.8	4.3	4.1	4.7	1.5	-0.1	-1.2	0.8	-0.1	-0.2	0
Turkey	8.8	-2.4	-18.5	48.8	-10.6	16.6	1.9	14.1	9.2	9.4	-1.1	0.8	8.0	4.5	3.8	5.4	-3.5	6.7	3.0	3.0
Total of smaller countries	5.8	3.9	2.1	8.6	1.1	4.2	2.5	4.4	4.1	3.2	1.7	2.6	3.8	3.1	2.0	1.4	0.9	0.6	0.1	0.9
Total OECD	3.1	2.5	2.2	3.4	1.8	2.4	1.9	3.2	3.8	2.3	2.1	1.9	2.4	1.8	1.3	0.8	0.7	0.6	0.1	0.5
OECD North America	1.6	1.5	2.2	2.2	1.9	2.1	1.9	4.4	4.1	1.9	2.0	2.6	2.4	1.3	0.1	0.1	0.2	-0.6	-1.1	-0.4
OECD Europe	3.9	3.0	1.6	4.3	1.3	2.7	1.6	3.0	3.0	2.9	2.2	1.2	2.7	2.2	2.4	1.1	0.6	1.1	0.8	0.9
EU	3.7	3.2	2.5	2.2	1.9	2.0	1.6	2.4	2.7	2.6	2.3	1.1	2.4	2.1	2.4	0.9	0.8	0.9	0.8	0.8
Total OECD *less* the United States	4.4	3.4	2.5	4.5	1.7	2.7	2.1	2.3	3.4	2.3	2.2	1.5	2.5	2.3	2.2	1.3	1.0	1.0	0.7	1.2

Annex Table 5. Real total gross fixed capital formation

Percentage changes from previous period

	Average 1971-78	1979	1980	1981	1982	1983	1984	1985	1986	1987	1988	1989	1990	1991	1992	1993	1994	1995	Projections 1996	1997
United States	4.3	4.7	-5.9	0.5	-7.0	7.9	15.6	6.0	2.1	0.4	1.5	2.0	-1.4	-6.6	5.2	5.1	7.9	5.4	5.3	2.7
Japan	3.5	5.9	-0.4	2.3	-0.2	-1.1	4.3	5.0	4.8	9.1	11.5	8.2	8.5	3.3	-1.5	-2.0	-1.0	0.8	5.6	3.2
Germany	-0.3	6.7	2.2	-5.0	-5.4	3.1	0.1	-0.5	3.3	1.8	4.4	6.3	8.5	6.0	3.5	-5.6	4.3	1.5	-2.4	2.5
France	1.7	3.1	2.6	-1.9	-1.4	-3.6	-2.6	3.2	4.5	4.8	9.6	7.9	2.8	0	-2.8	-6.7	1.3	2.8	1.5	3.3
Italy	0.8	5.4	8.5	-3.1	-4.7	-0.6	3.6	0.6	2.2	5.0	6.9	4.3	3.8	0.6	-1.7	-13.1	-0.1	5.7	5.1	5.2
United Kingdom	0.6	2.8	-5.4	-9.6	5.4	5.0	8.9	4.2	2.6	10.3	13.9	6.0	-3.5	-9.5	-1.5	0.6	3.0	-0.7	2.2	4.7
Canada	5.2	8.5	10.1	11.8	-11.0	-0.7	2.1	9.5	6.2	10.8	10.3	6.1	-3.5	-2.9	-1.5	0.6	7.2	0.2	2.5	6.2
Total of above countries	3.1	5.1	-1.7	-0.4	-4.3	3.7	8.7	4.6	3.1	3.9	5.9	4.6	1.9	-2.6	1.9	-0.1	4.4	3.4	3.9	3.3
Australia	1.1	4.0	5.5	9.1	-3.5	-8.5	10.5	9.6	-2.2	3.5	7.7	9.2	-8.1	-9.2	1.4	2.4	12.3	2.1	4.3	9.9
Austria	2.2	3.5	3.0	-1.4	-8.2	-0.6	2.1	5.0	3.7	3.1	6.0	6.2	5.7	6.3	1.7	-1.6	6.8	2.3	0.4	1.9
Belgium	3.1	-2.7	4.6	-16.1	-1.7	-4.4	1.7	0.7	4.4	5.6	15.4	12.3	10.1	-1.5	0.2	-6.7	0.5	2.7	2.9	4.2
Czech Republic	:	:	:	:	:	:	:	:	:	:	:	:	:	:	:	:	17.3	16.1	14.5	13.5
Denmark	0.6	-0.4	-12.6	-19.2	7.1	1.9	12.9	12.6	17.1	-3.8	-6.6	1.0	-1.7	-5.7	-4.2	-4.6	3.0	11.0	3.7	5.2
Finland	0.5	3.0	10.4	2.2	4.4	4.1	-2.1	2.9	-0.4	4.9	9.8	14.8	-4.1	-20.3	-16.9	-19.2	-0.3	8.1	8.0	10.1
Greece	1.8	8.8	-6.5	-7.5	-1.9	-1.3	-5.7	5.2	-6.2	-5.1	8.9	7.1	5.0	4.8	-1.4	-2.8	0.5	5.8	9.5	9.2
Iceland	3.1	-1.8	14.0	1.2	0.1	-12.6	9.3	1.0	-1.9	19.1	-0.1	-7.8	2.6	2.0	-11.1	-11.5	-1.1	3.0	16.8	7.2
Ireland	6.0	13.6	-4.7	9.5	-3.4	-9.3	-2.5	-7.7	-2.8	-1.5	-1.6	13.8	11.1	-7.1	-3.1	-0.8	7.3	10.8	8.2	6.5
Luxembourg	0	3.8	12.7	-7.4	-0.5	-11.8	0.1	-9.5	31.2	14.7	14.1	8.9	2.5	9.8	-2.1	3.9	2.4	3.5	3.0	4.0
Mexico	7.3	20.2	14.9	16.2	-16.8	-28.3	6.4	7.9	-11.8	-0.1	5.8	6.4	13.1	8.3	10.8	-1.2	8.1	-30.9	5.3	7.7
Netherlands	0.4	-1.5	-0.2	-9.9	-4.2	2.5	5.8	7.0	6.9	0.9	4.5	4.9	1.6	0.2	0.6	-3.1	3.0	4.9	2.8	2.5
New Zealand	0.9	-7.7	1.1	11.4	12.2	0.2	11.5	4.0	-1.7	1.7	0.2	6.5	-0.6	-16.0	5.2	17.7	23.3	18.0	6.4	6.8
Norway	2.5	-5.0	-1.5	17.9	-11.0	5.8	10.9	-13.9	23.9	-2.1	1.6	-8.8	-11.9	-1.3	-3.3	1.5	5.5	5.1	6.7	2.3
Portugal	3.0	-1.3	8.5	5.5	2.3	-7.1	-17.4	-3.5	11.4	16.8	11.2	4.3	6.8	2.4	5.4	-4.8	3.9	5.4	5.0	6.2
Spain	3.3	-4.4	0.7	-2.5	2.1	-2.4	-6.9	6.1	9.9	14.0	13.9	13.6	6.6	1.6	-4.2	-10.6	1.4	8.4	6.1	5.3
Sweden	-0.2	4.5	3.5	-6.0	-0.9	1.1	7.1	5.2	0.3	8.2	6.6	11.3	1.3	-8.9	-10.8	-17.2	-0.2	10.6	9.4	4.4
Switzerland	-2.1	5.1	9.8	2.7	-2.6	4.1	4.1	5.3	7.9	7.4	6.9	5.8	2.6	-2.5	-5.0	-2.5	5.9	5.3	2.0	2.6
Turkey	6.7	2.8	-16.7	31.6	-5.7	2.6	0.9	11.5	8.4	45.1	-1.0	2.2	15.9	1.2	4.3	24.9	-15.9	8.3	7.7	7.8
Total of smaller countries	3.4	3.6	2.3	4.1	-3.9	-5.2	2.2	5.7	3.3	8.8	7.0	7.6	5.2	-0.4	0.3	-1.8	3.3	1.2	5.6	6.2
Total OECD	3.2	4.8	-0.9	0.4	-4.2	2.1	7.5	4.8	3.1	4.8	6.1	5.2	2.5	-2.2	1.6	-0.4	4.2	3.0	4.2	3.8
OECD North America	4.6	6.0	-3.4	2.4	-7.9	5.0	14.0	6.4	1.5	1.2	2.4	2.6	-0.6	-5.4	5.1	4.3	7.8	2.7	5.1	3.3
OECD Europe	1.4	3.2	1.2	-2.9	-1.8	0.6	1.4	2.8	4.6	7.3	8.0	6.7	4.1	-0.3	-0.9	-5.1	1.8	4.0	2.8	4.3
EU	1.1	3.3	1.9	-5.0	-1.5	0.4	1.2	2.5	4.0	5.6	8.5	7.1	3.8	-0.3	-1.0	-6.7	2.2	3.5	2.3	4.1
Total OECD *less* the United States	2.4	4.9	2.0	0.3	-2.6	-1.4	2.7	4.1	3.8	7.5	8.8	7.1	4.8	0.5	-0.5	-3.6	2.1	1.5	3.6	4.5

Annex Table 6. **Real gross private non-residential fixed capital formation**

Percentage changes from previous period

	Average 1971-78	1979	1980	1981	1982	1983	1984	1985	1986	1987	1988	1989	1990	1991	1992	1993	1994	1995	Projections 1996	Projections 1997
United States	5.9	9.6	-0.5	5.3	4.4	-1.7	17.3	6.2	-3.5	-1.1	4.4	4.0	-0.6	-6.4	1.9	6.4	9.8	9.7	7.3	4.8
Japan	1.3	12.8	7.9	3.8	1.3	1.7	11.7	12.1	4.5	5.9	14.7	14.5	10.9	6.3	-5.6	-10.2	-6.0	2.9	5.2	5.6
Germany	-0.1	7.5	2.8	-3.9	-4.7	4.5	-0.4	5.0	4.3	3.8	5.6	7.4	10.1	7.5	-4.0	-10.0	0.7	1.4	-2.6	3.5
France	1.3	2.6	4.2	-2.5	0	-4.1	-2.1	4.4	6.6	6.0	9.6	8.6	4.7	0.4	-1.1	-8.2	1.5	4.0	2.1	4.4
Italy	2.6	7.2	9.3	-8.1	-7.2	-4.4	6.7	0.8	5.0	9.2	12.0	5.6	5.4	-0.3	-6.2	-18.4	3.7	9.3	6.0	5.8
United Kingdom	3.2	2.8	-4.3	-5.8	7.7	-0.6	14.3	13.2	0.5	17.3	17.8	6.2	-3.1	-9.5	-6.2	-18.4	1.8	2.3	6.5	7.0
Canada	6.9	18.7	20.5	15.5	-11.4	-7.0	2.0	8.9	4.5	9.7	15.8	6.2	-2.4	-0.2	-5.5	2.7	9.4	5.2	3.2	6.8
Total of above countries	3.8	9.2	3.1	2.2	-2.7	-1.0	11.4	7.2	0.8	3.7	8.8	7.0	3.2	-1.7	-1.2	-1.9	4.3	6.4	5.2	5.1
Australia	0.8	3.4	5.2	16.5	1.7	-9.6	5.6	13.2	-1.3	5.8	5.2	12.6	-8.0	-13.6	-2.4	-2.0	15.2	9.5	9.9	14.2
Austria	2.9	4.7	4.6	-2.7	-10.2	-0.9	4.1	8.6	3.7	5.8	7.3	8.8	8.3	5.1	-2.0	6.4	-4.1	2.9	0.6	2.5
Belgium	2.1	2.3	-0.5	-4.8	2.2	-5.1	6.6	2.4	6.3	7.3	15.0	15.5	11.3	-2.7	-4.5	-8.8	-0.8	5.0	3.9	4.3
Czech Republic	..	..	..	..	..	..	..	..	..	..	..	..	..	..	..	..	..	..	..	..
Denmark	2.6	-2.0	-9.6	-16.5	19.9	2.7	12.1	18.9	18.8	-5.4	-7.3	5.8	2.6	-4.5	-6.7	-5.1	1.4	14.6	5.1	6.0
Finland	-1.5	6.6	15.5	5.0	2.5	6.8	-1.7	6.3	3.6	5.2	8.5	19.1	-6.4	-24.2	-21.3	-22.6	1.8	19.5	14.7	10.7
Greece	0.7	18.3	7.2	3.0	1.7	-11.0	-1.8	9.1	-17.3	-7.0	15.5	16.0	6.5	3.1	0.1	1.4	5.3	10.4	14.0	10.5
Iceland	..	0	16.4	3.3	-4.8	-15.2	11.3	7.3	3.7	22.8	-10.0	-14.4	5.6	3.6	-17.1	-24.8	0.4	12.4	37.2	13.0
Ireland	5.7	13.5	-4.9	17.4	-3.7	-11.6	-2.9	-14.7	-2.9	7.1	8.2	15.3	15.3	-11.9	-8.3	-1.4	9.7	17.2	9.4	7.8
Luxembourg	..	..	..	..	..	..	..	..	..	..	..	..	..	..	..	..	..	..	..	..
Mexico	1.9	1.5	-3.3	13.1	-22.4	-31.4	10.1	15.4	-16.6	8.1	19.4	6.8	21.1	17.9	22.0	-2.9	8.0	-33.5	6.0	9.2
Netherlands	-0.8	0.3	..	-11.7	-2.5	6.4	5.9	13.8	11.6	0.2	1.6	7.8	2.3	2.0	-3.0	-4.2	0.5	6.5	4.0	2.4
New Zealand	1.4	..	11.6	12.8	8.8	-6.9	28.6	2.2	-5.1	13.1	1.1	11.8	-6.3	-16.2	12.3	28.1	29.1	23.7	6.9	7.5
Norway	1.4	-6.7	-1.9	28.9	-16.5	7.6	16.4	-20.4	30.6	-5.9	2.2	-8.3	-12.0	2.9	-3.4	5.2	3.9	3.7	7.5	2.3
Portugal	..	..	..	..	..	..	..	..	..	..	..	..	..	..	..	..	..	..	..	..
Spain	5.0	-1.2	1.4	-5.5	-2.1	-0.3	-10.6	0.1	14.0	21.1	13.9	13.5	3.9	2.6	-1.4	-15.1	4.6	14.0	8.0	6.5
Sweden	1.0	8.1	11.2	-7.1	1.3	2.7	7.2	12.7	2.3	9.3	5.8	15.0	-1.1	-15.2	-15.5	-13.0	14.4	24.5	10.0	5.0
Switzerland	-0.9	5.1	10.8	2.4	-3.6	3.4	4.1	10.6	13.3	10.8	8.9	5.2	3.3	-3.6	-8.5	-7.8	2.8	11.6	3.8	3.0
Turkey	..	..	..	..	..	..	..	..	..	..	..	..	..	..	..	..	..	..	..	..
Total of smaller countries	2.1	2.4	2.6	2.3	-4.5	-6.3	3.5	7.9	3.4	8.2	10.0	10.4	5.1	0.1	0.2	-5.8	5.9	3.6	7.0	7.0
Total OECD	3.5	8.1	3.0	2.2	-3.0	-1.9	10.1	7.3	1.2	4.4	9.0	7.5	3.5	-1.4	-1.0	-2.6	4.6	6.0	5.5	5.4
OECD North America	5.7	9.7	1.2	6.6	-6.1	-4.0	15.7	7.0	-3.7	0.3	6.2	4.4	0.6	-4.4	2.6	5.5	9.7	6.6	6.9	5.2
OECD Europe	2.0	4.5	3.0	4.4	-1.4	-0.4	3.1	5.6	5.7	8.5	10.1	8.2	4.4	-0.3	-3.3	-9.1	2.2	6.2	3.7	5.0
EU	2.1	4.7	2.8	-5.0	-1.1	-0.6	2.9	5.8	5.2	8.6	10.3	8.5	4.7	-0.3	-3.2	-9.3	2.2	6.1	3.6	5.1
Total OECD *less* the United States	2.0	7.1	5.1	0.2	-2.1	-2.0	5.7	8.0	4.1	7.8	11.8	9.7	6.0	1.7	-2.7	-8.1	1.4	3.7	4.3	5.7

Annex Table 7. **Real gross private residential fixed capital formation**

Percentage changes from previous period

	Average 1971-78	1979	1980	1981	1982	1983	1984	1985	1986	1987	1988	1989	1990	1991	1992	1993	1994	1995	Projections 1996	1997
United States	3.7	-3.7	-21.2	-8.0	-18.2	41.1	14.6	1.3	12.0	0.2	-2.0	-3.7	-9.3	-12.3	16.6	7.6	10.8	-2.3	2.7	-2.2
Japan	4.9	-0.9	-9.2	-2.3	-0.7	-5.9	-2.1	2.6	8.1	22.4	11.4	0.9	4.8	-8.5	-6.5	2.4	9.2	-6.1	0.8	0.6
Germany	-0.6	6.9	2.3	-5.0	-4.9	5.7	2.0	-9.9	-0.6	-1.2	3.7	4.9	8.5	4.3	9.4	3.8	13.1	3.0	-1.8	1.8
France	2.7	4.0	-0.3	-3.1	-6.3	-2.6	-4.4	-2.1	1.3	3.3	7.1	7.1	0.3	-4.1	-4.5	-7.8	2.0	3.0	0.6	2.0
Italy	-2.1	2.9	4.7	-0.1	-3.4	4.4	-0.5	-2.8	-2.1	-2.4	1.3	7.1	2.8	3.1	0.2	-0.9	-2.2	1.7	3.6	4.0
United Kingdom	-0.3	9.0	-5.5	-10.8	6.5	7.4	6.7	-2.7	12.0	8.1	20.5	-5.0	-16.7	-12.4	2.9	4.3	6.3	1.3	0.6	4.0
Canada	5.4	-1.0	-5.4	6.6	-16.3	17.0	0.5	9.8	13.3	16.4	2.8	4.8	-9.7	-12.5	7.9	-4.2	3.0	-13.8	-0.5	5.9
Total of above countries	3.0	0	-11.4	-5.3	-9.9	19.5	6.5	0	8.2	5.4	3.7	-0.4	-3.8	-8.2	7.5	3.7	8.5	-1.9	1.5	0.3
Australia	1.7	9.4	11.8	2.3	-13.7	-9.4	21.0	2.0	-8.2	1.3	22.1	2.4	-11.5	-4.1	10.7	11.0	11.0	-10.1	-6.3	2.7
Austria	1.6	3.7	4.8	2.0	-1.8	-1.7	-1.0	-1.5	2.4	1.8	8.4	-0.6	1.4	11.5	12.1	-22.4	51.6	1.7	0.2	1.0
Belgium	8.7	-14.4	13.0	-41.6	-5.8	-1.6	-0.3	4.6	4.7	7.7	22.3	19.0	8.5	-0.8	12.5	-3.9	2.2	1.0	1.9	2.6
Czech Republic	:																			
Denmark	-0.6	-0.8	-16.8	-25.7	-8.5	11.5	20.3	-2.1	21.3	-3.2	-9.4	-8.9	-13.7	-11.7	-4.2	-6.9	11.3	6.2	5.0	6.5
Finland	3.4	-1.5	4.7	-2.5	5.9	-0.3	-2.7	-3.0	-8.0	1.1	15.4	18.9	-5.7	-20.7	-16.1	-13.6	-4.1	-4.0	-3.8	9.2
Greece	3.8	4.7	-13.8	-22.7	-5.8	4.6	-19.7	-0.5	14.6	3.4	2.9	-1.9	5.5	1.0	-8.0	-7.0	-7.6	-3.5	1.0	2.5
Iceland	6.4	-1.9	7.5	-9.8	9.4	-9.1	10.4	-13.6	-13.8	14.2	14.8	2.8	-0.5	-4.9	-3.3	-5.8	0	-5.0	0	2.0
Ireland	10.3	17.3	-16.9	0.2	-5.5	-4.0	6.6	-1.8	3.5	2.2	-2.6	13.5	-0.6	0.2	9.4	-7.2	2.6	3.7	4.3	4.6
Luxembourg	:																			
Mexico	2.9	9.3	4.5	7.9	1.5	-5.9	5.0	8.1	-1.6	4.4	-1.2	8.3	1.7	4.5	3.5	4.8	7.9	-34.9	6.0	8.5
Netherlands	0.7	-5.0	4.7	-9.6	-5.6	-0.4	4.5	-0.4	3.7	1.9	11.3	0.7	-2.5	-5.4	6.4	-0.8	8.1	2.3	-0.6	2.4
New Zealand	-1.4	-3.4	-2.0	6.2	9.3	-1.6	18.3	-0.5	-2.9	-4.1	4.5	15.0	2.2	-15.9	6.2	17.3	12.3	2.1	4.1	6.9
Norway	4.6	2.4	-2.3	1.1	8.0	0.8	-1.4	4.1	9.6	4.0	-3.8	-17.0	-17.1	-27.3	-12.6	-1.4	25.9	14.0	8.7	3.1
Portugal	:																			
Spain	1.2	-7.6	-2.0	-0.8	-2.0	-5.5	-5.4	6.5	2.1	6.3	11.4	3.3	6.4	-3.7	-4.4	-4.3	0.2	7.5	7.0	7.0
Sweden	-1.4	1.8	-6.0	-5.1	-2.3	-0.5	11.2	-2.5	-2.2	8.8	8.4	4.8	7.2	-2.4	-7.3	-32.8	-35.3	-27.9	20.0	5.0
Switzerland	-4.0	12.1	17.4	2.5	-6.1	6.2	7.2	3.3	1.5	4.4	3.6	5.7	-1.0	-7.0	-3.6	5.3	26.9	-1.0	-1.0	2.0
Turkey	:																			
Total of smaller countries	2.4	1.1	2.6	-4.1	-3.2	-2.6	3.9	3.0	1.4	3.9	8.5	4.5	0.1	-3.1	1.3	-2.7	7.0	-6.6	3.4	5.0
Total OECD	3.0	0.2	-9.1	-5.1	-8.8	15.9	6.1	0.5	7.1	5.2	4.5	0.4	-3.2	-7.4	6.5	2.7	8.2	-2.7	1.8	1.0
OECD North America	3.9	-2.6	-18.3	-5.9	-16.8	36.3	12.9	2.4	11.2	1.7	-1.6	-2.3	-8.6	-11.3	15.1	6.5	10.0	-5.2	2.7	-0.9
OECD Europe	0.7	3.4	0.6	-5.8	-2.8	2.4	0.7	-2.8	2.7	2.5	8.0	3.0	0.2	-2.5	1.6	-2.1	5.6	1.9	1.6	3.3
EU	0.8	3.2	0.2	-6.1	-2.8	2.4	0.6	-3.0	2.7	2.4	8.3	3.2	0.5	-2.1	1.9	-2.3	4.8	1.9	1.6	3.3
Total OECD less the United States	2.2	2.5	-1.7	-3.3	-3.1	0.4	0.9	-0.1	4.1	8.2	8.5	2.8	0.6	-4.3	0.3	-0.3	6.7	-2.9	1.3	3.0

Annex Table 8. **Real total domestic demand**

Percentage changes from previous period

	Average 1971-78	1979	1980	1981	1982	1983	1984	1985	1986	1987	1988	1989	1990	1991	1992	1993	1994	1995	Projections 1996	1997
United States	3.3	2.1	-1.7	2.1	-1.1	5.3	7.9	4.0	3.4	2.7	2.9	2.7	0.9	-1.6	2.8	2.9	4.0	2.1	2.2	1.8
Japan	4.4	6.2	0.7	2.0	2.8	1.7	3.2	3.8	3.9	5.1	7.4	5.6	5.2	2.9	0.4	0.1	0.8	1.6	3.3	2.6
Germany	2.5	5.3	0.6	-2.3	-2.2	2.4	1.9	1.0	3.3	2.4	3.6	2.9	5.2	4.8	2.8	-1.3	2.8	1.7	0	2.1
France	3.1	3.8	1.6	-0.1	3.5	-0.7	0.4	2.5	4.5	3.3	4.7	3.9	2.8	0.6	0.2	-2.2	3.0	2.0	1.1	2.1
Italy	3.1	6.5	6.5	-1.1	0.6	0.2	3.5	2.8	3.0	4.2	4.4	2.8	2.5	1.9	0.8	-5.5	1.9	2.6	2.0	2.4
United Kingdom	2.0	3.6	-1.5	-1.1	1.2	4.8	2.8	2.9	4.9	5.3	7.9	2.9	-0.6	-3.1	0.2	2.1	3.0	1.6	2.3	3.0
Canada	5.1	4.5	2.4	4.4	-5.4	3.6	4.7	5.3	4.2	5.3	5.5	4.3	-0.5	-1.2	0.4	2.0	3.2	1.1	1.1	3.2
Total of above countries	3.4	3.8	-0.1	1.1	0	3.4	5.0	3.4	3.7	3.6	4.5	3.4	2.2	0.2	1.8	0.8	2.9	1.9	2.0	2.2
Australia	3.2	4.4	2.8	5.9	-0.7	-0.6	6.9	5.0	0.2	3.1	5.7	6.4	-0.8	-2.4	3.4	3.0	5.8	4.4	2.4	4.0
Austria	3.4	4.9	3.3	-2.2	-1.1	2.8	2.7	2.2	1.8	2.6	4.4	2.9	4.1	3.2	2.3	0.7	4.5	2.9	0.4	0.9
Belgium	3.7	3.7	2.1	-4.7	0.7	-2.4	2.3	0.5	2.8	3.8	4.4	4.7	3.3	2.0	2.2	-1.8	1.4	1.6	1.1	2.2
Czech Republic	..	..	..	..	..	..	..	..	..	..	..	..	..	..	..	..	7.3	12.1	9.3	7.7
Denmark	2.2	2.7	-4.3	-4.1	3.5	1.4	5.1	5.4	6.1	-2.2	-1.2	0.5	-1.0	-0.4	-0.1	0.8	5.8	4.6	1.4	2.6
Finland	2.1	9.2	5.6	-0.4	4.3	2.3	2.0	2.9	2.2	5.2	6.6	7.6	-1.3	-9.2	-6.4	-6.4	3.7	4.6	3.1	3.6
Greece	4.7	3.9	-0.5	1.4	2.4	0.7	0.7	5.1	0.5	0.6	4.5	5.3	2.9	3.8	0.3	-0.7	1.1	3.3	3.3	3.5
Iceland	4.7	3.5	5.9	5.6	5.0	-8.5	6.4	2.7	4.4	15.7	-0.5	-4.4	1.4	5.2	-5.3	-4.2	1.5	4.5	5.4	4.0
Ireland	5.4	7.1	-2.3	3.0	-2.5	-2.8	1.1	1.3	1.2	0.3	1.3	7.6	5.7	-0.1	-1.2	0.8	3.8	5.1	4.9	3.7
Luxembourg	2.6	-0.2	5.4	1.0	1.1	-0.1	2.9	0.5	7.6	4.0	6.7	5.9	4.8	7.4	0.7	-0.2	2.3	3.1	2.1	2.6
Mexico	6.3	10.7	11.1	9.6	-8.2	-9.5	4.2	4.7	-5.6	0.7	3.3	5.5	6.5	5.3	5.9	-0.3	4.4	-17.7	1.4	3.7
Netherlands	2.9	1.5	0.3	-4.6	-1.0	2.0	1.8	3.7	3.8	1.4	1.8	4.7	3.5	1.9	1.6	-1.2	3.3	2.4	1.5	2.2
New Zealand	1.4	4.7	-1.2	4.4	5.0	-2.3	11.2	-0.5	1.9	0.9	1.7	4.4	-0.8	-7.3	3.5	6.8	8.0	7.1	4.0	4.6
Norway	3.3	2.6	11.1	2.2	-0.6	-0.6	3.6	0.5	15.4	-5.6	-2.6	-2.4	-0.7	0.5	1.5	2.8	4.9	3.9	3.4	2.1
Portugal	4.4	2.9	5.9	3.2	2.2	-5.2	2.2	1.2	8.8	9.5	9.6	4.4	6.5	4.3	4.3	-0.9	1.5	2.7	2.5	3.2
Spain	4.2	0.9	1.5	-2.1	1.5	0.5	-1.0	3.4	5.4	8.1	7.0	7.8	4.8	2.9	1.0	-4.2	1.1	3.2	2.4	3.0
Sweden	1.5	5.0	1.9	-1.7	0.3	-0.5	3.6	3.3	2.4	4.0	3.0	3.5	1.1	-1.8	-1.8	-5.2	1.9	1.6	1.2	1.3
Switzerland	0.4	4.1	5.2	-0.8	-0.9	2.3	2.2	2.5	5.6	3.6	2.8	4.1	2.3	-0.5	-3.3	-1.8	3.8	2.5	1.1	1.7
Turkey	5.4	-0.8	3.4	2.4	1.4	5.8	6.4	3.2	7.0	8.9	-1.3	1.5	14.6	-0.9	5.2	13.5	-12.3	12.7	5.5	5.8
Total of smaller countries	3.9	4.0	3.7	1.2	-0.6	-0.8	3.0	3.3	2.8	3.8	3.7	4.8	4.3	1.2	2.0	0.3	2.0	1.3	2.5	3.3
Total OECD	3.5	3.8	0.6	1.1	-0.1	2.6	4.7	3.4	3.5	3.6	4.3	3.7	2.6	0.4	1.8	0.7	2.8	1.8	2.1	2.4
OECD North America	3.7	2.8	-0.6	2.8	-1.9	4.2	7.4	4.1	2.9	2.8	3.1	3.0	1.1	-1.1	2.8	2.6	3.9	0.8	2.1	2.1
OECD Europe	3.0	4.1	1.8	-1.3	0.8	1.4	2.1	2.4	4.2	4.0	4.5	3.6	3.4	1.3	1.1	-1.2	2.1	2.8	1.7	2.6
EU	2.9	4.3	1.6	-1.5	0.9	1.2	1.7	2.4	3.9	3.9	4.9	3.8	2.9	1.4	1.1	-1.9	2.6	2.2	1.4	2.4
Total OECD *less* the United States	3.6	4.9	2.0	0.5	0.6	1.0	2.8	3.1	3.6	4.1	5.2	4.3	3.6	1.6	1.2	-0.5	2.1	1.6	2.1	2.7

Annex Table 9. Real exports of goods and services

Percentage changes from previous period

	Average 1971-78	1979	1980	1981	1982	1983	1984	1985	1986	1987	1988	1989	1990	1991	1992	1993	1994	1995	Projections 1996	1997
United States	8.0	9.5	10.8	1.2	-7.1	-2.6	8.3	2.7	7.4	11.0	15.9	11.7	8.5	6.3	6.6	3.3	8.3	8.3	7.7	8.0
Japan	8.2	4.3	17.0	12.5	0.9	4.8	14.8	5.4	-5.7	-0.5	5.9	9.1	6.9	5.4	4.9	1.3	4.5	5.0	5.2	7.5
Germany	5.5	4.3	5.2	7.2	3.9	-0.8	8.2	7.6	-0.6	0.4	5.5	10.2	11.0	12.3	-0.3	-4.7	7.5	3.8	5.3	6.9
France	7.3	7.5	2.7	3.7	-1.7	3.7	7.0	1.9	-1.4	3.1	8.1	10.2	5.4	4.1	4.9	-0.4	6.0	5.9	1.6	6.6
Italy	7.3	8.3	-8.8	7.9	-2.4	2.3	8.5	3.2	2.5	4.7	5.4	8.8	7.0	0.5	5.0	9.4	10.9	11.1	3.4	5.7
United Kingdom	4.9	3.8	-0.2	-0.7	0.8	1.8	6.5	6.0	4.5	5.8	0.5	4.7	5.0	-0.7	4.0	3.3	9.0	5.7	5.0	6.1
Canada	5.9	5.0	2.7	4.4	-2.2	6.4	17.7	6.0	4.5	3.5	9.5	0.8	4.1	1.4	7.6	10.4	14.2	11.8	7.1	7.6
Total of above countries	7.5	7.2	8.2	4.5	-3.0	0.5	9.6	4.0	2.8	6.1	10.3	9.8	7.7	5.4	5.2	2.6	7.8	7.2	6.0	7.4
Australia	3.4	10.9	-1.1	-3.4	8.7	-4.5	16.1	11.0	5.0	11.3	3.2	3.2	8.3	13.0	5.0	7.4	8.5	4.0	9.0	6.0
Austria	6.6	11.7	5.2	4.9	2.7	3.2	6.1	6.9	-2.7	2.4	9.4	10.7	7.7	5.8	1.2	-1.6	5.2	5.0	3.0	3.7
Belgium	5.7	7.5	2.9	2.6	1.3	2.6	5.5	1.1	5.5	6.5	8.5	7.3	4.1	2.6	3.9	1.6	8.1	8.2	4.6	6.5
Czech Republic	:	:	:	:	:	:	:	:	:	:	:	:	:	:	:	:	0.2	7.9	10.2	10.2
Denmark	3.5	8.4	5.2	8.2	2.5	4.9	3.5	5.0	0	5.1	7.8	4.2	6.9	7.7	1.4	-1.6	7.9	1.0	2.1	5.0
Finland	5.9	8.8	8.4	4.9	-1.1	2.5	5.4	1.2	1.2	2.7	3.7	1.3	1.4	-6.6	10.0	16.7	13.3	7.6	3.7	6.2
Greece	12.7	6.7	6.9	-5.9	-7.2	8.0	16.9	1.3	14.0	16.0	9.0	4.8	-4.1	3.7	8.7	0.6	7.7	1.8	5.5	6.0
Iceland	8.4	6.3	2.7	3.2	-8.9	11.0	2.4	11.0	5.9	3.3	-3.6	2.9	0	-5.8	-1.7	6.7	9.7	-2.4	5.0	6.0
Ireland	8.1	6.5	6.4	2.0	5.5	10.5	16.6	6.6	2.9	13.7	8.9	10.3	8.6	5.1	13.8	9.2	13.9	13.6	9.8	9.0
Luxembourg	2.8	9.7	-1.4	-4.8	-0.3	5.3	18.0	9.5	3.2	6.5	7.5	6.9	2.6	3.6	1.3	-2.4	5.0	4.4	3.3	5.4
Mexico	8.8	12.1	6.1	11.6	21.8	13.6	5.7	-4.5	5.6	9.5	5.8	2.3	3.6	4.6	1.7	3.7	7.3	28.4	12.0	9.0
Netherlands	4.6	7.4	2.2	1.9	-0.9	3.2	7.5	5.1	1.8	4.0	9.0	6.7	5.3	4.7	2.9	1.6	5.8	6.1	3.3	5.7
New Zealand	3.1	6.5	3.8	3.7	1.6	7.8	7.4	8.0	-0.1	5.4	4.4	-2.4	6.4	7.1	1.0	6.0	9.6	2.2	3.5	7.0
Norway	7.5	2.6	2.1	1.4	-0.1	7.6	8.2	6.9	1.6	1.2	5.5	10.7	8.6	6.1	5.2	2.0	8.5	3.7	8.3	3.8
Portugal	0.2	33.0	2.2	-4.4	4.7	13.6	11.6	6.7	6.3	10.6	7.9	13.3	10.5	0.5	6.1	-5.1	10.7	11.4	9.7	7.5
Spain	7.0	5.6	2.3	8.2	5.0	10.0	11.7	2.7	1.9	6.3	5.1	3.0	3.2	7.9	7.3	8.5	16.2	9.3	7.3	7.3
Sweden	4.0	6.1	-0.5	2.1	5.8	9.8	6.8	1.4	3.7	4.3	2.5	3.1	1.6	-2.3	2.3	7.6	14.1	11.4	4.5	6.0
Switzerland	4.3	2.4	5.1	4.8	-2.9	1.1	6.3	8.3	0.4	1.7	5.8	5.0	3.0	-0.7	3.4	1.6	3.3	2.8	2.2	4.5
Turkey	4.9	-6.8	-4.5	63.5	34.0	13.1	25.4	-1.9	-5.1	26.4	18.4	-0.3	2.6	3.7	11.0	7.7	15.2	6.7	12.0	12.0
Total of smaller countries	6.1	7.5	2.5	9.9	8.6	7.2	10.7	2.9	2.6	8.8	7.3	4.3	4.4	4.9	5.0	4.6	9.8	9.9	7.4	7.2
Total OECD	7.3	7.3	7.2	5.5	-0.9	1.7	9.8	3.8	2.8	6.6	9.8	8.8	7.1	5.3	5.2	2.9	8.2	7.7	6.3	7.3
OECD North America	7.9	9.3	9.9	2.1	-4.9	-0.9	8.8	2.5	7.0	10.3	14.7	10.3	7.9	5.8	6.3	3.9	8.6	9.9	8.0	8.1
OECD Europe	6.2	6.0	0.9	7.0	2.3	3.6	8.8	4.3	1.2	5.0	6.1	7.4	6.2	4.4	4.0	2.3	9.0	6.6	4.7	6.6
EU	6.2	6.7	1.0	4.5	0.9	3.1	8.1	4.4	1.5	4.1	5.5	7.8	6.5	4.5	3.7	2.1	9.0	6.8	4.3	6.4
Total OECD less the United States	6.7	5.9	5.0	8.1	2.7	4.2	10.7	4.5	0	3.9	6.1	7.1	6.2	4.7	4.3	2.7	8.1	7.4	5.4	6.9

Annex Table 10. **Real imports of goods and services**
Percentage changes from previous period

	Average 1970-77	1979	1980	1981	1982	1983	1984	1985	1986	1987	1988	1989	1990	1991	1992	1993	1994	1995	Projections 1996	1997
United States	5.4	1.7	-6.7	2.6	-1.2	12.6	24.3	6.5	8.4	6.1	4.0	3.9	3.9	-0.7	7.5	9.9	12.0	8.0	6.1	5.6
Japan	6.2	12.9	-7.8	0.4	-2.5	-3.0	10.5	-1.4	2.0	9.5	20.9	18.6	7.9	-4.7	-1.1	1.7	9.0	13.5	14.7	9.5
Germany	4.5	9.2	3.6	-3.1	-1.1	1.4	5.2	4.5	2.7	4.2	5.1	8.3	10.3	12.8	2.2	-5.2	7.1	2.7	3.2	5.9
France	5.4	10.1	2.5	-2.1	2.6	-2.7	2.7	4.5	7.1	7.7	8.6	8.1	6.1	3.0	1.2	-3.5	6.7	5.0	1.9	5.7
Italy	3.8	11.7	2.9	-1.2	-0.3	-1.4	12.3	3.9	2.9	9.1	6.8	7.6	8.0	3.4	4.6	-7.8	9.8	9.8	4.5	5.9
United Kingdom	3.6	9.6	-3.6	-2.8	4.9	6.6	9.9	2.6	6.9	7.8	12.6	7.4	0.5	-5.3	6.5	2.8	5.1	3.1	5.2	5.9
Canada	7.6	11.4	4.9	8.5	-15.2	9.0	17.1	8.7	7.6	7.0	13.8	6.3	2.0	3.3	5.6	8.8	10.5	9.0	4.9	7.2
Total of above countries	5.4	6.8	-3.8	0.9	-1.2	5.8	16.0	4.3	6.0	7.0	8.8	8.0	5.4	0.3	4.5	3.9	9.8	8.0	6.8	6.5
Australia	4.5	2.2	5.0	9.7	5.5	-10.2	21.1	4.6	-4.9	1.9	16.6	20.1	-3.8	-2.4	7.8	5.2	15.3	9.7	6.1	9.4
Austria	6.6	11.7	6.2	-0.8	-3.3	5.5	9.9	6.2	-1.2	4.7	10.0	8.3	7.4	6.4	1.8	-0.7	8.2	7.1	2.0	2.3
Belgium	6.3	9.3	0	-2.9	0.2	-1.5	5.8	0.7	7.6	8.8	8.0	8.8	4.0	2.3	4.2	1.3	7.2	7.9	4.7	6.2
Czech Republic	..																7.8	19.2	15.0	12.0
Denmark	2.8	5.0	-6.8	-1.7	3.8	1.8	5.5	8.1	6.8	-2.0	1.5	4.5	1.2	4.1	0.8	-3.9	12.3	5.4	3.0	5.0
Finland	2.3	18.4	8.3	-4.7	2.5	3.0	1.0	6.8	2.6	9.2	11.1	8.9	-0.6	-11.7	1.1	0.8	12.6	9.6	5.9	7.0
Greece	7.6	7.2	-8.0	3.6	7.0	6.6	0.2	12.8	3.8	16.6	8.0	10.7	8.7	6.0	4.9	1.1	4.1	6.2	7.8	8.4
Iceland	5.2	2.5	3.0	7.1	-0.6	-9.7	9.2	9.4	1.0	23.3	-4.6	-10.3	1.0	5.5	-7.8	-8.6	4.1	4.4	11.0	8.0
Ireland	7.4	13.9	-4.5	1.7	-3.1	4.7	9.9	3.2	5.6	6.2	4.9	13.5	4.9	1.4	6.3	6.8	11.9	11.6	9.5	8.5
Luxembourg	2.5	6.4	3.9	-2.9	-0.3	1.2	13.9	7.0	6.1	7.8	8.5	6.1	4.3	8.1	0.2	-2.5	3.9	3.8	3.4	5.0
Mexico	8.0	29.9	31.9	17.7	-37.9	-33.8	17.8	11.0	-7.6	5.1	36.7	21.3	19.7	16.8	20.9	-1.3	12.9	-27.6	10.0	12.0
Netherlands	4.2	5.9	0.3	-5.9	-0.4	3.9	6.5	6.3	3.5	4.2	7.6	6.7	4.2	4.1	2.1	-1.1	7.5	6.5	3.3	5.3
New Zealand	2.4	17.4	-1.6	3.1	6.9	-7.7	16.5	0.6	2.6	10.0	-1.9	14.6	2.9	-3.9	8.9	8.9	17.9	12.6	7.5	8.4
Norway	3.6	-0.7	3.3	1.5	3.7	0	9.5	5.9	9.9	-7.3	-1.7	2.2	2.5	0.2	0.7	4.0	6.6	4.1	6.7	3.3
Portugal	2.0	12.6	6.9	2.3	3.9	-6.1	-4.4	1.4	17.3	20.2	16.5	7.9	13.7	5.4	11.1	-3.2	8.5	8.6	7.5	6.8
Spain	6.9	11.4	3.3	-4.2	4.8	-0.3	-1.8	7.9	14.4	20.1	14.4	17.3	7.8	9.0	6.9	-5.1	10.4	9.7	7.3	8.0
Sweden	2.3	11.6	0.4	-5.4	3.0	0.8	5.3	6.9	4.5	7.7	5.3	7.4	0.7	-4.9	1.1	-2.5	13.4	8.7	5.0	5.0
Switzerland	4.0	6.8	7.2	-1.3	-2.6	4.4	7.1	5.1	7.1	5.5	5.3	5.4	2.9	-1.7	-3.8	-0.8	9.0	6.4	3.2	4.2
Turkey	3.7	-7.3	69.3	12.5	8.3	16.9	19.7	-6.6	-3.5	23.0	-4.5	6.9	33.0	-5.2	10.9	35.8	-21.9	30.0	14.5	13.4
Total of smaller countries	5.7	10.4	13.2	3.2	-3.1	-3.7	9.0	5.5	3.2	10.0	12.6	12.5	9.3	4.0	7.4	2.8	7.6	5.3	7.3	8.2
Total OECD	5.5	7.5	-0.7	1.3	-1.5	4.1	14.7	4.5	5.5	7.6	9.5	8.8	6.1	1.0	5.0	3.7	9.4	7.5	6.9	6.8
OECD North America	5.8	4.2	-3.3	4.0	-4.6	9.4	23.3	6.9	7.3	6.1	6.8	5.2	4.7	0.8	8.2	9.1	12.0	5.8	6.3	6.1
OECD Europe	4.7	9.1	4.7	-1.8	1.8	1.7	6.6	4.2	5.4	8.7	7.8	8.5	7.4	3.6	3.8	-1.4	6.5	7.0	4.7	6.3
EU	4.7	10.1	1.6	-2.5	1.6	1.0	5.9	4.6	5.7	8.3	8.6	8.7	6.4	4.2	3.7	-3.2	7.8	5.8	4.1	6.0
Total OECD *less* the United States	5.4	10.9	2.9	0.5	-1.7	-1.0	9.0	3.4	3.8	8.5	12.7	11.7	7.4	2.0	3.6	0.1	7.9	7.3	7.4	7.5

Annex Table 11. **Output gaps**[a]

Deviations of actual GDP from potential GDP as a percentage of potential GDP

	1980	1981	1982	1983	1984	1985	1986	1987	1988	1989	1990	1991	1992	1993	1994	1995	Projections 1996	1997
United States	-0.9	-1.1	-5.5	-3.8	-0.2	0.2	0.1	0.2	1.2	2.1	1.1	-1.8	-0.9	-0.7	0.5	0.2	0.2	-0.1
Japan	1.2	0.5	-0.2	-1.7	-1.7	-1.5	-2.9	-3.1	-0.5	0.9	2.8	3.9	2.5	0.4	-1.6	-3.5	-3.7	-3.7
Germany	1.9	-0.3	-3.2	-3.3	-2.2	-1.8	-1.4	-1.9	-0.6	0.1	2.1	3.0	2.7	-1.3	-0.5	-0.6	-1.9	-1.6
France	0.7	-0.9	0.5	-1.0	-2.0	-2.4	-2.2	-2.4	-0.4	1.4	1.6	0.3	-0.5	-3.4	-2.3	-1.8	-2.6	-2.1
Italy	4.3	2.1	-0.7	-2.4	-2.6	-2.3	-1.6	-0.3	0.6	1.9	1.8	1.0	-0.2	-3.0	-2.5	-1.5	-1.8	-1.5
United Kingdom	-0.9	-3.8	-3.9	-2.2	-2.1	-0.6	1.2	3.7	6.1	5.7	3.6	-0.9	-3.4	-3.6	-2.2	-2.1	-2.0	-1.1
Canada	0.1	0.0	-6.4	-6.1	-2.8	-0.7	-0.3	1.1	3.3	3.1	0.8	-3.1	-4.5	-4.6	-2.5	-2.7	-3.1	-2.3
Total of above countries	0.3	-0.6	-3.4	-3.0	-1.3	-0.8	-0.8	-0.6	0.9	1.9	1.8	0.1	-0.1	-1.3	-0.7	-1.1	-1.4	-1.3
Australia	0.4	0.7	-3.2	-5.0	-0.8	0.2	-1.3	0.0	0.8	1.4	-0.2	-4.3	-4.2	-2.6	-0.4	-0.2	-0.2	-0.2
Austria	2.3	-0.8	-2.1	-2.1	-2.8	-2.2	-2.6	-2.6	-0.3	1.6	2.2	1.5	0.6	-1.7	-0.2	-0.3	-1.3	-1.6
Belgium	3.4	1.0	0.5	-1.0	-0.9	-1.8	-2.5	-2.8	-0.6	0.3	1.3	1.2	1.0	-2.5	-2.3	-2.4	-3.4	-2.9
Denmark	0.2	-2.6	-1.7	-1.0	1.1	2.9	3.9	1.8	0.8	-0.1	-0.6	-1.0	-2.7	-3.1	-1.5	-1.0	-2.2	-1.7
Finland	1.6	0.0	0.3	0.1	0.2	0.7	0.4	1.9	4.6	8.1	5.9	-3.3	-7.8	-9.5	-6.2	-3.3	-2.6	-1.5
Greece	3.6	0.3	-2.3	-4.2	-3.2	-1.9	-1.7	-3.1	0.0	1.7	0.3	1.4	0.5	-1.8	-2.0	-1.8	-1.7	-1.8
Ireland	2.1	2.6	0.0	-3.6	-2.7	-2.5	-5.2	-4.4	-4.9	-3.1	0.3	-1.9	-2.6	-4.2	-3.0	-0.6	0.1	0.1
Netherlands	0.7	-1.0	-3.1	-2.5	-0.6	0.8	0.8	-0.4	-0.7	1.0	2.3	1.7	1.1	-1.0	-0.4	-0.4	-1.2	-1.0
Norway[b]	2.8	2.0	0.6	-0.8	0.6	4.3	5.1	3.6	-1.0	-4.5	-5.0	-5.1	-4.4	-4.0	-1.2	0.0	0.2	0.6
Portugal	3.5	2.4	2.0	-0.7	-5.1	-5.2	-3.6	-1.6	0.7	3.1	4.3	3.8	2.5	-1.1	-2.7	-2.5	-2.6	-2.3
Spain	-2.8	-3.8	-3.2	-2.9	-3.3	-2.7	-2.0	0.7	2.6	3.9	4.4	3.5	1.3	-2.1	-2.4	-1.8	-2.1	-2.0
Sweden	0.5	-1.0	-1.5	-1.3	1.2	1.6	2.2	3.5	4.0	4.4	3.7	1.3	-1.0	-4.1	-2.9	-1.6	-2.0	-1.7
Switzerland	2.0	1.9	-0.4	-0.2	0.6	0.9	0.4	-0.9	-1.4	0.4	1.5	0.3	-0.7	-2.1	-2.0	-2.6	-3.3	-3.1
Total of above European countries	1.3	-0.7	-1.8	-2.2	-2.0	-1.5	-0.9	-0.4	1.0	2.0	2.3	1.2	0.0	-2.6	-1.8	-1.5	-2.1	-1.7
Total of above OECD countries	0.3	-0.6	-3.2	-2.9	-1.3	-0.8	-0.8	-0.5	0.9	1.9	1.8	0.2	-0.2	-1.5	-0.9	-1.2	-1.4	-1.4

a) For further details, see Giorno et al., "Potential output, output gaps and structural budget balances", OECD Economic Studies, No. 24, 1995/I.
b) Mainland Norway.

Annex Table 12. Compensation per employee in the business sector

Percentage changes from previous period

	Average 1970-78 [a]	1979	1980	1981	1982	1983	1984	1985	1986	1987	1988	1989	1990	1991	1992	1993	1994	1995	Projections 1996	1997
United States	7.6	8.8	9.4	9.2	6.7	5.1	5.0	4.0	4.0	4.5	4.8	3.2	4.9	3.9	5.6	2.7	2.5	2.8	2.9	3.3
Japan	14.7	6.0	5.8	6.8	4.2	2.4	4.2	3.4	2.4	2.5	3.0	3.8	5.1	4.3	1.0	0.6	1.3	1.1	1.6	1.9
Germany	8.9	6.1	6.9	4.8	4.8	3.8	3.8	3.1	3.7	3.3	3.2	3.0	4.2	-5.7	10.3	3.8	3.5	3.4	3.7	2.9
France	13.3	12.7	15.0	14.2	13.4	10.1	8.1	6.8	4.1	4.0	4.3	4.2	5.1	4.5	3.8	3.2	1.6	1.8	2.8	2.7
Italy	18.4	19.5	20.2	20.5	16.6	15.9	11.9	10.4	7.0	7.7	7.8	9.3	8.5	8.6	6.3	4.0	3.8	4.2	4.5	4.9
United Kingdom	15.7	16.6	19.1	13.2	8.9	7.9	6.1	8.6	8.4	6.5	8.2	8.5	10.0	8.2	4.8	2.3	2.5	2.4	3.5	3.7
Canada	10.1	6.9	9.5	12.2	10.2	4.7	5.1	5.4	3.0	6.7	6.6	5.2	4.2	5.0	3.1	1.5	1.8	1.1	2.7	2.5
Total of above countries	11.0	9.6	10.4	9.9	7.6	5.9	5.6	4.9	4.1	4.4	4.8	4.3	5.5	3.7	5.0	2.5	2.4	2.5	2.9	3.1
Australia	14.1	8.0	10.8	12.3	17.9	5.4	8.9	5.4	6.9	6.4	7.0	6.4	6.5	3.2	4.2	3.2	0.6	2.6	4.7	4.1
Austria	11.5	6.8	7.9	7.5	5.6	5.7	5.5	5.6	7.0	4.2	4.5	4.9	4.0	6.2	4.4	4.4	3.4	4.1	3.2	3.4
Belgium	13.6	6.5	10.2	6.8	7.4	5.5	8.5	5.3	4.3	3.4	1.9	4.3	6.3	7.5	6.0	3.2	3.1	1.4	1.9	2.7
Czech Republic	..	..	..	..	..	..	..	..	..	..	..	..	..	..	..	..	18.4	18.3	17.6	17.8
Denmark	12.8	10.5	11.1	8.7	11.2	9.0	6.0	4.9	5.0	7.3	3.5	4.5	5.4	4.9	4.2	2.2	3.3	3.7	3.8	3.9
Finland	17.3	11.9	14.0	14.2	9.0	9.3	10.1	10.4	7.6	8.0	9.8	10.5	9.4	3.8	4.8	3.7	5.3	3.8	2.9	2.9
Greece	17.9	21.6	14.7	20.4	27.6	21.4	18.6	21.5	13.0	10.0	16.0	23.0	14.6	16.9	10.4	7.3	13.8	13.7	10.2	8.2
Ireland	18.5	18.7	20.0	17.4	14.0	13.9	11.6	9.8	5.1	6.2	7.5	6.5	4.2	3.2	3.5	4.4	2.9	3.0	3.5	3.8
Mexico	..	..	..	33.2	49.3	58.9	56.0	58.2	72.0	124.2	96.6	23.9	29.4	25.1	22.1	12.8	9.3	25.0	27.0	19.0
Netherlands	12.1	6.0	5.9	4.3	6.4	3.8	0.9	2.1	2.6	1.5	1.2	0.8	3.2	4.4	4.2	2.9	2.5	2.6	1.8	2.7
New Zealand	13.8	13.8	17.0	20.6	11.3	3.9	3.3	12.0	19.2	13.8	9.9	6.2	1.9	0.9	4.1	1.0	1.7	2.0	3.1	3.1
Norway	12.0	4.4	12.7	9.4	11.4	7.6	7.4	7.0	10.3	9.5	6.2	5.0	5.3	4.7	3.8	1.2	2.9	2.5	2.8	5.7
Portugal	24.0	20.9	20.1	20.6	19.3	20.8	21.2	19.5	19.0	14.1	9.6	13.1	14.5	15.9	15.9	8.6	6.5	6.5	5.5	4.9
Spain	21.0	18.1	15.8	16.3	15.5	15.5	9.7	8.0	9.4	6.7	6.2	5.4	8.7	9.5	9.5	7.3	3.4	3.2	3.9	3.7
Sweden	12.3	8.3	14.7	10.5	5.5	8.0	9.8	8.4	8.3	7.4	8.1	12.2	9.8	6.3	3.3	5.2	5.6	4.7	5.2	4.9
Switzerland	8.7	4.8	5.8	5.6	6.1	3.4	2.8	3.5	4.8	5.0	4.9	5.5	6.2	7.6	5.7	4.1	1.4	1.4	1.4	1.9
Total of above smaller countries [b]	15.5	11.4	12.2	15.5	18.5	17.9	16.5	16.1	18.7	26.3	21.4	9.6	11.0	10.2	9.1	6.1	5.0	7.6	8.0	6.8
Total of above North American countries [b]	7.8	8.6	9.4	11.0	9.7	8.5	8.3	7.5	8.2	12.3	10.8	4.7	6.4	5.4	6.4	3.3	2.9	4.1	4.4	4.3
Total of above European countries [b]	14.0	12.4	13.6	12.0	10.6	9.3	7.4	7.0	6.1	5.4	5.6	6.1	6.8	4.4	6.6	3.8	3.4	3.4	3.8	3.8
Total of above OECD countries [b]	11.6	9.8	10.7	10.8	9.4	7.8	7.4	6.7	6.6	8.0	7.5	5.1	6.4	4.8	5.7	3.1	2.8	3.4	3.8	3.7

a) Average 1972-78 in the case of the United States and New Zealand.
b) Total excludes Mexico prior to 1981 and the Czech Republic prior to 1994.

Annex Table 13. Unit labour costs in the business sector

Percentage changes from previous period

	Average 1970-78 [a]	1979	1980	1981	1982	1983	1984	1985	1986	1987	1988	1989	1990	1991	1992	1993	1994	1995	Projections 1996	1997
United States	6.2	9.6	10.7	7.2	7.8	1.4	2.2	2.8	2.7	4.3	4.0	2.1	5.0	4.1	2.4	2.5	2.0	2.8	2.1	2.3
Japan	10.4	1.6	4.0	4.5	2.2	1.8	0.6	-0.6	0.3	-0.8	-1.6	0.8	1.6	1.9	0.9	0.6	0.9	0.2	-0.8	-0.3
Germany	5.3	3.1	7.6	4.6	4.5	0.1	0.8	1.6	2.6	2.4	-0.1	0.7	1.3	5.4	5.4	3.1	-0.5	1.0	2.0	0.5
France	9.5	8.8	13.0	11.8	10.4	8.7	5.0	4.0	1.5	1.9	0.4	1.1	3.5	3.4	1.4	2.5	-1.5	0.5	1.2	0.2
Italy	15.1	14.0	17.4	19.7	17.0	15.5	9.0	8.3	4.5	4.5	4.1	6.0	7.1	8.2	4.1	2.2	-0.5	0.3	2.6	2.5
United Kingdom	12.7	14.7	20.8	10.0	4.3	2.7	5.7	5.3	3.4	3.5	6.6	9.5	10.1	6.9	2.8	0.2	0.4	1.1	1.5	1.5
Canada	7.4	7.8	11.5	11.2	9.9	1.4	1.2	3.3	2.8	5.0	4.7	4.8	5.1	4.5	1.3	0.6	-0.8	0.8	2.2	1.3
Total of above countries	8.3	8.0	10.6	8.1	7.2	3.0	2.7	2.8	2.3	3.0	2.5	2.5	4.4	4.3	2.5	2.0	0.8	1.6	1.5	1.4
Australia	11.5	4.2	11.5	10.2	18.5	1.6	3.4	4.5	9.0	3.4	6.5	7.3	6.6	2.5	0.5	-0.8	-1.2	3.8	2.9	2.4
Austria	7.9	1.3	4.6	8.0	2.6	1.5	3.6	2.8	5.5	2.0	0.3	2.1	1.7	5.0	3.6	3.1	-0.3	1.5	1.5	1.4
Belgium	9.5	4.8	4.6	5.4	3.7	3.7	5.5	4.9	3.3	1.8	-1.7	2.4	4.1	5.3	3.4	3.9	0.0	-0.2	0.6	0.5
Czech Republic	..	..	..	..	..	..	..	..	..	..	..	..	..	..	..	..	16.8	14.9	12.7	12.5
Denmark	9.6	6.9	10.4	7.4	7.4	5.8	3.3	3.3	4.3	8.1	1.4	2.1	2.1	1.0	3.3	-1.1	-1.8	3.1	2.4	1.2
Finland	13.2	5.5	10.9	13.7	5.9	5.9	6.7	6.2	3.9	3.4	4.4	4.3	8.7	5.8	0.0	-3.1	-1.5	1.5	1.3	1.0
Greece	12.1	18.2	14.2	27.3	26.1	22.5	15.6	18.7	11.5	10.5	12.4	18.6	16.1	10.0	11.7	9.7	14.3	12.3	8.4	6.6
Ireland	12.7	17.2	19.4	11.5	13.8	12.6	4.8	3.9	5.4	2.9	3.6	1.3	-0.5	0.4	-0.5	2.9	-0.3	-1.7	-0.6	0.9
Mexico	..	..	..	..	..	..	52.5	56.2	82.6	123.7	97.5	23.2	27.2	23.9	23.4	16.7	7.0	35.2	24.3	16.5
Netherlands	8.1	4.9	5.3	3.0	4.6	-0.5	-2.8	0.4	1.9	1.9	0.2	-2.1	1.3	3.5	3.2	2.5	-0.4	1.0	1.0	0.9
New Zealand	14.2	13.7	16.4	15.4	8.5	0.0	-2.6	14.6	17.1	16.0	1.6	4.7	2.7	3.5	4.6	-2.6	2.1	5.2	2.7	1.5
Norway	8.3	-0.4	9.7	9.2	10.6	6.6	4.5	2.6	11.4	11.0	8.6	3.2	2.8	1.5	0.3	-1.5	-0.8	1.6	2.2	4.2
Portugal	20.2	15.3	17.1	19.1	16.5	25.7	23.5	15.2	12.6	10.7	5.8	8.7	12.1	16.9	4.6	7.7	5.4	2.8	2.7	1.9
Spain	15.8	15.9	10.4	12.7	11.9	11.3	5.8	3.8	8.0	3.9	3.6	4.5	7.3	6.9	6.3	3.5	0.1	2.6	2.3	2.1
Sweden	10.4	4.7	14.2	10.4	3.7	5.8	5.0	7.2	6.3	4.9	7.0	11.1	9.3	5.7	-0.7	0.9	1.6	3.8	4.3	3.6
Switzerland	7.4	3.3	3.5	6.6	7.8	2.2	1.9	1.7	4.2	5.5	4.5	4.2	7.3	9.0	4.2	4.3	-0.2	0.8	1.1	0.4
Total of above smaller countries [b]	11.7	8.4	9.7	10.5	10.2	6.9	13.0	13.7	19.7	24.9	19.7	8.0	9.7	8.8	6.9	4.9	2.3	8.4	6.3	4.7
Total of above North American countries [b]	6.3	9.5	10.7	7.6	8.0	1.4	5.4	6.2	7.8	12.0	10.0	3.7	6.4	5.4	3.7	3.3	2.1	4.7	3.5	3.1
Total of above European countries [b]	10.4	9.1	12.3	10.6	8.7	6.6	4.9	4.6	3.9	3.4	2.7	4.0	5.3	5.9	3.7	2.4	0.1	1.4	2.1	1.5
Total of above OECD countries [b]	8.8	8.1	10.4	8.4	7.6	3.6	4.4	4.6	5.2	6.6	5.3	3.4	5.3	5.0	3.2	2.4	1.1	2.7	2.3	1.9

a) Average 1972-78 in the case of the United States and New Zealand.
b) Total excludes Mexico prior to 1984 and the Czech Republic prior to 1994.

Annex Table 14. **GDP deflators**

Percentage changes from previous period

	Average 1971-78	1979	1980	1981	1982	1983	1984	1985	1986	1987	1988	1989	1990	1991	1992	1993	1994	1995	Projections 1996	1997
United States	6.8	8.5	9.2	9.2	6.3	4.2	4.0	3.3	2.7	3.1	3.7	4.2	4.3	4.0	2.7	2.6	2.3	2.4	2.1	2.2
Japan	9.3	2.8	5.4	4.1	1.8	1.8	2.6	2.1	1.8	0.1	0.7	2.0	2.3	2.7	1.7	0.6	0.3	-0.5	-0.3	0.3
Germany	5.1	3.8	5.0	4.2	4.4	3.2	2.1	2.1	3.2	1.9	1.5	2.4	3.2	3.9	5.5	3.8	2.3	2.2	1.5	1.3
France	10.1	10.1	11.4	11.4	11.7	9.7	7.5	5.8	5.2	3.0	2.8	3.0	3.1	3.3	2.1	2.5	1.5	1.6	1.8	1.3
Italy	15.3	15.5	20.2	19.0	17.2	15.1	11.6	8.8	7.9	6.0	6.6	6.2	7.6	7.7	4.5	4.3	3.6	4.8	4.3	3.1
United Kingdom	13.8	14.4	19.5	11.4	7.6	5.2	4.6	5.7	3.3	4.9	6.0	7.1	6.4	6.5	4.4	3.3	1.9	2.4	2.2	2.2
Canada	8.5	10.0	10.6	10.8	8.7	5.0	3.1	2.6	2.4	4.7	4.6	4.8	3.1	2.9	1.2	1.1	0.6	1.7	1.6	1.5
Total of above countries	8.6	8.1	9.8	8.9	6.7	5.0	4.4	3.7	3.2	2.8	3.3	3.9	4.1	4.1	3.0	2.5	1.9	2.0	1.7	1.7
Australia	11.8	10.1	11.0	9.5	11.3	8.2	6.4	6.0	6.9	7.5	8.3	7.5	4.4	2.3	1.3	1.3	1.3	2.6	2.7	2.6
Austria	6.9	4.1	5.2	6.5	6.2	3.9	4.9	3.1	4.3	2.4	1.6	2.9	3.3	4.0	4.2	3.4	3.4	2.1	1.7	1.6
Belgium	8.2	4.5	3.8	4.7	7.1	5.6	5.2	6.1	3.8	2.3	1.8	4.8	3.0	2.7	3.5	4.1	2.6	2.2	2.1	2.0
Czech Republic	..	..	..	..	..	..	..	..	..	..	..	..	..	..	..	..	11.1	11.5	11.0	10.5
Denmark	10.5	7.6	8.2	10.1	10.6	7.6	5.6	4.3	4.6	4.7	3.4	4.2	2.7	2.2	3.2	0.7	1.7	1.7	2.5	2.8
Finland	12.7	8.5	9.8	11.5	8.5	8.3	8.8	5.4	4.5	4.7	7.0	6.1	5.9	2.5	0.7	2.4	1.1	3.7	1.5	1.7
Greece	14.0	18.6	17.7	19.8	25.1	19.1	20.3	17.6	17.6	14.2	15.6	14.5	20.6	20.2	14.5	14.0	10.8	9.3	7.6	6.4
Iceland	34.2	40.9	52.5	49.8	53.3	76.1	25.4	31.3	25.4	19.6	22.9	19.8	16.8	7.6	3.7	2.4	2.2	2.9	2.4	2.9
Ireland	14.1	13.7	14.7	17.4	15.2	11.5	6.4	5.2	5.7	2.2	3.4	5.4	-0.8	1.7	2.0	4.1	1.2	1.4	1.5	1.4
Luxembourg	7.4	6.4	7.9	7.2	10.8	6.8	4.4	3.0	3.8	-1.0	4.0	6.0	3.0	3.0	4.5	4.7	1.9	3.1	1.9	1.9
Mexico	17.5	20.2	28.7	26.0	61.0	90.7	59.0	56.5	74.1	138.5	99.9	25.8	29.4	21.7	14.6	10.0	7.3	35.4	26.0	15.0
Netherlands	8.4	4.1	5.5	5.4	5.4	2.1	1.4	1.8	0.2	-0.7	1.2	1.2	2.3	2.7	2.3	2.0	2.3	1.9	1.3	1.9
New Zealand	12.2	15.7	15.8	16.6	12.0	4.6	6.2	15.6	14.1	15.5	6.8	7.9	3.2	2.6	2.2	1.3	1.6	2.0	2.2	1.9
Norway	8.1	6.6	14.6	14.0	10.2	6.1	6.4	5.0	-1.4	7.2	4.4	6.3	4.2	2.7	-0.5	2.6	0.2	2.8	2.4	2.2
Portugal	16.6	19.4	20.9	17.6	20.7	24.6	24.7	21.7	19.5	11.1	10.9	11.4	12.9	14.2	13.5	7.4	5.6	5.8	4.2	3.7
Spain	16.1	16.9	13.4	12.6	13.9	11.7	11.6	7.7	11.1	5.9	5.6	7.1	7.3	7.1	6.9	4.3	3.9	4.8	3.4	2.9
Sweden	10.0	7.9	13.0	9.5	8.3	10.0	7.6	6.6	6.9	4.8	6.5	8.0	8.9	7.6	1.1	2.6	2.7	4.1	1.6	2.8
Switzerland	5.3	2.0	2.9	6.9	7.1	3.0	2.8	3.1	3.8	2.6	2.4	4.2	5.7	5.5	2.6	2.0	1.4	1.4	0.9	1.2
Turkey	23.6	75.8	88.1	44.0	28.2	26.1	48.2	53.1	36.0	33.3	70.1	74.9	58.7	58.5	63.8	67.7	107.0	81.6	70.0	60.0
Total of smaller countries	13.7	18.0	20.7	16.0	20.4	23.0	19.8	18.9	20.1	28.2	25.9	15.8	14.6	13.1	11.6	10.7	13.5	15.6	12.5	9.9
Total OECD	9.5	9.9	11.8	10.2	9.2	8.3	7.2	6.5	6.3	7.4	7.4	6.1	6.0	5.7	4.5	3.9	4.0	4.5	3.7	3.2
Total OECD *less* Turkey	9.2	8.7	10.5	9.6	8.9	8.0	6.5	5.6	5.7	7.0	6.3	4.9	5.1	4.8	3.5	2.8	2.2	3.1	2.6	2.3
OECD North America	7.6	9.3	10.5	10.4	10.0	9.8	7.4	6.6	7.2	11.9	9.9	5.6	5.8	5.1	3.4	3.0	2.5	4.5	3.6	2.9
OECD Europe	11.5	13.2	15.7	12.3	11.1	9.1	8.7	7.9	6.8	5.3	7.2	8.0	7.7	7.8	6.9	6.4	7.2	6.4	5.4	4.7
OECD Europe *less* Turkey	10.9	10.3	12.4	10.8	10.3	8.4	6.9	5.8	5.5	4.0	4.3	4.9	5.3	5.5	4.4	3.6	2.7	3.1	2.6	2.2
EU	11.1	10.5	12.6	10.9	10.3	8.5	7.0	5.9	5.6	4.0	4.3	4.9	5.3	5.5	4.5	3.7	2.7	3.0	2.5	2.1
Total OECD *less* the United States	11.1	10.7	13.4	10.8	10.9	10.7	9.1	8.3	8.4	10.0	9.6	7.2	7.0	6.7	5.6	4.7	5.0	5.7	4.7	3.9

Annex Table 15. **Private consumption deflators**

Percentage changes from previous period

	Average 1971-78	1979	1980	1981	1982	1983	1984	1985	1986	1987	1988	1989	1990	1991	1992	1993	1994	1995	Projections 1996	1997
United States	6.7	9.0	10.9	8.9	5.8	4.5	3.8	3.7	2.9	3.8	4.1	4.9	5.1	4.2	3.3	2.6	2.4	2.3	2.0	2.3
Japan	10.1	3.6	7.5	4.6	2.7	2.1	2.6	2.3	0.7	0.5	0.5	2.0	2.6	2.5	1.9	1.2	0.7	-0.5	-0.4	0.6
Germany	5.0	4.2	5.8	6.2	5.1	3.2	2.5	1.8	-0.6	0.5	1.3	2.9	2.7	3.7	4.7	4.0	2.8	2.0	1.6	1.5
France	9.8	10.8	13.3	13.0	11.5	9.7	7.7	5.8	2.7	3.2	2.7	3.4	2.8	3.2	2.4	2.2	2.1	1.6	1.9	1.3
Italy	15.1	14.7	20.4	18.0	17.1	14.9	12.0	9.0	6.3	5.3	5.7	6.4	6.2	6.8	5.4	4.8	4.7	5.7	3.9	2.9
United Kingdom	13.5	13.6	16.2	11.2	8.7	4.8	5.0	5.3	4.0	4.3	5.0	5.9	5.5	7.4	4.7	3.5	2.5	2.6	2.5	2.5
Canada	7.7	8.5	10.0	11.2	10.2	6.3	3.9	3.7	3.8	4.0	3.8	4.7	4.3	4.8	1.3	1.7	0.7	1.6	1.4	1.4
Total of above countries	8.5	8.4	11.0	9.1	6.8	5.2	4.5	3.9	2.5	3.0	3.2	4.2	4.3	4.2	3.3	2.7	2.2	2.0	1.7	1.8
Australia	11.4	9.5	10.3	9.3	10.4	9.2	6.4	6.9	8.5	7.7	7.0	6.6	6.0	3.7	1.8	2.0	1.4	2.5	3.0	2.6
Austria	6.7	4.5	6.4	7.6	6.0	3.4	5.6	3.3	1.9	1.0	1.4	2.7	3.3	3.4	3.9	3.4	3.0	2.3	1.9	1.7
Belgium	7.9	3.9	6.4	8.7	7.8	7.1	5.7	5.9	0.7	1.9	1.5	3.7	3.5	2.5	2.0	3.1	3.0	1.5	2.1	1.8
Czech Republic	:	:	:	:	:	:	:	:	:	:	:	:	:	:	:	:	10.7	9.1	8.4	8.0
Denmark	10.6	10.4	10.7	12.0	10.2	6.7	6.4	4.3	2.9	4.6	4.0	4.3	2.7	2.4	2.0	0.2	1.7	1.7	2.2	2.5
Finland	12.8	7.7	11.2	11.9	9.4	8.7	7.4	6.1	3.1	3.6	4.6	5.0	6.0	5.6	4.1	4.2	1.4	1.1	1.5	2.0
Greece	13.1	16.5	21.9	22.7	20.7	18.0	17.9	18.2	22.3	15.7	14.2	13.5	20.0	19.7	15.0	13.7	10.8	9.3	7.8	6.5
Iceland	33.0	46.3	55.6	51.0	52.0	82.2	31.2	32.7	20.0	16.0	25.6	23.2	17.0	6.9	4.7	4.6	1.6	1.8	2.2	2.9
Ireland	13.8	14.9	18.6	19.6	14.9	10.2	7.4	5.0	3.7	2.4	3.9	4.0	2.0	2.8	2.5	1.7	2.7	2.5	2.3	2.4
Luxembourg	6.9	4.9	7.5	9.6	10.6	8.3	6.5	4.3	1.3	1.7	2.7	3.6	3.6	2.9	2.8	3.7	1.8	2.0	1.7	1.8
Mexico	16.7	17.6	24.8	26.3	56.9	90.5	65.3	59.0	83.1	133.5	109.6	23.4	28.3	21.8	14.0	9.3	6.6	39.1	33.0	17.0
Netherlands	8.0	4.9	6.8	6.4	5.0	2.9	1.9	2.4	0.3	0.2	0.5	1.2	2.2	3.2	3.1	2.3	2.4	1.0	1.8	1.8
New Zealand	11.4	14.0	17.9	14.7	15.4	7.5	7.2	17.2	12.2	13.9	6.9	6.4	5.8	2.9	1.9	0.3	1.3	1.6	1.9	2.0
Norway	8.6	5.1	10.0	13.5	11.0	8.4	6.4	5.9	7.7	7.9	6.2	4.8	4.7	3.9	2.7	2.2	1.3	2.4	1.7	2.4
Portugal	17.3	25.2	21.6	20.2	20.3	25.8	28.5	19.4	13.0	9.6	11.4	11.8	11.6	12.6	11.1	7.1	4.8	4.1	3.2	2.7
Spain	15.8	16.5	15.7	14.6	14.6	12.6	11.9	7.1	9.4	5.7	5.0	6.6	6.5	6.4	6.4	5.5	4.9	4.6	3.5	3.0
Sweden	9.8	7.9	13.8	12.1	10.5	10.8	7.7	7.0	5.2	5.6	6.1	7.0	9.9	10.3	2.2	5.7	3.1	2.7	1.8	2.8
Switzerland	5.2	4.5	4.5	6.6	5.5	2.6	3.3	3.7	0.3	1.5	2.3	3.5	5.3	5.7	4.2	3.1	1.0	1.3	0.9	1.3
Turkey	23.4	78.6	87.9	44.4	27.5	25.6	49.1	50.9	30.3	48.7	59.5	82.8	60.1	57.9	63.8	67.5	104.1	94.6	70.0	60.0
Total of smaller countries	13.4	18.1	21.1	17.2	19.7	23.4	21.1	19.2	20.3	28.9	26.0	15.7	14.7	13.3	11.6	10.9	13.3	16.9	13.6	10.2
Total OECD	9.4	10.2	12.8	10.6	9.2	8.5	7.5	6.7	5.7	7.7	7.4	6.3	6.2	5.8	4.8	4.2	4.3	4.7	3.9	3.4
Total OECD less Turkey	9.2	9.0	11.5	10.0	8.8	8.2	6.8	5.9	5.3	6.9	6.5	5.0	5.2	4.9	3.8	3.1	2.5	3.2	2.7	2.4
OECD North America	7.4	9.5	11.7	10.2	9.4	10.1	7.7	7.2	8.0	12.1	10.8	6.1	6.5	5.4	3.8	3.0	2.5	4.6	3.9	3.1
OECD Europe	11.3	13.4	16.2	13.3	11.3	9.2	9.1	7.7	4.9	5.5	6.2	8.2	7.2	7.8	7.1	6.7	7.6	6.9	5.4	4.7
OECD Europe less Turkey	10.7	10.4	12.9	11.9	10.5	8.4	7.3	5.7	3.8	3.6	3.8	4.8	4.8	5.5	4.5	3.9	3.3	3.0	2.5	2.2
EU	10.8	10.6	13.2	12.0	10.6	8.5	7.4	5.7	3.8	3.5	3.8	4.8	4.8	5.5	4.6	4.0	3.3	3.0	2.5	2.2
Total OECD less the United States	11.1	10.9	14.0	11.6	11.2	10.9	9.7	8.5	7.4	10.0	9.3	7.2	6.8	6.8	5.7	5.1	5.4	6.1	4.9	4.0

Annex Table 16. Consumer prices[a]

Percentage changes from previous period

	Average 1970-76	1977	1978	1979	1980	1981	1982	1983	1984	1985	1986	1987	1988	1989	1990	1991	1992	1993	1994	1995
United States	6.6	6.5	7.6	11.3	13.5	10.3	6.1	3.2	4.3	3.5	1.9	3.7	4.1	4.8	5.4	4.2	3.0	3.0	2.6	2.8
Japan	11.0	8.2	4.2	3.7	7.8	4.9	2.7	1.9	2.2	2.0	0.6	0.1	0.7	2.3	3.1	3.3	1.7	1.3	0.7	-0.1
Germany	5.8	3.7	2.7	4.0	5.4	6.3	5.2	3.3	2.4	2.1	-0.1	0.2	1.3	2.8	2.7	3.6	5.1	4.5	2.7	1.8
France	9.0	9.4	9.1	10.8	13.6	13.4	11.8	9.6	7.4	5.8	2.7	3.1	2.7	3.6	3.4	3.2	2.4	2.1	1.7	1.7
Italy[b]	11.6	19.3	12.4	15.7	21.2	19.3	16.4	14.9	10.6	8.6	6.1	4.6	5.0	6.6	6.1	6.5	5.3	4.2	3.9	5.4
United Kingdom	13.6	15.8	8.3	13.4	18.0	11.9	8.6	4.6	5.0	6.1	3.4	4.1	4.9	7.8	9.5	5.9	3.7	1.6	2.5	3.4
Canada	7.4	8.0	8.9	9.1	10.2	12.4	10.8	5.8	4.3	4.0	4.2	4.4	4.0	5.0	4.8	5.6	1.5	1.8	0.2	2.2
Total of above countries	8.3	8.4	7.2	9.8	12.7	10.3	7.2	4.7	4.6	3.9	2.1	2.9	3.3	4.5	5.0	4.3	3.1	2.7	2.2	2.4
Australia	10.8	12.3	7.9	9.1	10.2	9.6	11.2	10.1	3.9	6.7	9.1	8.5	7.3	7.5	7.3	3.2	1.0	1.8	1.9	4.6
Austria	7.3	5.5	3.6	3.7	6.3	6.8	5.4	3.3	5.7	3.2	1.7	1.4	1.9	2.6	3.3	3.3	4.0	3.6	3.0	2.2
Belgium	8.5	7.1	4.5	4.5	6.7	7.1	8.7	7.7	6.3	4.9	1.3	1.6	1.2	3.1	3.4	3.2	2.4	2.8	2.4	1.5
Czech Republic																			10.0	9.1
Denmark	9.2	11.1	10.0	9.6	12.3	11.7	10.1	6.9	6.3	4.7	3.7	4.0	4.5	4.8	2.6	2.4	2.1	1.3	2.0	2.1
Finland	12.1	12.6	7.8	7.5	11.6	12.0	9.6	8.3	7.1	5.9	2.9	4.1	5.1	6.6	6.1	4.3	2.9	2.2	1.1	1.0
Greece	12.4	12.4	12.6	19.1	24.7	24.5	21.0	20.2	18.5	19.3	23.0	16.4	13.5	13.7	20.4	19.5	15.9	14.4	10.9	9.3
Iceland[c]	25.4	30.3	43.8	44.4	58.5	51.8	50.2	84.0	30.9	32.0	22.1	18.3	25.7	20.8	15.5	6.8	3.1	4.0	1.6	1.7
Ireland	14.0	13.6	7.7	13.2	18.3	20.4	17.1	10.5	8.6	5.5	3.8	3.1	2.1	4.1	3.3	3.2	3.1	1.4	2.3	2.5
Luxembourg	7.6	6.7	3.1	4.5	6.3	8.1	9.4	8.7	5.6	4.1	0.3	-0.1	1.4	3.4	3.7	3.1	3.2	3.6	2.2	1.9
Mexico	12.7	29.1	17.5	18.2	26.4	27.9	58.7	102.3	65.3	57.8	86.2	131.8	114.2	20.0	26.7	22.7	15.5	9.8	7.0	35.0
Netherlands	8.7	6.4	4.1	4.2	6.5	6.7	5.9	2.7	3.3	2.3	0.1	-0.7	0.7	1.1	2.5	3.2	3.2	2.6	2.8	1.9
New Zealand	11.3	14.4	11.9	13.8	17.1	15.4	16.1	7.4	6.1	15.4	13.2	15.7	6.4	5.7	6.1	2.6	1.0	1.3	1.8	3.8
Norway	8.5	9.1	8.1	4.8	10.9	13.7	11.3	8.4	6.3	5.7	7.2	8.7	6.7	4.6	4.1	3.4	2.3	2.3	1.4	2.5
Portugal	16.0	27.2	22.5	23.9	16.6	20.0	22.4	25.5	28.8	19.6	11.8	9.4	9.7	12.6	13.4	11.4	8.9	6.5	5.2	4.1
Spain	13.0	24.5	19.8	15.7	15.6	14.5	14.4	12.2	11.3	8.8	8.8	5.2	4.8	6.8	6.7	5.9	5.9	4.6	4.7	4.7
Sweden	8.3	11.4	10.0	7.2	13.7	12.1	8.6	8.9	8.0	7.4	4.2	4.2	6.1	6.6	10.4	9.7	2.6	4.7	2.4	2.9
Switzerland	6.7	1.3	1.0	3.6	4.0	6.5	5.7	2.9	2.9	3.4	0.8	1.4	1.9	3.2	5.4	5.9	4.0	3.3	0.9	1.8
Turkey[d]	15.8	27.1	45.3	58.7	110.2	36.6	32.1	31.4	48.4	45.0	34.6	38.9	73.7	63.3	60.3	66.0	70.1	66.1	105.1	89.1
Total of above smaller countries	9.3	10.0	7.7	7.9	10.3	10.5	10.4	8.9	8.3	8.0	8.1	11.1	16.8	10.6	13.7	14.7	15.7	17.5	32.4	45.7
Total OECD[e]	8.8	10.1	8.7	11.0	14.6	11.6	10.0	9.3	8.1	7.0	5.9	7.8	8.6	6.2	6.8	6.1	4.9	4.3	4.4	5.5
Total OECD less Turkey[e]	8.7	9.8	8.0	10.1	13.0	11.1	9.6	9.0	7.4	6.2	5.4	7.3	7.5	5.2	5.9	5.1	3.7	3.1	2.6	3.8
OECD North America	6.6	6.6	7.7	11.1	13.3	10.5	6.5	3.5	4.5	3.8	2.7	5.5	7.4	5.7	6.8	5.8	4.1	3.6	2.9	6.4
OECD Europe[e]	10.2	12.6	10.2	12.3	17.1	13.4	11.5	9.4	8.9	7.8	5.2	5.0	6.7	7.8	8.1	7.8	7.5	6.4	7.6	7.6
OECD Europe less Turkey[e]	9.9	12.0	8.7	10.3	13.2	12.2	10.6	8.4	7.1	6.0	3.7	3.3	3.7	5.2	5.7	5.2	4.4	3.5	3.0	3.1
European Union	10.0	12.3	8.9	10.5	13.4	12.3	10.7	8.5	7.2	6.1	3.7	3.3	3.6	5.2	5.7	5.2	4.5	3.6	3.1	3.1
Total OECD less the United States[e]	12.7	15.1	10.0	10.6	15.9	13.3	14.8	16.3	12.0	10.2	9.5	11.2	12.1	7.3	7.8	7.4	6.2	5.1	5.4	7.2

a) Aggregates were computed using the previous year's consumer expenditure expressed in private consumption purchasing power parities.
b) Index for households of wage and salary earners.
c) Excluding rent.
d) Until 1981: Istanbul index (154 items); from 1982: Turkish index.
e) The Czech Republic is excluded from the aggregates.

Annex Table 17. Oil and other primary commodity markets

	1980	1981	1982	1983	1984	1985	1986	1987	1988	1989	1990	1991	1992	1993	1994	1995	Projections 1996	Projections 1997
Oil market conditions[a] (in million barrels per day)																		
Demand																		
OECD[b]	38.8	36.6	34.9	34.3	35.0	34.6	35.7	36.4	37.5	37.9	38.0	38.2	38.8	39.1	39.9	40.3	41.0	..
of which: North America[b]	19.4	18.5	17.6	17.2	17.7	17.6	18.1	18.6	19.2	19.3	18.9	18.6	18.9	19.2	19.7	19.8	20.2	..
Europe[b]	13.7	12.7	12.2	12.0	12.0	11.9	12.4	12.5	12.7	12.8	13.0	13.4	13.6	13.6	13.6	13.9	14.1	..
Pacific	5.7	5.4	5.1	5.1	5.3	5.1	5.2	5.3	5.6	5.8	6.1	6.2	6.3	6.3	6.6	6.7	6.8	..
Non-OECD	23.8	24.2	24.4	24.7	25.0	25.5	26.1	26.9	27.6	28.2	28.5	28.7	28.4	28.6	28.7	29.6	30.6	..
Total	62.6	60.8	59.3	59.0	60.0	60.1	61.8	63.3	65.1	66.1	66.5	66.9	67.2	67.6	68.6	69.9	71.6	..
Supply																		
OECD[b]	15.0	15.1	15.4	16.0	16.8	17.1	16.9	16.9	16.7	16.0	15.9	16.4	16.6	16.8	17.7	18.0	18.8	..
OPEC Total	27.6	23.6	19.9	18.6	18.8	17.6	19.9	19.7	21.8	23.8	25.1	25.4	26.5	27.0	27.4	27.7	..	..
Former USSR	12.1	12.3	12.3	12.4	12.3	12.0	12.3	12.6	12.5	12.2	11.5	10.4	9.0	7.9	7.2	7.2	7.2	..
Other non-OECD[c]	9.4	9.6	10.6	11.1	11.9	12.6	12.9	13.3	13.8	14.1	14.6	14.8	15.2	15.8	16.3	17.1	..	..
Total	64.1	60.6	58.2	58.1	59.8	59.2	62.0	62.4	64.8	66.1	67.0	66.9	67.2	67.4	68.5	70.0	..	..
Trade																		
OECD net imports[b]	24.3	21.4	19.0	18.0	18.5	17.3	19.1	19.8	20.7	22.0	22.3	21.8	22.2	22.5	22.5	22.0	..	..
Former USSR net exports	3.2	3.2	3.2	3.2	3.2	2.9	3.4	3.6	3.6	3.4	3.0	2.1	2.1	2.2	2.4	2.4	2.6	..
Other non-OECD net exports[c]	25.3	21.3	18.4	17.4	18.0	16.7	19.1	18.7	20.5	21.9	22.7	21.8	22.3	22.1	22.2	22.4	..	..
Prices																		
OECD crude oil import price (cif, $ per bl)[d]	33.9	37.3	34.9	30.0	29.0	27.5	15.0	17.9	14.8	17.5	22.3	19.3	18.5	16.4	15.6	17.2	17.6	16.8
Prices of other primary commodities[d] (US$ indices)																		
Food and tropical beverages	173	141	104	111	107	91	98	92	114	115	106	100	97	98	118	124	138	141
of which: Food	168	136	95	101	92	76	78	84	109	113	105	100	99	99	111	118	138	141
Tropical beverages	207	170	161	169	193	176	218	142	143	124	108	100	85	92	160	162	139	142
Agricultural raw materials	106	92	80	85	85	79	79	92	101	100	106	100	97	94	108	122	112	114
Minerals, ores and metals	107	90	78	84	78	75	71	84	123	123	111	100	96	82	93	112	106	106
Total	145	119	93	100	96	85	88	90	114	114	107	100	97	93	110	121	125	127
Memorandum item																		
Export prices of OECD manufactures (dollar index)	77	73	70	68	66	65	78	88	93	92	100	100	103	99	101	111	108	109

a) Based on data published in IEA, Oil Market Report, May 1996; Annual Statistical Supplement, September 1993.
b) Excluding Mexico and Czech Republic.
c) Including Mexico and Czech Republic.
d) Indices through 1995 are based on data compiled by IEA for oil and by UNCTAD for the prices of other primary commodities; OECD Secretariat projections for 1996 and 1997.

Annex Table 18. **Labour force**[a]

Percentage changes from previous period

	1992 Labour force (thousands)	1979	1980	1981	1982	1983	1984	1985	1986	1987	1988	1989	1990	1991	1992	1993	1994	1995	Projections	
																			1996	1997
United States[b]	128 099	2.7	1.9	1.6	1.4	1.2	1.8	1.7	2.1	1.7	1.5	1.8	1.6	0.4	1.4	0.8	1.4	1.0	1.0	1.1
Japan	65 768	1.2	1.0	1.0	1.2	2.0	0.7	0.6	1.0	1.0	1.4	1.7	1.8	1.9	1.1	0.6	0.4	0.3	0.2	0.3
Germany	38 821	1.2	1.5	1.3	0.9	0.2	0.2	0.8	1.0	0.7	0.8	0.7	2.2	1.7	-0.7	-0.5	0.1	-0.4	0.2	0.2
France	25 138	0.9	0.6	0.8	1.1	0	0.6	0.5	0.6	0.5	0.5	0.7	0.5	0.6	-0.4	0.2	0.9	0.3	0.2	0.4
Italy	23 023	1.4	1.4	0.1	0.3	1.0	1.1	0.4	1.8	0.1	0.8	-0.4	0	0.1	-0.6	-1.0	-0.5	0.2	0.4	0.1
United Kingdom	28 407	0.9	0.4	-0.3	-0.4	0.7	2.5	1.4	0.3	1.0	1.2	0.9	0.1	-0.6	-0.6	-0.4	-0.4	-0.5	0	0.1
Canada	14 481	3.2	3.0	2.9	0.6	1.6	1.9	2.1	1.9	1.9	2.0	1.8	1.3	0.6	0.5	1.3	1.1	0.7	1.2	1.7
Total of above countries	323 737	1.8	1.4	1.1	1.0	1.1	1.3	1.2	1.4	1.2	1.3	1.3	1.3	0.7	0.6	0.4	0.7	0.5	0.6	0.7
Australia	8 603	1.1	2.8	1.7	1.5	1.3	1.8	2.7	3.4	2.2	2.7	3.6	2.4	0.6	0.7	0.6	1.7	2.8	1.7	1.7
Austria	3 650	0.1	0.1	0.6	-0.1	-0.5	0	0.5	0.8	0.3	0.4	1.1	2.3	2.3	1.6	0.5	0	-0.3	-0.3	0.1
Belgium	4 188	1.2	0.3	0.6	0.6	0.5	-0.1	-0.5	-0.1	0.1	0.3	0.4	0.8	0.8	0.7	0.9	0.4	0.3	0	0.1
Czech Republic[c]		..	..	..	..	..	..	..	..	..	..	..	..	..	..	..	0.8	1.8	1.7	1.5
Denmark	2 828	0	0.4	1.0	1.2	1.0	1.3	1.4	1.3	0.8	0.2	0.2	-0.7	-0.5	0.2	0.2	-0.7	-0.6	-0.6	0.5
Finland	2 502	1.1	1.8	1.3	1.5	0.6	0.7	0.8	0.1	-0.6	-0.3	0.5	-0.1	-0.9	-1.2	-0.7	-0.2	0.7	0.2	0.6
Greece	4 034	1.1	2.3	6.6	1.0	3.4	0.7	0.6	-0.1	-0.1	2.0	0.2	0.8	-1.7	2.5	2.1	1.8	1.3	0.9	1.2
Iceland	129	1.0	3.2	4.9	3.0	1.2	1.7	3.2	2.8	5.6	-2.6	-0.5	-0.8	-0.6	2.0	1.0	1.4	1.3	1.0	1.0
Ireland	1 376	2.0	1.1	2.0	1.9	0.8	0	-0.3	0.3	0.6	-0.8	-0.6	1.7	1.5	1.4	2.0	1.9	1.3	1.8	1.8
Luxembourg	167	0.7	0.5	0.7	0	-0.1	0.6	-0.3	1.1	1.5	1.2	1.4	1.3	1.5	0.4	0.2	1.4	1.0	0.1	0.5
Mexico[d]	14 294	..	..	..	..	1.4	0.1	-0.2	1.6	1.2	4.3	2.9	1.7	5.4	5.6	5.1	1.7	1.7	1.7	2.0
Netherlands	6 221	1.3	1.6	0.8	1.1	0.7	1.9	2.5	2.1	1.2	2.1	0.9	2.0	2.0	1.6	1.9	1.0	1.0	1.1	1.1
New Zealand	1 635	1.6	0.7	1.5	1.1	0.7	1.0	1.8	2.7	0.9	-1.6	-1.0	1.6	1.4	0.4	1.1	2.7	2.6	2.1	2.0
Norway	2 130	1.2	0.2	1.8	1.1	0.9	1.0	1.7	2.9	2.0	0.6	-1.3	-0.6	-0.7	0.2	0	0.9	1.5	0.9	0.9
Portugal[e]	4 496	1.5	2.0	0.1	-0.2	4.3	0.7	-0.3	0.1	1.0	1.1	1.5	1.8	2.4	-6.4	-0.5	1.3	-0.3	0.3	0.3
Spain	15 155	0.1	0	0.2	1.2	1.1	0.6	0.8	1.7	2.4	1.6	1.3	1.4	0.4	0.5	1.1	1.0	1.0	0.7	0.8
Sweden	4 442	1.4	1.2	0.3	0.5	0.4	0.4	-0.5	0.4	0.6	1.0	1.2	1.1	-0.6	-1.9	-2.7	-1.2	1.3	0.2	0.3
Switzerland	3 901	1.1	2.2	2.3	0.7	0.5	1.2	1.8	2.1	2.4	2.5	2.5	3.2	1.7	-0.1	1.5	0	-0.4	0.2	0.3
Turkey[f]	20 663	0.2	0.6	-0.2	0.9	1.8	1.4	1.2	2.7	2.8	1.6	2.0	1.4	0.1	3.5	0.6	3.0	1.8	2.0	2.0
Total of smaller countries[g]	100 414	0.7	1.0	0.9	0.9	1.4	0.9	0.9	1.6	1.7	1.8	1.6	1.5	1.1	1.5	1.3	1.4	1.3	1.1	1.3
Total OECD[g]	424 150	1.6	1.3	1.1	1.0	1.2	1.2	1.1	1.2	1.3	1.4	1.4	1.4	0.8	0.8	0.6	0.9	0.7	0.7	0.8
OECD North America[g]	156 874	2.7	2.0	1.7	1.4	1.2	1.8	1.7	2.0	1.7	1.8	1.9	1.6	0.8	1.7	1.3	1.4	1.1	1.1	1.3
OECD Europe[g]	191 270	0.9	0.9	0.6	0.6	0.8	1.0	0.7	1.1	1.0	1.0	0.8	1.0	0.5	0.1	0	0.5	0.3	0.5	0.4
EU[g]	164 447	1.0	0.9	0.6	0.6	0.7	0.9	0.6	0.9	0.8	0.9	0.6	0.9	0.5	-0.3	-0.1	0.2	0.1	0.3	0.4
Total OECD *less* the United States[g]	296 051	1.1	1.1	0.9	0.8	1.2	1.0	0.8	1.2	1.1	1.3	1.2	1.3	1.0	0.6	0.5	0.6	0.5	0.6	0.7

a) For sources and definitions; see "Sources and Methods".
b) Break in series as of January 1994.
c) No data for 1992, the labour force in 1993 was 5 172 000.
d) Data based on the National Survey of Urban Employment; see "Sources and Methods".
e) Break in series in 1992.
f) The figures incorporate important revisions to Turkish data; see "Sources and Methods".
g) Totals exclude Mexico prior to 1988.

	Average 1971-78	1979	1980	1981	1982	1983	1984	1985	1986	1987	1988	1989	1990	1991	1992	1993	1994	1995	Projections 1996	1997
United States	67.4	70.7	71.0	71.3	71.6	71.7	72.3	72.8	73.6	74.3	74.9	75.8	76.5	76.2	76.6	76.6	77.0	77.1	77.1	77.2
Japan	71.1	71.8	71.8	72.1	72.3	73.0	72.7	72.5	72.4	72.5	72.8	73.3	74.1	75.2	75.8	76.1	76.4	76.5	76.8	77.2
Germany	68.5	68.1	68.3	68.1	67.8	67.3	67.0	67.4	68.0	68.4	68.7	68.6	69.1	71.1	70.2	69.3	69.1	68.6	68.5	68.5
France	68.0	68.7	68.4	68.0	67.8	66.9	66.6	66.4	66.5	66.5	66.4	66.5	66.6	66.7	66.8	66.6	67.1	67.1	67.0	67.1
Italy	58.4	59.5	60.1	59.8	59.2	59.0	58.7	58.5	59.4	59.4	59.3	59.4	59.2	59.2	58.7	59.0	58.9	59.1	59.4	59.6
United Kingdom	73.2	74.1	74.0	73.4	72.7	72.7	73.8	74.7	74.7	75.3	76.1	76.7	76.7	75.9	75.4	75.0	74.6	74.0	73.9	74.1
Canada	68.4	72.1	73.0	73.9	73.3	73.6	74.2	75.1	75.8	76.5	77.3	77.8	77.9	77.3	76.5	76.3	76.1	75.7	75.7	75.9
Total of above countries	68.1	69.8	70.0	70.1	70.0	70.1	70.3	70.6	71.0	71.5	71.8	72.4	72.9	73.1	73.1	73.1	73.2	73.2	73.3	73.5
Australia	70.0	69.7	70.5	70.4	70.1	69.8	69.9	70.6	71.7	71.9	72.4	73.6	74.2	74.0	73.7	73.5	73.9	75.1	75.5	75.8
Austria	69.1	69.2	68.6	68.1	67.2	66.2	65.6	65.5	65.9	65.9	66.1	66.7	67.4	68.1	68.8	68.0	67.8	67.1	66.5	66.2
Belgium	61.5	62.1	62.3	62.6	62.3	62.1	61.6	61.3	61.1	61.1	61.1	61.3	61.9	62.3	62.7	63.1	63.3	63.4	63.3	63.4
Czech Republic	..							..								83.3	84.1	84.7	85.8	86.7
Denmark	76.7	79.3	79.2	79.4	79.9	80.3	81.1	81.9	82.6	82.9	82.8	82.8	81.9	81.2	81.1	81.0	80.2	79.6	79.1	79.4
Finland	72.2	74.5	75.5	76.0	76.5	76.5	76.5	76.9	76.8	76.3	76.1	76.5	76.1	75.0	73.9	73.2	72.9	73.2	73.2	73.4
Greece	56.6	55.4	55.9	58.7	58.7	59.9	59.8	59.6	59.1	58.7	59.5	59.2	59.2	57.3	58.1	58.9	59.6	60.0	60.3	60.4
Iceland	72.1	73.1	74.3	76.7	77.6	77.3	77.6	79.3	80.8	84.0	80.1	78.7	77.5	76.0	77.2	77.7	78.4	79.1	79.6	80.0
Ireland	63.9	63.2	63.2	63.5	63.9	63.6	62.8	62.2	62.2	62.3	61.6	61.4	62.3	62.3	62.2	62.7	63.2	63.5	64.1	64.7
Luxembourg	..	61.7	61.5	61.4	61.2	60.6	60.7	60.1	60.3	61.0	61.2	61.8	62.2	62.1	61.9	61.6	62.1	62.3	61.8	61.5
Mexico[b]										51.0	51.5	51.7	51.8	53.2	54.3	55.7	54.7	54.5	54.3	54.3
Netherlands	59.7	57.6	57.7	57.4	57.3	57.4	56.8	56.0	56.4	56.5	57.2	57.4	58.2	59.1	59.6	60.4	61.0	61.3	61.7	62.0
New Zealand	65.1	66.4	66.0	66.5	66.2	65.3	65.4	66.4	66.2	66.1	64.6	63.5	63.8	63.7	63.3	63.3	64.1	64.8	65.2	65.6
Norway	71.0	75.6	75.3	76.1	76.4	76.5	76.7	77.5	79.2	80.3	80.1	78.7	78.0	77.1	76.9	76.5	76.8	77.6	78.0	78.4
Portugal	66.2	68.8	68.6	68.1	67.5	69.9	69.9	69.4	69.2	69.5	70.0	71.7	72.2	73.4	68.4	67.8	68.4	68.0	67.9	67.9
Spain	59.4	57.0	56.3	56.0	56.0	56.0	55.7	55.7	56.1	57.0	57.5	57.8	58.1	57.9	57.7	57.9	58.2	58.5	58.7	59.1
Sweden	77.3	80.4	81.1	81.0	81.1	81.3	81.4	81.0	81.2	81.5	82.0	82.5	82.6	81.8	83.2	77.6	76.3	77.1	77.0	77.0
Switzerland	75.5	73.7	74.4	75.1	74.7	74.4	74.7	75.5	76.5	77.7	79.0	81.7	83.6	84.0	83.2	84.0	83.5	82.7	82.4	82.0
Turkey[c]	71.5	69.2	68.2	65.8	64.1	62.9	61.6	60.2	60.9	60.9	60.1	59.6	58.8	57.1	57.5	56.3	56.5	57.0	56.7	56.5
Total of smaller countries[d]	66.5	65.7	65.5	65.1	64.6	64.4	64.0	63.6	64.0	62.3	62.3	62.5	62.6	62.3	62.3	63.0	62.9	63.2	63.1	63.2
Total OECD[d]	67.7	68.9	69.0	68.9	68.8	68.8	68.8	68.9	69.4	69.0	69.3	69.8	70.1	70.2	70.2	70.3	70.4	70.4	70.4	70.6
OECD North America[d]	67.5	70.8	71.2	71.5	71.7	71.9	72.5	73.1	73.8	71.8	72.4	73.1	73.6	73.5	73.9	74.0	74.1	74.0	74.0	74.1
OECD Europe	66.7	66.7	66.6	66.2	65.7	65.4	65.2	65.1	65.5	65.7	65.9	66.0	66.1	66.3	65.9	65.9	65.9	65.8	65.8	65.9
EU	66.0	66.1	66.2	65.9	65.6	65.4	65.3	65.4	65.7	66.0	66.2	66.5	66.6	67.1	66.6	66.4	66.4	66.2	66.3	66.4
Total OECD *less* the United States[d]	67.8	68.1	68.1	67.9	67.6	67.5	67.4	67.3	67.7	66.9	67.1	67.4	67.6	67.9	67.8	67.9	67.8	67.9	67.9	68.0

a) For sources and definitions; see "Sources and Methods".
b) Data based on the National Survey of Urban Employment; see "Sources and Methods".
c) The figures incorporate important revisions to Turkish data; see "Sources and Methods".
d) Totals exclude Mexico prior to 1987.

Annex Table 20. **Employment**[a]

Percentage changes from previous period

	1992 Employment (thousands)	1979	1980	1981	1982	1983	1984	1985	1986	1987	1988	1989	1990	1991	1992	1993	1994	1995	Projections 1996	1997
United States[b]	118 488	2.9	0.5	1.1	-0.9	1.3	4.1	2.0	2.3	2.6	2.3	2.0	1.3	-0.9	0.7	1.5	2.3	1.6	1.1	1.1
Japan	64 352	1.3	1.0	0.8	1.0	1.7	0.6	0.7	0.8	1.0	1.7	2.0	2.0	1.9	1.1	0.2	0.1	0.1	0.1	0.4
Germany	35 842	1.7	1.6	-0.1	-1.2	-1.4	0.2	0.7	1.4	0.7	0.8	1.5	3.0	2.5	-1.8	-1.8	-0.7	-0.2	-0.9	0.2
France	22 538	0.2	0.1	-0.5	0.4	-0.2	-0.9	-0.1	0.5	0.4	1.0	1.4	1.0	0	-0.6	-1.4	0.3	1.1	-0.3	0.2
Italy	20 989	1.1	1.5	-0.6	0.4	0.1	0.3	0.3	0.4	-0.3	0.5	-0.1	1.2	0.7	-0.9	-2.5	-1.7	-0.6	0.2	0.2
United Kingdom	25 607	1.4	-0.9	-3.4	-1.9	-0.2	2.3	1.0	0.3	2.4	3.5	2.7	0.4	-3.1	-2.4	-0.8	0.7	0.6	0.3	1.0
Canada	12 842	4.2	3.0	2.9	-3.2	0.6	2.7	3.0	3.0	2.7	3.2	2.1	0.6	-1.9	-0.6	1.4	2.1	1.6	1.4	2.1
Total of above countries	300 657	2.0	0.7	0.3	-0.6	0.7	2.0	1.3	1.4	1.7	1.9	1.8	1.4	0	-0.1	0.1	0.9	0.8	0.4	0.7
Australia	7 681	1.4	2.9	2.0	0	-1.8	2.9	3.6	3.5	2.2	3.8	4.7	1.5	-2.1	-0.7	0.3	3.1	4.1	1.5	1.8
Austria	3 457	0.2	0.2	0.1	-1.2	-1.2	-0.1	0.2	0.4	0	0.6	1.5	1.9	1.9	1.5	-0.3	0.2	-0.4	-0.6	-0.2
Belgium	3 753	1.0	-0.1	-1.9	-1.3	-1.0	-0.2	0.6	0.6	0.4	1.5	1.6	1.4	0.1	-0.4	-1.1	-0.7	0.4	-0.1	0.3
Czech Republic[c]	..	:	:	:	:	:	:	:	:	:	:	:	:	:	..	:	1.2	2.0	1.6	1.4
Denmark	2 510	1.2	-0.5	-1.3	0.4	0.3	1.7	2.5	2.6	0.9	-0.6	-0.6	-1.0	-1.5	-0.6	-1.0	-0.6	1.8	0.3	0.6
Finland	2 174	2.5	3.2	1.1	1.0	0.6	1.0	1.0	-0.3	-0.3	0.3	1.6	-0.1	-5.2	-7.1	-6.1	-0.8	2.2	1.1	1.7
Greece	3 685	1.1	1.4	5.2	-0.8	1.1	0.4	1.0	0.4	-0.1	1.6	0.4	1.3	-2.3	1.5	0.9	1.9	0.9	0.7	1.0
Iceland	125	1.0	3.3	4.8	2.6	0.9	1.5	3.6	3.1	5.8	-2.8	-1.5	-0.9	-0.4	0.5	-0.3	1.0	1.0	1.7	1.4
Ireland	1 163	3.2	1.0	-0.9	0.2	-2.1	-1.9	-2.0	0.2	1.0	-0.1	1.2	3.3	-0.2	0.4	1.8	3.5	3.0	2.3	2.1
Luxembourg	200	0.5	0.7	0.3	-0.3	-0.3	0.5	0.9	2.6	2.6	3.1	3.5	4.1	4.1	2.5	1.8	2.5	2.6	1.6	2.2
Mexico[d]	13 889	1.4	1.2	-1.1	-2.1	-1.3	0.5	1.3	2.5	1.6	4.7	3.6	1.9	5.5	5.4	4.5	1.4	-1.0	2.0	2.5
Netherlands	5 885	1.4	-0.1	0.7	0.9	-1.0	2.7	3.5	-0.4	0.8	2.3	1.8	3.0	2.6	0.4	0.7	-0.1	1.5	1.2	1.2
New Zealand	1 467	1.4	-0.1	0.9	-1.3	-1.0	-0.1	1.7	0.3	0.8	-3.2	-2.6	0.9	-1.4	0.4	2.0	4.2	4.7	2.2	1.8
Norway	2 004	1.1	0.5	1.5	0.4	0.1	1.3	2.3	3.5	1.9	-0.6	-3.0	-0.9	-1.0	-0.3	0	1.5	2.0	1.5	1.1
Portugal[e]	4 310	1.2	2.2	0.5	-0.1	4.0	-0.1	-0.5	0.1	2.6	2.6	2.2	2.2	2.9	-6.4	-2.0	-0.1	-0.6	0.1	0.2
Spain	12 366	-1.7	-3.0	-3.0	-1.3	-1.1	-1.8	-0.9	2.2	3.1	2.9	4.1	2.6	0.2	-1.9	-4.3	-0.9	2.7	0.7	1.1
Sweden	4 208	1.6	1.3	-0.2	-0.1	0.1	0.8	-0.3	0.8	1.0	1.4	1.5	1.0	-1.9	-4.3	-5.8	-0.9	1.6	0.3	0.7
Switzerland	3 805	1.1	2.3	2.3	0.5	0	1.0	2.0	2.3	2.5	2.6	2.7	3.2	1.2	-1.6	-0.6	-0.2	0.2	0.2	0.3
Turkey[f]	19 001	1.5	1.3	0.9	1.1	1.0	1.5	1.7	1.9	2.3	1.5	1.9	2.0	0.3	3.2	0.9	2.5	2.5	1.8	2.3
Total of smaller countries[g]	91 647	0.8	0.6	0.1	-0.2	-0.1	0.6	1.1	1.7	1.8	2.2	2.3	1.8	0.7	0.5	-0.2	1.0	1.5	1.2	1.5
Total OECD[g]	392 304	1.7	0.7	0.2	-0.5	0.5	1.7	1.2	1.5	1.7	2.0	1.9	1.5	0.1	0.1	0.1	0.9	1.0	0.6	0.9
OECD North America[g]	145 219	3.0	0.7	1.3	-1.1	1.2	4.0	2.1	2.4	2.6	2.5	2.2	1.2	-0.4	1.0	1.8	2.2	1.3	1.2	1.3
OECD Europe[g]	173 585	1.0	0.5	-0.8	-0.6	-0.2	0.4	0.6	1.0	1.2	1.6	1.6	1.6	0	-1.0	-1.4	0.1	0.8	0	0.8
EU	148 651	0.9	0.3	-1.1	-0.8	-0.4	0.2	0.4	0.9	1.1	1.6	1.7	1.6	0	-1.5	-1.8	-0.3	0.6	0	0.5
Total OECD *less* the United States[g]	273 816	1.2	0.8	-0.1	-0.3	0.2	0.6	0.8	1.1	1.3	1.8	1.9	1.7	0.6	-0.2	-0.5	0.3	0.7	0.4	0.9

a) For sources and definitions; see "Sources and Methods".
b) Break in series as of January 1994.
c) No data for 1992; the employment in 1993 was 4 988 000.
d) Data based on the National Survey of Urban Employment; see "Sources and Methods".
e) Break in series in 1992.
f) The figures incorporate important revisions to Turkish data; see "Sources and Methods".
g) Totals exclude Mexico prior to 1988.

Annex Table 21. **Unemployment rates: commonly used definitions**[a]

	1992 Unemployment (thousands)	1979	1980	1981	1982	1983	1984	1985	1986	1987	1988	1989	1990	1991	1992	1993	1994	1995	Projections 1996	1997
United States[b]	9 611	5.8	7.2	7.6	9.7	9.6	7.5	7.2	7.0	6.2	5.5	5.3	5.6	6.8	7.5	6.9	6.1	5.6	5.5	5.6
Japan	1 417	2.1	2.0	2.2	2.3	2.7	2.7	2.6	2.8	2.9	2.5	2.3	2.1	2.1	2.2	2.5	2.9	3.1	3.3	3.2
Germany	2 979	3.2	3.2	4.5	6.4	7.9	7.9	8.0	7.7	7.6	7.6	6.9	6.2	6.7	7.7	8.9	9.6	9.4	10.3	10.4
France	2 600	5.8	6.2	7.4	8.0	8.3	9.7	10.2	10.4	10.5	10.0	9.4	8.9	9.4	10.3	11.7	12.3	11.6	12.1	12.2
Italy	2 034	5.7	5.6	6.3	6.9	7.7	8.5	8.6	9.9	10.2	10.5	10.2	9.1	8.6	8.8	10.2	11.3	12.0	12.1	12.0
United Kingdom	2 801	4.0	5.3	8.3	9.7	10.5	10.7	11.0	11.0	9.8	7.8	6.0	5.8	8.2	9.9	10.2	9.2	8.2	7.9	7.5
Canada	1 639	7.5	7.5	7.6	11.0	11.9	11.3	10.5	9.6	8.8	7.8	7.5	8.1	10.4	11.3	11.2	10.4	9.5	9.3	9.0
Total of above countries	23 079	4.7	5.3	6.1	7.6	7.9	7.3	7.2	7.2	6.8	6.2	5.7	5.6	6.5	7.1	7.3	7.1	6.8	7.0	6.9
Australia	922	6.1	6.0	5.7	7.1	9.9	8.9	8.1	8.0	8.0	7.1	6.1	7.0	9.5	10.7	10.9	9.7	8.5	8.7	8.6
Austria	193	1.7	1.6	2.1	3.2	3.8	3.9	4.2	4.5	4.9	4.7	4.3	4.7	5.2	5.3	6.1	5.9	5.9	6.2	6.5
Belgium	435	7.6	8.0	10.3	12.0	13.3	13.4	12.4	11.8	11.5	10.4	9.4	8.8	9.4	10.4	12.1	13.1	13.0	13.2	13.0
Czech Republic[c]	..	..	..	..	..	..	..	..	..	..	..	..	..	..	..	3.6	3.2	3.0	3.1	3.2
Denmark	318	6.2	7.0	9.2	9.8	10.4	10.1	9.0	7.8	7.8	8.6	9.3	9.6	10.5	11.3	12.3	12.2	10.0	9.2	9.2
Finland	328	6.0	4.7	4.9	5.4	5.4	5.2	5.0	5.4	5.1	4.5	3.5	3.5	7.6	13.1	17.9	18.4	17.2	16.4	15.5
Greece	349	1.9	2.8	4.0	5.8	7.9	8.1	7.8	7.4	7.4	7.7	7.5	7.0	7.7	8.7	9.7	9.6	10.0	10.2	10.4
Iceland	4	0.4	0.3	0.4	0.7	1.0	1.3	0.9	0.6	0.5	0.6	1.7	1.8	1.5	3.0	4.3	4.7	5.0	4.4	4.0
Ireland	213	7.1	7.3	9.9	11.4	14.0	15.5	17.0	17.0	16.8	16.1	14.6	13.2	14.7	15.5	15.6	14.2	12.9	12.4	12.2
Luxembourg	3	0.7	0.7	1.0	1.3	1.6	1.7	1.7	1.5	1.7	1.5	1.4	1.3	1.3	1.6	2.1	2.7	3.0	2.9	2.8
Mexico[d]	405	..	4.7	4.2	4.2	6.1	5.6	4.4	4.3	3.9	3.5	2.9	2.7	2.6	2.8	3.4	3.7	6.3	6.0	5.5
Netherlands	336	3.6	4.0	5.8	8.5	11.0	10.6	9.2	8.4	8.0	7.8	6.9	6.0	5.5	5.4	6.5	7.6	7.1	7.0	6.9
New Zealand	169	1.8	2.5	3.3	3.6	5.3	4.5	3.5	4.0	4.1	5.6	7.1	7.8	10.3	10.3	9.5	8.1	6.3	6.2	6.4
Norway	126	1.9	1.7	2.0	2.7	3.4	3.2	2.6	2.0	2.1	3.2	4.9	5.2	5.5	5.9	6.0	5.4	4.9	4.3	4.1
Portugal	186	8.2	8.0	7.7	7.5	7.8	8.6	8.7	8.6	7.1	5.8	5.1	4.7	4.2	4.1	5.6	6.9	7.2	7.4	7.5
Spain	2 789	8.6	11.5	14.3	16.4	18.2	20.1	21.5	21.0	20.5	19.5	17.3	16.3	16.3	18.4	22.7	24.2	22.9	22.9	22.7
Sweden	234	2.1	2.0	2.5	3.1	3.5	3.1	2.9	2.5	2.1	1.7	1.5	1.6	3.0	5.3	8.2	8.0	7.7	7.6	7.2
Switzerland	96	0.3	0.2	0.2	0.4	0.9	1.1	0.9	0.7	0.7	0.6	0.5	0.5	1.0	2.5	4.5	4.7	4.2	4.2	4.0
Turkey[e]	1 662	8.6	8.1	7.1	7.0	7.7	7.6	7.1	7.9	8.3	8.4	8.5	8.0	7.7	8.0	7.7	8.1	7.5	7.7	7.4
Total of smaller countries[f]	8 767	6.1	6.5	7.2	8.3	9.5	9.8	9.6	9.5	9.4	8.3	7.7	7.4	7.8	8.7	9.7	10.0	9.8	9.8	9.5
Total OECD[f]	31 846	5.0	5.6	6.4	7.7	8.3	7.8	7.7	7.7	7.3	6.7	6.2	6.0	6.8	7.5	7.9	7.9	7.6	7.7	7.6
OECD North America[f]	11 655	6.0	7.2	7.6	9.8	9.8	7.9	7.5	7.3	6.5	5.6	5.3	5.6	6.8	7.4	7.0	6.3	6.0	5.9	5.9
OECD Europe	17 684	5.2	5.7	6.9	8.1	9.0	9.5	9.6	9.7	9.5	9.0	8.3	7.7	8.2	9.2	10.3	10.8	10.3	10.5	10.4
EU	15 796	5.0	5.6	7.2	8.4	9.4	10.0	10.2	10.3	10.0	9.4	8.5	7.9	8.5	9.6	11.1	11.6	11.2	11.4	11.3
Total OECD less the United States[f]	22 235	4.6	4.9	5.8	6.8	7.7	8.0	8.0	8.0	7.9	7.2	6.6	6.2	6.8	7.5	8.3	8.6	8.4	8.6	8.5

a) For sources and definitions; see "Sources and Methods".
b) Break in series as of January 1994.
c) No data for 1992, the unemployment in 1993 was 184 000.
d) Data based on the National Survey of Urban Employment; see "Sources and Methods".
e) The figures incorporate important revisions to Turkish data; see "Sources and Methods".
f) Totals exclude Mexico prior to 1988.

Annex Table 22. Standardised unemployment rates
Per cent of total labour force

	1976	1977	1978	1979	1980	1981	1982	1983	1984	1985	1986	1987	1988	1989	1990	1991	1992	1993	1994	1995
United States	7.6	6.9	6.0	5.8	7.0	7.5	9.5	9.5	7.4	7.1	6.9	6.1	5.4	5.2	5.6	6.8	7.5	6.9	6.0	5.5
Japan	2.0	2.0	2.2	2.1	2.0	2.2	2.4	2.6	2.7	2.6	2.8	2.8	2.5	2.3	2.1	2.1	2.2	2.5	2.9	3.1
Germany[a,b]	3.7	3.6	3.5	3.2	2.9	4.2	5.9	7.7	7.1	7.1	6.4	6.2	6.2	5.6	4.8	4.2	4.6	7.9	8.4	8.2
France[a]	4.4	4.9	5.2	5.8	6.2	7.4	8.1	8.3	9.7	10.2	10.4	10.5	10.0	10.9	8.9	9.4	10.3	11.7	12.3	11.6
Italy	6.6	7.0	7.1	7.6	7.5	7.8	8.4	8.8	9.4	9.6	10.5	10.9	11.0	10.9	10.3	9.4	10.5	10.2	11.1	12.2
United Kingdom[a]	5.6	6.0	5.9	5.0	6.4	9.8	11.3	12.4	11.7	11.2	11.2	10.3	8.6	7.2	6.9	8.8	10.1	10.4	9.6	8.7
Canada	7.1	8.1	8.3	7.4	7.5	7.5	10.9	11.9	11.2	10.5	9.5	8.8	7.7	7.5	8.1	10.3	11.3	11.2	10.3	9.5
Total of above contries	5.4	5.4	5.1	4.9	5.5	6.3	7.7	8.1	7.3	7.2	7.1	6.7	6.1	5.7	5.7	6.4	7.0	7.2	7.0	6.8
Australia	4.7	5.6	6.2	6.2	6.0	5.7	7.1	9.9	8.9	8.2	8.0	8.0	7.2	6.1	6.9	9.5	10.7	10.8	9.7	8.5
Belgium[a]	6.4	7.4	7.9	8.2	8.8	10.8	12.6	12.1	12.1	11.3	11.2	11.0	9.7	8.0	7.2	7.2	7.7	8.6	9.6	9.4
Finland	3.8	5.8	7.2	5.9	4.6	4.8	5.3	5.4	5.2	5.0	5.3	5.0	4.5	3.4	3.4	7.5	13.0	17.7	18.2	17.1
Ireland[a]	..	..	..	..	..	..	..	14.0	15.5	17.0	17.0	16.7	16.2	14.7	13.3	14.7	15.5	15.6	14.3	12.9
Netherlands[a]	5.5	5.3	5.3	5.4	6.0	8.5	11.4	12.0	11.8	10.6	9.9	9.6	9.1	8.3	7.5	7.0	5.6	6.2	6.8	6.5
New Zealand	..	..	..	..	..	..	..	..	..	..	4.0	4.0	5.5	7.1	7.7	10.3	10.2	9.4	8.1	6.3
Norway	1.7	1.4	1.8	2.0	1.6	2.0	2.6	3.4	3.1	2.6	2.0	2.1	3.2	4.9	5.2	5.5	5.9	6.0	5.4	4.9
Portugal	..	..	..	..	..	..	..	7.8	8.4	8.5	8.4	7.0	5.7	5.0	4.6	4.1	4.1	5.5	6.8	7.1
Spain	4.5	5.1	6.8	8.4	11.1	13.8	15.6	17.0	19.7	21.1	20.8	20.1	19.1	16.9	15.9	16.0	18.1	22.4	23.8	22.7
Sweden	1.6	1.8	2.2	2.1	2.0	2.5	3.5	3.9	3.4	3.0	2.8	2.3	1.9	1.6	1.8	3.3	5.8	9.5	9.8	9.2
Total OECD	5.4	5.4	5.2	5.1	5.8	6.7	8.2	8.6	8.0	7.8	7.7	7.3	6.7	6.2	6.1	6.8	7.5	8.0	7.9	7.5
Memorandum item																				
EU[c]	5.0	5.4	5.6	5.7	6.4	8.1	9.4	10.0	10.4	10.5	10.5	10.2	9.6	8.7	8.1	8.5	9.4	10.9	11.4	11.0

a) Series based on EU Labour Force Surveys: see corresponding notes in *Quarterly Labour Force Statistics*.
b) Up to and including 1992, data concern western Germany.
c) EU: only countries shown – Germany, France, Italy, United Kingdom, Belgium, Finland, Ireland, Netherlands, Portugal, Spain and Sweden – are included in the area total.
Note: These unemployment rates are based on the ILO/OECD Guidelines. The unemployed are defined as persons of working age who are without work, available for work and actively seeking employment; unemployment is expressed as a percentage of total labour force including all members of the armed forces. Break is marked by (l). The data above are averages of quarterly or monthly figures. For a detailed description of the sources and methods used, see *Standardised Unemployment Rates, Sources and Methods* (OECD, 1985).

Annex Table 23. **Labour force, employment and unemployment**

Millions

	1979	1980	1981	1982	1983	1984	1985	1986	1987	1988	1989	1990	1991	1992	1993	1994	1995	Projections 1996	1997
Labour force																			
Major seven countries	271.6	275.5	278.6	281.3	284.4	288.2	291.6	295.7	299.2	303.0	307.0	311.1	321.7	323.7	324.9	327.2	328.7	330.6	332.9
Total of smaller countries[a]	74.3	75.1	75.8	76.5	77.5	78.2	78.9	80.1	93.2	94.9	96.4	97.8	98.9	100.4	106.9	108.3	109.7	111.0	112.4
Total OECD[a]	345.9	350.6	354.4	357.8	361.9	366.4	370.4	375.9	392.5	397.9	403.4	408.9	420.6	424.2	431.8	435.5	438.4	441.5	445.3
OECD North America[a]	116.6	119.0	121.0	122.6	124.1	126.4	128.6	131.2	145.2	147.8	150.6	153.0	154.3	156.9	158.9	161.1	162.9	164.6	166.7
OECD Europe	165.3	166.9	167.9	168.9	170.3	171.9	173.2	175.2	177.0	178.8	180.2	182.0	191.1	191.3	196.4	197.4	198.1	199.1	200.4
EU	143.2	144.6	145.5	146.3	147.4	148.7	149.7	151.0	152.2	153.5	154.5	155.9	165.0	164.4	164.2	164.6	164.7	165.2	165.9
Total OECD less the United States[a]	241.0	243.6	245.7	247.6	250.4	252.8	255.0	258.0	272.6	276.2	279.5	283.1	294.3	296.1	302.6	304.5	306.0	307.9	310.1
Employment																			
Major seven countries	258.9	260.7	261.5	260.0	261.9	267.1	270.5	274.4	279.0	284.3	289.5	293.7	300.9	300.7	301.1	303.8	306.2	307.6	309.9
Total of smaller countries[a]	69.8	70.2	70.3	70.2	70.1	70.6	71.3	72.5	85.1	87.0	88.9	90.6	91.2	91.6	96.5	97.5	99.0	100.1	101.6
Total OECD[a]	328.7	331.0	331.8	330.2	332.0	337.7	341.8	346.9	364.1	371.3	378.5	384.3	392.1	392.3	397.6	401.3	405.2	407.7	411.5
OECD North America[a]	109.6	110.4	111.8	110.6	111.9	116.4	118.9	121.7	136.2	139.6	142.7	144.4	143.8	145.2	147.8	151.1	153.1	154.9	156.9
OECD Europe	156.7	157.4	156.2	155.3	154.9	155.6	156.5	158.1	160.1	162.6	165.3	168.0	175.4	173.6	176.1	176.2	177.6	178.1	179.5
EU	136.1	136.5	135.1	134.0	133.5	133.8	134.3	135.5	136.9	139.1	141.4	143.6	151.0	148.7	146.0	145.5	146.4	146.3	147.1
Total OECD less the United States[a]	229.9	231.7	231.4	230.7	231.2	232.7	234.7	237.3	251.7	256.3	261.2	265.5	274.4	273.8	277.3	278.2	280.2	281.4	283.9
Unemployment																			
Major seven countries	12.7	14.7	17.1	21.3	22.5	21.0	21.0	21.3	20.3	18.7	17.5	17.4	20.8	23.1	23.8	23.4	22.5	23.0	23.0
Total of smaller countries[a]	4.5	4.9	5.5	6.3	7.4	7.6	7.6	7.6	8.1	7.9	7.4	7.2	7.7	8.8	10.4	10.8	10.7	10.8	10.7
Total OECD[a]	17.2	19.6	22.6	27.6	29.9	28.7	28.6	28.9	28.4	26.6	24.9	24.7	28.5	31.8	34.2	34.2	33.2	33.8	33.7
OECD North America[a]	7.0	8.6	9.2	12.1	12.2	10.0	9.7	9.5	9.1	8.2	8.0	8.6	10.5	11.7	11.1	10.1	9.8	9.7	9.8
OECD Europe	8.6	9.4	11.7	13.6	15.4	16.4	16.7	17.1	16.9	16.2	14.9	14.0	15.7	17.7	20.3	21.2	20.5	21.0	20.9
EU	7.1	8.0	10.4	12.3	13.9	14.9	15.3	15.5	15.2	14.4	13.1	12.3	14.0	15.8	18.2	19.0	18.4	18.9	18.8
Total OECD less the United States[a]	11.1	11.9	14.3	16.9	19.2	20.1	20.3	20.7	21.0	19.9	18.4	17.6	19.9	22.2	25.3	26.2	25.8	26.5	26.2

a) The aggregate measures include Mexico as of 1987; there is a potential bias in the aggregates thereafter because of the limited coverage of the National Survey of Urban Employment.

Annex Table 24. **Capital income shares in the business sector**[a]

	Average 1970-78[b]	1979	1980	1981	1982	1983	1984	1985	1986	1987	1988	1989	1990	1991	1992	1993	1994	1995	Projections 1996	1997
United States	34.3	35.0	33.9	34.5	33.6	33.3	34.0	34.0	34.0	33.2	33.1	34.4	33.8	33.3	33.6	33.6	33.8	33.5	33.6	33.5
Japan	34.1	30.4	30.9	30.3	29.8	29.6	30.3	31.7	32.5	32.5	33.5	34.0	34.1	34.2	33.8	33.4	32.7	32.0	32.1	31.8
Germany[c]	29.6	30.5	28.5	28.2	28.6	30.8	31.8	32.4	33.1	32.7	33.8	34.6	35.6	34.0	33.3	33.4	35.0	36.0	35.8	36.3
France[c]	31.1	30.0	28.3	28.2	28.5	29.2	30.7	32.0	34.9	35.5	36.9	38.1	37.6	37.9	38.2	37.8	39.4	39.7	39.6	40.2
Italy[d]	31.4	35.5	36.0	35.3	35.4	34.5	36.4	36.6	38.6	38.4	38.8	38.3	37.3	36.6	36.6	36.9	39.8	42.5	43.7	44.0
United Kingdom[c]	30.0	31.3	29.2	28.9	30.7	32.3	31.9	32.2	31.0	31.4	30.9	29.6	28.2	26.8	27.7	29.9	31.0	31.5	31.7	31.9
Canada[d]	34.6	37.7	38.0	36.6	35.3	38.1	39.3	38.6	37.7	37.6	37.1	36.6	35.1	33.5	32.8	33.2	34.3	35.2	34.9	35.1
Total of above countries	33.0	33.2	32.4	32.4	32.0	32.3	33.1	33.5	34.0	33.7	34.0	34.7	34.3	33.7	33.8	33.9	34.4	34.6	34.7	34.7
Australia	32.4	35.1	34.1	33.5	28.6	33.0	34.8	35.2	35.1	37.3	38.8	38.9	37.3	37.0	37.5	38.5	39.2	38.3	38.1	38.2
Austria[d]	30.4	29.0	29.4	28.2	30.7	32.1	32.5	36.5	36.8	37.0	37.7	37.6	38.1	38.0	37.8	37.9	39.8	41.8	41.7	41.8
Belgium	33.4	29.5	28.2	27.4	29.7	31.5	31.8	32.8	33.6	33.4	35.9	36.8	36.3	34.3	33.9	33.4	34.2	36.0	36.5	37.4
Denmark	31.3	29.8	28.4	30.1	32.9	34.2	35.5	35.7	34.8	32.4	33.6	35.5	36.6	37.0	37.7	38.3	39.5	38.5	38.3	39.1
Finland[d]	27.1	31.3	30.4	28.7	30.1	29.7	29.9	28.4	28.2	28.4	29.1	29.9	27.7	24.6	25.1	29.8	31.6	33.8	32.2	32.3
Greece	51.8	46.2	47.9	44.5	41.4	41.1	43.1	42.7	45.9	46.5	47.1	45.4	44.4	48.2	49.3	51.7	50.5	49.4	48.5	48.2
Ireland	20.9	21.2	17.3	20.6	22.2	22.3	16.6	24.7	23.5	25.1	25.6	26.0	26.1	26.3	27.8	29.6	30.5	33.0	34.5	34.7
Netherlands[d]	29.8	29.6	30.3	32.6	33.4	35.4	38.2	39.2	37.8	37.9	38.4	40.5	40.8	40.0	38.8	37.9	39.3	39.1	38.9	39.3
New Zealand[d]	36.0	33.3	31.3	32.1	34.6	36.6	41.6	42.5	41.0	36.4	39.9	41.4	41.7	41.7	40.8	43.8	43.4	41.3	41.1	41.6
Norway[e]	31.1	33.9	33.6	33.9	33.3	33.8	34.1	34.4	34.0	33.6	32.8	34.3	34.6	36.1	36.8	39.0	39.7	38.2	38.5	38.6
Portugal[d]	27.1	31.1	30.4	28.3	28.1	26.9	27.3	29.5	30.8	29.1	30.0	30.8	30.0	27.7	31.2	31.7	31.2	32.7	32.9	33.6
Spain	31.6	30.7	32.3	31.5	33.0	32.5	36.0	37.6	38.2	38.9	40.0	40.9	40.6	40.3	39.9	40.8	42.5	43.4	43.9	44.2
Sweden	28.3	27.4	26.4	25.9	29.6	31.8	33.1	32.3	31.8	31.2	31.5	29.6	27.4	28.7	31.0	33.5	34.2	35.1	30.6	29.9
Switzerland[c]	26.2	20.7	20.1	20.2	19.8	20.1	20.7	21.7	21.3	19.2	17.5	17.6	16.4	13.8	12.4	10.3	11.7	12.3	12.0	12.5
Total of above smaller countries	31.4	30.7	30.7	30.4	30.8	31.9	33.7	34.7	34.8	34.9	35.7	36.3	35.7	35.3	35.4	36.2	37.2	37.6	37.3	37.6
Total of above North American countries	34.3	35.2	34.3	34.7	33.8	33.7	34.4	34.4	34.3	33.6	33.4	34.6	33.9	33.3	33.5	33.6	33.8	33.7	33.7	33.6
Total of above European countries	30.7	31.2	30.3	30.0	30.7	31.6	32.8	33.6	34.4	34.5	35.1	35.4	35.0	34.3	34.3	34.8	36.5	37.4	37.5	37.9
Total of above OECD countries	32.8	32.8	32.2	32.1	31.8	32.2	33.2	33.7	34.1	33.8	34.2	34.9	34.5	33.9	34.0	34.2	34.8	35.0	35.1	35.1

a) Difficulties in making an appropriate imputation for the labour income of the self-employed mean that great care is needed in interpreting cross-country differences in the level of capital income shares. For details, see "Sources and Methods".
b) Average 1972-78 in the case of the United States and New Zealand.
c) Excluding the employment adjustment for unpaid family workers for which data are not available.
d) Excluding the employment adjustment for unpaid family workers prior to: 1974 for Portugal; 1975 for Canada; 1977 for Italy and Finland; 1985 for Austria; 1986 for New Zealand and 1987 for the Netherlands.
e) Mainland business sector (i.e. excluding shipping as well as crude petroleum and gas extraction).

Annex Table 25. **Rates of return on capital in the business sector**[a]

	Average 1970-78[b]	1979	1980	1981	1982	1983	1984	1985	1986	1987	1988	1989	1990	1991	1992	1993	1994	1995	Projections 1996	1997
United States	15.3	16.0	14.9	14.8	13.8	14.1	15.6	15.9	16.0	16.0	16.3	17.3	17.1	16.6	17.4	17.8	18.3	18.3	18.7	18.8
Japan	18.3	14.4	14.2	13.7	13.3	13.2	13.6	14.3	14.8	14.7	15.5	15.8	15.7	15.6	14.8	14.2	13.8	13.3	13.4	13.3
Germany[c]	11.8	11.7	10.6	10.0	9.9	10.7	11.1	11.3	11.8	11.6	12.2	12.5	13.2	12.5	12.3	12.1	13.1	13.8	13.8	14.3
France[c]	12.7	11.5	10.5	10.3	10.2	10.4	10.9	11.4	12.8	13.1	13.9	14.7	14.5	14.4	14.5	14.1	15.0	15.2	15.1	15.5
Italy[d]	11.6	13.0	13.0	12.1	12.2	12.2	13.2	13.3	14.7	14.8	15.2	15.0	14.7	14.6	14.5	13.9	15.2	16.2	16.8	17.0
United Kingdom[c]	10.2	9.5	8.4	8.1	9.0	9.9	9.9	10.2	9.7	10.2	10.2	9.7	9.3	9.0	9.8	11.1	12.1	12.2	12.4	12.6
Canada[d]	14.8	17.3	18.7	18.0	15.7	17.7	19.2	19.2	18.9	19.5	19.9	19.3	17.8	17.3	17.1	17.5	18.4	19.2	19.3	19.4
Total of above countries	14.7	14.3	13.5	13.3	12.7	13.0	14.0	14.3	14.7	14.7	15.2	15.7	15.5	15.2	15.4	15.5	16.0	16.2	16.4	16.5
Australia	12.1	11.9	11.2	11.1	8.9	9.9	11.4	11.2	10.6	11.5	12.5	13.2	12.5	11.9	12.2	12.6	13.3	13.5	13.9	14.1
Austria[d]	12.1	10.4	10.2	9.3	9.9	10.3	10.3	11.5	11.6	11.5	11.8	11.7	12.0	12.0	11.9	11.5	12.3	13.3	13.0	13.0
Belgium	12.9	11.2	10.7	9.9	10.6	11.1	11.4	11.9	12.4	12.5	13.8	14.1	14.0	13.0	12.8	12.4	12.7	13.4	13.3	13.7
Denmark	10.5	9.0	8.1	8.0	9.1	9.5	10.2	10.3	10.1	9.1	9.5	9.9	10.3	10.0	10.4	10.2	10.7	10.5	10.3	10.5
Finland[d]	8.0	8.9	8.7	8.2	8.6	8.6	8.8	8.4	8.3	8.3	8.7	9.0	8.0	6.4	6.3	7.4	8.2	9.5	9.0	9.3
Greece	43.8	32.9	32.1	27.0	25.1	21.7	21.9	21.2	21.6	21.4	22.5	21.5	20.5	23.5	23.3	24.9	24.4	24.1	23.2	22.8
Ireland	6.4	6.6	5.2	6.3	7.0	6.9	4.8	7.8	7.6	8.7	9.1	9.4	9.9	9.8	10.5	11.4	12.2	13.7	14.5	14.7
Netherlands[d]	13.1	13.1	13.4	14.2	14.4	15.4	17.1	17.9	17.3	16.8	17.0	18.4	18.8	18.5	17.8	17.1	17.9	17.8	17.5	17.6
Norway[e]	14.9	13.5	13.2	12.6	11.8	11.8	12.3	12.2	12.1	12.0	10.7	10.2	10.1	10.5	10.4	10.9	11.2	10.6	10.5	10.8
Spain	18.5	15.9	15.4	14.1	14.8	13.9	15.5	15.7	17.0	18.0	18.9	19.5	19.4	19.1	18.6	18.5	18.9	19.1	19.2	19.1
Sweden	11.0	9.3	9.1	8.7	9.7	10.2	11.0	10.7	10.7	10.6	10.9	10.3	9.5	10.1	11.1	11.7	12.5	13.2	11.0	10.8
Switzerland[c]	11.3	9.0	8.6	8.6	8.3	8.4	8.8	9.2	9.3	8.5	7.5	7.4	7.0	5.8	5.1	4.2	5.0	5.2	4.9	5.1
Total of above smaller countries	15.0	13.2	12.8	12.1	12.1	12.1	13.1	13.3	13.6	13.8	14.3	14.6	14.4	14.2	14.0	14.0	14.6	14.9	14.7	14.7
Total of above North American countries	15.3	16.1	15.2	15.1	13.9	14.4	15.9	16.2	16.2	16.3	16.6	17.5	17.1	16.6	17.4	17.8	18.3	18.4	18.8	18.8
Total of above European countries	12.8	12.1	11.3	10.8	11.0	11.3	11.9	12.2	12.8	12.9	13.4	13.6	13.5	13.2	13.2	13.2	14.1	14.6	14.6	14.8
Total of above OECD countries	14.7	14.2	13.4	13.1	12.6	12.9	13.9	14.2	14.5	14.6	15.1	15.6	15.4	15.0	15.2	15.3	15.8	16.0	16.2	16.3

a) Difficulties in making an appropriate imputation for the labour income of the self-employed and in deriving a consistent measure of the capital stock across countries mean that great care is needed in interpreting cross-country differences in the levels of rates of return. For details see "Sources and Methods".
b) Average 1972-78 in the case of the United States.
c) Excluding the adjustment to employment for unpaid family workers for which data are not available.
d) Excluding the adjustment to employment for unpaid family workers prior to: 1975 for Canada; 1977 for Italy and Finland; 1985 for Austria and 1987 for the Netherlands.
e) Mainland business sector (i.e. excluding shipping as well as crude petroleum and gas extraction).

Annex Table 26. **Household saving rates**[a]

Percentage of disposable household income

	1978	1979	1980	1981	1982	1983	1984	1985	1986	1987	1988	1989	1990	1991	1992	1993	1994	1995	Projections 1996	1997
United States	7.3	7.5	8.4	9.3	9.0	6.8	8.6	7.1	6.4	5.2	5.3	5.0	5.2	5.8	5.7	4.7	4.2	4.7	4.8	5.0
Japan	20.8	18.2	17.9	18.4	16.7	16.1	15.8	15.6	15.6	13.8	13.0	12.9	12.1	13.2	13.1	13.4	12.8	13.4	13.1	12.9
Germany	12.1	12.7	12.8	13.6	12.7	10.9	11.4	11.4	12.3	12.6	12.8	12.4	13.8	12.7	12.8	12.2	11.6	11.6	11.7	11.5
France[b]	20.4	18.8	17.6	18.0	17.3	15.9	14.5	14.0	12.9	10.8	11.0	11.7	12.5	13.2	13.6	14.1	13.6	14.3	13.9	13.9
Italy[b]	26.9	26.1	23.0	21.8	20.4	22.3	20.6	18.9	18.2	17.8	16.9	16.7	18.2	18.2	17.7	15.8	14.8	13.1	12.8	13.0
United Kingdom[b]	10.9	12.1	13.4	12.6	11.3	9.7	11.1	10.7	8.7	7.0	5.6	7.1	8.1	10.1	12.2	11.4	9.6	10.2	10.1	9.7
Canada	12.6	13.2	13.6	15.4	18.2	14.8	15.0	13.3	10.7	9.2	9.7	10.4	9.7	9.9	10.3	9.6	7.9	7.4	7.0	6.9
Australia	11.2	12.3	10.8	9.7	8.3	8.6	9.9	7.3	6.9	5.5	6.1	6.4	6.8	5.0	4.2	2.7	2.5	1.3	1.3	1.2
Austria	11.3	11.2	10.5	8.1	10.3	8.3	8.2	8.3	10.9	12.4	11.5	12.6	13.7	14.1	12.6	12.2	13.6	13.4	12.7	12.4
Belgium	18.3	17.1	18.7	18.7	15.6	15.9	14.9	14.0	16.1	14.6	15.7	17.0	17.1	19.8	20.5	21.0	19.8	19.3	18.5	18.4
Czech Republic	..	..	..	..	..	..	..	..	..	..	..	..	..	..	..	..	..	..	..	..
Denmark	..	..	..	..	..	..	..	..	..	..	..	..	..	..	..	..	..	..	..	..
Finland	3.7	3.9	5.4	4.5	5.2	5.8	4.5	3.8	2.5	2.9	-1.2	-0.6	0.4	5.1	7.1	5.2	1.5	5.0	4.8	3.7
Greece	..	..	..	..	..	..	..	..	..	..	..	..	..	..	..	..	..	..	..	..
Iceland	..	..	..	..	..	..	..	..	..	..	..	..	..	..	..	..	..	..	..	..
Ireland	16.0	13.8	11.6	12.9	16.0	13.6	13.3	10.9	10.1	11.1	9.0	7.5	9.7	11.6	11.6	12.9	11.2	12.0	10.8	10.9
Luxembourg	..	..	..	..	..	..	..	..	..	..	..	..	..	..	..	..	..	..	..	..
Mexico	..	..	..	..	..	..	..	..	..	..	..	..	..	..	..	..	..	..	..	..
Netherlands[c]	1.7	1.3	1.8	3.3	3.4	-0.4	-0.6	0.1	2.8	2.3	2.2	4.0	5.8	1.1	2.3	0.9	0.7	1.8	0.8	0.6
New Zealand	..	..	..	..	..	..	..	..	..	..	..	..	..	..	..	..	..	..	..	..
Norway	8.4	4.6	3.4	4.5	3.8	4.3	5.2	-2.7	-6.1	-6.2	-2.4	0.9	0.9	2.9	5.4	5.6	6.3	5.2	4.3	4.9
Portugal	22.2	25.0	25.5	25.2	25.0	23.2	23.6	24.6	22.3	21.8	17.6	15.9	15.3	14.6	12.4	10.9	11.1	11.0	11.3	11.4
Spain[b]	13.9	12.5	10.8	11.8	12.8	12.3	11.4	11.2	11.5	8.8	10.1	8.4	10.5	11.6	9.8	12.5	10.6	11.7	11.5	10.9
Sweden	4.5	2.9	6.7	5.1	1.7	2.4	2.1	2.3	1.3	-2.8	-4.8	-4.9	-0.6	3.1	7.7	8.3	8.6	8.2	8.4	7.2
Switzerland	4.6	3.7	3.3	4.6	6.2	5.8	5.8	5.7	7.0	8.4	9.9	11.0	12.2	13.0	12.7	11.5	10.3	9.9	9.6	9.6
Turkey	..	..	..	..	..	..	..	..	..	..	..	..	..	..	..	..	..	..	..	..

a) National definition except the United States.
b) Gross saving.
c) Excluding mandatory saving through occupational pension schemes.

Annex Table 27. **Gross national saving**

As a percentage of nominal GDP

	1977	1978	1979	1980	1981	1982	1983	1984	1985	1986	1987	1988	1989	1990	1991	1992	1993	1994
United States	19.6	21.2	21.3	19.8	20.8	18.5	17.1	19.0	17.6	16.1	16.1	16.6	16.6	15.6	15.7	14.6	14.9	16.2
Japan	32.0	32.3	31.5	31.1	31.5	30.6	29.8	30.8	31.7	32.0	32.6	33.9	34.3	34.6	35.1	34.0	32.5	31.2
Germany	21.7	22.6	22.8	21.7	20.3	20.2	21.2	21.7	22.0	23.8	23.5	24.3	25.7	24.9	22.3	21.5	19.6	20.3
France	24.4	24.6	24.6	23.6	21.1	19.7	19.1	19.0	18.9	20.1	20.0	21.1	21.8	21.5	21.0	19.9	18.1	19.0
Italy	26.0	26.3	26.3	24.7	22.5	22.0	22.2	22.3	21.6	21.4	20.8	20.8	20.0	19.6	18.6	17.2	18.0	18.8
United Kingdom	18.5	18.4	19.0	17.7	16.7	16.7	17.1	16.8	17.6	16.0	16.0	15.5	15.4	14.3	13.5	12.8	12.6	13.5
Canada	20.9	21.1	23.1	22.9	22.6	19.5	18.8	20.2	19.6	18.1	19.0	20.6	19.4	16.4	14.3	13.2	13.7	16.0
Australia	20.6	21.5	22.1	21.6	20.5	17.5	19.8	19.6	18.9	19.4	21.1	22.4	20.7	17.5	15.4	15.5	16.7	16.8
Austria	24.3	25.3	25.7	25.8	24.3	24.0	22.6	23.5	23.2	23.8	23.8	24.5	25.2	26.3	26.0	25.3	24.3	25.3
Belgium	20.8	20.6	18.6	17.5	14.1	13.7	14.7	15.8	15.0	17.0	17.4	19.7	21.1	21.0	21.1	21.1	21.6	22.0
Denmark	18.9	18.8	16.6	14.9	12.4	12.1	13.4	15.1	14.9	16.1	16.1	16.6	16.9	17.8	17.5	17.7	17.1	16.3
Finland	22.9	23.2	25.2	26.0	24.9	23.3	22.8	23.8	22.8	22.5	22.1	24.0	24.8	23.0	15.1	12.1	13.0	16.7
Greece	24.5	26.3	28.3	29.1	24.6	16.7	16.8	15.4	13.1	14.5	14.5	17.3	15.9	13.8	15.2	15.3	15.5	..
Iceland	26.5	24.9	23.3	24.0	21.5	19.0	18.3	16.3	14.6	17.3	15.2	15.0	15.0	15.8	14.2	14.2	15.7	17.1
Ireland	20.5	20.4	18.2	15.2	13.0	16.1	15.9	15.8	15.0	14.9	16.3	15.5	16.3	20.0	20.7	18.5	19.3	19.5
Luxembourg	42.1	44.6	43.8	44.2	45.8	59.3	63.8	63.8	64.1	62.2	55.1	57.8	61.6	62.5	59.4	60.2	..	..
Mexico	19.7	19.8	20.8	22.2	21.4	22.4	24.7	22.5	22.5	18.2	22.0	19.3	18.8	19.2	17.8	16.1	15.8	15.1
Netherlands	23.0	21.5	20.7	20.9	21.5	21.4	22.1	23.5	24.3	24.3	22.6	24.2	26.1	26.0	24.8	23.7	23.3	24.4
New Zealand	20.9	19.5	20.1	18.6	20.7	19.7	20.9	20.2	18.1	19.3	19.1	18.7	16.4	14.9	14.6	17.0	19.2	20.7
Norway	22.3	23.4	25.3	29.6	29.4	27.7	28.3	31.0	29.6	23.0	23.4	22.7	24.6	24.1	23.6	21.0	21.9	..
Portugal	20.8	26.2	29.4	28.5	23.7	21.7	21.1	19.8	22.2	26.2	28.3	27.1	28.0	26.7	25.7	25.7	23.7	24.2
Spain	23.2	23.9	22.8	20.8	19.2	19.6	19.7	20.9	20.6	21.6	21.6	22.6	21.9	21.7	21.0	19.0	18.9	18.8
Sweden	17.8	17.6	17.8	17.8	15.6	14.2	16.1	17.9	17.5	18.1	18.2	18.8	19.2	17.7	15.8	13.4	12.3	13.7
Switzerland	26.5	27.0	26.6	26.7	28.4	28.1	27.9	28.9	29.8	31.1	31.7	32.8	33.7	33.1	31.6	29.7	29.6	29.3
Turkey	16.6	15.0	15.0	12.1	19.2	18.4	15.5	16.3	20.7	23.9	24.3	28.9	26.4	21.5	19.3	20.9	20.6	22.5
Total OECD	22.6	23.4	23.5	22.4	22.3	21.0	20.5	21.4	21.1	20.7	20.9	21.5	21.7	20.9	20.4	19.3	..	..
OECD North America	19.7	21.1	21.4	20.2	21.0	18.8	17.8	19.3	18.1	16.4	16.7	17.1	17.0	15.9	15.8	14.6	14.9	16.1
OECD Europe	22.4	22.7	22.8	21.7	20.3	19.8	19.9	20.3	20.5	21.2	21.0	21.7	22.1	21.3	20.1	19.1	..	..
EU	22.5	23.0	23.0	21.9	20.1	19.5	19.8	20.1	20.1	20.7	20.5	21.1	21.5	21.0	19.8	18.7	..	..

A30

Annex Table 28. **General government total outlays**[a]

As a percentage of nominal GDP

	1979	1980	1981	1982	1983	1984	1985	1986	1987	1988	1989	1990	1991	1992	1993	1994	1995	Projections	
																		1996	1997
United States[b]	29.5	31.4	31.7	33.4	33.9	32.4	32.9	33.1	33.0	32.1	31.9	32.8	33.4	34.4	33.9	33.0	33.3	33.1	32.9
Japan	31.1	32.0	32.8	33.0	33.3	32.3	31.6	31.9	32.1	31.3	30.6	31.3	30.9	31.7	33.7	34.3	35.6	36.7	37.1
Germany[c]	47.2	47.9	48.7	49.0	47.8	47.4	47.0	46.4	46.7	46.3	44.8	45.1	47.9	48.5	49.6	49.0	49.5	49.8	49.6
France[d]	45.0	46.1	48.6	50.3	51.4	51.9	52.1	51.3	50.9	50.0	49.1	49.8	50.5	52.2	54.8	54.2	53.7	54.2	53.7
Italy	41.6	41.9	45.9	47.6	48.7	49.3	50.9	50.7	50.2	50.3	51.3	53.2	53.5	53.6	56.9	54.1	51.9	51.3	50.3
United Kingdom	40.9	43.0	44.2	44.5	44.7	45.1	44.0	42.4	40.7	37.9	37.6	39.9	40.7	43.2	43.6	43.2	43.4	42.9	42.1
Canada	37.3	38.8	39.8	44.8	45.3	45.0	45.3	44.6	43.5	42.5	43.1	46.0	49.2	50.2	49.4	47.1	46.2	45.2	44.3
Total of above countries	34.8	36.2	37.1	38.5	38.6	38.0	38.2	38.1	37.8	37.0	36.6	37.6	38.4	39.4	40.1	39.4	39.6	39.7	39.4
Australia	31.4	31.4	31.4	32.9	35.1	35.4	36.5	37.5	35.4	33.8	33.1	35.0	37.3	37.8	37.5	37.0	37.1	37.1	36.7
Austria	48.2	48.1	49.5	50.1	50.4	50.0	50.9	51.6	51.9	50.2	49.0	48.6	49.8	50.4	53.1	51.8	52.8	52.5	51.5
Belgium	57.4	58.3	63.5	63.5	63.6	62.3	61.9	61.3	59.5	57.0	54.9	55.0	56.2	56.3	56.8	56.1	54.9	54.5	54.3
Denmark	53.2	56.2	59.8	61.2	61.6	60.4	59.3	55.7	57.3	59.4	59.6	58.6	59.2	61.1	63.7	63.6	62.4	62.9	61.9
Finland	38.4	38.1	39.0	40.8	42.4	43.9	43.8	44.7	45.0	44.0	42.0	45.3	53.9	59.1	60.2	59.4	57.6	56.0	55.1
Greece	30.1	30.4	34.8	35.6	37.5	39.9	42.9	42.4	42.3	42.2	43.6	48.3	44.3	45.9	48.5	48.0	46.0	45.5	44.8
Iceland	..	32.5	33.7	34.3	36.1	33.1	35.7	37.8	34.7	39.5	42.0	39.4	40.2	40.6	40.4	40.1	39.0	37.9	36.9
Ireland	45.5	49.3	50.6	53.4	53.0	51.3	52.3	52.5	50.6	47.3	40.6	41.2	42.2	42.9	42.8	43.7	42.0	41.5	40.9
Netherlands	53.9	55.8	57.6	59.8	59.9	58.8	57.1	57.0	58.5	56.7	53.9	54.1	54.6	55.1	55.3	53.1	50.9	50.5	49.5
Norway	45.2	43.3	43.0	43.3	43.4	41.5	40.9	44.6	46.0	49.6	49.2	49.8	50.7	52.0	51.3	49.6	47.4	46.2	44.7
Portugal	34.4	23.8	41.9	40.9	45.6	42.1	41.2	41.6	40.2	39.4	38.4	41.8	43.9	43.3	44.7	42.7	43.1	43.1	43.1
Spain	30.1	32.2	34.9	36.6	37.7	38.1	41.2	40.7	39.6	39.5	40.9	42.0	43.4	44.5	47.6	46.1	44.3	43.4	42.8
Sweden	60.0	60.1	62.6	64.8	64.5	62.0	63.3	61.6	57.8	58.1	58.3	59.1	61.3	67.2	71.0	68.7	66.2	66.6	63.9
Total of above smaller countries	41.6	42.1	45.1	46.4	47.4	46.9	47.9	47.8	47.0	46.3	45.7	46.9	48.3	49.6	51.2	49.9	48.7	48.2	47.4
Total of above EU countries	43.8	44.7	47.2	48.3	48.7	48.7	49.0	48.3	47.8	46.9	46.4	47.5	48.8	50.0	51.9	50.7	50.0	49.9	49.2
Total of above OECD countries	35.7	36.9	38.2	39.5	39.8	39.2	39.4	39.3	39.0	38.2	37.8	38.8	39.7	40.8	41.6	40.8	40.8	40.8	40.5

a) Current outlays plus net capital outlays.

b) Excludes deposit insurance outlays. Includes interest received (which is treated as a negative outlay in the National Income and Product Accounts) and payments made by federal, state and local employee pension schemes.

c) Includes outlays of the German Railways Fund from 1994 onwards and of the Inherited Debt Fund from 1995 onwards.

d) Break in series. As from 1992, the series differs from National Accounts data, having been adjusted by INSEE to exclude interest paid on "coupons courus" attached to government bonds.

Annex Table 29. General government current receipts[a]

As a percentage of nominal GDP

	1979	1980	1981	1982	1983	1984	1985	1986	1987	1988	1989	1990	1991	1992	1993	1994	1995	Projections 1996	1997
United States[b]	29.8	30.0	30.6	30.0	29.3	29.3	29.7	29.7	30.5	30.1	30.2	30.1	30.1	30.0	30.3	30.7	31.3	31.1	31.1
Japan	26.3	27.6	29.0	29.4	29.6	30.2	30.8	31.0	32.5	32.8	33.1	34.2	33.8	33.1	32.1	32.2	31.7	31.9	33.4
Germany	44.6	45.0	45.0	45.7	45.3	45.5	45.8	45.0	44.8	44.1	44.9	43.0	44.6	45.7	46.1	46.5	45.9	45.7	46.0
France	44.1	46.1	46.7	47.6	48.2	49.2	49.3	48.6	49.0	48.3	47.9	48.3	48.3	48.2	49.0	48.4	48.8	49.9	49.9
Italy	31.5	33.3	34.4	36.2	38.0	37.8	38.3	39.1	39.3	39.6	41.4	42.3	43.3	44.1	47.3	45.1	44.7	44.5	43.9
United Kingdom	37.7	39.6	41.6	42.1	41.4	41.3	41.2	40.0	39.3	38.9	38.4	38.7	38.2	36.9	35.8	36.4	37.6	38.1	38.4
Canada	35.3	36.1	38.3	38.8	38.4	38.5	38.5	39.2	39.7	40.0	40.3	41.9	42.6	42.8	42.1	41.9	42.1	42.4	42.5
Total of above countries	32.6	33.4	34.3	34.4	34.3	34.5	34.8	34.7	35.4	35.1	35.4	35.5	35.7	35.7	35.9	35.9	36.1	36.2	36.5
Australia	29.0	29.7	30.7	32.4	31.1	32.1	33.6	34.5	35.1	34.7	34.1	35.5	34.6	33.8	33.7	33.0	34.7	35.1	35.0
Austria	45.8	46.4	47.8	46.7	46.4	47.5	48.5	48.0	47.6	47.1	46.2	46.5	47.2	48.4	48.8	47.3	46.7	48.4	48.3
Belgium	50.3	49.5	50.4	52.5	52.0	52.9	52.9	51.9	52.0	50.2	48.5	49.1	49.6	49.3	50.1	50.9	50.5	51.3	50.6
Denmark	51.5	52.9	52.9	52.0	54.4	56.3	57.3	59.1	59.7	60.0	59.1	57.1	57.1	58.2	59.8	60.1	60.6	61.4	61.1
Finland	41.4	41.0	42.6	42.8	43.1	45.0	46.8	48.2	46.1	48.1	48.3	50.7	52.5	53.2	52.2	53.1	52.1	52.8	53.8
Greece	27.6	27.8	26.5	29.3	30.3	31.4	31.5	32.1	32.8	30.7	29.2	32.1	32.8	33.6	34.3	35.8	36.8	37.6	38.0
Iceland	..	33.8	34.9	36.0	34.1	35.4	34.0	33.8	33.9	37.4	37.5	36.1	37.3	37.8	35.9	35.4	35.6	35.6	34.9
Ireland	34.5	37.1	37.8	40.2	41.8	42.0	41.6	41.9	42.1	42.8	38.9	38.9	39.9	40.4	40.5	41.4	39.7	38.8	38.3
Netherlands	50.9	51.6	52.2	53.2	54.1	53.2	53.4	51.9	52.6	52.1	49.1	49.0	51.7	51.2	52.1	49.8	47.6	47.3	46.8
Norway	46.3	48.5	47.3	47.3	47.2	48.3	50.2	49.9	50.3	52.2	51.0	52.4	50.8	50.3	49.8	50.0	50.5	50.0	48.4
Portugal	28.1	29.4	31.2	33.1	35.4	35.0	33.7	35.2	34.5	35.7	36.0	36.4	37.5	40.0	37.6	37.0	38.0	38.7	38.9
Spain	28.3	29.9	31.2	31.2	33.1	32.8	34.2	34.7	36.4	36.3	38.1	37.9	38.6	40.3	40.2	39.1	38.1	38.1	38.1
Sweden	57.1	56.1	57.4	57.8	59.5	59.0	59.5	60.4	62.1	61.6	63.7	63.3	60.2	59.4	58.8	57.9	58.2	61.1	60.8
Total of above smaller countries	38.9	39.6	40.5	41.3	42.1	42.4	43.2	43.4	44.1	43.9	43.6	44.0	44.4	44.9	44.9	44.3	44.0	44.5	44.3
Total of above EU countries	40.0	41.2	42.1	43.0	43.5	43.7	44.1	43.8	43.9	43.6	43.8	43.7	44.4	44.8	45.4	44.9	44.8	45.2	45.1
Total of above OECD countries	33.4	34.2	35.1	35.3	35.3	35.5	35.9	35.9	36.5	36.3	36.5	36.6	36.9	36.9	37.0	37.0	37.2	37.3	37.5

a) Current receipts exclude capital receipts.
b) Includes contributions to federal, state and local government employee pension schemes.

A32

Annex Table 30. General government financial balances
Surplus (+) or deficit (−) as a percentage of nominal GDP

	1979	1980	1981	1982	1983	1984	1985	1986	1987	1988	1989	1990	1991	1992	1993	1994	1995	Projections 1996	1997
United States[a]	0.2	-1.4	-1.1	-3.5	-4.1	-3.0	-3.2	-3.5	-2.6	-2.1	-1.7	-2.7	-3.3	-4.4	-3.6	-2.3	-2.0	-1.9	-1.8
Japan	-4.7	-4.4	-3.8	-3.6	-3.6	-2.1	-0.8	-0.9	0.5	1.5	2.5	2.9	2.9	1.4	-1.6	-2.1	-3.9	-4.8	-3.7
Germany[b]	-2.6	-2.9	-3.7	-3.3	-2.6	-1.9	-1.2	-1.3	-1.9	-2.2	0.1	-2.1	-3.3	-2.8	-3.5	-2.5	-3.5	-4.1	-3.6
France[c]	-0.8	-0.0	-1.9	-2.8	-3.2	-2.8	-2.9	-2.7	-1.9	-1.7	-1.2	-1.6	-2.2	-4.0	-5.8	-5.8	-5.0	-4.3	-3.7
Italy	-10.2	-8.6	-11.6	-11.3	-10.7	-11.6	-12.6	-11.6	-11.0	-10.7	-9.9	-10.9	-10.2	-9.5	-9.6	-9.0	-7.2	-6.7	-6.4
United Kingdom	-3.3	-3.4	-2.6	-2.5	-3.3	-3.9	-2.8	-2.4	-1.4	1.0	0.9	-1.2	-2.5	-6.3	-7.8	-6.8	-5.7	-4.8	-3.7
Canada	-2.0	-2.8	-1.5	-5.9	-6.9	-6.5	-6.8	-5.4	-3.8	-2.5	-2.9	-4.1	-6.6	-7.4	-7.3	-5.3	-4.2	-2.9	-1.8
Total of above countries	-2.2	-2.7	-2.8	-4.0	-4.4	-3.6	-3.4	-3.3	-2.5	-1.8	-1.2	-2.1	-2.7	-3.8	-4.3	-3.5	-3.5	-3.4	-3.0
Australia	-2.3	-1.7	-0.7	-0.5	-3.9	-3.3	-2.8	-3.0	-0.3	1.0	1.0	0.6	-2.7	-4.0	-3.8	-4.0	-2.4	-1.9	-1.6
Austria	-2.4	-1.7	-1.8	-3.4	-4.0	-2.6	-2.5	-3.7	-4.3	-3.0	-2.8	-2.2	-2.6	-2.1	-4.3	-4.4	-6.2	-4.0	-3.2
Belgium	-7.1	-8.9	-13.1	-11.1	-11.6	-9.4	-9.0	-9.4	-7.6	-6.8	-6.5	-5.8	-6.7	-7.1	-6.7	-5.3	-4.4	-3.2	-3.7
Denmark	-1.7	-3.3	-6.9	-9.1	-7.2	-4.1	-2.0	3.4	2.4	0.6	-0.5	-1.5	-2.1	-2.9	-3.9	-3.5	-1.8	-1.5	-0.8
Finland	3.0	2.9	3.6	2.0	0.6	3.0	3.0	3.5	1.1	4.1	6.3	5.4	-1.5	-5.8	-8.0	-6.3	-5.6	-3.2	-1.2
Greece	-2.5	-2.6	-8.3	-6.3	-7.1	-8.4	-11.5	-10.3	-9.5	-11.5	-14.4	-16.1	-11.5	-12.3	-14.2	-12.1	-9.2	-8.0	-6.8
Iceland	..	1.3	1.3	1.7	-2.0	2.2	-1.7	-4.1	-0.9	-2.0	-4.6	-3.3	-2.9	-2.8	-4.5	-4.7	-3.4	-2.3	-1.9
Ireland	-11.0	-12.2	-12.8	-13.2	-11.2	-9.3	-10.7	-10.6	-8.5	-4.4	-1.8	-2.3	-2.3	-2.4	-2.4	-2.3	-2.4	-2.7	-2.6
Netherlands	-3.0	-4.3	-5.4	-6.6	-5.8	-5.5	-3.6	-5.1	-5.9	-4.6	-4.7	-5.1	-2.9	-3.9	-3.2	-3.2	-3.3	-3.2	-2.7
Norway	1.2	5.2	4.3	4.0	3.8	6.8	9.3	5.3	4.3	2.6	1.8	2.6	0.2	-1.7	-1.5	0.4	3.1	3.9	3.7
Portugal	-6.3	-5.6	-10.8	-7.7	-10.3	-7.1	-7.5	-6.5	-5.6	-3.6	-2.3	-5.5	-6.4	-3.3	-7.1	-5.6	-5.1	-4.4	-4.2
Spain[d]	-1.8	-2.2	-3.7	-5.4	-4.6	-5.2	-6.9	-6.0	-3.1	-3.3	-2.8	-4.1	-4.9	-4.1	-7.5	-6.9	-6.2	-5.2	-4.7
Sweden	-2.9	-4.0	-5.3	-7.0	-5.0	-2.9	-3.8	-1.2	4.2	3.5	5.4	4.2	-1.1	-7.8	-12.3	-10.8	-8.1	-5.5	-3.1
Total of above smaller countries	-2.8	-2.5	-4.6	-5.1	-5.4	-4.5	-4.6	-4.3	-2.8	-2.4	-2.1	-2.9	-3.9	-4.7	-6.3	-5.6	-4.7	-3.7	-3.1
Total of above EU countries	-3.8	-3.4	-5.1	-5.3	-5.1	-4.9	-4.9	-4.5	-3.8	-3.3	-2.5	-3.8	-4.4	-5.3	-6.5	-5.8	-5.3	-4.8	-4.1
Total of above OECD countries	-2.2	-2.7	-3.1	-4.2	-4.5	-3.7	-3.5	-3.5	-2.5	-1.9	-1.3	-2.2	-2.9	-3.9	-4.6	-3.8	-3.6	-3.5	-3.0
General government financial balances excluding social security																			
United States[a,e]	0.3	-1.3	-0.9	-3.3	-4.1	-3.1	-3.5	-3.8	-3.1	-2.9	-2.7	-3.7	-4.2	-5.2	-4.4	-3.2	-2.8	-2.8	-2.7
Japan[e]	-7.3	-7.0	-6.6	-6.3	-6.3	-4.8	-3.9	-4.1	-2.4	-1.6	-0.8	-0.7	-0.8	-2.0	-4.8	-5.0	-6.6	-7.4	-6.3

a) Excludes deposit insurance outlays. Includes cash flow surplus of federal, state and local government employee pension schemes.
b) Includes balances of the German Railways Fund from 1994 onwards and of the Inherited Debt Fund from 1995 onwards.
c) Break in series. As from 1992, the series differs from National Accounts data, having been adjusted by INSEE to exclude interest paid on "coupons courus" attached to government bonds.
d) Currently, the national accounts of Spain include social security payments and contributions on a cash basis, whereas recording them on an accrual basis would provide a measure more consistent with the principles of the System of National Accounts. The Spanish authorities estimate that if this accruals adjustment were made, the financial balance would be -6.2 per cent of GDP in 1994 and -5.8 per cent of GDP in 1995.
e) OECD Secretariat estimates, derived from fiscal year data converted to a calendar year basis. The coverage of the social security systems is not the same in the United States and Japan.

Annex Table 31. General government structural balances[a]

Surplus (+) or deficit (−) as a percentage of potential GDP

	1979	1980	1981	1982	1983	1984	1985	1986	1987	1988	1989	1990	1991	1992	1993	1994	1995	Projections 1996	1997
United States[b]	-0.7	-1.2	-0.7	-1.5	-2.6	-2.8	-3.3	-3.5	-2.6	-2.5	-2.4	-3.3	-3.3	-4.0	-3.3	-2.5	-2.1	-2.0	-1.8
Japan[c]	-5.6	-4.9	-4.1	-3.5	-2.9	-1.3	-0.2	0.4	1.9	1.7	2.1	1.7	1.5	0.4	-1.8	-1.4	-2.4	-3.1	-2.0
Germany[c,d]	-4.4	-3.9	-3.5	-1.6	-0.8	-0.8	-0.2	-0.6	-0.9	-1.8	0.1	-3.1	-4.4	-4.2	-2.9	-2.2	-3.2	-3.1	-2.8
France	-1.7	-0.4	-1.5	-3.0	-2.7	-1.7	-1.6	-1.5	-0.6	-1.4	-1.9	-2.4	-2.3	-3.7	-4.0	-4.5	-3.9	-2.9	-2.5
Italy	-10.9	-9.8	-12.2	-11.1	-9.9	-10.7	-11.7	-11.1	-10.9	-10.9	-10.6	-11.6	-10.6	-9.5	-8.3	-8.0	-6.6	-6.1	-5.8
United Kingdom	-4.8	-3.2	-0.7	-0.1	-1.8	-2.6	-2.3	-2.9	-3.2	-1.9	-2.0	-3.1	-2.3	-4.7	-5.9	-5.5	-4.6	-3.7	-3.0
Canada	-3.0	-2.9	-1.5	-2.8	-3.7	-5.0	-6.4	-5.2	-4.3	-4.1	-4.4	-4.5	-4.9	-4.8	-4.7	-3.9	-2.8	-1.3	-0.6
Total of above countries	-3.2	-2.9	-2.5	-2.7	-3.0	-2.9	-3.0	-3.0	-2.2	-2.2	-2.0	-2.9	-3.0	-3.7	-3.7	-3.1	-2.9	-2.8	-2.3
Australia	-2.6	-1.9	-1.0	0.5	-2.0	-2.8	-2.9	-2.6	-0.2	0.7	0.6	0.5	-1.2	-2.2	-2.5	-3.7	-2.3	-1.9	-1.6
Austria	-3.4	-2.8	-1.4	-2.3	-2.9	-1.2	-1.4	-2.3	-2.9	-2.9	-3.6	-3.2	-3.3	-2.4	-3.4	-4.3	-6.0	-3.4	-2.3
Belgium	-7.5	-11.0	-13.8	-11.4	-10.9	-8.8	-7.8	-7.7	-5.8	-6.4	-6.6	-6.6	-7.4	-7.7	-5.1	-3.8	-3.0	-1.1	-1.9
Denmark	-2.9	-3.4	-5.5	-8.1	-6.6	-4.6	-3.5	1.4	1.3	0.1	-0.5	-1.2	-1.6	-1.5	-2.0	-2.4	-1.1	-0.2	0.2
Finland	3.1	2.2	3.6	1.8	0.6	2.9	2.6	3.3	0.2	2.1	2.8	2.7	0.4	-1.2	-2.5	-2.7	-3.6	-1.8	-0.4
Greece	-4.2	-3.8	-8.5	-5.5	-5.6	-7.1	-10.6	-9.5	-8.2	-11.5	-15.2	-16.3	-12.1	-12.5	-13.3	-11.2	-8.3	-7.2	-5.9
Ireland	-13.6	-13.3	-14.3	-13.2	-9.1	-7.8	-9.3	-7.6	-6.0	-1.9	-0.4	-2.4	-1.4	-1.1	-0.2	-0.8	-2.1	-2.8	-2.7
Netherlands	-3.8	-4.8	-4.7	-4.4	-4.0	-5.1	-4.1	-5.6	-5.7	-4.1	-5.4	-6.6	-4.1	-4.7	-2.5	-3.0	-3.1	-2.4	-2.0
Norway[e]	-4.7	-4.5	-4.7	-4.6	-5.0	-2.9	-2.0	-0.2	0.0	1.5	0.3	-0.7	-3.3	-5.3	-5.6	-4.9	-2.3	-1.3	-1.5
Portugal	-6.9	4.8	-11.9	-8.6	-10.1	-5.2	-5.3	-4.9	-4.9	-3.8	-3.4	-7.3	-8.2	-4.5	-6.7	-4.5	-3.9	-3.2	-3.1
Spain	-0.7	-0.9	-1.8	-3.8	-3.0	-3.5	-5.4	-4.9	-3.5	-4.7	-5.1	-6.8	-7.1	-5.0	-6.1	-5.3	-5.0	-3.9	-3.5
Sweden	-3.7	-4.4	-4.5	-5.8	-4.0	-3.8	-5.0	-2.8	1.8	0.6	2.2	1.5	-2.1	-7.0	-8.9	-8.4	-6.7	-3.9	-1.8
Total of above smaller countries	-3.2	-3.1	-4.5	-4.5	-4.5	-4.1	-4.6	-4.1	-2.9	-3.0	-3.4	-4.4	-4.8	-4.7	-5.0	-4.7	-4.1	-2.9	-2.4
Total of above EU countries	-4.8	-4.0	-4.6	-4.3	-4.0	-3.9	-4.0	-4.0	-3.6	-3.9	-3.6	-5.1	-5.1	-5.3	-5.1	-4.8	-4.5	-3.7	-3.2
Total of above OECD countries	-3.2	-2.9	-2.8	-2.9	-3.2	-3.1	-3.2	-3.1	-2.3	-2.3	-2.2	-3.1	-3.2	-3.8	-3.8	-3.3	-3.1	-2.8	-2.3

a) OECD Secretariat estimates of the structural component of general government financial balances. The estimates are surrounded by large margins of error, reflecting uncertainty as to the present size and future growth of potential output, and the degree to which elimination of the output gap would translate into enhanced tax revenues and reduced expenditure. For a discussion of the methodology, see the section on fiscal policy in "Sources and Methods".

b) Excludes deposit insurance outlays. Includes cash flow surplus of federal, state and local government employee pension schemes. Receipts relating to Operation Desert Storm, amounting to 0.6 per cent of GDP in 1991, are excluded.

c) Excludes expenditure related to Operation Desert Storm in 1991 amounting to 0.2 per cent of GDP for Japan and 0.4 per cent of GDP for Germany.

d) Includes balances of the German Railways Fund from 1994 onwards and of the Inherited Debt Fund from 1995 onwards.

e) As a percentage of mainland potential GDP. The financial balances shown exclude revenues from oil production.

Annex Table 32. **General government primary balances**
Surplus (+) or deficit (−) as a percentage of nominal GDP

	1979	1980	1981	1982	1983	1984	1985	1986	1987	1988	1989	1990	1991	1992	1993	1994	1995	Projections 1996	1997
United States [a]	1.3	−0.3	0.4	−1.8	−2.5	−1.1	−1.2	−1.5	−0.6	−0.1	0.3	−0.7	−1.1	−2.3	−1.6	−0.3	0.4	0.3	0.4
Japan [b]	−4.0	−3.4	−2.6	−2.2	−2.0	−0.3	0.9	0.7	1.8	2.6	3.4	3.6	3.3	1.7	−1.4	−1.8	−3.4	−4.2	−3.0
Germany	−1.4	−1.6	−2.1	−1.3	−0.3	0.4	1.1	1.0	0.5	0.2	2.3	−0.1	−1.2	−0.2	−1.0	0.2	−0.6	−1.1	−0.5
France	0.0	0.8	−0.7	−1.6	−1.4	−0.9	−0.8	−0.6	0.3	0.5	1.0	0.8	0.4	−1.1	−2.7	−2.6	−1.6	−0.9	−0.3
Italy	−5.8	−3.9	−6.1	−4.8	−3.7	−4.1	−5.2	−3.8	−3.6	−3.1	−1.5	−1.8	−0.5	1.4	2.1	1.3	3.4	3.3	3.3
United Kingdom	−0.5	−0.3	0.7	0.7	−0.2	−0.5	0.5	0.7	1.6	3.6	3.3	1.2	−0.4	−4.2	−5.6	−4.2	−2.8	−1.5	−0.3
Canada	−0.3	−0.9	0.9	−3.0	−4.0	−2.9	−2.8	−1.2	0.4	1.8	1.9	1.3	−1.4	−2.3	−2.2	−0.2	1.5	2.8	3.6
Total of above countries	−0.8	−1.2	−0.9	−1.9	−2.1	−1.1	−0.8	−0.8	0.0	0.6	1.3	0.4	−0.1	−1.1	−1.6	−0.8	−0.5	−0.5	−0.1
Australia	−1.5	−0.8	0.2	0.4	−2.8	−1.7	−0.8	−0.8	1.8	2.8	2.9	2.3	−1.1	−2.4	−2.0	−1.6	0.0	0.5	0.8
Austria	−0.6	0.0	0.2	−1.1	−1.7	0.2	0.4	−0.8	−1.2	0.2	0.3	1.0	0.7	1.3	−0.8	−1.1	−2.7	−0.5	0.7
Belgium [b]	−2.5	−3.5	−5.9	−2.6	−2.9	−0.2	0.9	1.0	2.3	2.7	3.2	4.1	2.8	2.8	3.1	4.3	4.3	5.2	4.7
Denmark [c]	−1.2	−2.8	−5.1	−6.5	−2.9	1.7	4.1	8.5	6.9	4.8	3.3	1.8	1.4	0.0	−0.3	0.0	2.0	2.2	2.6
Finland	2.0	1.9	2.5	0.9	−0.4	2.1	2.1	2.4	0.2	3.2	5.1	3.6	−3.4	−7.8	−8.3	−5.5	−4.3	−1.4	0.5
Greece [b]	−0.4	−0.3	−5.3	−3.9	−3.6	−4.1	−6.4	−4.8	−2.7	−4.1	−6.8	−6.0	−2.1	−0.6	−1.4	2.1	3.7	3.9	4.0
Iceland	..	1.0	1.4	1.5	−2.2	2.4	−1.5	−3.4	−0.5	−0.8	−3.1	−1.4	−1.1	−0.9	−2.4	−2.5	−1.0	0.0	0.4
Ireland [b]	−7.7	−8.6	−8.3	−7.7	−5.7	−3.4	−4.2	−3.9	−1.8	1.9	4.3	3.8	3.4	2.7	2.4	2.2	1.8	1.3	1.2
Netherlands	−1.0	−1.9	−2.4	−2.8	−1.6	−1.1	1.0	−0.3	−1.0	0.3	−0.3	−0.7	1.7	0.8	1.6	1.5	1.4	1.5	1.9
Norway	1.2	5.4	4.2	3.7	3.5	5.9	8.0	3.5	1.9	−0.7	−0.4	1.1	−1.3	−3.1	−1.8	0.8	3.2	4.0	3.8
Portugal	−3.8	8.4	−6.0	−3.0	−4.7	0.2	0.9	2.3	2.2	3.5	4.1	3.2	2.1	4.4	−0.4	0.2	0.6	0.8	0.7
Spain [d]	−1.6	−1.9	−3.3	−5.0	−3.8	−3.8	−4.2	−2.7	−0.3	−0.3	0.3	−0.8	−1.3	−0.3	−2.6	−2.1	−1.1	−0.2	0.6
Sweden	−4.1	−4.4	−4.9	−5.4	−3.1	−0.5	−0.8	1.0	6.0	4.5	5.9	4.3	−1.0	−7.5	−11.2	−8.4	−5.1	−2.0	0.2
Total of above smaller countries	−1.6	−1.1	−2.7	−2.9	−2.7	−1.2	−0.8	−0.3	1.0	1.3	1.5	1.0	−0.1	−0.7	−1.8	−0.9	0.0	1.0	1.5
Total of above EU countries	−1.9	−1.3	−2.5	−2.3	−1.8	−1.3	−1.0	−0.5	0.0	0.5	1.3	0.2	−0.3	−0.7	−1.7	−1.1	−0.3	0.2	0.7
Total of above OECD countries	−0.9	−1.2	−1.2	−2.0	−2.2	−1.1	−0.8	−0.7	0.1	0.7	1.3	0.5	−0.1	−1.1	−1.6	−0.9	−0.5	−0.3	0.1

a) Excludes deposit insurance outlays. Includes contributions to and payments made by federal, state and local government employee pension schemes.
b) Where net interest payments are not available, net property income paid is used as a proxy.
c) The primary balance excludes not only net interest payments, but also dividends received.
d) Currently, the national accounts of Spain include social security payments and contributions on a cash basis, whereas recording them on an accrual basis would provide a measure more consistent with the principles of the System of National Accounts. The Spanish authorities estimate that if this accruals adjustment were made, the primary balance would be −1.4 per cent of GDP in 1994 and −0.7 per cent of GDP in 1995.

A35

Annex Table 33. **General government net debt interest payments**

As a percentage of nominal GDP

	1979	1980	1981	1982	1983	1984	1985	1986	1987	1988	1989	1990	1991	1992	1993	1994	1995	Projections 1996	1997
United States[a]	1.0	1.1	1.5	1.6	1.7	1.9	2.0	1.9	1.9	1.9	2.0	2.1	2.2	2.1	2.0	2.0	2.3	2.3	2.2
Japan[b]	0.8	1.0	1.2	1.4	1.6	1.7	1.7	1.6	1.4	1.1	0.9	0.7	0.4	0.2	0.2	0.3	0.5	0.6	0.7
Germany[c]	1.1	1.3	1.6	2.0	2.3	2.3	2.3	2.3	2.4	2.3	2.2	2.0	2.1	2.6	2.6	2.7	2.9	3.0	3.1
France[d]	0.8	0.8	1.2	1.2	1.7	1.9	2.1	2.1	2.2	2.1	2.2	2.4	2.5	2.8	3.1	3.2	3.4	3.5	3.5
Italy	4.4	4.7	5.5	6.6	7.0	7.5	7.4	7.8	7.4	7.6	8.4	9.1	9.7	10.9	11.6	10.3	10.5	10.0	9.6
United Kingdom	2.8	3.1	3.3	3.2	3.1	3.3	3.3	3.1	3.0	2.7	2.4	2.3	2.1	2.1	2.2	2.6	3.0	3.3	3.4
Canada	1.7	1.9	2.3	2.9	2.9	3.5	4.0	4.2	4.2	4.3	4.8	5.3	5.2	5.1	5.0	5.1	5.6	5.7	5.4
Total of above countries	1.4	1.5	1.9	2.1	2.3	2.5	2.6	2.5	2.5	2.4	2.4	2.5	2.6	2.6	2.7	2.7	2.9	2.9	2.9
Australia	0.8	0.9	0.9	0.9	1.2	1.6	2.0	2.2	2.1	1.8	1.9	1.8	1.7	1.7	1.8	2.4	2.4	2.4	2.5
Austria	1.8	1.7	1.9	2.3	2.3	2.7	2.9	2.9	3.1	3.2	3.1	3.2	3.3	3.4	3.5	3.4	3.5	3.6	3.9
Belgium[b]	4.6	5.4	7.2	8.5	8.7	9.2	9.8	10.4	9.9	9.4	9.7	9.9	9.5	9.9	9.8	9.6	8.8	8.3	8.3
Denmark[e]	0.5	0.5	1.8	2.6	4.3	5.8	6.1	5.1	4.5	4.2	3.8	3.4	3.5	2.8	3.6	3.5	3.7	3.7	3.4
Finland	-1.0	-1.0	-1.1	-1.0	-1.0	-0.9	-0.9	-1.0	-0.9	-0.9	-1.2	-1.8	-2.0	-2.0	-0.3	0.9	1.3	1.8	1.8
Greece[b]	2.1	2.3	3.0	2.5	3.5	4.3	5.1	5.5	6.8	7.5	7.6	10.2	9.4	11.7	12.8	14.2	12.9	11.9	10.8
Iceland	..	-0.3	0.1	-0.2	-0.2	0.2	0.1	0.6	0.4	1.2	1.5	2.0	1.9	1.9	2.1	2.2	2.4	2.3	2.3
Ireland[b]	3.3	3.6	4.5	5.5	5.5	5.9	6.5	6.7	6.7	6.3	6.0	6.1	5.7	5.2	4.8	4.5	4.2	4.0	3.9
Netherlands	2.0	2.4	3.0	3.8	4.2	4.5	4.7	4.7	4.9	4.9	4.4	4.4	4.6	4.7	4.8	4.8	4.7	4.7	4.6
Norway	0.1	0.2	-0.2	-0.3	-0.3	-1.0	-1.4	-1.9	-2.4	-3.3	-2.2	-1.4	-1.4	-1.4	-0.2	0.4	0.2	0.2	0.1
Portugal	2.6	2.8	4.8	4.8	5.5	7.4	8.4	8.7	7.9	7.1	6.4	8.7	8.5	7.7	6.7	5.8	5.7	5.2	4.9
Spain	0.2	0.3	0.3	0.4	0.7	1.5	2.7	3.3	2.9	3.0	3.1	3.3	3.6	3.9	4.8	4.8	5.1	5.1	5.3
Sweden	-1.1	-0.4	0.3	1.6	1.9	2.4	3.0	2.2	1.7	1.0	0.5	0.1	0.1	0.2	1.1	2.4	2.9	3.5	3.3
Total of above smaller countries	1.1	1.4	1.9	2.3	2.7	3.2	3.8	4.0	3.8	3.6	3.6	3.9	3.8	4.0	4.5	4.7	4.7	4.7	4.6
Total of above EU countries	1.9	2.1	2.6	3.0	3.3	3.7	3.9	4.0	3.8	3.8	3.8	4.0	4.1	4.5	4.8	4.8	4.9	4.9	4.9
Total of above OECD countries	1.3	1.5	1.9	2.1	2.3	2.6	2.7	2.7	2.6	2.6	2.6	2.7	2.7	2.8	2.9	2.9	3.2	3.1	3.1

a) Includes interest receipts of federal, state and local government employee pension schemes.
b) Where net interest payments are not available, net property income paid is used as a proxy.
c) Includes interest payments of the German Railways Fund from 1994 onwards and of the Inherited Debt Fund from 1995 onwards.
d) Break in series. As from 1992, the series differs from National Accounts data, having been adjusted by INSEE to exclude interest paid on ''coupons courus'' attached to government bonds.
e) Net interest payments including dividends received are used.

Annex Table 34. **General government gross financial liabilities**[a]

As a percentage of nominal GDP

	1979	1980	1981	1982	1983	1984	1985	1986	1987	1988	1989	1990	1991	1992	1993	1994	1995	Projections 1996	Projections 1997
United States	36.5	37.0	36.2	40.7	43.7	45.1	49.1	51.8	53.3	53.8	54.2	55.6	59.6	62.0	63.5	63.7	64.3	64.1[b]	63.8
Japan	45.6	51.2	55.5	59.4	63.8	65.8	67.0	70.5	72.5	70.9	68.7	65.1	62.3	63.5	67.9	73.2	81.3[b]	88.8	95.4
Germany[d,e]	30.8	32.8	36.5	39.6	41.1	41.7	42.5	42.5	43.8	44.4	43.2	45.5	44.4	45.8	52.0	51.6	61.6[b]	64.4	65.7
France	31.4	30.9	30.1	34.2	35.3	37.1	38.6	39.3	40.7	40.6	40.6	40.2	41.0	45.6	52.5	54.7	57.9[b]	60.3	62.1
Italy	60.3	57.7	59.9	64.9	70.0	75.2	82.3	86.3	90.5	92.6	95.6	106.4[c]	110.3	116.7	118.4	123.9	123.0[b]	123.1	123.3
United Kingdom	54.3	54.0	54.5	53.2	53.4	60.3[c]	58.9	57.9	55.6	49.3	42.9	39.3	40.6	47.7	56.9	54.6	57.6[b]	60.7	62.0
Canada	43.7	44.3	45.0	50.1	55.2	58.7	64.1	67.8	68.4	68.1	69.2	72.5	79.4	87.2	94.4	96.8	99.1	99.4[b]	97.9
Total of above countries	40.5	41.7	42.7	46.6	49.6	51.8	54.7	57.0	58.4	58.2	57.6	58.5	60.3	63.4	67.1	68.7	71.9	73.9	75.3
Australia[f]	..	..	..	..	..	..	..	..	31.1	24.6	22.6	21.3	22.9	27.8	32.0	42.7[b]	43.8	43.0	42.0
Austria	36.0	37.3[c]	39.3	41.8	46.5	48.6	50.5	54.9	58.7	59.5	58.9	58.3	58.7	58.3	62.8	65.0	69.4	72.3[b]	73.9
Belgium	70.6	78.7	92.9	102.9	113.7	118.4	122.6	127.3	131.8	132.1	128.9	130.9	130.3	131.5	137.9	136.0	133.5	132.4[b]	131.1
Denmark	..	44.7	54.9	67.0	77.9	79.3	76.6	73.4	70.2	68.2	66.9	68.0	69.1	73.2	86.0	80.2	80.1[b]	80.0	78.3
Finland	14.6	14.1	14.5	16.9	18.5	17.8	18.9	20.0	20.5	19.5	18.2	16.9	25.6	46.2	59.5	61.7	63.0[b]	64.1	64.2
Greece[e]	22.8	22.9	27.1	29.8	34.1	40.9	47.8	48.4	53.3	63.5	66.6	81.6	83.1	99.1	111.7	110.4	111.5	109.4[b]	107.3
Iceland	..	25.2	22.6	29.4	33.1	33.4	33.1	30.6	28.1	30.1	35.8	35.2	36.4	43.5	50.0	52.4	55.2[b]	54.6	53.7
Ireland	70.3	71.8	76.4	82.2	95.4	99.6	102.6	114.9	116.2[c]	113.3	103.3	97.1	96.7	94.2	97.3	91.5	85.8[b]	82.2	79.9
Netherlands	44.1	46.9	50.9	56.5	62.7	66.8	71.5	73.5	76.1	79.2	79.1	78.8	78.8	79.4	81.1	77.6	79.1	78.6[b]	78.2
Norway	57.4	47.6	43.3	38.4	35.4	35.3	37.1	46.6	39.0	35.1	34.9	31.6	29.4	35.0	43.3	40.2[b]	39.7	37.7	36.5
Portugal	22.6	33.0	41.6	44.6	49.7	55.4	58.5	56.5	63.6	65.0	62.8	68.6[c]	70.2	62.4	67.2	69.5	70.7	71.7[b]	72.5
Spain	16.5	18.3	24.0	30.4	38.7	45.4	45.4	51.4	50.7	46.9	48.4	54.3	51.5	54.3	65.8	68.4	71.1[b]	73.6	75.5
Sweden	39.6	44.3[c]	52.1	61.7	65.6	67.0	66.7	66.2	59.0	53.1	48.4	44.3	53.2	71.1	76.3	81.5	81.8[b]	83.2	81.5
Total of above smaller countries	33.9	36.2	40.9	46.2	52.0	55.8	58.9	60.2	60.7	59.2	58.3	59.2	60.8	65.2	72.6	74.4	75.5	76.0	75.9
Total of above EU countries	40.3	41.1	44.0	47.8	51.2	54.8	57.2	58.3	59.4	58.7	57.7	59.8	60.8	65.3	71.8	72.8	76.3	78.1	79.0
Total of above OECD countries	39.7	41.0	42.5	46.5	49.9	52.3	55.2	57.4	58.7	58.3	57.7	58.6	60.4	63.6	67.8	69.4	72.4	74.2	75.4

a) This table previously appeared under the title **Gross Public Debt**. The title has been changed to reflect more accurately the nature of the data shown, which includes all financial liabilities as defined by the System of National Accounts (where data permits) and covers the general government sector, which is a consolidation of central government, state and local government and the social security sector. It should be noted that the definition of debt applied under the Maastricht Treaty differs from the System of National Accounts definition shown here. Estimates of general government gross debt according to the Maastricht definition are shown in Annex Table 61.

b) Break in the series starting this year.

c) OECD Secretariat estimates starting from this year.

d) Includes the debt of the German Railways Fund from 1994 onwards and of the Inherited Debt Fund from 1995 onwards.

e) Assets held by one sub-sector of general government which constitute liabilities for another sub-sector of general government have not been fully consolidated.

f) Debt data refer to fiscal years ending 30 June. Data include indebtedness of local government towards other levels of general government.

Annex Table 35. General government net financial liabilities[a]

As a percentage of nominal GDP

	1979	1980	1981	1982	1983	1984	1985	1986	1987	1988	1989	1990	1991	1992	1993	1994	1995	Projections 1996	1997
United States	21.6	21.8	21.6	25.4	28.7	29.8	32.2	35.2	37.0	38.0	38.3	39.7	43.1	46.7	48.8	49.6	50.7b	50.4	50.2
Japan	13.3	16.4	19.2	21.8	24.5	26.1	25.9	25.0	22.0	18.3	14.9	10.6	5.4	3.7	4.6	6.8	10.7b	15.3	18.0
Germany[d]	11.6	11.8	15.0	17.8	19.5	20.4	20.8	21.2	22.4	23.4	22.0	20.6	22.2	26.7	35.1	39.6	44.1b	46.9	48.1
France	-0.2	-3.3	0.0	2.1	4.6	7.5	10.8	13.8	13.0	14.2	14.8	16.3	16.5	20.4	28.1	31.0	34.8b	38.2	40.6
Italy	54.7	52.7	56.0	62.3	67.2	72.7	80.0	84.1	88.4	90.7	93.8	84.3c	89.3	95.6	103.7	108.6	109.0b	110.1	111.3
United Kingdom[e]	36.0	36.2	37.8	37.3	37.5	30.0c	30.6	31.0	29.3	23.7	19.1	18.8	19.2	26.1	35.5	35.5	39.6b	42.7	44.0
Canada	13.0	13.3	11.7	17.7	24.1	28.5	34.7	38.7	38.8	37.7	39.9	43.1	48.5	56.5	62.5	67.5	69.8b	70.1	68.5
Total of above countries	20.5	20.8	22.1	25.4	28.4	29.6	31.8	33.8	34.3	34.0	33.4	32.7	34.0	37.3	41.4	43.4	45.8	47.4	48.2
Australia[f]	..								19.1	14.9	11.3	10.6	11.8	16.9	22.3	27.4b	28.4	29.1	29.4
Austria[g]	..	20.0	21.9	23.3	28.1	29.3	31.0	34.1	37.0	38.9	38.6	38.6	38.5	39.6	44.4	45.3	49.7b	52.5	54.1
Belgium[h]	63.1	69.6	84.3	94.2	105.2	109.6	112.6	117.5	121.7	122.1	119.5	119.3	120.3	122.0	128.2	127.6	127.6	127.6b	126.3
Denmark	..	14.2	25.0	38.1	46.6	49.9	46.3	38.7	34.4	36.2	34.1	34.0	38.9	40.8	45.6	46.0	45.8b	45.7	44.1
Finland	-31.0	-30.7	-30.4	-28.1	-26.5	-26.3	-27.6	-28.5	-28.3	-29.8	-33.9	-36.1	-34.8	-26.3	-18.2	-13.7	-7.1b	-3.6	-2.2
Iceland	..	3.3	3.1	0.5	5.8	5.8	6.1	9.0	8.2	8.5	16.4	17.6	17.5	23.6	31.2	33.6	34.7b	34.4	33.7
Netherlands	21.6	24.6	26.9	30.9	35.9	39.4	42.3	45.5	28.2c	32.2	35.9	36.9	37.7	41.3	42.5	42.7b	43.3	44.3	44.1
Norway	8.9	0.4	-2.0	-4.3	-7.7	-11.4	-14.6	-19.2	-19.5	-33.6	-33.2	-33.4	-31.1	-28.7	-26.0	-24.8b	-26.3	-28.5	-31.0
Spain	5.8	6.1	9.2	13.0	18.5	22.0	27.5	30.1	30.7	31.4	30.9	31.7	33.4	35.7	43.1	47.6	50.3b	52.8	54.7
Sweden	-19.8	-13.9c	-5.6	4.2	10.8	13.7	14.3	12.9	6.6	0.2	-6.2	-8.1	-5.2	4.7	11.0c	21.9	27.8b	32.3	34.0
Total of above smaller countries	13.2	14.9	18.7	22.7	27.8	30.2	32.5	33.9	31.2	30.3	29.0	29.0	30.5	34.2	39.7	43.0	45.1	46.8	47.3
Total of above EU countries	21.5	20.9	24.4	27.8	31.1	32.4	35.1	37.0	36.9	37.0	36.3	34.6	36.1	40.9	48.6	51.9	55.0	57.4	58.8
Total of above OECD countries	19.8	20.1	21.7	25.1	28.3	29.7	31.9	33.8	33.9	33.6	32.9	32.2	33.6	37.0	41.2	43.4	45.7	47.3	48.1

a) This table previously appeared under the title **Net Public Debt**. The title has been changed to reflect more accurately the nature of the data shown, which includes all financial liabilities less all financial assets, as defined by the System of National Accounts (where data permits) and covers the general government sector, which is a consolidation of central government, state and local government and the social security sector.
b) OECD Secretariat estimates starting from this year.
c) Break in the series starting this year.
d) Includes the debt of the German Railways Fund from 1994 onwards and of the Inherited Debt Fund from 1995 onwards.
e) Financial assets exclude shares and holdings in public corporations.
f) Debt data refer to fiscal years ending 30 June.
g) Financial assets exclude shares, holdings in public corporations and financial assets of the social security system.
h) Financial assets exclude shares, holdings in public corporations and lending.

Annex Table 36. **Short- and long-term interest rates**[a]

	1982	1983	1984	1985	1986	1987	1988	1989	1990	1991	1992	1993	1994	1995	Projections 1996	Projections 1997
Short-term rates																
United States	10.6	8.6	9.5	7.5	6.0	5.8	6.7	8.1	7.5	5.4	3.4	3.0	4.2	5.5	5.1	5.3
Japan	7.0	6.7	6.5	6.6	5.1	4.2	4.5	5.4	7.7	7.2	4.3	2.9	2.3	1.2	0.7	0.9
Germany	8.9	5.8	6.0	5.4	4.6	4.0	4.3	7.1	8.5	9.2	9.5	7.3	5.4	4.5	3.3	3.5
France	14.6	12.5	11.7	9.9	7.7	8.3	7.9	9.4	10.3	9.6	10.3	8.6	5.8	6.6	3.9	3.8
Italy	19.9	18.3	17.3	15.3	13.4	11.3	10.8	12.6	12.0	12.0	14.4	10.7	8.5	10.3	9.9	8.9
United Kingdom	12.3	10.1	9.9	12.2	10.9	9.7	10.3	13.9	14.8	11.5	9.6	5.9	5.5	6.7	6.0	6.0
Canada	14.4	9.5	11.2	9.6	9.2	8.4	9.6	12.2	13.0	9.0	6.7	5.0	5.4	7.0	4.9	4.8
Australia	16.6	12.2	12.2	16.2	16.4	13.5	12.9	17.7	14.4	10.1	6.5	5.1	5.7	7.7	7.5	7.5
Austria	8.8	5.4	6.5	6.2	5.3	4.3	4.6	7.5	8.5	9.1	9.3	7.2	5.0	4.3	3.3	3.4
Belgium	14.0	10.4	11.4	9.5	8.1	7.1	6.7	8.8	9.6	9.4	9.4	8.2	5.7	4.8	3.4	3.6
Denmark	16.8	12.7	11.7	10.2	9.1	10.1	8.5	9.8	10.8	9.7	11.5	10.3	6.2	6.0	3.9	4.1
Finland	11.8	14.6	16.5	13.5	12.7	10.0	10.0	12.6	14.0	13.1	13.3	7.8	5.4	5.8	3.8	4.0
Ireland	16.3	13.2	13.2	11.9	12.5	10.8	8.0	10.0	11.3	10.4	14.3	9.1	5.9	6.3	5.1	5.0
Mexico	45.7	59.5	49.7	63.7	90.5	102.8	62.1	44.8	35.0	19.8	15.9	15.5	14.7	48.4	36.0	22.0
Netherlands	8.4	5.6	6.1	6.3	5.7	5.4	4.8	7.4	8.7	9.3	9.4	6.9	5.2	4.4	3.1	3.4
New Zealand	17.0	13.1	15.0	23.3	19.1	21.1	15.4	13.5	13.9	10.0	6.7	6.3	6.7	9.0	9.1	8.6
Norway	15.4	13.3	13.0	12.5	14.4	14.7	13.5	11.4	11.5	10.6	11.8	7.3	5.9	5.5	4.5	4.8
Spain	16.3	20.0	14.9	12.2	11.7	15.8	11.7	15.0	15.2	13.2	13.3	11.7	8.0	9.4	7.5	6.8
Sweden	13.3	11.4	11.9	14.2	9.8	9.4	10.1	11.5	13.7	11.6	12.9	8.4	7.4	8.7	6.5	6.0
Switzerland	5.1	4.1	4.3	4.9	4.2	3.8	3.1	6.9	8.8	8.1	7.8	4.8	4.0	3.0	1.6	1.9
Long-term rates																
United States	13.0	11.1	12.4	10.6	7.7	8.4	8.8	8.5	8.6	7.9	7.0	5.9	7.1	6.6	6.6	6.6
Japan	8.3	7.8	7.3	6.5	5.1	5.0	4.8	5.2	7.0	6.4	5.3	4.3	4.4	3.4	3.4	3.7
Germany	8.9	8.2	8.1	7.2	6.3	6.4	6.6	7.1	8.7	8.5	7.9	6.5	6.9	6.9	6.5	6.4
France	16.0	14.4	13.4	11.9	9.1	10.2	9.2	9.2	10.4	9.5	9.0	7.0	7.5	7.7	6.6	6.4
Italy	20.2	18.3	15.6	13.7	11.5	10.6	10.9	12.8	13.5	13.1	13.7	11.3	10.6	11.8	10.2	9.9
United Kingdom	13.1	11.3	11.3	11.1	10.1	9.6	9.7	10.2	11.8	10.1	9.1	7.5	8.2	8.2	8.0	8.0
Canada	14.4	11.8	12.7	11.1	9.5	9.9	10.2	9.9	10.8	9.8	8.8	7.9	8.6	8.4	7.8	7.3
Australia	15.3	14.1	13.6	13.9	13.4	13.2	12.1	13.4	13.2	10.7	9.2	7.3	9.0	9.2	8.8	8.6
Austria	9.9	8.2	8.0	7.8	7.3	6.9	6.7	7.1	8.7	8.6	8.3	6.6	6.7	6.5	6.2	6.0
Belgium	13.4	11.9	12.2	11.0	8.6	8.2	8.0	8.6	10.1	9.3	8.7	7.2	7.7	7.4	6.9	6.7
Denmark	21.4	15.1	14.5	11.6	10.1	11.3	9.6	9.8	10.6	9.3	8.9	7.2	7.9	8.3	7.1	6.7
Finland	11.0	10.8	11.1	10.7	8.9	7.9	10.3	12.1	13.2	11.9	12.1	8.2	8.4	7.9	6.8	6.7
Ireland	17.1	13.9	14.6	12.6	11.1	11.3	9.5	8.9	10.1	9.2	9.1	7.7	8.2	8.3	7.7	7.5
Mexico	..	56.3	56.3	63.7	90.5	102.8	62.1	44.8	34.9	19.7	16.1	15.5	13.8	39.8	34.0	22.0
Netherlands	9.9	8.2	8.1	7.3	6.3	6.4	6.4	7.2	8.9	8.7	8.1	6.4	6.9	6.9	6.5	6.4
New Zealand	12.9	12.2	12.6	17.6	16.7	15.7	13.1	12.8	12.5	9.9	8.4	6.9	7.7	7.7	8.1	7.4
Norway	13.2	12.9	12.2	12.6	13.3	13.3	12.9	10.8	10.7	10.0	9.6	6.9	7.4	7.4	6.8	6.7
Spain	16.0	16.9	16.5	13.4	11.4	12.8	11.7	13.8	14.6	12.8	11.7	10.2	10.0	11.3	9.6	9.2
Sweden	13.3	12.6	12.5	13.2	10.5	11.7	11.4	11.2	13.2	10.7	10.0	8.5	9.5	10.2	8.5	8.0
Switzerland	4.8	4.4	4.5	4.7	4.2	4.0	4.0	5.2	6.4	6.2	6.4	4.6	5.0	4.5	4.1	4.1

a) For sources and detailed definitions, see "Sources and Methods".

Annex Table 37. **Nominal exchange rates (*vis-à-vis* the US dollar)**

Average of daily rates

	Monetary unit	1983	1984	1985	1986	1987	1988	1989	1990	1991	1992	1993	1994	1995	Projections[a] 1996	1997
United States	Dollar	1.000	1.000	1.000	1.000	1.000	1.000	1.000	1.000	1.000	1.000	1.000	1.000	1.000	1.000	1.000
Japan	Yen	237.5	237.6	238.6	168.5	144.6	128.2	138.0	144.8	134.5	126.7	111.2	102.2	94.1	105.6	105.3
Germany	Deutschemark	2.553	2.846	2.944	2.172	1.797	1.756	1.880	1.616	1.659	1.562	1.653	1.623	1.433	1.515	1.534
France	Franc	7.621	8.739	8.984	6.927	6.009	5.956	6.380	5.446	5.641	5.294	5.662	5.552	4.991	5.146	5.193
Italy	Lira	1519	1757	1909	1491	1297	1302	1372	1198	1241	1232	1572	1613	1629	1569	1568
United Kingdom	Pound	0.660	0.752	0.779	0.682	0.612	0.562	0.611	0.563	0.567	0.570	0.666	0.653	0.634	0.662	0.666
Canada	Dollar	1.232	1.295	1.366	1.389	1.326	1.231	1.184	1.167	1.146	1.209	1.290	1.366	1.373	1.364	1.363
Australia	Dollar	1.109	1.141	1.432	1.496	1.429	1.281	1.265	1.282	1.284	1.362	1.473	1.369	1.350	1.273	1.255
Austria	Schilling	17.97	20.01	20.69	15.27	12.64	12.34	13.23	11.37	11.67	10.99	11.63	11.42	10.08	10.67	10.82
Belgium-Luxembourg	Franc	51.13	57.76	59.43	44.69	37.34	36.77	39.40	33.42	34.16	32.15	34.56	33.46	29.50	31.13	31.51
Czech Republic	Koruny	..	..	..	..	..	..	..	..	29.47	28.26	29.15	28.79	26.54	27.57	27.75
Denmark	Krone	9.14	10.36	10.59	8.09	6.84	6.73	7.31	6.19	6.40	6.04	6.48	6.36	5.60	5.85	5.91
Finland	Markka	5.565	6.003	6.196	5.070	4.396	4.186	4.288	3.823	4.043	4.486	5.721	5.223	4.367	4.748	4.831
Greece	Drachma	87.9	112.7	138.1	139.5	135.2	141.6	162.1	158.2	182.1	190.5	229.1	242.2	231.6	243.9	249.0
Iceland	Krona	24.85	31.73	41.54	41.10	38.68	43.03	56.68	58.36	59.10	57.62	67.64	70.00	64.77	67.04	67.37
Ireland	Pound	0.805	0.923	0.946	0.747	0.672	0.657	0.706	0.605	0.622	0.588	0.683	0.670	0.624	0.642	0.645
Mexico	Peso	0.155	0.192	0.327	0.639	1.418	2.281	2.495	2.841	3.022	3.095	3.115	3.389	6.421	7.486	7.475
Netherlands	Guilder	2.854	3.209	3.322	2.450	2.026	1.977	2.121	1.821	1.870	1.758	1.857	1.820	1.605	1.694	1.714
New Zealand	Dollar	1.496	1.767	2.026	1.917	1.695	1.529	1.674	1.678	1.729	1.860	1.851	1.687	1.524	1.460	1.450
Norway	Krone	7.296	8.160	8.594	7.392	6.737	6.517	6.903	6.258	6.482	6.214	7.092	7.057	6.337	6.539	6.591
Portugal	Escudo	110.8	146.4	169.9	148.2	140.8	143.9	157.1	142.3	144.4	134.8	160.7	166.0	149.9	155.9	157.4
Spain	Peseta	143.5	160.8	170.1	140.0	123.5	116.5	118.4	101.9	103.9	102.4	127.2	134.0	124.7	126.1	127.0
Sweden	Krona	7.667	8.273	8.602	7.124	6.340	6.129	6.446	5.918	6.045	5.824	7.785	7.716	7.134	6.825	6.856
Switzerland	Franc	2.099	2.350	2.457	1.798	1.491	1.463	1.635	1.389	1.434	1.406	1.477	1.367	1.182	1.230	1.246
Turkey	Lira	224	363	520	669	855	1419	2120	2606	4169	6861	10966	29778	45738	82231	135848
Chinese Taipei	Dollar	40.07	39.60	39.85	37.84	31.92	28.57	26.28	26.63	26.55	25.02	26.35	26.45	26.49	27.23	27.17
Hong Kong	Dollar	7.265	7.818	7.791	7.804	7.795	7.806	7.799	7.789	7.770	7.739	7.735	7.728	7.734	7.734	7.735
Korea	Won	775.7	806.0	870.0	881.0	825.0	730.3	669.2	708.0	733.2	780.0	802.4	804.3	771.4	779.4	778.1
Singapore	Dollar	2.113	2.133	2.200	2.177	2.106	2.013	1.949	1.812	1.727	1.628	1.615	1.527	1.417	1.408	1.407
ECU		1.125	1.272	1.322	1.019	0.867	0.846	0.908	0.788	0.809	0.773	0.854	0.843	0.765	0.797	0.805
SDR		0.936	0.975	0.986	0.853	0.774	0.742	0.780	0.738	0.731	0.710	0.716	0.699	0.659	0.689	0.692

a) On the technical assumption that exchange rates remain at their levels of 2 May 1996, except for Greece and Turkey where exchange rates vary according to official exchange rate policy.

Annex Table 38. **Effective exchange rates**[a]

Indices 1991 = 100, average of daily rates

	1983	1984	1985	1986	1987	1988	1989	1990	1991	1992	1993	1994	1995	Projections[b] 1996	1997
United States	116.5	124.1	130.6	114.0	105.3	100.1	102.8	101.0	100.0	98.6	100.7	100.0	100.5	106.0	106.3
Japan	62.7	65.8	68.3	90.0	97.6	106.5	99.9	91.8	100.0	105.4	126.5	136.2	143.6	128.9	129.7
Germany	80.8	80.4	81.2	89.9	96.0	95.9	95.1	100.4	100.0	103.5	107.3	108.8	115.3	113.1	113.0
France	98.4	95.0	96.4	99.7	99.9	98.1	97.0	101.6	100.0	103.3	106.5	107.9	111.5	112.0	112.0
Italy	107.5	103.1	98.2	100.8	100.9	98.1	99.0	101.1	100.0	97.3	81.9	78.9	71.5	77.7	78.6
United Kingdom	111.5	107.1	107.4	99.6	98.0	103.8	100.5	99.1	100.0	96.4	88.2	88.9	85.1	84.3	84.5
Canada	98.6	95.7	91.8	86.1	87.5	93.0	97.9	98.2	100.0	94.1	88.8	83.5	83.0	84.6	84.7
Australia	149.8	152.9	125.1	100.8	94.9	100.5	105.4	101.3	100.0	92.4	86.3	90.1	86.6	95.6	97.1
Austria	89.7	89.6	90.4	94.9	98.0	97.9	97.3	100.3	100.0	102.0	104.4	105.0	108.6	107.0	106.7
Belgium–Luxembourg	86.2	84.7	85.7	91.8	96.2	95.2	94.4	99.9	100.0	102.6	103.7	106.0	111.3	109.4	109.1
Czech Republic								..	100.0	101.1	106.9	107.6	107.6	108.2	108.9
Denmark	91.1	88.6	90.0	95.4	98.9	97.2	94.9	101.3	100.0	102.5	105.9	106.3	111.2	110.3	110.0
Finland	96.1	98.1	98.6	96.6	97.2	98.6	102.1	103.8	100.0	87.0	76.0	82.5	91.2	86.3	85.4
Greece	288.0	249.3	211.9	162.0	144.0	133.6	123.8	112.6	100.0	92.4	84.8	79.5	77.5	76.0	75.1
Iceland	319.6	271.8	213.4	173.9	161.7	140.9	112.6	99.3	100.0	99.3	93.1	88.5	88.4	88.3	88.5
Ireland	95.0	91.4	92.6	98.9	97.9	95.9	94.8	101.4	100.0	103.6	97.9	98.1	99.1	100.1	100.3
Mexico	2 111.1	1 758.1	1 115.4	528.5	232.2	132.9	123.1	106.5	100.0	96.9	97.3	89.5	46.6	40.1	40.2
Netherlands	85.2	83.9	84.3	92.2	97.4	97.1	96.1	100.6	100.0	102.8	105.9	106.9	112.4	110.7	110.4
New Zealand	141.6	127.5	116.5	105.7	109.1	113.0	105.9	103.9	100.0	92.4	96.0	101.4	107.9	114.7	115.3
Norway	117.4	115.2	113.1	106.4	102.2	102.0	101.9	101.8	100.0	101.2	99.4	98.2	100.9	100.7	100.6
Portugal	177.1	147.3	130.9	120.2	110.2	104.5	101.4	99.1	100.0	103.6	97.9	94.1	96.2	95.5	95.3
Spain	94.9	93.5	91.5	89.5	88.8	91.8	96.0	99.7	100.0	97.9	86.6	81.0	80.7	82.6	82.6
Sweden	101.9	104.0	103.7	102.0	100.8	101.1	101.6	100.0	100.0	101.4	82.5	81.7	81.3	88.5	88.9
Switzerland	89.7	88.9	88.5	96.7	101.5	100.8	95.5	101.3	100.0	98.4	101.4	108.5	116.3	115.9	115.4
Turkey	2 429.2	1 639.1	1 189.5	747.1	513.3	303.2	210.6	154.8	100.0	58.4	39.5	15.4	8.6	5.0	3.0
Chinese Taipei	77.8	81.8	83.2	77.7	86.2	92.7	104.3	99.9	100.0	104.2	100.7	98.4	94.1	95.0	95.6
Hong Kong	129.1	125.6	129.5	113.5	104.3	100.0	103.5	99.5	100.0	98.4	101.9	100.3	95.8	99.5	99.9
Korea	114.6	114.7	108.8	93.7	92.2	100.3	113.2	104.3	100.0	91.8	90.2	88.1	87.9	90.9	91.4
Singapore	97.5	101.2	100.6	89.4	85.4	86.1	91.4	95.1	100.0	104.1	107.9	112.2	115.8	120.8	121.4

a) For the details on the method of calculation, see the section on effective exchange rates and competitiveness indicators in "Sources and Methods".
b) On the technical assumption that exchange rates remain at their levels of 2 May 1996, except for Greece and Turkey where exchange rates vary according to official exchange rate policy.

Annex Table 39. **Export volumes**

Total goods, customs basis, percentage changes from previous period

	1978	1979	1980	1981	1982	1983	1984	1985	1986	1987	1988	1989	1990	1991	1992	1993	1994	1995	Projections 1996	1997
United States[a]	11.2	11.8	11.9	-1.0	-9.1	-2.9	7.9	3.6	5.1	11.0	18.8	12.5	8.3	7.0	7.0	3.5	10.1	10.7	9.2	9.3
Japan	-2.8	0.4	19.2	10.7	-2.3	8.1	15.8	5.0	-0.5	0.4	4.2	4.6	4.9	2.4	1.7	-1.9	1.7	3.3	2.6	6.9
Germany	3.4	5.1	1.7	6.8	-1.9	-0.5	9.1	6.0	1.4	2.9	6.7	8.2	1.4	1.6	0.8	-6.4	9.0	3.6	3.9	7.0
France	4.9	8.3	3.3	3.9	-2.8	3.6	7.0	2.4	-1.1	3.7	9.0	9.1	5.3	3.9	4.7	-1.0	6.5	7.6	1.6	7.0
Italy	9.3	8.7	-3.4	4.4	0.9	4.5	5.1	6.3	1.8	3.1	8.6	5.5	2.6	0.8	3.6	11.6	10.5	8.5	4.7	5.8
United Kingdom	2.7	4.0	1.2	-1.3	3.2	1.8	8.5	5.8	4.0	5.5	2.5	5.4	6.5	0.5	2.1	0.2	12.9	5.9	3.6	6.1
Canada	10.2	1.8	-0.3	3.4	-0.5	7.4	18.6	6.4	3.8	3.6	9.3	1.2	4.6	1.6	8.1	11.2	14.7	12.3	7.2	7.8
Total of above countries	4.8	6.0	5.8	4.1	-2.6	2.3	10.1	5.0	1.8	4.3	8.7	7.5	4.8	3.0	3.7	0.9	8.8	7.2	5.1	7.4
Australia	0.7	13.0	-0.2	-5.8	9.6	-5.9	16.4	11.4	3.7	10.8	-0.4	4.3	7.7	15.2	4.8	5.7	8.4	5.0	10.1	6.6
Austria	10.0	12.4	4.7	4.9	1.7	4.3	9.4	9.6	1.1	2.1	7.6	14.4	10.2	6.5	3.8	-2.5	11.1	10.8	4.3	3.7
Belgium-Luxembourg	3.6	6.0	0.0	0.5	1.6	4.0	5.4	4.2	4.2	6.2	7.5	8.1	3.1	4.0	0.0	6.7	10.1	8.5	4.7	6.6
Czech Republic																	3.0	7.7	10.1	10.4
Denmark	2.4	9.6	9.0	7.0	2.0	7.6	5.4	4.6	1.4	2.4	4.9	7.5	5.9	7.5	4.9	-3.4	8.9	-1.4	1.6	4.9
Finland	7.0	10.1	9.7	2.5	-2.9	4.0	9.7	0.9	0.4	1.6	3.3	-0.1	2.9	-9.1	9.0	18.6	14.0	4.6	3.0	6.0
Greece	18.1	2.1	12.9	-15.9	0.4	16.5	18.1	-0.1	17.9	11.1	-32.3	39.3	-5.8	11.4	18.2	4.8	2.5	-0.5	4.0	5.5
Iceland[b]	12.2	10.2	6.3	5.2	-17.0	15.2	-0.5	13.3	15.2	14.4	-2.0	0.3	4.1	-0.7	-4.9	3.7	17.5	-2.6	6.3	6.8
Ireland	10.5	7.9	7.8	0.7	7.2	12.1	18.4	6.5	3.7	14.5	7.1	11.2	8.5	5.6	14.7	10.2	15.2	13.8	10.3	9.3
Mexico	53.3	16.1	35.7	22.2	12.7	25.8	9.1	-5.8	4.0	-12.9	-10.4	2.2	1.5	3.4	-2.9	9.5	12.1	28.4	11.1	9.1
Netherlands	2.8	10.0	1.1	0.6	-0.6	4.5	7.4	5.9	2.1	4.5	9.2	6.4	5.2	4.8	2.6	6.0	6.8	5.8	3.4	6.2
New Zealand	2.0	7.2	5.1	1.3	3.1	5.3	4.7	10.7	-1.7	2.7	4.2	-3.1	6.0	10.5	2.2	4.4	10.1	1.2	4.6	7.4
Norway	23.7	5.5	5.5	-1.7	-0.8	12.5	9.1	3.5	1.8	13.9	4.6	15.0	6.7	6.6	8.0	5.2	12.4	4.6	8.8	3.6
Portugal	9.9	26.3	6.9	-2.5	11.8	19.1	14.5	10.6	7.8	11.7	9.3	20.5	12.6	0.6	7.7	-4.3	14.7	10.6	9.2	7.3
Spain	15.1	11.1	0.3	10.0	9.4	8.7	17.5	2.8	-3.5	8.0	6.4	4.5	12.4	11.4	5.0	11.8	21.2	10.9	7.8	7.9
Sweden	6.6	8.9	1.3	1.1	4.0	12.0	7.8	3.2	2.8	2.6	3.3	2.5	0.1	-2.5	1.1	10.5	15.8	14.3	4.2	6.1
Switzerland	3.1	4.2	4.5	2.6	-5.0	-0.5	7.9	7.8	0.0	1.7	7.4	7.8	3.4	-2.6	3.5	1.0	3.9	1.9	2.0	4.6
Turkey[b]	17.4	-11.7	14.4	80.9	29.8	5.2	29.2	14.8	-20.8	21.9	8.9	0.6	0.9	6.7	5.4	14.2	16.6	7.6	14.2	12.7
Total of smaller countries	7.4	8.5	4.5	3.2	2.8	7.1	9.4	4.5	1.9	4.2	4.4	6.9	4.8	4.1	3.4	6.6	10.9	8.5	5.9	6.6
Total OECD	5.5	6.7	5.4	3.9	-1.2	3.7	9.9	4.9	1.8	4.3	7.4	7.3	4.8	3.3	3.6	2.5	9.4	7.6	5.4	7.2
OECD North America	12.8	9.5	10.6	1.8	-5.1	2.7	10.6	3.0	4.6	6.1	13.4	8.9	6.9	5.6	6.6	5.6	11.3	12.3	8.9	8.9
OECD Europe	5.1	6.8	1.8	3.6	0.1	3.3	8.3	5.2	1.5	4.4	6.4	7.4	4.0	2.4	2.9	2.1	10.1	6.6	4.2	6.5
European Union	4.9	7.1	1.5	3.5	0.2	3.3	8.2	5.0	1.7	4.1	6.4	7.4	4.0	2.5	2.8	1.7	10.3	6.8	4.0	6.5
Total OECD less the United States	4.7	5.9	4.3	4.8	0.2	4.7	10.1	5.0	1.4	3.3	5.7	6.4	4.2	2.6	3.0	2.3	9.3	7.0	4.5	6.7

a) Derived from values and unit values on a national accounts basis.
b) OECD Secretariat estimates.

Annex Table 40. **Import volumes**
Total goods, customs basis, percentage changes from previous period

	1978	1979	1980	1981	1982	1983	1984	1985	1986	1987	1988	1989	1990	1991	1992	1993	1994	1995	Projections 1996	1997
United States [a]	9.0	1.7	-7.4	2.0	-2.5	13.6	24.2	6.3	10.2	4.6	4.0	4.2	3.0	-0.1	9.6	10.6	13.5	9.1	6.0	6.0
Japan	4.6	11.6	-4.9	-2.4	-0.7	1.3	10.6	0.7	9.7	9.0	16.9	7.7	5.0	3.8	-0.6	3.8	13.6	12.5	8.6	10.7
Germany	6.2	7.5	0.4	-4.6	-7.1	3.8	5.1	4.9	5.4	5.3	6.4	7.3	12.7	12.0	1.3	-9.8	7.9	2.1	2.8	6.4
France	3.7	10.6	2.4	-3.7	2.9	-2.7	2.6	4.7	7.4	7.7	9.0	8.0	5.7	2.9	0.9	-4.1	7.3	5.7	2.0	5.9
Italy	5.1	13.7	10.2	-8.3	-0.1	1.2	7.5	8.6	2.8	10.2	3.7	9.6	4.1	2.9	3.3	-9.1	10.5	6.1	4.9	6.3
United Kingdom	3.9	8.0	-6.0	-4.8	5.1	6.4	10.7	3.9	7.1	7.1	13.6	7.9	0.5	-5.4	6.4	0.4	6.3	2.4	5.5	6.2
Canada	3.8	9.3	-4.4	1.4	-16.4	11.0	19.7	10.4	7.6	6.3	14.2	5.4	0.4	3.1	7.1	11.0	13.6	9.8	4.8	7.2
Total of above countries	5.9	7.5	-2.1	-2.6	-2.4	5.6	12.5	5.4	7.7	6.5	8.2	6.7	4.9	2.9	4.5	1.1	10.8	7.0	5.1	6.8
Australia	4.2	3.0	7.1	10.6	4.9	-12.5	22.0	7.1	-4.3	1.0	16.4	20.3	-4.8	-1.5	9.0	6.5	12.8	11.0	6.5	10.1
Austria	-2.2	10.7	7.7	-4.0	-0.8	7.9	8.4	5.4	5.2	5.3	7.8	10.2	11.0	2.9	3.2	-1.0	12.8	6.2	2.6	2.1
Belgium-Luxembourg	2.5	6.0	2.6	-3.7	1.7	-1.4	6.1	4.4	6.9	6.9	6.2	6.8	5.2	4.1	1.0	0.6	3.1	7.3	5.0	6.4
Czech Republic	‥	‥	‥	‥	‥	‥	‥	‥	‥	‥	‥	‥	‥	‥	‥	‥	15.6	21.4	15.7	11.6
Denmark	-0.3	4.9	-6.9	-2.4	2.3	3.0	3.9	8.0	6.7	-1.8	-1.8	2.4	2.9	5.2	4.1	-6.9	12.5	1.0	3.6	5.2
Finland	-4.4	19.1	12.4	-6.3	1.3	3.3	-0.1	5.8	5.5	9.0	9.0	10.6	-4.0	-16.9	-2.1	-3.6	20.0	12.7	6.1	6.8
Greece	8.7	8.3	-12.0	1.1	12.8	3.7	2.0	13.0	5.9	13.0	-13.5	31.1	14.4	9.9	7.7	2.4	4.0	9.4	7.6	9.3
Iceland [b]	-2.0	2.3	6.4	8.7	-2.4	-9.3	4.5	10.9	10.0	26.9	-4.7	-12.2	6.8	6.6	-5.1	-8.1	9.7	7.4	13.7	9.3
Ireland	14.4	14.7	-4.9	2.2	-3.5	3.3	10.2	3.3	2.9	6.3	4.7	13.0	6.8	0.8	4.8	7.0	12.6	10.1	9.7	9.5
Mexico	27.8	33.2	39.7	27.7	-37.9	-26.5	36.8	13.8	-18.0	-22.3	40.1	14.9	21.7	31.4	22.8	0.7	11.2	-21.6	10.5	13.0
Netherlands	6.1	6.5	-1.2	-6.2	0.9	4.5	5.5	7.2	3.7	4.7	8.0	6.8	4.7	4.3	1.9	-4.4	8.0	6.3	3.5	5.7
New Zealand	-8.6	18.1	-2.3	2.9	6.3	-6.7	19.9	0.0	-1.6	10.3	-7.7	21.4	7.8	-9.5	10.5	4.1	16.3	11.5	6.6	8.4
Norway	-11.1	4.8	11.2	-3.8	3.5	-3.4	13.5	11.6	14.6	-2.2	-9.3	-5.8	10.3	2.5	3.4	0.6	16.3	8.2	7.3	2.9
Portugal	-1.9	7.1	11.9	6.9	5.9	-10.4	-5.5	6.7	19.3	27.9	22.2	8.3	15.8	6.0	13.4	-9.9	11.5	5.8	7.9	6.8
Spain	-3.4	15.7	4.7	-4.4	0.9	-1.4	-0.9	8.0	19.8	27.8	19.1	16.8	9.8	11.5	6.9	-5.8	15.2	10.4	7.4	7.9
Sweden	-10.8	19.1	1.6	-5.0	4.6	2.2	3.3	9.3	3.8	6.1	4.5	6.5	0.5	-5.8	0.6	1.9	12.9	9.2	6.0	5.1
Switzerland	9.7	7.8	8.3	-4.9	-2.2	5.9	8.5	3.8	8.5	6.0	4.5	7.0	1.9	-1.4	-5.1	-0.9	8.4	4.0	2.9	4.3
Turkey [b]	-30.6	-9.3	19.0	24.7	3.5	11.8	24.2	7.8	-5.0	14.1	-1.1	8.1	26.6	-3.1	7.2	38.9	-20.7	31.8	14.6	13.8
Total of smaller countries	1.7	9.4	4.5	-1.0	-1.6	-0.2	7.7	6.8	5.0	6.2	7.5	9.2	6.1	3.7	4.2	-0.3	9.3	6.2	6.0	6.9
Total OECD	4.6	8.1	-0.1	-2.1	-2.1	3.7	11.0	5.8	6.9	6.4	8.0	7.4	5.3	3.2	4.4	0.7	10.3	6.8	5.4	6.8
OECD North America	8.7	4.6	-4.0	4.1	-8.9	10.3	24.0	7.4	8.2	3.8	6.9	4.9	3.4	2.2	10.1	9.9	13.4	7.1	6.1	6.6
OECD Europe	3.2	9.1	1.8	-4.5	0.0	2.2	5.9	5.8	6.3	7.4	7.3	8.1	6.3	3.6	2.6	-3.9	8.3	5.7	4.5	6.2
European Union	3.5	9.4	1.2	-4.7	0.0	2.1	5.5	5.8	6.1	7.6	7.9	8.5	6.3	4.0	2.9	-4.8	8.5	5.3	4.3	6.2
Total OECD *less* the United States	3.6	9.6	1.5	-2.9	-2.0	1.6	7.9	5.7	5.9	6.9	9.1	8.3	5.8	4.0	3.1	-1.9	9.4	6.1	5.2	7.1

a) Derived from values and unit values on a national accounts basis.
b) OECD Secretariat estimates.

Annex Table 41. **Export prices (average unit values)**

Total goods, percentage changes, national currency terms

	1978	1979	1980	1981	1982	1983	1984	1985	1986	1987	1988	1989	1990	1991	1992	1993	1994	1995	Projections 1996	1997
United States	5.7	13.2	9.8	7.0	-1.1	-0.7	0.9	-5.0	-3.3	2.6	6.5	1.4	-1.0	0.0	-1.7	-1.1	0.6	3.0	0.1	0.2
Japan	-2.2	8.4	9.9	2.8	5.5	-6.3	-0.2	-0.7	-15.4	-6.0	-2.5	6.9	4.3	-0.3	-0.1	-4.7	-0.9	-0.7	6.0	1.4
Germany	0.9	5.3	9.6	6.2	4.5	1.5	3.4	3.9	-3.3	-2.7	0.9	4.5	-1.1	-0.8	0.6	0.0	1.0	1.7	1.6	1.0
France	6.5	10.2	11.4	13.4	12.8	10.0	9.6	4.2	-3.5	-0.6	2.7	4.9	-1.9	-0.1	-2.3	-2.5	2.2	1.3	0.6	1.4
Italy	8.0	16.9	19.3	22.9	15.1	6.2	11.1	9.2	-4.3	0.3	2.2	9.6	2.4	2.7	0.8	8.8	3.9	13.6	-0.7	0.7
United Kingdom	7.6	10.1	15.2	8.3	6.4	7.5	7.0	5.2	-10.5	3.9	0.4	8.4	3.9	0.5	1.3	9.6	0.4	6.9	4.7	2.2
Canada	8.8	20.8	17.2	6.5	0.5	-0.1	3.7	0.5	-2.7	1.3	-0.2	1.5	-1.7	-5.1	2.4	4.9	4.7	3.7	0.8	1.1
Total of above countries	3.9	10.8	11.8	8.3	5.1	1.4	4.0	1.4	-6.3	-0.6	1.8	4.9	0.5	-0.3	-0.2	0.7	1.2	3.2	1.9	1.0
Australia	2.3	19.8	13.8	3.6	3.7	9.4	3.7	12.0	-0.7	4.2	10.3	5.8	-0.1	-7.0	2.2	1.7	-4.0	6.1	-2.4	1.5
Austria	-0.7	4.0	5.0	6.1	4.2	-0.4	3.7	2.7	-4.2	-2.1	4.0	-1.6	-1.4	-3.6	-1.8	-1.8	-0.2	0.4	0.4	0.5
Belgium-Luxembourg	1.3	11.1	10.8	8.8	13.7	7.2	7.0	1.6	-6.9	-4.7	2.7	7.9	-3.1	-1.9	-1.4	-1.4	-0.8	1.2	1.2	1.1
Czech Republic																		5.6	4.8	5.5
Denmark	5.6	7.8	13.8	11.9	11.1	4.9	6.1	3.4	-4.3	-0.9	0.2	5.7	-1.5	-0.4	-1.7	-2.3	0.8	0.7	2.5	2.7
Finland	6.4	12.4	10.8	11.1	7.3	6.4	6.3	2.6	-2.2	2.1	4.9	7.7	-1.2	0.8	6.1	5.4	0.8	8.2	1.3	2.3
Greece	2.3	16.0	33.3	22.2	20.7	16.2	19.5	15.7	6.9	7.3	16.0	14.2	12.7	12.8	1.3	6.5	6.9	6.8	7.0	4.5
Iceland[a]	51.6	46.4	50.6	36.8	57.2	91.3	24.3	30.2	15.7	2.8	18.9	28.2	12.3	0.8	-0.3	8.1	5.6	5.3	2.6	2.2
Ireland	6.7	9.3	10.0	15.0	10.8	8.3	8.6	2.9	-6.9	-0.5	7.1	6.8	-9.3	-1.0	-3.3	7.6	0.2	1.9	1.5	1.2
Mexico	-3.3	20.9	29.8	13.5	116.2	96.8	37.9	49.1	79.0	178.1	83.4	19.3	28.7	6.5	6.4	3.3	9.0	84.9	12.9	4.2
Netherlands	-2.7	8.7	13.3	15.6	4.1	-0.2	5.9	1.3	-17.1	-5.7	0.4	5.1	-1.2	-0.6	-2.9	-2.8	0.6	1.4	0.9	1.3
New Zealand	6.3	21.3	15.4	13.1	10.4	5.6	13.5	8.8	-2.3	5.9	6.3	13.1	-1.4	-4.2	8.3	2.5	-4.0	1.0	-0.1	0.9
Norway	5.8	16.8	30.6	15.3	7.3	3.7	9.4	5.1	-24.9	-3.5	0.0	12.3	3.7	-3.3	-8.5	0.8	-3.9	3.9	3.5	0.8
Portugal	24.3	31.2	23.4	13.6	15.3	29.0	30.7	15.7	3.3	8.4	10.4	5.8	2.9	0.2	-2.2	4.3	5.2	4.5	3.0	1.4
Spain	12.3	9.6	19.1	16.4	7.8	16.7	12.5	6.7	-4.0	2.5	5.1	4.6	-2.2	-1.1	1.1	5.2	4.2	5.7	1.6	2.1
Sweden	7.8	10.3	9.8	10.2	10.0	13.5	7.0	4.1	-1.0	3.3	5.1	6.6	2.1	0.4	-3.0	7.9	4.6	7.5	-3.6	0.8
Switzerland	-3.9	1.0	5.7	6.0	4.9	2.5	4.7	2.0	0.5	-1.0	2.2	5.6	1.3	2.2	1.0	0.1	-0.7	-1.8	0.6	1.2
Turkey[a]	49.7	77.1	124.7	29.4	37.2	31.8	55.9	39.7	52.1	43.1	74.3	48.2	35.9	56.4	69.5	46.0	182.5	70.4	70.4	59.9
Total of smaller countries	3.3	11.8	15.3	11.5	13.0	11.0	9.7	6.7	-2.9	5.6	8.2	7.4	1.3	0.6	0.1	1.7	2.6	7.2	2.3	2.3
Total OECD	3.7	11.1	12.8	9.2	7.2	4.0	5.5	2.8	-5.3	1.1	3.5	5.6	0.7	0.0	-0.1	0.9	1.6	4.3	2.0	1.4
OECD North America	5.7	15.3	12.7	7.3	4.7	4.5	3.8	-0.7	1.0	9.9	9.3	2.6	0.7	-0.7	-0.3	0.5	2.0	7.5	1.1	0.7
OECD Europe	4.3	9.7	13.4	11.3	8.6	5.9	7.4	4.7	-5.6	-0.7	2.4	6.4	0.1	0.5	-0.1	2.3	2.1	4.1	1.7	1.7
European Union	4.2	9.5	12.7	11.4	8.6	5.9	7.2	4.5	-5.8	-0.9	2.1	6.0	-0.3	-0.1	-0.4	2.1	1.5	4.0	1.3	1.3
Total OECD *less* the United States	3.4	10.6	13.4	9.6	9.0	5.0	6.5	4.5	-5.8	0.8	2.9	6.4	1.1	0.0	0.2	1.4	1.8	4.6	2.4	1.6

a) OECD Secretariat estimates.

Annex Table 42. **Import prices (average unit values)**
Total goods, percentage changes, national currency terms

	1978	1979	1980	1981	1982	1983	1984	1985	1986	1987	1988	1989	1990	1991	1992	1993	1994	1995	Projections 1996	1997
United States	6.6	18.0	26.3	5.4	-4.0	-4.2	-0.7	-4.0	-2.2	7.1	4.8	2.8	1.8	-1.4	-0.8	-1.6	0.6	2.6	-0.9	0.5
Japan	-16.4	29.4	38.9	0.7	4.6	-9.4	-2.6	-4.5	-36.6	-7.9	-5.3	11.8	11.3	-9.1	-6.9	-12.4	-7.9	-0.3	8.7	0.8
Germany	-2.9	11.3	17.0	13.8	0.6	-0.3	5.9	2.6	-16.0	-6.1	0.9	7.5	-2.6	1.9	-2.4	-1.5	0.8	0.5	1.5	0.8
France	2.7	12.0	22.6	19.5	12.6	8.2	10.1	1.5	-14.3	-1.1	2.5	7.1	-2.0	-0.6	-3.4	-3.7	2.0	1.7	0.3	1.2
Italy	6.6	18.9	26.0	32.1	12.5	3.5	12.9	7.4	-15.9	-1.6	7.5	6.4	-0.5	0.9	-0.7	10.6	4.9	16.2	-1.9	0.5
United Kingdom	4.3	9.2	11.2	7.9	7.2	7.9	8.4	3.8	-5.8	2.5	-0.3	5.9	3.0	-0.4	-0.5	7.7	3.5	8.9	4.6	2.4
Canada	13.6	14.2	16.3	12.0	3.5	-1.3	4.6	1.7	0.0	-1.9	-1.9	-0.3	0.7	-3.2	1.9	3.8	3.8	1.3	-0.3	1.1
Total of above countries	1.3	15.9	22.9	11.2	3.2	-0.4	4.3	0.2	-13.0	-0.4	1.7	5.8	1.3	-1.4	-2.0	-0.9	0.7	3.5	1.4	1.0
Australia	6.7	14.2	14.8	4.7	7.3	6.9	2.2	17.0	12.7	4.0	-2.9	-1.6	2.6	0.6	3.2	5.3	-2.7	1.2	-5.1	0.6
Austria	0.7	5.3	8.9	10.2	0.2	-2.8	3.9	4.2	-10.0	-4.2	1.8	3.6	-2.7	3.5	-2.7	-4.0	0.9	0.9	0.9	0.8
Belgium-Luxembourg	1.8	10.3	13.8	13.8	13.3	7.4	7.7	-0.2	-13.2	-5.4	3.1	7.1	-1.8	-1.3	-3.2	-5.1	1.0	0.5	1.4	1.1
Czech Republic	..																0.0	4.7	3.1	3.0
Denmark	2.6	13.4	21.4	16.7	9.5	3.2	8.0	2.5	-9.8	-4.3	2.5	7.1	-3.0	0.0	-3.0	-3.2	2.5	3.1	2.0	2.5
Finland	10.7	13.9	18.0	12.3	4.3	7.1	4.4	3.6	-9.7	-2.4	1.8	3.6	1.8	2.5	10.3	12.9	-2.9	0.3	2.7	3.3
Greece	6.6	16.8	41.8	14.6	27.0	14.5	19.4	22.7	12.6	0.5	9.6	13.7	10.0	10.8	7.5	6.7	8.2	6.9	4.6	4.1
Iceland[a]	55.0	55.5	55.2	40.8	59.7	94.1	22.8	30.8	10.8	5.1	17.4	31.9	14.1	-0.1	-0.7	6.9	4.4	2.8	2.7	2.6
Ireland	4.9	13.1	18.3	18.7	6.9	4.7	9.7	2.6	-11.0	-0.1	6.5	6.6	-4.9	2.2	-2.0	5.4	2.3	3.0	2.8	2.5
Mexico	13.8	17.6	12.0	5.9	120.9	111.6	36.8	50.0	164.2	152.7	80.4	9.6	21.8	5.2	5.0	0.0	8.0	118.1	16.6	5.8
Netherlands	-2.8	11.6	14.9	14.9	1.0	0.1	5.7	0.9	-18.1	-3.1	-0.6	5.2	-1.7	-0.3	-2.7	-0.4	0.2	0.0	1.1	1.3
New Zealand	3.6	12.9	29.2	14.1	11.6	8.4	13.6	10.8	-2.4	-4.4	-0.9	7.8	0.8	1.1	6.6	-0.3	-3.6	-4.1	-2.4	0.6
Norway	4.9	10.2	12.9	6.7	4.4	3.8	3.0	6.5	0.0	2.9	2.9	6.1	1.0	-1.6	-2.1	1.0	0.7	1.3	2.0	2.2
Portugal	23.1	34.4	28.0	19.8	17.0	34.3	35.4	7.1	-8.7	6.3	7.0	7.8	3.2	0.3	-5.1	5.0	3.4	1.9	2.9	1.6
Spain	9.5	2.6	36.4	29.0	16.0	22.0	11.9	1.3	-18.9	-4.0	-2.0	2.1	-3.4	-2.7	-1.2	5.2	5.8	5.2	2.0	2.3
Sweden	14.8	10.7	14.2	9.5	11.6	15.2	5.8	2.6	-8.6	4.2	4.3	5.9	1.9	-1.1	-4.2	12.4	4.1	5.5	-2.1	0.5
Switzerland	-10.5	6.7	11.9	7.2	-1.2	-0.7	4.2	4.3	-9.3	-3.6	4.9	8.1	-0.4	0.1	2.0	-1.9	-4.8	-2.1	0.6	1.2
Turkey[a]	54.3	92.8	154.9	35.6	40.4	29.6	52.6	40.1	32.3	44.2	69.1	53.0	37.2	55.0	67.7	48.0	173.7	77.7	70.4	59.0
Total of smaller countries	4.4	12.1	19.7	14.1	12.9	12.1	10.2	6.3	-4.5	4.3	6.5	6.5	1.1	1.5	0.2	1.6	3.5	7.5	3.0	2.8
Total OECD	2.2	14.7	21.9	12.1	6.1	3.3	6.1	2.0	-10.5	1.0	3.1	6.0	1.3	-0.5	-1.3	-0.1	1.5	4.7	1.9	1.5
OECD North America	8.4	17.2	23.4	6.6	3.0	1.9	2.6	0.0	5.1	12.0	7.7	2.7	2.9	-1.2	0.1	-0.5	1.7	7.9	0.4	1.0
OECD Europe	2.4	12.0	19.4	16.2	7.4	5.5	8.8	3.4	-12.7	-2.1	2.7	6.8	-0.6	0.9	-1.3	1.7	2.9	4.2	1.8	1.8
European Union	2.5	11.6	18.9	16.7	7.6	5.6	8.7	3.0	-13.5	-2.5	2.0	6.3	-1.1	0.4	-2.0	1.5	2.3	3.9	1.3	1.3
Total OECD less the United States	1.2	14.0	20.9	13.8	8.6	5.2	7.8	3.5	-12.4	-0.4	2.8	6.8	1.1	-0.3	-1.5	0.3	1.8	5.2	2.6	1.7

a) OECD Secretariat estimates.

Annex Table 43. **Competitive positions: relative unit labour costs**

Indices, 1991 = 100

	1978	1979	1980	1981	1982	1983	1984	1985	1986	1987	1988	1989	1990	1991	1992	1993	1994	1995	Projections 1996	1997
United States	111	115	120	126	137	146	155	160	134	114	105	107	103	100	96	95	92	90	92	91
Japan	121	101	89	95	83	90	90	88	121	123	125	109	95	100	106	129	138	144	125	123
Germany	88	89	90	82	86	87	86	84	93	103	102	99	103	100	107	114	114	121	118	116
France	103	104	109	107	104	103	104	107	109	108	102	98	101	100	99	102	100	103	104	103
Italy	91	90	88	88	89	95	92	90	92	91	90	94	99	100	95	79	76	67	73	74
United Kingdom	80	95	116	120	113	103	99	101	95	96	102	101	97	100	98	89	91	90	90	92
Canada	85	81	82	85	94	94	86	83	80	84	91	96	96	100	91	84	80	79	82	83
Australia	108	101	103	115	123	116	122	102	85	84	93	103	102	100	90	83	87	87	97	100
Austria	119	114	111	111	111	111	107	107	112	112	106	102	102	100	100	100	97	98	96	94
Belgium-Luxembourg	149	146	135	122	101	92	90	92	98	100	96	93	101	100	100	99	102	106	103	103
Denmark	99	100	87	82	81	81	82	85	94	103	100	96	105	100	101	105	105	109	110	111
Finland	91	90	90	94	98	95	98	98	95	93	95	99	104	100	77	62	67	76	71	69
Mexico	130	136	146	173	133	67	82	77	62	63	78	85	89	100	113	124	125	82	83	94
Netherlands	133	129	122	110	114	111	100	98	106	111	107	100	102	100	104	106	103	106	103	103
New Zealand	122	122	119	120	117	114	96	94	94	106	114	104	102	100	89	92	99	105	112	113
Norway	106	98	92	96	98	99	97	97	97	98	102	103	99	100	97	96	97	102	102	103
Portugal	79	72	76	83	82	78	76	76	77	76	79	82	89	100	110	108	110	116	117	120
Spain	87	104	98	93	91	79	81	80	79	79	84	91	99	100	101	89	82	83	85	86
Sweden	106	99	99	101	88	79	81	85	85	85	89	93	96	100	98	72	72	80	80	82
Switzerland	85	81	72	71	78	86	85	83	90	94	95	91	98	100	98	100	109	117	116	116
Korea	71	78	68	62	68	69	66	69	57	61	73	101	100	100	94	91	96	96	100	102
Chinese Taipei	58	65	71	76	78	74	87	82	74	83	93	107	103	100	107	104	106	103	106	108
Hong Kong	84	80	79	109	109	95	93	108	84	75	77	87	93	100	102	116	127	125	133	137
Singapore	75	76	75	81	96	107	114	119	88	80	81	89	93	100	107	106	107	109	115	115

Note: Indices are expressed in a common currency and concern the manufacturing sector. The relative unit labour cost indices take into account both export and import competitiveness. For the details on the method of calculation, see the section on effective exchange rates in "Sources and Methods".

Annex Table 44. Competitive positions: relative export prices

Indices, 1991 = 100

	1978	1979	1980	1981	1982	1983	1984	1985	1986	1987	1988	1989	1990	1991	1992	1993	1994	1995	Projections 1996	1997
United States	114	116	117	131	139	142	143	141	122	110	105	105	100	100	97	96	93	87	88	86
Japan	95	86	82	87	83	83	84	86	95	96	98	96	92	100	106	119	127	130	124	125
Germany	98	98	96	89	90	91	88	89	98	102	99	97	102	100	104	106	106	110	107	107
France	102	103	102	99	96	95	97	99	103	104	103	100	103	100	100	99	101	102	101	101
Italy	83	84	87	90	90	89	89	90	92	92	89	94	99	100	99	88	86	87	92	93
United Kingdom	88	94	105	104	99	97	94	97	92	94	98	97	98	100	98	98	99	99	102	103
Canada	98	95	96	96	95	99	99	98	94	98	101	104	102	100	96	95	95	96	98	99
Australia	124	122	121	117	109	112	116	103	96	102	115	116	107	100	92	90	90	89	92	94
Austria	116	113	111	107	109	108	106	105	109	111	114	104	105	100	99	100	98	99	96	95
Belgium-Luxembourg	105	107	105	98	94	95	94	94	98	98	98	100	103	100	101	100	99	102	100	99
Denmark	103	99	92	88	87	90	88	91	98	101	98	96	102	100	102	101	103	103	103	104
Finland	81	81	83	88	91	88	89	91	91	93	96	101	101	100	92	82	87	101	96	96
Mexico	85	88	87	84	90	63	71	65	82	91	97	96	102	100	102	111	111	108	104	110
Netherlands	111	110	108	104	106	105	100	96	97	104	104	100	102	100	100	100	100	104	102	102
New Zealand	97	100	100	103	105	105	103	100	94	100	113	112	107	100	97	100	107	113	120	120
Norway	102	100	104	104	101	99	104	100	95	96	112	116	105	100	95	91	89	99	99	99
Portugal	107	107	110	112	107	104	107	107	105	103	103	98	99	100	102	97	96	99	99	100
Spain	80	84	84	76	78	74	77	79	86	88	91	91	96	100	102	94	89	87	88	89
Sweden	95	97	98	98	90	88	90	92	93	95	97	98	99	100	99	86	87	90	92	92
Switzerland	86	82	76	77	82	86	84	82	92	96	95	91	98	100	99	101	107	107	106	106
Korea	90	96	90	94	93	92	97	95	92	93	100	110	100	100	96	96	96	95	97	98
Chinese Taipei	81	85	86	89	87	85	91	89	84	92	98	104	100	100	99	99	97	92	93	94
Hong Kong	121	117	117	116	115	107	116	118	108	104	99	102	98	100	99	102	101	97	100	100
Singapore	123	118	116	126	128	133	130	127	99	98	95	101	101	100	98	98	97	97	100	100

Note: Indices are expressed in a common currency and concern manufactured goods. The relative export price indices take into account both export and import competitiveness. For the details on the method of calculation, see the section on effective exchange rates in "Sources and Methods".

Annex Table 45. **Export performance for total goods**[a]

Percentage changes from previous period

	1978	1979	1980	1981	1982	1983	1984	1985	1986	1987	1988	1989	1990	1991	1992	1993	1994	1995	Projections 1996	1997
United States	4.4	1.8	4.6	-6.6	-3.6	-1.8	-2.0	0.3	1.6	6.4	6.4	3.6	3.7	-0.9	0.0	-1.7	-1.0	2.9	1.7	0.6
Japan	-8.6	-5.0	12.1	4.7	-2.6	3.5	2.1	0.5	-5.5	-5.3	-4.5	-3.6	-0.4	-5.1	-6.8	-9.5	-10.3	-7.3	-5.9	-1.5
Germany	0.0	-2.7	-5.1	7.9	-3.2	-1.4	1.4	2.2	-4.8	-3.7	-1.0	0.1	-3.0	-1.0	-1.6	-9.5	0.1	-4.4	-2.2	0.0
France	0.5	1.9	-2.8	2.8	-2.0	2.9	0.5	-0.3	-6.4	-3.1	0.5	0.9	-0.5	-1.1	0.4	-0.2	-2.9	0.2	-4.1	0.0
Italy	4.9	3.1	-7.8	3.2	0.7	4.9	-0.6	3.1	-5.3	-3.1	0.1	-2.8	-4.0	-4.0	0.3	12.9	1.5	0.4	-1.1	-1.3
United Kingdom	-2.0	-4.4	-3.3	-4.1	2.5	-0.3	1.6	2.4	-1.7	0.5	-3.2	-2.5	1.1	-3.8	-2.1	1.2	2.9	-2.6	-2.5	-1.1
Canada	-0.3	3.1	4.1	-0.1	-0.5	-3.8	-0.6	-0.3	-2.5	1.5	3.7	-3.8	1.0	0.2	-0.7	1.2	2.0	3.3	0.7	1.3
Total of above countries	-0.5	-0.9	0.2	1.3	-1.5	0.6	0.5	1.2	-3.5	-1.2	0.0	-0.6	-0.2	-2.2	-1.7	-2.9	-1.7	-1.4	-1.7	-0.2
Australia	-2.9	5.8	-0.3	-8.1	9.2	-5.3	5.9	9.9	2.1	6.2	-7.1	-2.6	6.1	10.0	0.4	-0.2	-0.9	-5.0	1.1	-2.3
Austria	5.5	3.8	-1.6	7.9	3.7	3.1	2.4	5.5	-5.1	-4.3	0.1	5.8	3.1	1.4	4.1	1.4	1.0	2.9	-1.5	-3.5
Belgium-Luxembourg	-1.2	-1.7	-4.5	1.2	1.6	1.9	-1.1	-0.8	-1.7	-0.5	-1.6	-0.5	-3.5	-1.4	-2.8	9.5	-0.1	1.3	-0.4	-0.2
Czech Republic																				
Denmark	1.0	1.1	6.2	8.0	1.2	5.2	-0.6	-0.9	-3.8	-3.2	-0.6	0.3	1.0	3.7	1.8	-1.7	-5.1	0.4	2.7	1.9
Finland	11.0	-2.8	7.1	2.8	-1.6	2.6	0.2	-2.7	-6.7	-4.2	-1.9	-6.8	-0.3	-11.4	6.8	21.9	10.4	-6.3	-3.9	-1.4
Greece	13.4	-3.9	9.0	-15.6	0.7	14.7	12.7	-3.9	14.3	5.9	-35.7	29.8	-9.0	6.7	15.4	6.5	-5.7	-6.2	-1.8	-1.5
Iceland	7.6	4.7	9.2	2.3	-19.1	12.5	-5.5	8.9	9.0	8.6	-6.7	-3.9	-1.2	-4.2	-9.0	4.6	8.7	-6.1	1.5	0.9
Ireland	6.5	-1.0	6.7	-1.0	4.9	7.0	9.1	1.9	-1.9	9.0	-3.9	3.8	4.7	3.5	7.0	15.6	5.0	7.0	4.7	2.6
Mexico	36.8	7.1	38.0	21.1	12.6	28.0	-6.7	-9.2	-1.8	-17.9	-9.9	-0.4	-1.2	7.4	-9.0	0.3	-0.3	18.6	4.7	2.8
Netherlands	-1.2	2.6	-1.7	3.3	0.7	2.9	2.5	2.0	-2.7	-1.0	2.4	-0.8	-1.0	-0.2	-0.3	4.1	-2.3	0.2	-0.7	-0.3
New Zealand	-5.0	1.5	2.1	-6.3	1.8	4.7	-4.2	7.8	-0.4	-0.5	-4.5	-11.7	6.6	6.4	-3.2	-1.1	1.6	-7.2	-2.9	-1.1
Norway	23.2	-1.0	10.9	7.8	3.5	12.2	-0.2	1.7	-5.8	8.5	0.0	8.7	2.5	4.0	5.6	4.0	7.4	1.9	3.2	-2.3
Portugal	7.0	17.4	1.9	-2.5	12.7	15.1	7.5	5.6	0.1	3.4	0.6	11.5	7.0	-2.8	4.6	-0.4	3.2	3.2	3.9	0.8
Spain	12.0	4.7	-6.0	10.0	2.0	5.4	13.1	-2.6	-14.2	-0.3	-0.1	-1.1	2.2	1.3	-0.5	13.6	12.0	6.1	2.5	1.2
Sweden	4.6	1.2	-3.5	2.9	3.4	9.2	-0.1	-1.7	-3.6	-2.4	-2.4	-4.3	-4.4	-5.1	-2.8	11.2	4.6	6.2	-1.7	-0.6
Switzerland	-0.8	-7.8	-0.7	2.0	-3.4	-5.1	-3.4	5.0	-4.6	-4.1	-0.8	-0.8	-1.9	-8.7	1.1	1.6	-7.1	-4.3	-3.7	-2.8
Turkey	9.5	-17.7	10.9	82.4	32.6	2.2	22.1	10.9	-24.9	14.8	2.5	-7.0	-5.5	-0.1	2.8	18.0	5.8	1.0	8.1	5.4
Total of smaller countries	3.7	0.3	1.2	4.2	2.7	5.0	1.7	0.7	-3.9	-1.4	-2.2	-0.2	-0.5	-0.3	0.0	6.6	1.3	1.8	0.2	-0.3
Total OECD	0.7	-0.6	0.5	2.2	-0.4	1.8	0.8	1.0	-3.6	-1.3	-0.6	-0.5	-0.3	-1.7	-1.2	-0.4	-0.9	-0.5	-1.2	-0.3
OPEC	-5.2	-1.7	-12.4	-10.9	-5.5	-10.4	-6.1	-0.4	9.5	-4.8	5.3	-3.5	1.9	1.9	-4.6	11.7	-2.8	0.2	0.0	-1.4
ANIEs[b]	8.1	-0.3	6.6	3.2	4.5	7.6	4.2	-4.0	9.1	12.6	1.5	-5.8	0.1	2.0	2.0	1.2	1.4	1.8	3.1	1.2
Other Asia[c]	1.2	4.3	1.8	1.8	8.4	0.1	-0.1	2.3	4.1	2.8	-2.3	5.2	2.2	6.1	5.6	8.1	4.8	3.2	3.6	2.5
Latin America[c]	4.9	2.8	3.0	1.5	-0.6	1.6	3.7	-3.2	-15.2	8.1	7.6	1.5	-3.8	-1.0	-1.2	1.5	-3.2	-3.6	-0.5	-0.1
Africa[c]	2.7	1.2	33.7	-7.7	0.8	4.7	-2.9	-2.8	1.3	1.2	-4.7	-1.8	0.2	-0.3	-4.4	2.0	-3.2	3.3	2.2	-0.1
Central and Eastern Europe	-1.2	3.4	9.8	-2.3	0.9	-0.8	2.1	-5.0	-3.1	2.6	-4.2	-1.4	0.3	-7.8	-8.4	10.8	0.1	3.4	-1.2	-2.8
Total of non-OECD countries	-1.4	0.7	0.7	-4.2	0.6	-0.7	0.1	-2.7	2.5	4.1	0.2	-2.0	0.3	0.5	-0.6	5.8	0.6	1.8	1.9	0.5
World	0.0	-0.2	0.6	0.3	-0.1	1.1	0.7	0.1	-2.0	0.2	-0.3	-0.9	-0.1	-1.1	-1.1	1.4	-0.5	0.2	-0.2	0.0
OECD North America	4.5	2.4	6.1	-3.5	-1.4	1.1	-1.7	-0.9	0.4	2.3	4.0	1.5	2.7	-0.1	-0.8	-1.0	-0.2	4.0	1.7	0.9
OECD Europe	1.5	-0.9	-3.1	3.9	-0.1	1.8	1.4	1.5	-4.6	-1.8	-1.0	-0.4	-1.5	-1.9	-0.3	1.9	0.8	-0.8	-1.5	-0.5
European Union	1.2	-0.4	-3.7	3.6	-0.2	1.9	1.5	1.2	-4.4	-2.1	-1.0	-0.5	-1.5	-1.7	-0.5	1.6	0.9	-0.7	-1.6	-0.4
Total OECD *less* the United States	0.1	-0.9	-0.1	3.9	-0.1	2.2	1.3	0.1	-4.4	-1.6	-1.6	-1.2	-1.0	-1.8	-1.5	-0.1	-0.9	-0.5	-1.8	-0.5

a) Export performance is the ratio between export volumes and export markets for total goods. The export volume concept employed is the sum of the exports of food, raw materials, energy and manufactures. The calculation of export markets is based on a weighted average of import volumes in each exporting country's markets, with weights based on trade flows in 1991. The export market for total goods facing each country is calculated as the weighted sum of the individual export markets for food, raw materials, energy and manufactures, where the weights correspond to the commodity export structure of the exporting country in the previous year.
b) ANIEs include Chinese Taipei; Hong Kong, Korea and Singapore.
c) Not including OPEC countries.

Annex Table 46. **Shares in world exports and imports**

Percentage, values for total goods

	1978	1979	1980	1981	1982	1983	1984	1985	1986	1987	1988	1989	1990	1991	1992	1993	1994	1995	Projections 1996	1997
A. Exports																				
United States	11.0	11.0	11.1	11.9	11.5	11.4	11.7	11.5	10.6	10.3	11.5	12.1	11.5	12.1	12.0	12.3	12.1	11.7	12.1	12.2
Japan	7.5	6.2	6.5	7.6	7.5	8.2	8.9	9.2	10.0	9.3	9.4	9.1	8.4	9.0	9.2	9.8	9.5	9.0	8.2	8.2
Germany	11.7	11.2	10.3	9.6	9.8	9.7	9.2	9.8	11.9	12.2	11.8	11.6	11.9	11.5	11.7	10.4	10.3	10.4	9.8	9.6
France	6.0	6.0	5.7	5.3	5.2	5.2	5.0	5.8	5.8	5.9	5.9	5.8	6.2	6.1	6.3	5.7	5.6	5.7	5.4	5.3
Italy	4.1	4.2	3.8	3.8	4.0	4.0	3.8	4.1	4.6	4.7	4.6	4.6	4.9	4.8	4.8	4.6	4.5	4.7	4.8	4.7
United Kingdom	5.2	5.2	5.4	5.1	5.2	5.1	4.9	5.2	5.0	5.3	5.2	5.0	5.4	5.3	5.1	4.8	4.9	4.9	4.8	4.8
Canada	3.7	3.5	3.4	3.7	3.9	4.3	4.7	4.7	4.3	4.0	4.1	4.1	3.8	3.6	3.6	4.0	4.0	3.9	4.0	4.0
Other OECD countries	18.2	18.3	17.7	17.3	18.3	18.3	18.4	18.7	19.7	20.2	19.9	19.7	20.6	20.3	20.3	19.7	19.9	20.7	20.2	19.9
Total OECD	67.5	65.5	63.9	64.3	65.4	66.2	66.6	68.4	72.0	71.9	72.4	72.0	72.7	72.7	73.1	71.2	70.9	71.0	69.3	68.7
Non OECD Asia[a]	7.7	7.9	8.1	8.9	9.5	10.4	11.3	11.0	11.3	12.5	13.3	13.4	12.9	14.1	14.6	15.9	16.7	17.0	18.4	19.2
Latin America[a]	3.3	3.3	3.3	3.3	3.1	3.3	3.4	3.0	2.6	2.4	2.6	2.6	2.4	2.4	2.4	2.5	2.6	2.5	2.6	2.6
OPEC	11.2	13.4	14.4	13.4	11.6	9.6	8.6	7.9	5.1	4.9	4.2	4.7	5.4	4.9	4.6	4.8	4.5	4.1	4.1	4.0
Other non OECD countries	10.3	9.9	10.3	10.1	10.4	10.4	10.1	9.6	9.0	8.2	7.5	7.3	6.6	6.0	5.3	5.6	5.4	5.4	5.6	5.5
Total of non-OECD countries	32.5	34.5	36.1	35.7	34.6	33.8	33.4	31.6	28.0	28.1	27.6	28.0	27.3	27.3	26.9	28.8	29.1	29.0	30.7	31.3
B. Imports																				
United States	13.6	13.0	12.4	13.5	13.5	15.2	17.7	17.9	17.5	16.9	16.2	16.0	14.8	14.2	14.5	16.1	16.3	15.5	15.4	15.0
Japan	5.6	6.1	6.4	6.5	6.4	6.4	6.5	6.2	5.5	5.6	6.1	6.3	6.2	6.1	5.7	5.9	6.0	6.2	6.2	6.3
Germany	9.6	10.0	9.7	8.5	7.9	8.1	7.6	7.9	8.6	8.8	8.5	8.4	9.6	10.3	10.2	8.7	8.5	8.4	7.8	7.6
France	6.3	6.6	6.8	6.1	6.3	5.9	5.5	5.6	6.1	6.4	6.4	6.3	6.8	6.5	6.4	5.6	5.6	5.7	5.3	5.1
Italy	3.8	4.2	4.6	4.2	4.3	4.1	4.1	4.3	4.3	4.7	4.5	4.6	4.9	4.7	4.6	3.7	3.7	3.9	3.9	3.8
United Kingdom	5.4	5.6	5.3	4.7	5.0	5.1	5.1	5.2	5.5	5.8	6.2	6.1	6.0	5.5	5.4	5.1	5.1	5.0	4.9	4.9
Canada	3.4	3.3	3.0	3.3	3.0	3.4	3.8	4.0	3.8	3.6	3.8	3.9	3.5	3.5	3.4	3.7	3.6	3.4	3.4	3.4
Other OECD countries	21.4	21.9	21.6	20.2	20.2	19.4	19.1	19.1	21.2	22.1	21.8	21.8	22.9	22.5	22.5	20.8	20.7	21.1	20.6	20.4
Total OECD	68.9	70.6	69.6	67.1	66.6	67.5	69.4	70.9	72.5	73.9	73.5	73.4	74.6	73.3	72.6	69.5	69.5	69.3	67.4	66.6
Non OECD Asia[a]	8.0	8.4	8.7	9.6	9.8	10.7	10.8	11.3	10.7	11.2	12.5	13.1	13.0	14.5	15.4	17.9	18.6	19.0	20.5	21.3
Latin America[a]	4.0	4.0	4.3	4.4	3.8	3.4	3.0	2.7	2.7	2.6	2.3	2.4	2.3	2.5	2.9	3.5	3.7	3.8	3.9	3.9
OPEC	6.3	5.2	5.7	6.8	7.5	6.6	5.6	4.6	3.8	3.2	3.2	3.1	3.0	3.4	3.7	3.5	2.9	2.7	2.7	2.7
Other non OECD countries	12.9	11.7	11.7	12.1	12.2	11.8	11.2	10.6	10.3	9.1	8.5	8.1	7.1	6.3	5.3	5.6	5.2	5.2	5.4	5.5
Total of non-OECD countries	31.1	29.4	30.4	32.9	33.4	32.5	30.6	29.1	27.5	26.1	26.5	26.6	25.4	26.7	27.4	30.5	30.5	30.7	32.6	33.4

a) Excluding OPEC countries.

Annex Table 47. **Trade balances**
$ billion

	1978	1979	1980	1981	1982	1983	1984	1985	1986	1987	1988	1989	1990	1991	1992	1993	1994	1995	Projections 1996	1997
United States	-33.9	-27.6	-25.5	-28.0	-38.5	-67.1	-112.5	-122.2	-145.1	-159.6	-127.0	-115.2	-109.0	-74.1	-96.1	-132.6	-166.1	-174.5	-158.6	-150.9
Japan	24.6	1.8	2.1	20.0	18.1	31.5	44.3	56.0	92.8	96.4	95.0	76.9	63.5	96.1 *a*	124.6	139.5	144.2	132.1	103.0	101.7
Germany	23.0	15.2	8.0	15.5	24.2	19.4	21.7	27.9	54.1	67.7	76.4	75.1	69.4	18.0	26.5	39.8	49.1	68.7	73.1	81.8
France	0.0	-3.2	-13.5	-9.9	-15.5	-8.1	-4.3	-5.0	-1.5	-7.8	-7.6	-10.2	-13.1	-9.4	2.4	7.5	7.7	11.7	10.2	14.0
Italy	3.4	-0.1	-15.9	-10.8	-7.9	-1.7	-5.2	-5.5	4.7	0.2	-0.7	-1.7	1.2	-0.2	3.1	33.1	35.3	44.0	50.0	52.8
United Kingdom	-3.1	-7.1	3.2	6.5	3.3	-2.3	-7.1	-4.3	-14.0	-18.9	-38.2	-40.4	-33.4	-18.1	-23.0	-20.1	-16.6	-18.2	-21.8	-24.2
Canada	4.2	4.2	8.0	6.4	14.8	14.8	16.0	12.6	7.7	9.0	8.1	6.0	8.3	3.9	5.8	7.9	12.2	21.9	30.0	33.7
Total of above countries	18.2	-16.8	-33.6	-0.2	-1.4	-13.5	-47.1	-40.5	-1.2	-13.1	6.0	-9.6	-13.1	16.2	43.3	75.1	65.9	85.7	85.8	108.9
Australia	0.1	2.5	1.4	-2.2	-2.1	0.0	-0.8	-1.0	-1.8	0.3	-0.6	-3.4	0.4	3.5	1.5	-0.1	-3.2	-4.3	-1.0	-2.7
Austria	-3.3	-4.3	-6.3	-4.5	-3.1	-3.4	-3.3	-2.7	-3.5	-4.2	-4.6	-5.0	-5.9	-7.6	-7.7	-4.6	-4.9	-4.9	-3.6	-2.8
Belgium-Luxembourg	-1.3	-3.1	-4.0	-3.6	-2.2	-0.7	-0.3	0.5	2.3	1.3	2.8	2.3	1.6	1.9	3.5	5.9	6.6	9.7	9.1	9.9
Czech Republic																-0.3	-0.9	-3.9	-5.1	-5.6
Denmark	-2.4	-3.4	-2.0	-0.9	-0.8	0.2	-0.2	-0.7	-1.1	0.8	1.9	2.4	4.9	4.7	7.2	8.0	7.4	6.8	6.9	7.3
Finland	1.1	0.4	-0.6	0.3	0.2	0.2	1.5	0.9	1.6	1.4	1.1	-0.2	0.7	2.3	3.8	6.3	7.5	10.7	9.1	9.1
Greece	-3.5	-5.0	-5.6	-5.4	-4.8	-4.3	-4.2	-5.1	-4.4	-5.5	-6.1	-7.4	-10.2	-10.1	-11.6	-10.6	-11.4	-14.5	-15.6	-17.6
Iceland	0.0	0.0	0.0	0.0	-0.2	0.0	0.0	0.0	0.1	-0.1	0.0	0.1	0.1	0.0	0.0	0.2	0.3	0.2	0.1	0.1
Ireland	-1.1	-2.3	-2.2	-2.2	-1.1	-0.2	0.3	0.6	1.1	2.6	3.8	4.0	4.0	4.2	7.0	8.1	9.5	12.4	13.3	14.1
Mexico	-1.7	-2.1	-3.1	-3.9	7.0	14.1	13.2	8.4	5.0	8.8	2.6	0.4	-0.9	-7.3	-15.9	-13.5	-18.5	7.1	5.2	1.3
Netherlands	-0.8	-0.6	-0.2	5.6	6.2	5.5	6.6	6.7	7.6	6.2	10.0	9.8	11.9	11.9	12.3	15.5	15.8	19.9	19.2	21.0
New Zealand	0.5	0.4	0.3	0.2	-0.3	0.3	-0.5	0.0	0.1	0.6	2.1	1.0	0.9	2.1	1.6	1.7	1.4	0.9	1.0	1.0
Norway	-0.5	0.1	1.9	3.0	2.4	4.4	5.2	4.7	-2.1	-0.7	-0.5	3.5	5.6	7.4	8.3	6.9	6.8	8.3	10.0	10.1
Portugal	-2.1	-2.6	-4.0	-7.0	-4.8	-3.0	-2.1	-1.5	-1.7	-3.6	-5.5	-4.9	-6.8	-7.9	-9.5	-6.8	-6.7	-6.9	-7.0	-7.5
Spain	-4.1	-5.7	-11.7	-10.0	-9.3	-7.6	-4.3	-4.2	-6.4	-12.8	-18.0	-24.6	-29.5	-30.8	-30.8	-15.7	-14.4	-17.6	-18.9	-20.9
Sweden	2.6	-0.7	-2.2	0.1	-0.4	1.9	3.4	2.3	5.0	4.5	4.8	4.0	3.4	6.3	6.7	7.5	9.6	15.1	13.7	15.5
Switzerland	0.6	-1.7	-5.0	-2.5	-1.3	-2.3	-2.3	-2.0	-2.0	-3.1	-3.2	-4.4	-3.5	-2.5	2.4	4.9	5.2	4.3	3.4	3.8
Turkey	-2.1	-2.6	-4.6	-3.9	-2.7	-3.0	-2.9	-3.0	-3.1	-3.2	-1.8	-4.2	-9.6	-7.3	-8.2	-14.2	-4.2	-13.2	-14.5	-15.9
Total of smaller countries	-18.4	-30.9	-48.0	-36.7	-17.0	2.5	9.5	4.2	-3.5	-7.0	-10.9	-26.5	-33.9	-29.4	-31.1	-0.7	5.8	30.1	25.4	20.4
Total OECD	-0.2	-47.7	-81.5	-36.9	-18.3	-11.1	-37.6	-36.3	-4.7	-20.2	-5.0	-36.1	-47.0	-13.2	12.2	74.4	71.7	115.8	111.1	129.3
OECD North America	-31.5	-25.5	-20.5	-25.5	-16.6	-38.2	-83.3	-101.2	-132.4	-141.8	-116.3	-108.9	-101.6	-77.5	-106.3	-138.2	-172.3	-145.5	-123.4	-115.9
OECD Europe	6.1	-26.9	-64.8	-29.4	-17.5	-4.7	2.7	9.9	36.6	24.4	14.8	-1.7	-10.2	-37.4	-9.3	71.5	101.7	132.6	131.5	145.1
European Union	8.6	-22.5	-57.0	-26.2	-15.9	-4.1	2.5	10.0	44.0	31.7	20.1	3.3	-1.7	-34.8	-10.1	74.1	94.5	136.9	137.6	152.6
Total OECD *less* the United States	33.8	-20.1	-56.0	-8.9	20.1	56.0	74.9	85.9	140.3	139.4	122.0	79.1	62.0	60.9	108.3	207.0	237.8	290.3	269.7	280.2

a) Break in series starting this year.

Annex Table 48. **Non-factor services, net**

$ billion

	1978	1979	1980	1981	1982	1983	1984	1985	1986	1987	1988	1989	1990	1991	1992	1993	1994	1995	Projections 1996	1997
United States	4.2	3.0	6.1	11.9	12.3	9.3	3.3	0.3	5.5	6.9	11.6	23.9	29.0	44.7	56.6	57.8	59.9	63.0	63.8	68.9
Japan	-8.3	-11.5	-12.2	-12.8	-11.6	-12.2	-12.0	-12.0	-14.4	-22.4	-32.3	-39.0	-45.5	-41.8 *a*	-44.0	-43.0	-48.0	-57.2	-62.3	-70.1
Germany	-5.8	-9.4	-9.3	-7.0	-6.0	-5.5	-3.7	-3.0	-4.3	-8.0	-10.9	-9.4	-13.2	-17.4	-27.2	-31.5	-37.7	-44.2	-41.4	-43.7
France	9.1	10.2	10.0	7.1	7.1	8.2	8.0	9.2	9.0	9.1	9.9	12.8	14.6	15.7	18.7	16.3	18.7	18.4	18.7	20.6
Italy	4.1	5.7	4.7	3.6	3.8	5.0	4.6	4.6	5.3	5.1	2.9	0.8	-1.2	-0.1	-4.6	-0.1	1.2	1.1	2.0	2.4
United Kingdom	7.1	8.3	8.5	7.6	5.3	5.8	5.6	8.2	9.1	10.2	7.0	5.5	6.6	6.5	8.9	8.5	7.3	8.9	10.2	12.0
Canada	-3.2	-2.6	-3.2	-3.2	-3.5	-3.8	-4.1	-4.1	-4.3	-5.3	-5.7	-7.8	-10.3	-10.8	-10.8	-10.4	-8.1	-7.8	-8.2	-9.1
Total of above countries	7.2	3.7	4.6	7.1	7.5	6.9	1.7	3.1	5.9	-4.3	-17.4	-13.3	-20.0	-3.2	-2.4	-2.4	-6.6	-17.9	-17.2	-18.9
Australia	-2.2	-2.3	-2.6	-3.0	-3.1	-2.6	-3.5	-3.4	-2.9	-2.7	-2.5	-4.5	-3.7	-2.8	-2.8	-1.8	-1.1	-1.0	-1.1	-1.5
Austria	3.1	3.6	5.2	3.7	4.3	4.1	3.5	2.9	4.4	5.0	5.3	6.3	8.1	9.2	9.8	6.0	4.8	3.3	2.6	3.0
Belgium-Luxembourg	0.5	0.5	0.3	0.7	1.2	1.5	1.1	0.9	1.5	2.5	2.0	1.9	1.9	1.9	2.9	3.3	3.9	4.1	3.9	3.8
Czech Republic																1.0	0.7	1.6	1.7	1.8
Denmark	1.3	1.4	1.3	1.2	0.9	0.8	0.7	0.7	0.3	0.5	1.2	0.9	2.6	3.9	4.1	2.9	1.8	0.6	-0.1	0.0
Finland	0.3	0.3	0.3	0.4	0.3	0.1	-0.2	-0.4	-0.6	-1.0	-1.5	-2.1	-3.0	-3.3	-2.6	-2.0	-1.2	-1.3	-1.3	-1.6
Greece	1.7	2.1	2.5	2.3	1.9	1.4	1.4	1.2	1.7	2.7	2.9	2.4	3.6	4.1	5.0	4.8	5.6	5.3	5.4	6.0
Iceland	0.1	0.0	0.0	0.0	0.0	0.1	0.0	0.0	0.1	0.0	0.0	0.0	0.0	0.0	0.0	0.0	0.1	0.1	0.1	0.1
Ireland	-0.1	-0.2	-0.4	-0.2	-0.2	-0.2	-0.2	-0.2	-0.5	-0.8	-1.1	-1.4	-1.2	-1.2	-1.8	-1.8	-2.3	-3.3	-3.8	-4.0
Mexico	1.2	1.1	-1.9	-3.5	-1.9	-0.4	-0.4	-0.7	-0.6	0.1	-0.2	-0.7	-2.2	-2.1	-2.7	-2.5	-2.6	1.2	1.9	2.0
Netherlands	0.3	-0.9	-1.4	-1.0	-0.6	-0.9	-0.8	-1.4	-1.5	-1.7	-2.6	-1.1	0.2	-1.2	-0.5	0.0	0.9	0.6	0.8	0.7
New Zealand	-0.5	-0.6	-0.8	-0.8	-0.8	-0.5	-0.4	-0.3	-0.5	-0.5	-0.6	-0.8	-0.8	-0.9	-1.0	-0.6	-0.3	-0.3	-0.3	-0.3
Norway	0.1	1.1	1.6	1.4	0.7	-0.1	-0.2	0.0	-0.5	-1.1	-0.1	0.2	2.1	2.2	0.5	0.7	0.7	0.5	0.5	0.5
Portugal	0.3	0.5	0.6	0.5	0.2	0.4	0.5	0.8	0.9	1.2	1.0	1.2	1.4	1.1	0.9	0.7	0.6	0.8	1.3	1.5
Spain	5.1	6.1	6.0	5.9	5.8	6.3	7.6	7.6	11.2	12.9	13.3	12.0	12.2	12.9	13.2	11.8	14.2	17.8	19.1	20.0
Sweden	-0.9	0.2	0.5	0.2	-0.4	0.0	-0.1	-0.6	-1.9	-1.8	-2.4	-3.2	-3.5	-2.8	-3.0	-0.9	-1.1	-0.9	0.2	0.6
Switzerland	0.6	0.2	0.2	0.3	0.4	0.9	0.8	1.7	2.4	2.8	2.0	1.4	0.8	1.5	1.9	3.4	3.1	3.1	3.1	3.3
Turkey	0.2	0.3	0.1	0.8	0.9	0.8	0.9	1.3	1.3	1.8	3.3	3.4	4.2	4.4	4.8	5.6	5.7	7.3	7.0	7.7
Total of smaller countries	11.4	13.9	12.0	9.3	10.2	12.2	11.4	10.7	15.5	20.7	21.0	16.5	22.8	27.6	30.5	30.5	33.4	39.7	41.1	43.6
Total OECD	18.6	17.6	16.6	16.4	17.8	19.0	13.1	13.8	21.4	16.3	3.6	3.2	2.8	24.5	28.1	28.1	26.8	21.8	23.9	24.7
OECD North America	2.2	1.5	1.0	5.2	6.9	5.1	-1.2	-4.6	0.7	1.7	5.7	15.4	16.5	31.8	43.2	44.9	49.2	56.4	57.4	61.9
OECD Europe	27.4	30.5	31.2	27.8	26.2	29.2	30.2	34.1	38.5	40.1	33.3	32.1	36.3	38.2	32.8	28.7	27.0	23.9	30.2	34.7
European Union	26.0	28.5	28.9	24.9	23.6	27.1	28.1	30.5	34.7	35.9	27.2	26.5	28.8	29.4	23.7	18.0	16.8	11.2	17.8	21.3
Total OECD *less* the United States	14.4	14.6	10.5	4.5	5.4	9.8	9.8	13.5	15.9	9.5	-8.0	-20.6	-26.2	-20.2	-28.5	-29.7	-33.1	-41.2	-39.9	-44.3

a) Break in series starting this year.

A51

Annex Table 49. Investment income, net

$ billion

	1978	1979	1980	1981	1982	1983	1984	1985	1986	1987	1988	1989	1990	1991	1992	1993	1994	1995	Projections 1996	1997
United States	20.4	30.9	30.1	32.9	29.8	31.1	30.0	20.6	12.9	9.5	13.3	13.7	20.7	15.1	10.1	9.0	-9.3	-11.4	-17.5	-21.9
Japan	0.9	2.0	0.9	-0.8	1.7	3.1	4.2	6.8	9.5	16.7	21.0	23.4	23.2	26.0[a]	35.8	40.4	40.5	44.8	51.4	56.3
Germany	1.4	0.4	1.0	-0.4	-2.0	1.1	3.1	2.7	4.0	3.3	3.7	11.1	16.8	17.9	14.4	10.8	5.1	-1.4	-1.3	-1.7
France	1.2	2.2	3.5	2.3	0.7	-1.1	-2.0	-1.9	-1.1	-0.9	-0.4	0.3	-3.2	-5.1	-8.3	-8.5	-10.3	-6.0	-8.8	-8.2
Italy	-1.1	-0.5	-0.6	-3.2	-3.9	-3.9	-3.9	-4.0	-6.2	-6.6	-7.1	-8.3	-14.7	-17.5	-20.8	-16.2	-15.3	-14.9	-11.5	-8.1
United Kingdom	1.5	2.6	-0.4	2.5	2.5	4.3	5.8	2.9	6.8	6.1	7.9	5.5	1.7	-0.4	6.5	2.8	14.3	10.5	10.8	9.9
Canada	-5.2	-6.1	-6.7	-9.5	-10.3	-12.6	-12.3	-12.8	-13.7	-15.4	-19.8	-21.2	-19.6	-16.7	-16.5	-20.2	-21.2	-23.9	-24.9	-25.6
Total of above countries	19.2	31.4	27.6	23.9	18.6	22.0	24.9	14.5	12.1	12.7	18.7	24.7	25.0	19.3	21.2	18.1	3.8	-2.4	-1.8	0.7
Australia	-2.0	-2.5	-2.7	-2.9	-2.6	-3.3	-4.3	-4.7	-5.0	-6.0	-8.4	-11.4	-13.3	-12.4	-10.4	-8.8	-11.2	-14.0	-14.2	-14.6
Austria	-0.5	-0.5	-0.5	-0.5	-0.4	-0.4	-0.4	-0.3	-0.7	-0.9	-0.9	-0.9	-1.0	-1.5	-1.2	-1.0	-0.9	-1.0	-1.2	-1.5
Belgium-Luxembourg	0.8	0.5	0.1	0.0	-0.2	-0.1	0.0	-0.1	0.3	0.5	0.5	1.3	2.4	3.3	2.9	4.9	5.3	6.4	5.9	6.1
Czech Republic																-0.1	0.0	-0.1	-0.1	-0.1
Denmark	-0.9	-1.3	-1.8	-2.0	-2.2	-2.0	-2.2	-2.6	-3.5	-4.1	-4.2	-4.3	-5.7	-5.6	-5.6	-4.7	-5.1	-5.0	-4.7	-4.4
Finland	-0.7	-0.7	-0.9	-1.1	-1.3	-1.2	-1.1	-1.1	-1.4	-1.6	-1.8	-2.7	-3.7	-4.6	-5.3	-4.9	-4.4	-4.4	-3.2	-3.6
Greece	-0.1	-0.2	-0.3	-0.6	-0.6	-0.8	-0.9	-1.1	-1.3	-1.4	-1.5	-1.5	-1.6	-1.7	-2.0	-1.5	-1.3	-1.7	-1.9	-1.8
Iceland	-0.1	-0.1	-0.1	-0.1	-0.1	-0.1	-0.2	-0.1	-0.2	-0.2	-0.2	-0.2	-0.3	-0.3	-0.2	-0.2	-0.2	-0.2	-0.2	-0.2
Ireland	-0.5	-0.7	-0.8	-1.0	-1.5	-1.6	-1.9	-2.2	-2.8	-3.2	-4.2	-4.7	-5.3	-4.7	-5.7	-6.0	-6.3	-7.4	-7.6	-8.2
Mexico	-2.8	-3.8	-6.3	-9.9	-12.0	-9.0	-10.0	-8.9	-7.4	-6.6	-7.0	-8.1	-8.3	-8.3	-9.2	-11.0	-11.7	-13.0	-13.8	-14.1
Netherlands	0.2	2.3	1.5	0.4	0.4	1.1	1.3	-0.2	-0.2	-1.3	1.1	2.8	-0.6	0.5	-0.9	0.6	1.4	1.4	1.4	1.4
New Zealand	-0.6	-0.5	-0.5	-0.6	-0.7	-0.9	-1.1	-1.3	-1.5	-2.0	-2.1	-1.9	-1.6	-2.5	-2.0	-2.3	-3.5	-4.4	-4.4	-4.4
Norway	-1.4	-1.8	-1.9	-1.8	-1.9	-1.7	-1.5	-1.0	-1.1	-1.2	-2.5	-2.8	-3.4	-3.9	-2.8	-2.6	-2.9	-1.8	-1.8	-1.4
Portugal	-0.3	-0.4	-0.6	-1.0	-1.3	-1.1	-1.2	-1.2	-1.0	-0.9	-0.9	-0.7	-0.2	0.1	0.6	0.2	-0.3	-0.9	-0.6	-0.4
Spain	-1.0	-1.1	-1.5	-2.3	-2.3	-2.5	-2.4	-1.8	-2.0	-2.8	-3.5	-3.0	-3.8	-4.8	-6.6	-5.1	-7.9	-4.0	-7.8	-9.0
Sweden	-0.7	-0.8	-1.4	-2.2	-1.7	-1.8	-1.9	-2.0	-1.9	-1.4	-1.6	-2.2	-4.3	-6.2	-9.8	-8.6	-5.8	-6.4	-5.5	-5.0
Switzerland	4.1	5.0	5.3	6.0	6.0	6.2	6.7	6.8	8.5	10.5	13.3	11.7	13.7	14.2	13.7	14.0	13.6	16.5	17.0	17.0
Turkey	-0.4	-1.0	-1.1	-1.4	-1.5	-1.4	-1.4	-1.3	-1.6	-1.8	-2.0	-1.7	-1.8	-1.9	-1.6	-1.5	-2.0	-1.0	-1.0	-1.4
Total of smaller countries	-7.2	-7.8	-13.9	-21.5	-24.3	-20.7	-22.6	-23.1	-22.8	-22.0	-26.1	-30.5	-39.0	-40.3	-46.2	-38.7	-43.3	-40.9	-44.0	-45.5
Total OECD	12.0	23.6	13.7	2.4	-5.6	1.3	2.2	-8.6	-10.7	-9.3	-7.4	-5.9	-14.0	-21.0	-25.0	-20.6	-39.5	-43.2	-45.8	-44.8
OECD North America	12.3	21.0	17.1	13.6	7.5	9.5	7.7	-1.0	-8.2	-12.6	-13.5	-15.6	-7.2	-9.9	-15.7	-22.2	-42.2	-48.3	-56.2	-61.6
OECD Europe	1.3	3.6	-0.9	-6.8	-11.5	-7.1	-4.3	-8.4	-5.5	-5.4	-4.3	-0.4	-15.1	-22.3	-32.8	-27.6	-23.1	-21.4	-22.4	-20.5
European Union	-0.7	1.7	-2.8	-9.0	-13.7	-9.8	-7.7	-12.6	-11.0	-12.6	-12.8	-7.2	-23.2	-30.3	-41.8	-37.1	-31.6	-34.8	-36.2	-34.4
Total OECD *less* the United States	-8.4	-7.3	-16.3	-30.5	-35.4	-29.8	-27.8	-29.2	-23.6	-18.8	-20.6	-19.5	-34.7	-36.1	-35.1	-29.6	-30.2	-31.8	-28.3	-22.9

a) Break in series starting this year.

Annex Table 50. **Current account balances**
$ billion

	1978	1979	1980	1981	1982	1983	1984	1985	1986	1987	1988	1989	1990	1991	1992	1993	1994	1995	Projections 1996	1997
United States	-15.1	-0.3	2.3	5.0	-13.4	-44.5	-99.8	-124.2	-150.9	-166.3	-127.1	-103.8	-92.7	-7.4	-61.5	-99.9	-151.2	-152.9	-149.8	-138.9
Japan	16.5	-8.8	-10.8	4.8	6.8	20.8	35.0	49.2	85.8	87.0	79.6	57.2	35.8	68.3[a]	112.7	131.8	130.6	111.9	81.7	76.9
Germany	9.1	-5.3	-13.2	-3.6	5.0	4.5	9.8	17.0	40.5	46.1	49.5	57.2	48.9	-19.2	-21.5	-16.3	-21.4	-17.4	-11.3	-6.1
France	7.0	5.2	-4.2	-4.7	-12.2	-4.8	-1.2	-0.3	1.8	-5.0	-4.8	-4.7	-9.8	-6.1	3.9	9.3	8.1	17.4	13.9	19.5
Italy	6.0	5.8	-10.4	-9.6	-7.0	0.9	-2.9	-4.0	2.0	-2.2	-6.3	-11.8	-17.0	-23.6	-27.8	11.3	15.5	27.4	38.0	44.4
United Kingdom	2.2	5.8	6.6	13.6	8.1	5.3	2.0	2.9	-1.3	-8.1	-29.6	-36.8	-33.8	-14.4	-16.6	-16.6	-3.2	-10.7	-17.0	-19.4
Canada	-4.3	-4.1	-1.0	-5.1	2.3	-1.4	-0.6	-4.5	-10.1	-11.8	-17.1	-22.8	-21.6	-23.6	-21.4	-22.3	-16.3	-9.6	-2.8	-0.6
Total of above countries	21.4	-8.4	-30.5	0.4	-10.4	-19.1	-57.7	-64.0	-32.1	-60.4	-55.8	-65.6	-90.3	-26.2	-32.3	-2.7	-37.9	-33.8	-47.5	-24.2
Australia	-4.4	-2.6	-4.1	-8.3	-7.9	-5.9	-8.6	-8.7	-9.2	-7.4	-10.0	-17.4	-14.8	-9.8	-10.6	-10.5	-15.4	-18.7	-15.8	-18.3
Austria	-0.7	-1.1	-1.7	-1.3	0.7	0.2	-0.2	-0.1	0.2	-0.2	-0.2	0.2	1.2	0.1	-0.1	-0.7	-1.8	-4.7	-3.8	-3.1
Belgium-Luxembourg	-0.8	-3.1	-4.9	-4.2	-2.4	-0.4	0.0	0.7	3.1	2.8	3.5	3.6	3.6	4.9	6.6	11.3	12.3	16.5	15.1	15.7
Czech Republic																0.1	-0.1	-1.9	-3.1	-3.5
Denmark	-1.4	-3.0	-2.5	-1.9	-2.2	-1.2	-1.6	-2.7	-4.5	-3.0	-1.3	-1.1	1.3	2.2	4.8	5.6	3.0	1.4	1.1	1.9
Finland	0.7	-0.2	-1.4	-0.5	-1.0	-1.1	0.0	-0.8	-0.7	-1.7	-2.7	-5.8	-6.9	-6.6	-4.9	-1.1	1.4	4.5	4.0	3.4
Greece	-1.0	-1.9	-2.2	-2.4	-1.9	-1.9	-2.1	-3.3	-1.7	-1.2	-1.0	-2.6	-3.5	-1.6	-2.1	-0.7	-0.1	-2.9	-3.1	-3.6
Iceland	0.0	0.0	-0.1	-0.2	-0.3	-0.1	-0.1	-0.1	0.0	-0.2	-0.2	-0.1	-0.1	-0.3	-0.2	0.0	0.1	0.1	-0.1	-0.1
Ireland	-0.8	-2.1	-2.1	-2.6	-1.9	-1.2	-1.0	-0.7	-0.8	-0.1	0.1	-0.5	0.1	1.5	2.5	3.1	3.1	4.4	4.4	4.5
Mexico	-3.2	-4.6	-10.4	-16.2	-5.9	5.9	4.2	0.8	-1.4	4.2	-2.4	-5.8	-7.4	-14.9	-24.4	-23.4	-28.8	-0.7	-2.7	-6.5
Netherlands	-1.2	0.1	-1.2	3.5	4.7	4.7	6.1	4.1	4.3	3.8	6.7	9.6	8.6	7.0	6.6	11.6	12.8	15.6	15.2	15.9
New Zealand	-0.5	-0.7	-0.9	-1.2	-1.7	-1.0	-1.9	-1.6	-1.7	-1.8	-0.5	-1.6	-1.2	-0.9	-0.9	-0.5	-1.5	-2.5	-2.2	-2.2
Norway	-2.1	-1.0	1.1	2.2	0.6	2.0	2.9	3.1	-4.5	-4.1	-4.0	-0.1	3.1	4.4	4.7	3.6	3.0	5.1	6.7	6.8
Portugal	-0.4	0.0	1.1	-4.6	-3.1	-1.5	-0.6	0.3	1.2	0.4	-1.0	0.2	-0.2	-0.7	-0.2	0.9	-1.1	0.0	-0.3	-0.4
Spain	1.6	1.1	-5.1	-4.8	-4.2	-2.5	2.0	2.7	3.9	-0.1	-3.7	-10.9	-16.9	-16.7	-18.3	-4.2	-6.0	1.3	-1.3	-2.8
Sweden	-0.2	-2.4	-4.4	-2.9	-3.5	-0.8	0.5	-1.3	-0.1	-0.2	-0.8	-3.4	-6.6	-4.8	-8.7	-3.7	0.9	4.9	5.4	8.2
Switzerland	4.4	2.4	-0.6	2.8	4.1	3.8	4.4	5.7	7.8	8.7	10.4	7.0	8.6	10.6	15.1	19.4	18.4	19.8	19.1	19.4
Turkey	-1.3	-1.4	-3.4	-1.9	-1.0	-1.8	-1.4	-1.0	-1.5	-0.8	1.6	1.0	-2.6	0.3	-0.9	-6.4	2.5	-2.3	-3.8	-4.7
Total of smaller countries	-11.7	-20.6	-45.1	-44.4	-26.7	-2.1	3.2	-2.2	-5.5	-0.3	-4.7	-27.0	-34.6	-24.7	-31.8	4.3	2.7	39.8	34.9	30.8
Total OECD	9.6	-29.0	-75.7	-44.1	-37.1	-21.2	-54.5	-66.3	-37.5	-60.7	-60.5	-92.6	-124.9	-50.8	-64.1	1.6	-35.2	6.0	-12.5	6.5
OECD North America	-22.6	-9.0	-9.1	-16.3	-17.0	-40.0	-96.2	-128.0	-162.3	-173.9	-146.6	-132.4	-121.7	-45.9	-107.4	-145.6	-196.4	-163.1	-155.4	-146.0
OECD Europe	20.6	-8.0	-50.8	-23.0	-17.2	4.9	17.2	22.8	49.9	35.3	17.0	1.6	-22.9	-62.5	-57.8	26.4	47.4	78.3	79.1	96.2
European Union	19.9	-7.7	-47.7	-26.1	-21.0	0.4	10.8	14.6	47.9	31.3	8.3	-6.9	-31.0	-78.1	-76.0	9.7	23.4	57.6	60.2	78.2
Total OECD *less* the United States	24.8	-28.7	-78.0	-49.1	-23.6	23.2	45.2	58.0	113.3	105.7	66.6	11.3	-32.2	-43.4	-2.5	101.5	116.1	158.9	137.3	145.4

a) Break in series starting this year.
Note: The balance-of-payments data in this table are derived from OECD countries' submissions and publications. They are based on the concepts and definitions of the IMF *Balance of Payments Manual*.

Annex Table 51. **Current account balances as a percentage of GDP**

	1978	1979	1980	1981	1982	1983	1984	1985	1986	1987	1988	1989	1990	1991	1992	1993	1994	1995	Projections 1996	1997
United States	-0.7	0.0	0.1	0.2	-0.4	-1.3	-2.6	-3.0	-3.4	-3.5	-2.5	-1.9	-1.6	-0.1	-1.0	-1.5	-2.2	-2.1	-2.0	-1.8
Japan	1.7	-0.9	-1.0	0.4	0.6	1.8	2.8	3.6	4.3	3.6	2.7	2.0	1.2	2.0a	3.0	3.1	2.8	2.2	1.8	1.6
Germany	1.4	-0.7	-1.6	-0.5	0.8	0.7	1.6	2.7	4.5	4.2	4.2	4.8	3.3	-1.1	-1.1	-0.9	-1.0	-0.7	-0.5	-0.3
France	1.4	0.9	-0.6	-0.8	-2.2	-0.9	-0.2	-0.1	0.2	-0.6	-0.5	-0.5	-0.8	-0.5	0.3	0.8	0.6	1.1	0.9	1.2
Italy	2.0	1.6	-2.3	-2.3	-1.7	0.2	-0.7	-0.9	0.3	-0.3	-0.8	-1.4	-1.6	-2.1	-2.3	1.2	1.5	2.5	3.2	3.5
United Kingdom	0.7	-0.2	1.2	2.5	1.7	1.2	0.4	0.6	-0.2	-1.1	-3.5	-4.4	-3.5	-1.4	-1.6	-1.8	-0.3	-1.0	-1.5	-1.7
Canada	-2.0	-1.8	-0.4	-1.7	0.8	-0.4	-0.2	-1.3	-2.8	-2.8	-3.5	-4.1	-3.8	-4.0	-3.7	-4.0	-3.0	-1.7	-0.5	-0.1
Total of above countries	0.4	-0.1	-0.5	0.0	-0.2	-0.3	-0.8	-0.8	-0.3	-0.6	-0.5	-0.5	-0.6	-0.2	-0.2	0.0	-0.2	-0.2	-0.3	-0.1
Australia	-3.8	-2.0	-2.7	-4.8	-4.7	-3.6	-4.7	-5.4	-5.4	-3.7	-4.0	-6.2	-5.0	-3.3	-3.6	-3.7	-4.7	-5.4	-4.0	-4.4
Austria	-1.2	-1.6	-2.1	-2.0	1.1	0.3	-0.3	-0.2	0.3	-0.2	-0.2	0.2	0.7	0.0	-0.1	-0.4	-0.9	-2.0	-1.7	-1.3
Belgium-Luxembourg	-0.9	-2.8	-4.2	-4.4	-2.7	-0.5	-0.1	0.9	2.8	2.0	2.3	2.3	1.9	2.5	3.0	5.4	5.4	6.1	5.7	5.8
Czech Republic																0.4	-0.1	-4.1	-6.0	-5.8
Denmark	-2.5	-4.5	-3.7	-3.2	-4.0	-2.1	-3.0	-4.6	-5.5	-2.9	-1.2	-1.1	1.0	1.7	3.4	4.1	2.0	0.9	0.6	1.0
Finland	1.9	-0.3	-2.7	-1.0	-2.0	-2.3	-0.1	-1.4	-1.0	-2.0	-2.6	-5.1	-5.1	-5.4	-4.6	-1.3	1.5	3.5	3.3	2.7
Greece	-2.5	-4.0	-4.5	-5.4	-4.2	-4.5	-5.2	-8.1	-3.5	-2.2	-1.5	-3.8	-4.3	-1.7	-2.2	-0.8	-0.2	-2.5	-2.6	-2.8
Iceland	0.9	-0.8	-2.3	-4.3	-8.1	-2.1	-4.7	-4.0	0.5	-3.5	-3.6	-1.5	-2.2	-4.6	-3.0	0.0	1.9	0.8	-0.8	-1.3
Ireland	-6.2	-12.4	-10.6	-13.5	-9.4	-5.9	-5.5	-3.4	-3.1	-0.3	0.2	-1.3	0.2	3.3	4.9	6.6	5.8	7.2	7.0	6.8
Mexico	-2.9	-3.3	-5.4	-6.5	-2.2	5.1	2.6	0.8	-0.9	3.0	-1.4	-2.9	-3.1	-5.2	-7.4	-6.5	-7.8	-0.2	-1.0	-2.0
Netherlands	-0.9	0.1	-0.7	2.5	3.3	3.5	4.8	3.1	2.4	1.7	2.9	4.2	3.0	2.4	2.1	3.8	3.8	3.9	3.9	4.0
New Zealand	-2.9	-3.5	-4.4	-5.0	-7.2	-4.4	-8.8	-7.1	-6.3	-5.1	-1.1	-3.7	-2.8	-2.2	-2.3	-1.1	-3.0	-4.3	-3.5	-3.3
Norway	-4.7	-2.0	1.7	3.4	1.0	3.4	4.8	4.9	-5.9	-4.4	-4.1	-0.1	2.6	3.7	3.7	3.1	2.4	3.5	4.4	4.3
Portugal	-2.1	-0.2	-3.8	-16.8	-11.7	-6.1	-2.6	1.4	3.4	1.1	-2.2	0.3	-0.3	-0.9	-0.2	1.0	-1.2	0.0	-0.3	-0.3
Spain	1.0	0.6	-2.4	-2.6	-2.4	-1.6	1.3	1.6	1.7	0.0	-1.1	-2.9	-3.4	-3.2	-3.2	-0.8	-1.2	0.2	-0.2	-0.5
Sweden	-0.3	-2.2	-3.5	-2.6	-3.6	-0.9	0.6	-1.4	-0.1	-0.1	-0.4	-1.8	-2.8	-2.0	-3.5	-2.0	0.4	2.1	2.2	3.2
Switzerland	5.1	2.6	-0.5	3.0	4.2	4.0	4.8	6.0	5.7	5.1	5.6	4.0	3.8	4.6	6.2	8.4	7.1	6.5	6.5	6.5
Turkey	-1.8	-2.0	-5.0	-2.6	-1.4	-2.9	-2.4	-1.5	-1.9	-0.9	2.0	0.9	-1.7	0.2	-0.6	-3.5	2.1	-1.6	-2.3	-2.8
Total of smaller countries	-1.0	-1.5	-3.0	-3.0	-1.9	-0.2	0.2	-0.2	-0.3	0.0	-0.2	-1.1	-1.2	-0.8	-1.0	0.1	0.1	1.1	0.9	0.8
Total OECD	0.2	-0.4	-1.0	-0.5	-0.4	-0.3	-0.6	-0.7	-0.3	-0.5	-0.4	-0.6	-0.7	-0.3	-0.3	0.0	-0.2	0.0	-0.1	0.0
OECD North America	-0.9	-0.3	-0.3	-0.4	-0.5	-1.0	-2.2	-2.7	-3.3	-3.3	-2.6	-2.1	-1.9	-0.7	-1.5	-2.0	-2.5	-2.0	-1.8	-1.7
OECD Europe	0.9	-0.3	-1.8	-0.8	-0.6	0.2	0.6	0.8	1.2	0.7	0.3	0.0	-0.3	-0.8	-0.7	0.4	0.6	0.9	0.9	1.0
European Union	0.8	-0.3	-1.4	-0.9	-0.7	0.0	0.4	0.5	1.3	0.7	0.2	-0.1	-0.5	-1.1	-1.0	0.1	0.3	0.7	0.7	0.9
Total OECD *less* the United States	0.7	-0.7	-1.7	-1.0	-0.5	0.5	0.9	1.2	1.7	1.3	0.7	0.1	-0.3	-0.4	0.0	0.8	0.8	1.0	0.9	0.9

a) Break in series starting this year.

Annex Table 52. Structure of current account balances of major world regions[a]

$ billion

	1978	1979	1980	1981	1982	1983	1984	1985	1986	1987	1988	1989	1990	1991	1992	1993	1994	1995	Projections 1996	1997
Trade balance																				
OECD	0	-48	-82	-37	-18	-11	-38	-36	-5	-20	-5	-36	-47	-13	12	74	72	116	111	129
Non-OECD *of which:*	24	84	125	64	22	23	53	47	16	55	40	50	50	26	13	-19	7	-5	-11	-26
OPEC	50	118	175	125	64	45	54	53	7	30	18	44	73	42	39	36	54	58	66	64
ANIEs[b]	-4	-8	-11	-11	-9	-4	4	10	20	27	25	21	11	7	6	7	0	-9	-9	-8
Other Asia[c]	-14	-19	-28	-31	-27	-30	-25	-35	-28	-20	-24	-23	-20	-22	-27	-47	-34	-38	-45	-49
Latin America[c]	-1	-4	-8	-8	-4	6	14	15	-9	8	20	20	16	11	-5	-5	-9	-20	-20	-20
Africa[c]	-5	-3	-3	-13	-12	-6	-7	-3	2	-3	-7	-8	-9	-10	-13	-12	-13	-9	-8	-8
Central and Eastern Europe	-2	0	1	3	11	13	14	6	9	13	8	-4	-20	-2	5	2	9	12	6	-4
World[d]	24	36	44	27	4	12	16	10	11	35	35	14	3	12	26	56	78	111	100	104
Services and private transfers, net																				
OECD	28	39	29	16	6	12	8	-2	1	-2	-14	-11	-22	-11	-14	-9	-32	-44	-45	-44
Non-OECD *of which:*	-49	-60	-76	-94	-87	-71	-76	-74	-61	-59	-67	-75	-64	-86	-78	-77	-66	-74	-74	-81
OPEC	-44	-51	-64	-74	-68	-53	-52	-49	-34	-35	-38	-45	-52	-72	-67	-66	-60	-59	-59	-61
ANIEs[b]	4	4	3	5	6	6	4	2	6	4	7	6	7	8	14	10	16	18	10	17
Other Asia[c]	4	4	10	11	12	12	9	8	6	4	-1	-2	4	-17	5	2	4	1	0	-1
Latin America[c]	-9	-12	-14	-22	-27	-25	-26	-23	-24	-22	-23	-23	-20	8	-13	-16	-15	-19	-18	-19
Africa[c]	-4	-5	-10	-11	-10	-9	-10	-7	-9	-8	-7	-9	-7	-3	-2	-3	-3	-5	-5	-4
Central and Eastern Europe	1	0	-1	-3	-2	-1	-1	-5	-5	-5	-6	-1	3	-9	-10	-6	-9	-9	-10	-13
World[d]	-21	-21	-47	-77	-81	-58	-68	-76	-60	-62	-81	-86	-86	-96	-91	-86	-98	-118	-119	-125
Official transfers, net																				
OECD	-18	-20	-23	-23	-25	-23	-25	-28	-34	-38	-42	-46	-55	-27	-63	-64	-75	-66	-78	-78
Non-OECD *of which:*	-2	5	2	5	5	6	8	7	8	11	13	14	4	-13	22	21	20	21	23	22
OPEC	-6	-6	-9	-8	-6	0	-5	-6	-6	-4	-3	-3	-11	-34	1	1	1	-1	-1	-1
ANIEs[b]	0	0	7	0	0	0	0	0	0	0	0	0	0	0	0	0	0	0	0	0
Other Asia[c]	5	7	7	8	8	7	7	7	7	7	8	7	5	4	8	8	8	8	8	8
Latin America[c]	0	1	1	1	1	1	1	1	1	6	2	2	2	3	8	2	2	3	8	3
Africa[c]	3	3	4	4	3	4	4	5	6	6	7	8	9	9	9	9	9	9	11	11
Central and Eastern Europe	0	0	0	0	0	0	0	0	0	0	0	0	0	6	4	1	2	2	11	2
World[d]	-15	-15	-21	-19	-19	-16	-17	-21	-26	-28	-28	-32	-51	-40	-41	-43	-54	-45	-56	-56
Current balance																				
OECD	10	-29	-76	-44	-37	-21	-55	-66	-38	-61	-60	-93	-125	-51	-64	2	-35	6	-13	7
Non-OECD *of which:*	-22	29	52	-25	-60	-41	-15	-21	-37	6	-14	-11	-9	-73	-43	-75	-39	-58	-62	-84
OPEC	0	61	101	43	-10	-14	-4	-2	-34	-9	-22	-3	10	-63	-30	-29	-6	-2	5	2
ANIEs[b]	0	-4	-8	-6	-2	2	8	12	25	33	32	27	18	14	16	21	16	10	9	9
Other Asia[c]	-6	-7	-11	-12	-7	-11	-8	-20	-15	-8	-17	-18	-11	-10	-14	-37	-22	-29	-38	-42
Latin America[c]	-10	-15	-21	-30	-30	-18	-11	-7	-13	-12	-1	-2	-3	-3	-7	-19	-22	-36	-35	-36
Africa[c]	-6	-5	0	-21	-19	-11	-13	-4	4	-9	-7	-9	-7	-4	-6	-6	-7	-5	-2	-1
Central and Eastern Europe	-1	0	0	1	8	11	13	1	4	8	2	-6	-16	-6	-1	-3	2	4	-3	-15
World[d]	-13	0	-24	-69	-97	-62	-70	-87	-74	-54	-74	-103	-134	-123	-107	-73	-74	-52	-75	-77

a) Historical data for the OECD area are aggregates of reported balance of payments data by each individual country. Because of various statistical problems as well as a large number of non-reporters among non-OECD countries, trade and current balances estimated on the basis of these countries' own balance of payments records may differ from corresponding estimates shown in this table.
b) ANIEs include Chinese Taipei, Hong Kong, Korea and Singapore.
c) Not including OPEC countries.
d) Reflects statistical errors and asymmetries. Given the very large gross flows of world balance of payments transactions, statistical errors and asymmetries easily give rise to world totals (balances) that are significantly different from zero.

Annex Table 53. Stocks of foreign assets and liabilities

$ billion, end period

Assets[a]

	1982	1983	1984	1985	1986	1987	1988	1989	1990	1991	1992	1993	1994
Major seven countries													
United States	999	1 129	1 141	1 218	1 377	1 509	1 677	1 874	1 964	2 039	2 055	2 291	2 378
Japan	227	271	340	437	726	1 070	1 468	1 770	1 857	2 005	2 034	2 180	2 423
Germany	249	238	239	336	495	657	682	856	1 091	1 138	1 168	1 269	1 433
France[b]	180	179	182	215	255	337	339	472	707	724	802	887	979
Italy	87	95	103	119	156	195	203	262	343	386	372	416	478
United Kingdom	667	700	716	853	1 058	1 295	1 395	1 531	1 747	1 771	1 773	2 047	2 191
Canada	74	76	83	86	98	117	143	161	179	195	189	202	211
Selected other OECD countries													
Australia[c]	14	17	20	20	26	42	56	64	73	73	78	77	92
Austria	..	..	..	51	65	80	76	86	101	104	111	115	130
Belgium-Luxembourg	102	105	108	147	199	259	268	319	389	415	431	458	527
Denmark	15	17	18	30	38	53	59	68	94	109	109	120	114
Finland	11	11	14	18	21	30	32	36	47	46	42	44	52
Netherlands	136	132	131	167	214	271	275	324	391	423	431	..	..
Norway	18	17	20	28	32	41	38	41	49	50	48	50	56
Spain	33	31	39	41	51	75	83	100	133	161	168	217	223
Sweden[d]	21	24	23	28	34	48	56	55	81	83	73	76	88
Switzerland	..	..	173	247	334	441	429	468	556	580	578	639	733
Total of above countries	..	..	..	4 043	5 177	6 520	7 280	8 487	9 801	10 303	10 462	..	..

Liabilities

	1982	1983	1984	1985	1986	1987	1988	1989	1990	1991	1992	1993	1994
Major seven countries													
United States	740	867	991	1 171	1 434	1 648	1 919	2 230	2 317	2 487	2 658	2 939	3 159
Japan	203	235	267	308	547	831	1 178	1 478	1 530	1 623	1 522	1 570	1 735
Germany	223	210	201	289	405	496	480	594	744	819	887	1 036	1 230
France[b]	191	198	203	227	254	334	348	497	761	824	866	985	1 067
Italy	108	113	120	151	192	239	258	342	465	530	516	535	587
United Kingdom	602	625	631	755	916	1 187	1 287	1 450	1 763	1 780	1 766	2 032	2 168
Canada	186	192	198	210	235	272	318	356	392	427	421	444	455
Selected other OECD countries													
Australia[c]	56	62	71	74	95	130	159	182	210	224	231	227	270
Austria	..	..	..	59	75	94	90	98	115	123	128	134	153
Belgium-Luxembourg	109	113	120	158	211	271	279	328	392	409	417	438	503
Denmark	34	36	39	58	75	99	104	114	143	165	158	163	156
Finland	20	21	24	28	34	48	53	63	84	90	89	92	107
Netherlands	108	103	101	137	179	229	233	282	343	373	389	..	..
Norway	32	29	29	35	43	57	57	61	67	64	58	58	59
Spain	54	52	55	60	69	95	110	139	203	256	263	294	317
Sweden[d]	39	44	43	53	63	84	101	124	183	190	182	182	203
Switzerland	..	..	101	144	209	257	250	290	347	353	351	404	467
Total of above countries	..	..	..	3 916	5 035	6 371	7 223	8 629	10 060	10 736	10 903	..	..

a) Excluding monetary gold.
b) As from 1989 due to change in concept and definitions, the figures are not comparable with those of previous periods.
c) Fiscal year ending end-June.
d) Excluding direct investment.

Annex Table 54. **Semiannual demand and output projections**

Percentage changes from previous period, seasonally adjusted at annual rates, volume

	1995	1996	1997	1995 I	1995 II	1996 I	1996 II	1997 I	1997 II
Private consumption									
United States	2.4	2.5	2.0	2.0	2.5	2.7	2.2	1.9	2.1
Japan	1.6	2.4	2.2	0.4	3.6	2.0	2.2	2.3	2.0
Germany	1.7	1.3	2.0	2.5	0.4	1.3	2.1	2.0	2.0
France	1.8	1.4	1.9	1.6	1.2	1.6	1.3	2.0	2.2
Italy	1.6	1.4	2.1	1.8	1.2	1.4	1.7	2.2	2.3
United Kingdom	2.3	3.0	3.2	2.4	2.3	3.2	3.2	3.2	3.2
Canada	1.4	2.2	3.0	0.9	1.4	2.1	3.1	3.0	3.1
Major seven countries	2.0	2.2	2.2	1.7	2.2	2.3	2.2	2.1	2.2
OECD North America	1.4	2.4	2.2	0.2	2.3	2.4	2.5	2.0	2.1
OECD Europe	2.1	1.9	2.4	2.6	1.6	2.0	2.2	2.5	2.6
EU	1.8	1.7	2.3	2.1	1.3	1.8	2.1	2.3	2.4
Total OECD	1.8	2.2	2.3	1.3	2.3	2.2	2.4	2.3	2.3
Public consumption									
United States	-0.3	-0.9	-0.5	-1.1	-1.1	-0.8	-0.7	-0.5	-0.3
Japan	2.0	1.7	2.1	5.0	-1.0	2.7	2.3	2.1	2.0
Germany	2.1	1.4	1.4	3.0	2.3	1.1	1.2	1.4	1.4
France	0.9	1.1	1.1	0.6	1.2	1.1	1.1	1.1	1.0
Italy	-0.3	-0.1	0.4	-0.5	-0.7	-0.1	0.4	0.4	0.4
United Kingdom	0.9	0.8	0.8	1.0	1.0	0.7	0.8	0.8	0.8
Canada	-0.9	-1.6	-0.2	0.7	-3.8	-1.0	-0.7	-0.1	0
Major seven countries	0.5	0.1	0.5	0.8	-0.5	0.3	0.4	0.5	0.5
OECD North America	-0.6	-1.1	-0.4	-1.2	-1.5	-1.1	-0.8	-0.3	-0.1
OECD Europe	1.1	0.8	0.9	1.7	0.6	1.0	0.8	0.9	0.9
EU	0.9	0.8	0.8	1.1	1.0	0.6	0.8	0.8	0.8
Total OECD	0.6	0.1	0.5	1.1	-0.6	0.4	0.4	0.6	0.7
Investment									
United States	5.4	5.3	2.7	5.3	2.9	7.0	4.2	2.0	2.5
Japan	0.8	5.6	3.2	-1.2	7.7	6.4	2.0	3.3	4.5
Germany	1.5	-2.4	2.5	0.2	-0.9	-4.3	0.2	3.3	3.4
France	2.8	1.5	3.3	2.8	-0.9	2.1	2.7	3.3	3.7
Italy	5.7	5.1	5.2	8.4	4.9	5.3	5.1	5.1	5.4
United Kingdom	-0.7	2.2	4.7	0.1	-1.4	3.3	3.7	5.0	5.0
Canada	0.2	2.5	6.2	-0.9	-1.8	3.4	5.2	6.5	6.5
Major seven countries	3.4	3.9	3.3	3.0	2.7	4.8	3.4	3.1	3.6
OECD North America	2.7	5.1	3.3	1.4	1.1	7.1	5.3	2.6	2.7
OECD Europe	4.0	2.8	4.3	5.3	2.4	2.7	3.5	4.6	4.7
EU	3.5	2.3	4.1	4.3	1.6	2.3	3.3	4.3	4.5
Total OECD	3.0	4.2	3.8	2.6	2.6	5.2	4.2	3.6	3.9
Total domestic demand									
United States	2.1	2.2	1.8	1.5	1.5	2.5	2.3	1.5	1.9
Japan	1.6	3.3	2.6	0.5	4.5	3.3	2.0	2.8	2.9
Germany	1.7	0	2.1	1.6	-0.1	-0.7	1.5	2.3	2.3
France	2.0	1.1	2.1	1.7	0.6	1.2	1.4	2.3	2.5
Italy	2.6	2.0	2.4	0.6	4.2	0.9	2.2	2.4	2.6
United Kingdom	1.6	2.3	3.0	0.8	2.4	2.0	2.8	3.0	3.1
Canada	1.1	1.1	3.2	2.0	-1.4	1.4	3.1	3.2	3.3
Major seven countries	1.9	2.0	2.2	1.3	2.0	2.0	2.2	2.1	2.4
OECD North America	0.8	2.1	2.1	-0.4	0.6	2.4	2.8	1.7	1.9
OECD Europe	2.8	1.7	2.6	2.9	2.4	1.2	2.1	2.7	2.9
EU	2.2	1.4	2.4	1.8	1.7	1.0	2.0	2.5	2.6
Total OECD	1.8	2.1	2.4	1.2	2.0	2.1	2.4	2.3	2.5

Percentage changes from previous period, seasonally adjusted at annual rates, volume

	1995	1996	1997	1995 I	1995 II	1996 I	1996 II	1997 I	1997 II
Exports of goods and services									
United States	8.3	7.7	8.0	6.1	7.9	7.0	9.0	7.9	7.4
Japan	5.0	5.2	7.5	6.1	2.0	6.0	7.0	7.5	8.0
Germany	3.8	5.3	6.9	1.0	7.4	4.0	6.0	7.0	7.5
France	5.9	1.6	6.6	9.2	−3.7	2.5	5.2	6.8	7.4
Italy	11.1	3.4	5.7	16.7	0.7	4.1	4.5	5.8	6.5
United Kingdom	5.7	5.0	6.1	5.0	3.4	5.4	5.8	6.2	6.3
Canada	11.8	7.1	7.6	7.8	6.5	7.0	7.9	7.5	7.4
Major seven countries	7.2	6.0	7.4	6.6	5.0	5.8	7.4	7.4	7.4
OECD North America	9.9	8.0	8.1	9.1	7.9	7.5	8.8	8.0	7.5
OECD Europe	6.6	4.7	6.6	7.2	2.8	5.2	5.9	6.7	7.0
EU	6.8	4.3	6.4	7.7	2.9	4.4	5.5	6.5	6.9
Total OECD	7.7	6.3	7.3	7.8	5.0	6.4	7.4	7.3	7.3
Imports of goods and services									
United States	8.0	6.1	5.6	8.6	2.7	7.4	6.9	5.0	5.6
Japan	13.5	14.7	9.5	12.6	17.8	15.7	10.0	9.4	9.3
Germany	2.7	3.2	5.9	−0.7	3.8	2.2	4.5	6.3	6.6
France	5.0	1.9	5.7	6.3	−0.6	2.2	3.8	6.0	7.0
Italy	9.8	4.5	5.9	9.1	7.0	3.3	4.5	6.0	7.3
United Kingdom	3.1	5.2	5.9	1.1	5.0	5.0	5.7	6.0	6.0
Canada	9.0	4.9	7.2	9.5	2.2	5.2	7.1	7.2	7.2
Major seven countries	8.0	6.8	6.5	7.7	5.8	7.4	6.7	6.2	6.7
OECD North America	5.8	6.3	6.1	5.4	1.5	7.9	8.0	5.5	5.7
OECD Europe	7.0	4.7	6.3	7.1	6.1	3.9	5.2	6.6	7.0
EU	5.8	4.1	6.0	4.9	4.4	3.6	4.9	6.2	6.7
Total OECD	7.5	6.9	6.8	7.2	5.8	7.5	7.2	6.6	6.9
GDP									
United States	2.0	2.3	2.0	1.2	2.0	2.4	2.5	1.8	2.0
Japan	0.9	2.2	2.4	0	2.8	2.2	1.7	2.5	2.7
Germany	1.9	0.5	2.4	2.0	0.8	−0.3	1.9	2.5	2.6
France	2.2	1.0	2.4	2.4	−0.3	1.3	1.8	2.5	2.6
Italy	3.0	1.7	2.3	2.8	2.3	1.1	2.2	2.4	2.3
United Kingdom	2.4	2.2	3.0	2.0	2.0	2.1	2.8	3.1	3.1
Canada	2.2	2.1	3.4	1.5	0.6	2.1	3.5	3.4	3.4
Major seven countries	1.9	1.9	2.3	1.4	1.8	1.9	2.3	2.3	2.4
OECD North America	1.5	2.3	2.3	0.3	1.6	2.5	2.8	2.0	2.2
OECD Europe	2.7	1.6	2.7	3.0	1.4	1.5	2.2	2.8	2.8
EU	2.5	1.4	2.5	2.5	1.3	1.2	2.1	2.6	2.7
Total OECD	1.9	2.1	2.5	1.4	1.7	2.0	2.4	2.4	2.6
Nominal GDP									
United States	4.5	4.4	4.3	4.0	4.1	4.5	4.5	4.1	4.3
Japan	0.3	1.9	2.7	−0.6	2.7	1.9	1.2	3.1	3.4
Germany	4.2	2.1	3.8	4.4	3.1	0.9	3.4	3.9	4.0
France	3.9	2.8	3.7	4.3	1.4	3.3	3.2	3.8	4.0
Italy	8.0	6.1	5.5	7.1	9.9	4.6	5.3	5.6	5.5
United Kingdom	4.8	4.5	5.3	4.8	4.1	4.4	5.1	5.3	5.3
Canada	4.0	3.8	5.0	3.5	2.5	3.8	5.1	4.9	5.0
Major seven countries	3.9	3.7	4.1	3.5	3.9	3.5	3.8	4.1	4.3
OECD North America	6.1	6.0	5.3	6.0	5.9	6.1	5.9	5.1	5.1
OECD Europe	9.3	7.1	7.5	9.7	7.0	7.1	7.3	7.7	7.3
OECD Europe *less* Turkey	5.6	4.1	4.8	5.8	4.7	3.7	4.4	4.9	5.0
EU	5.5	3.9	4.7	5.8	4.5	3.5	4.3	4.8	4.9
Total OECD	6.5	5.8	5.8	6.5	5.9	5.9	5.8	5.8	5.7
Total OECD *less* Turkey	5.0	4.6	4.7	4.9	4.9	4.5	4.6	4.7	4.8

Annex Figure 1. **Recent consumer-price developments**

OECD area[1]

Consumer prices, all items

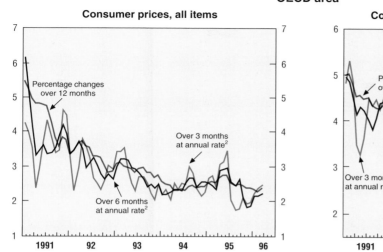

Percentage changes over 12 months

Over 3 months at annual rate[2]

Over 6 months at annual rate[2]

Consumer prices, non-food non-energy

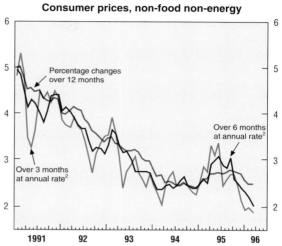

Percentage changes over 12 months

Over 3 months at annual rate[2]

Over 6 months at annual rate[2]

Individual countries

Non-food non-energy prices
Percentage changes from corresponding month of previous year

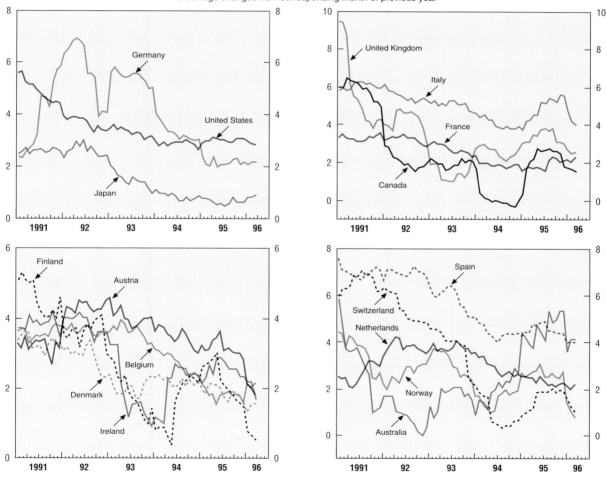

Germany

United States

Japan

United Kingdom

Italy

France

Canada

Finland

Austria

Belgium

Denmark

Ireland

Spain

Switzerland

Netherlands

Norway

Australia

1. Excluding Mexico and Turkey.

2. Seasonally adjusted.

Annex Table 55. **Semiannual price, cost and unemployment projections**

Percentage changes from previous period, seasonally adjusted at annual rates

	1995	1996	1997	1995 I	1995 II	1996 I	1996 II	1997 I	1997 II
Private consumption deflator									
United States	2.3	2.0	2.3	2.5	1.7	2.1	2.0	2.3	2.4
Japan	−0.5	−0.4	0.6	−0.6	−0.5	−0.4	−0.4	0.9	1.0
Germany	2.0	1.6	1.5	1.8	2.1	1.4	1.4	1.5	1.5
France	1.6	1.9	1.3	1.8	1.5	2.4	1.4	1.3	1.2
Italy	5.7	3.9	2.9	6.3	5.7	3.5	3.0	2.9	2.9
United Kingdom	2.6	2.5	2.5	2.9	2.0	2.7	2.6	2.5	2.4
Canada	1.6	1.4	1.4	1.8	1.5	1.3	1.5	1.4	1.5
Major seven countries	2.0	1.7	1.8	2.1	1.6	1.7	1.6	1.9	2.0
OECD North America	4.6	3.9	3.1	5.5	4.7	3.9	3.3	3.1	3.0
OECD Europe	6.9	5.4	4.7	7.5	5.1	5.8	5.0	4.8	4.2
OECD Europe *less* Turkey	3.0	2.5	2.2	3.1	2.9	2.5	2.3	2.2	2.2
EU	3.0	2.5	2.2	3.1	2.8	2.5	2.2	2.2	2.1
Total OECD	4.7	3.9	3.4	5.3	4.0	4.0	3.5	3.5	3.2
Total OECD *less* Turkey	3.2	2.7	2.4	3.6	3.1	2.7	2.3	2.4	2.4
GDP deflator									
United States	2.4	2.1	2.2	2.7	2.1	2.1	2.0	2.2	2.2
Japan	−0.5	−0.3	0.3	−0.6	−0.1	−0.4	−0.5	0.6	0.6
Germany	2.2	1.5	1.3	2.4	2.3	1.2	1.4	1.3	1.4
France	1.6	1.8	1.3	1.8	1.6	2.0	1.4	1.3	1.3
Italy	4.8	4.3	3.1	4.2	7.4	3.4	3.0	3.1	3.1
United Kingdom	2.4	2.2	2.2	2.7	2.1	2.3	2.2	2.2	2.1
Canada	1.7	1.6	1.5	2.0	1.8	1.6	1.5	1.5	1.6
Major seven countries	2.0	1.7	1.7	2.1	2.1	1.7	1.5	1.8	1.8
OECD North America	4.5	3.6	2.9	5.7	4.2	3.6	3.0	3.0	2.9
OECD Europe	6.4	5.4	4.7	6.5	5.6	5.6	5.0	4.8	4.3
OECD Europe *less* Turkey	3.1	2.6	2.2	3.2	3.3	2.4	2.2	2.2	2.3
EU	3.0	2.5	2.1	3.2	3.2	2.3	2.1	2.1	2.2
Total OECD	4.5	3.7	3.2	5.0	4.1	3.8	3.3	3.3	3.1
Total OECD *less* Turkey	3.1	2.6	2.3	3.7	3.2	2.5	2.1	2.3	2.3
Unit labour costs (total economy)									
United States	2.9	2.0	2.3	4.1	2.7	1.8	1.8	2.5	2.3
Japan	0.7	−0.2	0	3.8	−1.1	−0.2	0.6	−0.1	−0.2
Germany	1.3	1.7	0.3	2.2	1.8	2.4	0.4	0.1	0.8
France	1.6	1.9	0.7	2.3	2.3	2.0	1.1	0.5	0.6
Italy	−0.1	2.5	2.3	−0.2	1.4	3.2	2.3	2.4	2.4
United Kingdom	1.3	1.8	1.5	1.5	1.6	2.0	1.7	1.4	1.4
Canada	0.7	1.5	1.1	1.1	1.7	1.6	1.0	1.1	1.1
Major seven countries	1.8	1.6	1.4	3.1	1.7	1.6	1.4	1.5	1.4
OECD North America	4.5	3.3	3.1	6.3	4.4	3.1	2.7	3.3	3.0
OECD Europe	5.2	5.1	4.0	5.5	5.4	5.2	4.7	4.0	3.6
OECD Europe *less* Turkey	1.8	2.2	1.5	2.3	2.6	2.4	1.6	1.5	1.6
EU	1.6	2.1	1.4	2.2	2.3	2.3	1.5	1.3	1.5
Total OECD	4.2	3.5	3.0	5.6	4.0	3.5	3.2	3.1	2.7
Total OECD *less* Turkey	2.9	2.3	2.0	4.4	2.8	2.3	2.0	2.0	2.0
				Per cent of labour force					
Unemployment									
United States	5.6	5.5	5.6	5.6	5.6	5.5	5.5	5.6	5.6
Japan	3.1	3.3	3.2	3.0	3.3	3.3	3.2	3.2	3.2
Germany	9.4	10.3	10.4	9.3	9.5	10.2	10.5	10.5	10.3
France	11.6	12.1	12.2	11.7	11.5	11.9	12.2	12.2	12.2
Italy	12.0	12.1	12.0	12.0	12.0	12.1	12.2	12.1	12.0
United Kingdom	8.2	7.9	7.5	8.3	8.0	7.9	7.9	7.6	7.3
Canada	9.5	9.3	9.0	9.6	9.4	9.5	9.2	9.1	8.9
Major seven countries	6.8	7.0	6.9	6.8	6.9	6.9	7.0	7.0	6.9
OECD North America	6.0	5.9	5.9	6.0	6.1	5.9	5.9	5.9	5.9
OECD Europe	10.3	10.5	10.4	10.4	10.3	10.5	10.6	10.5	10.3
EU	11.2	11.4	11.3	11.2	11.1	11.4	11.5	11.4	11.2
Total OECD	7.6	7.7	7.6	7.6	7.6	7.7	7.7	7.6	7.5

Annex Figure 2.   **Capacity utilisation in manufacturing**

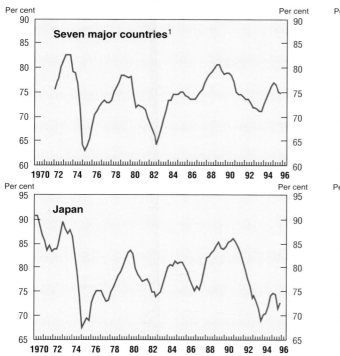

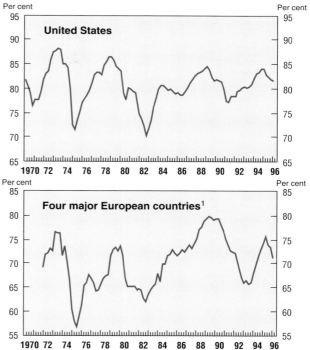

1.   Data for Germany concern western Germany.
Note: Cross-country comparisons of capacity utilisation levels may be misleading owing to conceptual and methodological differences in the construction of the indices. For further details, see Methodological notes of *Main Economic Indicators* and *Sources and Methods,* No. 37 (Business Surveys), April 1983.

Annex Figure 3.   **Real commodity prices**[1]
Index 1960 = 100

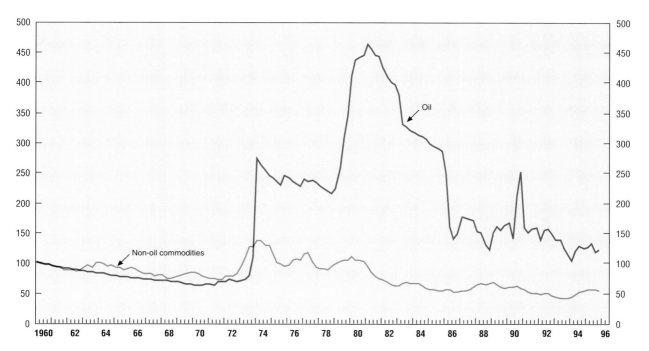

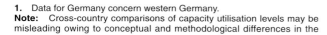

1.   Deflated by the GDP deflator for the seven major countries.

Annex Table 56. Contributions to changes in real GDP in major OECD countries

As a per cent of real GDP in the previous period, seasonnally adjusted at annual rates

	1993	1994	1995	1996	1997	1995 I	1995 II	1996 I	1996 II	1997 I	1997 II
United States											
Final domestic demand	2.7	3.4	2.5	2.5	1.8	2.1	2.0	2.9	2.1	1.6	1.8
Stockbuilding	0.2	0.6	−0.4	−0.3	0.1	−0.5	−0.5	−0.4	0.2	0.0	0.1
Net exports	−0.7	−0.5	−0.1	0.1	0.2	−0.4	0.5	−0.2	0.1	0.3	0.1
GDP	2.2	3.5	2.0	2.3	2.0	1.2	2.0	2.4	2.5	1.8	2.0
Japan											
Final domestic demand	0.3	1.0	1.4	3.3	2.5	0.3	4.2	3.3	2.1	2.5	2.7
Stockbuilding	−0.1	−0.2	0.2	0.0	0.1	0.2	0.1	−0.1	−0.1	0.2	0.1
Net exports	0.0	−0.3	−0.7	−1.0	−0.2	−0.5	−1.6	−1.0	−0.3	−0.2	−0.2
GDP	0.1	0.5	0.9	2.2	2.4	0.0	2.8	2.2	1.7	2.5	2.7
Germany											
Final domestic demand	−1.1	1.6	1.7	0.5	2.0	2.0	0.5	0.0	1.5	2.1	2.2
Stockbuilding	−0.2	1.2	0.0	−0.5	0.1	−0.5	−0.6	−0.7	0.1	0.2	0.1
Net exports	0.1	0.1	0.3	0.5	0.3	0.4	0.9	0.5	0.4	0.2	0.3
GDP	−1.2	2.9	1.9	0.5	2.4	2.0	0.8	−0.3	1.9	2.5	2.6
France											
Final domestic demand	−0.7	1.3	1.8	1.4	2.0	1.7	0.8	1.6	1.5	2.1	2.3
Stockbuilding	−1.5	1.7	0.1	−0.3	0.1	0.0	−0.2	−0.4	−0.2	0.2	0.2
Net exports	0.9	−0.2	0.2	−0.1	0.2	0.8	−0.9	0.1	0.4	0.2	0.1
GDP	−1.3	2.8	2.2	1.0	2.4	2.4	−0.3	1.3	1.8	2.5	2.6
Italy											
Final domestic demand	−4.4	1.0	2.1	1.9	2.4	2.6	1.5	1.9	2.1	2.4	2.6
Stockbuilding	−1.4	0.8	0.5	0.1	0.0	−1.9	2.6	−1.0	0.1	0.0	0.0
Net exports	4.6	0.3	0.4	−0.3	−0.1	2.1	−1.9	0.3	0.0	0.0	−0.2
GDP	−1.2	2.2	3.0	1.7	2.3	2.8	2.3	1.1	2.2	2.4	2.3
United Kingdom											
Final domestic demand	1.8	2.6	1.5	2.4	3.0	1.7	1.4	2.7	2.8	3.0	3.0
Stockbuilding	0.4	0.4	0.2	−0.1	0.0	−0.9	1.0	−0.7	0.0	0.0	0.0
Net exports	0.1	0.9	0.7	−0.1	0.0	1.0	−0.5	0.1	0.0	0.0	0.1
Compromise adjustment	0.0	−0.1	0.1	0.0	0.0	0.1	0.0	0.0	0.0	0.0	0.0
GDP	2.3	3.8	2.4	2.2	3.0	2.0	2.0	2.1	2.8	3.1	3.1
Canada											
Final domestic demand	1.2	3.0	0.7	1.5	3.1	0.5	−0.3	1.8	2.8	3.1	3.2
Stockbuilding	0.9	0.3	0.4	−0.4	0.1	1.5	−1.1	−0.4	0.3	0.1	0.0
Net exports	0.3	1.1	1.0	0.9	0.3	−0.6	1.7	0.8	0.4	0.2	0.2
Error of estimate	−0.1	0.2	0.1	0.1	0.0	0.0	0.3	0.0	0.0	0.0	0.0
GDP	2.2	4.6	2.2	2.1	3.4	1.5	0.6	2.1	3.5	3.4	3.4
Total of above countries											
Final domestic demand	1.0	2.3	2.0	2.2	2.1	1.7	2.0	2.4	2.1	2.1	2.3
Stockbuilding	0.2	0.8	0.1	−0.1	0.1	−0.1	0.0	−0.3	0.1	0.0	0.1
Net exports	−0.2	−0.3	−0.2	−0.2	0.1	−0.2	−0.2	−0.3	0.1	0.2	0.1
GDP	1.0	2.8	1.9	1.9	2.3	1.4	1.8	1.9	2.3	2.3	2.4

Note: Components may not add to GDP due to rounding.

Contributions to changes in real GDP in other OECD countries

As a per cent of real GDP in the previous period

	1994	1995	1996	1997		1994	1995	1996	1997
Australia					**Netherlands**				
Final domestic demand	6.0	3.6	2.9	4.1	Final domestic demand	2.0	2.3	1.9	1.8
Stockbuilding	−0.4	0.7	−0.5	−0.1	Stockbuilding	1.1	0.0	−0.5	0.2
Net exports	−1.1	−1.1	0.6	−0.7	Net exports	−0.4	0.2	0.2	0.6
GDP	5.2	3.1	3.1	3.3	GDP	2.7	2.4	1.6	2.6
Austria					**New Zealand**				
Final domestic demand	3.6	2.1	0.6	0.9	Final domestic demand	8.6	8.0	5.0	5.6
Stockbuilding	1.0	0.9	−0.3	0.0	Stockbuilding	−0.2	−0.2	−0.4	−0.2
Net exports	−1.5	−1.2	0.4	0.6	Net exports	−4.4	−5.6	−1.9	−2.0
GDP	3.0	1.8	0.8	1.5	GDP	4.1	2.2	2.7	3.4
Belgium					**Norway**				
Final domestic demand	1.2	1.5	1.3	2.1	Final domestic demand	3.7	2.5	3.2	2.0
Stockbuilding	0.3	0.1	−0.2	0.1	Stockbuilding	0.9	1.1	0.0	0.0
Net exports	0.8	0.3	−0.1	0.3	Net exports	1.2	0.1	1.1	0.5
GDP	2.2	1.9	1.0	2.4	GDP	5.7	3.7	4.2	2.4
Czech Republic					**Portugal**				
Final domestic demand	7.0	7.6	9.1	9.0	Final domestic demand	1.6	3.2	3.1	4.0
Stockbuilding	0.4	5.2	1.4	0.0	Stockbuilding	0.2	0.2	−0.1	0.0
Net exports	−4.8	−7.9	−4.9	−3.2	Net exports	−1.0	−0.8	−0.7	−1.3
GDP	2.6	4.8	5.6	5.8	GDP	0.8	2.5	2.3	2.7
Denmark					**Spain**				
Final domestic demand	4.3	2.9	1.9	2.6	Final domestic demand	0.8	3.1	2.7	3.1
Stockbuilding	1.0	1.3	−0.6	−0.1	Stockbuilding	0.3	0.2	−0.2	0.0
Net exports	−0.9	−1.6	−0.2	0.3	Net exports	1.0	−0.4	−0.2	−0.5
GDP	4.4	2.6	1.1	2.7	GDP	2.1	3.0	2.3	2.7
Finland					**Sweden**				
Final domestic demand	1.1	3.7	3.0	3.3	Final domestic demand	0.3	1.1	1.9	1.1
Stockbuilding	2.3	0.5	−0.2	0.0	Stockbuilding	1.5	0.5	−0.8	0.1
Net exports	1.0	0.0	−0.4	0.1	Net exports	0.9	1.4	0.2	0.7
GDP	4.4	4.2	2.4	3.5	GDP	2.6	3.0	1.3	2.0
Greece					**Switzerland**				
Final domestic demand	1.4	2.7	3.7	4.1	Final domestic demand	2.3	1.6	0.9	1.5
Stockbuilding	−0.1	1.0	0.0	0.0	Stockbuilding	1.5	0.9	0.2	0.3
Net exports	0.2	−1.7	−1.6	−1.8	Net exports	−2.6	−1.8	−0.7	−0.1
GDP	1.5	2.0	2.2	2.3	GDP	1.2	0.7	0.5	1.7
Iceland					**Turkey**				
Final domestic demand	1.6	3.5	5.6	3.9	Final domestic demand	−8.6	7.9	5.7	6.0
Stockbuilding	−0.2	0.6	−0.4	0.0	Stockbuilding	−4.6	4.7	0.0	0.0
Net exports	2.1	−2.2	−1.6	−0.5	Net exports	8.6	−5.1	−1.2	−1.1
GDP	3.5	2.0	3.6	3.4	GDP	−5.5	7.3	4.5	5.0
Ireland					**OECD Europe**				
Final domestic demand	4.1	4.1	4.0	3.0	Final domestic demand	1.3	2.3	1.9	2.5
Stockbuilding	−0.8	0.2	0.0	0.0	Stockbuilding	0.5	0.4	−0.3	0.0
Net exports	3.1	3.4	2.0	2.0	Net exports	0.7	0.0	0.1	0.2
GDP	6.4	7.7	6.0	5.0	GDP	2.5	2.7	1.6	2.7
Luxembourg					**Total OECD**				
Final domestic demand	2.5	2.7	2.3	2.8	Final domestic demand	2.2	1.7	2.3	2.3
Stockbuilding	−0.1	0.5	−0.2	−0.1	Stockbuilding	0.7	0.2	−0.1	0.1
Net exports	0.9	0.5	−0.2	0.3	Net exports	−0.2	0.0	−0.2	0.1
GDP	3.3	3.7	1.9	3.0	GDP	2.7	1.9	2.1	2.5
Mexico									
Final domestic demand	4.4	−15.7	1.0	3.2					
Stockbuilding	0.0	−1.8	0.2	0.0					
Net exports	−0.9	10.8	1.8	0.7					
GDP	3.5	−6.8	3.0	4.0					

Note: Totals may not add-up due to statistical discrepancy.

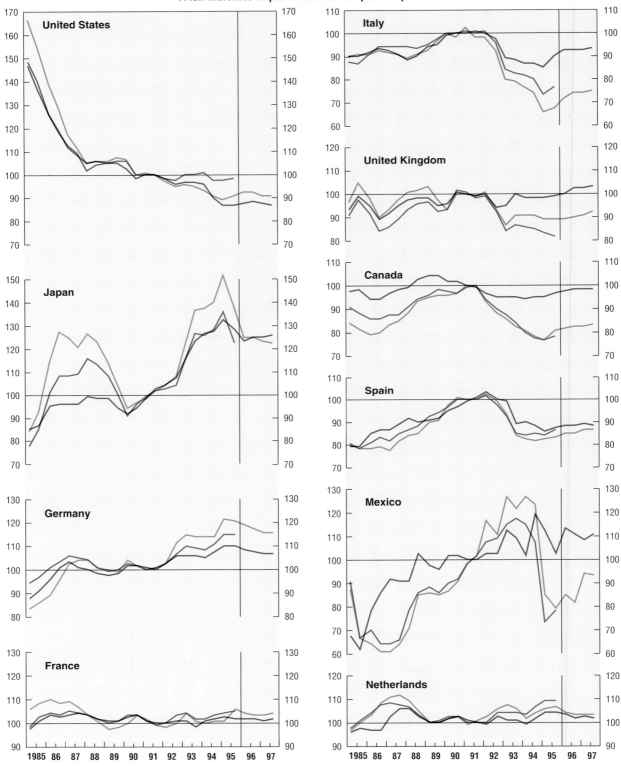

Annex Figure 4. **Measures of relative competitive position**

Indices in US$ terms; 1991 = 100

Relative average value of manufactured exports
Relative unit labour costs in manufacturing
Relative consumer prices

A fall indicates improvement in competitive position

United States

Italy

United Kingdom

Japan

Canada

Spain

Germany

Mexico

France

Netherlands

1985 86 87 88 89 90 91 92 93 94 95 96 97

1985 86 87 88 89 90 91 92 93 94 95 96 97

Note: The vertical line indicates the end of the historical period and the beginning of the projection period.

Annex Figure 4 *(cont'd).* **Measures of relative competitive position**

Indices in US$ terms; 1991 = 100

Relative average value of manufactured exports
Relative unit labour costs in manufacturing
Relative consumer prices

A fall indicates improvement in competitive position

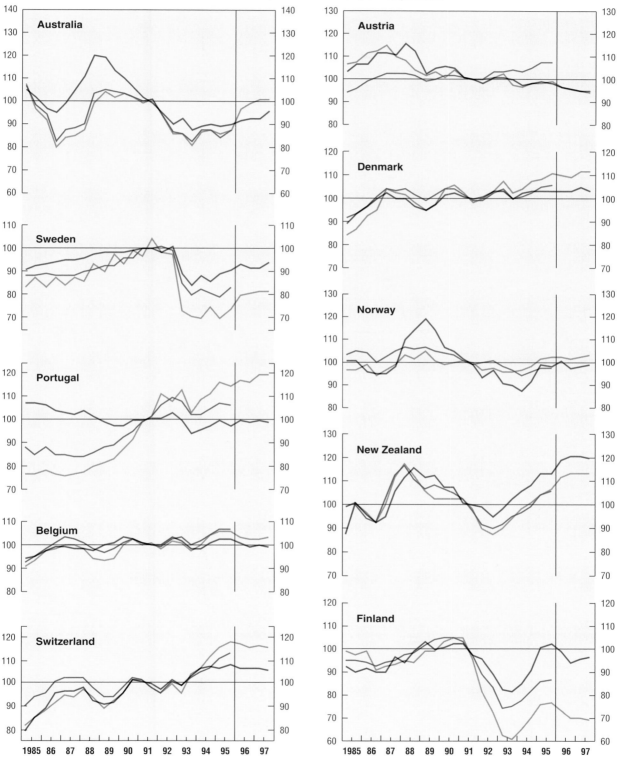

Note: The vertical line indicates the end of the historical period and the beginning of the projection period.

Annex Table 58. **Household saving, net wealth and indebtedness**[a]

	1983	1984	1985	1986	1987	1988	1989	1990	1991	1992	1993	1994	1995
United States													
Saving ratio	6.8	8.6	7.1	6.4	5.2	5.3	5.0	5.2	5.8	5.7	4.7	4.2	4.7
Net wealth	488.0	464.9	478.9	491.3	495.8	488.1	502.7	470.8	495.1	488.7	493.1	483.4	..
of which: Net financial wealth	256.5	239.1	252.0	261.5	261.1	259.2	272.5	254.1	275.1	275.2	279.6	268.4	..
Real assets	231.5	225.8	226.9	229.9	234.6	229.0	230.2	216.8	220.0	213.5	213.5	214.9	..
Financial assets	330.0	313.1	332.2	345.7	348.8	348.9	364.9	346.4	368.0	367.8	375.1	366.8	..
of which: Corporate equities	45.5	38.7	48.2	55.6	53.2	53.2	59.8	53.6	72.5	79.2	87.0	80.6	..
Liabilities	73.5	74.0	80.2	84.2	87.6	89.7	92.4	92.4	92.9	92.5	95.5	98.4	..
of which: Home mortgages	46.6	46.8	49.5	53.2	57.5	60.1	62.8	64.1	65.5	65.9	67.5	68.4	..
Japan													
Saving ratio	16.1	15.8	15.6	15.6	13.8	13.0	12.9	12.1	13.2	13.1	13.4	12.8	13.4
Net wealth	543.9	550.4	561.9	636.9	758.3	797.3	866.4	849.0	775.6	697.5	679.7	674.3	..
of which: Net financial wealth	146.6	156.9	164.7	184.0	202.4	222.6	251.6	222.2	221.5	210.3	215.7	224.8	..
Real assets	397.2	393.5	397.2	452.9	555.9	574.7	614.8	626.8	554.1	487.3	464.0	449.5	..
Financial assets	231.2	244.4	253.4	275.7	303.3	330.1	363.1	338.7	336.5	320.8	325.7	336.7	..
of which: Corporate equities	23.7	27.0	29.8	41.8	52.4	70.2	89.9	58.1	54.4	34.7	32.7	36.4	..
Liabilities	84.6	87.5	88.7	91.6	100.9	107.5	111.5	116.5	115.0	110.6	110.0	111.9	..
of which: Home mortgages	34.8	35.3	35.6	37.1	40.1	42.7	45.8	47.8	48.0	48.7	50.4	52.5	..
Germany													
Saving ratio	10.9	11.4	11.4	12.3	12.6	12.8	12.4	13.8	12.7	12.8	12.2	11.6	11.6
Net wealth	..	..	..	..	..	..	..	..	..	..	..	..	..
of which: Net financial wealth	159.7	164.8	172.8	177.6	175.9	182.1	185.4	178.3	..	..	..	..	..
Real assets	..	..	..	..	..	..	..	..					
Financial assets	175.6	180.9	189.3	194.2	192.8	199.2	203.1	196.1					
of which: Equities	8.7	9.2	13.3	14.8	10.7	12.9	15.1	12.5	..	..	..	..	..
Liabilities	15.9	16.1	16.5	16.6	16.9	17.1	17.8	17.7	..	..	..	..	..
of which: Long-term bank credit	10.1	10.1	10.4	10.7	11.2	11.6	12.1	12.1	..	..	..	..	..
France													
Saving ratio	15.9	14.5	14.0	12.9	10.8	11.0	11.7	12.5	13.2	13.6	14.1	13.6	14.3
Net wealth	385.7	384.4	388.3	413.8	400.8	416.2	424.2	395.6	415.9	414.1	440.8	425.2	422.3
of which: Net financial wealth	86.0	86.9	98.4	124.4	111.6	130.8	147.5	123.6	142.5	147.8	179.2	167.4	169.4
Real assets	299.7	297.5	289.8	289.4	289.1	285.4	276.8	272.0	273.4	266.2	261.7	257.7	252.9
Financial assets	143.9	150.4	161.7	188.3	184.8	211.8	230.7	207.2	221.5	225.5	252.2	238.8	239.7
of which: Equities	25.4	32.0	43.4	66.3	60.5	85.4	103.1	82.6	97.4	96.7	115.1	95.7	88.7
Liabilities	57.9	63.5	63.3	63.9	73.2	81.0	83.2	83.6	79.1	77.6	73.0	71.4	70.3
of which: Medium- and long-term credit	39.4	41.3	42.9	43.3	47.0	49.4	48.9	49.1	48.0	45.8	49.0	47.5	45.8
Italy [b]													
Saving ratio	22.3	20.6	18.9	18.2	17.8	16.9	16.7	18.2	18.2	17.7	15.8	14.8	13.1
Net wealth [c]	487.7	487.6	503.7	489.7	504.0	510.6	534.5	531.3	546.7	584.4	..	..	..
of which: Net financial wealth	113.9	122.4	138.9	155.8	155.2	165.0	195.9	196.1	202.9	208.6	250.7	248.4	..
Real assets [c]	373.8	365.1	364.8	333.9	348.8	345.7	338.6	335.2	343.7	375.8	..	..	..
Financial assets	121.5	131.0	148.2	166.0	166.0	176.9	224.3	225.1	232.8	239.5	283.2	281.3	..
of which: Equities	6.5	7.7	14.9	22.6	16.2	17.3	48.8	46.0	48.0	48.2	72.1	67.1	..
Liabilities	7.6	8.6	9.3	10.2	10.8	11.9	28.4	29.0	29.9	30.9	32.5	32.9	..
of which: Medium- and long-term credit	5.2	6.2	6.5	7.0	7.7	8.6	13.1	13.7	14.3	14.5	15.1	..	..
United Kingdom													
Saving ratio	9.7	11.1	10.7	8.7	7.0	5.6	7.1	8.1	10.1	12.2	11.4	9.6	10.2
Net wealth	465.6	477.8	491.2	530.3	566.3	632.1	641.7	575.2	561.0	536.0	570.1	540.2	..
of which: Net financial wealth	162.7	173.8	179.2	202.2	200.6	197.9	219.0	184.9	198.8	213.0	256.8	239.7	..
Real assets	302.9	304.0	312.0	328.1	365.7	434.2	422.7	390.3	362.3	323.0	313.3	300.6	..
Financial assets	237.0	254.2	265.0	293.5	300.3	305.6	331.0	302.1	315.4	325.0	366.1	350.8	..
of which: Domestic equities	26.1	27.0	26.7	35.0	39.8	37.5	41.4	33.3	34.7	34.2	41.7	37.8	..
Liabilities	74.3	80.4	85.8	91.3	99.7	107.7	112.0	117.2	116.6	112.0	109.3	111.1	..
of which: Mortgages	46.6	48.4	52.3	58.2	64.1	70.2	72.9	77.6	78.8	77.5	77.2	78.9	..
Canada													
Saving ratio	14.8	15.0	13.3	10.7	9.2	9.7	10.4	9.7	9.9	10.3	9.6	7.9	7.4
Net wealth	404.4	400.4	399.4	418.0	426.4	427.3	428.7	428.0	437.8	448.8	461.4	476.7	487.5
of which: Net financial wealth	157.4	161.8	165.2	171.7	170.1	167.4	167.7	169.7	177.4	185.1	191.7	199.0	205.4
Real assets	247.0	238.6	234.2	246.3	256.3	259.9	261.0	258.3	260.5	263.7	269.7	277.7	282.0
Financial assets	232.7	234.5	240.3	252.6	257.7	258.6	260.4	264.8	273.5	283.0	291.8	302.1	309.6
of which: Equities	53.1	53.1	55.3	59.4	61.4	59.1	56.3	55.8	59.4	61.8	68.8	73.8	75.1
Liabilities	75.2	72.7	75.2	80.9	87.6	91.2	92.6	95.1	96.2	97.9	100.1	103.1	104.1
of which: Mortgages	46.8	45.4	46.4	50.4	54.6	57.1	58.8	60.9	63.4	66.3	68.1	70.2	71.1

a) Households and private unincorporated enterprises. The series are expressed as a percentage of household nominal disposable income. Assets and liabilities refer to year-end nominal values. Real assets and net wealth include durable goods for the United States, Italy, the United Kingdom, and Canada. Data for Germany exclude acquisition of real assets and associated liabilities; it is estimated that inclusion of household mortgages would increase the ratio of total liabilities to income to about 0.70 per cent in 1985.
b) Beginning in 1989, the financial accounts statistics for Italy are constructed with new sources and with a new methodology. They are, therefore, not comparable with the historical series.
c) Do not include the real assets of private unincorporated enterprises.
Sources: United States, Federal Reserve, *Balance Sheets for the US Economy;* Japan, Economic Planning Agency, *Annual Report on National Accounts;* Germany, Deutsche Bundesbank, *Ergebnisse der gesamtwirtschaftlichen Finanzierungsrechnung der Deutschen Bundesbank;* France, INSEE, *25 ans de Comptes de Patrimoine (1969-1993)* and *Rapport sur les Comptes de la Nation;* Italy, Banca d'Italia, *Supplementi al Bolletino Statistico;* Ando A., Guiso L., Visco I.(1994), *Saving and the Accumulation of Wealth;* OECD, *Financial Accounts of OECD countries;* United Kingdom, Central Statistical Office, *United Kingdom National Accounts, Financial Statistics;* Canada, Statistics Canada, *National Balance Sheet Accounts.*

Annex Figure 5. **Stock prices and long-term interest rates**

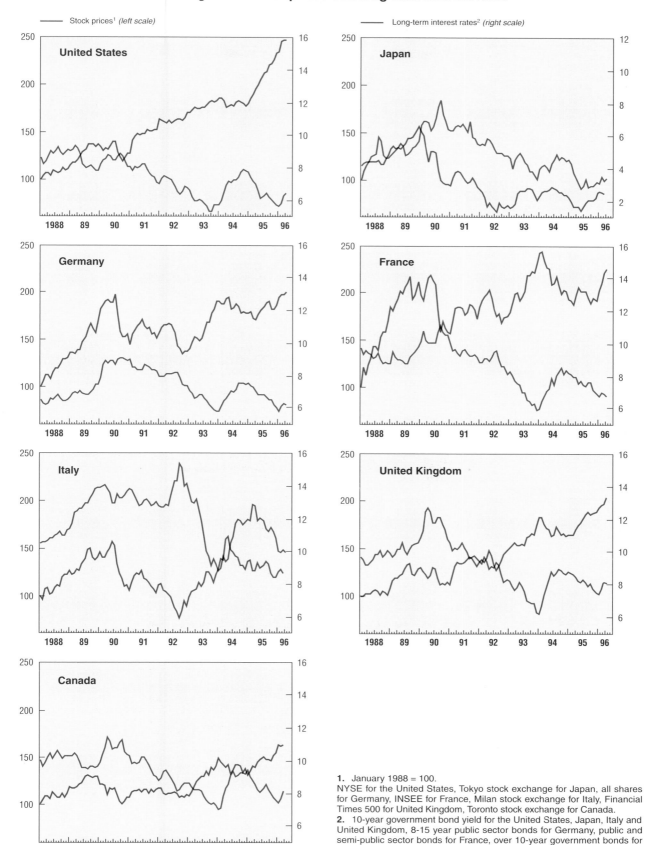

—— Stock prices[1] *(left scale)*   —— Long-term interest rates[2] *(right scale)*

1. January 1988 = 100.
NYSE for the United States, Tokyo stock exchange for Japan, all shares for Germany, INSEE for France, Milan stock exchange for Italy, Financial Times 500 for United Kingdom, Toronto stock exchange for Canada.
2. 10-year government bond yield for the United States, Japan, Italy and United Kingdom, 8-15 year public sector bonds for Germany, public and semi-public sector bonds for France, over 10-year government bonds for Canada.

Annex Table 59. **Productivity in the business sector**

Percentage changes at annual rates

	Total factor productivity[a]			Labour productivity[b]			Capital productivity		
	1960[c]-73	1973-79	1979-95[d]	1960[c]-73	1973-79	1979-95[d]	1960[c]-73	1973-79	1979-95[d]
United States	2.5	0.2	0.5	2.6	0.4	0.9	2.3	−0.2	−0.2
Japan	5.4	1.1	1.1	8.4	2.8	2.2	−3.3	−3.7	−2.1
Germany[e]	2.6	1.8	0.4	4.5	3.1	0.9	−1.4	−1.0	−0.6
France	3.7	1.6	1.3	5.3	2.9	2.3	0.6	−1.0	−0.6
Italy	4.4	2.0	0.9	6.3	2.9	1.8	0.4	0.3	−0.9
United Kingdom	2.6	0.6	1.5	3.9	1.5	2.0	−0.3	−1.5	0.5
Canada	1.9	0.6	−0.1	2.9	1.5	1.1	0.2	−1.0	−2.4
Total of above countries[f]	3.3	0.8	0.8	4.5	1.6	1.4	0.3	−1.1	−0.7
Australia	2.2	1.1	0.8	3.3	2.4	1.4	0.1	−1.4	−0.2
Austria	3.1	1.0	0.9	5.5	3.0	2.1	−2.0	−3.1	−1.7
Belgium	3.8	1.3	1.2	5.2	2.6	2.1	0.6	−1.9	−1.0
Denmark	2.3	0.9	1.3	3.9	2.4	2.2	−1.4	−2.6	−0.9
Finland	4.0	1.9	2.5	5.0	3.2	3.5	1.4	−1.6	−0.4
Greece	2.5	0.7	−0.3	9.0	3.3	0.6	−8.8	−4.2	−2.0
Ireland	4.6	3.4	2.6	5.1	4.1	3.3	2.3	0.5	−0.2
Netherlands	3.4	1.7	1.1	4.8	2.7	1.6	0.8	−0.1	0.1
Norway[g]	2.0	1.7	−0.1	3.8	3.1	1.5	0.0	0.2	−1.8
Portugal	5.4	−0.2	1.6	7.4	0.5	2.4	−0.7	−2.5	−0.8
Spain	3.2	0.9	1.7	6.0	3.2	2.9	−3.6	−5.0	−1.5
Sweden	2.0	0.0	1.0	3.7	1.4	2.0	−2.2	−3.2	−1.3
Switzerland	2.1	−0.3	−0.2	3.2	0.8	0.3	−1.4	−3.5	−1.6
Total of above smaller countries[f]	3.0	1.0	1.1	5.1	2.5	2.0	−1.5	−2.7	−1.0
Total of above North American countries[f]	2.5	0.2	0.4	2.6	0.5	0.9	2.1	−0.3	−0.4
Total of above European countries[f]	3.3	1.4	1.0	5.1	2.6	1.8	−0.7	−1.4	−0.6
Total of above OECD countries[f]	3.3	0.8	0.8	4.6	1.7	1.5	0.1	−1.3	−0.8

a) TFP growth is equal to a weighted average of the growth in labour and capital productivity. The sample-period averages for capital and labour shares are used as weights.

b) Output per employed person.

c) Or earliest year available, *i.e.* 1961 for Australia, Greece and Ireland; 1962 for Japan and the United Kingdom; 1964 for Spain; 1965 for France and Sweden; 1966 for Canada and Norway; 1970 for Belgium and the Netherlands and 1972 for the United States.

d) Or latest available year, *i.e.* 1991 for Norway; 1992 for Ireland and Portugal; 1993 for Germany, Austria, Belgium, Finland, Sweden and Switzerland and 1994 for Japan, France, the United Kingdom, Australia, Denmark, Greece, the Netherlands and Spain.

e) The two first averages concern western Germany. The percentage changes for the period 1979-95 are calculated as the weighted average of western Germany productivity growth between 1979 and 1991 and total Germany productivity growth between 1991 and the latest year available.

f) Aggregates are calculated on the basis of 1992 GDP for the business sector expressed in 1992 purchasing power parities.

g) Mainland business sector (*i.e.* excluding shipping as well as crude petroleum and gas extraction).

Annex Table 60. **Central government financial balances**

Surplus (+) or deficit (−) as a percentage of nominal GDP

	1989	1990	1991	1992	1993	1994	1995	1996	1997
United States[a]	−2.4	−3.0	−3.5	−4.7	−3.9	−2.7	−2.1	−1.9	−1.8
excluding social security[a,b]	−3.4	−4.0	−4.4	−5.5	−4.7	−3.5	−2.9	−2.8	−2.7
Japan[c]	−1.2	−0.3	−0.2	−2.1	−2.8	−3.5	−4.2	−4.3	−3.9
Germany	−0.9	−2.0	−1.9	−1.3	−2.1	−1.5	−1.5	−1.9	−1.8
France	−1.5	−1.5	−1.7	−2.9	−4.4	−4.8	−4.1	−3.6	−3.1
Italy	−9.4	−9.9	−9.9	−10.2	−10.2	−8.8	−7.2	−6.7	−6.4
United Kingdom	+1.2	−1.1	−2.2	−7.0	−8.0	−6.5	−5.5	−4.6	−3.5
Canada	−3.2	−3.9	−4.6	−4.2	−4.9	−3.8	−3.5	−2.2	−1.3
Total of above countries	−2.3	−2.7	−3.0	−4.3	−4.4	−3.6	−3.2	−3.0	−2.7

a) Excludes deposit insurance outlays. Includes cash surplus of federal government employee pension schemes.

b) OECD Secretariat estimates, derived from fiscal year data converted to a calendar year basis.

c) For the fiscal years beginning 1 April of the year shown.

Annex Table 61. **Maastricht definition of general government gross public debt**[a]

As a percentage of nominal GDP

| | 1990 | 1991 | 1992 | 1993 | 1994 | 1995 | Projections | |
							1996	1997
Austria	58.3	58.7	58.3	62.8	65.0	69.4	72.3	73.9
Belgium	130.9	130.3	131.5	137.9	136.0	133.5	132.4	131.1
Denmark[b]	59.6	64.6	68.7	80.1	76.0	72.0	72.1	70.9
Finland	14.5	23.0	41.5	57.3	59.5	59.5	60.8	61.0
France	35.4	35.8	39.8	45.4	48.3	52.4	55.0	56.9
Germany	43.8	41.5	44.1	48.2	50.4	58.1	61.0	62.4
Greece	81.6	83.1	99.1	111.7	110.4	111.5	109.4	107.3
Ireland	96.5	96.7	94.4	97.5	91.5	86.3	82.7	80.3
Italy	97.9	101.3	108.4	119.4	125.4	124.7	124.8	124.8
Luxembourg	5.5	4.9	6.1	7.6	7.37	7.4	..	..
Netherlands	78.8	78.8	79.4	81.1	77.6	79.1	78.6	78.2
Portugal	68.6	70.2	62.4	67.2	69.5	70.7	71.7	72.5
Spain	45.1	45.8	48.4	60.5	63.1	65.7	68.5	70.7
Sweden	43.5	53.0	67.1	76.0	79.3	79.9	81.3	79.8
United Kingdom	..	35.5	41.8	48.3	50.2	54.0	57.2	58.7

a) General government gross debt according to the definition applied under the Maastricht Treaty is based on estimates in national currencies provided by the Commission of the European Communities for 1990 to 1995 and projected forward in line with the OECD Secretariat's projections for general government financial balances and GDP. These data may differ from the gross financial liabilities figures shown in Annex Table 34. For further details, see *OECD Economic Outlook 55*, page 17.

b) In accordance with the Maastricht definition, government deposits held at the central bank, securities (other than government securities) held by the Social Pension Fund and public debt on behalf of public enterprises are included.

Annex Table 62. **Monetary and credit aggregates: recent trends and targets**[a]

Percentage changes, seasonally adjusted at annual rates

| | | Annual change (to 4th quarter) | | | | Latest twelve months | | From target base period | Current target or projection |
		1992	1993	1994	1995				
United States	M2	2.0	1.7	−1.9	4.0	5.1	(Mar. 1996)	6.7	1-5
	M3	0.6	1.0	1.6	5.9	6.6	(Mar. 1996)	8.0	2-6
	BC	0.1	3.5	7.5	10.8	8.3	(Mar. 1996)		
Japan	M2 + CD	−0.5	1.6	2.8	3.1	3.1	(Feb. 1996)	2.8	around 3
	BC	2.1	0.7	−0.6	0.7	1.0	(Feb. 1996)		
Germany	M3	9.6	7.5	5.7	1.3	5.4	(Mar. 1996)	12.2	4-7
	BC	8.2	7.8	5.5	5.6	7.1	(Mar. 1996)		
France	M3	5.5	−2.3	0.8	4.0	4.0	(Feb. 1996)	1.0	5
	BC	3.9	0.6	−1.1	0.0	0.2	(Nov. 1995)		
Italy	M2	6.2	8.5	1.6	2.4	1.5	(Feb. 1996)	−1.1	5
	BC	11.6	7.6	6.2	5.2	4.7	(Feb. 1996)		
United Kingdom	M0	2.8	5.5	7.2	5.4	5.6	(Mar. 1996)	5.3	0-4
	M4	4.4	3.6	4.4	9.5	10.3	(Mar. 1996)	9.9	3-9
	BC	−2.6	2.9	2.4	7.6	7.6	(Nov. 1995)		
Canada	M2	3.5	3.1	2.6	3.9	4.2	(Mar. 1996)		
	BC	0.7	3.5	8.1	5.4	9.0	(Mar. 1996)		

a) BC = commercial banks credit to economy. For more details see ''Sources and Methods''.

Annex Table 63. **Export market growth and performance in manufactured goods**

Percentage changes from previous year

	(1) Import volume				(2) Export market growth[a]				(3) Export volume				(4) Export performance[b]			
	1994	1995	1996	1997	1994	1995	1996	1997	1994	1995	1996	1997	1994	1995	1996	1997
United States	15.6	11.2	6.7	6.5	12.8	8.8	7.6	8.9	12.3	11.9	10.8	10.1	−0.5	2.8	3.0	1.1
Japan	19.9	21.9	10.9	13.2	13.2	11.4	8.6	8.5	1.3	3.2	2.4	6.9	−10.5	−7.4	−5.8	−1.4
Germany	10.1	4.0	3.4	6.8	10.4	9.3	6.2	7.1	10.4	5.0	3.6	7.3	0.1	−3.9	−2.4	0.1
France	8.8	8.0	2.1	6.1	10.5	8.8	6.2	7.2	9.1	8.8	1.8	7.2	−1.3	0.0	−4.2	0.0
Italy	16.1	8.2	4.5	6.0	9.8	8.9	6.0	7.4	12.0	8.8	4.6	5.8	2.0	−0.1	−1.3	−1.4
United Kingdom	8.6	2.5	5.4	6.2	10.9	9.8	6.5	7.5	12.7	6.5	3.7	6.2	1.6	−2.9	−2.6	−1.2
Canada	15.8	11.0	5.0	7.3	15.0	11.1	6.9	6.9	16.3	14.1	7.6	8.0	1.0	2.8	0.7	1.0
Total of the above countries	13.4	9.3	5.6	7.2	11.8	9.7	7.1	7.9	9.8	7.9	5.4	7.7	−1.8	−1.6	−1.5	−0.1
Australia	12.3	10.9	6.4	10.6	14.6	14.1	9.9	10.0	11.0	5.6	9.6	6.5	−3.0	−7.5	−0.3	−3.2
Austria	14.0	6.3	2.7	2.2	10.1	7.9	5.9	7.5	11.7	11.0	4.3	3.6	1.3	3.0	−1.5	−3.7
Belgium-Luxembourg	2.3	8.7	5.3	7.0	10.7	8.0	5.4	7.1	11.3	9.0	4.8	6.8	0.6	0.9	−0.5	−0.3
Czech Republic	15.2	22.8	17.0	12.3	8.9	8.1	7.4	8.5	3.3	7.9	10.8	11.1	−5.1	−0.2	3.2	2.4
Denmark	16.4	2.8	3.6	5.5	11.9	8.7	6.2	6.7	7.7	−0.4	−0.4	4.5	−3.7	−8.4	−6.2	−2.1
Finland	19.2	16.4	6.7	6.8	11.8	8.8	6.4	7.1	14.0	3.8	2.5	6.0	2.0	−4.5	−3.7	−1.0
Greece	4.6	11.0	8.2	9.7	10.3	8.2	5.9	7.2	4.6	−0.6	4.6	6.6	−5.3	−8.0	−1.2	−0.6
Iceland	9.4	8.6	16.0	10.6	11.3	7.8	5.4	6.7	18.8	0.1	4.0	2.0	6.9	−7.1	−1.4	−4.4
Ireland	13.6	10.6	10.2	9.8	10.8	7.2	5.4	6.8	16.1	14.3	10.9	9.6	4.8	6.6	5.1	2.7
Mexico	12.1	−22.3	10.9	13.0	15.3	11.2	6.6	6.8	13.4	29.9	10.9	9.3	−1.6	16.7	4.1	2.4
Netherlands	10.5	6.7	3.9	6.1	9.5	7.7	5.4	6.9	8.5	7.2	4.6	6.9	−0.9	−0.5	−0.8	0.0
New Zealand	17.5	12.1	7.9	9.2	14.2	13.3	8.9	10.5	14.0	3.0	5.1	5.6	−0.1	−9.1	−3.5	−4.4
Norway	17.8	8.7	7.9	2.9	12.2	9.1	6.2	7.0	11.9	5.2	3.8	3.6	−0.2	−3.5	−2.3	−3.2
Portugal	10.9	6.5	8.8	7.1	11.7	8.3	5.1	6.5	13.9	11.3	9.9	7.3	1.9	2.7	4.5	0.7
Spain	19.8	15.2	7.2	7.5	10.1	7.5	5.3	6.9	24.6	16.7	8.2	8.1	13.2	8.5	2.8	1.1
Sweden	15.7	11.2	6.3	5.4	12.0	8.6	6.3	6.9	18.6	15.5	4.2	6.2	5.9	6.4	−2.0	−0.7
Switzerland	8.4	7.9	3.2	4.5	11.4	9.2	6.4	7.6	3.3	4.3	2.5	4.6	−7.3	−4.4	−3.7	−2.8
Turkey	−22.1	31.4	15.1	14.8	11.3	8.0	5.7	7.3	18.0	7.7	14.3	11.8	6.0	−0.1	8.1	4.2
Total of smaller countries	10.4	7.4	6.3	7.2	11.3	8.7	6.1	7.3	12.3	10.3	5.8	6.8	0.9	1.5	−0.3	−0.5
Total OECD	12.5	8.8	5.8	7.2	11.7	9.5	6.9	7.7	10.4	8.6	5.5	7.5	−1.1	−0.8	−1.2	−0.2
OPEC	−7.4	5.7	5.1	5.8	12.5	12.2	8.7	9.1	8.2	7.6	7.1	5.1	−3.8	−4.1	−1.5	−3.7
ANIEs[c]	16.9	15.5	12.7	11.0	13.9	12.6	9.2	9.2	16.5	14.7	12.7	10.5	2.3	1.7	3.2	1.2
Other Asia	14.2	15.7	13.8	11.9	14.5	13.2	9.7	9.6	18.3	15.1	13.1	11.9	3.3	1.7	3.1	2.1
Latin America	15.6	13.1	4.7	6.0	13.2	10.9	6.7	7.5	7.3	3.3	4.4	5.0	−5.2	−6.9	−2.2	−2.3
Africa	4.1	9.2	6.7	5.0	10.9	9.8	6.4	7.5	1.7	8.8	8.0	5.6	−8.3	−1.0	1.5	−1.7
Central and Eastern Europe	5.0	7.7	10.4	11.0	8.9	8.8	8.2	9.1	7.4	10.8	5.9	4.5	−1.4	1.8	−2.1	−4.2
Total of non-OECD countries	11.0	13.2	10.8	9.9	13.2	12.1	8.9	9.1	14.3	13.2	11.2	9.6	0.9	1.0	2.1	0.5
World	12.0	10.1	7.3	8.0	12.0	10.1	7.3	8.0	11.3	9.7	7.0	8.0	−0.6	−0.3	−0.3	0.0
OECD North America	15.4	8.7	6.6	7.0	13.4	9.4	7.4	8.3	13.1	13.5	10.1	9.6	−0.2	3.7	2.5	1.2
OECD Europe	10.2	7.3	4.7	6.4	10.5	8.8	6.1	7.2	11.4	7.8	4.2	6.7	0.8	−1.0	−1.8	−0.5
European Union	10.7	6.8	4.4	6.4	10.5	8.8	6.0	7.2	11.8	8.0	4.1	6.7	1.2	−0.8	−1.8	−0.4
Total OECD less the United States	11.5	8.0	5.5	7.4	11.4	9.6	6.7	7.5	10.0	7.8	4.3	6.9	−1.3	−1.6	−2.2	−0.6

a) The calculation of export markets is based on a weighted average of import volumes [panel (1) above] in each exporting country's markets, with weights based on manufacturing trade flows in 1991.

b) Export performance is calculated as the percentage change in the ratio of export volumes to export markets.

c) ANIEs include Chinese Taipei, Hong Kong, Korea and Singapore.

Sources: Direction of Trade data – United Nations Statistical Office; OECD, *Foreign Trade By Commodities.*

Annex Table 64. **Geographical structure of OECD trade**

Percentage of nominal GDP

Area or country	Source/destination		Source of imports						Destination of exports					
			1962	1972	1982	1992	1993	1994	1962	1972	1982	1992	1993	1994
OECD	**OECD**		**6.06**	**7.98**	**10.32**	**11.14**	**10.14**	**10.72**	**5.79**	**7.83**	**9.97**	**10.97**	**10.30**	**10.86**
	of which:	Europe	3.83	5.20	6.61	7.39	6.34	6.70	3.97	5.27	6.87	7.54	6.69	6.95
		North America	1.80	2.02	2.65	2.53	2.58	2.79	1.39	2.05	2.38	2.72	2.91	3.14
		Other	0.43	0.76	1.06	1.22	1.22	1.23	0.42	0.51	0.71	0.71	0.70	0.77
	Non-OECD		**2.39**	**2.46**	**4.77**	**3.45**	**3.55**	**3.73**	**2.39**	**2.35**	**4.33**	**3.33**	**3.57**	**3.69**
	of which:	DAEs[a] + China	0.18	0.35	0.85	1.39	1.49	1.62	0.25	0.40	0.84	1.32	1.50	1.65
		OPEC	0.66	0.81	2.14	0.72	0.67	0.63	0.33	0.41	1.41	0.56	0.50	0.44
USA	**OECD**		**1.84**	**3.47**	**4.91**	**5.81**	**6.04**	**6.51**	**2.22**	**2.94**	**4.18**	**5.14**	**4.99**	**5.23**
	of which:	Europe	0.78	1.27	1.65	1.86	1.84	1.96	1.09	1.25	1.89	1.96	1.81	1.77
		North America	0.74	1.37	1.97	2.25	2.41	2.68	0.81	1.19	1.44	2.20	2.27	2.48
		Other	0.31	0.84	1.29	1.71	1.79	1.86	0.33	0.49	0.84	0.98	0.92	0.97
	Non-OECD		**1.02**	**1.12**	**2.83**	**3.13**	**3.24**	**3.48**	**1.55**	**1.18**	**2.56**	**2.40**	**2.43**	**2.48**
	of which:	DAEs[a] + China	0.08	0.33	0.87	1.75	1.84	2.02	0.11	0.22	0.67	1.08	1.14	1.21
		OPEC	0.26	0.22	0.99	0.56	0.53	0.50	0.18	0.23	0.73	0.37	0.33	0.29
Japan	**OECD**		**5.37**	**3.99**	**4.41**	**3.11**	**2.76**	**2.89**	**3.94**	**5.23**	**6.22**	**5.14**	**4.55**	**4.46**
	of which:	Europe	1.00	0.82	0.93	1.04	0.88	0.94	1.11	1.57	2.01	1.97	1.55	1.43
		North America	3.60	2.37	2.77	1.68	1.55	1.60	2.56	3.36	3.71	2.94	2.78	2.81
		Other	0.77	0.80	0.72	0.39	0.33	0.34	0.27	0.29	0.50	0.22	0.21	0.22
	Non-OECD		**3.88**	**3.72**	**7.67**	**3.26**	**2.98**	**3.10**	**4.13**	**4.17**	**6.49**	**4.15**	**4.06**	**4.16**
	of which:	DAEs[a] + China	0.84	0.73	1.61	1.52	1.47	1.63	1.29	1.67	2.39	2.82	2.86	3.03
		OPEC	1.12	1.50	4.45	1.06	0.89	0.83	0.52	0.61	2.00	0.52	0.41	0.36
Europe	**OECD**		**11.38**	**13.56**	**17.81**	**17.81**	**16.63**	**17.53**	**10.29**	**13.25**	**16.85**	**17.12**	**16.89**	**18.05**
	of which:	Europe	8.61	11.22	14.50	14.94	13.78	14.62	8.48	11.22	14.59	14.96	14.50	15.39
		North America	2.22	1.73	2.41	1.77	1.79	1.87	1.36	1.66	1.81	1.63	1.81	1.98
		Other	0.55	0.61	0.90	1.10	1.07	1.04	0.45	0.38	0.46	0.53	0.58	0.67
	Non-OECD		**4.20**	**3.79**	**6.30**	**3.84**	**4.05**	**4.22**	**3.43**	**3.25**	**5.65**	**3.69**	**4.25**	**4.43**
	of which:	DAEs[a] + China	0.23	0.27	0.61	1.06	1.19	1.24	0.25	0.26	0.46	0.78	1.03	1.18
		OPEC	1.16	1.33	2.77	0.74	0.71	0.66	0.54	0.59	2.08	0.74	0.72	0.62

a) DAEs are the Dynamic Asian Economies (Chinese Taipei, Hong Kong, Korea, Malaysia, Thailand and Singapore).

SOURCES AND METHODS

The analysis in the *OECD Economic Outlook* and the projections on which it is based are the work of the OECD Economics Department. The following notes describe various technical aspects of the projection methods used, and underlying statistical concepts, sources and methods.

PROJECTION METHODS

While taking into account official and unofficial national projections for Member countries, the *OECD Economic Outlook* projections are based on the OECD Secretariat's independent assessment of the world economy. This draws on individual country, general economic and area analyses. Emphasis is placed on the role of international trade and financial linkages, to ensure that projections for each country are consistent with global developments.

The *OECD Economic Outlook* projections are conditional on technical assumptions about exchange rates, energy prices, and the choice of economic policies – fiscal, monetary and structural:

– Exchange rates against the US dollar are generally assumed to remain constant over the projection period, at the level prevailing on a prespecified cut-off date, chosen in the course of the exercise, except for those countries with stated or *de facto* policies.
– The price of crude oil is set on the basis of a methodology described in the text.
– Fiscal and monetary policy assumptions for individual countries are generally based upon stated official policies, with public sector expenditure and revenue projections being based upon the most recent budgetary statements.

The OECD Secretariat's world macroeconomic model, INTERLINK,[1] is used to help to ensure national and international consistency, though a considerable amount of country-specific expertise and judgement is brought to bear in the construction of the underlying individual country assessments.

A preliminary version of the *OECD Economic Outlook* projections is presented to and discussed by the OECD Working Group on Short-Term Economic Prospects, where Member country delegates provide their analyses and detailed comments, drawing on national authority evidence and projections.

In presenting half-yearly demand, output and price projections, all estimates reported in the *OECD Economic Outlook* are seasonally adjusted and shown in terms of percentage changes at annual rates. Further definitional notes relating to reporting conventions, in particular the measurement of semiannual rates of growth, are given below.

The domestic economy

Macroeconomic developments reflect the interaction of many economic variables and relationships. The following paragraphs describe those which are particularly important to OECD Secretariat projections.

Domestic expenditure

Two broad categories of domestic expenditure are distinguished, consumption and investment, subdivided into various private and public sector components. The projections of private consumption typically depend on real personal disposable income, changes in the rate of inflation, monetary and financial conditions, and also leading indicators of consumer confidence and retail sales. Particular attention is given to current trends in personal and business sector saving rates and asset holdings. Private investment is, for most countries, subdivided into business fixed investment, residential construction and stockbuilding. Business fixed investment is typically assessed in relation to non-financial variables (sales, output and capacity utilisation) and financial variables (cash flow and interest rates). Business survey information is also taken into account. Projections for residential construction take account of demographic trends, housing stocks, real income and financial conditions, and also draw on cyclical indicators for the construction sector. Projections of stockbuilding are usually made with reference to relevant stock-output and stock-sales ratios, taking account of recent trends, financial factors and specific supply-side influences.

Government non-wage expenditures, divided into non-wage consumption and investment, are treated as being exogenous policy variables, specified in either nominal or real terms. In a number of cases, an independent assessment is made of expected out-turns versus stated policy goals. Government wage expenditures may be set either in terms of nominal targets for the total wage bill or as the product of government employment and associated wage projections.

Methods involved in the analysis of external influences on output and real GDP, *i.e.* those coming from goods and services trade, are described below in the section concerning foreign trade.

Employment, wages and prices

Employment and other labour market trends are commonly assessed in relation to changes in the levels of actual and expected output. Important additional elements relate to labour and factor productivity trends, capacity constraints and real factor costs. Unemployment rate projections are computed from employment and labour supply projections, with the latter assessed judgmentally on the basis of demographic trends and participation rate assumptions.

Wage and earnings assessments take into account a number of key factors. Extensive use is made of the pattern of current wage settlement as a leading indicator, with pressure of demand in the labour market, productivity rates and the terms of trade also influencing the overall projection of real wages and compensation per employee. The projections of unit labour costs used in the assessment of prices and inflation take account of those for employment, productivity growth, wage rates and social contributions. Public sector wage projections are generally based on announced policies but may also be assumed to adjust in line with private sector wages.

The assessment of domestic prices and inflation trends depends crucially on unit costs, the levels of demand and supply potential (see below) and foreign prices. In making individual price projections, allowance is also made for a number of special factors affecting prices in individual countries – harvest yields, changes in taxes and subsidies and administered price regimes. The overall set of domestic expenditure deflators in conjunction with goods and services trade prices and corresponding real expenditure components are then combined to give projections of total domestic demand and output deflators. The specific treatment of trade prices is discussed in more detail in the section concerning foreign trade.

Supply potential and output gaps (Annex Table 11)

As outlined in the relevant chapter of *OECD Economic Outlook 56*, the OECD Secretariat has recently carried out a major reassessment of its methods for measuring potential output and output gaps for use in its analyses of inflation pressure and structural budget balances. The revised output gap measures, reported now in Annex Table 11, are based on the methodology set out in ''Potential Output, Output Gaps and Structural Budget Balances'', by Claude Giorno, Pete Richardson, Deborah Roseveare and Paul van den Noord, *OECD Economic Studies*, No. 24, 1995/1.

The output gap is measured as the percentage difference between actual GDP in constant prices, and estimated potential GDP. The latter is based on a production function approach, taking into account the capital stock, changes in labour supply, factor productivities and underlying non-accelerating wage rates of unemployment or the NAWRU for each Member country. It should be stressed that the estimated levels of potential are subject to significant margins of error.

Sectoral accounts

Appropriation accounts for the household and government sectors are projected for the seven major OECD economies and some smaller countries. Both accounts are constructed by identifying the different sources of income and expenditures, saving and net lending.

Household income consists primarily of the wage compensation of employees, self-employment income, and transfers. Property and other income – essentially dividends and inter-

est – are evaluated in the light of business income and debt interest flows. The sum of these elements is adjusted for direct taxes and transfers paid to give household disposable income. The latter is then split between household consumption and saving. Household taxes and transfers are typically projected on the basis of movements in the appropriate nominal bases and corresponding marginal tax and transfer rates. There is some variation in the detail of the treatment of transfers as between the larger and smaller economies. Social security receipts are projected on the basis of the unemployment rate, prices and wage compensation levels. Household net lending is obtained by subtracting housing investment from household saving.

For the United States a full disaggregation of revenues and expenditures is made as between State and Local and Federal accounts, with wage and non-wage expenditures also split between defence and non-defence spending. For the other major economies a relatively standardised total general government approach (described below) is adopted, while for some smaller economies there is a less detailed treatment of transfers, subsidies and property income. For a number of countries, specific allowance is made for revenues and tax receipts from sectors of specific importance, for example, oil and gas.

The current receipts of the government sector are in general defined as the sum of direct taxes on household and business sectors, indirect taxes, social security, and other transfer receipts and interest-related property income. Indirect taxes are projected on the basis of weighted expenditures, combined with corresponding tax elasticities. Business sector taxes are assessed on the basis of projected business income, making allowance for the lags between accruals and payments. Social security and other transfer receipts are linked directly to the corresponding household sector payments, while property income is in general assumed to grow broadly in line with nominal GDP.

Current disbursements are the sum of current consumption, transfer payments, subsidies and interest payments. For the major economies, interest payments are assessed on the basis of the stocks of outstanding debt, the rate of roll-over in the stock and the relevant interest rates. Government net lending is then derived as current saving, less nominal investment, capital consumption and other miscellaneous capital transactions. The stock of government net financial liabilities is finally obtained as the cumulation of net lending, subject to statistical discrepancies.

Domestic monetary policies

For the major economies, prevailing monetary policies are examined against a range of monetary indicators. Typically, assumptions are made about the choice and stance of policy, taking into account recent policy announcements with respect to the choice of monetary targets, associated target ranges and instruments, by national authorities. Increasingly, this involves a strong interdependent element, given for example the importance of interest rates, exchange rates, output and prices to international transmission mechanisms. Effectively this means that international financial linkages are increasingly important in the overall global assessment, and hence the assumptions for short- and long-term interest rates and/or monetary aggregates for virtually all OECD countries may hinge critically on the assessment of monetary policy in the three largest ones.

Further details of a wider range of statistical and methodological issues are described below in the Monetary Aggregates and Interest Rates section.

Foreign trade and balance of payments

Particular attention is given in the forecasting exercise to ensuring the consistency of international trade volume and price projections, trade representing a principal channel through which developments in one country affect other economies. Six categories of international trade are customarily distinguished: manufactures; energy; food; raw materials; non-factor services; and other services. Various adjustment and reconciliation procedures are involved in linking customs-basis foreign trade projections to the national-accounts basis projections for individual countries.

The projections for total goods trade are based on a split into the following specific SITC categories:

– food: 0 + 1
– raw materials: 2 + 4
– energy: 3
– manufactures: 5 + 6 + 7 + 8 + 9

Projections for these components are weighted together using moving weights based on 1991 trade flows. These are approximately comparable to figures published in the OECD's *Monthly Statistics of Foreign Trade* (Series "A"). The paragraphs below summarise how projections for these components are prepared. The structural specifications of equations used in the foreign trade projections are set out, for each country, in the OECD Secretariat's INTERLINK Reference Manual.

a) *Goods: volumes*

i) *Manufactures*

The initial projections of import volume growth for manufactured goods are derived from equations (in logarithm level form) in which the main explanatory variables are activity (demand) and lagged competitive positions. The activity variable in the import equations is specified so that a distinction is made for most countries between the short-and long-term response of imports to a change in demand (*i.e.* demand is split into two components: a moving average, and the ratio of actual demand to this moving average). In addition, for some countries a lagged dependent variable is included in the specification. Export volume projections are based on developments in export markets and competitive positions. For each exporting country, export market growth is defined as a weighted average of real import growth in other countries, while competitiveness effects are proxied by changes in relative prices. These are measured by the ratio of each country's export prices to a weighted average of its competitors' export prices. The weights are derived through a double weighting procedure described in the section on effective exchange rates below.

Expenditure elasticities for imports are, in general, estimated in the range of 1.5 to 2.5, while most of the price elasticities (import prices relative to domestic prices) range from –0.4 to –0.9, the response being lagged over two to three years. For export volumes, price elasticities (export prices relative to competitors' prices) are typically taken to be in the range of –1.0 to –2.0, lagged over three years, while market growth elasticities for most countries are close to unity.

ii) *Energy*

International trade in energy is concentrated in oil, and the forecasting effort is focused accordingly. It is assumed that OPEC is the marginal supplier, with other producers setting prices relative to those of OPEC such that they are always able to sell their full capacity output.

The demand for oil is projected, in collaboration with the International Energy Agency, from relationships which link oil consumption to the real cost of imported oil. Judgmental adjustment is then made to reflect any unusual weather conditions and new developments in energy substitution.

With oil demand determined, net oil imports are obtained by subtracting expected domestic production and adjusting for any expected change in stocks. The movement in oil imports is then added to the projected movements of imports of other forms of energy.

iii) *Food and raw materials*

Import volumes of food are assumed to follow projected movements in real private consumption; import volumes of raw materials are assumed to follow movements in industrial production. While some allowance is made for the effects of large changes in competitiveness, trade volumes of food and raw materials are generally assumed to be relatively insensitive to changes in competitiveness over the projection period. Food and raw material exports are based on, *inter alia,* export market growth for these commodities, with an allowance for factors affecting supply.

b) *Goods: unit values*

i) *Manufactures*

Projections for unit values of exports of manufactured goods are based initially on movements in unit labour costs, import prices, and competitors' export prices – the first two being subject to lags of up to one year. Some allowance is made for exceptionally high or low rates of capacity utilisation.

Import unit values are derived as weighted averages of foreign costs and domestic prices. The resulting import price projections are then modified to reflect time lags in the translation of exchange rate changes into import prices. In those countries where competitiveness has changed sharply, an allowance is made for price discrimination by foreign suppliers in the first half-year, partly reversed over the next two half-years. The export and import price equations have been estimated to ensure consistency at the world level. (For more details, see "Import and export price equations of manufactures", *OECD Economics and Statistics Department Working Papers,* No. 43, Richard Herd.)

ii) *Energy*

The customary technical assumption is that, in the near term, oil prices are determined by market conditions, including announced OPEC decisions, and thereafter follow prices of OECD exports of manufactured goods. Adjustments are made to reflect natural gas and coal contracts and thereby allow for the lag between the movements of other fossil fuels and oil prices.

iii) *Food and raw materials*

In general, food and raw material unit values (in dollars) are derived from projected movements of spot commodity prices. Current OECD Secretariat estimates suggest that about three-quarters of the change in spot industrial materials prices is passed through into OECD import unit values of raw materials within about six months.

Equations for OECD export unit values for food and raw materials utilise domestic cost pressure variables as well as world spot commodity prices as explanatory variables. In addition, food export unit value equations for EC countries are adjusted for the effects of the Common Agricultural Policy.

Import unit values for food and raw materials are trade-weighted averages of partner-country export unit values.

c) *Non-factor services and investment income*

Projections of non-factor services (which cover transportation, travel, communications, construction, insurance, financial, computer and information services, royalties and license fees, other business services, personal, cultural and recreational services, and government services) are based on equations of broadly similar specification to those used for manufactures trade. Volumes of non-factor service debits depend both on projected movements of import-content-weighted real expenditure, and the price of import of services relative to domestic prices. Non-factor service credits depend on market growth for services and each country's export prices of services relative to those of its competitors. A service trade share matrix based on 1989 flows is used to calculate market growth and competitors' prices. Export prices of services for each country are assumed to move in line with its total expenditure price deflator. Service export prices for non-OECD zones are assumed to move with the average for the OECD area. Import prices are then calculated from export prices using the service trade share matrix. Import elasticities of non-factor services with respect to import-content-weighted expenditure components are around 1.2, with price elasticities of –0.7 to –0.8 lagged over 1 1/2 years. Non-factor service export projections are based on market growth in partner countries, with market growth elasticities around unity and price elasticities of –0.4 to –0.5 lagged over 1 1/2 years. Projections for investment income (which includes foreign workers' remittances and income arising from foreign investment) are based on equations that take account of external assets and liabilities and rates of return. Movements in external assets and liabilities are linked to capital outflows and current-account balances.

The current account balance is derived as the sum of the balance of goods and invisibles. Invisibles are defined as the sum of non-factor services, investment income and current transfers (which consist of all transfers that are not transfers of capital).

d) *Non-OECD*

Trade volumes and prices of the non-OECD area are projected on the basis of six country groupings (see Country Classification for details). Individual projections are made for some important non-OECD countries. Import and export prices for each group reflect world prices weighted according to the commodity structure of trade. Export volumes for each group are projected on the basis of the growth of their markets, with account taken, in some cases, of changes in competitiveness. For groups with large external assets, import volumes are in line with assessment of development plans. For other groups, import volumes are projected taking account of export revenues, the level of external financing and import prices.

INDICATORS OF EXPORT MARKET GROWTH AND PERFORMANCE

Indicators of export market growth represent the potential export growth for a country assuming that its market shares are unchanged. Market growth indicators for each country are then calculated as a weighted average of import volume growth in all

its markets, with the weighting pattern being derived from the share of its exports going to that market in a chosen base year.

Indicators of export performance are calculated for each country by comparing the growth of its export volumes with that of its export market. This shows whether the country's exports grow faster or slower than its market, *i.e.* if over time it is experiencing market share gains or losses.

For all OECD countries, the Secretariat calculates market growth and export performance indicators for 4 groups of commodities, which cover SITC categories 0-1, 2-4, 3, 5 to 9, and for the total of merchandise (SITC 0 to 9).

EFFECTIVE EXCHANGE RATES AND COMPETITIVENESS INDICATORS

The Secretariat calculates three different measures of relative competitive positions. These are based on the ratio between domestic and competitors' average values of manufacturing exports, manufacturing unit labour costs and consumer prices. The latter corresponds to the real effective exchange rate published in the OECD's *Main Economic Indicators.*

The calculation of competitiveness indicators and effective exchange rates uses a system of weights based on a double-weighting principle, which takes account of the structure of competition in both export and import markets. A discussion of other measures of competitiveness is given in ''OECD's indicators of international trade and competitiveness'', *OECD Economics Department Working Papers,* No. 120, Martine Durand, Jacques Simon and Colin Webb.

Twenty-five OECD Member countries (Belgium-Luxembourg is treated an one country) and four of the Dynamic Asian Economies (Hong Kong, Korea, Singapore and Chinese Taipei) are included in the calculation of effective exchange rates (nominal and real). The Czech Republic is included in the index only since January 1991. The introduction of the Czech Republic does not substantially alter the effective exchange rates for other countries. Twenty OECD countries and the four Dynamic Asian Economies are included in the calculation of competitiveness indicators based on export prices and unit labour costs (the Czech Republic, Greece, Iceland, Ireland and Turkey are excluded because of lack of data). Thirty-one markets are considered: the twenty-five OECD countries and the six non-OECD zones.

For each year, starting in 1970, a country by market matrix has been constructed for the calculations. The diagonal elements represent the production of manufactured goods (net of exports) of individual countries and the off-diagonal elements represent the exports of manufactured goods from one country (row) to other OECD countries or non-OECD zones (column). These basic matrices are then used to compute intermediate shares matrices for each country which give a measure of the relative importance of the other competitors in the domestic and foreign markets. These intermediate matrices are then weighted by the relative share of the markets in the exports of the country involved. This gives global weighting systems for each year since 1970 with the weights reflecting the importance of the other countries as competitors in domestic and third markets.

The effective exchange rate index is a chain-linked index. First, changes in the index are calculated as a geometric weighted average of changes in nominal exchange rates using the weighting matrix of the previous year. The levels of indices of nominal effective exchange rates are then calculated from a starting period by cumulating the change in the index. This gives a set of effective exchange rates based on moving weights.

Also the competitiveness indicators are calculated by chain-linking percentage changes in the three cost and price measures from a starting period. Relative indices are computed as the ratio of the index for the country concerned (expressed in US$ at market exchange rates) to a weighted average of indices of the other 19 OECD countries included in the calculation and of the four Dynamic Asian Economies (also expressed in US$).

FISCAL POLICY

Government financial liabilities

The figures for gross financial liabilities (Annex Table 34) refer to the debt and other liabilities (short and long-term) of all of the institutions contained in the general government sector of the national accounts. Liabilities are those defined in the System of National Accounts, subject to data availability. The general government sector is the aggregate of the central and local government sectors and the social security sector. The gross data are consolidated within and between the sub-sectors of the general government sector, national sources permitting. The figures for net financial liabilities (Annex Table 35) measure the gross financial liabilities of the general government sector less the financial assets of the general government sector. Such assets may be cash, bank deposits, loans to the private sector, participations in private sector companies, holdings in public corporations or foreign exchange reserves, depending on the institutional structure of the country concerned and data availability.

Gross debt according to the convergence criteria set out in the Maastricht Treaty (Annex Table 61) comprises currency and deposits, bills and short-term bonds, other short-term loans and other medium and long-term loans and bonds, defined according to the European System of Integrated Economic Accounts (ESA). Financial liabilities such as trade credits extended to the government are not included.

Cyclical and non-cyclical components of general government financial balances (Annex Table 31)

The budget balance can be decomposed into a cyclical and a non-cyclical, or structural, component. The decomposition is aimed at separating cyclical influences on the budget balances resulting from the divergence between actual and potential output (the output gap), from those which are non-cyclical. Changes in the latter can be seen as a cause rather than an effect of output fluctuations and may be interpreted as indicative of discretionary policy adjustments. It should be noted, however, that changes in resource revenues – as a result of oil price changes, for example – and in interest payments – as a result of past debt accumulation or changes in interest rates – are neither cyclical nor purely discretionary. Yet these changes are reflected in the evolution of the structural component of the budget balance.

The structural budget balance is derived by (re-)calculating the items on the government appropriation account which would be obtained if output (GDP) were at its potential level.

Denoting a cyclically-adjusted variable by an asterisk, revenues (T) and expenditures (G) are recalculated as follows:

$$T_t^* = T_t \ (GDP_t^*/GDP_t)^\alpha \qquad \alpha > 0$$
$$G_t^* = G_t \ (GDP_t^*/GDP_t)^\beta \qquad \beta < 0$$

where α and β are respectively the elasticity of current receipts and expenditure with respect to nominal output growth. The cyclical adjustment is carried out for the main revenue items separately (*i.e.* corporate taxes, personal income taxes, indirect taxes and social security contributions), and for the unemployment-related expenditure.

The structural budget balances are reported as a percentage of potential output as described earlier. It should be stressed that the estimated structural budget balances are surrounded by large margins of uncertainty. This is due not only to the usual risks to the projection of actual output, but also reflects uncertainty as to the present size and future growth of potential output, and the degree to which elimination of the output gap would translate into enhanced tax revenues and reduced expenditures. For a further discussion of these issues, see ''Potential Output, Output Gaps and Structural Budget Balances'' *op. cit.*

The primary balance (Annex Table 32) is obtained by netting net interest payments from the overall balance.

MONETARY AGGREGATES AND INTEREST RATES

Monetary and credit aggregates (Annex Table 62)

M1 is the narrowly defined money supply, *i.e.* currency plus domestic demand deposits. M2, M2 + CD, M3 and M4 are broadly-defined money stocks, which add to M1 domestic savings deposits and other managed liabilities of banks and other financial institutions, and certificates of deposit (CD) in Japan, France and the United Kingdom. In the United Kingdom, M0 is currency in circulation with the public plus bankers' operational balances with the central bank. Monetary aggregates are obtained from national data sources.

Bank credit: United States: commercial banks loans; Japan: commercial banks loans and discount; Germany: bank credit to economy, excluding Central Bank, short-, medium- and long-term; France: bank credit to economy, total; Italy: commercial and saving banks, credit to private sector; United Kingdom: bank credit to industry and other sectors; Canada: chartered banks, credit to economy. Bank credit information is obtained from OECD, *Main Economic Indicators.*

Latest twelve-month changes are calculated from the most recent 3-month average relative to the corresponding 3-month average a year earlier. Changes from target base period are calculated as the latest monthly figure relative to the fourth quarter of the previous year, except for the United Kingdom and Japan which are changes over the previous twelve months and for Germany the rate is the one published by the Bundesbank, where the fourth quarter average is calculated on selected return days (end of month level included with a weight of 50 per cent). For the United States and Germany, targets are for Q3 to Q3 annual growth rates; for Japan, the figure is not a target but a projection for growth from Q3 to Q3; for France, the figure is a medium-term objective; for the United Kingdom, the current target or monitoring range is expressed in terms of changes over the previous 12 months.

Interest rates

The following interest rates are reported in Annex Table 36.

Short-term rates: United States: 3-month Treasury bills; Japan: 3-6 month CD; Germany, France, United Kingdom: 3-month interbank rates; Italy: interbank deposits; Canada: 90-day finance company paper; Austria: day-to-day money; Belgium: 3-month Treasury certificates; Denmark: 3-month interbank rate; Finland: 3-month Helibor; Ireland: 91-day Exchequer bills up to 1983, 3-month interbank rate from 1984; Mexico: 3-month Treasury certificates; Netherlands: 3-month Aibor; Norway: call money rate; Spain: 3-month interbank loans; Sweden: 3-month Treasury discount notes; Switzerland: 3-month euro-deposits; Australia: 90-day bank-accepted bills; New Zealand: 90-day bank bills.

Long-term rates: United States, Japan and United Kingdom: 10-year government bonds; Germany: 8-15 year public sector bonds; France: public and semi-public sector bonds; Italy: long-term government bonds, gross rate; Canada: over 10-year long-term federal government bonds; Austria: public sector bonds (more than 1 year); Belgium: central government bonds (more than 5 years); Denmark: central government bonds (10 years); Finland: non-central government taxable public bonds (as from 1994, taxable 5-year central government bonds); Ireland: 15-year government bonds; Mexico: 1-year Treasury certificates; Netherlands: 10-year government bonds; Norway: 6-10 year central government bonds; Spain: government bonds (more than 2 years); Sweden: 10-year government bonds; Switzerland: 10-year federal government bonds; Australia: 10-year bonds; New Zealand: 10-year government bonds.

Sources: OECD, *Main Economic Indicators* and *OECD Financial Statistics.* Some series are not strictly comparable over time due to changes in definitions or in institutional arrangements. For further details, see *OECD Financial Statistics, Methodological Supplement, 1991-92.*

LABOUR FORCE DATA

This section outlines the sources and definitions of the data concerning labour markets. Where different series are available, those chosen are the ones which the OECD Economics Department finds most useful for policy analysis and forecasting, usually because they are the most commonly cited, and are frequently published. The data are not always consistent with the national authorities' definitions and those published in the OECD's quarterly and annual publication *Labour Force Statistics* (LFS). Exceptions are noted below.

For most countries the source of these data is a labour force survey of a sample of households in which both components of the unemployment rate (UNR), unemployment levels (UN) and labour force (LF), are measured simultaneously. For the remaining countries, one of the components of the identity LF = UN + ET (employment) is derived from the other two, which are generally estimated from different sources. The term "total" is used with reference to labour force and employment to indicate that all armed forces (conscripts as well as professional military) are included. In some countries (indicated below), employment and labour force include professional military, but exclude conscripts. "Civilian" labour force and employment data exclude all military personnel. Participation rates are calculated as the labour force divided by the total working-age population, where the count of the working-age population, the labour force, the employed and the unemployed is normally restricted to individuals 16 through 64 years of age. Unless otherwise specified, annual data refer to the average of either monthly or quarterly data; semiannual data shown for the seven largest countries are averages of monthly or quarterly seasonally-adjusted figures.

United States

Unemployment, civilian employment and civilian labour force are from the monthly *Current Population Survey* of persons aged 16 and over. The data are seasonally-adjusted by the Bureau of Labour Statistics. All layoffs are included in unemployment. Since January 1994, the data have been based on a new survey methodology, and are not directly comparable with data for previous years. For a full discussion of the implications of the change see Box 1 in the *OECD Economic Survey of the United States* (November 1994).

Japan

Unemployment, employment and labour force (including national "self-defence" forces) are from the monthly Labour Force Survey of persons aged 15 and over. The data are seasonally adjusted by the OECD Secretariat.

Germany

Data on employment (GDP basis) and unemployment are based on national accounts statistics. The labour force is derived as the sum of total employment (dependent and self-employed) and unemployment. Seasonal adjustment is done by the OECD Secretariat. Up to 1991, data refer to western Germany only.

France

INSEE provides the OECD with quarterly series on civilian employment. They are seasonally adjusted by the OECD and an interpolated annual series of the armed forces is added in order to arrive at total employment. Monthly seasonally-adjusted unemployment data corresponding to ILO guidelines are also sent by INSEE. The labour force is the sum of total employment and unemployment.

Italy

Employment, unemployment and labour force are from the quarterly Labour Force Survey of persons aged 15 and over. The definitions of unemployment and the labour force were revised in 1986 and in 1992 to be more in line with ILO and Eurostat guidelines. The national Labour Force Survey data are adjusted by the OECD for seasonal variations and for statistical breaks since 1981. The employment figures from the quarterly Labour Force Survey differ from those in the national accounts source, *Conti Economici Trimestrali,* ISTAT. The latter are used for derived variables such as labour productivity and labour costs. A standard labour unit has been defined which measures the average volume of work carried out by a full-time worker.

United Kingdom

Seasonally-adjusted unemployment, total employment and total labour force (working population) are from the *Labour*

Market Trends published by the Office for National Statistics. The unemployment figures refer to those claiming unemployment related benefits at Employment Service Offices. They exclude students seeking vacation work and those persons temporarily stopped from work. Employment data are based on quarterly surveys of employers and households. Self-employment is derived from the 1981 Census of Population and the Labour Force Surveys; it excludes unpaid family workers. Total employment equals the sum of employees, participants in work-related government training programmes, self-employment and the armed forces. The national unemployment rate refers to unemployed claimants aged 18 and over as a percentage of the total labour force.

Canada

Unemployment, civilian employment and civilian labour force are from the monthly Labour Force Survey of persons aged 15 and over. Unemployment also includes persons who, while not actively looking for work in the preceding four weeks, were available for work, but were on temporary layoff or had a new job to start in four weeks or less. The data are seasonally adjusted by the national authorities.

Australia

Data for unemployment, employment and the labour force are taken from the monthly Household Labour Force Survey. Though the survey covers persons aged 15 and over, the OECD Secretariat extracts and publishes data based on persons aged 16 to 64, in order to provide for comparability with other countries. Only persons laid-off for less than four weeks (because of bad weather or plant breakdown) are included among the employed; all other layoffs are considered as unemployed or out of the labour force. The national unemployment rate is calculated with reference to the civilian labour force.

Austria

Data on unemployment and employment are from the labour office. The unemployment series is corrected for statistical breaks and follows ILO definitions. The labour force is derived as the sum of dependent employment, self-employment and unemployment.

Belgium

Data on unemployment are based on administrative sources, complemented by surveys. They refer to end-of-June, and comprise fully unemployed persons entitled to benefits, other unemployed obliged to register and voluntarily registered persons. The mid-year estimate of the total labour force comprises domestic employment (including all armed forces), plus unemployment.

Czech Republic

From the first quarter of 1993, employment data refer to the labour force survey. The survey is conducted every week and the sample undergoes a rotation of one-fifth of the panel every quarter. Unemployment data refer to the unemployed registered at labour offices. The labour force is derived from the identity LF = ET + UN.

Denmark

Unemployment refers to the registered unemployed aged 16 to 66 years and includes the partially unemployed converted to full-time equivalents. Unemployment and total employment figures, corresponding to national accounts concepts, are compiled from the Danish Central Register of Labour Market Statistics (CRAM). Total labour force is then derived from the identity LF = ET + UN. The national rate refers to all registered unemployed expressed as a percentage of the CRAM estimate of total labour force. The *OECD Economic Outlook* statistics differ from those published in LFS, which are based on the spring Labour Force Survey.

Finland

Unemployment, civilian employment and civilian labour force are from the monthly Labour Force Survey of persons aged 15 to 74. The labour force concept underlying the national unemployment rate includes the professional military but excludes conscripts. Unemployment figures exclude persons over the age of 56 receiving a preretirement unemployment pension and not actively seeking work.

Greece

Unemployment, total employment and total labour force are compiled from the annual Labour Force Survey. The figures are completed or revised in line with the latest census results. All data refer to the second quarter of each year.

Iceland

The unemployed are registrations. Civilian employment, expressed in person-years (that is, full-time equivalents), is compiled from accident insurance statistics. The labour force is derived from the identity LF = ET + UN.

Ireland

Unemployment, total employment and total labour force figures are derived from the annual Labour Force Survey and relate to mid-April of each year. The national unemployment rate is calculated by the Irish Statistical Agency in line with ILO and Eurostat guidelines.

Luxembourg

National employment excludes non-resident persons working in Luxembourg and includes nationals working over the border and international civil servants. Data are those provided by the Administration de l'emploi and the national statistical agency (STATEC). Unemployment refers to those registered at the employment agencies and resident in Luxembourg. The labour force is calculated as the sum of national employment and unemployment.

Mexico

Data for unemployment, total employment, labour force and the working-age population are from the National Survey of Urban Employment covering in 1995 39 urban areas, *i.e.* some 15.5 million persons, compared to 35.5 million in the 1995 National Employment Survey. The sample of the Urban Survey has been enlarged over the years: it covered 16 urban areas in 1987, increasing to 32 urban areas in January 1992,

34 in July of the same year; 35 in April 1993, 36 in July and 37 in October of that year; 38 in July 1994, 39 in October of that year; 41 as from January 1996. The data are rebased before 1992 using growth rates from the constant sample of the 16 main urban areas. As of 1993, growth rates of the labour market variables reflect a growing sample size. Data from the Urban and National Employment Surveys also differ from those in the national accounts. The latter, which put employment around 23 million in 1993, records the number of dependent jobs in the economy; it is used to derive labour costs. Data for general government employees are from the national accounts. Self-employment is derived as the difference between total employment from the National Employment Surveys of 1988, 1991, 1993 and 1995 – interpolated for the years between two successive surveys – and dependent employment from the national accounts.

Netherlands

Unemployment refers to persons registered at employment offices who do not work at all or who work fewer than 12 hours per week, and who are available for paid work for at least 12 hours per week. The series is based on the monthly survey undertaken by the Central Bureau of Statistics. Total employment is taken from the national Labour Force Survey and refers to persons aged between 15-64 and working more than 12 hours per week. The total labour force is then derived from the identity LF = ET + UN. The employment figures from the Labour Force Survey differ from those in the national accounts source. The latter, expressed in full-time equivalents, are used for derived variables such as labour productivity and labour costs.

New Zealand

Data on unemployment, employment and the labour force are from the Household Labour Force Survey of persons aged 15 and above. Data prior to 1986 have been chain-linked with the new series.

Norway

Data on unemployment, employment and labour force are taken from the Quarterly Labour Force Survey of persons aged 16 to 74. The seasonally-adjusted rate of unemployment is calculated by the OECD Secretariat on the basis of national aggregate statistics, and differs somewhat from the corresponding figure published by the Central Bureau of Statistics, Oslo, which is based on an aggregation of labour force statistics seasonally-adjusted at the regional and occupational levels.

Portugal

Unemployment, civilian employment and civilian labour force are derived from the quarterly Labour Force Survey of persons aged 14 and over. There are breaks in the series in 1973/74, 1982/83 and 1991/92. The data shown are not seasonally adjusted and refer to continental Portugal; the professional army is included, conscripts are excluded. Figures reported in the *Economic Outlook* adopt the narrow definition of unemployment which applies a one-month reference period for job search.

Spain

Unemployment, employment and labour force are from the quarterly Labour Force Survey of persons aged 16 and over. Permanent inmates at institutions, notably religious establishments, are excluded from the survey. Temporary inmates are included in their original household (approximately 1 per cent of inmates are missed by the survey) as are professional military. Prior to 1988, data exclude the provinces of Ceuta and Melilla. Starting in 1995, labour force survey data is adjusted in line with the results of the 1991 census.

Sweden

Unemployment and employment data are from the monthly Labour Force Survey of persons aged 16 to 64. There is a break in the series in 1986. The labour force is derived from the identity LF = ET + UN. Both the numerator and the denominator of the national unemployment rate and the Swedish labour force data published in LFS are based on the results of the Labour Force Survey.

Switzerland

Unemployment refers to the monthly registered unemployed. Civilian employment figures, including permanent military personnel, are established using the labour force survey and the central register of foreigners. The labour force is derived from the identity LF = ET + UN.

Turkey

In 1989, the State Planning Organisation revised the labour market statistics from 1978 onwards. The new series on civilian employment, civilian labour force and unemployment are based on the provisional results of the 1988 Household Labour Force Survey and sectoral value-added and productivity statistics. Since 1988, labour market statistics are derived from the biannual household Labour Force Surveys. Annual figures refer to the results of the October surveys.

COST AND PRICE DATA

Average compensation (Annex Table 12)

Average compensation is calculated as wage and non-wage labour costs, as estimated in the national accounts, per employed person.

Capital income shares and rates of return on capital
(Annex Tables 24 and 25)

The estimates of capital income are derived from OECD's *National Accounts* statistics. They refer to income generated from production, and hence exclude inflation gains and losses accruing to enterprises from holdings of tangible and financial assets and liabilities. The difference between value-added calculated at factor cost (*i.e.* excluding net indirect taxes) and labour income – the gross operating surplus of enterprises – is taken as the measure of income from capital. A labour income componentequal to average business-sector compensation has been imputed to self-employed persons after excluding from the latter unpaid family workers. For those countries where data on numbers of unpaid family workers are not available either for the whole or part of the period covered (see notes to the tables), the bias due to this inclusion is unlikely to be significant.

An adjustment to exclude the operating surplus of the housing sector has not been made owing to the paucity of data; however, estimates based on available data suggest that excluding this item might typically reduce capital income shares by around 6 percentage points, and the estimated rates of return on capital by around 3 percentage points.

The capital stock estimates which are used to compute the rates of return cover only assets included in non-residential gross fixed capital formation and hence exclude dwellings, inventories, monetary working capital, land and natural resources. The historical capital stock data are obtained from national sources whenever possible. For the projection period they have been extrapolated using the perpetual inventory method, which involves accumulating past investment and dropping out assets at the end of their service lives.

Evaluation of the capital stock is based on replacement cost. It should be noted that cross-country differences exist in respect to the assumed service lives of the different capital assets (structures and plant/equipment) and the deflation methods applied.[2]

USE OF NATIONAL STATISTICS

National accounts

The figures shown in the country tables on Demand and Output follow, in general, the OECD's *Standardised System*[3] definitions. One important deviation from the *Standardised System* is the line "public investment" which includes, whenever possible, fixed capital formation by both general government and government-owned and controlled enterprises. The latter's definition and coverage may vary as between countries.

a) *United States*

Official quarterly national accounts, published by the Bureau of Economic Analysis of the US Department of Commerce, are available through the first quarter of 1996. The OECD Secretariat uses the chain-type measures of real output and prices. The appropriation account for households is based on OECD definitions and differs slightly from official US figures. Briefly, OECD disposable income equals US disposable income minus consumer interest payments and net foreign transfers. OECD Secretariat estimates of the savings ratio may thus differ by one- or two-tenths of a percentage point from estimates based on the official US definition.

b) *Japan*

Annual and quarterly national accounts are published by the Economic Planning Agency. Figures from the second quarter of 1995 to the fourth quarter of 1995 are preliminary estimates published by the Economic Planning Agency.

c) *Germany*

The historical figures for Germany are based on official data published by the Statistisches Bundesamt. Historical quarterly components of demand and GDP for western Germany are available through the fourth quarter of 1994. National accounts data for eastern Germany are available from the third quarter of 1990 through the fourth quarter of 1994. National accounts for unified Germany are available from the third quarter of 1990 through the fourth quarter of 1995. Seasonal adjustment of unified German accounts follows the method of the Bundesbank but without adjustment for working days.

d) *France*

Quarterly accounts based on the *Enlarged System of National Accounts* (ESNA) are available through the fourth quarter of 1995. Industrial production figures refer to the official quarterly index of industrial production and not to the value added in the industrial sector.

e) *Italy*

The definitions used are those of the OECD's *System of National Accounts*. Half-yearly series, in constant 1985 prices, through the second half of 1995, are based on quarterly national accounts published by the *Istituto Centrale di Statistica* (ISTAT).

f) *United Kingdom*

National accounts data through the fourth quarter of 1995 are taken from *Economic Trends,* CSO. The three official estimates of GDP, output, expenditure and income are averaged to yield a "compromise" GDP estimate.

g) *Canada*

Official quarterly national accounts through the fourth quarter of 1995 are published by Statistics Canada. Over the projection period, the residual error is assumed to remain constant from the second half of 1995.

Current statistics

Unless otherwise stated, all the national statistics quoted in the *OECD Economic Outlook* are taken from the *Main Economic Indicators* (MEI) published monthly by the OECD Secretariat. Starting in September 1967, supplements to MEI have been published describing in detail the sources and methods of these statistics. The following notes are therefore confined to some methodological points of special importance for the understanding of the text.

Index of industrial production

The figures shown include, as far as possible, mining, manufacturing and public utilities (electricity, gas and water), but exclude construction. The exact coverage, the weighting system and the methods of calculation vary from country to country but the divergences are less important than in the case of the price and the wage indices.[4] With the exception of certain smaller countries, the indices are seasonally adjusted by national statistical offices using different methods usually derived from the US Bureau of the Census Method II.

Seasonal adjustment

Some of the series used have been seasonally adjusted, notably in the area of foreign trade but also in some cases for industrial production, unemployment and consumer prices. The method used is the X-11 variant of the US Bureau of the Census Method as programmed for computer use by the Agency. (Further details may be found in Technical Paper No. 15 of the Bureau of the Census.) Where appropriate, series are also corrected for calendar variations.

CALCULATION AND DEFINITION OF SEMIANNUAL GROWTH RATES

Although quarterly and higher frequency data are commonly shown in the *OECD Economic Outlook* for some countries and variables, most of the data reported are either annual or semiannual and are presented in terms of percentage growth rates. The calculation and presentation of growth rate information, particularly that relating to semiannual series, is sometimes a source of confusion and the following paragraphs therefore provide specific clarification on the measurement principles involved.

Annual growth rates are commonly defined as the percentage change in a variable between two consecutive years. Similarly, semiannual growth rates can be calculated as the percentage changes between two consecutive half-years. It is often convenient, however, to convert such measures of semiannual growth into a form which is more readily comparable with annual growth figures, *i.e.* to express them at *annual rates*. Mathematically, this is done by squaring the semiannual growth factor (which is obtained by dividing the current value of a variable by its value in the preceding half year), subtracting unity and multiplying by 100. In effect, the semiannual growth rate is *compounded* over two half-years to provide the annual rate of growth which would result from the continuation of the semiannual rate of growth over a one-year period.

In terms of simple algebra, if a variable has a value of X_t in one half-year and X_{t+1} in the next, the formula for the semiannual rate of growth for period $t + 1$, expressed at an *annual rate,* is given by:

$$g(t + 1) = [(X_{t+1}/X_t)^2 - 1.0]*100$$

For example, if the statistics for the Industrial Production index in the United Kingdom are as follows:

	1988		1989		1990	
	I	II	I	II	I	II
Industrial production (1985 = 100 basis)	111.7	116.4	118.8	119.0	119.9	116.7

Given the above formula, the growth between the first and second halves of 1989 expressed at an *annual rate,* is computed as $[(119.0/118.8)^2 - 1.0]*100$, or 0.3 per cent. Corresponding rates of growth for each of the years and half-years in question are, on a similar basis, as follows:

	1989	1990	1988		1989		1990	
			I	II	I	II	I	II
Industrial production (growth rates)	4.3	−0.5	5.2	8.6	4.2	0.3	1.5	−5.3

Such a numerical example helps illustrate the usefulness of semiannual growth rates in highlighting movements in an economic variable during the course of a year. It also demonstrates that annual growth rates for a specific year do not usually correspond to the average of the semiannual growth rates *during* that year. In the above example, the annual rate of growth for 1989, at 4.3 per cent, is higher than the average of the two semiannual rates of growth experienced during 1989, at 2.2 per cent. This is because year-on-year rates of growth are influenced by the levels of a variable in both halves of the preceding year, whereas the average of the corresponding two semiannual rates are influenced only by the level achieved in the second half of the preceding year. This feature is known as a "carry over" effect.

There is however a useful rule of thumb which can be used to approximately convert semiannual rates of growth to corresponding year-on-year growth rates. Known as the "quarter-half-quarter" rule, this approximates the year-on-year growth rate by weighting together the semiannual growth rates for the second semester of the preceding year and those of the first and second semesters of the year in question, with weights of one quarter, one half and one quarter, respectively. Applying this rule to the above example gives annual rates of growth for 1989 and 1990 of 4.3 per cent (*i.e.* 8.6/4 + 4.2/2 + 0.3/4) and −0.5 per cent (*i.e.* 0.3/4 + 1.5/2 − 5.3/4), respectively, coinciding with the actual measured rates. In using this rule, it is important to bear in mind that some degree of approximation is involved, particularly where large variations in semiannual growth rates are concerned.

Other measures of growth rates are, of course, used in commenting and presenting economic statistics. Quarter-on-quarter growth rates are often referred to, which may in turn be expressed at annual rates, by raising the quarterly growth factor to the power four, subtracting unity and multiplying by 100. Analogous measures also exist for monthly rates of growth and inflation, expressed also at annual rates. In some countries, notably the United States, public interest may also focus on growth rates between the final quarters of successive years, commonly referred to as the growth rate *in* the year in question. In others, growth rates measured in relation to the corresponding month, quarter or semester of the previous year are also commonly used and referred to as "year-on-year" growth rates.

NOTES

1. Descriptions of the scope, structure and properties of the OECD Secretariat's INTERLINK model and the underlying empirical studies are given by Richardson (1988), OECD (1988), and associated *OECD Economics Department Working Papers.*
2. A full description of the sources and methods for the capital stock data is contained in Keese *et al.* (1991).
3. For detailed definitions, see United Nations, *A System of National Accounts,* New York, 1968.
4. A quarterly supplement to OECD's *Main Economic Indicators* provides an internationally comparable selection of industrial output indices for branches and a number of categories.

REFERENCES

Giorno C., P. Richardson, D. Roseveare, P. van den Noord (1995), "Potential output, output gaps and structural budget balances", *OECD Economic Studies,* No. 24, 1995/1.

Keese, M., G. Salou and P. Richardson (1991), "The measurement of output and factors of production for the business sector in OECD countries", *OECD Department of Economics and Statistics Working Papers,* No. 99.

OECD (1988), "OECD INTERLINK system, Reference Manual" (January).

Richardson, P. (1988), "The structure and simulation properties of OECD's INTERLINK model", *OECD Economic Studies,* No. 10 (Spring).

MAIN SALES OUTLETS OF OECD PUBLICATIONS
PRINCIPAUX POINTS DE VENTE DES PUBLICATIONS DE L'OCDE

ARGENTINA – ARGENTINE
Carlos Hirsch S.R.L.
Galería Güemes, Florida 165, 4° Piso
1333 Buenos Aires   Tel. (1) 331.1787 y 331.2391
Telefax: (1) 331.1787

AUSTRALIA – AUSTRALIE
D.A. Information Services
648 Whitehorse Road, P.O.B 163
Mitcham, Victoria 3132   Tel. (03) 9210.7777
Telefax: (03) 9210.7788

AUSTRIA – AUTRICHE
Gerold & Co.
Graben 31
Wien I   Tel. (0222) 533.50.14
Telefax: (0222) 512.47.31.29

BELGIUM – BELGIQUE
Jean De Lannoy
Avenue du Roi 202 Koningslaan
B-1060 Bruxelles   Tel. (02) 538.51.69/538.08.41
Telefax: (02) 538.08.41

CANADA
Renouf Publishing Company Ltd.
1294 Algoma Road
Ottawa, ON K1B 3W8   Tel. (613) 741.4333
Telefax: (613) 741.5439
Stores:
61 Sparks Street
Ottawa, ON K1P 5R1   Tel. (613) 238.8985
12 Adelaide Street West
Toronto, ON M5H 1L6   Tel. (416) 363.3171
Telefax: (416)363.59.63

Les Éditions La Liberté Inc.
3020 Chemin Sainte-Foy
Sainte-Foy, PQ G1X 3V6   Tel. (418) 658.3763
Telefax: (418) 658.3763

Federal Publications Inc.
165 University Avenue, Suite 701
Toronto, ON M5H 3B8   Tel. (416) 860.1611
Telefax: (416) 860.1608

Les Publications Fédérales
1185 Université
Montréal, QC H3B 3A7   Tel. (514) 954.1633
Telefax: (514) 954.1635

CHINA – CHINE
China National Publications Import
Export Corporation (CNPIEC)
16 Gongti E. Road, Chaoyang District
P.O. Box 88 or 50
Beijing 100704 PR   Tel. (01) 506.6688
Telefax: (01) 506.3101

CHINESE TAIPEI – TAIPEI CHINOIS
Good Faith Worldwide Int'l. Co. Ltd.
9th Floor, No. 118, Sec. 2
Chung Hsiao E. Road
Taipei   Tel. (02) 391.7396/391.7397
Telefax: (02) 394.9176

**CZECH REPUBLIC –
RÉPUBLIQUE TCHÈQUE**
Artia Pegas Press Ltd.
Narodni Trida 25
POB 825
111 21 Praha 1   Tel. (2) 242 246 04
Telefax: (2) 242 278 72

DENMARK – DANEMARK
Munksgaard Book and Subscription Service
35, Nørre Søgade, P.O. Box 2148
DK-1016 København K   Tel. (33) 12.85.70
Telefax: (33) 12.93.87

EGYPT – ÉGYPTE
Middle East Observer
41 Sherif Street
Cairo   Tel. 392.6919
Telefax: 360-6804

FINLAND – FINLANDE
Akateeminen Kirjakauppa
Keskuskatu 1, P.O. Box 128
00100 Helsinki

Subscription Services/Agence d'abonnements :
P.O. Box 23
00371 Helsinki   Tel. (358 0) 121 4416
Telefax: (358 0) 121.4450

FRANCE
OECD/OCDE
Mail Orders/Commandes par correspondance :
2, rue André-Pascal
75775 Paris Cedex 16   Tel. (33-1) 45.24.82.00
Telefax: (33-1) 49.10.42.76
Telex: 640048 OCDE
Internet: Compte.PUBSINQ @ oecd.org
Orders via Minitel, France only/
Commandes par Minitel, France exclusivement :
36 15 OCDE

OECD Bookshop/Librairie de l'OCDE :
33, rue Octave-Feuillet
75016 Paris   Tel. (33-1) 45.24.81.81
(33-1) 45.24.81.67
Dawson
B.P. 40
91121 Palaiseau Cedex   Tel. 69.10.47.00
Telefax: 64.54.83.26

Documentation Française
29, quai Voltaire
75007 Paris   Tel. 40.15.70.00

Economica
49, rue Héricart
75015 Paris   Tel. 45.78.12.92
Telefax: 40.58.15.70

Gibert Jeune (Droit-Économie)
6, place Saint-Michel
75006 Paris   Tel. 43.25.91.19

Librairie du Commerce International
10, avenue d'Iéna
75016 Paris   Tel. 40.73.34.60

Librairie Dunod
Université Paris-Dauphine
Place du Maréchal-de-Lattre-de-Tassigny
75016 Paris   Tel. 44.05.40.13

Librairie Lavoisier
11, rue Lavoisier
75008 Paris   Tel. 42.65.39.95

Librairie des Sciences Politiques
30, rue Saint-Guillaume
75007 Paris   Tel. 45.48.36.02

P.U.F.
49, boulevard Saint-Michel
75005 Paris   Tel. 43.25.83.40

Librairie de l'Université
12a, rue Nazareth
13100 Aix-en-Provence   Tel. (16) 42.26.18.08

Documentation Française
165, rue Garibaldi
69003 Lyon   Tel. (16) 78.63.32.23

Librairie Decitre
29, place Bellecour
69002 Lyon   Tel. (16) 72.40.54.54

Librairie Sauramps
Le Triangle
34967 Montpellier Cedex 2 Tel. (16) 67.58.85.15
Telefax: (16) 67.58.27.36

A la Sorbonne Actual
23, rue de l'Hôtel-des-Postes
06000 Nice   Tel. (16) 93.13.77.75
Telefax: (16) 93.80.75.69

GERMANY – ALLEMAGNE
OECD Publications and Information Centre
August-Bebel-Allee 6
D-53175 Bonn   Tel. (0228) 959.120
Telefax: (0228) 959.12.17

GREECE – GRÈCE
Librairie Kauffmann
Mavrokordatou 9
106 78 Athens   Tel. (01) 32.55.321
Telefax: (01) 32.30.320

HONG-KONG
Swindon Book Co. Ltd.
Astoria Bldg. 3F
34 Ashley Road, Tsimshatsui
Kowloon, Hong Kong   Tel. 2376.2062
Telefax: 2376.0685

HUNGARY – HONGRIE
Euro Info Service
Margitsziget, Európa Ház
1138 Budapest   Tel. (1) 111.62.16
Telefax: (1) 111.60.61

ICELAND – ISLANDE
Mál Mog Menning
Laugavegi 18, Pósthólf 392
121 Reykjavik   Tel. (1) 552.4240
Telefax: (1) 562.3523

INDIA – INDE
Oxford Book and Stationery Co.
Scindia House
New Delhi 110001   Tel. (11) 331.5896/5308
Telefax: (11) 332.5993
17 Park Street
Calcutta 700016   Tel. 240832

INDONESIA – INDONÉSIE
Pdii-Lipi
P.O. Box 4298
Jakarta 12042   Tel. (21) 573.34.67
Telefax: (21) 573.34.67

IRELAND – IRLANDE
Government Supplies Agency
Publications Section
4/5 Harcourt Road
Dublin 2   Tel. 661.31.11
Telefax: 475.27.60

ISRAEL – ISRAËL
Praedicta
5 Shatner Street
P.O. Box 34030
Jerusalem 91430   Tel. (2) 52.84.90/1/2
Telefax: (2) 52.84.93

R.O.Y. International
P.O. Box 13056
Tel Aviv 61130   Tel. (3) 546 1423
Telefax: (3) 546 1442

Palestinian Authority/Middle East:
INDEX Information Services
P.O.B. 19502
Jerusalem   Tel. (2) 27.12.19
Telefax: (2) 27.16.34

ITALY – ITALIE
Libreria Commissionaria Sansoni
Via Duca di Calabria 1/1
50125 Firenze   Tel. (055) 64.54.15
Telefax: (055) 64.12.57
Via Bartolini 29
20155 Milano   Tel. (02) 36.50.83

Editrice e Libreria Herder
Piazza Montecitorio 120
00186 Roma   Tel. 679.46.28
                              Telefax: 678.47.51

Libreria Hoepli
Via Hoepli 5
20121 Milano   Tel. (02) 86.54.46
                              Telefax: (02) 805.28.86

Libreria Scientifica
Dott. Lucio de Biasio 'Aeiou'
Via Coronelli, 6
20146 Milano   Tel. (02) 48.95.45.52
                              Telefax: (02) 48.95.45.48

JAPAN – JAPON
OECD Publications and Information Centre
Landic Akasaka Building
2-3-4 Akasaka, Minato-ku
Tokyo 107   Tel. (81.3) 3586.2016
                              Telefax: (81.3) 3584.7929

KOREA – CORÉE
Kyobo Book Centre Co. Ltd.
P.O. Box 1658, Kwang Hwa Moon
Seoul   Tel. 730.78.91
                              Telefax: 735.00.30

MALAYSIA – MALAISIE
University of Malaya Bookshop
University of Malaya
P.O. Box 1127, Jalan Pantai Baru
59700 Kuala Lumpur
Malaysia   Tel. 756.5000/756.5425
                              Telefax: 756.3246

MEXICO – MEXIQUE
OECD Publications and Information Centre
Edificio INFOTEC
Av. San Fernando no. 37
Col. Toriello Guerra
Tlalpan C.P. 14050
Mexico D.F.
          Tel. (525) 606 00 11 Extension 100
                    Fax: (525) 606 13 07

Revistas y Periodicos Internacionales S.A. de C.V.
Florencia 57 - 1004
Mexico, D.F. 06600   Tel. 207.81.00
                              Telefax: 208.39.79

NETHERLANDS – PAYS-BAS
SDU Uitgeverij Plantijnstraat
Externe Fondsen
Postbus 20014
2500 EA's-Gravenhage   Tel. (070) 37.89.880
Voor bestellingen: Telefax: (070) 34.75.778

NEW ZEALAND – NOUVELLE-ZÉLANDE
GPLegislation Services
P.O. Box 12418
Thorndon, Wellington   Tel. (04) 496.5655
                              Telefax: (04) 496.5698

NORWAY – NORVÈGE
NIC INFO A/S
Bertrand Narvesens vei 2
P.O. Box 6512 Etterstad
0606 Oslo 6   Tel. (022) 57.33.00
                              Telefax: (022) 68.19.01

PAKISTAN
Mirza Book Agency
65 Shahrah Quaid-E-Azam
Lahore 54000   Tel. (42) 353.601
                              Telefax: (42) 231.730

PHILIPPINE – PHILIPPINES
International Booksource Center Inc.
Rm 179/920 Cityland 10 Condo Tower 2
HV dela Costa Ext cor Valero St.
Makati Metro Manila   Tel. (632) 817 9676
                              Telefax: (632) 817 1741

POLAND – POLOGNE
Ars Polona
00-950 Warszawa
Krakowskie Przedmieácie 7   Tel. (22) 264760
                              Telefax: (22) 268673

PORTUGAL
Livraria Portugal
Rua do Carmo 70-74
Apart. 2681
1200 Lisboa   Tel. (01) 347.49.82/5
                              Telefax: (01) 347.02.64

SINGAPORE – SINGAPOUR
Gower Asia Pacific Pte Ltd.
Golden Wheel Building
41, Kallang Pudding Road, No. 04-03
Singapore 1334   Tel. 741.5166
                              Telefax: 742.9356

SPAIN – ESPAGNE
Mundi-Prensa Libros S.A.
Castelló 37, Apartado 1223
Madrid 28001   Tel. (91) 431.33.99
                              Telefax: (91) 575.39.98

Mundi-Prensa Barcelona
Consell de Cent No. 391
08009 – Barcelona   Tel. (93) 488.34.92
                              Telefax: (93) 487.76.59

Llibreria de la Generalitat
Palau Moja
Rambla dels Estudis, 118
08002 – Barcelona
               (Subscripcions) Tel. (93) 318.80.12
               (Publicacions) Tel. (93) 302.67.23
                              Telefax: (93) 412.18.54

SRI LANKA
Centre for Policy Research
c/o Colombo Agencies Ltd.
No. 300-304, Galle Road
Colombo 3   Tel. (1) 574240, 573551-2
                              Telefax: (1) 575394, 510711

SWEDEN – SUÈDE
CE Fritzes AB
S–106 47 Stockholm   Tel. (08) 690.90.90
                              Telefax: (08) 20.50.21

Subscription Agency/Agence d'abonnements :
Wennergren-Williams Info AB
P.O. Box 1305
171 25 Solna   Tel. (08) 705.97.50
                              Telefax: (08) 27.00.71

SWITZERLAND – SUISSE
Maditec S.A. (Books and Periodicals - Livres
et périodiques)
Chemin des Palettes 4
Case postale 266
1020 Renens VD 1   Tel. (021) 635.08.65
                              Telefax: (021) 635.07.80

Librairie Payot S.A.
4, place Pépinet
CP 3212
1002 Lausanne   Tel. (021) 320.25.11
                              Telefax: (021) 320.25.14

Librairie Unilivres
6, rue de Candolle
1205 Genève   Tel. (022) 320.26.23
                              Telefax: (022) 329.73.18

Subscription Agency/Agence d'abonnements :
Dynapresse Marketing S.A.
38, avenue Vibert
1227 Carouge   Tel. (022) 308.07.89
                              Telefax: (022) 308.07.99

See also – Voir aussi :
OECD Publications and Information Centre
August-Bebel-Allee 6
D-53175 Bonn (Germany)   Tel. (0228) 959.120
                              Telefax: (0228) 959.12.17

THAILAND – THAÏLANDE
Suksit Siam Co. Ltd.
113, 115 Fuang Nakhon Rd.
Opp. Wat Rajbopith
Bangkok 10200   Tel. (662) 225.9531/2
                              Telefax: (662) 222.5188

TUNISIA – TUNISIE
Grande Librairie Spécialisée
Fendri Ali
Avenue Haffouz Imm El-Intilaka
Bloc B 1 Sfax 3000   Tel. (216-4) 296 855
                              Telefax: (216-4) 298.270

TURKEY – TURQUIE
Kültür Yayinlari Is-Türk Ltd. Sti.
Atatürk Bulvari No. 191/Kat 13
Kavaklidere/Ankara
                Tel. (312) 428.11.40 Ext. 2458
                              Telefax: (312) 417 24 90
Dolmabahce Cad. No. 29
Besiktas/Istanbul   Tel. (212) 260 7188

UNITED KINGDOM – ROYAUME-UNI
HMSO
Gen. enquiries   Tel. (171) 873 8242
Postal orders only:
P.O. Box 276, London SW8 5DT
Personal Callers HMSO Bookshop
49 High Holborn, London WC1V 6HB
                              Telefax: (171) 873 8416
Branches at: Belfast, Birmingham, Bristol,
Edinburgh, Manchester

UNITED STATES – ÉTATS-UNIS
OECD Publications and Information Center
2001 L Street N.W., Suite 650
Washington, D.C. 20036-4922 Tel. (202) 785.6323
                              Telefax: (202) 785.0350

Subscriptions to OECD periodicals may also be
placed through main subscription agencies.

Les abonnements aux publications périodiques de
l'OCDE peuvent être souscrits auprès des
principales agences d'abonnement.

Orders and inquiries from countries where Distributors have not yet been appointed should be sent to:
OECD Publications Service, 2, rue André-Pascal,
75775 Paris Cedex 16, France.

Les commandes provenant de pays où l'OCDE n'a
pas encore désigné de distributeur peuvent être
adressées à : OCDE, Service des Publications,
2, rue André-Pascal, 75775 Paris Cedex 16, France.

1-1996

OECD PUBLICATIONS, 2, rue André-Pascal, 75775 PARIS CEDEX 16
PRINTED IN FRANCE
(12 96 59 1) ISBN 92-64-14713-6 – No. 48705 1996
ISSN 0474-5574

OECD ECONOMIC OUTLOOK

Statistics and projections on microcomputer diskette

The full set of historical time series data and projections underlying the *OECD Economic Outlook* is regularly available on microcomputer diskette at the same time as its publication. A basic version of the *OECD Economic Outlook* diskette contains approximately 3 500 macroeconomic time series for OECD countries and non-OECD zones, beginning in 1980 and extending to the end of the published forecast horizon. In addition, the *OECD Economic Outlook Reference Supplement* contains data for most OECD countries and the majority of National Accounts and other country-specific statistics, starting as early as 1960. This supplement provides data in a form which is fully compatible with other *OECD Economic Outlook* files, permitting a wide variety of analyses and statistical applications, *e.g.* for modelling and longer-term comparative and graphical analyses.

The general subject and country coverage for both versions are as follows:

Subject coverage

- Gross national product and its components
- Government and households appropriation accounts
- Fiscal and monetary indicators
- Labour market and supply indicators
- Wages, prices and profitability
- International trade and payments

Country coverage

- 26 OECD countries
- OECD area aggregations
- Non-OECD zones

Prices and subscription information

Annual subscription, two issues per year, in June and December:

including *Reference Supplement:*	£375	US$620	FF 3 400	DM 1 030
excluding *Reference Supplement:*	£250	US$410	FF 2 250	DM 680

Subscriptions, which also include the printed version of the *OECD Economic Outlook,* may be made at any time of the year. For special conditions (Academics, Government Agencies, and Commercial Redistribution Rights) contact OECD Publications.

Diskette format

Data are provided on 3½-inch diskettes suitable for IBM PC-compatible microcomputers. These include a simple programme to translate these series into a variety of formats which can be read and used by most PC software packages.

Send your order to:

OECD Publications
2, rue André-Pascal
75775 Paris Cedex 16
FRANCE

Other OECD Statistical Series on Diskette

International Trade and Competitiveness Indicators (ITCI)

The *International Trade and Competitiveness Indicators* statistical series are designed for use in a wide range of empirical analyses related to the international trade performance of OECD Member countries. The set of diskettes includes principal series for external trade classified by four broad SITC commodity groups (basic materials, food, fuels and manufactures) in nominal and constant-price value terms, along with corresponding price deflators, market shares and competitiveness indicators. These statistics are available in a consistent quarterly form for OECD countries. The length of individual series is determined by the availability of individual country source information, but in general all series are available from 1975 onwards.

ITCI diskettes are accompanied by relevant user instructions and detailed Sources and Methods material based upon *Working Paper*, No. 120. The set of diskettes is updated to take account of new information and data revisions on a twice-yearly basis, at an annual subscription rate of £250, US$410, FF 2 250, DM 680.

Business Sector Data Base (BSDB)

The *Business Sector Data Base* contains data for 25 OECD Member countries related to business-sector value added, employment, investment, factor prices and capital stocks, from 1960 to the present day, and are stored in quarterly form. The underlying data base was developed for use in the analysis of production and supply issues in the context of the OECD's regular surveys and assessments, and related empirical studies.

The BSDB diskettes are accompanied by relevant user instructions and detailed Sources and Methods material, based upon *Working Paper*, No. 99. The BSDB is available in two issues per year, with an annual subscription of £275, US$455, FF 2 500, DM 755.

Fiscal Positions and Business Cycles (FPBC)

The **Fiscal Positions and Business Cycles** (FPBC) diskettes contain detailed quantitative information on potential output and output gaps, on actual and cyclically-adjusted government revenues, outlays and balances, and on government financial liabilities (including debt series consistent with the Maastricht criterion). Historical annual data from 1970 onwards and the projections of the *OECD Economic Outlook* are given for 19 OECD countries. The diskettes are a valuable data source for those interested in fiscal policy and in potential output and output gaps.

The FPBC diskettes are accompanied by relevant user instructions and detailed Sources and Methods material based upon *Working Paper,* No. 152. The set of diskettes is updated on a twice-yearly basis to take into account data revisions and to make available new projections. The annual subscription rate of: £275, US$455, FF 2 500, DM 755.

OECD electronic books

Economics Department Publications in Electronic Form

Recognising the growing importance of multimedia electronic publications, the OECD is in the process of producing a new range of electronic books corresponding to many of its key economic publications. A special version of the *OECD Economic Outlook* (excluding the statistical Annex) is now available and electronic book versions of the OECD and Centre for Co-operation with the Economies in Transition (CCET) *Economic Surveys* will shortly be released based on the 1995-96 series. These typically provide the text, tables and figures of the relevant publication on screen and in an identical format to that of the printed version, including the use of colour in graphs.

The electronic book, which retains the quality and readability of the printed version throughout, will enable readers to take advantage of the new tools that the ACROBAT software (included on the diskette) provides by offering the following benefits:

- User-friendly and intuitive interface;
- Comprehensive index for rapid text retrieval, including a table of contents, as well as a list of numbered tables and figures;
- Rapid browse and search facilities;
- Zoom facility for magnifying graphics or for increasing page size for easy readability;
- Cut and paste capabilities;
- Printing facility;
- Reduced volume for easy filing/portability.

Working environment: DOS, Windows or Macintosh.

OECD Economic Outlook (June and December 1996)

1996 Subscription	£40	US$65	FF 355	DM 107

OECD and CCET *Economic Surveys*

Complete 1995-96 series:	£200	US$317	FF 1 800	DM 545
Complete 1994-95 series on CD-ROM: (Available early 1996)	£220	US$365	FF 2 000	DM 600

The OECD sells a large number of its publications or statistical data on diskette, magnetic tape or CD-ROM. The catalogue of OECD Electronic publications is available free of charge upon request to OECD publications.

For further information contact OECD Publications Centres in Bonn, Mexico, Tokyo and Washington, or your local distributor, or write to:

OECD Publications
2, rue André-Pascal
75775 Paris Cedex 16
FRANCE